CRITICAL MASS

Also by James Wolcott

*Lucking Out: My Life Getting Down and
Semi-Dirty in Seventies New York*

*Attack Poodles and Other Media Mutants:
The Looting of the News in a Time of Terror*

The Catsitters: A Novel

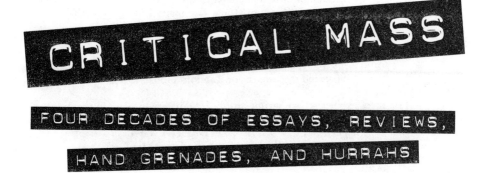

CRITICAL MASS

FOUR DECADES OF ESSAYS, REVIEWS, HAND GRENADES, AND HURRAHS

James Wolcott

DOUBLEDAY
New York   London   Toronto
Sydney   Auckland

All rights reserved. Published in the United States by Doubleday, a
division of Random House LLC, New York, and in Canada
by Random House of Canada Limited, Toronto,
Penguin Random House Companies.

www.doubleday.com

DOUBLEDAY and the portrayal of an anchor with a dolphin
are registered trademarks of Random House LLC.

The pieces appeared, sometimes in slightly different form, in the
following publications: *Esquire, Harper's, The London Review of Books,
The New Republic, The New Yorker, The New York Review of Books,
Texas Monthly, Vanity Fair, The Village Voice, What's This Cat's Story?:
The Best of Seymour Krim* (Paragon House, 1991).

*Book design by Michael Collica
Jacket design by Emily Mahon*

Library of Congress Cataloging-in-Publication Data
Wolcott, James, 1952–
[Prose works. Selections]
Critical mass : four decades of essays, reviews, hand grenades,
and hurrahs / James Wolcott.
pages cm
I. Title.
PS3573.O4575A6 2013
814'.6—dc23   2013015290

ISBN 978-0-385-52779-8

MANUFACTURED IN THE UNITED STATES OF AMERICA

1 3 5 7 9 10 8 6 4 2

First Edition

In memory of Norman Mailer, Dan Wolf, Clay Felker,
Pauline Kael, and Gore Vidal

Contents

III. PUNK, POP, ROCK

Patti x Two

Johnny Rotten x Two

Introduction

＊

Allow me to set the scene, the way fiction writers used to do before they went all meta-conceptual and self-annotating. Picture the screened-in back porch of a yellow bungalow on the southern tip of the Jersey shore. A small parish of mourning doves make their stately way across the scrubby lawn, pecking at fallen seeds from the bird feeder while squirrels conduct their own food-gathering choreography. It is late autumn, not long after Hurricane Sandy paid a tumultuous call, making landfall a few miles northeast, upheaving many of the resort towns. Here I sit cross-legged on a zigzag rug, but not in meditation. Arrayed around me like a drum kit are stacks of gray, dark-streaked clips of nearly every review, essay, and article I've written over four decades. If I were ever inclined to ask the question, "Where did my life go?," I'd be able to say with a sweep of my hand: "This is where it went." It wouldn't be the complete answer, of course. I did other things too, those special things that separate man from the mollusk, but so much of my irretrievable past was poured in and out of this cement mixer. The amount of reading, researching, writing, re-writing, worrying, procrastination, answering copy queries and fact-checking questions, poring over successions of galleys and still managing to miss that typo on page four; the beaded string of sleepless nights and panicky mornings that went into meeting those countless deadlines (which never seems to get easier, no matter how many times you've done it)—in terms of accumulated word-count and distilled bulk alone, the result is prodigious. It's impressive how much you can get done when you don't go anywhere, or take any wild swerves. I've never knocked off for a year or six months or even three months to discover the romance of Barcelona or the subtle fragrances of Istanbul, retreat to a rustic cabin to "clear my head," taken the time to schedule a nervous collapse, become calcified with writer's block. Even after an attack of vertigo in Miami Beach that left me walking with a cane for months, on the constant teeter of nausea due to a lingering inner-ear imbalance, I managed to put together a column, pushing out a sentence or two at a time between lurching pitches that cured me of any desire to run away to sea.

And yet, like every hag-ridden writer I know, I carry needling traces of guilt and self-reproach, feeling as if I could have done more, dove deeper, wrestled larger crocodiles. It seems to be an occupational trait, this sigh of the slacker. Samuel Johnson used to chastise himself for his sloth and irresolution, and all *he* ever achieved was authoring the first English language dictionary, the mini-biographies that make up *The Lives of the Poets*, the dense ruminations of the essays in *The Rambler* and *The Idler*, the philosophical allegory *Rasselas*, a small heap of poetry, and conversational sallies that have lasted three centuries, thanks to his biographer-pest James Boswell. If Johnson succumbed to sea-slug accidie, what hope is there for the rest of us short-order cooks? But such self-chastisement carried to extremes can also be a form of vanity, a penitential pride, and besides, nobody wants to hear it. Non-practitioners envy the life of a writer, even if that life isn't what it used to be, because for all of its anxieties and discouragements, writing is the greatest form of aviation that you can perform while firmly planted: the freedom, the vistas, the right word snapping a sentence to attention like the click of a gun, the passages that stretch into long solos, the nights when everything recedes and you feel as if you're the only one awake in the world: welcome to the pros. And, like Norman Mailer said when asked the best thing about being a writer, "You can't beat the hours."

Descending into the archives combines an archeological dig with a biographical regression as the professional and the personal overlap like a double exposure, a blurred collage of what-you-did and who-you-were reintroducing you to a familiar stranger: your former self. I had gotten reacquainted with my former self, my junior edition, while working on the memoir *Lucking Out* (2011). Even so, some of the pieces I drew from the stacks around me seemed the work of a double agent. They bore my byline, they sounded like me, but I had no recollection of writing them, none. The ghost of amnesia had effaced them in white fog. And some of the articles weren't bad, either! It was reassuring to discover that I had a doppelgänger (or was it a guardian angel?) I could depend on. Such blanks were exceptions. Most of the pieces I sifted through carried associations, memory ticklers. They brought back smiles of recognition along with a few wounded winces. What strikes me most about the earliest pieces of mine in *The Village Voice*, the downtown paper where I went through boot camp as a journalist, having arrived as a sophomore-year dropout in New

York in 1972 with a letter of recommendation from Norman Mailer, is how much poise and confidence there was at the outset, to the point of obnoxious. I was such a precocious snot, quick-drawing my cap pistol as the new gunslinger in town, but being young and full of myself was a novelty for me, being otherwise so old-souled, solitary, and repressively armored. I had to enjoy it while I could, and I should have enjoyed it more than I did.

Leaving aside the mesa formations of my personality, what I'm struck by going through my back pages is the incredible room I had to roam along the sidelines as a rookie writer, interviewing everyone from William F. Buckley, Jr., to comedy team Peter Cook and Dudley Moore (in Tuesday Weld's apartment, no less) to Sissy Spacek (fresh from destroying the prom in *Carrie*) to future president Jimmy Carter to rampaging jazz drummer Buddy Rich, covering porn in Times Square, the bawling birth of punk on the Bowery, an intellectual Olympiad at Skidmore College, the infernal tunnel of ego and desperation at the stand-up club the Improv. It was a more spread-eagle decade, the seventies, the meritocracy hadn't fully sunk its Vulcan death-grip on journalism, the culture.

Although the Internet is reckoned a wild frontier by those who've made the mistake of venturing into the psycho ward of the average *Huffington Post* or YouTube comments sections, journalism and criticism on the heavy-traffic ad-busy sites tend to be more conventional, trend-humpy, and narrowly slatted than the underground/countercultural papers of the sixties and seventies and magazine renegades such as *Evergreen Review, Ramparts, New Times, Creem,* and *Rolling Stone* before it became a boomer nostalgia rag. *The New Yorker* under William Shawn was an ecclesiastical order that inspired awe, loyalty, and fond exasperation, a much more experimental, multitrack magazine than was understood at the shaggy time (its exquisite formalities and sedative cover art providing a deceptive glaze). Also, it wasn't the only game in town then (*The New York Review of Books* was at full battleship strength, each issue an intellectual throwdown), whereas today *The New Yorker* nearly monopolizes the collective mind-space of what's left of the cultural terrarium. Although we live in a culture of uncircumcised snark, it actually seems a more deferential time to me, the pieties and approved brand names—Cindy Sherman, Lena Dunham, Quentin Tarantino, Junot Diaz, Mark Morris, Judd Apatow, John Currin (feel free to throw other names into the pot)—more securely clamped down over our ears. When a major reputation is taken on, it's often done more with self-consciously contrarian attitude than with gut conviction or temperamental force—a calculated provocation fed into the wood chipper of Twitter, Facebook, and the blogs for buzz dispersal. Critics cared much less about being buddy-roo then, today's social media making even the meanest rattlesnakes mend their ways in the hope of being liked, friended, and followed in numbers sufficient enough not to be mortifying.

Then again, I've been accused of going soft, and if by "soft" you mean becoming a more loving, caring, dulcimer-strumming individual: guilty as charged. I am more aware of the injury a review can do and not just because I've since been on the receiving end, but because a writer's morale and position are much more precarious in the digital age when words have never been so promiscuously flung and cheaply held. It's so much harder to get anything published and publicized, so what's the point of swooping down on something struggling for sunlight? (If you make a happy discovery, that's different: strike up the band.) Older big-name novelists no longer command as vast a proscenium stage and the younger stars all seem on antidepressants or fed through an eyedropper, robbing the literary world of so much reviving libido. I have no hesitation in reprinting here the negative notices of the novelists Joyce Carol Oates and Richard Ford, since they've prospered in the interim—she's been bruited about as a Nobel Prize possibility, psycho-pulp's answer to Pearl Buck, and he was awarded the Pulitzer Prize for fiction in 1995—while retaining their integrity and remaining as platitudinous (in his case) and sado-cataclysmic (in hers) as they were when the pieces were published. After the Ford review came out, dark mutterings reached me of Ford's unhappiness and of the disgruntlement of some of his novelist buds, one of whom said what I needed was "a walk in the woods." This was an allusion to a passage in John Seabrook's profile of Ford in *Interview* when Seabrook asked if Ford would like to take a walk in the woods, to which Ford uttered, like Hemingway with a sententious hard-on, "I don't walk. I hunt. Something dies when I stroll around outside." I later spotted Ford at the Strand Book Store, and he me, but he wasn't packing heat and there was no convenient forest nearby, so there it ended, in a swift exchange of averted glances rather than a Duel at Diablo. Joyce Carol Oates wrote a letter to *Harper's* after "Stop Me Before I Write Again!" was published, a standard grievance-department memo of high-minded sniffiness, and years later we were introduced at a dinner party hosted by Gloria Vanderbilt, where we rose above the earlier unpleasantness by not alluding to it, sharing a cool and perfunctory handshake that signaled that no further conversation was necessary, or desired. It is by such evasive maneuvers that a semblance of civilization is able to proceed so that the entrée may be served.

Other reviews and essays I've chosen not to reprint because doing so would only administer additional hurt to the hurt already done and I don't want to be "that guy," as comedian Marc Maron would put it. In particular, the *Vanity Fair* column that caused the rupture with my friend and mentor Pauline Kael is too awful an episode for me to fold into the collection unless I never intended to open the book; that I was never able to make peace with Pauline is a source of pitchforked remorse, if I could expunge the article I would. It was less than my finest hour, to put it ever so gently, and I want this collection to represent the writing that I'm proudest of, happiest with, the pieces that carry a lift even if they're taking a contra position.

Even so, a slew of pieces that still have a bop to them didn't make it past the first elimination round because either the subjects they addressed have now fallen into antiquity, requiring a raft of footnotes and brackets to explain the references, or involved running gags that, out of context with no setup, would have the reader going "Huh?" This is especially true of the television reviews I did for *The Village Voice*—preliminary cuts that were particularly hard to make since it was at the *Voice* that so many people first read me, and that I first developed any following. Even now, after so many lilac springs and winter snows, I run into someone who says, "You did a hilarious review of X, do you remember that?" To which the honest answer is often, "Nope, complete blank," but the important thing is that this particular reader remembers, and that's what counts. But not enough to warrant inclusion for the book if the TV special or miniseries itself is lost to time, nowhere to be found on Hulu, a chunk of space debris. One exception I made is a piece I wrote about the local New York talk show host and seventies sensation Stanley Siegel, who, each Friday, would recline on a psychiatrist's couch on the set with his actual therapist and air his reflections and regrets on how the interviews had gone that week, which ones he had socked home and which ones he had fumbled and wished he could re-do. He would chastise himself, then forgive himself, his therapist barely getting in a word. I've included the column not only because it preserves the original flavor of the Me Decade but because Siegel's name remains in small circulation, resurfacing whenever there's a discussion of Truman Capote's post–*La Côte Basque* dishabille. (It was on his morning program that Capote came infamously, slurrily undone, ripping into his former friend and swan Lee Radziwill with a barrage of insults and indiscretions that made worldwide news.) The same selection process applied to the book pieces, some of the authors I reviewed who were salient in their time and prime—John Hawkes, for example, with his prose-painterly studies of fruited flesh, or John Gardner, the professorial, mythopoeic novelist complete with hobbit pipe—having since receded into the marsh mist. Others peaked early as fiction writers and downtown dandies (some of the eighties' "Brat Pack" nighthawks), while in the case of Mary Gaitskill I'm dissatisfied with the writing I did on her and feel I owe her more due. My pleasantest surprise was going through the movie columns I wrote for *Texas Monthly* in the eighties and seeing what a roll I was on then—those reviews really bammed along, a testament to Pauline's close-by influence and my own leaning into the windshield as everything came rushing forward.

It was at *Vanity Fair*—a national magazine with an international outlook, one of the few remaining luxury pavilions left in journalism—that I was able to wide-out as a writer, the James Bond jet pack lifting me over the toy village rooftops, or so I like to pretend in moments of intense, hand to hand combat with a paragraph. It was in 1983 that the courtly Leo Lerman was installed as editor of *Vanity Fair* after starfleet commander Richard Locke had fallen victim to a media swarm attack on the magazine's much-publicized relaunch. The inaugural issues of the plump glossy were savaged as if they represented the return of Marie Antoinette riding a Rose Bowl float, the prolonged buildup of hype and expectations triggering a punishing backlash. It's a sobering education to re-look at those issues today and realize the quality and amplitude on sumptuous display—what was missing was a unifying gleam in the editorial eye to pull it all together, an overarching personality. When Leo, whom I had written for at *Vogue*, asked me to consider coming aboard *Vanity Fair*, the magazine didn't seem long for this wicked world, according to the gowned Greek chorus standing on the risers: a silent deathwatch countdown had commenced. But, what the hell, I said Yes, mostly because I revered Leo, and Pauline (who knew and liked Leo immensely) said it would be fun; it was, it is. Apart from an extended sojourn at *The New Yorker* in the mid-nineties, *Vanity Fair* has been my home ever since the Reagan presidency, *insert historical montage of the Clinton-Bush-Obama eras, Madonna, Tom Cruise, the collapse of the Berlin Wall, the cast of* Friends, *Brad and Angelina, 9/11, Tony Soprano raiding the refrigerator like a bear in a bathrobe, Lady Gaga, Hurricane Sandy washing through Lower Manhattan . . .* , and there's nowhere higher to go, unless there are newsstands in heaven, doubtful.

I don't want to give the impression that I think I'm manning the last outpost of a certain type of informal criticism, yet I do feel lonesome sometimes, depending on the hour and mood, surrounded by the legion of the lost. Norman Mailer, Gore Vidal, Pauline Kael, Dwight Macdonald, Mary McCarthy, Seymour Krim, Marvin Mudrick, Susan Sontag, Edmund Wilson, Alfred Kazin, Irving Howe, Manny Farber, John Leonard, Wilfrid Sheed, Alexander Cockburn, Albert Goldman, Gilbert Sorrentino, James Dickey, Lester Bangs, Veronica Geng—all of them now gone, along with so many writers and editors I knew at *The Village Voice* . . . one by one, the bleachers have emptied, to borrow a haunted metaphor from John Updike, himself now gone, the absence of his voice on the page perhaps the most grievous of all because it gave the illusion of being most immortal. But there's solace in knowing that I learned and stole from the best, and there's still more to learn. One of the upsides to being a college dropout is that it's made me feel like a student ever since, forever feeding my head to fill the gap of an incomplete education. For a writer, there's no better hunger to have.

I : TALKING FURNITURE

O.K. Corral Revisited

Be advised, this piece is not for most of you, since it is concerned mostly with literary matters, the clash of two altogether large egos (indeed one of them is leviathan in its proportions), and the pyrotechnics of existential theater. A veritable cornucopia of conflicts. So, if you are intelligent (and patient) the sound of artillery should keep you awake.

I

VIDAL: As far as I am concerned, the only crypto-Nazi I can think of is yourself, failing that, I would only say that we can't have . . .

HOWARD K. SMITH: Now let's not call names.

BUCKLEY: Now listen, you queer. Stop calling me a crypto-Nazi or I'll sock you in your goddamn face and you'll stay plastered—

SMITH: Gentlemen! Gentlemen! Let's not call names.

The exchange printed above was the famous ad hominem crossfire between William F. Buckley and Gore Vidal on ABC-TV during the near-to-apocalyptic Democratic Convention of 1968. Keep the exchange in mind; we will return to it later; the symmetry of the argument will delight you.

II

Enough mystery. *The Dick Cavett Show* recently featured Gore Vidal, novelist and playwright; Janet Flanner, correspondent in France for *The New Yorker*; and Norman Mailer, American writer numero uno. Now television talk shows tend to be witty and vacuous (as is usually the case with Dick Cavett), dumb and vacuous (cf. Merv Griffin and Johnny Carson), or unctuous and vacuous (cf. the analingual David Frost). Talk shows, that is, usually are showcases for mediocre comedians telling dreadful jokes, politicians pontificating, writers pushing new books, singers doing new Bacharach material; a showcase of remarks and entertainments meant to be lively but not galvanizing, quick but never penetrating. When social issues—dread the term— are discussed, the discussion is carried on in tone and language so plastic and so pious that one would think the ghost of Adlai Stevenson was whispering in the wings.

But this particular show was different, extraordinarily different. It started as a more or less typical show, clever and safe as milk: Cavett did an extremely amusing monologue, Gore Vidal was introduced and spoke about Eleanor Roosevelt, ecology, and his new play enti-tled *An Evening with Richard Nixon*; Janet Flanner followed with little snack cakes of stories perfectly suited for any small cocktail party. All very nice, amiable, and dull.

After Mailer's introduction, however, the mood-temperature of the show went from lukewarm to warm (and it was to reach torrid before the evening was through). Mailer's entrance on stage was done with such swagger and streetfighter toughness that he appeared to be the baddest gunfighter ever to kick open the doors of the Silver Dol-lar Saloon. When he got to his chair, he neglected all too obviously to shake hands with Vidal. Cavett, noting this, asked if there was animosity between the two. Indeed, there was. A short explanation follows.

III

In the first winter of this year, Mailer published a book-length essay entitled *The Prisoner of Sex*, the work being a rebuttal to Kate Mil-lett's *Sexual Politics* and exploration of the issues involved in Women's Liberation—sexual technology, the family orgasm, homosexuality, the literature of Henry Miller and D. H. Lawrence (Mailer's defense of Lawrence soars like a windhover). The effect on Mrs. Millett was devastating—she was so badly lacerated that she is still bandaging the wounds. In the essay was a short slicing reference to Vidal: "The subject"—i.e., women's lib—"was too large for quick utterances: The need of the magazine reader for a remark he could repeat at the eve-ning table was best served by writers with names like Gore Vidal . . ." Vidal, not without pride, to say the least, did not enjoy being trivial-ized. So in an article in *The New York Review of Books*, Vidal formu-lated a prototype male called M3; M3 being an equation for Henry Miller–Norman Mailer–Charlie Manson and representing the sort of male who thinks that women are ". . . at best, breeders of sons;

at worst, objects to be poked, humiliated, killed." Comparing Mailer to Manson was hyperbolic enough, but consider this datum: Mailer, married four times, non-fatally stabbed his second wife. All right? Back to the show.

IV

After admitting he had just come from a bar, Mailer added that he hesitated to break the jovial mood of the show, but that he was furious with Vidal for what he had written and that it was obvious that Vidal as a writer was slipping badly. (Note: From this point on, all dialogue is printed as close to the facticity and spirit of the show as memory permits. The quotes, that is, are composed from memory and should not be taken as actual transcript.) He chastised Vidal for being so decadent as to write a play about Nixon; it was "too easy" and it could very well get Nixon re-elected because such a play, coupled with Philip Roth's *Our Gang*, would only generate sympathy for the president—"It's *overkill*, Gore," remonstrated Mailer. Vidal responded weakly, Cavett did not get the conversation going, and Mailer told him, in effect, do your job (that is, don't let silence set in). When Janet Flanner saw that the mood was going to be contentious, she made some puerile remark about talking sensibly and not dredging up old problems. Mailer, in street-cop staccato, fired back, "Listen, after vomitation, examining the contents of Gore Vidal's stomach would be no more interesting than examining the insides of an intellectual cow." Murder was in the air. And Mailer was not finished—he was to escalate the attack the rest of the evening in order to get Vidal out from under the table.

Vidal did attempt to defend himself, of course. He said a) that the attack by him on *The Prisoner of Sex* was not personal, b) that Mailer was in constant metamorphosis, and c) he took exception to Mailer's argument that good sex makes good babies (to be precise, Mailer wrote "Good fucks make good babies") and d) despaired of Mailer's love of the violent as revealed in Mailer's statement that "murder . . . is never unsexual."

To which Mailer replied that comparing him to Charlie Manson was personal, and intellectually shoddy—indeed lumping in Henry Miller, "America's greatest living writer," multiplied the insipidity of Vidal's equation. Mailer charged that the comparison to Manson was a calculated smear—the parallel between the murder of Sharon Tate and Mailer's wife-stabbing would escape no knowledgeable reader. And since Vidal's approach to sex was so superficial, he would never know if good fucks make good babies, the question being was Muhammad Ali conceived in a good fuck or a bad one? To Vidal's last point, Mailer asked, "How do you know murder is not sexual?" Vidal: "Well, seeing that I haven't killed anyone lately . . ." Mailer: "You killed Kerouac."

You killed Kerouac. No doubt 90 percent of the audience missed the reference. Kerouac, of course, was one of the most famous of the Beat writers, the author of *On the Road*. If we quote from Vidal's most recent book, a novel-memoir entitled *Two Sisters*, we will see where the homicide took place: ". . . Jack Kerouac's *The Subterraneans* in which he describes . . . (with) astonishing accuracy an evening he spent with William Burroughs and me. Everything is perfectly recalled until the crucial moment when Jack and I went to bed together at the Chelsea Hotel . . ." Now note: Vidal is a missionary bisexual, Kerouac was never known to be bisexually inclined until this passage was published, and the passage was written and published after Kerouac's death . . . it was Kerouac's reputation as a man that was murdered in print, ambushed when it was impossible for Kerouac to defend himself.

V

So Norman Mailer kept hammering away, his "Retaliator in and out of Vengeance Mews." The audience was against him, Janet Flanner was interrupting with comments worthy of a doughty truck stop waitress on the morning shift, Vidal was attempting to stay Above It All, Cavett was pandering to the mood of the audience. After one of Miss Flanner's more odorous bird droppings in defense of Vidal, Mailer in indignation worthy of Carroll O'Connor's Archie Bunker demanded, "Miss Flanner, are you the referee or are you Vidal's manager?" A perfect short, direct hit, the first time in remembrance a meddling guest was told by another guest to, for the love of Jesus, keep your mouth shut.

Cavett, repelled by Mailer's chutzpah, asked if he wouldn't like two more chairs brought onstage to contain his giant intellect; Mailer replied, "As long as they bring out fingerbowls for the rest of you." And Cavett, in an embarrassing charade, pretended not to understand what Mailer meant. But Cavett also got off the funniest line—there was a silence and Mailer said, "Why don't you look at your question-card?" Cavett: "Why don't you fold it five ways and shove it where the moon don't shine?" The timing was exquisite, the studio audience exploded with laughter . . . but it made one somewhat ill to hear it. The line was freeze-dried, stored away to be a smartass counterpunch, it was as programmed as Johnny Carson's cute comments as Carnac the Magnificent. The line was sharp, very sharp, but it betrayed Cavett's small nightclub comic core.

But if Cavett was a comic with a zip-gun, Vidal was a priest with a rosary. We have been, he said, divided enough and listened to enough heated rhetoric and nothing was served by hateful dialogue, etc. Did I say he sounded like a priest? No, Vidal sounded worse than that . . . his voice echoed Rrrammsey Clark. It was the audience, however, that was most hostile to Mailer. Mailer asked for five minutes to address the audience.

VI

"Listen," he said, head raised to address the balcony, "are you all truly, really idiots or is it me?" "*You!*" the audience hooted almost in unison, to which Cavett quipped, "Oh, that was the easy answer." Mailer invited the audience to yell their condemnations to determine why *HE* was the idiot. "You're rude!" yelled one. "Male chauvinist pig!" bellowed a woman. One female's thin, liberal, shaky, despondent voice rose above the others: "You come on the show and insult everyone and the other guests are polite and dignified and calm and you're rude and boorish." "Okay," said Mailer, "the reason I am rude and boorish is because I'm rude and boorish and the reason they're polite and dignified is because they are polite and dignified—and they would slit my throat in the alley if they could. All right?" The hostilities out in the open, Mailer asked the audience, "Can I talk to you now? Can I reach you?"

Mailer then delivered a five-minute peroration for himself, a short speech cauterizing with existential brilliance. It was a speech that the best English professor on the best day of his life could not give, because the nuances of Mailer's voice spoke of the frustrations, victories, and attrition of pursuing the Great Bitch, that mother-woe of a novel not meant to be written. The difference between an English professor and Norman Mailer describing the quest of the writer is the difference between a war correspondent and a weary battle-wise lieutenant describing a military siege—one writes of skin, the other of blood.

So Mailer communicated the knowledge that comes from going

over the ridge. "Great writers," he began, "were traditionally men of letters, they respected tradition and literary punctilios even when they transgressed them in order to further their work. But it was Hemingway who first knew that writers, especially American writers, take as much abuse and punishment as prizefighters, and, moreover, he, Hemingway, wanted to be champion. Hemingway wanted to be the best American writer, he wanted to be the champion, BECAUSE THAT'S ALL HE CARED ABOUT. He wasn't just the lute that the sweet winds of Art played—he was a writer with an existential quest, he wrote to deliver himself as a man. I wrote a book called *The Prisoner of Sex* and found that my ideas about sex were terribly complex and, in a sense, Gore is correct in saying that my style is becoming unreadable because the ideas are so complex that it is getting more and more difficult to express them on paper. But after the book was published, it was as if it had never been written: it was taken as an anti–women's lib diatribe and dismissed. Which is why some libber will shout 'male chauvinist pig.' Well that's dull, it's DULL, it's beneath us as Americans to use frozen rhetoric, to pollute the intellectual rivers while everyone howls over ecology. Bad enough when the ignorant do the polluting, but it is enraging when someone like Gore Vidal, who's been around in the literary world and knows what he's doing, intentionally misrepresents my work. Because, understand, like Hemingway, I want to be the champion because that's all I care about, and after twenty-five years of working and writing to be the best American writer of our time, I am not going to let myself get kicked in the balls by Gore Vidal."

VII

So what are we to make of all this? Was it just a fencing match, a shoot-out, an intellectual slugfest? It would appear that way perhaps to the unperceptive, but something more profound, something closer to the nerve took place. The question is whether or not one's work is important; is one's writing merely an activity, a way of making one's way economically through the world, an exercise in self-expression, a means of achieving fame? Because if that is all there is, then to be a good writer is knowing best how to toss impure pearls before swine (the more the swine, the greater the writer by this logic). But if writing is a pilgrimage across the fever-swamps of experience in search of the Hemingwayesque big two-hearted river, if it is that great a mission, then one had damn well better carry a revolver fully loaded.

Yes, if Lord Byron wrote to save himself from suffocating on cum [decades later, I have no idea what I mean by this—JW], and D. H. Lawrence out of fear that he was less than a man, and Hemingway from his sense of mission, then in our time, even as crass and cheap and cynical as it is, Norman had an imperative to destroy the intellectual pretensions of Gore Vidal.

But a defense of Mailer rests on a crucial assumption—that ideas have importance. Of course, most would say in the abstract, of course they do. But we are not talking abstractly and we are not talking of ideas as opinions chewed over at faculty dinners, solemnized at seminars, buried in textbooks, carried around compartmentalized in the head of a near-dead scholar. In such a context, Vidal's gamesmanship and charlatanism are nothing to be concerned about. But if ideas and language have meaning, if they are as much in the blood and gut as sex and love, then those who knowingly and proudly defecate in the river have got to stand trial.

VIII

When William F. Buckley reflected on his bazooka blast at Gore Vidal—the physical threat, the vicious epithet—he reached the initial conclusion that his "response was the wrong one if it is always wrong to lose one's temper . . ." But later he came across a passage from theologian C. S. Lewis: "The higher the stakes, the greater the temptation to lose your temper . . ." Not to note such transgressions as being called a crypto-Nazi, or in Mailer's case being made kin to Charles Manson, "argues a terrible insensibility . . . Thus the absence of anger, especially that sort of anger we call indignation, can, in my opinion, be a most alarming symptom. And the presence of indignation may be a good one. Even when that indignation sharpens into personal vindictiveness, it may still be a good symptom, though bad in itself. It is a sin; but it at least shows that those who commit it have not sunk below the level at which temptation to that sin exists . . ."

So Norman Mailer, Lucifer of a sinner, with revolver in hand and murder in the heart, emptied a revolver into the corpulent reputation of Gore Vidal, vivisected the corpse, and thus delivered across the dull gray void of television a message transcending any medium and catalyzing the ever so long article that you have just finished reading.

State to Date. Frostburg State University, December 13, 1971

Liv and Let Die

Scenes from a Marriage

Once, while driving through a sequoia forest, Igor Stravinsky and Christopher Isherwood stopped to look at the trees. Standing near a skyscraper sequoia, Stravinsky was silent for a moment, then turned to Isherwood and said gravely, "That's serious." Several score of sequoias must have met the ax in order to publish Liv Ullmann's *Changing*, for every page is toweringly solemn about life, art, and the mournful joys of being a woman. Ullmann introduces each episode of Ingmar Bergman's *Scenes from a Marriage* (now showing on WNET-13) with splinters from *Changing*, and she says things like, "No relationship between people is perfect," and "Love, to a great extent, has been a feeling of dependency," in hushed, somber tones, as if offering prayer in a small, quiet chapel. Critics—who have almost unanimously hailed *Scenes* as a masterpiece—treat Ullmann's introductions as a peripheral annoyance. They're wrong: *Scenes from a Marriage* is at the core as banal and didactic and humorlessly dull as Liv Ullmann's sermonettes.

Scenes is a six-part chronicle of a middle-class marriage on the smash-up. Johan (Erland Josephson), an associate professor of science, is a smug little scuzz with weak, sloping shoulders, mischievous eyes, and a beard that never quite reaches Hemingwayesque fullness. He's a cheerful culture-philistine—when he rips into women's liberation, he says: "Imagine 110 women with menstrual periods trying to play Rossini—" and as confident of his charm as a rich courtesan. Marianne (Ullmann) works for a law firm, is a devoted wife and mother, and shoulders all her responsibilities with wan, stoical grace. Her portrayal of a modern Nora is impressive. Ullmann is all trembling fingers, pinched smiles, and flickering anguish (she has the most eloquent eyes of any actress alive); she has no color, but she's grayly brilliant. Other people appear—married friends, their children, Marianne's mother—but mostly it's a two-character drama, expertly photographed (by Sven Nyquist), masterfully directed. The crack-up is captured almost completely in close-ups, and many respond to *Scenes*

from a Marriage not only as a work of art but as a pentecostal illumi-
nation of their lives.

I confess I didn't feel the fire of recognition. Wilfrid Sheed once
wrote, "To lay a huge flopping and kicking prejudice right out on the
table—I do not believe that Ingmar Bergman can make a bad movie.
If I see one I don't like, that's my mistake." To lay my own experiences on the copy desk, I've never been married or lived with anyone
or summered in chill, dingy cottages, and the six hours of *Scenes from
a Marriage* have only braced me in my decision not to become an
adult. Moreover, if by "bad" one means corpse-cold and pretentious,
then Bergman has made a slew of bad movies, among them *Winter
Light, Hour of the Wolf, The Silence.* Several years ago there was a movie
starring Toshiro Mifune and Lee Marvin called *Hell in the Pacific* in
which the characters, not understanding each other's language, mum-
ble and mutter for two endless hours. Bergman's chamber dramas,
with their cosmic breakdowns of connections and gothicized dread,
also made one feel stranded—Hell in the Baltic. *Scenes* is talkier, but
it's also maddeningly ascetic. Its setting is visually astringent—like
an ice-white hospital ward—and inhumanly uncluttered, as if extras
would have violated the movie's purity. No strays appear, not even a
kitten or two. Early into *Scenes* my heart sank because I knew Bergman had returned us to that damned island.

When an artist as enigmatic as Ingmar Bergman does something
as straightforward as *Scenes*, it's understandable that such simplicity
is confused with artistic rigor; what's stripped away is assumed to be
flab and plumage. Bergman's strategy is undisguisedly banal—that is,
to peel away the layers of a Perfect Marriage so that we can see the
blight of rancor and deceit beneath—*Scenes* clunks along from crisis to teary crisis, like a hobbled horse between waterholes. Bergman
writes, "I have felt a kind of affection for those people. . . . They have
grown rather contradictory, sometimes anxiously childish, sometimes
pretty grown-up." Unlike Ozu or O'Neill, he treats his characters as
if they were lovable, squabbling children, and the poetry of stillness
or delirium is beyond his intentions.

The banality here is teacherly: every nuance has a point. In the first
two segments, Bergman sets off tremors of disaffection (Marianne's
conversation with a divorce client mirrors her own anxieties; Marianne and Johan have a rhetorical sparring after seeing *A Doll's House*),
and each didactic detail falls cleanly into place. Indeed, the effect is
doubly didactic since Liv Ullmann's introductions explain the char-

acters and why they behave as they do. In the third episode, the marriage hits the reef when Johan announces he is leaving Marianne for a younger woman, Paula. Paula never appears and the rest of *Scenes* is starved by her absence.

The series is at its most soapily self-regarding in its reconciliation of Marianne and Johan. In both Liv Ullmann's introduction and Bergman's published commentary, that conclusion is described as truer to life and art than a contrived "happy ending." At the end of segment five, Marianne and Johan, after an ugly, bloody quarrel, sign the divorce papers, their hands trembling with rage. It's a smashing denouement, the crest of the series. Then, years later, both married to others, they rendezvous for a weekend at a summer cottage, and *Scenes from a Marriage* ends with Johan and Marianne cuddling under the blankets, wishing each other good night as darkness snowily descends. The tableau has a sleepy, kissy tenderness, but it's as trite as any RKO fade-out. Their embrace—their shared acceptance of life's meaningful meaninglessness—is an art-movie banality that has traveled from Antonioni's *La Notte* to Fassbinder's *Mother Kusters*. It's intended as a sort of existential affirmation, but shared loneliness in the midst of spiritual desolation isn't much to look forward to, is it? Liv Ullmann writes that Hollywood's rhyming plots present "a dream world that is treacherous because it incites people to march off to ever new tunes." Well, I would have preferred a few new tunes to slogging through Bergman's six-hour leper-colony dirge only to arrive at a poignant cuddle-up.

After the showing of segments five and six, WNET-13 is going to have a phone-in session, in which counselors and psychologists will field questions about marriage and its discontentments. Somehow it's dismally appropriate; *Scenes from a Marriage* is a telephone pole pretending to be a sequoia.

The Village Voice, April 4, 1977

Hartman Is the Best Thing About Lear

Confession: *Mary Hartman, Mary Hartman* caught me almost completely by surprise. It doesn't broadly parody soap operas, and it isn't the sort of flamboyantly "controversial" sitcom that one has come to expect from Norman Lear; which is to say that *Mary Hartman* doesn't signal its comedy in any of the usual ways. On even the best TV comedies—*The Mary Tyler Moore Show, Happy Days*—you can hear the gears meshing as the jokes are being prepared, and frequently the preparation is more amusing than the kicker (that is, the anticipation of the joke is better than the joke itself). *Mary Hartman* has its awful jokey spasms, as when a character is called a "prevert" (a line older than the dust on Terry Southern's shoes), but when the residents of Fernwood are so involved in themselves that the laughter comes leaking out of their self-absorption, it's the most subtly, disconcertingly funny show ever to appear on television.

Mary Hartman is played with groggy charm by Louise Lasser, who has intent, earnest eyes and a ludicrously toothful smile: she's a suburban rabbit in a beleaguered hutch. Her husband resists her strokings of sexual affection, her grandfather is a compulsive exhibitionist (he's known in the community as the Fernwood Flasher), and her daughter, crossing the edge of puberty, is about to be questioned about a mass murder in which a family of five were slaughtered along with their goats and chickens. ("What kind of maniac would kill goats and chickens?" asks an incredulous Mary. "And what kind of man would keep *goats?*" replies her husband.) Even more distressing, Mary H. just can't seem to control the growth of waxy yellow buildup on her kitchen floor.

Fortunately for the show's dynamics, it isn't Entropy that lives next door, but an aspiring country singer named Loretta, who practices her act in the living room for her bald-headed, beaming-with-pride husband. After winning his praise, she coos, "Honey, you make me feel bigger than Janis Joplin . . . when she was alive, that is." Loretta echoes the Gwen Wells character in *Nashville*—a novice so ebulliently eager to please that she's simply not going to let a little thing like lack of talent get in her way. In her bowling-alley gig, she does her honky-tonk so spiritedly that she drowns out the sound of falling pins.

The loopiness of the characters is treated with genial matter-of-factness—only Dody Goodman, doing her dumb cluck number as Mary's mother, is overwrought—and *that* is what makes the show so liberating, not the "frank" subject matter. For nothing would have been more tiresomely predictable than a nightly farrago of abuse and hurled dirt. Lear has gone as far as he can go (at least I hope he has) with the almost Homeric sarcasm of *Maude* and *All in the Family*, and the gentle, laconic absurdity of *Mary Hartman* shows that TV adults don't have to blister each other's eardrums in order to be heard. Ingenious, then, to place *Mary Hartman* within a soap-opera ambience; in the absence of studio audience and laugh track, the relationship between the actors and the camera can be more intimate, quieter. A nice balance is struck: You don't have the strident theatricality of a filmed-before-a-live-audience show like *Maude*, but you don't have the claustrophobic close-ups and leaden pauses that you get in the soaps. What *Mary Hartman* takes from the soaps is the sense that the camera is another character in the room, indeed that the camera is the most observant character of all.

And what is that camera attentive to? Not sin, really, but the discovery of sin: embarrassment. Embarrassment is the experience of being trapped in one's own lies or, even worse, discovering that one is inadequate in dealing with society's demands. There isn't any television genre more concerned with social rank, privilege, and style than the soap opera—the soaps are quite severe with a character who wears the wrong dress to a swank party. This is the appeal of soaps—their novelistic appeal—they deal with ambitious professional people moving through a circumscribed world, a world with boundaries, duties, treacheries, comforts, and responsibilities . . . a world of rooms. Embarrassment is the tension that comes with having the wrong door opened.

Then think of prime-time TV heroes: could one imagine Starsky and Hutch embarrassed? by anything? Of course not, their jaggedly dynamic world of gunplay, screeching cars, and furtive junkie killers is a narrative flux which recognizes no social restraints. And police hard-ons like Baretta and Kojak could never feel anything akin to embarrassment, not only because as actors Robert Blake and Telly Savalas are such beribboned showboats, but because if you're given free use of a revolver, a superego is unnecessary equipment.

If you're watching *Joe Forrester* or *Harry O* or *Police Story*, and then tune in, the shift from the door-crashing crime-fighters to Fernwood sets up the context of violence impinging from the outside. The nihil-istic edge to *Mary Hartman* is that though the characters are trapped in those soap-opera rooms, the viewer is always aware of the cha-otic world outside. Mary's knocked-out quizzicality seems almost a response to, and a comment on, all the pounding action that is on prime time before 11; she's been so battered by the violence on *Hawaii Five-0* that a mass-murder in her neighborhood just doesn't connect with her feelings.

What *does* connect with her feelings is sex, or rather, the lack of it. Mary feels sorrowful embarrassment not for something she's done, but for something she can't bring herself to do: masturbate. The bed-room scene in which she confessed to her husband that she doesn't masturbate, that she's never been able to masturbate, wasn't shocking; it was sad, achingly sad. When her husband nervously changes the subject, Louise Lasser's Mary sighs, "I can't do it and you can't talk about it," and the line was charged with the pain of disconnectedness, and it was like watching a spacey American *Scenes from a Marriage*. It was a piercingly tender moment, one that didn't have to endure hours of schematic plotting, studied drabness, and deadening Bergmanian sobriety to reach.

As in *Scenes from a Marriage*, the center of the narrative is a per-plexed woman who finds the scaffoldings of her life giving way. Liv Ullmann is a great actress, but I couldn't respond to her in *Scenes*—she is too alertly intelligent for the character she portrayed, and you could sense Ullmann holding herself in. Louise Lasser, though a lesser actress, is a more quiescent and vulnerable presence; her need for affection seems so genuine that her marital travails have true emotional pull. Ullmann has a firm spine of self-esteem, but Lasser's Mary is so battered by bruising setbacks (sexual and otherwise) that at times she seems almost lost in a barbituated fog—out of focus. If *Mary Hartman* fulfills its promise, Lasser will sharpen as the show progresses, and the confusions of her character's life will slowly crystallize.

So far, *Mary Hartman, Mary Hartman* is loose and fitful, ham-handed at times, and often too close to the edge of Carol Burnett burlesquerie, but it has verve, affection, and a loving attentiveness to the nuanced banalities of everyday talk, and in its best moments the comedy reveals the raw nerves of love's loneliness. It's not only more entertaining than *Scenes from a Marriage*, it's better art.

The Village Voice, January 19, 1976

Stanley Siegel
Jack Paar in the Age of est

At 9:00, Stanley Siegel strides from his dressing room with the soaring confidence of a Paddy Chayefsky cartoon and opens WABC's *A.M. New York* by asking, "Is anyone havin' any fun? The British economist said in the long run we're all dead: D-E-A-D. Well," he says, raising his hand in a swear-to-God gesture, "I'm having fun . . . I've been to Hong Kong, China, and two world's fairs." Enthusiasm is percolating in Siegel like java in a Mr. Coffee because this morning his only guest is that Bathsheba of bathos, Barbara Walters. His combative charm and her cagey graciousness make for fizzy on-the-air chemistry: when Siegel asks if her professional relationship with Harry Reasoner has a hostile, hot-friction edginess, Walters says, No, that's not true, but there's no way to prove otherwise "unless [he] and I go up and fornicate on the air." By the end of the show, they are garlanding each other with compliments: he praises her straight-arrow sanity (". . . because I've seen most of the big stars and most of them are *whacked* out"), and she salutes his geniality, which she suggests will lead to a starry future in television. That stokes Siegel's appetite. "I'm hungry," he tells Barbara Walters. "You're talking to a *hungry lion.*"

Each morning, the ratings arrive on a single sheet of sickly yellow paper. "Look at these figures . . . this is what I would see every day for the first few weeks," says Siegel, running his finger along a column of impoverished decimals. He then points to the show's current ratings—the numbers squiggle like healthy red corpuscles. Without much station promotion or critical attention (John J. O'Connor of the *Times* still has not reviewed him; Siegel says O'Connor has his dial locked on Channel 13), he has raised the show from terminal convalescence into ruddy prosperity, and his success has spurred speculation that he will soon go network to take on Tom Snyder.

"You have to be pretty fuckin' plucky here," says Siegel. When he first took over *A.M. New York* (after a three-year stint as a talk-show host in Nashville), every episode was an apache dance, and often he was the one dragged by the hair and hurled against the wall. Now, a year later, he's still crazy, but no longer is there a kamikaze gleam in his eye. Recently, during an interview with Heinz Eiermann of the Food and Drug Administration, he asked what specific chemicals in cosmetics can do damage to the skin, and Eiermann retreated into foggy bureaucratese. Siegel kept in pursuit, Eiermann kept fudging, and soon the air in the studio was bristling with tension. "My function is that if someone is going to belly up on me, I still have the power to do something about it," Siegel said afterward. "I made something of his circumlocutory responses to my questions, the fact that he was using these big fuckin' technical words—if he's the best spokesman for the FDA, well fuck, we *know* we're in trouble."

Guests unprepared for his coiled-heat questioning often curdle on the air. "In a teasing way—it was not meant to be salacious—I said to [Joan Mondale]: If your husband is the vice-president, he could become the president, which means one day you might wake up in bed with the president of the United States. She put her hands up to her face; she was so embarrassed . . . she reacted very poorly. I think she's a strange woman, I really do." Yet when confronted with the formidable feminist polemicist Flo Kennedy, Siegel could not rouse himself into argument. "I just found her pathetic. She's not very intelligent, not very interesting; she's not very funny: she's a horse's ass."

In his fisted brashness, Siegel has often been compared to Tom Snyder, but he lowers his guard in a way Snyder never does, absorbing punches to keep the show's adrenaline flowing. What was once mere cockiness in Snyder has now become a smirky loftiness: a recent interview with Telly Savalas was like a small-screen *Twilight of the Gods* because both were so imperially self-satisfied that they had nothing to say to us lesser mortals. What distinguishes Siegel is that he isn't reluctant to play a self-mocking clown.

This harlequinade comes in many forms: there is Uncle Stan, who buddies up to his guests; there is show-business-is-my-life Stanley, who puts on a scuba suit and immerses himself in a vat of Jell-O (a stunt which got him fired as a news anchorman in Green Bay, Wisconsin); there is Stanley the party boy, who spends New Year's Eve at Hal Prince's and reports that everyone there was engrossed in making peanut butter with a Mr. Peanut machine ("It was the kinkiest thing ya ever saw"). There is also Stanley the klutzy rake, who says one of the reasons he's on television is to meet "wimmen." On a recent show with Katharine Ross, he gurgled, "You're one of the most smashing women I've ever seen." She said thank-you with the metallic politeness of a woman deft at fending off Binaca breath at singles' bars. Then Siegel said he read in the paper about cases of pregnancy in men—"I've got to check out my dates, this could ruin my career."

The camera came in tight on her as he added, "Is there anything you'd like to ask *me*?" Katharine Ross's face was as beautifully cold and expressionless as Nico's voice in a forest of violins. With a regal toss of her hair, she looked at Stanley and replied, "I can't think of anything right now." A BB pellet would have looked like Jupiter compared to Stanley Siegel's ego at that moment.

Then again, his sense of absurdity may serve as carapace. "Sometimes in the green room before the show, a cameraman will say so-and-so's an asshole, and I'll have to go out there and do the show . . . I just find it funny. I'm self-amused." Siegel can also shake off such ice-water dousings because his career is on an upward trajectory; he says talk of a network slot is "premature" but that "I've watched all my colleagues, and although I have respect for them, I feel I'm better." He then launches into a Cosell harangue: "As I've said on the air, I want a talk-show Olympiad: I want Dick *Cavett* there, Tom *Snyder*, Johnny *Carson*—we'll battle it out before a jury of nine wise Argentinians. . . ."

Stanley Siegel's rodomontade isn't all steam either. He's going to be a megastar on TV, not only because of his ebullience, impudent charm, and spacey wit, but because the way he waves and unfurls his personality like a toreador's cape is perfect for the therapy-junkie seventies. "I'm trying to bring my life on television, as much as I can. It's television reality, but there's a lot of reality to it." Siegel's TV antecedent is Jack Paar, who waged feuds with the press, showed home movies of lion cubs and daughter Randy, and wept copiously enough to raise the ark from that Turkish mountaintop. Like Paar, Siegel's heart-on-the-sleeve effusions are edged with charlatan cunning. What he has done on *A.M. New York* is bring Paar's confessional style into the est–Arica–T.M.–let-all-birds-be-uncaged zeitgeist.

Hence the most popular segment on the show is Stanley and the Shrink. "Every Friday I go on the couch. Have you seen this? Well, I get on the goddam couch, and you know what I said last week?—My family was in town, and I wanted to murder my mother." Do you feel better afterward? "Absolutely." Siegel, who off-camera is in therapy three times a week, says that the most letters he's ever received have been for the Stanley-and-the-Shrink segments, which suggests that perhaps the Ice Age of Johnny Carson is nearing its end. Even though in recent weeks Carson has had some uncharacteristic outbursts—tearing up traffic tickets, setting fire to his notes, invading the set of *CPO Sharkey*—he still allows not a drop of emotion to leak out. What

Siegel said of Dick Cavett applies to Carson as well: "[He] came off as a guy who was pretty cold and could not cry, could not put his arms around anybody, couldn't reveal personal secrets." Referring to Cavett's "knowing coolness," Siegel says, "Wit is . . . ," and he can't find a word to express his contempt for bloodless wit, so he says simply, *"Be human."*

After the Katharine Ross interview, Stanley went on the couch while Dr. Elizabeth Thorne sat vigilantly near. "Whenever I'm in the presence of a beautiful woman, I panic." With one arm in the air, he grappled with a paradox: in his relations with women, he feels that "if they like me, there's something wrong with them; if they don't like me, there's something wrong with me." But professionally, he said, he feels good, he feels stronger all the time, and the camera closed in until the only image on the screen was Stanley Siegel's clenched fist.

The Village Voice, February 7, 1977

Postscript

Despite my bold prediction, Stanley Siegel did not achieve next-big-thingness as a talk show host. After his initial streak across the sky, his comet went cold and there would be no triumphant career rebound for him as there was for Regis Philbin, who caromed around after serving as Joey Bishop's sidekick on Bishop's late night show to nag his way into household status as the beloved "Reege." So why include the column? Because Siegel's flourishing on the New York scene captures the wacky, driven narcissism of the Me Decade and the high-roller bravado that even a local-TV phenomenon could boast. Glue a swinger's mustache on Stanley and knock off twenty or thirty IQ points and he could be Manhattan's answer to Anchorman's *Ron Burgundy. After his WABC talk show was canceled, Siegel seemed to dematerialize into the Phantom Zone, nothing was heard about him for decades, and then he resurfaced, contacting me to let me know that he was now hosting a travel show on cable's RLTV channel called* Stanley on the Go, *where he jaunts around the world making an amiable nuisance of himself. It's a show aimed at the AARP generation, making Siegel one of the few TV performers to leap from youthful insouciance to senior adventurousness while skipping middle age altogether. He has lost none of his lusty love of attention in the interim. In the* Stanley on the Go *episode devoted to his trip to Jordan, he makes his entrance in a Ben-Hur chariot. He is, in his own perverse fashion, an inspiration to us all.*

The Vindication of Vanessa Redgrave
Playing for Time

INTERVIEWER: *Do you think people should watch* [Playing for Time]?

FANIA FENELON: No, exactly not. Boycott, complete boycott. It will give a false impression of concentration camps. I know that some of our enemies, the fascists and the Nazis, still exist. Everywhere in the whole world they will say, "You see? We were right. A concentration camp was like a sanitarium. They could be very happy there. . . ."

—Los Angeles Herald Examiner, *October 30, 1979*

On a boxcar shipping Nazi Germany's undesirables to Auschwitz, mothers rock their weeping children, bits of light and scenery blink through the slats, and a pailful of urine tips over, provoking cries of distress, disgust. The train stops, the doors slide open: and a long season in Hell begins for French-Jewish nightclub singer Fania Fenelon (Vanessa Redgrave). She and the other female passengers are herded to the reception block of Birkenau, Auschwitz's extermination camp. Stripped of their clothes and belongings, the women are branded on the arm with an identification tattoo—Fenelon's number: 74862—and their hair is chopped off by jeering, piggish Polish girls clicking blunt scissors. Trickles of blood run down their brows as their hair is hacked into patches of scrubby fuzz. Skeletons draped in striped rags stare with dead eyes at the newcomers: the newcomers punctuate the night with coughs, moans, sobs. Where, asks Fenelon, are the people we came in with? And, as the camera peers through a miasmic haze, a Polish girl points to a building in which the windows are red with flame and smoke is heaving from the chimney. "There are your friends," she says. "Cooking."

Based on Fania Fenelon's memoir, *Playing for Time* (September 30, CBS) picks through the rubble of Auschwitz for three hours, trying futilely to make sense of history's most tragic moment of senselessness. After films like *Seven Beauties* and *The Night Porter*, after mini-series like *Holocaust* and bestsellers like *Sophie's Choice* and documentaries like Alain Resnais's *Night and Fog*, concentration-camp imagery comes almost too easily: the curling loops of barbed wire, corpses piled like sticks of firewood, the gleaming boots of the SS, the tattoos, smoke rising in mounds from the crematoria. In this controversial production, director Daniel Mann and screenwriter Arthur Miller have spared us the grisly, gut-wrenching worst: we never see bodies roasted, children tormented. And yet Fenelon's claim that the drama makes concentration-camp life look like a holiday simply doesn't stick. *Playing for Time* lurches from scene to scene, its acting is often stilted and drab, and the dialogue is aimed at the lowest rungs in the audience. ("Her uncle was Gustav Mahler, the great composer," says one inmate to another—as if we wouldn't know who Mahler was.) Yet with all its inept awkwardnesses, the film never loses its grip on our feelings and conscience—and for that full credit must go to its embattled star. Vanessa Redgrave gives a brave, stirring performance; she vindicates the film—she vindicates herself.

Not everyone will agree. When the casting of Redgrave as Fenelon was first announced, there were angry objections from Jewish organizations like the Simon Wiesenthal Center of Holocaust Studies and the Anti-Defamation League of B'nai Brith, Hollywood writers and producers (Larry Gelbart, David Wolper, the late Dore Schary), and, of course, Fenelon herself. In part, the objections were personal: Redgrave was too old for the role, it was argued, too old and too toweringly tall. In a complaint which itself bordered on anti-Semitism, some argued that Redgrave didn't have the right conformation—or as producer Bud Yorkin put it, "If Vanessa Redgrave looks Jewish, I look Swedish." But of course the greatest objection was to Redgrave's fierce and unwavering support of the PLO. Said Howard M. Squadron of the American Jewish Congress: "The idea that Vanessa Redgrave, who publicly supported the terrorist cause and the PLO goal of destroying Israel, has been cast in the role of a concentration-camp inmate is grotesque. It is bound to be regarded as offensive by the Jewish community." It was; it still is.

But as soon as Redgrave appears on the screen one's reservations float away like wisps of milkweed. Regal and top-lofty in most of her roles, Redgrave here reduces herself to a pair of red, raw knuckles and a gray-stubbled skull; she *diminishes* herself heroically, into a charcoal sketch of walking death. In the opening sequence, Fenelon performs at the piano in some shadowy, murmurous dive in Paris, and with her lacquered hair and tired, wise eyes, Redgrave looks oddly like the young Lillian Hellman (an homage to her role in *Julia*?). After aiding the French resistance, Fenelon—who's half-Jewish—is sent to Auschwitz, where she thirsts and starves into semiconsciousness until a voice in the barracks shriekingly asks if anyone there can sing *Madame Butterfly*. Fenelon is nudged into volunteering. Frightened, groggy, confused, she falteringly taps away at a Bechstein keyboard, but the audition is a success; she's accepted into the Auschwitz orchestra along with her friend Marianne (Melanie Mayron, who starred in *Girlfriends*). Led by a proud violinist named Alma Rose (Jane Alexander), the orchestra plays outdoors for inmates who are being marched to their deaths and indoors for SS officers who pride themselves on their refined tastes. One of the connoisseurs enraptured by Fenelon's music is the infamous Dr. Mengele, played with foxy understatement by Max Wright, an actor better known for his comedy performances (he was one of the screwball scientists in Marshall Brickman's *Simon*).

Some of the casting and acting are a touch off-pitch. When Alma conducted, writes Fenelon, she "gave off an extraordinary sensuality; her relaxed mouth softened, half-opened; her eyes misted over; her body trembled." Jane Alexander is an intelligent, capable actress, and she was classily sexy in a recent *Dick Cavett Show* interview; but as Alma she never persuades the viewer that she is enthralled by music— eroticized by it. The schoolteacherly edge of impatience Alexander brings to the role isn't enough to capture Alma's blind pride, her near-fanatical resolve. As camp chief Lagerfuehrerin Mandel, Shirley Knight also fails to strike the sharpest chords. In the book, Mandel is tall and slender and radiant, almost a parody of the ideal Aryan woman. Knight looks less like a Nazi valkyrie than a piece of glazed pastry, and she lacks Mandel's commanding poise. In a small bit as a resistance fighter, model Maud Adams uses her marvelous cheekbones to suggest unyielding heroism and—almost miraculously—carries it off. Unfortunately, the most cartoonishly written and performed part is that of the orchestra's token Zionist, who wants to bear children in Jerusalem and cries things like, "The voices of innocent Jews cry out against her treason!" She doesn't have the great spirit of a Mala or Alma; she's a righteous little fussbudget—Lucy of *Peanuts* bossing around Linus and Charlie Brown on the kibbutz.

Blame for the shrill shallowness of her role must be pinned on screenwriter Arthur Miller, who's also responsible for a number of other wincers. A concentration-camp handyman (?) wanders into the barracks to inform Fania that twelve thousand Jews have just been gassed . . . pointing to the sky, he sagely reports, "The air is full of angels." Since no such character turns up in Fenelon's account, I assume that this wise gnomic handyman, like the dwarf Michael Dunn played in *Ship of Fools*, is meant to represent the Vagabond Spirit of Man. He pays witness to man's bloody follies, then toddles off into the future, carrying hope over his shoulder in a knapsack. This, to put it mildly, is a sentimental conception we should have been spared. And Miller should never, never have had another inmate congratulate Fania for being so popular in the barracks with these words: "Maybe it's because you have no ideologies; you're happy just to be a person." How can any actress look Vanessa "Zionist hoodlums" Redgrave in the eye and praise her for not burdening herself with ideological convictions? If Miller intended this as irony, well, it's foolishly out of place.

What Miller most grievously fails to dramatize is the moral disintegration of Fania's friend, Marianne. Trading her body for scraps of food and a brassiere (a luxury item in Auschwitz), Marianne skids down the slope to bestiality with every act of barter. She's so determined to survive that she even copulates with "an enormous flat-skulled brute of a German" whose sadism wins high marks from the SS. By the end of Fenelon's memoir, she's turned into a sadistic ogre herself, torturing a French girl for the grim sport of it. In the TV-adaptation, the torture incident is missing and Miller has added something not in the book: a shot of Marianne leaping into a truck to be carted off with the German prisoners after the British have liberated the area. Doubtless Miller added this sequence to show how deeply Marianne had gone over to the other side, but it's too little too late. Since Marianne's fate is a mirror-reversal of Fania's—since she symbolizes everything Fania refuses to become—we need to see the horror of her betrayal slowly, graphically unfold. Instead, like so much of *Playing for Time*, the mushroomy growth of damp rot in Marianne's character is presented in a slapdash, side-swiping manner. Close-ups never come when they're most pitilessly needed.

Playing for Time was a trouble-plagued production, which may explain why continuity between scenes is wobbly—why some minor characters seem to tumble down trap doors while others drop in out of nowhere, like puppets unexpectedly lowered from the curtain-top of a toy stage. Tony Richardson was originally scheduled to direct the telefilm; he was replaced by Joseph Sargent (*MacArthur, The Taking of Pelham One Two Three*), who was in turn replaced by Daniel Mann, who inherited a thankless chore. Wisely, Mann doesn't try to bedazzle us with splintery technique, as Wertmuller did in *Seven Beauties;* he gives the actresses quiet room to find the truthful moments in their scenes—and is often rewarded. The scene in which the orchestra women stand around the piano and belt out "Stormy Weather" is movingly comic, as is the moment when Lagerfuehrerin Mandel kneels at Fania's feet to lace up her new shoes. The most daringly successful moment comes when the camera swiftly closes in on the plump, bland face of a British soldier when he liberates a camp and sees before him women who have been reduced to goblins, bony heaps, scarecrows. The stunned, disbelieving look on his face could serve as an emblem for the moment when the British stumbled upon Bergen-Belsen and saw (in the famous words of the London *Times* correspondent) "something beyond the imagination of mankind."

Yet it's Vanessa Redgrave's Fania around whom the camera most often hovers and probes, searching for tiny cracks in her pride, her composure. From the bridge of her nose to the first frown-line of her brow, Redgrave gives an eloquently searching performance—her eyes tell you immeasurably more than Miller's words ever could what it's like to wake up in Hell in a shattered daze. Smacking the side of her head like a frustrated infant, Fania tries to make sense of her life in the orchestra, tries to justify to herself entertaining the very monsters who are driving thousands upon thousands into the slaughterhouse. As the threads of Fania's health and sanity begin to fray, Redgrave rings tricky changes on her voice, lowering it so hollowly that it seems to be coming from a different body. Which of course makes inspired sense: after months at Auschwitz, Fenelon's body is a battered shell, her voice a fading echo. One sequence—Fania debating whether or not to eat a piece of sausage the whorey Marianne has left for her—is too much like an acting-class exercise, with Redgrave picking up the sausage, pushing it aside, picking it up again, etc.; but the scene is capped with Redgrave guiltily banging her head against the wall—and the slight scrape of her hair-stubble against the wood is so woeful and eerie that I felt a knot tighten in my throat.

A knot which never loosened. The book ends with Fania and her fellow inmates, finally freed, wading in a sunlit meadow against a "cool, soft tide" of wild flowers near a woody patch of birch and fir. The film denies us that warmth and camaraderie, ending instead with a shot of the freed Fania shivering in the chill gray. Yes, it was rude provocation to cast Vanessa Redgrave as a concentration-camp survivor, but I don't see how anyone could argue after seeing her performance that she has "defamed" the memory of those who perished in the Holocaust. As a pro-PLO propagandist, Redgrave needs to be questioned, quarreled with, ridiculed, attacked; but it's probably pointless trying to divide her talent and her political convictions into neat piles. Perhaps Redgrave's political passion and her passion as an artist spring from the same rich source; perhaps the gall and energy which propel her all over the globe to spout Marxist rubbish are also what enable her to enter so deeply into a role that she becomes transfigured—luminously possessed. She becomes so possessed with Fania Fenelon's sickness and fatigue that she snuffs her own luminousness, leaving the viewer with loose pale skin, numbness, ashes. Controversy over Redgrave's casting will and should continue, but without her this film would have been just another guided tour of the Nazi inferno. The racked, haunted look in Vanessa Redgrave's eyes gives *Playing for Time* its only moments of near-greatness.

The Village Voice, September 24, 1980

The Crane-Shot That Captured Christmas
SCTV

Sitting cross-legged on a snow-frosted street curb in downtown Melonville, thunderheads of vapor escaping from his vasty lungs, the once-promising film director Johnny La Rue (John Candy) used the Christmas editions of NBC's *SCTV* to uncork all of his pent-up bitterness and grief. ". . . so that basically sums up my life. I'd just like to say that I apologize to everyone who ever met me, or knew me, or wanted to meet me. Oh, I had talent. I had more talent in this little finger," he said, raising his right pinky, "than I had in *this* little finger."

As *SCTV* fans know, Johnny La Rue's career began its inglorious slide when he blew a wad of money for a showy crane-shot at the end of the made-for-TV movie *Polynesian-town*. "Can I be candid with you folks? Do you think the Oliviers of this world, the Andy Devines of this world—do you think they had to beg for a crane-shot? I think not . . . therefore I am not." Racked by cold and self-pity, La Rue began to sing Negro spirituals and babble insanely about Admiral Byrd ("Maw, maw, I can't feel my feet . . . ate the last mule yesterday, maw") before collapsing in a heap on the curb. Suddenly a pool of light fell upon his crumpled fame. Hauling himself up, La Rue stumbled toward a swirl of blue mist where to his astonishment (and ours) he saw, gleaming in the starless night, a camera-crane ringed with Christmas lights. It was a booze-woozy miracle: Santa had given Johnny La Rue a crane-shot celestial beyond his wildest imaginings.

"Beautiful" is not a word often applied to comedy, but *SCTV*'s December 18 Christmas special was such a seamless wave of wit and dream logic and affection that a lesser word won't serve. As a tightly wrapped Catholic spinster checked passes at the door, the camera poked its head into the *SCTV* staff Christmas party, where familiar faces were freshening their tonsils and casting wayward glances at the leggy numbers draping themselves at the fringes. Bobby Bittman sauntered through, the clink of his medallions announcing his presence like a bell ribboned around a kitten's throat. Edith Prickly, copping a snort at the bar, chortingly teased the butch bartender ("What

are you doin' here tonight?—your Nautilus equipment break down?")
while Lola Heatherton and Dr. Tongue rehearsed the lyrics to a new
3-D musical. The party was a daisy-chain of "in" jokes, and the jokes
blossomed in rich abundance as the show rolled on.

Intercut with the cast-party shenanigans were scenes from the
SCTV network's own Christmas specials. John Candy, fitted with a
lion's wig and fake breasts the size of dirigibles, shivered his timbers
as Divine in a "naughty" special hosted by Dusty Towne (Catherine
O'Hara) while Doug and Bob Mackenzie offered recipes for beer-nog
from the set of *Great White North*. On the set of *The Sammy Maudlin Show*, a whooshing fire claimed a plastic Christmas tree and—
mercifully—cut short an interview with owlish Neil Simon and his
wife Marsha Mason, who were visiting Sammy to promote their latest
collaboration, *Neil Simon's Nutcracker Suite*. After the conflagration
came the *Nutcracker Suite* itself, a brilliant parody of Neil Simon's
movies which speared all of his snuggy conceits and mannerisms on
the same shish-kebab. Nearly all the Neil Simon familiars poked their
heads through the door. Eugene Levy, peering down the crooked
cliff of his rubbery nose, did a note-perfect deadpan take-off of Judd
Hirsch, Rick Moranis chewed up the carpet as Richard Dreyfuss, and
Andrea Martin undammed a cataract of tears as the acutely sensitive
Marsha Mason. Maggie Smith and Alan Alda also were represented.
Having the hugest fun of all perhaps was John Candy's James Coco,
who pounded on his desk and fumigated the room when his nostrils
were assaulted by a Neil Simon script that was truly stinkeroo. He
had Coco's mincing-penguin mannerisms down cold.

The Christmas special consummated with a kiss the strange, daring direction *SCTV* has taken since occupying the late-night berth
on NBC. One local critic recently chided *SCTV* for the toothless-
ness of its satire, but the fact is that *SCTV* has long since given up
satire—indeed, most of its humor now doesn't even have (a phrase I
never thought I'd use in television criticism) an "objective correlative."
Except for the Neil Simon send-up, the Christmas special was an
interlocking series of confidential jokes about the vanities and eccentricities of the *SCTV* team: Jerry Todd's kid-like avidity for the state-
of-the-art video gear, Lola Heatherton's nerve-shot petulance, Guy
Caballero's *Godfather* vision of turf-consolidating strife and rule. The
entire shebang ended with the *SCTV* staff waving "Merry Christmas"
at the audience as the camera pulled back and Johnny La Rue, in the
director's chair, was able to savor his yuletide crane-shot. Later, Bob

and Doug Mackenzie wandered through the empty, confetti-strewn studio, with Doug staring upward and muttering, "We worship you, O Crane."

SCTV is now so deep into its fun-world warp that it's developing its own deities, its own totems. Can they continue burrowing without running the risk of leaving audiences high above-ground scratching their heads in befuddlement?—it'll be interesting to see. In the meantime, happy new year, hose heads, and may all your crane-shots be smooth and celestial, eh. Just like Johnny La Rue's.

The Village Voice, December 30, 1981

Potter's Reel

The Singing Detective

Dennis Potter is a busy devil. He writes with a hot fork. Raised in England's Forest of Dean, his boyhood a D. H. Lawrence pastoral of coalpits and church hymns, Potter has pumped forth a steady fury of stage plays, movie scripts, and mystery novels. He has a multimedia imagination. But it is as a TV playwright that he has left his biggest signature. Unlike those dullards still chained to Mom's ankle and the kitchen sink, Potter runs rings around handed-down realism. His *Blue Remembered Hills* used adult actors to play children—big hulking men stuck behind wooden desks and sniveling. *Dreamchild* was a charming hallucinogen about the real-life "Alice" of Lewis Carroll's classic. In his masterpiece, *Pennies from Heaven*, a sheet-music salesman played by Bob Hoskins—who went off like a grenade onscreen—briefly shed the drab fabric of his existence by bursting into lip-sync song. (Steve Martin peddled the notes in the movie version, written by Potter and directed by Herbert Ross.)

Early this year, public television is broadcasting *The Singing Detective*, Potter's medical musical mystery comedy drama. Imported from England, the mini-series offers the full dashboard of Potter effects: freaky-deaky production numbers, shards of shock fantasy, Freudian flashbacks. Despite its title, *The Singing Detective* isn't très debonair. A gyroscopic drop into a diseased psyche, it spares no soft spot in its antihero's defenses. Or ours. But it isn't a monster mash, either, grinding us into submission. Happiness whistles weakly from the wings.

The Singing Detective takes its title from a paperback thriller being read by a ducktailed dude in a hospital ward populated mostly by heart patients with weak tickers. In the ward is the book's author, Philip Marlow (Michael Gambon), whose name has rendered him fit only for pop fiction. Like Potter himself, Marlow suffers from a horrible case of psoriasis and arthritis. He's a crippled ball of raw pain. His fingers have been fused into futile clubs, leaving only his thumbs free and able. (Fumbling to light a cigarette, he seems to be wearing boxing gloves.) But it's his epidermis that has taken the worst hit. Pocked and peeling, his skin looks as if it's been carpet-bombed.

Skin is a disguise that can't be discarded, and Marlow has nowhere to hide from his own repugnance. Yet feeling sorry for himself not only doesn't help but palpably hurts. His very tears burn upon his cheeks. He resembles a huge flayed boiled baby, and lets fly with an ire worthy of John Osborne's soreheads. His only respite is a grease job of his delicate parts by a pretty nurse (Joanne Whalley, and what eyelashes!) employing generous globs of ointment. Otherwise—sheer hell.

To calm the queasy, I should note that Marlow's skin condition *improves* as the series proceeds, until it acquires the sheen of a glazed ham. (This is not meant as a sly knock on Michael Gambon's performance, which is out there on the ledge.) And it's also worth noting that Potter has said that his own psoriatic attack was *worse* than the one shown in *The Singing Detective*. Bad as things get, we've been somewhat spared.

Two rivers of reverie run through Marlow's mind as he lies ill. One takes him back to his youth, where he climbed the tall branches of a wind-swollen tree to hold a conference with God. His boyhood was a glum, drab phase, a period of bad haircuts, phlegm spat upon the stovetop, crowded parlors, scarecrows. In interviews, Potter has said that nostalgia isn't a real emotion but a cover-up, and the childhood sequences in *The Singing Detective* convey true ache and dolor. (The hangdog expression of Marlow's father, played by Jim Carter, casts a sweet, lingering poignance.) The second river in the story is the murky one from which a dead woman is fished, her nude body blue in the moonlight. Investigating her death is the Singing Detective (Michael Gambon again), who sports a white jacket on the bandstand and a trench coat on the prowl.

"The detective story is a parable of the triumph of reason," observes Paul Coates in his book *The Story of the Lost Reflection*. "Wisdom outwits the Harlot Mystery: the metropolitan mist that veils the causes of things is drawn back to reveal the true perpetrators of actions." *The Singing Detective* certainly has its Harlot Mystery—a garter-belted Russian beauty named Sonia (Kate McKenzie) who stuffs torn five-pound notes into her lipsticked mouth and spits them on the carpet. She's the blue nude hauled from the Thames. For all of Sonia's beware-of-a-holy-whore bravura, however, this pastiche of Raymond Chandler proves the weakest strain in the series. It's become hoary, breaking the gat and fedora out of the cupboard and sending a freelance dick on yet another spoofy stroll through the wet alleys of pulp fiction. Why bother? We all know that tough guys don't dance and dead men don't wear plaid. That metropolitan mist has worn thin. The business of having two nonentities trail Marlow (they're like Rosencrantz and Guildenstern in matching trench coats) also wears thin, though there is a neat moment when one of them says of a victim sprawled on the floor with a knife through his throat, "I thought his voice sounded funny on the phone." As Marlow's wife, Janet Suzman is Medusa with a wealthy mane of blood-red hair. If Sonia is Harlotry, Suzman represents Adultery—the epitome of all those rich dames Chandler's Marlowe wanted to kiss with his knuckles. Pity her hauteur isn't better exploited.

Where *The Singing Detective* is riveting is in its excavated hurt and musical transports. "Life is first boredom, then fear," wrote Philip Larkin. Potter sees it somewhat differently. For him, life is first fear, then shame. The fear is of adult authority and jeering classmates; the shame derives from inconstancy. In the woods, Marlow, aged nine, catches his mother screwing someone, an incident mirroring the pivotal moment in Potter's play *Brimstone and Treacle* where a teenage girl stumbles upon her father giving it to an employee. Both sights traumatize. You can't trust your parents, you can't trust your classmates; worst of all, you can't trust yourself. In a scene that is a virtual reprise from his 1965 TV drama, *Stand Up Nigel Barton* (and echoed in *Pennies from Heaven*), a fat boy is blamed for a prank, and harshly, stupidly punished. Only this time the fat boy is punished because Marlow himself is the lying fink. The classroom inquisition is too drawn out, and the spinster conducting this terror looks like Monty Python's Terry Jones in drag—she's too campy. But the moment that Marlow breaks through the crust to spill his guilty guts to a shrink (Bill Paterson, the sane, genial D.J. in Bill Forsyth's *Comfort and Joy*) is truly cathartic. It has a primal crack of pity completely absent from most TV. No TV writer on this side of the Atlantic digs for the buried child within the adult psyche. Characters on American TV are born at adolescence with a skateboard under their feet and a shiny set of values. Their hymens are pure plastic.

The Singing Detective continues the musical innovation of *Pennies from Heaven*. The hospital ward becomes a revue stage, with doctors and nurses playing dem dry bones like xylophones. For Potter, popular music is our dream spin on the dance floor—our democratic portion of immortality. Musical fantasy doesn't discriminate against the old or ugly. In the make-believe ballroom of the mind, rusty vocal pipes sound peach-fed, pitted skin becomes smooth and pearly, a romantic shine returns to rheumy eyes. Potter loves to crank up the gramophone on his sound tracks. The static of golden oldies, the fuzz in the grooves, seems as at home in his head as the rustle of leaves in the Forest of Dean. It's the aural fallout, the ground-level crackle, of once green hopes and wishes. *The Singing Detective* isn't as sustained as *Pennies from Heaven*, but there's a hypnotic rhythm to its musical and visual motifs (recurring images of a scarecrow upon the hill, a train pulling into the station, a boy atop a tree, Dad taking tired footsteps). And there's an added hook in seeing how these intriguing pieces fit into the grand puzzle of Marlow's mind. *The Singing Detective* is the very opposite of plastic. It's steep and rocky underfoot. But when it's all over, you feel as if you've trekked through major terrain.

Reading Dennis Potter has its kicks, too. His mystery novels are cardiac machines on the blink, all indicators showing rapid blips of distress. Unlike his teleplays, they monitor the present tense. But it's a wildly gyrating present tense—the breathing is quick and faint. Widely praised in England, his amnesiac thriller, *Ticket to Ride*, seems to me too existentially anxious, coated and injected with Sartrean nausea: "He had to step around an already slicked torpedo of dog shit on the edge of the gutter. A warning spurt of nausea from an empty stomach told him to look away . . ." The novel chases its own tail (and chews it ragged). But his latest spooker, *Blackeyes*, is a diabolical success, Nabokovian in its haunted mazes and reflected depths. *Blackeyes* is about a former model named Jessica whose experiences have been done up in print by her uncle, a musty literary moth named Maurice James Kingsley. His novel about her, *Sugar Bush*, is a surprise best-seller which gives his bygone career a second wind. He needs that wind to bore everyone in the vicinity with his fustian airs. "The old man was using what his few acquaintances had learnt to recognize with misery as his Literary Voice. There had also been times late of an evening when distraught strangers had yelled *Shut up!* across the entire length of a saloon bar when subjected to it. Declamatory, nasal, swooping and trembling, and above all trumpetingly loud, Kingsley's Literary Voice suggested antique spellings and tadpole-sized commas." Foul old bugger, too. Like W. H. Auden, he pees in the sink.

Blackeyes and *The Singing Detective* are both studies in how writers retroactively clean the muck out of their lives only to add their own. "You don't know writers," Marlow tells the shrink. "They'll eat their own young." Jessica certainly feels she's been half-digested. In her uncle's novel, she's portrayed as the model Blackeyes, from whose opaque orbs men conjure enigma, allure. A passive wet dream and martyr, Blackeyes becomes to readers and critics alike an all-purpose symbol of Empty Hedonism, a raven edition of Julie Christie in *Darling*. Blackeyes's supine passivity plus Jessica's personal sense of travesty fuels our heroine to a murderous tizzy. From this fuck doll Kingsley has created in her image, Jessica wishes to reclaim her soul. And to reclaim her soul, she must rewrite the book's suicidal finish, which has Blackeyes dream-walking like a ghostly pinup to her death as she proceeds to drown without a ripple in a pond at Kensington Gardens. In her radical revision, Jessica intends to leave quite a ripple. "Deconstruct though she might, putting the truth back into Kingsley's subversions" presents, ahem, problems.

As in *The Singing Detective*, Potter plays peekaboo with storytelling, using competing narratives—Kingsley's, Jessica's—to create a contrapuntal tension while leaving himself lots of elbow room for authorial fiat. "Her silky little panties, the last to go, fell across Kingsley's face in an irony she had not so precisely intended, but which I certainly did." As with Nabokov, such lordly caprice and chess-master cunning send a chill up the kilts of some critics. *The Spectator*'s reviewer, for example, accused the novel of lacking heart. Other critics may have wearied of novels that play reflexive games with fiction in the manner of Borges, Calvino, Eco. English writers have certainly gotten the bug. They're lining up at the mirror to take a metatextual look. (Julian Barnes's *Flaubert's Parrot* and Peter Ackroyd's *Chatterton* are two examples, and even Clive James seems to be popping his head out of the shower curtain in *The Remake*.) But I found the crosscutting ingenuity and daggered thrust of *Blackeyes* exciting, and its fierce energy far from heartless—there's a bloom of anger beneath its ivory mask.

Because of his psoriasis, Potter has an acute feel for the price put on flesh. In *The Singing Detective*, Marlow investigates a neon dive called Skinskape's, and skinscapes are what Potter explores too, knowing how thin a shield they afford against the world's spiky teeth. Marlow's body is a subject, a backed-up toilet of inner turmoil; Blackeyes's body is an object, a tiny chapel of prostitution. (Blackeyes at an audition: "Her nipples had spoken to them. Have we got the job? they asked. Yes, we've got the job, they said.") Both bodies are occupied and betrayed, Marlow's by disease, Blackeyes's by sex. Perhaps it's not a surprise then that in Potter's badlands of skin and blood to be a writer is to be a bit of a bastard. It's a preemptive position: use others before they use you. Establish a high bounty on your hide. But Potter also knows that this Hemingwayesque show of tough hide is mostly pose. (It was for Hemingway.) Stripped of bluff, Philip Marlow is a scared boy with skinned knees. As for Maurice James Kingsley—he becomes frantic when he can't find his teddy bear. No wonder those old songs Potter loves are poured onto the sound track like warm milk. They're lullabies floating on the surface of fever and dread. *The Singing Detective* breaks into a sweat and awakens into day. *Blackeyes*, cool and laminated, plunges into the dark deep.

Vanity Fair, February 1988

Designing Couple
Designing Women

In the first autumn of Jimmy Carter's presidency, ABC fastened together a sitcom called *Carter Country*, set in a small town down the road a piece from Carter's home in Plains, Georgia. If Bill Clinton is elected, he won't have to wait even that little while for homage. Thanks to the creative team of Harry Thomason and Linda Bloodworth-Thomason, chunks of the prime-time schedule could already be dubbed Clinton Country—*Designing Women, Evening Shade*, and now *Hearts Afire*, all on CBS. Fellow Southerners (their company is Mozark Productions, a contraction of "Missouri" and "Arkansas"), the Thomasons belong to the inner circle of longtime official FOBs—Friends of Bill. They not only huddle with the Clintons but often call the signals as media advisers. "There's a definite connection between entertainment and politics, and the line is definitely getting more blurred," Bloodworth-Thomason has said. "I don't think that's a bad thing." It certainly hasn't been a bad thing for Bill Clinton. The Thomasons have helped blur the line to his benefit.

Under their tutelage, Clinton, the policy wonk's policy wonk, has used the talk show to demonstrate that his lawyer suit isn't lined with cardboard. It was the Thomasons who got Clinton on *The Tonight Show* to kid himself after he developed runaway tongue during the keynote speech at the 1988 Democratic Convention. (A speech so long it's still running in some time zones.) And they can take credit for what may prove to be the turnaround moment in the 1992 campaign—his soul-man sax blow on *Arsenio*. They supervised *The Man from Hope*, the video CARE package of Clinton shown at this year's Convention, with JFK's apostolic laying-on-of-hands of young Bill. Indeed, the Convention was practically a Mozark production, from the Clintons' Kennedyesque stroll across Seventh Avenue the night of his nomination (Bloodworth-Thomason's idea) to his reprise of the "comeback kid" line in the hall (ditto). Harry Thomason even cued the confetti shower for Clinton's arrival.

When the Republicans under Reagan became pointillistic masters of the photo op, liberals were all supposed to deplore the elevation of image over substance. How could reason prevail over that procession of raised moments? Next stop in the twilight zone: the movie star as messiah, presiding over the faceless many. So why aren't libs concerned when Democrats stage-manage reality down to the tiniest sincerity? Perhaps it's because after so many presidential dunkings they're relieved to find *anything* that works, anything that erases the shame of poor Dukakis poking his head out of the tank like Snoopy. But it may also be because the TV culture, in which the Thomasons are preeminent, has taught us to accept politics as part of the general buzz. Like Clinton, the Thomasons are technocratic populists, preaching a gospel of change which doesn't orate from an angry gut but seems to travel via fiber optics. Their shows reflect the opportunism of smart people seizing their chance to expound. And smart people are like anybody else when they expound—hard to shove back into the trunk.

The primary pulpit for the Thomasons remains *Designing Women*, now in its seventh season. The designing women have never done much designing. Their interior-decorating firm is simply a forum that enables them to dish. The characters seem sandbagged on the set, baying to each other from the far reaches of the Naugahyde. In the first few seasons, their idle blab had enough bounce to disguise how stationary the show was. The major draw was Delta Burke. Big-round, Burke settled into the sofa as if it were her baby bath. The echo in her features of Elizabeth Taylor's suggested a luxury fund of food-libido. Her pampered conceits clashed with the loftier social austerities of Dixie Carter's Julia, who was Bloodworth-Thomason's ongoing op-ed page on the issues of the day. AIDS, battered wives, pornography, breast implants, sexual harassment—she always had an opinion to peel. But whenever she began to drape herself too grandly across the screen a quick cut of Burke creating a thought balloon above her head with a tuck of her chin would salvage the scene. Burke and Carter balanced each other—the public and the private sectors in separate cartons.

One carton began to spoil. After bad-mouthing the producers in print, Burke, who seemed to expand into an International House of Pancakes before our eyes, was wedged off the sofa. Replacements were hired, but the indent remained. Absent Burke, Dixie Carter anchored the spotlight as queen of the cold cream. Delivering every directive like Tallulah Bankhead descending a staircase, she became the show's political spokesmodel, speechifying to the masses. Let others grub in the gutter—her Julia Sugarbaker upholds the honor of noblesse oblige.

As Bloodworth-Thomason became more confident in her outgoing messages, Julia wasn't the only one sounding like an op-ed page. Everyone began vibrating at the same frequency. In the series' most famous episode, the designing women took time out from their vacant schedules to debate the Anita Hill–Clarence Thomas controversy, leaving no question about where the show's sympathies lay. "We just gave poor Anita Hill a little twenty-minute pat on the back after they took her down for six nights," said Bloodworth-Thomason. This was a first: using fictional characters in an entertainment show to rectify a perceived political wrong. It put Washington on notice that prime time was now a policy player, part of the news loop. For me, the Anita Hill episode was a pill to watch, not because of its pamphleteering but because of its snitty tone. It's tricky squeezing comedy out of indignation; the actor is reduced to a placard. (This season, Judith Ivey has been added to the cast, shaking her jewelry as a brassy dame inspired by the liberal Texas icons Molly Ivins and Governor Ann Richards.) A similar stiffness befell this season's *Murphy Brown* big-deal comeback at Dan Quayle, in which Candice Bergen introduced single-parent families as if they were Easter Seal posters. The screen went inactive, as it often does on *Designing Women.*

The limp staging in *Evening Shade* often reflects the lack of anything better to do. If *Designing Women* is the Thomasons' soapbox, this show, with Burt Reynolds as a high-school football coach, is their footrest. It's meant to mend that part of the mind which politics has callused. A plywood piece of pastoral, *Evening Shade* (the original title was *Arkansas*—Hillary Clinton suggested the evocative name change) is set in a town off the main drag, where time has its own slow strum. "Every day that passes is slower than molasses," Dr. John rasps in the theme song. Sunset is spent on the front porch, waiting for the crickets to lay down a sound track. The air is so thick with nostalgia and night thoughts that the present seems to be happening in the past. The characters have already become their former selves.

It's tempting to divvy *Designing Women* and *Evening Shade* between the Thomasons. With Julia Sugarbaker as her megaphone, *Designing Women* is Bloodworth-Thomason's baby. Since Harry Thomason coached football in Little Rock (he met Bill Clinton through his brother, Danny, who was a teacher), *Evening Shade* would seem to occupy his side of the ledger. The relation between the two series is dialectical. Where *Designing Women* takes a step forward, *Evening Shade* takes a step back. The characters on *Evening Shade* try to cope with the changes that the ones on *Designing Women* advocate. In the season premiere, Coach Reynolds chained himself to a fence to prevent the razing of an old store of his daddy's to make room for a car wash. This quixotic protest against progress was a prelude to a sensitive-man monologue about the coach's not knowing whether his father had really loved him. There were pieces of Reynolds's autobiography in the story—especially in the mention of how his dad filled the entire doorframe. But the monologue also wore the unmistakable shadow of Clinton's acceptance speech in its eulogizing of a father too early dead. The show had enough subtext to float a sympathy vote.

With *Hearts Afire*, the Thomasons are operating in open daylight. Hammocked between *Evening Shade* and *Murphy Brown* on Monday nights, it's one of the few can't-fail entries on the fall schedule. A romantic comedy set in the nation's capital, it fields John Ritter as a Senate aide to a Foghorn Leghorn filibusterer played by George Gaynes. Into Ritter's office, as if fresh from *Casablanca*, materializes Georgie Ann Lahti (Markie Post) in a trenchcoat. Post (a close friend of Bloodworth-Thomason's) waves her cigarettes around with the weary shrug of a woman who has been places, done things, faced some crummy dawns. Like the recovering alcoholic Murphy Brown, the nicotined Georgie is an addictive personality accustomed to glitz. But she hasn't forgotten her humble roots. (Who has, these days?) Traveling with Georgie is the black woman who raised her, Beah Richards's Miss Lula, whom Ritter refers to as her mammy. Miss Lula explains that she has to keep her legs elevated, a-cause of her diabetes.

Like Miss Lula's complaint, everything about *Hearts Afire* seems a bit "Huh?" Why would someone with Georgie's famous connections be reduced to acting as press secretary for a senator whose politics she abhors? Why does she move into Ritter's town house, Miss Lula again in tow? Given the simple premises of other Mozark productions, the disjointed foundation of *Hearts Afire* is a jolt.

The show feeds on distraction until its eyeballs deviate. A raucous party at Ritter's town house in the hourlong premiere (directed by Harry Thomason) was as chaotic as a bad Blake Edwards comedy, with Georgie interviewing a homeless couple in the kitchen and pecking their responses into a laptop while guests flee a bee attack in the living room. Later, as Ritter soaks in a bathroom equipped with a water-god spout and a built-in fireplace, Georgie slides fully clothed into the tub to give him a French kiss, only to stop him from further

ado. She just isn't . . . ready. His probing manhood raises boundary
issues for her. I know it does for me.

This being the nineties, Ritter doesn't take rejection like a gent; he
complains about her sticking her tongue down his throat. You can tell
he's upset by how tight he ties his bathrobe sash. Why is *Hearts Afire*
so hung up on hopping the bunny? The hitch, I suspect, is that CBS
insisted that the series not be overtly partisan during the election year.
Which leaves the Thomasons stuck with trying to make an apolitical political comedy. Since they don't have the patience or the knack
to mimic the pitter-patter of the bureaucratic process (think of the
caterpillarish tickle of England's *Yes, Minister*), they're leaning on that
old reliable, sex. (They're not FOBs for nothing.) But if the politics
are muted, class consciousness seeps through the cracks. The choicest
sneers in *Hearts Afire* are directed at Beth Broderick's Dee Dee Starr,
a blowsy Senate receptionist, whose night-club-stripper name sums
up her bimbo status. Barely able to focus, Dee Dee is described as
being so dumb she thinks Mount Rushmore is a natural rock formation (old joke, by the way). It isn't her lack of morals or brains that the
show disapproves of. What the digs against her represent is a kind
of class snobbery, with which *Designing Women* is also rife. (And the
sentimental condescension of *Evening Shade* isn't much better.)

On race, the Thomasons tread more carefully. (Who wouldn't?)
Like Clinton himself, wooing what *The Economist* calls "that elusive
white beast, the Reagan Democrat," the Thomasons' sitcoms are
a touch standoffish about blacks, a bit rote in their rhetoric. They
include black characters, make the right noises about their awful
plight, but bar them from full access to the action. These characters
seldom go one-on-one with the camera. The function of Meshach
Taylor on *Designing Women* and of Ossie Davis, using his Ol' Man
River voice, on *Evening Shade* is to occupy the catbird seat and provide a wise, rueful chuckle about the foolish antics of these white
folks. Perhaps the addition of Sheryl Lee Ralph (from *Mistress*) to
Designing Women will help curb this sense of tokenism, but at the
moment it's as if each show allotted one Black Friend to authenticate
its characters' liberal credentials. Miss Lula, on *Hearts Afire*, isn't even
that. In the first episode, she's an exhibit from the Colored Museum,
stored upstairs for safekeeping.

TV programmers, like politicians, have to learn to juggle constitu-
encies, jolly them along. The knock on Clinton is that he's too eager
to be liked by everyone he meets, that there's no man inside, nothing but stuffed politician. But the beating he took in the primaries

left lumps that bare themselves on C-SPAN in the letdown moments between campaign stops. He doesn't come across as complacent. For all their frantic endeavor, the Thomasons do. As political advisers, the Thomasons have proved themselves invaluable. They may have earned their own wing in the White House. But the cant of *Designing Women*, the corn of *Evening Shade*, the crust of *Hearts Afire*—it's Hollywood liberalism laying down the cultural law on everyone's behalf. Sitcoms such as these want to tell you not only what to think but how to feel. At least they don't shout at us, as Norman Lear did. They're content to nag us to death.

The New Yorker, October 12, 1992

"X" Factor

The X-Files

Certain responses are guaranteed. In biology class, there was always some jokester who would try to gross out his lab partner by hiding dissected frog parts in his or her desk—usually hers. The girl would open a candy wrapper only to find a frog's eye staring back at her. Advances in special effects have enabled filmmakers to elevate silly pranks into schlock horror. HBO's campy anthology series *Tales from the Crypt*, also syndicated on Fox, dangles a buggy eyeball in almost every episode, topping a cannibal platter of guts, stumps, and slimy gunk. Its Grand Guignol doesn't stick to the mind. Playing with one's food and making a mess is easy. What's hard is giving shape to the shadows on the ceiling—creating horror not out of human meat but out of the unresolved business of the unconscious. *The X-Files* (Fox, Fridays), which is the work of Chris Carter, employs scare tactics—blood spitting from a face slapped by an invisible hand, a locustlike plague infesting a courtroom—but it doesn't let them upstage its speculative purpose. Each episode is a mood piece—a queasy odyssey. It's television's first otherworldly procedural. Although its ratings have been in the basement, *The X-Files* has been building a cult audience and has the makings of a classic. (The show has been renewed for a second season.) *The X-Files* is as scary as *The Twilight Zone*, and much sexier.

Like *The Twilight Zone*, *The X-Files* expresses a national unease, which helps explain its hold on our nerves. *The Twilight Zone*, first broadcast in 1959, was the dark negative of the sunny snapshots of suburbia shown on sitcoms like *Ozzie and Harriet* and *Leave It to Beaver*. Created by Rod Serling, who also acted as its host, the show served as a night watchman to the anxieties of the atomic age. It presented worst-case scenarios of what might happen if the launch buttons were pushed: neighbors beat on the doors of bomb shelters closed to outsiders; Norman Rockwell villages became ghost towns, a tattered calendar telling us when time stopped; on bare plains, survivors shriveled in the sun like bugs under a magnifying glass. Whether the threat was missiles or flying saucers, our skies were not safe. Other planets offered no refuge, as astronauts found themselves wriggling in air, tweezered between giant fingers.

The cardboard construction of *The Twilight Zone* didn't cheapen its sense of dread; it functioned as thin insulation against the abyss. The show's very lack of production values promoted a stark-bare allegorical staging. I remember having nightmares over an episode in which doll-like characters were trapped in a barrel, verbally abusing one another for what seemed like eternity—a pocket version of Sartre's *No Exit*. (Hell is other puppets.) That toy barrel, like the show's bomb shelters, reflected a bunker mentality. The question posed by *The Twilight Zone* was: Who will survive the next blast? And will survival be anything more than death warmed over?

The Cold War is absent from *The X-Files*, replaced by a more cosmic paranoia. The show reflects the end of the millennium, the flip side of the New Age. Beneath the soothing cover of incense, mantras, and Tibetan chants, rude beasts are awakening—Gnosticism reborn. The term *X-Files* refers to hush-hush, top-secret FBI case studies of paranormal activity. Investigating new outbreaks are the FBI agents Fox "Spooky" Mulder (David Duchovny), a believer, and Dana Scully (Gillian Anderson), a skeptic. Their partnership achieves a rare parity between the sexes, a personal regard shown in subtle body shifts and a steady rebound of eye contact. They're more than ghostbusters. All escapees from the netherworld are in their jurisdiction, be they vampires, poltergeists, astral projections, firestarters, telekinetics, satanic cultists, psychic surgeons, alien abductees, possessed animals, replicants, reincarnated spirits, shape shifters, or local chapters of the international brotherhood of zombies. Occult signs abound. Pentagrams. Crop circles. Crucifixes. The show's Sherlock Holmes satisfactions derive from its forensic zeal in the face of garish horror, its refusal to be ruffled or bumped off course. This refusal also accounts for the show's deadpan humor, as each eruption in the energy field is met with dry-ice understatement by Mulder or capped by an inspired sick joke. (At the end of the firestarter episode, the human torch—sealed in a hyperbaric tube, his body blistered with burns—was asked by a nurse if there was anything she could get him. Turning his charred face to the camera, he said, "I'm just dying for a cigarette.")

What's distinctive about *The X-Files*, apart from its ingenious story lines and gun-swivel camerawork, is its suffused atmosphere. Shot in Vancouver, the show's exteriors seem familiar yet anonymous—muted. David Lynch wrecked the trance of *Twin Peaks* when he abandoned all interest in even a quaint semblance of normality and began to strobe the screen in a fit of expressionism. (His feature film *Twin Peaks: Fire Walk with Me* was even trippier.) *The X-Files* doesn't make the mistake of elevating its sensibility at the expense of its subjects. It takes time to seep into its surroundings. An episode about a bisexual succubus stalking the disco scene evoked the warehouse purgatory of the porn director John Leslie's *Catwoman* films, with their deep blues, prowling shadows, and industrial din.

Once an episode earns your faith, no avenue seems too far out. One outstanding *X-File* episode began with a camera pan of suburban backyards across isolated squares of pasture. A young girl clutching a stuffed animal draws the attention of a passing couple, who follow her into her backyard. On the swing set, her father sits slumped, his back to us. In his neck are a pair of puncture wounds. "Daddy?" No answer. Daddy's been drained of blood. Vampires? Cattle mutilators upgrading to human prey? No, this blood tap proves to be the by-product of a cloning experiment that resulted in a spate of bad seeds. All the female clones were named Eve and were endowed with extra chromosomes that made them super-smart, super-strong, psychotic, and prone to suicide. (There's an amazing shot of all the identical Eves posed for a group portrait—at a swing set.) The episode ends with the last remaining clones, Eve 9 and Eve 10—telepathic twins, played with spooky calm by sisters Erika and Sabrina Krievins—imprisoned in an institution for the criminally insane, an iron dungeon fit for Hannibal Lecter. (Visitors are issued panic buttons.) They appear to be there for the duration. But the last shot is of their clone mother, the Eve of Eves, come to claim her daughters. "How did you know I'd come for you?" she asks. Eve 9: "We just knew." Eve 10: "We just knew."

Nothing is put to rest on *The X-Files*. The open-endedness of the Eve episode and others indicates not only the untrappable nature of these forces but the show's refusal to pronounce final judgment. Where *The Twilight Zone* was wrapped tight, everything tied together with an O. Henry twist, *The X-Files* is suspended. Its adversaries aren't evil; they're "genetically driven"—damaged from within. Absolution was even granted to a serial killer on death row, played by Brad Dourif as if he himself had been kept in a box. Claiming that he could channel the voice of a kidnap victim, the killer tried to cut himself a deal: I help catch the kidnapper, you spare me the gas chamber. As Dourif dialed into different psyches, he worked his face like a quick-change artist—you could see his pale features bubble and form lumps before they set into the face of someone new. What made the performance more than a technical feat was the passionate overflow he brought to his plight—his redneck fury to hold on to the last inch of life. In league with the dead, he had the cracked karma that Norman Mailer claimed for Gary Gilmore.

The show squirms most when it is closest to the fetal position. Stenciled across the stormy sky at the beginning of each *X-File* episode are the words "THE TRUTH IS OUT THERE." But the show is much more of an inward journey than even the hunkered-down *Twilight Zone* was. The truth is that the general population shows less interest in studying the sky for answers than it did in the early days of the space race. The fascination with UFOs has flagged as the focus has shifted to alien abduction, which is more of a psychological event. Even the starship voyages on *Star Trek* look nostalgic now—rides on a riverboat. As the world becomes more wired, a giant cranium webbed with computer lines, it becomes too enmeshed in its own mental processes to extend an eye into the universe. Constant self-monitoring can lead to sick thought, hypochondria. *The X-Files* is the product of yuppie morbidity, a creeping sense of personal mortality. (The sense of mortality in *The Twilight Zone* was the prospect of mass annihilation—*We're all gonna die!*) It tries to cheat the big sleep by prying open so many doors into the beyond. Where middlebrow culture has begun to ponder angels again, pop culture courts immortality through soul migration or in hologram images or through the rejuvenation of cells or conversion into electrical charges. Nobody on *The X-Files* is ever *dead* dead. People die with a shudder, their souls removed like luggage, to be rerouted elsewhere. Perhaps the afterlife will be part of the information superhighway, a hub in cyberspace. What's erotic about the show is its slow progression from reverie to revelation, stopping just short of rapture. It wants to swoon, but swooning would mean shutting its eyes, and there's so much to see.

The New Yorker, April 18, 1994

Prime Time's Graduation

After I fell out of love with movies (new movies, that is—classic Hollywood I still adulate), I realized during my rare visits to the multiplex that what I missed wasn't the big screen, that Mount Rushmore larger-than-lifeness, but the short vacation in the receptive dark, the comfort and calm of the blinds being lowered on the city outside. But even that respite is too often tattered by the cell-phone compulsives texting and checking their messages, whatever spell the filmmakers attempted to cast spoiled by these mousy little screens flashing their gray pallor. As movie theaters switch from film to digital projection, home flat-screens take up a wall, Blu-Ray discs exhume masterpiece-painting volumes of color and intricate detail from popular releases, and the unholy moviegoing experience cries out for human-pest control, cinema has lost its sanctuary allure and aesthetic edge over television, which as a medium has the evolutionary advantage. Movies will never die, not as long as a director like Terrence Malick can make every green blade of grass sway like the first dance of creation, but TV is where the action is, the addictions forged, the dream machine operating on all cylinders. As I write this, the Academy Awards are a few days away, with *The Artist* the odds-on best-picture winner. Does *anyone* think *The Artist* is better than *Mad Men*?

Even in cine-mad Manhattan, where the admonitory ghost of Susan Sontag haunts theaters by night, the new movie that everybody's talking about is being talked about by a shrinking number of everybodies. It's seldom the presiding topic of cocktail chat and intellectual quarrel, as it was when critic Pauline Kael led the wagon train. (Her successors at *The New Yorker*, David Denby and Anthony Lane, might as well be tinkling the piano in the hotel lobby for all the commotion they create.) Movies divide and stratify; television, like sports, is the democratic includer. Mention *Breaking Bad*, Madonna's Super Bowl halftime Cleopatra-a-go-go procession, Abby Lee Miller's latest volcanic diatribe on *Dance Moms*, or *Downton Abbey* and all the birdies start to pipe up, except for the one pill present (there's always at least one), who takes pride in declaiming that he or she never watches television—they only listen to NPR. Pity these poor castaways. They must stand there with glassy, uncomprehending eyes while the rest of us tongue-flap about the latest installment of a favorite series down to the last crumb, like Proust scholars. A sophisticated sensation such as public television's creamy soap *Downton Abbey* (*Upstairs Downstairs* with fancier airs and more elbow room) corrals an audience and achieves a critical mass that explodes and expands beyond its actual viewership, the series's cast, costumes, and signature strokes (most of them executed from on high by Maggie Smith, as if she were a pithy Lady Bracknell Pez dispenser) inspiring tributaries of parodies, homages, fan fiction, fashion shoots, and tweedy commentary. Like *Twin Peaks, 24, Mad Men,* and *The Sopranos* before it, *Downton Abbey* enriches the iconography and collective lore of pop culture. It replenishes the stream. (It also provides the perfect layup for PBS's next prestige import, starting in April: the BBC adaptation of Sebastian Faulks's best-selling novel *Birdsong,* which will once again elegantly chuck us into the WW I trenches.) By contrast: for those of us who have fallen out of romance with movies, its franchise blockbusters seem to be leeching off the legacy of pop culture and cinema history, squandering the inheritance with endless superhero sequels and video-game emulations that digitize action stars into avatars and motion-capture figures, a mutant species with an emotive range running strictly in shades of bold. And those films that aren't aiming for an opening-weekend monster kill seem to dwell solely within a realm of discourse dominated by film bloggers and Twitter twitchers, these configurations of loyalists and lost-causers adopting a film that they fell for at some festival and cradling it like a football as they chug downfield in a deserted stadium. *Margaret, Bellflower, Martha Marcy May Marlene, The Future, Shame, Take Shelter*—these are quality titles (so I assume, I haven't seen most of them, I shall Netflix them in the fullness of time) that become objects of obsession for a few but float in limbo for those not on screening or "screener" lists. The controversial, heavily anticipated spooker *We Need to Talk About Kevin* fizzed out at the box office from too much foreplay; by the time civilians got to see it, it had already been pre-gnawed to death in the press and online. Arty entries may accrue a cult status over time that collects more disciples into the fold, but they lose the catalytic moment to set the culture humming.

Whereas those who missed out on what all the initial fuss was about with *Breaking Bad*, *The Walking Dead*, *Game of Thrones* (it and *Spartacus* spearheading premium cable's brawny-buxom pagan revival), and *Dexter* are able to catch up with past seasons on DVD—an immersion course of binge viewing—and bring themselves up to speed in time for the next season's debut, fully conversant with the workings of Walt's woefully understaffed meth lab, say, or the latest trend lines in zombie migration. And those who missed out completely on *The Wire* can get hold of the boxed set and ingest the entire drug saga, boring all their friends with revelations about plot twists that everyone else marveled at five years ago.

The characters in a thick-tapestried, treachery-strewn series such as *The Wire* acquire dimensions, depths, personal flaws, moral failings, and discordant quirks that seem integral and variable, not pinned on like prom corsages. They're given enough time to sit and stew, to mull over the next move, a luxury seldom extended to movie characters (with a few notable exceptions—Brad Pitt's Billy Beane in *Moneyball*, for one). These beats of downtime are how TV protagonists and those in their orbit take a novelistic hold on viewers, each story arc unveiling another aspect of their personality without extinguishing the inner shadow of a Don Draper, the ruthless ingenuity of Walt in *Breaking Bad*. The slowly etched outlines of psychological terrain are what endow ambiguous heroes with their own 3-D quality, a by-product of excellent scriptwriting that doesn't feel the compulsion to connect every ridiculous dot. Actors, in turn, don't have to serve as pointers, message carriers. Because Hollywood movies have so much more money riding on them, casting usually becomes a case of making a sure bet—casting against type or gambling on an unknown quantity can jeopardize financing. Television allows more leeway and chanciness, especially pay cable. It took Starz's original series *Boss* to transmute the pedantic comic vanity and élan of Kelsey Grammer into Tony Soprano tainted pork—to bring out the bully. It took HBO's *Boardwalk Empire* to turn Steve Buscemi, a cranky fixture of indie film (the boho in the bowling shirt), into a bootleg kingpin whose dark circles under the eyes add volume to his glowering, insomniac glare. It also took *Boardwalk Empire* to properly forefront the phosphorescent glamour of Gretchen Mol, whom too many had relegated to a joke after her notorious nipple cover for this magazine, despite the terrific performances she later gave in *The Notorious Bettie Page* and lesser flings. But then, television is a far more hospitable medium to women than movies, where glamour is now a goner.

Movie actresses may receive the red-carpet treatment for iconic portraiture (Helen Mirren as Queen Elizabeth in *The Queen*, Michelle Williams as Marilyn Monroe in *My Week with Marilyn*, Meryl Streep as Margaret Thatcher in *The Iron Lady*) in star vehicles where everyone else seems to recede—roles that sop up most of the juice. But each of the films parenthesized above could have just as easily been done as an HBO or Showtime docudrama without suffering any loss of scale or density of detail. It's the contemporary woman that movies don't know what to do with, other than bathe her in a bridal glow in romantic comedies where both the romance and the comedy are artificial sweeteners. (And it's not even a sumptuous bridal glow. The flight attendants on ABC's *Pan Am* are more flatteringly lit, framed, and costumed than the female stars of most movies, whose tensely toned emaciation cries out for a cookie.) To trace the arc of Reese Witherspoon from *Legally Blonde* to *This Means War* is a depressing business, and the overpraise for *Bridesmaids*—a lumpily paced, indifferently shot, distended exercise with funny scenes fending off plotty inertia—reflected a craving for something more real and bumptious from the rom-com formula. Beyond the rom com, however, it's a famine zone, apart from a few indies and whatever screenwriter Diablo Cody (*Young Adult*) has brewing. If it's complex, prickly women you find wanting—the successors to the unlikely 1970s feministas played by Jane Fonda (*Klute*), Ellen Burstyn (*Alice Doesn't Live Here Anymore*), Jill Clayburgh (*An Unmarried Woman*)—then it's TV that'll hook you up.

The crafty survivalism and bureaucratic finagling of Edie Falco's Nurse Jackie, that angel of mercy as pillhead junkie. The sly devilry of Mary Louise Parker's pot-peddling suburban mom on *Weeds*. The slack-jawed incredulity and crusader indignation of Laura Dern in the minimalist corporate-drone parable *Enlightened*. The wicked machinations of Glenn Close on *Damages*, the echidna on wheels that is Katie Sagal's vengeance-is-mine matriarch on *Sons of Anarchy*, the whiplash malice of Jane Lynch on *Glee*. And, for the young and the listless, the quartet of twentysomethings scraping by in the upcoming HBO series *Girls*. An attempt to create a rookie division in the *Sex and the City* genre (signaled by a *Sex and the City* poster in the premiere episode), *Girls* doesn't cater to the shiny pretty richy-bitchy stick-figure expectations of a CW audience bred on *Gossip Girl* and the rebooted *90210;* it's moored to the pokier manner and metabolism of its writer-director-star, Lena Dunham, whose low-budget, tightly enclosed, first-personal debut film, *Tiny Furniture,* made a critical splash that helped get her profiled in *The New Yorker,* which means we're stuck with her. How you react to *Girls* will depend heavily on how you respond to Dunham as a screen presence. Some may find Dunham's Hannah something of a slow load, passive, shapeless, and self-infantilizing, a clogged-sinus throwback to Rhoda Morgenstern's sister Brenda, whom Julie Kavner played in the old *Mary Tyler Moore Show* spinoff. But if the show notches any notoriety, it should inspire a decent skit on *Saturday Night Live,* which has had a bang-up season so far.

In fact, anyone looking for comedy should just nest at home, because Hollywood comedy has become a plague, a blight, and an affront to humanity. The gross-out element in film comedy (puke, poop, sperm, breast milk—any bodily fluid with projectile possibilities) has gotten so prevalent and predictable that it's as if filmmakers had their heads diapered. It's pointless complaining about it now—it makes one sound like such a church lady—but can't movie comedies at least be rudimentarily, technically competent? Whenever I catch a chunk of an Adam Sandler comedy on cable, it looks as badly shot and goofily tossed off as a Jerry Lewis gag reel once he hit the late downslide with *Hardly Working* and *Cracking Up.* Feature-length film comedy is harder to pull off than the episodic sitcom—it doesn't have the same factory machinery up and running, teams of writers putting familiar characters through permutations—but that doesn't explain the widening quality gap that makes movie humor look like a genetic defective. (Check out *Bucky Larson: Born to Be a Star* if you doubt my word.) There's more imaginative attack, ensemble mesh, unmuzzled personality, and exuberant id in *Arrested Development* (rerunning on IFC, with talk of a TV revival and a film to follow), *It's Always Sunny in Philadelphia, Curb Your Enthusiasm, 30 Rock, Modern Family, The Office, Community, Parks and Recreation, The Big Bang Theory* (Jim Parsons's Sheldon: the Niles Crane of nerd-dom), the cellular regeneration that is *The Simpsons,* and the crazed rapport between late-night host Craig Ferguson and his gay robot sidekick, Geoff, than in almost any recent Hollywood comedy I've seen, apart from *Horrible Bosses,* which has the makings of a reprobate classic. Its three male leads all came from TV: Jason Bateman (*Arrested Development*), Jason Sudeikis (*Saturday Night Live*), and Charlie Day (*It's*

Always Sunny in Philadelphia), which only reinforces whatever point I'm trying to make. TV also found the perfect fairy jar for Zooey Deschanel (the Fox sitcom *New Girl*), providing a role model for a new generation of Tinker Bells, something even a manly man like me can appreciate.

Vanity Fair, May 2012

Who's Laughing Now?
Is Stand-Up Comedy Dead on Its Feet?

According to recent reports in *New York* and *The Washington Post*, once-bustling comedy clubs resemble the mouths of abandoned mine shafts. It's desolate inside their doors, the laughter is thin and lonely. Where'd everybody go? "Comedy is the rock of the eighties" was the boast of that decade—not an absurd claim given that flamethrowers like Sam Kinison and Andrew Dice Clay were filling arenas and enjoying the raucous adulation once reserved for guitar gods. Where Lenny Bruce aspired to jazz virtuosity, Kinison and Clay strove for heavy-metal hegemony, hitting their punch lines like power chords. And club comics required a lot less upkeep than the average rock band: they didn't need piles of amplifiers, tedious sound checks, and numerous backstage amenities (blow jobs, etc.) to keep them operational. In the eighties, it seemed, every building with a liquor license stuck a microphone in front of a brick wall and called itself a comedy club. These new venues sported cute names like Giggles, Yuk-Yuks, the Funny Bone, the Laff Trak, and Stitches. The more established spots, like Caroline's and the Improv, became the sites of cable stand-up showcases (which are still shown in endless repeats). Comics also hit the college circuit. But, to paraphrase Kingsley Amis, More means Worse. The product became diluted as too many peppy faces rolled off the assembly line with their eight-by-ten glossies, and the club boom proved a boon for mediocrity. The élite talents stuck to movies (Robin Williams, Eddie Murphy, Michael Keaton), landed their own sitcoms (Roseanne Barr, Jerry Seinfeld, Brett Butler, Garry Shandling, Martin Lawrence, Tim Allen), frazzled themselves frail (Richard Pryor), or met their deaths (Andy Kaufman, Kinison), leaving the B-squad players to line up against the brick wall. The audience also dwindled: the mobs of yuppies that once hunched over drink-filled tables began nesting at home, treating themselves to Blockbuster nights. Gradually, as the club scene has lost its flash, pockets of "alternative" comedy have popped up in places like Rebar, the downtown-Manhattan hangout that offers weekly workshops where novice and pro stand-ups take practice cuts at new material. (They're like poetry jams, with a lot less posturing.)

Television, too, is flirting with alternatives. This summer, cable's Comedy Central is staging stand-up in unorthodox formats in an attempt to revive it. The results are spotty, as results often are. A mere distraction called *Comedy del Sol*, hosted by Richard Jeni (the star of the really bad sitcom *Platypus Man*), is taped on the beach in Santa Monica, which has proved to be a mistake. Stand-up comedy needs the contained energy of a nocturnal pit in which to feed and free-associate. It thrives in strip joints and nightclubs, where money and sex provide extra friction. As *Comedy del Sol* demonstrates, humor dissipates in an al fresco environment friendly to Frisbee-tossing and watching the sunset: whatever, man. By contrast, *The Real Deal*, which plunks five top comics—Allan Havey, Robert Wuhl, Kevin Pollak, John Mendoza, and John Caponera—around a poker table in Lake Tahoe, couldn't be more of a sealed crate, its crew of smart mouths jousting for bragging rights as they swap jokes and compete for real money. The jokes they tell—too long to repeat and raunchy enough to turn Philip Roth pink—involve parrots, penis implants, and basic infidelity. Comedy is delivered in such abstract shorthand today that it's easy to forget the structural pleasures of the "Bolero" buildup, the incidental detail, and the payoff of a traditional joke. The body English these pros put into their jokes, even while sitting down, suggests the avid zeal of pool hustlers anticipating the carom. *The Real Deal* also features very funny impressions, such as Robert Wuhl's Broderick Crawford of *Highway Patrol* attempting a stand-up act— "Two Jews walk into a bar, *gimme a big ten-four!*" This riff session of guy humor achieves a retro Rat Pack/Cassavetes-cast squad-house camaraderie as the comics scatter chips and flirt with the cocktail waitress (it's like eavesdropping on the rough draft of a David Mamet play), but there's too much self-conscious jabber and awkward camera work once they get over the humps of their best stories. It's an experiment worth repeating, with a different set of guys.

The most self-consciously alternative series is *Comedy Product*, hosted and co-produced by Janeane Garofalo, who's an odd duck. A pie-faced comic actress—she appeared in *Reality Bites*, endured a dismal season on *Saturday Night Live*, plays a talent booker on *The Larry Sanders Show*, and has joined Michael Moore's mischief-makers on *TV Nation*—Garofalo has a full platter of what might be called self-image issues. She is, in short, her own biggest bringdown. Her production company is called I Hate Myself, and that sentiment is expanded upon in her introductory remarks: "I smell bad, as a rule. . . . And I think that it's because I hate myself so much that the odor comes from the inside and just goes out, and it's like kind of hummus meets vinyl, just pours off of me, and it's just the stench of utter defeat and unrealized goals. And with that, let me bring on your first act." Try following that, Tonto.

The format for *Comedy Product* is modeled on the workshops at Rebar, where the comics perform in an informal setting, sometimes pausing to consult their notes, which are always crumpled, for that authentic creative look. At both places, the comics who fall flat are the slackers who come so unprepared that their faces appear sleep-lined, as if they had arrived late for class with their mouths full of lint. They tend to meander. It's one thing to perform new material; it's another thing to perform no material. Some comedians not only make a personal impression but poke fun at the very concept of alternative comedy. Andy Kindler, for example, has a helpful suggestion: "A lot of people want to know how can we make this alternative comedy more popular, and my theory is, Make it more mainstream—that's my theory right there. Alternative comedy means talking about yourself. 'I woke up today and I read the paper and forget-about-it, right?'" The curly-haired Kindler is a tight-wound comic with a well-developed persecution complex. His humor is based on his own imbalance; he's so touchy that the least little remark makes him emphatic. On being warned by a commercial director not to be "shticky," he says, "You know how I hear that? 'I hate the *Jews*,' that's how I hear that. 'You are a *Jewy* Jew Jew. I hate you, Jew.' Nobody hates the Jews more than the Jews, though, I'll tell you that." A Pez dispenser of passive aggression (he and Garofalo are soul mates), Kindler fantasizes about starring in his own Jean-Claude Van Damme–style action vehicle, pointing his finger at the camera and issuing such macho threats as "Don't get in Andy's way, unless you're willing to play the role of caretaker" and "If you're gonna hang out with Andy, bring a sweater—'cause it's gonna get *chilly*."

Comedy Central doesn't have a monopoly on the new stand-ups. The top cat of the alternative scene in Manhattan is Marc Maron, who performs regularly at Rebar and will headline his own special on HBO on September 7. Unlike the typical alternative comic, Maron doesn't content himself with hovering over the morning paper; he incarnates the news. He's that New York specialty—the well-informed wise guy. Dressed in black, and sporting John Lennon granny glasses and sideburns, Maron looks more like a seventies protest singer than like a stand-up; pretending to be stoned onstage, he does a Mr. Natural cakewalk, his eyes glinty with pothead greed. His HBO special, taped at San Francisco's Fillmore Auditorium, leans heavily toward the hippie-yippie left, literally flipping the middle finger at Rush Limbaugh, Newt Gingrich, and the Christian Coalition. "Fuckin' crazy-ass Republicans," he thinks aloud. Like Kindler, he also explodes Jewish stereotypes from the inside: "The great thing about being Jewish is that we got all the money—all of it—and we run the media. I'm surprised I have time to do this [gig]." In his tendentious moments, though, he often hammers his points too hard, as if trying to ring the bell at the county fair. His humor works better in looser imaginative sorties, such as his agnostic take on the information superhighway. His theory of the paradigm shift is that we're moving out of a "petroleum-based phallic era," defined by missiles and hardware, "into an information-based scrotal era." Ergo, "it's not about big cocks, it's about information storage—it's about big balls." Since, as Maron notes, no woman has ever been heard to moan in breathy admiration, "Wow, that's a lot of memory," techno geeks will have to invent their own play doll. The day isn't far off when science will create "a fuckable computer": "Imagine walking in on somebody and they got virtual-reality glasses on, some sort of weird keyboard, and this genital mitt. 'Hey, get outta here, son, Daddy's working!'" In the meantime, he has a friend who spends eight hours a day playing video games with some guy in France. When his friend says, "The computer's a tool," Maron replies, "No, the computer's a toy—*you're* a tool. It's using you to get to me."

Comics like Maron are right to resist surfing the Third Wave. Surrendering to technology nullifies their unique impact. At Rebar, you sometimes see comics consulting material stored on their PowerBooks before they take their turn, and comics will no doubt be doing their acts in cyberspace cabarets. But without the sweaty urgency of the comic, the contorted Kabuki faces concealing a sniper's eye, the hint of sacrificial flesh, the words might as well come by Western Union. The brick walls of the classic comedy club served as a reminder that every comic who takes the stage faces a potential firing squad. This risk of public rejection gives comedy its existential edge, even to comics who perform by rote. The attitude of the ringside cynic is, Anybody can be funny—what makes you special? Unable to formulate a gut response, a lot of the younger stand-ups seem to be abdicating their bodies and marketing themselves as mild antidepressants— shying away from the effort of imposing too much, in a period double-glazed with irony and deadpan cool. They're so depersonalized that they're already half adrift in cyberspace. They'll be the ones wiped off the slate when the next rebound in comedy occurs. And it will. Watching these programs, you feel that, although the current scene may be directionless, the best comics—Maron, Kindler, the poker buddies on *The Real Deal,* even Garofalo (when she isn't acting skanky)—haven't lost their drive or their killer instinct. There's no dearth of talent. Stand-up comedy in the nineties is suffering from a case of charisma deficiency. Andrew Dice Clay had more charisma than these guys, and he wasn't even that good! As if to atone for his trespasses, Andrew Clay—he's dropped the "Diceman" moniker and attitude—is starring in his own CBS sitcom this fall, playing a lovable lug. Quite a comedown for a man who would be king.

The New Yorker, August 14, 1995

Late Night

What Keeps Johnny on Top? Insincerity!

Quiet, please: Carnac must have silence. "Johnny Carson." (He rips open the envelope.) And the question is: Who is the most enigmatic performer on television? (Silence from the audience.) May your next haircut be performed with a Texas Chain Saw. . . .

On that night at the Westchester Premier Theatre, a traffic-choking blizzard descended. Yet despite the arctic assault, empty seats were surprisingly few, and after a greasily frenetic performance by the Manhattan Transfer the *Tonight* theme blared and Johnny Carson made his entrance. He looked great: handsome in his smooth-fitting tux and coppery California tan, vigorous in his stride, commandingly confident in his comportment. As thunderclaps of applause swept over him, Carson crooned, "Like a rhinestone cowwwwwwwwwwwwwboy," and the crowd hi-yo'd like a multitude of Ed McMahons. Their cattle calls were acknowledged with radiant regal cool, as if strained humility would be unbecoming from television's self-proclaimed prince.

And yet there is a shadowiness to Carson's princemanship. He refuses interviews, his biographers circle around his personality without being able to alight, and despite his place in the routine of our lives, he has so masterfully managed an off-air aloofness that there is something essentially enigmatic about his fame. For over thirteen years—following the abdication of *Tonight*'s apoplectic king, Jack Paar—Carson has reigned supreme on late-night television. Under Jerry Lester, the *Tonight* show (then called *Broadway Open House*) was a rowdy vaudeville showcase; Steve Allen, Lester's successor, turned the show into a nightly party which could be either sober-minded (Allen being the epitome of a *Saturday Review* intellectual) or swoopingly silly (Allen also being the most brilliant of TV Dadaists). That vervey spontaneity became encounter theater therapy under the direction of the Marquis de Paar, who was peerless at grittily vapid chatter, misty bathos, and scenery-chewing controversy. Dick Cavett, who wrote for Paar, said that working for him was like having an alcoholic in the family.

Unsurprising, then, that Carson, who began his career as a magician (The Great Carsoni) and whose previous TV credits included hosting game shows like *Who Do You Trust?* and *Earn Your Vacation*, appeared too lightweight a presence to dominate video space the way Paar so recklessly did. However, from the outset Carson's ratings were better than Paar's, under his helmsmanship *The Tonight Show* has become a fabulously prosperous institution, and Carson himself one of the most influential performers in the history of the medium. A jokey clue to the cultural contradictions of Carsonism was slipped across by Jack Benny, who said at a Friars Roast that Johnny Carson is living proof that Lincoln was wrong: "that you *can* fool all of the people all of the time."

As a comedian, Carson is unquestionably a master, but a perplexing one. In his only movie, *Looking for Love* (starring a cantilever-chested Connie Francis), Carson played (unsurprisingly) a talk-show host and every pause, inflection, and facial nuance was etched with the influence of Jack Benny. On television, as Dick Cavett points out in his book, nearly all of his bits have been lifted from other comedians—Aunt Blabby from Jonathan Winters, Art Fern the tea-time movie host from Jackie Gleason, Carnac from Steve Allen, the Mighty Carson Art Players from Fred Allen—and his salient mannerisms are borrowed as well (for example, Carson's stare-into-the-camera "take" comes from Oliver Hardy). Carson has distilled all of these influences into a style which is perfectly calibrated to the scale of the video medium; he has a gift akin to David Bowie's for copping from others and yet appearing totally self-invented. Like Bowie, Carson absorbs voices without losing his own: his pauses are Bennyesque without being as long as Benny's, his rhythm is Hope-quickened but not as nervously fleet, his Hardy "takes" are not as broad as Hardy's . . . Carson has learned how to miniaturize their theatricality. Where Bowie and Carson converge is in their ability to be culturally omnivisible while being characterologically cloudy; where they diverge is that Bowie releases himself while Carson is the prisoner of a Waspish timidity.

That timidity, that fear of spontaneity and growth, is shaped by Carson into a dramaless drama in which he always emerges the victor. His monologues now are as much a commentary on the jokes as they are a succession of jokes, and this enables him to turn the sourest of lines into sweet advantage. He reassures ("Don't worry, I can get out of this . . . there are always valleys before you reach the peaks"), he mock-pleads ("Is that any way to treat a veteran of the big war?"), and he mock-insults ("May a crazed leper fondle your daughter's hope chest"). McMahon's presence is crucial here for his horsey laugh is loudest when Carson's jokes take their deepest dives, and Carson's confidence rebounds off McMahon's Yahoo whinnying. For without that whinnying, silence. And silence is what freezes a comedian's blood.

McMahon's function as a surrogate fan and the carefully monitored space-module atmosphere of the studio insure Carson against the sort of sepulchral yawn which haunts a loser-comic like John Osborne's Archie Rice. Carson has so skillfully orchestrated his television audience's responses over the years that when he faces them in person, they howl like a well-paid claque, and there is no smell of the arena hanging in the air. Which is what makes him a comedian in the mandarin manner of Hope, Benny, and George Burns—the ability to involve an audience while keeping it at an emotional distance. Recently on Dinah Shore's show, a woman asked Bob Hope why comedians seem to have the longest career span of all entertainers, and Hope quickly chortled, "Because we're not *sincere*." Insincerity is their charm and armor and the shield which separates their public identities from their emotions. The mandarin comedians are like politicians who have learned to live with their lies; certainly, Bob Hope hustles himself these days with the edgy ebullience of a Hubert Horatio Humphrey. Now that Carson has quit dyeing his hair, the color has gone from inky-dark to senatorial silver, and with that transformation has come a surrounding nimbus of eminence.

Echoing Will Rogers's "Well, all I know is what I read in the papers," Johnny Carson often cushions a political barb by assuring his audience that "all I'm doing, folks, is reporting the news." Charmingly, Carson's inspired tactic is to emulate the apolitical political stance of Rogers—Everyman musing over morning-edition follies— and yet slice through the skin of a politician's pretensions in a way Rogers never did. Will Rogers, twirling his lariat and aw-shucksing his thoughts about life's passing carnival, clearly never meant to ruin anyone's sleep. He sedulously scanned the papers for material so that his remarks always had a tart newsworthiness, yet the sentiments which are anthologized are usually mild nebulosities like: "Most all new senators are earnest and mean well. Then the air of Washington gets into their bones and they are just as bad as the rest."

Carson makes similar innocuous complaints, but with the steady hand of an assassin. He has said that President Ford reminds him "of the guy at the Safeway who okays your check," and for a time his portrayal of Ford as President Dumb was so effective that Ron Nessen whined about it during a ski slope press conference. Carson and his writers were even tougher on Ford's predecessor, leaving all protestations of innocence in shreds as Nixon groveled his way to his ignominious endgame.

And yet in politics, as in commerce, Carson works with deft discretion. After thirteen years on the air, all of the show's rough edges have been smoothed and lacquered. The moguls also tell us that the decade is more apolitical than the previous, that people are now less "issue-oriented" and "activist-minded." Like all corporate rationales, the argument has the stench of cant, yet it's probably true that *The Tonight Show* will acknowledge distress signals only when the smell of smoke reaches the studio. Here is Terry Galanoy's account of how *The Tonight Show* reacted to the murder of Martin Luther King: "Sammy Davis, Jr., asked Carson if he could come on the show and talk to his black brothers. Carson opened up the time for him. The cameras moved in very tight on Davis when he asked the young Negroes around the country for calm and restraint in this, their hour of tragedy. He pointed out that there was nothing to be gained from violence. . . . He finished by asking the blacks to 'cool it.' . . ."

Since the property of the Republic is presently in no combustible danger, *The Tonight Show* now has the gleaming smugness of an institution which has washed the blood from the walls and sees no new threats approaching the palisades. Except for the affectionate treatment accorded to fellow comedians (particularly Rodney Dangerfield, Joan Rivers, and John Byner), all *Tonight* guests are treated with courtly disinterest. Unlike former rival Cavett, Carson doesn't try to prod his guests, or draw them out. He seems more comfortable with dimpled dulloids like John Davidson or Burt Convy because he can give their salesmanship a keener luster, and do so without surrendering any of his own thoughts. With them Carson can be congenial, and yet remote. He also keeps a decent distance from the more vulgar forms of the show's merchandising—it's McMahon who wrestles with the dog in the Alpo commercial.

Perhaps Carson's greatest influence has been in the field of sexual politics, where he has had a liberalizing influence not unlike that of Hugh Hefner. Like Hefner, Carson has successfully packaged glossy, sophisticated entertainment while conveying (or betraying) a boy's sniggery wonder at the fleshy treasures of middlebrow hedonism. The two of them have salubriously loosened up sexual attitudes and given an artfulness to suburban blue humor yet Hefner, unlike Carson, hasn't acquired a sense of dignity in the seventies; with that pipe in his mouth Hef still doesn't look like an adult, he looks like a teenager awkwardly trying to imitate Dad. On the air, Johnny Carson still indulges in anal jokes (prunes and Preparation H are his faves) and gets juvenilely giggly around starlets, but in his graying reticence he no longer seems so smutty-minded. The only bluish moment at Westchester came when he railed against banks which penalize depositors for early withdrawals, then mused: "That's what got me in trouble with one of my ex-wives, early withdrawal . . . of course, I didn't leave it in the full six years."

Such jokes are inoffensive coming from Johnny, not only because they are pale blue, but because with his Johnny Carson suit (a line of men's wear bears his name), precise articulate gestures (pointed trigger finger, stiffly bent arms, swiveling spine), and passionless ice-blue eyes, Johnny C. doesn't look like a dirty-fingernailed midwestern populist, or a smalltown lech, but an ex-astronaut, an athletic Wasp more adept with a steely tether than a lariat. That glimmer of hard-won discipline gives even his silliest jokes an underlying severity.

Despite the mercantilism of *The Tonight Show*, and the timidity of the functionaries who program the show (who, of course, ulcerate that timidity in the fear of Carson's wrath), I watch it often, enjoy it, enjoy it as much as anyone . . . probably more. It's not just the pleasure of watching a cool professional at work, though Carson at his most graceful reminds one of Brooks Robinson holding down third base for the Orioles; much of one's interest in Carson lies in speculating about those vectors of his personality where no one has been allowed to trespass. There's mystery in Carson's genius, a wan, pinched mystery. As with media figures like Jimmy Carter, Jerry Brown, David Bowie, and Neil Armstrong, it's difficult to bring the motives into sharp focus or clearly hear their emotional tonalities, yet there's also the suspicion that what's hidden from us may not be teeming and vast, but thin and sparse. The realm behind the dry Jesuitical calm of Jerry Brown may not be a sprawling city with winding streets, salons, whorehouses, and broken glass in the back-alleys but a small room, badly lit, with dusty furniture. These men lack the feverish obsessiveness which gives heroic dimension to a Mailer, Peckinpah, Bruce Lee, and Nureyev, but their very tentativeness and thin-voiced reserve are harmonious with the undramatic disquietude of the seventies.

So it is with Johnny Carson, a midwestern ex-magician who keeps his feelings so deeply pocketed that one can only approach him through analogues like Hefner, Rogers, Bowie, et al. Faintly filtering through Carson's steel-mesh detachment is a vague sense of sorrow which is more palpable to those who have worked for him. All through Robert Lardin's paperback bio of Carson are quotes from Carson's associates who fault him for his aloofness, parsimony, and paranoia, yet the book ends with a friend saying, "I considered Johnny the most unhappy individual I have ever met in my life. . . . He's constantly seeking gaiety without ever quite finding it." Even with a happy marriage (after two failed ones) and a coruscatingly successful career, the corrosive bitterness is still there.

For though Carson's Babbittry is gashed with melancholia, there's a mean-spiritedness in his genius which makes folly out of a metaphysical inquiry. In a recent ninety-minute Bob Hope special called *Joys,* dozens of America's most prestigious comedians were systematically stabbed, garroted, and bludgeoned by a shadowy figure who Zorroed across the screen with fleet stealth. At the end of the show—after Dean Martin, Steve Allen, Phyllis Diller, and Harry Ritz (Harry Ritz!) have gone to smithereens—the killer unmasks, and it's Johnny Carson, beamingly pleased with his murderous triumph.

Though none of the comedians liquidated in *Joys* could top Carson as a monologist, a gleeful maniac like Harry Ritz is finally more liberating a performer—he leaps off the top of his id. Carson is the comedic virtuoso of the superego, which is why he's heir to Bob Hope, which is why his triumphant insincerity is rimmed with bleakness.

The Village Voice, March 29, 1979

Johnny, We Hardly Knew Ye

"That plastic character on the Coast" is how S. J. Perelman dismissed Johnny Carson during one of his snit fits. Like most word-men, Ol' Picklepuss preferred rival Dick Cavett, who could play patty-cake with puns, lines of poetry, anagrams, palindromes. Carson? A mere cue-card reader.

America's night-light. A test pattern for lonely hearts. To culture's snooty squires, Carson has always been antiseptic to anything smacking of pungency. Even Kenneth Tynan in his famous adulatory profile of Carson in *The New Yorker* felt obliged to sigh, "It is depressing to reflect that if Rabelais were alive today he would not be invited to appear on *The Tonight Show*."

Over the years such once fashionable put-downs have receded into the annals of received opinion. Perelman's fang marks and Tynan's love bites have both faded. The man has shown through.

"He's the cream of middle-class elegance, yet he's not a mannequin," the director Billy Wilder told Tynan. No life-size plastic replica could have hosted NBC's *Tonight Show* for nearly thirty years without becoming warped beyond recognition. No reasonable facsimile could have sustained such high wattage in the dismal hours of divorce, drunken arrest, and the death of a son. If Johnny Carson solos in the jet stream of American comedy—the earth below cigarette-burned with the crash sites of Cavett, Merv Griffin, Regis Philbin, Joey Bishop, Alan Thicke, Pat Sajak, and every other talk-show host who has engaged him in dogfight—it isn't because he's been on autopilot. His reign, which spans JFK to *JFK*, reflects a washboard stomach of Wasp stamina and character. His professionalism has paved a shining path.

On May 22, Johnny Carson (born 1925) will pass the mike to a new generation, in the person of Jay Leno. Before *The Tonight Show* under Johnny Carson became a lost bit of Americana, I hithered to the NBC studios in Burbank, California, to pay homage. I journeyed to "beautiful downtown Burbank" with my head bowed, as befits a pilgrim. I only hoped I wouldn't mope home disillusioned. (I'm still at that impressionable stage.)

Aside from a few people of color, it's a long loaf of white bread formed in front of Studio One. The audience queued for *The Tonight Show* looks like Carson cloned. Or, rather, Carson if he had remained a bumpkin from Nebraska. The men shuffle as if they'd left their lawn mowers behind. Their wives inch forward with locked hips. America being a land of crazed loners (before killing John Lennon, Mark David Chapman considered targeting Carson), we're herded single file through a metal detector. Flashlights probe the inner recesses of women's handbags.

As NBC pages seat us cattle, members of the *Tonight Show* band trickle from the wings. Gray of hair and ashen of skin, the band members look like the board of directors of an insolvent bank. Providing a palette of color is their conductor, Doc Severinsen, who prances like a show pony in harem jammies. He introduces Ed McMahon, who's been Johnny's loyal echo since the game show *Who Do You Trust?* During the warm-up, we're shown a highlight tape of Johnny's greatest hits, from the hippy-dippy sixties to the polyester seventies to the Armani eighties. The last clip includes Leno, underscoring the orderly transition through the nineties.

"Let's get this baby cranked up," says Ed, taking his position at the announcer's stand. Tension ticks in the air. "These last few minutes are exciting, aren't they?" he says. The stage director raises his hand for the countdown. Three, two, one—go. The band slams into the *Tonight Show* theme, Ed reels off the guest list, and with a vocal sweep cries:

"HERRRRE'S—Johnny!"

The curtain parts, and after a pause, out bounds Carson. His appearance sends a jolt. On TV he looks light as a kite. In person he projects power. With his albino hair, flagpole spine, and thumblike head, he carries the smack of Lee Marvin in *Point Blank*. (Between marriages Carson dated *Point Blank* co-star Angie Dickinson.) Glancing at a joke board slanted at knee level, he does a newswire rip of the day's events—the primary races, the Michelangelo computer virus, the repackaging of fat from Geraldo Rivera's fanny to his face. "He may have overdone it. Today he stuck his head out of the car window, and was arrested for mooning."

The TV screen flattens the field of Carson's stand-up routine. Shields him, to an extent. Seeing him live reveals how much more exposed he really is. Beneath the boom mike he works a naked circle of space. He has nothing to lean on or hide behind. Even with his crack timing and prepared "savers" (booed after a bad joke, he'll retort, "You didn't boo me when I smothered a grenade at Guadalcanal"), he's one step away from a clifflike drop into deaf air. No wonder his heart rate used to double before he did the monologue. He's auditioning for death every time he steps on the mound. Even when the monologue zips by like a slick bird, as it did when I saw him, failure isn't far from the forefront.

After his trademark golf swing takes us into commercial, Carson entertains questions from the audience. What are you going to do after retiring? someone asks. "I'm going to become a Jehovah's Witness. I like rejection." A joke to ward off a jinx.

He stations himself at the desk. Nearly all of the copy on Carson describes him as cool, aloof, armored (Tynan: "You get the impression that you are addressing an elaborately wired security system"), irritable, and, when crossed, shark-toothed. Longtime associates have sunk without a trace. He had Joan Rivers for fish bait when she defected as *Tonight*'s guest host to head her own show. Certainly he was no ride on the merry-go-round during his drinking days. Alcohol made him cocky, abusive, unstable. He allegedly abused his first wife, bullied his sons. Once, while sitting in a bar, he even dared tear a strip off Frank Sinatra:

> The door swung open, and Frank Sinatra walked in with more bodyguards and hangers-on than an Arab potentate. An aura of uncertainty, of danger, surrounded Sinatra. The room grew so quiet that you could hear the flattery drop. Johnny waited until the singer reached *his* table. He looked at Sinatra, then at his watch, and back at the singer. "Frank," Johnny said, "I told you twelve-thirty."
>
> —From *King of the Night*, by Laurence Leamer

It was Ed who was deputized to clamp Carson in a bear hug and carry him to safety. Alcohol was the one release valve from the pressure cooker holding Carson prisoner during *Tonight*'s early heyday. Now he seems in no need of pissing his name in acid. On the set it's the supposedly bonhomous Ed who seems down, perched on the sofa like a parrot under a drop cloth. Congratulating Ed on his recent marriage, the comedian Don Rickles turns to Johnny and confides, "I give it about a week, tops." During the commercial breaks Carson doesn't lower the Cone of Silence, as I'd so often heard, but jollies up a storm with his guests, beating time on the desk with a pencil. The entire show, he vicariously jams with the band.

Carson's nonstop drumming is the key to his persona. He's always had a drum set in the house. He was once filmed behind the skins for *60 Minutes.* Profiles of Carson usually describe his drumming as a way of blowing off steam, flexing his chops. But it's more than a habit or hobby; it's image-defining. Significantly, the most undone Carson's staff remembers seeing him was when his friend, the riotous jazz drummer Buddy Rich, died. It was one of the rare times he canceled a show. Rich's death hit him hard because Rich was his unrepressed alter ego. For Carson is comedy's last practitioner of white jazz. Such jazz is often derided for not clawing to the raw bottom of experience, the syringe-littered hellhole of Charlie Parker, Lenny Bruce. Angst-ridden it's not. It belongs more to the bachelor pad of passé legend, where the cocktail hour unfolds against a *Playboy After Hours* skyline. But time has given Carson's pristine jazz touch steel tips. Early on he mastered the knack of lying back and adding casual fill to an interview rather than flailing away with all fours. His staying power is due in part to his steady pistons. When Jay Leno assumes the top spot on *The Tonight Show,* it will be more than one comedian succeeding another. It will represent the rock generation's completing its long coup d'état of pop culture, finally putting the jazz influence of the forties and fifties out to pasture. (If Bill Clinton becomes president, we'll have an Elvis in the White House, and an Elvis on *Tonight.*)

Factory-made though it is, *The Tonight Show* has its awkward patches. As Carson authenticates himself, he's less able to fake prefab hype. He floundered with twin-injected Melanie Griffith, asking her if she was a good homemaker. Although Elizabeth Taylor was a hoot, squeezed into leather like a Swiss-roll motorcycle moll, Carson blanked when she announced she was tossing herself a sixtieth-birthday bash at Disneyland to celebrate her inner child. (Although a reformed drinker, Carson never has peddled AA-speak.)

It's also become tedious hearing one celebrity after another eat up the clock offering him farewell testimonials, although I suppose such thanks are inevitable. Carson may become choked up the closer he gets to sayonara, but so far he's kept his emotions in check. He always has. One of his chief attributes is that he's never been a pimp for cheap schmaltz or personal pain. The clown-mask pathos of Jerry Lewis or Joan Rivers is beneath him. Unlike most comics, he's never seemed to bleed for audience love. He's more like Sinatra, tucking his ego into a holster. "You just get moody and walk away," gibed Don Rickles, who knows them both. Which enables him to leave the greatest gig and longest grind in American television with his mystique intact. Because of his self-containment, we'll probably miss Johnny Carson more than he'll miss us. Not to be maudlin, but I miss him already.

Vanity Fair, May 1992

The Swivel Throne

Has David Letterman had a personality implant? Letterman suffered a deep burn when NBC chose Jay Leno to fill Johnny Carson's seat as the host of *The Tonight Show*. After hosting *Late Night* for more than a decade, Letterman felt that he had earned the nod. Eleven years is a long time to warm up in the bullpen. In the biggest defection since Barbara Walters switched networks, he ditched NBC to headline his own late-night show for CBS, setting up a grudge match against *The Tonight Show*—may the best Nielsens win. In the press conferences and interviews preceding the launch of the *Late Show*, Letterman was his usual deliberate-jerk self, blowing cigar smoke as he took jabs at Joey Buttafuoco and at his new boss, Larry Tisch. But ever since he hit the stage of the Ed Sullivan Theater for his August 30 premiere and received a standing ovation, which has been repeated almost every night, he's had the look of love. He's lost weight, his eyes are clear, his problem hair has a manageable shine. He's become a regular sunbeam. Gone is the grump who would pout at his desk on *Late Night* about lumps in his Slurpee, or plunge into a protracted hacking cough just to annoy everyone. He's gracious with his guests now, extending the hand of fellowship.

Not everyone enjoys this miracle makeover. The actress Ellen Barkin told him to his orange face that she didn't like the new Dave; she preferred the old, "fat and sour" Dave. ("Fat and Sour—new from Nabisco," Letterman replied.) But he hasn't had all the poisons pumped from his system. There are still traces of his former snot. He left Jeff Goldblum nonplussed by praising his acting in *The Accidental Tourist*, which almost immediately seemed less like a mistake than like a put-down: not only was Goldblum not in the film but his ex-wife, Geena Davis, was—indeed, won an Academy Award for her performance. But this is trivial compared with the hostile outbreaks on *Late Night*, where Cher called him an asshole and Shirley MacLaine wanted to scalp him alive. He has real authority now, and it rests lightly on his shoulders. The new king of late-night comedy, he has ascended to the swivel throne.

Late-night shows used to offer the braking power of a train slow-
ing into the station, a big band coasting into the end of a tune. They
were heavy but efficient, easing the viewer into bed like a letter into
an envelope. With *Late Night*, Letterman turned the talk show
into a tacky clubhouse where the pace was more erratic. From the
moment Larry (Bud) Melman first waddled onto the set to flub his
lines, *Late Night* prided itself on being just amateur enough to subvert
slick formula. Planting Chris Elliott under the seats as a mole person
("Greetings, surface-dwellers"), playing pranks on other NBC shows,
using trick cameras like the Monkey-cam, holding dogsled races and
archery contests in the halls, *Late Night* was a small guerrilla action
directed mostly at itself. A lot of its silly high jinks originated on Steve
Allen's old Westinghouse show, but where Allen himself was often
genuinely giddy Letterman was always somewhat distant. Distance
was the lens that allowed the viewer to think of the comedy not just
as a laugh opportunity but as a loose, ongoing installation—an art
piece. Like the music of the B-52's, the comedy of *Late Night* was col-
legiate kitsch. Letterman's writing staff, many of them recent Harvard graduates, injected just enough *Lampoon/Spy* inside knowledge
into its smart-dumb humor to make critics feel like accessories to the
action. (Strike enough ironic poses in the mirror and you, too, can be
called self-reflexive.)

Once Letterman had set up shop at CBS, a strategy change was in
order. He more than built himself a better Dave; he remodeled the
talk-show format into a modern-reproduction antique. He and his
staff must have realized that they had deconstructed talk-show idioms
on *Late Night* down to the last dot. They reversed the process, magnifying their vision. The new show would be a ritzy affair. It would
have the brassy fanfare and bright lights of an opening night. CBS's
expensive decision to buy, gut, and renovate Broadway's Ed Sullivan
Theater to house the *Late Show* made this gala idea possible. The purchase united two gold mother lodes of popular culture. Establishing
a link to Ed Sullivan's CBS variety series summoned the glory days
of network TV. Placing Letterman on Broadway near *Cats* and *Miss
Saigon* cast him as the unlikely continuer of theatrical tradition. ("Hi,
I'm Dave Letterman—Mr. Broadway.") So unsentimental is Letterman that he could draw on both pasts without seeming to dabble
in nostalgia. Boasting a monster neon marquee, a stage with a wide
sweep, and music provided by Paul Shaffer and the CBS Orchestra
(another grand touch, since his band has no string section), the *Late*

Show is a cheerful blast of pseudo bombast. Where *Late Night* was a nontraditional talk show, the *Late Show* is neotraditional, a mixture of glitz and broken glass.

This consolidation effort has left Letterman's rivals fighting over vacant property. They're trying to subvert and parody a format that he's moved uptown. On *The Tonight Show*, which used to set the standard, Jay Leno tries to emulate the Letterman of *Late Night* by doing all sorts of wacky stunts—man-in-the-street polls ("Who's the new surgeon general?" he asked Los Angeles airheads), celebrity look-alikes planted in the audience, funny phone calls. It is a sorrow to behold. The supporting players seem stuck to the screen like refrigerator magnets. The audience-participation segments resemble something you'd be subjected to on a cruise ship. (Let's put Harry in a dress.) Leno has lost whatever ability he may have had to ad-lib his way out of Death Valley. His voice gets yappier as the microphone goes limp in his hand. Aside from the poor writing, the problem is that Leno limits himself to being a joke dispenser. In a backstage look at *The Tonight Show* for the E! Entertainment Network, he said that the formula for being a talk-show host is simple: "Write joke, tell joke, get check." And the jokes can't be mean or personal. Mustn't make Mom mad.

The rap on Leno has been that he's too nice. Nice doesn't cut it on the streets. Nice doesn't get you top bunk in the cell. If Leno reminded everyone that it's his show, he might earn a little more respect. He's often ignored by his guests, especially broody-intense actor types like Andy Garcia, Richard Gere, and Alec Baldwin, who seemed to be staring inward for a glimpse of their own images as Leno tried to be their interviewer-pal. He apparently can't even impress his staff. It's embarrassing to watch him buddy up to his bandleader, Branford Marsalis, whose body droops with can't-be-bothered disregard. The brother seems downright cold. These are minor slights.

Far weightier is the approval that has been withheld by Johnny Carson. Although technically Leno is Johnny Carson's heir as the host of *The Tonight Show*, performing in the same studio where Carson held court during his entire West Coast reign, it's Letterman who has emerged as the chosen son. (Keeping a significant silence concerning Leno, Carson let it be known that he had watched Letterman's opening show.) It must frustrate Leno, having his inheritance devalued by the very man who made it possible. It must smart. Perhaps that explains the moment in the E! special when Leno, escorting the viewer on a tour of the Burbank facilities, pointed to lobby photo-graphs of NBC stars that he labeled "the wall of the dead." The next shot featured three photographs of Johnny Carson.

The set of the new Conan O'Brien show offers its own gallery of the (un)dead. Premiering on September 13, NBC's *Late Night with Conan O'Brien* places the Harvard graduate and former *Simpsons* producer in a bachelor hangout surrounded by framed black-and-white photo-graphs of Ernie Kovacs, Tom Snyder, and Joe Franklin. The bumpers between commercials feature O'Brien's Jimmy Olsen face pasted over publicity shots for *The Love Boat, I Love Lucy,* etc. He's being primped as Generation X's media spokesmodel: Conan O'Brien—TV Boy. Like Leno, O'Brien must wrestle with the ghost of Host Past, taping in the same Rockefeller Center studio where Letterman did his show. It's mostly a tickling match. "He's no Let-ter-man," an old souse com-plains in a staged bit before being hauled away by security. Conan O'Brien and his brain trust clearly believe in preemptive criticism. For the first few weeks, he harped on his inexperience and obscurity. "I promise I will get better, America. Just give me a little time."

A tall, lanky redhead who wears his hair in an Edd (Kookie) Byrnes flip, O'Brien bounces from the blue curtain each night ready to boogie down to the music of the house band, the Max Weinberg Seven. When he dances, he's all arms. His legs are like arms. Once he begins to speak, however, his motor burps. His monologues are gawky, ingenuous, like the opening remarks of the guest hosts on *Saturday Night Live.* (Which shouldn't surprise, since the show's pro-ducer is *SNL*'s Lorne Michaels, who picked Conan out of a chiffon swirl of ingénues.) Puttering at his desk, O'Brien sits oddly aslant from his guests, his left side forming a solid abutment. A writer by vocation, O'Brien doesn't have the broadcast experience or the knack to get jazzy byplay going. When the interview hits a snag, it's like watching a loser on a bad date, digging himself a deeper hole. He gets whiny. When he chatted with the actress Daphne Zuniga, part of the time was spent discussing how going-nowhere the interview was. "Oh, come on, this is enjoyable," O'Brien protested before asking that irresistible question "Was Rob Reiner fun to work with?"

He does try to add a little depth, as they say in Hollywood. One night, his distinguished guest was David Halberstam, the judicious, noble-jawed author of *The Fifties.* Exhausted by his efforts to free the slaves and preserve the Union, Halberstam lowered himself into the chair and launched into an Ice Age account of how Elvis was booked on the Ed Sullivan show. The earth began to open. Halberstam's delivery was so ponderous that for the first time in my thirty years of watching talk shows (I would sneak over to Alan Dunn's house to watch Steve Allen), I could hear people *coughing* in the studio, like an audience at a bad play. An interview with another Ancient Mariner, Gore Vidal, was interrupted by a visit from Conan's make-believe next-door neighbor. Even more than Leno's *Tonight*, O'Brien's *Late Night* jitters with distractions—a Greek chorus of dumb guys doing variations on Conan's name ("Conan the—veterinarian"), visits from a Bruce Springsteen impostor and the late William Howard Taft, taped remotes, more funny phone calls, Irish tunes not so much sung as gargled. Thus far, O'Brien's show is a junior version of Letterman's—*Late Night Lite*. But the writing can be clever, and I don't mind O'Brien's much picked-on sidekick, Andy Richter. There's something sweet about how he tries to help.

It's a patriarchal contest being played out on late night. With Johnny Carson standing aloof as the Absent Father, we have David Letterman (born 1947) as the oldest son, the one who feels the pre-rogative; Jay Leno, the middle son (born 1950), puzzled that he isn't the favorite; and Conan O'Brien (born 1963), the youngest, mimicking the oldest brother, just wanting to be included. At first glance, Chevy Chase wouldn't seem to fit into this chart. Yet Chase is the host most openly, acutely imitative of Carson himself. An original alumnus of *SNL*, the star of the *Fletch* and *National Lampoon's Vacation* films, Chase belongs to a poker club that includes Neil Simon, Steve Martin, and Carson. Between shuffles, he must have studied Carson's every sandpapery move. Behind the desk in the Hollywood studio that once housed Ed McMahon's *Star Search*, Chase leans in his chair, yanks his head, tugs on his ear, and scratches his nose like Carson; he even blinks like him. He blinks a lot on his show, as if trying to tell himself that this is all a terrible dream.

For catastrophe buffs, Fox's *The Chevy Chase Show* is a godsend equal to the Jerry Lewis telethon—a crackup for the ages. Once in a lifetime does show biz contain this much psychodrama. The flubs, cheesy insults, stutter-step conversations ("You talk," "No, you talk"), gross slapstick (spewing vomit, drooling blood), insincere flattery, and wounded sulks are all rolled into one time bomb. The impending doom holds you fast. You can't watch, and yet you can't not watch. Every show yields a fresh wince. When a fan asked what color underwear he wore, Chase answered, "My underwear changes color, depending on what I had for lunch. In fact, right now I think I'm wearing Rocky Road." Beverly D'Angelo pretended to snore during her interview. During a dull stretch in his interview, Ron Silver asked the audience, "Does anyone have a newspaper I can read?"

It is, of course, wrong to revel in someone's misfortune. Yet what's oddly heartwarming about this fiasco is that it was so clearly in the wind. It restores your faith in fate. After Fox announced it had signed Chevy Chase to host a late-night talk show, many media experts issued the same caveats about Chase: scant interviewing experience, rusty physical skills, stuck-up attitude, beady eyes. Fox's stock answer was that he had Q ratings up there with the gods. (The Q ratings measure a performer's likability.) The show's high ratings its first night justified such faith in numbers. But a strong recognition factor couldn't paint over the flaws in Chase's persona, a persona that wasn't even totally his. The posters for *The Chevy Chase Show* featured Chase with a fake gap in his teeth, a takeoff on Letterman.

Aside from Arsenio Hall, trying to rally the faithful few, all the talk-show hosts are copying Letterman. There's an overlapping quality to late-night now. The guests are in quick rotation. The reclusive Robert De Niro appears with Jay, then with Chevy. The more available Jamie Lee Curtis, looking like one of those scary nymphos in *Shock Corridor*, plugs her children's book on Jay, Chevy, and Conan. It isn't just the whirling Rolodex that makes these shows seem same-ish; it's the pervasive boyishness of the programs. Late-night has become the newest American device to prolong adolescence. So much frivolity. On those evenings when I'm feeling virtuous, I find myself returning to PBS's *Charlie Rose*, where at least there are adults present.

The New Yorker, October 18, 1993

Letterman Unbound

When the king stumbles, the flunkies take the fall. After defecting from NBC to CBS, David Letterman dominated late-night show biz with the launching of the *Late Show*, in 1993. Hosted by a leaner, almost boulevardier Dave, the *Late Show* restored Broadway glitz to the bat cave of the old Ed Sullivan Theater and made cult figures of merchants in the area. Letterman looked unbeatable. Meanwhile, at NBC, *The Tonight Show*, hosted by Jay Leno, staggered through an identity crisis as it grappled with the phantom of Johnny Carson. Trying to placate everyone at once, Leno lost his bop in the opening monologues and jerked around onstage like a puppet tangled in its own strings. Slowly, cautiously, Leno moved to emancipate himself, agreeing to let the network dump his manager-turned-producer Helen Kushnick, having the Burbank studio remodeled into a nightclub setting, and cutting loose his pouty band-leader, Branford Marsalis; he also took full advantage of a booking coup when Hugh Grant gave *The Tonight Show* his first interview after his inglorious blow job. A plow horse who never gets winded, Leno pulled ahead of Letterman in the ratings and has refused to take a breather since, doing five new shows a week, with few vacations. Letterman's slide into second place, coupled with the plastering that he took over his hosting of the 1995 Academy Awards, cost him his media-darling status and put him and his show on the defensive. He could no longer afford to let the *Late Show* run on cruise control. It was now out with the old. His longtime director, Hal Gurnee, departed, and so did his announcer, Bill Wendell. Writers and other staffers jumped overboard. Some of this was normal attrition. But in March Letterman fired his executive producer, Robert Morton (Morty, as he's known), replacing him with the show's former head writer Rob Burnett. At first, Letterman tried to issue diplomatic murmurs regarding the popular Morton, but in an interview in the current issue of *Rolling Stone* he blurted, "It was just—we had a little infection, and the limb had to come off." He also expressed the fear that Morton might become his enemy for life. (If

I were Morty, being compared to an infected limb might leave me a little miffed.)

The purge hasn't pacified the *Late Show* itself. On any given night, the difference between Letterman and Leno isn't one of talent or material but one of temperament. Leno is a man of no discernible psychology. He doesn't seem given to high or low moods. He's a Las Vegas vending machine of predictable jokes. Letterman is less containable. As a recent article in the *New York Observer* reported, Letterman has flared up over technical flubs and miscues that have dragged out the taping of his show, and has indulged in acts of self-loathing bordering on masochism, the most blatant example being the time he pummelled a life-size dummy of himself on the air, giving it repeated shots to the head. His neurosis has achieved classical dimensions. I happened to be reading Dr. Karen Horney's *The Neurotic Personality of Our Time* recently, and (except for the pages that reminded me of me) almost every chapter cried out, *Dave, Dave, Dave.* The grandiosity with which Letterman habitually touts himself as "the most powerful man in American broadcasting" in his opening remarks and then bashes his own image reflects an inflated yet blighted sense of self, in which he is both overlord and loser, potent yet pathetic. As Horney writes of this kind of highfalutin defeatist, "He tends to feel that he is nothing, but is irritated when he is not taken for a genius." It has often been reported how Letterman will beat up on himself after a bad show. (From *USA Today:* "'It sucked,' he said of that night's show. 'Not very good tonight, because I was not very good tonight.'") According to Horney, such self-criticism is disproportionate, beyond the call of duty, a pseudo martyrdom. It's a way of saying, No matter what anyone does, it's never enough; I alone suffer. She writes:

> In such suffering there are no apparent advantages to be gained, no audience that might be impressed, no sympathy to be won, no secret triumph in asserting his will over others. Nevertheless, there is a gain for the neurotic, but of a different kind. Incurring a failure in love, a defeat in competition, having to realize a definite weakness or shortcoming of his own is unbearable for one who has such high-flown notions of his uniqueness. Thus when he dwindles to nothing in his own estimation, the categories of success and failure, superiority and inferiority cease to exist; by exaggerating his pain, by losing himself in a general feeling of misery or unworthiness, the aggravating experience loses some of its reality, the sting of the special pain is lulled, narcotized.

The difference between David Letterman and the average neurotic is that the latter doesn't ride his seesaw of misery in front of millions of people. The average neurotic can keep his nothingness to himself. Even a professional neurotic, like Woody Allen, babies himself onscreen with protective blankets of culture, irony, and high-mindedness, which tend to render him a blinking figure of bafflement. Others, like Jerry Seinfeld or Paul Reiser, channel their neuroses into hypochondria or neatnik fixations. Letterman, the ninja of neurosis, is more openly embattled. It's Dave contra mundum. He has even offered to box network executives. In a recent show, he upped the ante and offered to fight the entire studio audience, except for one neatly groomed guy. Whether he's knocking himself around or pretending to bait the audience, he's seeking a muscular release for his frustration. Johnny Carson, Letterman's role model in the art of aloofness, was content to play the drums.

Despite the snit fits, Letterman seems in no danger of full mental meltdown on camera. Under Rob Burnett, the *Late Show* has regained some of its former funkiness. There are still lame bits, such as Gene Siskel wandering around the studio with a bucket of popcorn, searching for Roger Ebert (he should stay lost); and sadistic streaks, such as Letterman bullying his announcer to scream out the numbers in the mailbag segment (*"Letter Number One!"*). But Burnett, understanding that if you leave Letterman alone too much he begins to prey on himself, has increased the number of oddball Dave activities, which translates into boosting the number of remote bits—i.e., segments shot outside the studio, where Dave is loosed from his own echo chamber. On a recent visit to San Francisco, for example, Letterman linked up with a roly-poly young man named Manny, whose ditzy comments made Beavis and Butt-head sound like Leavis disciples. For Manny, everything was either "dank" (praise) or "schwag" (putdown). Together, he and Dave rode around and ranked people. "Roseanne— dank or schwag?" "Schwag!" A really hot babe would receive the ultimate accolade: "Diggity-dank." What made the segment good TV was that it brought out a bemused, sarcastic-older-brother side of Letterman, which is probably about as far as he can be drawn into the family of man.

Burnett also knows how to stage Letterman's personal hangups so that they become theater of the absurd. Back from San Francisco, Letterman began complaining about how a recent dental procedure had left him with a whistle. He compared himself to a teakettle in a tie. He needled the audience for laughing about it, saying, "You're looking at a man who whistles when he talks. You act like it's a good thing. No. You're looking at a man in his darkest hour." (Letterman believes in exaggerating his pain until it becomes our pain.) Finally, after much whining by Dave, the show brought on a dentist to take a look at the offending tooth; a mini-camera peered inside Letterman's mouth, offering a red-cavern perspective of the interior. Letterman looked like a horse about to chomp into an apple, if the apple were the audience's head. It was a funny-awful spectacle, almost pornographic in its engulfing grossness. "Oh, did that make you sick?" he asked the revolted audience. "You babies!" The weird grace note of the segment was when the visiting dentist (who looked like Henny Youngman's younger brother) dropped his mask to congratulate Helen Hunt on her success in *Twister*. Freaked her out.

Letterman doesn't seem observably happier on the air post-Morty. His eyes still gun from beneath his slanted brow when he fixes his tie. It's questionable whether he can ever be happy on the air, given his irreconcilable desires to be the magnetic center and to be left the hell alone. He's forty-nine years old, single (although he makes half-hearted noises about marrying his longtime girlfriend), and tries to make comedy out of his loner status. (One of the show's segments involves finding Dave a "friend.") He has all the makings of an old fussbudget. Since Burnett has taken the helm, however, Letterman's nervous energy isn't as free-floating and quick to sour. He's forcing himself to focus, as if trying to will himself back to the early days of late-night, when the Top Ten List and Stupid Pet Tricks and goofy pranks were still fresh. A trouper, he's battling through his battle fatigue, which is an arduous way to have fun. Once you reach Letterman's age, holding on to your immaturity is hard work. His triumph as a comic performer is that his efforts, unlike Leno's, never look mechanical. Out among the people in the remote segments, he adopts the loose, droopy manner of a bumbling jerk on holiday. His top half sinks into itself, like a wheezed-out accordion. With his floppy clothes and crumpled face, he's anti-charisma in action, taking a break from fame. He looks sleepy, half shucked. Watching Dave at such moments, you feel that his idea of bliss would be to leave his body behind and join the silver shade of Johnny Carson somewhere in the distant sunlight. He would gladly be rid of himself if he didn't have a show to do.

The New Yorker, June 3, 1996

Great Carson's Ghost!

He retired as host of NBC's *Tonight Show* in 1992, concluding a thirty-year run that began when John Fitzgerald Kennedy was president and color TV was a toddler. Upon retirement, he made only a few evanescent public appearances, a silver phantom whose craving for privacy never wavered. A chain-smoker for most of his adult life (sneaking puffs at the *Tonight Show* desk during commercial breaks), he died of emphysema-related respiratory failure in 2005. And yet the spectral presence and kingly mien of Johnny Carson loom like Hamlet's father's ghost over the late-night talk-show wars that volcano'd this winter. It is over Carson's throne that the daggers are drawn, his troubled spirit that must be honored and avenged. And it's so hard to win Daddy's approval when Daddy's long gone.

Although the late-night war of mouth-to-mouth combat has many smaller players to-ing and fro-ing, chewing bits of scenery for roughage, at its thorny heart is a trinity competing for karmic advantage—a contender, a pretender, and a defender.

Conan O'Brien is the contender, or was, until he was so rudely toppled. A herky-jerky jackanapes who triumphed over naysayers as the host of NBC's *Late Night with Conan O'Brien*, O'Brien and company delighted dormitories across America with beloved characters such as the Masturbating Bear, Triumph the Insult Comic Dog, and the mustachioed Spanish soap-opera heartthrob Conando. In 2009, O'Brien and his family and followers made the covered-wagon journey to reach the promised land, Universal City, California, site of his new home at *The Tonight Show*. And after only seven months, barely enough time to acclimate to the sound of Vin Scully's voice lullabying the settlers to sleep, O'Brien was made an offer he couldn't but refuse if he had a trace of pride within his balsa frame (to roll the starting clock on *Tonight* back to 12:05 A.M.), and refuse it he did, in an open letter addressed to the People of Earth: "Six years ago, I signed a contract with NBC to take over The Tonight Show in June of 2009. Like a lot of us, I grew up watching Johnny Carson every night and the chance to one day sit in that chair has meant everything to me.

I worked long and hard to get that opportunity . . . and since 2004 I have spent literally hundreds of hours thinking of ways to extend the franchise long into the future." But now that franchise's future squirms in the grubby, grabby hands of the windup stand-up comic who is both his predecessor *and* successor: Jay Leno, the pretender.

As every amateur scholar of pop media knows, the bad blood now bubbling and spilling over the brim anew began in 1991, after Carson's retirement was announced and the war over who would win custody of the *Tonight Show* desk was joined. Carson had two vying and viable heirs, one of them long of jaw, the other gapped of tooth. The behind-the-scenes campaign to assume command of *Tonight* became the basis for Bill Carter's 1994 book, *The Late Shift*, and a subsequent HBO movie, the latter an entertaining ruckus that made the main players look like braying cartoon critters with prosthetic attachments. One of *The Late Shift*'s wild revelations was that Leno hid in an office closet during a negotiating session, like Kyle MacLachlan spying in *Blue Velvet*, or do I mean Polonius fidgeting behind the arras in *Hamlet*? Whatev. Honor thy father was not high on Leno's priority list once he took over *Tonight*. He notably did not mention Johnny Carson's name on his first broadcast and salted the wound when, after one rousing applause moment, he exclaimed, "This is not your father's *Tonight Show*!" Sacrilege!

In 2004, NBC, not wanting to have O'Brien warming up in the bull pen until his arm fell off, set up a succession plan that was almost too sensible to work: Leno agreed to step aside for O'Brien in 2009, affording *The Tonight Show* a seamless transition that would avoid the savage infighting and carpet stomping of 1991. In a 2004 statement that, as a YouTube clip, has since been draped like a toilet seat around Leno's neck, Leno said, regarding the host job, "Here it is, Conan. It's yours. See you in five years, buddy." Yeah, see you *in hell*. For, unlike Carson, Leno refused to exit through the door exuding white light, instead succumbing to a new arrangement with NBC to host a nightly prime-time *Tonight* knockoff that would be cheaper to produce than hour-long dramas and keep his mug front and center. It was a bold experiment, composed of equal portions of hubris and folly. It wasn't simply that the migration from late night to prime time seemed to produce a jet-lag effect in which Leno's punch lines died before they got over the net, but that his sub-par ratings pulled down the ratings of the local-news programs of the network's affiliates, which in turn pulled down the ratings of O'Brien's *Tonight Show*, creating a huge drainage problem. Apparently working with clay models of the principals on his desk, NBC head Jeff Zucker then authorized the late-night reclamation plan that Leno accepted with lackey alacrity and O'Brien spurned. Leno emerged as the winner-loser. Although he has always positioned himself as a regular guy, a glorified grease monkey with a fleet of vintage autos, it was his head that seemed the most swollen with helium, vanity, and neediness—an unwillingness to let go that blinded him to the damage he was doing to his image and reputation.

Helpfully, David Letterman was available to point out Leno's flaws, magnify them to gigantic, grainy size, and smash them with the palm of his hand with grouchy gusto. If O'Brien is the contender and Leno the pretender, Letterman is the defender in this Oedipal drama—the defender of the Carson faith. Although Carson had too much class to disparage Leno explicitly, it was obvious that he considered Letterman his true heir, making one of his rare post-retirement appearances on Letterman's show and, we later learned, submitting jokes for Letterman. (After Carson died, Letterman did an entire monologue of Carson-supplied material.) The two even appeared on the cover of *Rolling Stone*'s comedy issue together, with Carson's hand jauntily draped over Letterman's shoulder, a significant gesture, given the much-vaunted armored-vault thickness of Carson's frosty reserve. (Before he retired, Carson joked in a monologue that former staffers were trying to copyright the words "cold" and "aloof" for use in their memoirs.)

What comedians admired about Carson was his poise, steely resilience, generosity to younger comics, Swiss-watch timing, and ability to mask his true emotions despite the camera's stark examination, always maintaining a keen aura of ellipsis and enigma. Ironically, most of these qualities are what all of the late-night stars in this multi-sided kung fu cabaret—contender, pretender, and defender alike—have lacked. They have been incontinent, spilling their spleens, personalizing everything at a lowball level. (And then Letterman and Leno making cute with that dorky-looking Super Bowl stunt ad.) It will continue to make for great TV as Leno and Letterman face off on the ice again in competing time slots and O'Brien knits a network deal, but the adult supervision that Carson embodied will become further a relic of the past. The nearest cousin to Carson's irritable, opaque cool can be found on television today only in *Mad Men*'s Don Draper, and he's a fictional creation. Oh, and Barack Obama, equally lean, quick, and unrattleable, and there are those who think he's fictional, too.

Vanity Fair, April 2010

Jerry Lewis
Last Tuxedo Standing

Remember the old joke about bandleader Guy Lombardo—"When Guy Lombardo dies, he's taking New Year's Eve with him"? Oh sure you don't. Every December 31, Guy and his Royal Canadians would ring out the old / ring in the new to the shipboard sway of "Auld Lang Syne" in a national broadcast that made the conductor synonymous with balloons dropping at midnight and wheezing kazoos. Then death stilled Guy's baton, deputizing Dick Clark and Ryan Seacrest to carry on the holiday tradition, and so America's decline began. Could this be the year when Jerry Lewis takes Labor Day as we know it with him? Not because Jerry's due to join Lombardo in that big ballroom in the sky, though at the age of eighty-five he has to be careful how hard he blows out the birthday candles, but because this will be the last Labor Day weekend that he will be hosting the Jerry Lewis Muscular Dystrophy Telethon, raising millions for "Jerry's Kids." When Lewis sings "You'll Never Walk Alone" at this year's close, as he has tearfully, raggedly, undauntedly done for the last forty-five years, it will be the end of a showbiz era, a proud reign of pomade. A performer since the age of five, Lewis himself embodies the end of an era stretching from vaudeville to Las Vegas—the last surviving clown prince of nightclub comedy and movie slapstick mime. His former partner Dean Martin, that golden raisin whose crooning voice poured like a pitcher of caramel goo, died in 1995 and was the subject of a crackling bromantic memoir by Lewis (co-written with James Kaplan), called *Dean and Me: A Love Story*. (A one-sided love story, Dean's cool indifference being as tough as Naugahyde. The emotional bullet of the book comes when Lewis tells Dean about the love that glued their teamwork, and Martin fires back point-blank: "You can talk about love all you want. To me, you're nothing but a fucking dollar sign.") Jerry's sidekick announcer for the telethon, Ed McMahon, whose copper pipes and heigh-o ebullience seemed immortal, passed away in 2009. The telethon will be less of a marathon this Labor Day, shortened to six hours from the twenty-one-hour gruelers of the past. Its former duration imbued it with psychodrama and suspense as Jerry, racked by fatigue and frustration, would start laying a super-heavy guilt trip on those sitting on their wallets and reluctant to give. As Harry Shearer wrote in his epic piece "Telethon," published in *Film Comment*, "It's a Jewish-Puritan spectacle. You should enjoy; then you should feel bad; then you should give money to feel good again."

The telethon is the one TV formula that has worked for Lewis since he and Dean divorced. In 1963, Lewis presided over a live, two-hour variety show on Saturday night that became a fabled shambles. It aspired to class, elegance, sophistication, and all that good stuff. Dick Cavett, hired as a young writer for the extravaganza, recalled that the premiere resembled a Hollywood gala from the golden age. "[Lewis] dressed himself and all the guests in tuxedos. But not only the guests. Camera operators, stage hands, ushers, off-camera crew, men invisible up in the flies wore, many for the first time, no doubt, black tie." Unfortunately, the nation's television critics, many of them probably sitting at home in their un-darned socks, cried phooey. "The first show got reviews comparable to the account of the attempted mooring of the Hindenburg at Lakehurst," observed Cavett. Then President Kennedy was assassinated and the nation was in even less of a mood for an uproarious romp. Two decades later Lewis tried again on TV in a more manageable format, a syndicated talk show for Metromedia where, flanked by master of mimicry Charlie Callas (he of the iguana tongue), he invited other showbiz luminaries into his make-believe living room so that they could tell one another how great they were. In Jerry Lewis's universe, every kindred star was not only a phenomenal talent but a great humanitarian, a humble peasant at heart, and a complete, total pussycat. My personal favorite highlight from the series' brief run was when Lewis told singer Mel Tormé from the bottom of his gourd, "You have driven your theatrical prowess through the galaxies and back," and the Velvet Fog didn't even blush or act abashed, accepting such tribute as his due. If the show had been giddier in its soapy back scrubbing of ego and less of a comedy seminar, it might have achieved the groovy schmaltz of Sammy Davis Jr.'s weekly talk show, *Sammy and Company*, which inspired the classic *SCTV* send-up "The Sammy Maudlin Show," where Joe Flaherty's host Sammy Maudlin would slap his thigh silly from uncontrollable laughter at some lame joke. No, the *SCTV* sketch that *Lewis* inspired was the beyond twisted "Martin Scorsese's Jerry Lewis Live on the Champs-Élysées," where, between infantile gags and tearful outbursts, Martin Short's Jerry would gnomically reflect, "Where are you, the public, expected to find the love and the caring and the feeling and the good and the nice? And even if you did, it wouldn't be the good kind, because of the difference caused by the earlier thing." At the finale, baguettes bombarded the stage as part of the audience ovation.

The acclaim of the French has become a horse collar around Lewis's neck, a source of domestic ridicule from our own tastemakers. How many millions of times have you heard someone scoff, "What do the French know? They think Jerry Lewis is a genius." The French know a lot (Jeanne Moreau's smoky silences contain multitudes), and perhaps to French cinéastes Lewis's comedy possesses an abstract, askew formalism—a klutzy Kabuki quality that to Americans is simply the candy machine of kiddie entertainment going tilt. On the sets of film comedies such as *The Ladies Man*, *The Bellboy*, and *The Errand Boy*, in his canvas throne as actor-screenwriter-director-producer (his guidebook for aspiring multi-talents was titled *The Total Film-Maker*), he presided over a giant dollhouse, his personal puppet theater—the precursor to *Pee-wee's Playhouse*. In his schlemiel roles, Lewis adopts a stooped, knock-kneed posture, as if his body were collapsing inwardly, the Cubistic angles unable to bear the load of the next mishap to befall him. He's a defective beta product aspiring to be an alpha-male Big Man on Campus. This duality was the basis for his most enduring character, the Nutty Professor, a Jekyll-and-Hyde figure who was an ineffectual, milquetoast mutterer until he swallowed the potion that transformed him into Buddy Love, the lounge-lizard lady-killer whose kiss-off arrogance literally blew cigarette smoke into the faces of squares. The perfect name, because love for Lewis is always laced with lippy demand—Come on, baby, give. (The string of stations that broadcast his fund-raising telethon are known as the Love Network, as if asking the viewers to pucker up and deliver.)

For his films' sentimental interludes, those muffled pleas for love, Lewis would inflict Pagliacci sad-sackness on the camera, much as Jackie Gleason did as the "Poor Soul" and the mute in *Gigot*, or Red Skelton did putting on the clown paint and Emmett Kelly rags. In 1972, Lewis went all out, directing *The Day the Clown Cried* and starring as the broken-down circus clown who entertains Jewish children en route to the extermination camp, eventually joining them in the gas chamber. The feel-bad movie of the century, it was unfinished and never released, growing in rumor and legend into the most talked-about, apocrypha-shrouded film for fortune hunters everywhere, along with Orson Welles's uncompleted *The Other Side of the Wind*. Harry

Shearer, one of the few to have laid eyes on a rough cut of *The Day the Clown Cried*, compared it to flying to Tijuana and finding a painting of Auschwitz on black velvet, an act of bad taste that defies reason.

Given such follies, not to mention his Paleolithic attitude toward female comics and gross lapses into stereotypical ethnic humor, it's easy to be derisive of Jerry Lewis, to regard *him* as black-velvet kitsch. I've always found Lewis more fascinating than ha-ha funny, and the source of his fascination is the core power he possesses, his prodigious boiler system. So many comedians seem to shrink into themselves when they're not going for laughs, the light in their refrigerator going out once the door closes. When Jim Carrey and Robin Williams go the sincere route, they lose their elasticity as performers, become ordinary. Lewis is the opposite. When he isn't "on," he's the opposite of off; his presence intensifies with an increase of dark matter, transmitting scary-dad authority even when trussed up and immobile, as he was playing the talk-show host held hostage in Martin Scorsese's *The King of Comedy* (1983). His seething undercurrent isn't solely a matter of temperament. For years it was also rooted in physical anguish. In 1965, Lewis took a spill on a wet spot on the set of the Andy Williams variety show that fractured his skull and knocked a chip out of his spinal column. He was tormented by misery and nausea until he was given Percodan, which lofted away the pain but also inflated his sense of well-being and eventually curtained him behind a thick haze. Performing was like flying through fog. "In fact," Lewis says in *Dean and Me*, "I'm ashamed to say that there's an entire block of MDA Telethons—some four or five years in the mid- and late-seventies—that I have no recollection of whatsoever." Those were the telethons whose run-on monologues and flares of temper made voyeur fiends out of Harry Shearer and TV junkies. It was the punk era, and in his own way Jerry fit right in.

In past years, part of the Telethon's lure was the opportunity to see this beautiful humanitarian turn self-pitying and nasty as the hours dragged by. You could count on a really ugly rampage if you held out till five or six in the morning. "Where are all my so-called good friends in Las Vegas?" he once demanded in the doldrums of a New York telethon. "They say, 'Jerry, God bless you, you're doing great things,' but I would really like to hear where the hell these people are when I need them . . ."

—Harry Shearer, "Telethon," *Film Comment*, 1979

There'll be none of that this year. Jerry won't be working a grave-yard shift, there's no one left to harangue, and the mood will be valedictory. Jerry will continue until he drops, driving his theatrical prowess through the galaxies and back, because that's what those in his entertainment generation do, and his will be the last tuxedo standing.

Vanity Fair, September 2011

Christopher Guest
Mystery Guest

A hard guy to figure (he looks like the winner of a staring contest), Christopher Guest may be the most familiar unfamiliar face in comedy today—and its most inconspicuous *auteur*. His career has been a series of below-the-radar strikes that have left his secret identity intact, despite his being (a) a half-brother of journalist and Pac-Man partygoer Anthony Haden-Guest, (b) a baron, a title inherited from his late father, Peter Haden-Guest, a member of the British House of Lords who died in 1996 (Guest dropped the "Haden" part after his first audition, when his full name got a sniffy response—casting directors can be so cruel), and (c) the husband of actress Jamie Lee Curtis, no stranger to hullabaloo. Despite all that potential "Page Six" fodder, he has managed to stay aloof. He's the caretaker of an opaque face—a Buster Keatonesque mask—that seldom divulges unnecessary information or cracks a public smile. Simulating a blank cartridge, he's always in deadpan disguise.

Born in 1948, Guest started on the Broadway stage in the early seventies in *Room Service* and *Moonchildren*, but found his calling as a writer-performer in the Off Broadway satirical revue *National Lampoon's Lemmings*. He wrote for comedy specials starring Lily Tomlin and Martin Short, and became a cast member of *Saturday Night Live* for one season, perhaps his most memorable segment being an Olympics spoof in which he coached Short and Harry Shearer in their quest to become members of the first all-male synchronized-swim team. Splashing like ducks, the undaunted duo kept thrusting their arms as if reaching for Olympic gold. His film career ranges from bit parts in gritty urban dramas such as *The Hospital*, *The Hot Rock*, and *Death Wish* to fleshier roles in *Beyond Therapy*, *The Princess Bride*, and *A Few Good Men*. He made his biggest notch in a fluky success that has achieved cult status and become a franchise: Rob Reiner's 1984 "mockumentary," *This Is Spinal Tap*, where he played Nigel Tufnel, the snail-brained lead guitarist of the bad-luck heavy-metal band Spinal Tap, those lumbering Druids of schlock rock. Since its original release, *This Is Spinal Tap* has spun followups such as the Spinal Tap album *Break Like the Wind*, a reunion tour, and a special DVD edition of the movie being released this month—evidence that dinosaurs still roam the earth.

It is as a director that Guest has spun wonders with an invisible hand. His first feature, *The Big Picture* (1989), was a genial Hollywood satire about studio politics and artistic compromise raised to a higher plane by Martin Short's crazed, boomerang performance as a queeny agent with his own personal line of showbiz schmooze. The embodiment of Hollywood temptation was a starlet played by a ripe-for-picking Teri Hatcher, wielding a Dustbuster as an erotic device during a fantasy seduction. Stocked with other kooky elements (Jennifer Jason Leigh as a lyrically ditsy filmmaker—a West Coast copy of a Tama Janowitz artiste), *The Big Picture* nevertheless had a conventional look and story structure. You sensed Guest was hemming himself in to keep everything neatly folded. His forte as a performer-director is in the *This Is Spinal Tap* arena of put-on docudrama, where loose ends can be left untucked. *Waiting for Guffman* (1997), a comedy about an amateur theatrical group staging a musical tribute to their hometown's sesquicentennial, is a stunning ensemble piece capped by Guest's own ionospheric performance as Corky St. Clair, a local Diaghilev who dreams big and burns with more ardor than talent. (And we do mean burns. His stage adaptation of *Backdraft* resulted in a fire that torched the theater.) With the bangs of his monkish bowl-cut establishing a cutoff line above his gleaming, demented eyes, Corky practices spaz moves and Frankenstein lurches alone in his apartment that he later translates into "choreography." A colorful dresser, Corky is a refugee from the audition grind of New York, where even Off Off Off *Off* Broadway didn't want him, a painful odyssey he recounts as if still pulling out the thorns. Vain, temperamental, silly, he's redeemed by his determination to put on a good show—whatever else, he *cares*. (The Guffman in the title is a Godot figure—a New York talent scout whose delayed arrival keeps everyone in suspense.)

Like Mike Judge's *Office Space* and the Coen brothers' *The Big Lebowski*, *Waiting for Guffman* is a sleeper that has gained "legs" on video and cable, expanding its in-crowd following into an admiration society. Working with many of the oddballs from *Waiting for Guffman* (Eugene Levy, Catherine O'Hara, Parker Posey, and Bob Balaban, among others), Guest now presents *Best in Show*, a "dogumentary" about competitive purebreds and the neurotic owners tugging at the other end of their leashes. Premiering at the Toronto International Film Festival in September, *Best in Show* extends Guest's reach into the realm of the normal, everyday weird. I interviewed Guest, that elusive butterfly, at the Beverly Hills office of Castle Rock Entertainment the morning after a screening of the film at Sony Studios. I was too shy to remind him we had met before. After I had interviewed his wife at their home in Beverly Hills regarding her starring role in the cop melodrama *Blue Steel*, he got stuck driving me back to the hotel. Our efforts at small talk during the ride were a small trial for us both, a discomfort I tried to dispel by babbling.

Seating himself in the spare, bare room at Castle Rock, which looks like the office of a failed business or a political campaign that has pulled up stakes, he makes no mention of our former meeting. His hair has grayed over the years, but otherwise he looks unchanged. Like most directors, he's watchful, but he also has the odd, neutral calm of a pod person, able to replicate a host body and assume its identity, leaving behind a dead husk. A *Vogue* interviewer in 1987 noted that during their chat Guest so dissolved into the personae of two characters he was imitating that he himself seemed to vanish. I had the eerie sensation he could exit the interview room looking like me, which would certainly make Jamie Lee drop the Hamburger Helper when he got home.

The idea for *Best in Show*, says Guest, sprouted from his experience walking his own pooches in a local dog park and observing the other owners' "religious fervor for their breeds." Even the canine world has its caste system. Guest began attending blue-ribbon dog shows, studying their rituals and gamesmanship and the qualities that separate a true champion from the rest of the bowwows. Take that papillon Kirby that won the Westminster Kennel Club show in 1999—what a trouper. "I'm certainly no expert, even though I've done a lot of research for this film, but that dog was a very animated dog. I mean, I wouldn't go so far as to say [that] dog is any more motivated than a Saint Bernard, but it certainly was a peppy little item. Of course, you could say that about certain actors."

The peppy actors in *Best in Show* include *SCTV* alumni Levy and O'Hara as Gerry and Cookie Fleck, a cheerfully tacky twosome from Fern City, Florida ("Don't water the plants, they're plastic!" Gerry yells to the house sitters); Guest himself in a hunting cap as a bucolic goober who seems to have undergone a mind-meld with his bloodhound, Hubert; a wealthy dope and her adept dog handler, played by Jennifer Coolidge and a sparkling Jane Lynch; a gay couple with kimonos for every occasion (John Michael Higgins and Spinal Tapper Michael McKean); and Michael Hitchcock and Parker Posey as a highly caffeinated couple whose tense shallowness is like a sheet of glass about to shatter. As in a Robert Altman film, the showcase finale in *Best in Show*—a prestigious dog show modeled on the annual Westminster Kennel Club event, with Fred Willard wringing every atom of jolly inanity out of the role of a Joe Garagiola–like commentator—is a pretext for setting the characters into motion and connecting the dots between them until the moment of crash-pile convergence. But where the clueless subjects of Altman's *Health* and *Ready to Wear* wander foggily through the director's free-floating dyspepsia (the last one standing wins the booby prize), Guest's misfits and dreamers enjoy his full hospitality. His humor isn't based on humiliation. When one of the dogs misbehaves and has to be disqualified, it's comic without being cruel. He doesn't dole out punishment by playing nasty tricks on his characters.

Guest, in his own undemonstrative way, loves his characters because he loves the actors who invest them with their pent-up vitality and invention. Although he and co-scenarist Eugene Levy prepared a basic blueprint for *Best in Show*, the scenes themselves, as in *Waiting for Guffman*, are totally impromptu. "It's 100 percent improvised," Guest says. "There is no script. There's no dialogue written." This puts the burden and the glory on the actors, who have to navigate a behavioral strait between the anomic numbness of Andy Warhol superstars and the blowhard posturing of John Cassavetes's cinéma-vérité loudmouths (see *Husbands*). Steeped in improv comedy, Guest knows how to pick actors who can handle a lobbed pass and wing a scene without becoming mannered and camera-conscious. "They're the best people at this I think that there are. And that is my joy in doing this. These are not moneymaking propositions. These are small movies, but I think the value for people working in them is that they get to do what they do, and they're not given the chance to do that in a conventional movie." (*Waiting for Guffman* cost $1.9 million and grossed $8.1 million.)

This fosters an esprit de corps that's missing from many, if not most, movie sets, where the size and specs of the stars' trailers can trigger power plays. "Nobody shows up late," Guest says of his shoots. "Everyone gets the same amount of money. Everyone has the same trailer. Everyone has the same everything, including me." When it all cooks and the actors hit a high groove, it's like Christmas. "It's a gift that these people have that is to me one of the most satisfying things to watch because I'm a musician as well. It's like having someone solo and then you back out a little bit, and then they solo, and it's just . . . they're soaring. They're making these words up, and to me it's the ultimate. It's acting at the highest level in many ways, because these moments are literally real and happening for the first time. And maybe subliminally the audience can know that. I don't know. I hope."

This let-'er-rip approach has been a boon to the great Catherine O'Hara, whose other film work—mom parts in *Beetlejuice* and *Home Alone*—hasn't touched the highs of her *SCTV* creations, such as the ultra-needy nightclub legend Lola Heatherton, a lethal combination of Lola Falana and Joey Heatherton in a vinyl mini. (Similarly, Levy, who did inspired work for *SCTV*, is better known to mainstream audiences as the dad in *American Pie*.) Guest's films have released the carbonation in O'Hara. One of the peak moments in *Waiting for Guffman*, where her Sheila is married to Fred Willard's unflappable Ron, is her drunken tirade in a Chinese restaurant. Ignoring Ron's shushing, Sheila blurts out comments about his penis-reduction operation and uncircumcised member. It's an uncomfortably funny bit spilling over into hysteria, like watching a tipsy Lucille Ball completely lose it and begin to snarl. When Guest edited *Waiting for Guffman*, O'Hara's pouty tantrum was the first scene he screened. "I looked at the scene, I thought, This is really scary. This is dark. This is insane, it's absolute madness." Living in London at the time, he invited the actor Tom Conti over to take a gander. "And he liked it. But it really is on the edge of going way over. And that representation of her drunk is the greatest thing. I mean, I've never seen anything like that in a movie where it says so much about so many things."

In *Best in Show*, O'Hara's Cookie, dressed like another Erin Brockovich, with cleavage you could yodel into, is a happily married woman who mowed men down like tenpins in her bachelorette days. Wherever she goes, she bumps into a former lover who grows amorous at the fond memory of the bedsheets they scorched together. "I banged a lot of waitresses in my time, but you were the best," says one old beau, a testimonial that brings no cheer to hubby. (Levy's fuming reaction indicates a blood-pressure gauge needling toward the danger zone.) What's wonderful about these encounters is the mixture of pride, embarrassment, and still-hot-to-trot eagerness that percolates through Cookie's bloodstream and surfaces in an abashed blush. "She just melts," Guest says, "as if she's just melting, and remembering. You can just see that happen. Well, that never happened before. That had never been rehearsed." Sometimes it takes veteran talent to generate virgin responses.

Guest's comedies simulate not only the look of mundane life (the fake-wood paneling, the souvenir knickknacks) but also the sound. He prefers conversation au naturel to the blustering dialogue of screenplays. Like the British dramatist Alan Bennett, he has a connoisseur's appreciation for the banal remark dropped like a glove, the vacant pause. "That's what I like about real conversations when I eavesdrop, the fact that there's no pace. I love the boredom in between those moments, where people look at each other and there's nothing happening." A choice example of nothing happening occurs in *Waiting for Guffman* when Parker Posey's Libby Mae Brown—who auditions for Corky's theatrical with a rousing nymphet rendition of "Teacher's Pet"—reflects on her job at Dairy Queen. Trying to recall how long she's worked at "the DQ," she draws a blank. She stares into inner space for what seems like a long ellipsis . . . Guest: "It takes something like ten seconds for her to come up with [an answer], and I think that to me is really fearless in the best way for an actor, because that's the kind of moment you can't have in a conventional movie because they say you got to tighten up."

In *Best in Show*, Posey is the extreme opposite of Libby Mae's daydream believer. Once the Princess Pocahontas of indie cinema, based on her spin-the-dial omnipresence in films such as *Party Girl*, *The House of Yes*, and *The Daytrippers*, Posey has gone from a cutie-pie phase into savage case-study mode. Scarily thin, she plunges bladelike into every scene. She and Michael Hitchcock play Meg and Hamilton Swan, the distraught owners of a Weimaraner named Beatrice. In the film's opening scene they explain to a pet therapist that Beatrice is still reeling from the shock of witnessing them coupling in a Kamasutra position known as "the Congress of the Cow." This primal scene was too much for Bea's fragile psyche: she lolls her head like a Victorian maiden overby the vapors. We soon surmise that what's bumming the poor canine is not a Freudian complex but the burden of her owners' expectations. Fanatically committed to winning, Meg and Hamilton ride each other's patience to the breaking point, reaching a screaming crescendo when they misplace Beatrice's favorite chew-toy before the dog show and, unable to replace it, turn on each other like snapping cobras. It's as if the only thing keeping them together is their tangled nerves. As psychodramatic as their freak-outs are in the film, they represent only the tip of their profound dysfunction. "Oh, my God, this is so deeply disturbing, this relationship, this hate," thought Guest, modulating their *Who's Afraid of Virginia Woolf?* grudge matches so that they wouldn't warp the rest of the movie. Now he feels he's achieved the right balance of sweet lunacy and shooting sparks. Unfortunately, this taming of the shrews meant losing Meg and Ham's deeply considered rumination on shopping catalogues and the mental states they conjure. Holidays and fireplaces . . . so L.L. Bean, and mornings—mornings are pure J. Crew. (This notion derives from an idea Guest had years ago of staging a party scene in a movie where all of the extras would be catalogue models, a casualwear layout come to life.)

"You could make a hundred movies. If you were to give this footage to someone who was independent of this initial process, you could make a hundred different films. Yes. You could stress one character over another. You could obviously eliminate things. In all these movies, there have been subplots which have disappeared." (A missing subplot in *This Is Spinal Tap* explains how the band members contracted their mysterious herpes sores.) This stockpile of alternative angles and directions to pursue is made available by the superabundance of film shot. *This Is Spinal Tap*, eighty-two minutes long, was mined from fifty-five hours of material. *Waiting for Guffman* and *Best in Show*, both of which run under an hour and a half, were each whittled down from sixty hours of footage. It's sifting through a mountain of sand to fill a popcorn bag. But in the age of DVD, nothing discarded is irretrievably lost. I was happy to hear that a DVD version of *Waiting for Guffman* is planned.

Regardless of how Guest's movies are divvied up on the plate, they appeal to a minority taste, a situation he recognizes and accepts. "Obviously, I mean, if you look at what I've done, I'm not exactly going to jump on any bandwagons. I can't think that way. I'm not good at that." Even if he were so inclined, there's an age gap hindering him from surfing the latest fads. Guest is a baby-boomer working mostly with other baby-boomers, a guild of experienced pros. Maturity is a liability in today's comedy market, where the characters spurt enough liquid and gas to create a new smog cover and the screenwriters try to keep pace with the arms buildup in dildo jokes. Filmmakers, critics, and audiences are infantilizing themselves, risking diaper rash and establishing incontinence as an artistic credo. (The reviewer for *Slate* lauded *South Park: Bigger, Longer & Uncut* by saying that he hadn't felt such bliss since he was potty-trained, a joy shared by a colleague at *Salon*, who tried to sink the Tidi-Bowl man with her essay "Shit-Eating Grins: In Defense of Adam Sandler, *South Park*, and the Proud Tradition of Poop Humor.") The ideal viewer for Guest's films isn't an arrested child digging for buried treasure in the litter box; it's a grown-up capable of appreciating the mileage on Guest's mixed nuts and the widening lane between what they wanted from life and what they got.

His "mockumentaries" are about middle-aged, middle-class also-rans who've deluded themselves into thinking that the only thing separating them from stardom is a lucky break. They still dream of hitting it big even as their bouffants continue to deflate. Their refusal to give up their illusions accounts for the films' lingering melancholy. After his characters' brush with celebrity, they go their separate ways back into obscurity. In the coda to *Waiting for Guffman*, Libby Mae is working at a Dairy Queen in a different state to be near her father, who just got out of jail; Corky opens a movie-memorabilia store in New York City which sells *My Dinner with André* action figures and Brat Pack dolls; Ron and Sheila, once the royal couple of their town's theater scene, become Hollywood extras in cowboy suits. There's a sadness to everyone's perseverance. *Best in Show* has a similar soft landing, leavened by a few parting laughs.

If some of Guest's characters seem to be wearing goldfish bowls on their heads to fend off reality, it may be because their director purposely inhabits his own bubble. With superhuman restraint he steers clear of reading reviews of his work or articles about the entertainment business, not only because he doesn't want the *Daily Variety–Hollywood Reporter* seismograph of who's up/who's down wired into his nervous system, but also, perhaps, so that he can people his films with characters whose existences are independent of media stereotypes. The implication of his remarks, delivered off the record, is unmistakable: he won't be reading the article I'm writing about him, either. Fine, deprive yourself of my salient insights and plush imagery! Like Gloria Gaynor, I will survive. Besides, I've interviewed enough comedians to know each has his own method of maintaining his inner weirdness. Guest's just happens to be more tamper-resistant than most. He preserves his talent under a tight lid.

Vanity Fair, October 2000

Mort Sahl
Mort the Knife

May I commit an act of cultural blasphemy and abject philistinism?

I never found Lenny Bruce that funny. He never set my attic ablaze.

Yes, I'm aware, as are we all, that he was a Swiftian satirist, a renegade demiurge in *Reader's Digest* America, a nightclub shaman performing psychic surgery on a sick society, a human torpedo on a suicide run against encrusted authority, pious hypocrisy, and Puritan taboo. Unjustly persecuted and prosecuted for obscenity, he died for our sins and all that. (The photo of Bruce's body lying dead on the floor following a drug overdose is as iconic a portrait of Christ-bearded martyrdom as the grubby presentation of Che Guevara's bony cadaver by Bolivian officials.) Bruce's inspirational impact and influence are undeniable—it's near impossible to imagine Richard Pryor, the Philip Roth of *Portnoy's Complaint*, the Stanley Kubrick of *Dr. Strangelove*, or the power of the Ramones being uncapped if Bruce's id hadn't unlocked so many forbidden drawers. Listening to his old routines, I can appreciate the switchblade flick of his attack, the quick-change artistry of his shifting personas ("He do the police in different voices," to quote the evocative line from Dickens), and his jackpot glee when his shock tactics strike home—his proto-punk bravado as agent provocateur. But as I make mental clicks of recognition for each point he scores or verbal pivot he executes, I don't find myself actually *laughing* that much. A lot of Bruce's routines today are like the punny gags in Shakespeare—fustian hairballs.

Mort Sahl was always more my guy. If I didn't already have a father, Mort could be my father, my sarcastic, honorary dad. I'd watch him on now defunct talk shows hosted by Steve Allen, Jack Paar, and Merv Griffin, and his staccato phrasing and scratchy contempt in the service of honesty would switch on the Christmas-tree lights in my head like the first deluge of Bob Dylan's sneerings and snarlings on *Highway 61 Revisited*. Here was the unshaven voice of democracy! And so I still believe, even though traditional pop-criticism dogma has decreed that St. Lenny of Bruce was the more authentic prophet of the atomic age, the true shaggy mouth of the inferno. As Albert Goldman neatly formulated it in his gonzo biography (with Lawrence Schiller), *Ladies and Gentlemen, Lenny Bruce!!*: "Mort Sahl was hip; Lenny Bruce was a hipster." What Mort riffed about secondhand, Lenny lived, man. According to the gospel, Mort was a mohair dabbler and dilettante who shunned hazardous excess. He didn't curse or drink, and would have paled at the prospect of a heroin needle violating his limpid veins. His jazz-aficionado tastes ran to Stan Kenton and Dave Brubeck, neither of whom was associated with the netherworld. Whereas Lenny, the Jewish prince of perdition, had the sacrificial courage of his convictions. He cursed, drank, did drugs, and dug jazz on a deep, substratum, superspade level of sponge-worthiness. "[Lenny] hung out with the heavy cats—got right down with them," Goldman wrote with obvious approval. Sahl didn't hang out and/or get down with the heavy cats. He failed the heavy-cat test of white negritude.

Far be it from me to condemn those who decline to walk on the wild side for fear of ruining their penny loafers. One can admire the daredevilry of Bruce's diving nerve while also wondering why Sahl or any other vital container of talent should be penalized—docked points on the hip scoreboard—for observing the guardrail and practicing self-preservation, not to mention proper hygiene. Death may be a good career move, as in the cases of Elvis Presley and Kurt Cobain, but on a personal level it doesn't get you anywhere; for those with long-range plans, early demise is rather counterproductive. Me, I like it when artists that I admire manage to stick around awhile. A lifestyle which eschewed alcohol and narcotics, coupled with an avoidance of heavy cats and the humid dramas they drag indoors, may help account for Sahl's patent-leather resilience—the happy fact that instead of dying before his time in a dopey haze, he marked his eightieth birthday on May 11 and was fêted on June 28 at Brentwood's Wadsworth Theatre with a "Sahlebration" whose prospective list of toastmasters featured Jay Leno, Bill Maher, Richard Lewis, Sydney Pollack, David Steinberg, Shelley Berman, and Woody Allen, along with a few surprise guests whose identities were being held in reserve as we went to press. It's a long-overdue tribute to a lean cat who never lost a sense of mission and whose tale, as *The New Yorker*'s Adam Gopnik rightly discerned, "would make a better movie than Lenny Bruce's did."

A founding member of the banner generation of stand-up comics, satirical sketch artists, and professional fidgets whose roster includes Allen, Berman, Bob Newhart, Dick Gregory, cartoonist Jules Feiffer, and the team of Mike Nichols and Elaine May (the Rudolf Nureyev and Margot Fonteyn of exquisitely turned-out neuroses), Mort Sahl was the one who introduced air, light, and news-with-attitude into the isolation booth of cornball stand-up. "He totally restructured comedy," Allen is quoted saying in Gerald Nachman's *Seriously Funny: The Rebel Comedians of the 1950s and 1960s*. From his first performance at San Francisco's hungry i, in 1953, Sahl revolutionized the monologue by informalizing it and relaxing the dress code, spurning the snappy attire of overgrown Borscht Belt bar mitzvah boys for a campus-intellectual V-necked sweater, comfortable slacks, and a mock-pedantic air. (Later he would get downright professorial, diagramming political dynamics on a chalkboard.) With his imperative sense of forward motion ("Onward," he would say by way of transition, charging ahead to the next topic), Sahl was to the spoken word what Jack Kerouac was to the written word—the great emancipator of extemporaneity.

Unlike the bleary king of the Beats, Sahl didn't succumb to sentimental blubber. From the outset he was trim, astringent, paradoxical. Absorbing the lefty, low-rent boho *mise en scène* of the Berkeley campus following a tour of duty in the air force ("Things were simple then," he would later muse about his scroungy Berkeley days, adding, "All there was to worry about was man's destiny"), Sahl sauntered onstage with a folded newspaper and swatted current events around ("keeping up on current events" being a prime directive of the postwar era) as if it were the most natural thing in the world to do. He introduced muscle relaxant into the body language of stand-up. Rejecting the rivet-gun rhythms of traditional nightclub jokesters, he adopted a conversational, thinking-aloud approach, the first comic to address the audience as educated adults capable of laughing at their own nasal pretensions and Freudian hangups. He was adversarial to society at large and advocational with the audience. Where Lenny Bruce played existential ringmaster with two-drink-minimum patrons, seducing and taunting them with a cobra stare and a lewd dart of his tongue (as the critic Pauline Kael observed, "He vamped the audience with a debauched, deliberately faggy come-hither that no one knew quite how to interpret; he was uncompromisingly not nice"), Sahl practiced sympathetic magic as the Pied Piper of the highly strung, enlisting his camp followers—or, as he half ironically called them, "my people"—in a varsity fellowship.

It wasn't that Sahl lacked a killer instinct or intestinal fire. In a profile published in *The New Yorker* titled "The Fury" (1960), Robert Rice found his subject as "uncompromising" as Kael considered Bruce, capable of devouring Little Red Riding Hood in a single gulp: "[Sahl] hurls his words ferociously at his listeners, almost without pausing to breathe. He has big white teeth, which, when he says something destructive enough to amuse even him, suddenly glare from his lean and sardonic face in a wolfish grin, and if he becomes truly transported by the damage he is doing, he erupts into a staccato two-syllable bark of triumph." To my ear, that wolf bark is less a note of vainglory than a climactic release of nervous energy—an exclamation mark shot from an electric grate. (Sometimes Sahl laughs in *anticipation* of what he's about to say, as if what just popped into his head strikes him as funny, too.) Similarly, Rice seems to be trying to give *The New Yorker*'s prudential readers a hearty scare when he portrays Sahl as a nouveau riche "nihilist" relishing every ounce of havoc he uncorks. For all its toothy flare, Sahl's humor was never a negation device, a homemade bomb intended for the palace. "In truth," the social historian Stephen E. Kercher writes in *Revel with a Cause: Liberal Satire in Postwar America*, "Sahl during the 1950s was less a revolutionist than a liberal Democrat." Sahl was hardly a locked-in-cement, doctrinaire liberal: he later befriended former general Alexander Haig and boosted his presidential delusions, christening the campaign with the memorable one-liner that Haig had thrown his helmet into the ring. But he was so associated with liberalism in its heyday, so closely identified with the flap of its eagle wings, that as it fell out of fashion, he lost his halo status, his echo of Camelot.

Worse, Sahl became a casualty of the Kennedy curse. While enjoying his highest cruising altitude as a performer (he even cohosted the Academy Awards show in 1959!), Sahl, Kercher relates in *Revel with a Cause*, received a request from patriarch Joseph Kennedy "to write some things for Johnny," who was ramping up for a presidential run. "Over the next year and a half, Sahl honored Joseph Kennedy's request and forwarded—without a fee—a steady supply of jokes for his son." The jokes were seldom used but relations remained cordial until Sahl asserted his independence. After JFK accepted the nomination for president, at the Democratic convention in Los Angeles, Sahl claimed that rival Richard Nixon had sent a congratulatory telegram to Joseph Kennedy reading, YOU HAVEN'T LOST A SON, YOU'VE GAINED A COUNTRY. Allusions to Kennedy's wealth were a no-no in Hyannis Port circles. After Kennedy defeated Nixon, the entire clan became satirical fair game. Sahl showered the New Frontier with flaming arrows. He zinged the zealousness of Attorney General Bobby Kennedy ("Little Brother is watching you") and mocked the new administration's Cuba policy. Warned through intermediaries to lay off,

Sahl typically, perversely cranked up the volume. Kercher: "These warnings only prompted Sahl to do 'three times as much material' on the Kennedy family—some of it particularly hard-hitting. During a monologue on ABC-TV's short-lived 'Jerry Lewis Show,' for example, Sahl even jokingly referred to a connection between President Kennedy, mobster Sam Giancana, and the singer Frank Sinatra." Taking such names in vain was worse than dabbling in the occult! That's when the phones went dead and Sahl's career suffered its first frost. For fear of being tax-audited, nightclubs refused to book Sahl. One owner who did defy the ban—the loyal Enrico Banducci of the hungry i, the holy manger where Sahl began—saw his business go under after an IRS audit. (Happily, Banducci, a papa bear in a sporty beret, has been able to witness the hungry i's elevation into lost-legend countercultural-landmark status. He was the guest of honor this March for the opening-night celebration of the San Francisco Performing Arts Library & Museum's exhibition documenting the glory days of the club that made history.)

Like many comedians who specialize in being touchy, Sahl was capable of nursing a grudge and raising it into a fine, strapping vendetta. But when President Kennedy was assassinated in 1963, he put aside career rancor and turned crusader. "November 1963 was when the country began to unravel," he later explained to the *San Diego Jewish Journal*, "because it was then OK to shoot the president." He joined District Attorney Jim Garrison in New Orleans and plunged headfirst into the investigation of a possible conspiracy behind the events in Dallas. To some, once in, Sahl never came back up for air. "I wish I had a cause, because I have a lot of enthusiasm," he had famously joked. Now he had found a cause, only to mislay his compass. Just as Lenny Bruce read aloud from his court transcripts during his act, provoking a constant trickle to the exits, Sahl quoted extensive absurdities from the Warren Commission report that baffled and alienated the uninitiated. He also professed in a *Playboy* interview, "I certainly do believe a single conspiratorial group—call it an assassination bureau—was involved in the murders of President Kennedy, Dr. King, and Bobby Kennedy." His evangelism, coupled with his swanky hedonism (his taste in shiny toys—sunglasses, watches, hi-fi sets, cars—and flashy babes), spurred mutterings around the punch bowl that Sahl had "sold out." Today, "selling out" is so acceptably commonplace it doesn't even seem like a syndrome, but in the sixties being called a sellout carried some sting. It was a synonym for betrayal, as Dylan discovered after he was heckled as a "Judas" for going electric. By the mid-sixties, Sahl didn't need to fend off accusations of selling out, because fewer and fewer were buying. Once at the red-hot center, he found himself in the floating leper colony for lost entertainers. According to *Revel with a Cause*, "In 1965 [Sahl] earned $13,000—a steep drop from the $600,000 to $1 million annual incomes he formerly enjoyed."

In a career buffeted with highs and lows, splashy acclaim and pissy requiems, in-crowd acceptance and cold-shoulder snubbings, outliving the bastards can be the best revenge. Surviving ten presidential administrations in his career (so far), Sahl continues to perform and get laughs, firing off one-liners that retain the crack and ricochet of a rifle shot. He did a one-man show on Broadway in 1987, where he had to introduce himself to a new generation of jaded journalists ("In many of their faces he saw himself mirrored as some kind of Abominable Snowman of American Comedy shaking off a quarter century of hoarfrost as he shuffled toward Broadway's lights," wrote Lawrence Christon in the *Los Angeles Times*), covered the political conventions for *Imus in the Morning* in 1996, returned to Manhattan for a brief stint at Joe's Pub, fielded Larry King's ding-a-ling questions on CNN. His delivery betrays little buildup of rust or erosion, the intellectual turbines still whir, but a wit of Sahl's range, experience, sophistication, and voluminous files of mental information faces the same predicament confronting teachers, editors, and TV producers alike as they try to seize and hold an audience's attention in the Digital Age—the acute shrinkage of the audience's frame of reference. When Sahl first swooped, in the fifties, there was a much more homogenized, middlebrow media landscape—fewer than a handful of television networks, no Internet, no satellite radio, no iPods. Except for cable-news junkies, keeping up on current events is practically an aristocratic pursuit these days. And cultural allusions?—forget it. You can't assume the audience knows *anything* beyond the latest thong-snappings in the supermarket tabloids. Fewer and fewer ticket buyers may go to Lindsay Lohan's movies, but everyone knows who she *is*. But when Sahl mentions Estes Kefauver during a *Fresh Air* interview with Terry Gross on NPR, he's drawing a name from an abandoned well. Even I, a phony student of history, have to rub a couple of dry sticks together in my head before the name Estes Kefauver computes.

By remaining faithful to his expansive frame of reference, however esoteric it may be for those who think anything that happened the day before yesterday is ancient myth, Sahl is declining to dumb down his act or coarsen his monologues into a cartoon version of himself and the rest of humanity, as Joan Rivers and Jackie Mason have done. Their routines have degenerated into insults and put-downs of celebrities and politicians—jabbings of voodoo-doll pins. Sahl has always striven to map out something larger and wider, to get beyond personalities into the unspoken assumptions that bind us as a people and animate us to allow ourselves to be led merrily, monstrously, tragically astray. This fall Sahl will be teaching a course in critical thinking at Southern California's Claremont McKenna College (a private liberal-arts school) which will incorporate screenings of classic American movies with a social message. The movies will provide a measure of what we have lost. "I was always an optimist," he told the *Marin Independent Journal*. "I believed that movie *Mr. Smith Goes to Washington*. But the country feels like it's finished. If it isn't, it's breathing in a very shallow fashion." He, however, is still breathing fire.

Onward.

Vanity Fair, August 2007

III: PUNK, POP, ROCK

Patti x Two

Patti Smith
Mustang Rising

Patti Smith moves through a room like a shark through the lower depths. Sharp features, oilblack hair, dark intense eyes. A lithe toughness.

So her smile catches you by surprise, not only because it's switchblade quick, but because it's *not* the smile of a killer. So many reports on Patti Smith have made her sound demonic, word-crazed—a cocaine Ophelia—that I was surprised to see her so poised a performer. Her flakiness is legendary but her smile carries the weight of professional confidence.

She's spending her weekends performing with her band at CBGB sharing the bill with Television, a group led by Tom Verlaine, who has also coauthored a number of songs with her. Verlaine to her Lady Rimbaud—a good matching. And the songs themselves are better than good, the theme of all of them being: Penetration draws blood.

Sexual penetration first of all. Without working very hard at it, Patti is perhaps the most macho performer in the macho-obsessed rock scene. One night, in between songs, she casually played with the zipper on her jeans, zipping and slowly unzipping, and the gesture was vaguely disturbing. Even threatening. Is Patti the prisoner of penis envy or some vanguard heroine of pussy power? Not too difficult to imagine high school boys envious of her stray-cat cool.

The confusion is complicated further by the influence of William Burroughs on her work. In the realm of *Naked Lunch*, sex is pain, sex is sadism—every caress is a laceration. Virginal blood is spilled: thrust and flow. Penetration draws blood and not just the penetration of flesh into flesh, but of needle into flesh. During one of Patti's sets I lost count of all the references to horse, sugar, snow, tracks, snow on the tracks, tracks in the snow, "body and brain it spell cocaine," and at one point she half-chanted, "The blackest thing in Harlem is white," savoring the paradox of evil and black transcendence being bred in a white virginal powder. Perhaps this smack celebration is her way of linking herself with her heroes (Rimbaud, Burroughs, Dylan) because like them, Patti Smith is a navigator across ever-changing inner landscapes.

Which doesn't make her sound like a good time. Yet she is, she's a knockout performer: funny, spooky, a true off-the-wall original. Like the character in Dickens, she do the police in different voices. One moment she's telling an agreeably dopey joke about kangaroos ("... and Momma Kangaroo looked down and exclaimed, 'Oh, my pocket's been picked!'") and in the next she's bopping into the scatological scat of "Piss Factory."

Because of her notorious poetry readings, her reputation is largely as a crazy-as-birds stage speaker, but it's clear that she's going to be an extraordinary rock singer, maybe even a great one. Not that her voice has richness or range—there might be two hundred female rockers with better voices—no, Patti possesses a greater gift: a genius for phrasing. She's a poet of steely rhythms—her work *demands* to be read aloud—so language is her narcotic, her lover, her mustang.

And her body is as eloquent as her voice. Scrawny and angular in repose, it becomes supple and expressive when the music sways. Dressed in black jeans, black coat, and loose torn T-shirt, she dances with a smooth sassiness, her boyish hips tenderly pistoning, her bamboo-thin arms punctuating the air for emphasis. The performing area at CBGB is as tiny as a bathroom tile so it'll be interesting to see her hit stride on a larger stage.

Also interesting to speculate as to how her work will come off on record. She has a great repertoire: "Piss Factory," several UFO songs (including one about Wilhelm Reich's son), male-supremacist rock songs which are even meaner when she does them (she brings a swaggering conviction to them which Jagger & Co. just don't have anymore). Inspired reworkings of rock classics (some Smokey Robinson stuff, "Gloria," the Patty Hearst "Hey Joe"). Rock fans are going to be enraptured making all the allusive connections in her work: one of the best songs—which begins with the entrance of the four horsemen of the Apocalypse and ends with a burial in the horse latitudes—is a surreal fusion of rock mythos and horse/heroin imagery.

So would it be too awful to say that Fame is her steed if Patti Smith chooses to mount? Well, the horse might be the perfect emblem for her career. "I ride the stallion thru the dust storm" is the way she begins a poem entitled "Mustang." "Get off your mustang, Sally," is what the women told her at the Piss Factory. But Patti didn't listen, Patty said screw it, and skinny schizzy Patti is on her way to becoming the wild mustang of American rock.

The Village Voice, April 14, 1975

Tarantula Meets Mustang
Dylan Calls On Patti Smith

A copy of *Witt* was slid across the table to Patti Smith. "Would you sign this for me, please?" "Sure," said Patti, "what's your first name?" He told her. "Like in New Jersey?" Patti asked, and he said no: with a *z*. "Well, I'll draw you a map of New Jersey," and so on the inside page Patti scratched its intestinal boundaries, in the middle labeled it Neo Jersey, signed her name, and passed the copy of *Witt* back to Jerzy Kosinski.

The night before, after the second set at the Other End, the green-room door opened and the remark hanging in the air was Bob Dylan asking a member of Patti's band, "You've never been to New Jersey?" So, all hail Jersey. And in honor of Dylan's own flair for geographical salutation ("So long New York, hello East Orange"), all hail the Rock and Roll Republic of New York. With the Rolling Stones holding out at Madison Square Garden, Patti Smith and her band at the Other End, and Bob Dylan making visitations to both events, New York was once again the world's Rock and Roll Republic.

Patti Smith had a special Rimbaud-emblematized statement printed up in honor of Stones week, and when her band went into its version of "Time Is on My Side" (yes it is), she unbuttoned her blouse to reveal a Keith Richards T-shirt beneath. On the opening night she was tearing into each song and even those somewhat used to her galloping id were puzzled by lines like, "You gotta lotta nerve sayin' you won't be *my* parking meter." Unknown to many in the audience, parked in the back of the room, his meter running a little quick, was the legendary Bobby D himself. Dylan, despite his wary, quintessential cool, was giving the already highly charged room an extra layer of electricity and Patti, intoxicated by the atmosphere, rocked with stallion abandon. She was positively *playing* to Dylan, like Keith Carradine played to Lily Tomlin in the club scene from *Nashville*. But Dylan is an expert in gamesmanship and sat there crossing and uncrossing his legs, playing back.

Afterwards, Dylan went backstage to introduce himself to Patti. He looked healthy, modestly relaxed (though his eyes never stopped burning with cool blue fire), of unimposing physicality, yet the corporeal Dylan can never be separated from the mythic Dylan, and it's that *other* Dylan—the brooding, volatile, poet-star of *Don't Look Back*—who heightens or destroys the mood of a room with the tiniest of gestures. So despite Dylan's casual graciousness, everyone was excitedly unsettled.

And there was a sexual excitation in the room as well. Bob Dylan, the verdict was unanimous, is an intensely sexual provocateur—"he really got me below the belt," one of the women in the room said later. Understand, Dylan wasn't egregiously coming on—he didn't have to. For the sharp-pencil, slightly petulant vocals on *Blood on the Tracks* hardly prepared one for the warm, soft-bed tone of his speaking voice: the message driven home with that—Dylan offhand is still Dylan compelling. So with just small talk he had us all subdued, even Patti, though when the photographers' popping flashbulbs began she laughingly pushed him aside, saying "Fuck you then, take *my* picture, boys." Dylan smiled and swayed away.

The party soon broke up—Dylan had given his encouragement to Patti, the rest of us had a glimpse from some future version of *Don't Look Back* (but with a different star)—and the speculation about Dylan's visit commenced. What did his casual benediction signify?

Probably nothing was the reasonable answer. But such sensible explanations are unsatisfying, not only because it's a waste of Dylan's mystique to interpret his moves on the most prosaic level, but because the four-day engagement at the Other End convincingly demonstrated that Patti and the band are no small-time cult phenomenon. Not only was Patti in good voice, but the band is extending itself confidently. Jay Daugherty, the newly acquired drummer (he played with Lance Loud's group and lived to tell the tale) provides rhythmic heat, and Lenny Kaye has improved markedly on guitar—his solo on "Time Is on My Side" for example moves Keith Richards riffing to Verlaine slashing. The band's technical improvement has helped revivify the repertoire: "Break It Up" is not more sharply focused, "Piss Factory" is dramatically jazzy, and their anthem, "Gloria" ends the evening crashingly. Missing were "Free Money" and "Land"— the Peckinpahesque cinematic version of "Land of 1000 Dances"— which is being saved for the forthcoming album.

Something is definitely going on here, and I think I know what it is. During one of her sets Patti made the seemingly disconnected remark, "Don't give up on Arnie Palmer." But when the laughter subsided, she added, "The greats are still the greatest." Yes, of course! All her life

Patti Smith has had rock and roll in her blood—she has been, like the rest of us, a fan; this is part of her connection with her audience—and now she's returning what rock has given her with the full force of her love. Perhaps Dylan perceives that this passion is a planet wave of no small sweep. Yet what I cherished most about Patti's engagement was not the pounding rock-and-roll intensity, but a throwaway gesture of camaraderie. When Lenny Kaye was having difficulty setting up his guitar between numbers, Patti paced around, joked around, scratched her stomach, scratched her hair—still Kaye was not quite ready. "I don't really mind," she told the audience. "I mean, Mick would wait all night for Keith."

The Village Voice, July 7, 1975

The Ramones
Chord Killers

Loud, hard, and relentless, the Ramones are pagan-cult rockers whose sole god is the inviolable Chord. They function totally as a unit—I've seen ten sets and have yet to hear a solo—and when they're at their fierce, assaultive best, they remind one of Pauline Kael's description of "The Wild Bunch": "a beautiful self-destroying machine." Like the Wild Bunch, the Ramones leave nothing behind them but scorched earth.

According to their press bio, the Ramones "originate from Forest Hills and kids who grew up there either became musicians, degenerates, or dentists." More information they're not eager to give. I once left my notepad on the bar at CBGB's and asked the drummer to write down the names of the group's members and their respective instruments; later, when I looked at the notepad, all I had were first names (Dee Dee—bass, Johnny—guitar, Joey—vocals, Tommy—drums), which suggests that these guys are so function-oriented that they consider last names unnecessary equipment. The song titles are equally blunt: "Loudmouth," "I Don't Care," and "Judy Is a Punk." Such solid-component macho allows no texture or irony or ambiguity, but clearly the Ramones could care less—all they want to do is rock you dead in your tracks.

And they do. A typical set begins with Joey curled around the mike stand announcing, "I Don't Want to Go Down to the Basement," a romp quickly followed by "California Sun" and "Beat on the Brats," the set ending ferociously with "I Want to Be Your Boyfriend," all songs played with a chopping freneticism, the pace so brutal that the audience can barely catch its breath, much less applaud. A Ramones rampage is intoxicating—it's exciting to hear the voltage sizzle—but how long can they keep it up? Maybe that's why their sets average twenty minutes.

While other bands use irony as a heat shield, the Ramones aren't insulated from the fire they create. They argue a lot on stage, taking their aggression out on each other in tantrum bursts. Lou Reed's wan detachment probably wouldn't serve them well anyway: they're trying to rocket themselves into AM radio. The Ramones have a group concept and (to use Tom Wolfe's distinction) they dress not for work but for *role*, the role being a singles band with menace. I think they'll succeed, though when really revved-up the Ramones resemble a perilously overheated chopper. Catch them before they go up in flames.

The Village Voice, July 21, 1975

A Conservative Impulse in the
New Rock Underground

Arabian swelter, and with the air-conditioning broken, CBGB resembled some abattoir of a kitchen in which a bucket of ice is placed in front of a fan to cool the room off. To no avail of course, and the heat had perspiration glissading down the curve of one's back, yeah, and the cruel heat also burned away any sense of glamour. After all, CBGB's Bowery and Bleecker location is not the garden spot of lower Manhattan, and the bar itself is an uneasy oasis. On the left, where the couples are, tables; on the right, where the stragglers, drinkers, and loveseekers are, a long bar; between the two, a high double-backed ladder, which, when the room is really crowded, offers the best view. If your bladder sends a distress signal, write home to mother, for you must make a perilous journey down the aisle between seating area and bar, not knock over any mike stands as you slide by the tiny stage, squeeze through the piles of amplifiers, duck the elbow thrust of a pool player leaning over to make a shot . . . and then you end up in an illustrated bathroom which looks like a page that didn't make *The Faith of Graffiti.*

Now consider the assembly-line presentation of bands with resonant names like Movies, Tuff Darts, Blondie, Stagger Lee, the Heartbreakers, Mink de Ville, Dancer, the Shirts, Bananas, Talking Heads, Johnny's Dance Band, and Television; consider that some nights as many as six bands perform, and it isn't hard to comprehend someone declining to sit through a long evening. When the air gets thick with noise and smoke, even the most committed of us long to slake our thirst in front of a Johnny Carson monologue, the quintessential experience of bourgeois cool.

So those who stayed away are not to be chastised, except for a lack of adventurousness. And yet they missed perhaps the most important event in New York rock since the Velvet Underground played the Balloon Farm: CBGB's three-week festival of the best underground (i.e., unrecorded) bands. The very unpretentiousness of the bands' style of musical attack represented a counterthrust to the prevailing baroque theatricality of rock. In opposition to that theatricality, this was a music which suggested a resurgence of communal faith.

So this was an event of importance but not of flash. Hardly any groupies or bopperettes showed up, nor did platoons of rock writers with their sensibilities tuned into Radio Free Zeitgeist brave the near satanic humidity. When the room was packed, as it often was, it was packed with musicians and their girlfriends, couples on dates, friends and relatives of band members, and CBGB regulars, all dressed in denims and loose-fitting shirts—sartorial-style courtesy of Canal Jeans. The scenemakers and chic-obsessed were elsewhere, wherever that was.

Understandable. Rock simply isn't the brightest light in the pleasure dome any longer (my guess is that dance is), and Don Kirshner's "Rock Awards" only verifies the obvious; rock is getting as arthritic, or at least, as phlegmatic, as a rich old whore. It isn't only that the enthusiasm over the Stones tour seemed strained and synthetic, or that the Beach Boys can't seem able to release new material until Brian Wilson conquers his weight problem, or that the album of the year is a collection of basement tapes made in 1967. "The real truth as I see it," said the Who's Peter Townshend recently, "is that rock music as it was is not really contemporary to these times. It's really the music of yesteryear."

He's right and yet wrong. What's changed is the nature of the impulse to create rock. No longer is the impulse revolutionary— i.e., the transformation of oneself and society—but conservative—to carry on the rock tradition. To borrow from Eliot, a rocker now needs an historical sense; he performs "not merely with his own generation in his bones" but with the knowledge that all of pop culture forms a "simultaneous order." The landscape is no longer virginal—markers and tracks have been left by, among others, Elvis, Buddy Holly, Chuck Berry, and the Beatles—and it exists not to be transformed but cultivated.

No, I'm not saying that everyone down at CBGB's is a farmer. Must you take me so literally? But there is original vision there, and what the place itself is doing is quite extraordinary: putting on bands as if the stage were a cable television station. Public access rock. Of course not every band which auditions gets to play, but the proprietor, Hilly Kristal, must have a wide latitude of taste since the variety and quality of talent ranges from the great to the God-condemned. As with cable TV, what you get is not high-gloss professionalism but talent still working at the basics; the excitement (which borders on comedy) is watching a band with a unique approach try to articulate its vision and still remember the chords.

Television was once such a band; the first time I saw them everything was wrong—the vocals were too raw, the guitar work was relentlessly bad, the drummer wouldn't leave his cymbals alone. They were lousy all right but their lousiness had a forceful dissonance reminiscent of the Stones' *Exile on Main Street*, and clearly Tom Verlaine was a presence to be reckoned with.

He has frequently been compared to Lou Reed in the Velvet days, but he most reminds me of Keith Richards. The blood-drained bone-weary Keith on stage at Madison Square Garden is the perfect symbol for Rock '75, not playing at his best, sometimes not even playing competently, but rocking swaying back and forth as if the night might be his last and it's better to stand than fall. Though Jagger is dangerously close to becoming Maria Callas, Keith, with his lanky grace and obsidian-eyed menace, is the perpetual outsider. I don't know any rock lover who doesn't love Keith; he's the star who's always at the edge and yet occupies the center.

Tom Verlaine occupies the same dreamy realm; like Keith, he's pale and aloof. He seems lost in a forest of silence and he says about performing that "if I'm thinking up there, I'm not having a good night." Only recently has the band's technique been up to Verlaine's reveries and their set at the CBGB festival was the best I've ever seen: dramatic, tense, tender ("Hard on Love"), athletic ("Kingdom Come"), with Verlaine in solid voice and the band playing *as a band* and not as four individuals with instruments. Verlaine once told me that one of the best things about the Beatles was the way they could shout out harmonies and make them sound intimate, and that's what Television had that night, loud intimacy.

When Tom graduated from high school back in Delaware he was voted "most unknown" by his senior class. As if in revenge, he chose the name Verlaine, much as Patti Smith often invokes the name Rimbaud. He came to New York, spent seven years writing fiction, formed a group called Neon Boys, then Television. The name suggests an aesthetic of accessibility and choice. It also suggests Tom's adopted initials: T.V.

"I left Delaware because no one wanted to form a band there," he says. "Then I came to New York and no one wanted to form a band here either." Verlaine came to New York for the same reason every street-smart artist comes to New York—because it's the big league—even though he realizes "New York is not a great rock and roll town."

Still, they continue to arrive. Martina Weymouth, bassist, born in California; Chris Frantz, drummer, in Kentucky; David Byrne, singer and guitarist, Scotland. All attended the Rhode Island School of Design, and according to their bio, "now launching career in New York"—a sonorous announcement, yes?

These people call themselves Talking Heads. Seeing them for the first time is transfixing: Frantz is so far back on drums that it sounds as if he's playing in the next room; Weymouth, who could pass as Suzi Quatro's sorority sister, stands rooted to the floor, her head doing an oscillating-fan swivel; the object of her swivel is David Byrne, who has a little-boy-lost-at-the-zoo voice and the demeanor of someone who's spent the last half hour whirling around in a spin dryer. When his eyes start Ping-Ponging in his head, he looks like a cartoon of a chipmunk from Mars. The song titles aren't tethered to conventionality either: "Psycho Killer" (which goes "Psycho Killer, que'st-ce c'est? Fa-fa-fa-fa-fa-fa-fa"), "The Girls Want to Be With the Girls," "Love Is Like a Building on Fire," plus a cover version of that schlock classic by ? and the Mysterians, "96 Tears."

Love at first sight it isn't.

But repeated viewings (precise word) reveal Talking Heads to be one of the most intriguingly off-the-wall bands in New York. Musically, they're minimalists. Byrne's guitar playing is like a charcoal pencil scratching a scene on a notepad. The songs are spined by Weymouth's bass playing which, in contrast to the glottal buzz of most rock bass work, is hard and articulate—the bass lines provide hook as well as bottom. Visually, the band is perfect for the table-TV format at CBGB; they present a clean, flat image, devoid of fine shading and color. They are consciously antimythic in stance. A line from their bio: "The image we present along with our songs is what we are really like."

Talking to them, it becomes apparent that though they deny antecedents—"We would rather achieve a new sound rather than be compared to bands of the past"—they are children of the communal rock ethic. They live together, melting the distinction between art and life, and went into rock because as art it is more "accessible." They have an astute sense of aesthetic consumerism, yet they're not entirely under the Warholian sway for as one of them told me, "We don't want to be famous for the sake of being famous." Of all the groups I've seen at CBGB, Talking Heads is the closest to a neo-Velvet band, and they represent a distillation of that sensibility, what John Cale once called "controlled distortion." When the Velvets made their reputation at the Balloon Farm they were navigating through a storm of multimedia effects, mirrors, blinking lights, strobes, projected film images. Talking Heads works without paraphernalia in a cavernous room projecting light like a television located at the end of a long dark hall. The difference between the Velvets and Talking Heads is the difference between phosphorescence and cold gray TV light. These people understand that an entire generation has grown up on the nourishment of television's accessible banality. What they're doing is presenting a banal facade under which run ripples of violence and squalls of frustration—the id of the vid.

David Byrne sings tonelessly but its effect is all the more ominous. This uneasy alliance between composure and breakdown—between outward acceptance and inward coming-apart—is what makes Talking Heads such a central seventies band. A quote from ex-Velvet John Cale: "What we try to get here (at the Balloon Farm) is a sense of total involvement." Nineteen sixty-six. But what bands like Television and Talking Heads are doing is ameliorating the post-sixties hangover by giving us a sense of detachment. We've passed through the Dionysian storm and now it's time to nurse private wounds. Says Tina Weymouth, quite simply: "Rock isn't a noble cause."

More than thirty bands played at the CBGB festival. There seemed to be a lot of women in these groups, and none of them were backup singers. I asked Tina (who once introduced herself as a "bassperson") whether it was difficult to work with men in a band, and she gave me a look which said, "Don't you have any better questions to ask?" Albeit, here are some additional notes on the musicianpersons I saw performing during the three weeks:

The Shirts. Annie Golden, lead singer of this Park Slope septet, is a self-proclaimed "street punk." Her hard-skiing voice is the chief attraction in this technically proficient and equipment-abundant group (on stage they refer to themselves as the Average Cramped Band). They share an artistic commune in Brooklyn and the salient virtue of the band is that the sense of companionship comes through in the texture of the music. The very chords seem bonds of friendship.

The Heartbreakers. Totally different problem here. This band has rockers who have made names for themselves—Jerry Nolan and Johnny Thunders formerly of the New York Dolls, Richard Hell formerly of Television—and the place was crowded with other band members curious about how they would/wouldn't resemble the Dolls. By the third song, when it was clear they weren't the Dolls redux, people began streaming out. Actually, they weren't that bad, certainly better than the advance reports. They've managed to give their don't-give-a-fuck crumminess a certain coherence, and they know how to draw the groupies (no small consideration for a beginning outfit). In rock, talent is only half of it. Sometimes not even that much.

Ruby and the Rednecks. Ruby threw out an oversized teddy bear, shrieked, stomped on the bear, kicked it, clawed at the audience, while her claque (from *Interview Magazine* I was told) roared back their delight. Meanwhile, Michael Goldstein, of the *Soho Weekly News*, was telling Tina Weymouth, Trixie A. Balm, and myself that Ruby was going to make it big because she has what it takes. To quote Chico Marx, she can keep it.

Blondie. Someone ought to tell the guitarist that the way to sing harmony is to sing into the microphone.

The Ramones. The Ramones recently opened at a Johnny Winter concert and had to dodge flying bottles. During one of their CBGB sets, they had equipment screw-ups and Dee Dee Ramone stopped singing and gripped his head as if he were going to explode and Tommy Ramone smashed the cymbal shouting, "What the FUCK's wrong?" They went offstage steaming, then came back and ripped into "Judy Is a Punk." A killer band.

"Playing with a band is the greatest way of feeling alive," says Tom Verlaine. But the pressures in New York against such an effort—few places to play, media indifference, the compulsively upward pace of city life—are awesome. Moreover, the travails of a rock band are rooted in a deeper problem: the difficulty of collaborative art. Rock bands flourished in the sixties when there was a genuine faith in the efficacious beauty of communal activity, when the belief was that togetherness meant strength. It was more than a matter of "belonging": it meant that one could create art with friends. Playing with a band meant art with sacrifice, but without suffering: Romantic intensity without Romantic solitude.

What CBGB is trying to do is nothing less than to restore that spirit as a force in rock and roll. One is left speculating about success: Will any of the bands who play there ever amount to anything more than a cheap evening of rock and roll? Is public access merely an attitude to be discarded once stardom seems possible, or will it sustain itself beyond the first recording contract? I don't know, and in the deepest sense, don't care. These bands don't have to be the vanguard in order to satisfy. In a cheering Velvets song, Lou Reed sings: "A little wine in the morning, and some breakfast at night/Well, I'm beginning to see the light." And that's what rock gives: small unconventional pleasures which lead to moments of perception.

Flashes like the way Johnny Ramone slouches behind his guitar, Patti Smith and Lenny Kaye singing "Don't Fuck With Love," on the sidewalk in front of CBGB's, the Shirts shouting in unison in their finale number, Tina Weymouth's tough sliding bass on "Tentative Decisions," the way Tom Verlaine says "just the facts" in "Prove It." One's affection goes out to Lou Reed for such moments *are* like wine in the morning. Shared wine.

The Village Voice, August 18, 1975

Lou Reed Rising

No "legendary" rock band of the 1960s has proven more legendary than the Velvet Underground. The name alone (before it was abbreviated by fans into "the Velvets") carried a special resonance, evoking Genet decadence, whip-and-leather s&m, Warhol chic, and European ennui. And even though other urban bands (the Lovin' Spoonful, the Rascals) were more commercially successful at the time, the best songs of the Velvets ("Sweet Jane," "Candy Says," "Waiting for the Man," "Beginning to See the Light") have an emotional texture and a sharply defined drive which propel the songs beyond the time in which they were written.

Yet when one tries to think of the Velvet Underground photographically, one draws a grainy blur. The great rock stars of the sixties live vividly in our memories through their photos; one thinks of the Beatles first in their suit-uniforms, then in their glossy Sgt. Pepper outfits, of Hendrix in his black-nimbus Afro and layers of scarves, of countless shots of Jagger pouting and preening and hip-thrusting. Yet the Velvets, except for the imperially lovely Nico, seemed not to occupy visual space at all. Even when one listens to their live albums now, it's impossible to imagine what they looked like playing their instruments—they don't come into focus. This shadowiness makes the power of their music all the more provocative since it means that not theatricality but its absence is what gives that music its current urgency. The Velvets didn't have a strong stud-star at center stage (as did the Stones and the Doors) and didn't provide a good-vibes community atmosphere (as did the Dead and the Airplane) and didn't attempt to stagger the audience with histrionics (as did Alice Cooper and just about everybody else).

I first heard the Velvet Underground in the record library of Frostburg State College in western Maryland; the album, their first (with a jacket painting by Warhol), was the only rock album in the entire collection, and that distinction intrigued me. Yet, except for their chanteuse, Nico, and her ghostfloating vocals on "Sunday Morning" and "I'll Be Your Mirror," except for Reed's quirky phrasing and John

Cale's merciless viola on "Black Angel's Death Song," the music was unenthralling. The liner-note quotes about "three-ring psychosis" and "Warhol's brutal assemblage" described a realm of experience that was for me as faraway and nocturnally exotic as Apollinaire's Paris, or Brecht's Berlin. At a time when the most popular bands on campus were corporate entities like Grand Funk Railroad, Chicago, and Crosby, Stills, Nash & Young, it was difficult to connect with a band that dedicated songs to Delmore Schwartz. What I didn't know at the time was that the Velvet Underground had already disbanded, that they had left behind not one studio album but four; only when I came to New York and discovered a dingy copy of *White Light/White Heat* in a Canal Street 99¢ bin did the music of the Velvets hit me with its careening bloodrushing force.

Now, three years later, their music is even more compelling. And though the Velvets were either ignored or denounced in their prime—they go undiscussed in Charlie Gillett's *The Sound of the City* and Carl Belz's *The Story of Rock*, and even in Stephen Koch's vertiginously brilliant book about Warhol their music is described as "the hideous 'acid' maundering . . . of insufferable navel-gazing guitars"—it's clear now that they were the supreme American avant-garde band. With the Warhol affiliation no longer impinging upon their aesthetic, the music can be freshly heard and appreciated for its radical primitivism. "Sister Ray" is still throbbingly dissonant, a river of electronic fever, and the best of "Loaded" is as vibrantly alive as if it had been recorded last week at CBGB by white-shirted kids with virginal Stratocasters. This is true precisely because the music of the Velvet Underground was in no way formally innovative. The Beatles, the Mothers of Invention, the Grateful Dead—all were more experimental, eclectic, and orchestrally inventive, yet there's something wanly dated about their music now . . . it's as pale and faded as old Peter Max posters, or discarded copies of the *East Village Other*. Once the values and sentiments of the psychedelicized counterculture lost their sway, the audaciousness of the music seemed sheer pretentiousness—intricate toys being passed off as sacerdotal gifts. The desire for community was so fervent, and the reverence for pop stars so fanatically intense, that when John Lennon sang, "I don't believe in Elvis . . . don't believe in Beatles," people reacted as if he had said something shattering, something revolutionary. If someone next week sang, "I don't believe in Aretha . . . don't believe in *Roxy*," he'd earn a tempest of derisive laughter. And rightly so.

Well, the Velvets never fell for the platitudes of transcendence (via acid) and community (via rock) which distance us from so much of the *Sgt. Pepper*–era rock. The dynamics of the Velvets' music—its disorderliness, loneliness, melancholy, abrupt joyfulness, claustrophobia (contrasted with the wide blue vistas of much post-Woodstock rock), chiaroscuro shadings (contrasted with the Peppery psychedelicized rainbows), antihedonism, and druggy wistfulness—are consonant with the tensions of the Ford era. Though there's a pull of litany in their songs, the Velvets were never purveyors of salvation—they were always too thoughtful, too tentative. Their modest expectations, their distrust of charisma (both political and cultural), and their disdain for grand gestures are attitudes congruent with the apolitical politics of Jerry Brown. It's a leaderless time, and the Velvets never believed in leaders; their music always stressed survival over community. Even their most beautiful love songs ("Pale Blue Eyes," "I'll Be Your Mirror") were about the distances between people—about the inability to penetrate the mystery of the other. The drug they sang about was not a vision-inducing agent like acid, or a partytime pass-it-around substance like pot, but the drug that most completely isolates one from others: heroin. The Velvets' music was about nihilism, the nihilism of the street, and this barely bridled energy—what John Cale called "controlled distortion"—is expressed cinematically by Martin Scorsese and Sam Peckinpah, novelistically by William Burroughs, musically by post-Velvet rockers like Patti Smith (who sings "Pale Blue Eyes" more passionately than Lou Reed ever did), Roxy Music, David Bowie, the Dolls, Talking Heads, and Television.

The Heads and Television may even be more commercially successful than the Velvets originally were because both are more melodic, more visible (unobscured by multimedia effects), and more photogenic. The Heads look like a still from a Godard movie (*La Chinoise*, maybe) and Tom Verlaine looks like Artaud from Dreyer's *The Passion of Joan of Arc*. But since they're as yet unsigned, the underground-rock breakthrough which is most precipitous is embodied in a wonky little wacker named Jonathan Richman, the *auteur*-alumnus of a Velvet-influenced band called the Modern Lovers.

This Jonathan Richman, a feral child of Rocky and Bullwinkle, will soon be shuffling his way across the FM dial and into America's bruised bosom. Richman has already received moderate airplay and modest notoriety with his soupy contributions to *Beserkley Chartbusters, Vol. 1*, particularly his witty celebration of highway life called "Roadrunner," which offers a fine antidote to Springy's over-ripe imagery. An album of keen documentary interest has just been released which may make Jonathan Richman a household name in every household in which Mary Hartman is the smiling madonna. It's called *Modern Lovers* and it's a demo tape produced by ex-Velvet John Cale for a Warner Bros. album which was never made. The Velvet influence is reflected not only in the music (the organ work, for example, is strongly reminiscent of "Sister Ray") but in the expression of angst.

Fascinating is the contrast between the New York of *Loaded* and the Boston of *Modern Lovers*. Where the cityscape of the Velvet Underground is cluttered yet lonely, Richman's ironic rhapsodies about Boston conjure up a city which is somnolently empty, a city visually and aurally impoverished.

> *I'm in love with the modern world*
> *Massachusetts when it's late at night*
> *And the neon when it's cold outside*
> *I got the radio on*
> *Just like a roadrunner*
> ("Roadrunner"/Jonathan Richman/Jonathan's Music)

And here is Richman faced with the mysteries of amour at his local bank:

> *There's only three in the other lines*
> *In my line, well, I count eleven*
> *Well, that's fine cause I'm in heaven*
> *I got a crush on the new bank teller*
> *She looks at me and she knows*
> ("The New Teller"/Jonathan Richman/Jonathan's Music)

When Susan Sontag wrote that new art is painful because it hurts having your sensorium stretched, she was anticipating Richman's effect. For he has an unforgettable voice: off-key, off-pitch, so achingly widehorizonly *flat* that it makes a Rothko painting resemble a lunar landscape by comparison. When he performed last year at CBGB, he lazily strummed his acoustic guitar and yammered mindlessly on about Love, wonderful Love, and how wonderful it is to have a girlfriend to share Love in the Modern World with, strum strum strum, and after the audience gave him exaggerated bravos, he performed his special version of "Rudolph the Red-Nosed Reindeer" for the third or fourth time.

Wedded to such an instrument of torture, Richman's Weltschmerz pose could make him a sui generis rock star, though we'll have to wait until his first solo album is completed for Beserkley Records before we'll know if he can stretch himself, or if he's just a dandy with a gift for punky pinched irony.

Punk humor, a healthy parody of rock machismo, can be found in the music of the Dictators (who sing: "The best part of growing up/ Is when I'm sick and throwing up/It's the dues you got to pay/For eating burgers every day . . .") and the leather-jacketed Ramones, in the Daffy Duckery of Patti Smith, in magazines like *Punk* and *Creem*, and in television heroes like Fonzie and Eddie Haskell. It's a style of humor which reverses banality, thrives upon it, and enjoys juxtaposing it with high culture references in order to create a comically surreal effect.

Of course, the rock-and-roll regent of punkish irony is ex-Velvet Lou Reed whose solo albums include *Transformer* (with Reed's most popular song, "Walk on the Wild Side"), two live collections, *Sally Can't Dance*, *Berlin* (my favorite Reed work, a misery-drenched masterwork: sunless, spiteful, and cold-bloodedly cruel), and *Metal Machine Music*, a two-record set of such triumphant unlistenability that it crowned Reed's reputation as a master of psychopathic insolence. What Reed learned from Warhol (though he could have learned it equally well from Mailer or Capote) is careermanship: making yourself such a commanding media figure that even when your latest work is a pathetic package of retread riffs and coffee-grind lyrics, people will still be intrigued by the *strategy* behind it.

In the forging of an emblematic identity, Reed not only turned himself into a clown but into a cartoon. When he played with the Velvets, he looked like a bright brooding college kid in sweater and slacks; now, in the premiere issue of *Punk* magazine, a hilarious interview with him is interpolated with cartoons showing him grumbling, sneering, wrecking television sets—transformed from Joe College into a methamphetamine W. C. Fields. The diva of American rock critics, Lester Bangs, has described the decline of Reed's artistry thusly: "Lou Reed is the guy who gave dignity and poetry and rock 'n' roll to smack, speed, homosexuality, sadomasochism, murder, misogyny, stumblebum passivity, and suicide, and then proceeded to belie all his achievements and return to the mire by turning the whole thing into a monumental bad joke. . . ." Bangs sees Reed's post-Velvet career as one long graveyard stroll, noting that after the breakup of the Velvets, "People kept expecting him to die."

Instead, he became a death-artist, a performer in pursuit of ultimate separateness (a pursuit very much like Warhol's futile quest for perfect pristine stillness), and after absorbing chemical cannonades which left his brain as battered as Charles Bukowski's face, Lou Reed survived and parodied Death on the Installment Plan. "Heroin," for example, was a song which was dropped from the Velvets repertoire for a while because too many people embraced it as being pro-smack, when in fact Reed intended the song as a sort of exorcism. Yet only a few years later Reed would not only perform "Heroin" in his solo act but would take out a syringe, wrap the microphone cord around his arm, pretend to shoot up, and hand the syringe to someone in the audience. When Cher said that the music of the Velvet Underground would replace nothing except suicide, she was unknowingly anticipating the rue-morgue antics of Lou Reed and his progeny. Just last week I heard one of New York's underground bands, the Miamis, do a song glamorizing the La Guardia bombing incident, and at one point the lead singer proclaimed, "There's no such thing as an innocent bystander!" Maybe he and Reed should take a ride in De Niro's taxi. . . .

Where Lou Reed used to stare death down (particularly in the black-blooded *Berlin*), he now christens random violence. Small wonder, then, that his conversation ripples with offhanded brutality: though he probably couldn't open a package of Twinkies without his hands trembling, he enjoys babbling threats of violence. One night, when a girl at CBGB clapped loudly (and out of beat) to a Television song, Reed threatened to knock "the cunt's head off"; she blithely ignored him, and he finally got up and left. No one takes his bluster seriously; I even know women who find his steely bitterness sexy.

After dumping all this dirt, I have to confess that this walking crystallization of cankerous cynicism possesses such legendary anticharisma that there's something princely about him, something perversely impressive. There's a certain rectitude in Lou Reed's total lack of rectitude: one can imagine him sharing a piss with Celine in some smoky subterranean chamber, the two of them chuckling over each other's lies.

In the absence of Celine, it's encouraging news that Reed and John Cale may soon team up again, for Cale could force Reed to exert himself, and Reed's presence could help raise Cale's visibility. Though Cale is currently touring with the Patti Smith Group, doing a rambunctious miniset along with the encore numbers, he's still a tiny figure in the rock tapestry. The post-Velvet career of the classically trained Cale (he studied with Aaron Copland) has been stormy, flamboyant, and fueled by alcohol. But his output has been prolific: *Vintage Violence, Church of Anthrax* (with avant-garde composer Terry Riley), *Fear, Slow Dazzle*, and, most recently, *Helen of Troy*. Where Reed did his deathwalk by looking like an emaciated survivor out of *The Night Porter*, Cale went the rock-Dada route—performing cunnilingus on a mannequin during a concert, playing guitar in a goalie's mask, lurching around with Frankensteinian menace. Like Reed, Cale has been treated as a joke yet, unlike Reed, his latest work is worthy of serious attention—*Helen of Troy* is a classic of drunken genius. The album lacks the stylishness of his earlier work and at first listen, everything seems askew—the mixing is odd (the bass dominates, the vocals seem distanced), the pacing seems muscle-pulled, the lyrics offhand then arrowy—and then the sloppiness shapes itself into force and beauty. Island Records has not yet decided whether or not to release *Helen of Troy* in America. Which is indecision bordering on criminal negligence. In the meantime, seek out the album through stores which deal in English imports and see if it doesn't haunt your nights like a reeling somnambulist from the cabinet of Dr. Caligari.

Indeed, the Velvets and their progeny are all children of Dr. Caligari—pale-skinned adventurers of shadowy city streets. Richard Robinson, author of *The Video Primer*, has a videotape which shows Lou Reed and John Cale rehearsing for a concert to be performed in Paris with Nico. After Reed runthroughs "Candy Says," they perform "Heroin" together: Reed's monochromatic voice, Cale's mournful viola, the dirgeful lyrics ("heroin . . . be the death of me . . ."), the colorless bleakness of the video image . . . a casual rehearsal had become a drama of luminous melancholia. What was blurry before became indelibly vivid, and the Reed/Cale harlequinade melted away so that one could truly feel their power as prodigies of transfiguration. For them—as for Patti Smith, Eno, Talking Heads, and Television—electricity is the force which captures the fevers, heats, and dreamily violent rhythms of city life, expressing urban disconnectedness and transcending it. Electricity becomes the highest form of heroin . . . listening to the Velvets, you may have been alone, but you were never stranded.

The Village Voice, March 1, 1976

John Cale Refuses to Die

Squinting eyes, craned necks. Like Velikovsky cultists, some pop true-believers still stare skyward in the hope that the Beatles will make a deus ex machina return to rock. Soon they'll get discouraged, slip their sun visors into their shoulder bags, and head on home. One such Pepperite—Steve Simels, a staffer at *Stereo Review*—published a column recently in which he expressed "the unfashionable, unrealistic hope that the time is now right for Our Boys to get together again. . . ." He wears *his* sun visor around the office. Then: "Moving from the sublime to the ridiculous, I'd like to put my two cents in [big spender] about the current media focus on the New York Rock Scene, which embarrassingly refuses to die," and then goes on to dismiss the Dolls, the Ramones, et al. Well, not only does the scene refuse to die in order to accommodate the nostalgic longings of professional Beatlemaniacs, but last week a real reunion took place, one which did more than unfurl the flag of the past.

At the Lower Manhattan Ocean Club, John Cale—producer, performer, founding father of the Velvet Underground—led an informal jam session, sharing the stage with Patti Smith, David Byrne of Talking Heads, and ex-Velvet Lou Reed. (The Heat Lightning Revue?) (Never mind.) At one level it was a social event—the cameras chirped cheerfully at such rock-scene notables as Mick Ronson, Clive Davis, and Lisa-Danny-and-LennyK, not to mention the ubiquitous Sylvia Miles and Archbishop Warhol. There was also an historical echo since Ocean is managed by Mickey Ruskin, who presented the Velvet Underground during their last, legendary engagement at Max's Kansas City.

As a *musical* event, Cale & company wasn't volcanic entertainment, but there were many pleasing tiny explosions. Most of those bursts came when Cale soloed on his own songs: "I Keep a Close Watch," "Gun," "Fear Is a Man's Best Friend," and "Buffalo Ballet." His grizzly Welsh voice carried more power than it does on record, and when he began one song with "The bugger in the short sleeves fucked my wife . . . ," one could imagine Cale's angry hands around a woman's throat doing an Othello choke. Since Cale's best music is lurching and unruly—some of his outbursts on *Helen of Troy* are worthy of Ray Milland in *Lost Weekend*—the jams were less successful because, working without rehearsal and with modest technical abilities, the others were timorous, and Cale was forced to hold himself back. Only on the Velvets classic, "Waiting for the Man," did they feel enough confidence to romp.

Even when the music was at its messiest, however, there were visual delights: not only the pleasing symmetry of two ex-Velvets/two neo-Velvets on the same stage but the quirky choreographic movements of each. Cale hulked like a yeti with an acoustic guitar, Smith sashayed around as if she had wandered in from another movie, David Byrne did a swiveling, bent-elbow dance which suggested a Martian chicken, and Lou Reed . . . well, Deborah Jowitt should have seen *him*. Though Reed didn't sing (too bad), he played Earth, Wind and Fire licks, and did a modified Funky Robot with his eyes bulging out like twin Easter eggs. Flash I've always expected from Reed, but this sneaky wit was a funny surprise.

Yet Reed never burlesqued; he never upstaged Cale. Since Cale (along with Eno) was dropped by Island Records just before the company commenced its Reggae Got Soul promotional campaign, it was fitting that center-stage was his so that he could play before an audience (however small) that knows him only through underground reputation, and advertise himself to record executives who know him only as the bass-wielding maniac on the Patti Smith tour. He's still a maniac, of course, but at least his mania isn't past-imprisoned. Rather than check into the Memory Motel (which is really just another name for the Tarantula Arms), I prefer to see John Cale at his roaring-lion best, singing lustily and pounding his piano into splinters and scatteration.

The Village Voice, August 2, 1976

Richard Hell Comes in Spurts

Richard Hell—bassist and vocalist, formerly of Television and the Heartbreakers—has been a cult luminary from the earliest CBGB days, his hip tatterdemalion look (ripped T-shirt, Godard sunglasses, choppy disheveled hair) has been hugely influential, and not just in New York. The Sex Pistols, the most volatile of the British new-wave bands, have a scummily charismatic singer named Johnny Rotten who has taken the Hell style to its dissolute extreme. The Sex Pistols' "Anarchy in the U.K.," which was played last week before Hell's set at Max's, is not only a great record—the best piece of Rock-operatic anger since "I Can See for Miles"—but it points up how Hell has been overshadowed by his admirers.

Which is too bad. Though technically his new EP is a sorry brew—it sounds as if it were mixed in a laundromat—it has a snapping, scissory energy which keeps the listener alert even during the sloppier passages. "(I Could Live With You) (In) Another World"—Hell has a fetish for parentheses—is fitful, jagged, with scraping guitars and nostrily vocals; "You Gotta Lose" opens with a thick, plodding bass line (sounds like a junkie's pulse) and then gets perversely playful as Hell sings of the joys of being a pinhead's son. But it's on "(I Belong to) The Blank Generation" that Hell's reputation as a songwriter rests. It's certainly a good song, but as a punk anthem, pretty dubious. Johnny Rotten may be full of rant, but when he sings of anarchy as ecstasy, his Dionysian fury is far more compelling than Hell's beyond-cool attitudinizing. When Hell sings, "I belong to the blank generation/I can take it or leave it each time," one can't help but wonder: Is that anything to *brag* about?

Fortunately, when Hell and his Void Oids performed at Max's they didn't peddle such stylized vacancy. Though the Oids are a ragged crew, they play fast and tight, and with "Love Comes in Spurts" the set leaped to feral life. On the other gas-pedal-to-the-floor rockers ("New Pleasure," "Time Stands Still") the band displayed muscular speed, but the slower numbers were embarrassingly flat, and the fault was not in the guitars. In the rockers, Hell's voice is just another knife in the attack, but when the tempo slows Hell proves to be such a miserably ungifted singer that it's a wonder he isn't gonged. It's also troubling that the strongest numbers in the set were the oldest ones.

When Hell was playing with Television, Patti Smith wrote: "His bass is total trash. . . . He has a driving monotonous way of playing it that comes on real sexy." In that compliment is Hell's curse. Like Johnny Rotten, he has the embattled ferocity of a star, but unlike David Byrne or Tom Verlaine, Hell hasn't yet given any indication that he has the makings of a major rock artist. When he's rawly ripping along, he's a swaggering sewer-prince, but his effectiveness becomes monotonous, and when his music goes quiet, it also goes flaccidly dull. So far, Richard Hell has mastered his come-on but hasn't yet learned to consummate.

The Village Voice, February 7, 1977

Johnny Rotten x Two

Kiss Me, You Fool
Sex Pistols 77

With a rage so rabid that you can feel the spittle hitting the microphone, Johnny Rotten snarls, "She was an animal—she was a *bloody disgrace!*" The song is "Bodies" from the album *Never Mind the Bollocks, Here's the Sex Pistols* and the "she" is not Ilse Koch or the Empress of Iran but a nameless girl from Birmingham who has just had an abortion. "Gurgling bloody mess," is how he describes the doomed fetus; "Look at it squirm," he says. The song climaxes with Rotten pretending to be the fetus pleading for its life—"Mummy!" he cries, then a crash of cymbals, and a brief deathly moan. . . . Except for some of Lou Reed's *Berlin*, nothing in rock equals the hatefulness of "Bodies." Why is Rotten so wired up? And why does he insist on establishing his superiority by repeatedly sneering "I'm not an animal"? Answers emerge from the next track, "No Feelings," in which Rotten threatens to beat a groupie black and blue. He sings "I got no emotion for anybody else/You better understand I'm in love with myself/My self/My beautiful self, bitch." It's a declaration worthy of the Me Decade and it's not a joke: *Here's the Sex Pistols* is a celebration of Johnny Rotten's beautifully rotten self.

Three of the tracks here were top ten chartmakers in England—"Anarchy in the U.K.," "God Save the Queen" (a.k.a. "No Future," in which the queen is called a moron, a potential H-bomb), and "Pretty Vacant," their we-belong-to-the-blank-generation statement. "Holidays in the Sun," currently on the charts, lifts the hook riff from the Jam's "In the City," but it's a brilliant rip-off. It opens with the sound of marching feet. An army marching through wet leaves? No: British tourists heading off to their vacations at the seashore. Rotten, however, decides to holiday in Germany (which he calls "the New Belsen") so that he can visit the Berlin Wall—"Didn't ask for sunshine and I got World War III/I'm lookin' over the wall and they're lookin' at me!" As the marching feet pound in the background—tourists this time, or the Berlin troops?—Rotten babbles ecstatically, "I wanna go *over* the Berlin Wall!" The troops are louder now, and Rotten is singing of paranoia, of too many closets, all around him he sees "Cheap dialogue/Cheap essential scenery," and he admits, "I don't understand this bit at all." Neither do I, but I love the song—it's like watching a home movie narrated by a speed freak. Cinematically, it works, but the satirical point is elusive. The Belsen reference for example. A spokesman for Virgin Records (which released the album in England) says that the Belsen refers to holiday camps—which, if true, is a breathtakingly stupid comparison for the Pistols to make. Belsen after all was an internment camp in which an estimated forty thousand died, most of them Polish and Hungarian Jews. When British troops liberated the camp in April 1945, they were confronted with thirteen thousand unburied corpses. And if "the New Belsen" is in fact Germany, is it East or West Germany? According to London's *New Musical Express*, the Pistols have a song in their repertoire written by bassist Sid Vicious entitled "Belsen Was a Gas." So the Belsen crack seems to be there only to shock.

Another finger-pointing number, "EMI," is even more muddled, and its confusions don't have the looney-tune craziness of "Holidays." The Pistols were signed by EMI, who later dropped them after they said "fuck" on the BBC and became front-page bad news: EMI paid them £30,000 in a termination settlement, then melted down the remaining copies of *Anarchy in the U.K.* Rotten's account of the break-off is completely unconvincing. "I tell you it was all a frame/ They only did it cause of fame/Who/EMI!" he says. But the controversy made the *Pistols* famous, not EMI. Later they were signed by A & M, then dropped, £75,000 richer; and the song ends with Rotten groaning, "Good-bye, A and Emmmmmm." All the song really is is an opportunity for Rotten to acidly spit out the initials of record companies.

And I won't deny he's sensational at it. When the Pistols' singles first came out, I thought Johnny Rotten was destined to become the greatest rock singer since Dylan went electric. Like Dylan, he's the master of the put-down and the piss-off. In "New York," as the band mimics the famous Dolls song "Looking for a Kiss," Rotten taunts a rocker from the halcyon days of Max's Kansas City for being a loser, a has-been, a "poor little faggot"; "Kiss me," he commands, sounding as full of humanity as Caligula addressing a eunuch. But he lacks Dylan's cruel precision—his squalling and hissing are too often hoarsely baroque. In part, this is due to the Pistols' musical limitations: the band behind Rotten consists of three stooges who play raw power chords, and one song ("Submission") is actually an aquatic version of Iggy's "I Wanna Be Your Dog," with dolphin love calls instead of barks. His tantrummy vocals are meant to carry one over the band's gear meshing, and too often he becomes an operatic brutalist, making every syllable die an agonizing death.

Musically, this record is too monotonously tense and abrasive, and I'd measure it below *Marquee Moon* and *Rocket to Russia* and *My Aim Is True*. Worse, Rotten already seems too delighted by his own vomity villainy; he's becoming *smugly* nihilistic. He dramatizes himself as anarchistic id surrounded by bores, fools, and parasites, and sings of No Fun, No Feelings, No Future. Johnny Rotten embodies an apocalyptic narcissism—his mocking, gloating laughter echoes across the ruins. He's scabrously charismatic: the murderous gleam in his eye is a turn-on, and droogy cultists will imitate his every trashing move. *Never Mind the Bollocks, Here's the Sex Pistols* is an indispensable record, perhaps even a great one, but I want to see the Pistols live before hailing them as the punk messiahs. I want to see Johnny Rotten laugh unmockingly. I want to see him burst into flames. The record alone is a windowless vision of the future and the claustrophobic fury is more—and less—than I can live with. Unlike the Clash, the Sex Pistols deny any possibility of solidarity, of a community rooted in hope, pop, and affection. Behind them they leave nothing but scorched earth.

The Village Voice, November 21, 1977

Rotten and Vicious

Rotten, John Lydon

For a band that divorced after just one album, undone by drugs, greed, and violence, the Sex Pistols have left a long paper trail. Their punk exploits, which spanned three years in the mid-seventies, have been documented down to the last puncture hole. Managed by Malcolm McLaren, who prided himself on being the Diaghilev of pop decadence, a pimp of piss elegance, the original Sex Pistols consisted of Glen Matlock on bass, Paul Cook on drums, Steve Jones on guitar, and, on vocals, John Lydon, whose green teeth earned him the nickname Johnny Rotten. The mild-mannered Matlock was soon bounced from the band and replaced by Rotten's friend and schoolmate Sid Vicious (who was named after a hamster Rotten once had)—a personnel switch that proved to be both the making and the unmaking of the Sex Pistols. With Matlock, the Pistols might have become a tight squad, toting their guitars like rifles, in the style of the Clash or the Jam; God forbid, they might have achieved *musicianship*. In Vicious, whose trash presence transcended talent, the Pistols found the living vehicle of their autodestruct nihilism. His very roughness suited McLaren's scheme of creating a subversive craze from scratch. Sid also represented Rotten's ideal of "shambolic chaos." Once Sid had mastered his onstage sneer, he became—in a kind of parody of Ringo's role in the Beatles—the band's punchy mascot.

The Pistols' 1978 campaign to conquer America was the Beatles' story replayed as farce, with McLaren substituting for Brian Epstein, and springing on the world not four happy, head-bobbing lads but a loutish crew that looked like a box of bloody Kleenexes. Where the Beatles inspired an epic outpouring of joy, the Pistols expired in a fit of pique and a volley of vomit; they were both the perpetrators and the victims of a scam that went sour. "Ever get the feeling you've been cheated?" Rotten asked the audience at the end of the Sex Pistols concert in San Francisco, the final stop on their nightmarish American tour. (In San Antonio, the band was barraged with beer cans and hot dogs. In Dallas, Vicious mutilated himself onstage with a broken bottle.) After the San Francisco show—a bad-vibes event, during which Rotten exhorted the audience, "Be a man, be someone, kill someone, be a man, kill yourself!"—the band dissolved. It made sense that the Sex Pistols should break up at the end of their first American tour, the critic Lester Bangs wrote; it showed a perverse integrity on their part—as he put it, "we do our work and go." But go where? Sid Vicious had nowhere to go but down. As if taking Rotten's advice to heart, he died of a heroin overdose a year later in New York, after fatally plunging a knife into his girlfriend Nancy Spungen. Zombie lovers, Sid and Nancy were the Kurt Cobain and Courtney Love of their day, giving the lie to the phrase "too dumb to die."

Punk rock, a call to smash authority and treat the body as a tribal battlefield, ended up smacking itself in the face. It left the larger world unmoved. It didn't topple Margaret Thatcher, excite revolution in the streets, or rid the music world of false gods, despite the Clash's declaring "No Elvis, Beatles, or Rolling Stones!" in their song "1977." But, as T. S. Eliot observed, there are no lost causes, because there are no won causes; and the nasty scrawl that punk made in the seventies has thickened into a jungle of intellectual graffiti. Punk has its own library, in which the Sex Pistols have their own section. The British journalist Jon Savage strove to play Thomas Carlyle with *England's Dreaming: Anarchy, Sex Pistols, Punk Rock, and Beyond*, an apocalyptic political overview of that sweaty phase. (Sample sentence: "'Punk didn't do much to challenge male sexuality or image,' says Lucy Toothpaste, whose fanzine *Jolt* explicitly dealt with feminist ideas.") Even more exhaustive was Greil Marcus's *Lipstick Traces*, which featured Johnny Rotten on the cover of the paperback version and read like a garbled radio broadcast from a catacomb of rival sects. Malcolm McLaren was the subject of a biography, and Glen Matlock published a memoir, as did Nancy Spungen's mother. The American tour was given documentary-like treatment in *12 Days on the Road*, the definitive account of trying to keep Sid on the bus. Now Rotten himself, never known for his reticence, has decided to set the record straight and get in some additional licks. In *Rotten: No Irish, No Blacks, No Dogs*, a book riddled with misspellings and repetitions yet alive at the core, John Lydon (with the assistance of Keith and Kent Zimmerman, and with additional testimonies by, among others, Chrissie Hynde and Billy Idol) revels in his role as irritant and scourge. "We were very good at being sarcastic," he says of his fellow Sex Pistols, "and I think my qualities in this area can speak for themselves." They do. He's quite the humorist.

In all the furor over punk at the time, and in all the effort to read

significance into it since, we have often overlooked how funny-awful
the whole thing was. One needed a face of stone not to laugh at rockers calling themselves Rotten, Vicious, Rat Scabies, Cheetah Chrome,
Richard Hell, and Poly Styrene, or at bands with names like the Slits,
the Cramps, the Sic F*cks. Or at the provocations of punk fashion,
which had pale young poseurs looking like crashed UFOs, bondage
queens, and Iroquois warriors. The magazine *Punk*, created in New
York in 1975 by John Holmstrom and Legs McNeil, captured the
slapstick spirit of the period, with its pasteups of cartoons, photographs, and inane interviews. (The first *Punk* Q & A, with Lou Reed,
was a classic.) Comedy is an antiheroic device, a deflater of hopes and
assumptions. And, as Lydon says in *Rotten*, what made the Pistols a
great band is that they were the most antiheroic of all. They flunked
every crunch test. "I really do think the crown and glory of the Sex
Pistols is that we've always managed to disappoint on big occasions.
When the chips were down, we never came through. We were so bad,
it was gloriously awful." (This opinion is echoed by Savage in *England's Dreaming*. As he puts it, "the Sex Pistols did what they always
did when they were under intense scrutiny: they stank.") And, when
it came to not coming through, Sid Vicious was a true champion. He
was the opposite of a natural performer. He was an unnatural performer. He couldn't sing, he couldn't play, he could barely stand. It
took him forever simply to learn how to dress the part of a punk.

"Sid was an absolute fashion victim—the worst I'd ever known,"
Lydon recollects. "He'd wear sandals in the snow with no socks when
he wanted to show off his toenail varnish." He'd try bits of Rotten's
gear, to no better effect. "I was rushed to the hospital after a gig in
Walthamstow supporting Kilburn and the High Roads because I
foolishly walked on stage in a rubber T-shirt. Three songs in, I collapsed, and then it was oxygen tent time. I ended up selling what was
left of that same shirt to Sid, and precisely the same thing happened
to him. Midsummer madness. The fool walked outside, and it was
eighty-five degrees. Fashion-first Sid. He collapsed." Sid never quite
found the knack. At one point, Lydon had agreed to marry Chrissie Hynde, the moody-lipped lead singer of the Pretenders, only to
chicken out before the ceremony. Sid went instead. "She wouldn't
have him," Lydon claims. "He was so filthy, Sidney did not believe in
washing at the time. This was his antifashion period. He'd gone the
other way from the prissy nail varnish to total hound-dog of the first
degree. Really bad but with a punk hairdo. Chrissie took one look at
that and wouldn't have it!"

Lydon might have played Butt-head to Vicious's Beavis indefinitely if Vicious had not impaled himself on the fingernails of the punk groupie Nancy Spungen. Seldom has a person been so aptly named. Money, drugs, cosmetics: Spungen sponged off everyone, since she couldn't get paid for her true talent—whining. "When she started up with that incessant whining she was more than the human mind could bear," Chrissie Hynde recalls in *Rotten*. Like many members of the punk scene, Spungen behaved like an Andy Warhol superstar, creating phony hysteria around her during the wait between fixes. Lydon says, "Sid's idea of fun at the time was taking drugs with Nancy. My idea of fun was taking drugs with anyone but her, and the two didn't tarry well." Fun is fun, but for Sid and Nancy it became fatal. I've always thought that hard-core addiction is a kind of negative nurturing—an attempt to mother oneself, to reenact the dreamy dependency of being a newborn attached to a feeding machine. The needle functions as a sharp nipple, and with each injection the junkie breastfeeds himself, seeking a sustenance that eventually sickens. Sid and Nancy's crash pad at the Chelsea Hotel became a squalid playpen as they took turns at the crystal tit. Their antics, like scenes from a Warhol film, became a skit that went on too long. Like all junkies, they had to work harder and harder at pretending to be alive. Lydon considers the Alex Cox movie *Sid and Nancy*, which starred Gary Oldman and Chloe Webb, a glorification of their last, gutted days. "To me this movie is the lowest form of life. I honestly believe that it celebrates heroin addiction. It definitely glorifies it in the end when that stupid taxi drives off into the sky. That's such nonsense." But, when most people think of punk, Sid and Nancy is what they picture.

It's a shame. If you listen to the Sex Pistols now, it's amazing how usurping they still sound. The subjects of the songs may have dated ("God Save the Queen," the infamous anti-Jubilee anthem; "EMI," an attack on their former record company), but the door-slam rudeness remains. Lydon's singing supplies the driving lash. One publicity shot had him posing in a straitjacket, and his vocals were an urgent catcall, a burst of Adam's apple, as if he couldn't reach the source of the rash eating him alive. (He's still a bundle of raw nerves. "I'm claustrophobic," he confesses in *Rotten*. "I can't ride in subways, and I don't like heights. I'm epileptic as well, but I'm not on any medication. Strobe lights really set me off, also afternoon sun between the trees as you drive along in the car. I can't take that constant flash.") With a stage persona that he has likened to Richard III, wringing wiry changes from his one-note harangues, Lydon belonged to that line of ranters stretching from the poet Richard Savage to Jimmy Porter in *Look Back in Anger.* His psychodramatic highs included "Holidays in the Sun," with its crunchy marching feet and paranoid babble, and a cover of the Stooges' "No Fun," in which he sounds as if he were singing from the scaffold, fashioning his own noose.

After the Pistols disbanded, he junked Rotten, reverted to his real name, and formed a group called Public Image, Limited—PiL for short. His monochromatic effects acquired a dark lacquer: the foreground percussion on the album *Flowers of Romance* propels an Islamic prayer chant. PiL's masterwork, *Metal Box*, is a three-record set in which Lydon languishes in the soul of a dead machine. Heavy bass lines thread through a profitless land. It's an art movie on vinyl, only Lydon is too ornery to settle for anomie. He manages to whip isolation, weariness, and leftover mockery into a stay against suicide, an affirmative shrug. A song called "Death Disco," which borrows a melody line from *Swan Lake*, ends with his most passionate utterance: "Seeing in your eyes / I'm seeing through my eyes /—Words cannot express, words cannot express . . ."

"Death Disco" was written by Lydon for his mother, who died of cancer in 1979. As if to show that Lydon isn't a complete ferret, the penultimate chapter of *Rotten* features Lydon's father testifying to his son's filial devotion: "Johnny sat with his mum all through her illness. He sat by her side for ten weeks—never spoke to anybody—never left her day or night. He washed in the hospital, slept on the seat. He was that close to her." It was a watch that Lydon now wishes he had kept on Sid. "I could have helped Sid more," he reflects. "If only I hadn't been lazy and washed my hands of him like Pontius Pilate. That's something I'll have to carry to the grave with me. I don't know what I could have done, but I know I should have done something. There are always ways. You must never be lazy when it comes to your friends."

A flicker of humanity! An expression of remorse! It's not a sympathy that extends very far—annoyed, during his book tour, at being asked so many questions about Kurt Cobain's suicide, Lydon finally snapped, "I don't give a fuck about Kurt Cobain"—but, after all the cut marks of wit and ego found in *Rotten*, this admission counts as an emotional breakthrough. He risks sounding corny—and that, for a master of ridicule like Lydon, is no small risk. If I didn't admire him so much, I might accuse him of maturity.

The New Yorker, May 16, 1994

The Noise Boys
Lester Bangs and Richard Meltzer

Three decades after Elvis Presley anointed Eros with hair oil, rock criticism has grown rather grim and jowly. While rock music has replenished its roster with glossy new faces to reflect light on the old (best example: Whitney Houston paying homage to Aretha Franklin in her "How Will I Know" video), rock writing has had the same stoic slabs of cheese striking Rodin's *The Thinker* pose for lo, these many years. John Rockwell, Jon Pareles, Jay Cocks, Ben Fong-Torres, Stephen Holden, Robert Palmer, Robert Hilburn, Robert Christgau, Dave Marsh—these are just a few of the living statues capable of tearing open record cartons with their bare hands. When some of these older scribes raise a hurrah for the Replacements or the Beastie Boys, it's because such slobbo rowdies take them back to what they wish were their own glory days of spewed beer and fondled titty, to the days when they were the boys of noise, piling up review copy at *Cheetah, Creem, Rolling Stone*. And what of the women? Female rock critics are a vanishing few. Ellen Willis, the former rock correspondent for *The New Yorker* and once considered the Rosa Luxemburg of riffs and body politics, has opted out of the current tumult to become a bobby-soxer for the peace-love music of the sixties. With the noise boys locked in a huddle, rock criticism has become a mode of discourse as coded and insular as semiotics, a mantra for the elect—a catechism for those who write by rote. Wasn't always so.

In the heyday of rock writing, critics didn't dispense eyedropper opinions; words were poured like paint upon a pinwheel, for a psychedelic swirl. A rock mag named *Crawdaddy!* used to peer at rock albums as if through a stained-glass window, seeking celestial design and acid-trip revelation. Doubtless this resulted in impressionistic spill and overkill, every crack in Janis Joplin's voice traced to a dry riverbed in Texas, every guitar lick from Jefferson Airplane a brush-stroke twig on the tree of life, but there was a heady kick to language and analysis gone happily amok. It was similar to the show of colors that the New Journalism briefly unfurled.

As if to kick-start rock criticism's sluggish system, yet another practitioner, Greil Marcus—the author of *Mystery Train* and currently a glowing tapeworm in the dank bowels of postmodernism for *Artforum*—has consulted the archives and dusted off a pair of rock writers renowned for their raucous disdain of tact, decorum, and tidy expression. Earlier this year Marcus supplied the intro to a reissue of Richard Meltzer's *The Aesthetics of Rock* (Da Capo), seeking to cast upon the book the aura of a status object. First published in 1970, "*The Aesthetics of Rock* does not read like an artifact of some vanished time, but like an oddly energized version of real cool academic discourse. . . . It will soon be, in certain circles, the coolest book to be seen carrying." Marcus has also introduced and edited a major chunk of collected rockcrit by the late Lester Bangs punkily titled *Psychotic Reactions and Carburetor Dung*, which Knopf made available for cool display last month. Of the two, Bangs is the prize exhibit. Full of bullinsky as Bangs could be (and he was the first to admit it), his was a unique, unsilenceable voice.

It's a voice that manages to bulldoze its way even through Marcus's editorial misjudgments. Putting together this anthology was clearly a labor of love for Marcus, who was Bangs's friend and colleague, but he sets up a lot of clutter that the reader needs to discard to get to the real buzz. In *The Book of Rock Lists*, the citation for Lester Bangs under the heading "The 10 Best Rock Critics" reads in part: "Most influential critic, best stylist, renegade taste that frequently doubles back on itself"—which seems fair enough. Marcus goes further. "Perhaps what this book demands from a reader is a willingness to accept that the best writer in America could write almost nothing but record reviews." Such hyperbole is a hindrance to appreciating Bangs, who was not America's greatest writer (dream on) but a novalike talent who exploded the record-review personality-piece formats of hack rock journalism. And when Marcus confides, "As a writer who has often fantasized his own death, I imagine that all writers fantasize their own deaths," the logic is dubious, the disclosure presumptuous. If Marcus wants to get *personally weird*, let him do it in the pages of *Artforum*, where no one cares. Lester Bangs hardly fantasized the death he received, as Marcus himself admits. (An addictive personality who wrote reams on speed and swigged Romilar at parties, Bangs expired quietly in his sleep in 1982 at the age of thirty-three from complications involving influenza and an intake of Darvon. His overdose was a tragic fluke, coming at a point in his life when he had fallen in love and kissed off his Charles Bukowski barfly flexes of brain waste. Death snuck up on him like a thief.)

One could also quibble with Marcus's selections. He omits Bangs's scathing put-down of Bob Dylan's ode to the gangster Joey Gallo, in which Bangs contrasted Dylan's lyrics with Gallo's actual deeds to demonstrate how dumb and falsifying Dylan's mythmaking was. Instead, Marcus clots the text with hollow chest thumps from Bangs's unpublished, unfinished novel and a book proposal that reads like a loose transistor from Norman Mailer's *Why Are We in Vietnam?* It's Lester Bangs the bebop artist of scat-man prose that Greil Marcus wishes to preserve, but a lot of Lester's solos went nowhere fast for lack of subject. When he had a subject worth his powerhouse wit, however, he could muster a flurry of notes to gale force.

What special gust did Lester Bangs bring to the party that's been missing from rock criticism since? For one thing, an impudent humor. The impudence carries over to Bangs's attitude toward rock stars, most of whom he considered to be sequined carcasses spouting cosmic inanities. The major tiff in *Psychotic Reactions* is the feud Bangs carried on with Lou Reed in the pages of *Creem* (where Bangs was editor and star writer), which reads like Fred Allen and Jack Benny exchanging insults on Dexedrine. Lou Reed, the naked skull that skulked, and Lester Bangs, the conscience that laughed, were a perfect comic match. Not even the Freudian section heading, "Slaying the Father" (groan), can take away from the fun. Warming up, Bangs calls Lou Reed a liar and a lummox and a Judas to his own cause. "Lou Reed is the guy that gave dignity and poetry and rock 'n' roll to smack, speed, homosexuality, sadomasochism, murder, misogyny, stumblebum passivity, and suicide, and then proceeded to belie all his achievements and return to the mire by turning the whole thing into a monumental bad joke." Yet it is a howling wind that whistles through Lou Reed's bones. "Lou Reed is my own hero principally because he stands for all the most fucked up things that I could ever possibly conceive of. Which probably only shows the limits of my imagination." When Reed released *Metal Machine Music*, a two-record sonic migraine that appeared on the scene like the black slab from *2001*, an opaque herald awaiting an inscription, Bangs entered the outer limits of his imagination. In a state of rapt Nirvana, he burst forth with thousands of words on Lou Reed's buzz-saw baby, including a list of reasons *Metal Machine Music* was the greatest album ever made. "If you ever thought feedback was the best thing

that ever happened to the guitar, well, Lou just got rid of the guitars."
Lester was fond of feedback. Like the legendary producer Phil Spector, he erected in his mind immense walls of sound. Raw spires of
dissonance above a dense fortress. It was Lester Bangs, after all, who
popularized the phrase "heavy metal."

Indeed, the most apt epitaph for Lester Bangs and his brand of
mondo-bondage manic-depressive criticism comes in the book from
the guitarist Bob Quine (he played with Richard Hell's band), who
says to Lester, "I've figured you out. Every month you go out and
deliberately dig up the most godawful wretched worthless unlisten-
able offensive irritating unnerving moronic piece of horrible racket
noise you can possibly find, then sit down and write this review in
which you explain to everybody else in the world why it's just wonderful and they should all run right out and buy it. Since you're a good
writer, they're convinced by the review to do just that—till they get
home and put the record *on*, which is when the pain sets in. They
throw it under the sink or somewhere and swear it'll never happen
again. By the next month they've forgotten . . . so the whole process is
repeated again with some other even more obnoxious piece of hideous
blare. . . . You know, I must say, I have to admit that's a noble thing to
devote your entire life to."

Yet it would be a mistake to chalk up Bangs's brand of rockcrit
excess as Dadaism with a dental drill. There's a humanism in *Psychotic
Reactions* that reaches much deeper than mere politics. (Which is what
most rock critics practice today: socialism with a stony face.) This
fellow feeling animates the passages about touring with the Clash,
the farewell to Elvis, the achingly vivid portrait of Iggy Pop, and the
obit on the punk-rocker Peter Laughner, who shriveled in fast motion
before Bangs's eyes and died of drugs. This one-on-one sympathy is
what distinguishes *Psychotic Reactions* from *The Aesthetics of Rock*. Richard Meltzer's wired work habits had certain similarities to Bangs's:
"I'd get up in the morning, smoke some dope, put on an LP, enter its,
uh, *universe*, take profuse notes, play another album, jump from cut
to cut, make the weirdest of plausible connections (no professors—
wheeee!—to monitor the hidebound topicality of my thoughts anymore), more notes, more records, occasional meals and masturbation,
more more, then hop in the car and drive to Boston for Jefferson
Airplane—or Asbury Park for the Doors—and home to write it up on
my sister's diet pills." (They never talk this way in *The Paris Review*.)
And Meltzer's free-associative meltdown in the very grooves of the
album he was listening to also recalls Bangs. "Like Lester Bangs,"

blurbs John Rockwell, "Richard Meltzer writes about rock with prose that aspires to the spirit of the music."

But where Bangs, all heart and bear hug, wrestled with rock in the palpable present (he always wanted to know, "What does this make me *feel*?"), Meltzer superimposes his blown mind on the music in order to conjure up fleeing phantoms from The History of Western Thought. "The Angels' 'My Boyfriend's Back' presents the entire panorama of the arrival of Orestes." "Moreover, 'Ain't That Just Like Me' by the Searchers can be examined for its affinities to Marcel Duchamp's sex machine metaphor." Greil Marcus isn't completely screwy when he claims that *The Aesthetics of Rock* approximates the spirit of academic discourse (deconstruction, semiotics): this book, so packed with allusions, thorny formulations, and oracular asides, *is* kinda Derrida. It's a thin-air book, a dizzy penthouse view of pop culture, a ghostly body just barely supporting a jack-o'-lantern head. Meltzer's province isn't rhythm or emotion but, as Marcus himself notes, words—*verbal* noise. Meltzer is brilliant in spades, but how far can you go? Language having a self-conscious nervous breakdown has been done to death in literary criticism, and it's hardly a more appealing spectacle when the subject is rock lyrics. Pedantry and put-on combined make for a project as dead-end as Flaubert's dictionary of clichés in *Bouvard et Pécuchet*. The mind is a terrible thing to fritter.

Which both Bangs and Meltzer in their different ways understood. Meltzer has pretty much given up writing about rock, and before his death Bangs was trying to phase himself into more personal graffiti. Both have left a large residue of influence on the outskirts of pop journalism. Hard-core fanzines devoted to punk and heavy metal owe their scrawling bravado to these two, and there is a cadre of writers at the *Village Voice* (RJ Smith, Chuck Eddy, Greg Tate) trying awfully hard to be the noise boys of the eighties. But, face it, the thrill is gone. (Perhaps for the musicians too—T-Bone Burnett recently lamented that "it's all become professional now. Rock 'n' roll is a *museum*.") Not only has rock writing become doctrinaire, reflecting the opinions and priorities of its commissars, but it's been superseded by music video. In 1987, one would deconstruct pop music not linguistically, à la *The Aesthetics of Rock*, but imagistically, via MTV. (And already we've had decodings of Madonna's lingerie and Dwight Yoakam's rodeo finery.) Rock videos don't allow the viewer and listener to free-associate; they supply the associations for you. The looming pictures of ice-capped mists and dinosaur bogs that Led Zeppelin once conjured in the imagination are now plopped down in plain sight and photographed at *Caligari*-askew angles. Rock videos are a series of retinal quickies, too punchy to be subliminal, too scattered to have true impact. One thing about noise is that it has heft and duration. It's a beast that sits on your chest and stays awhile. It generates obsession rather than distraction. From this behemoth of feedback and squalling guitars Bangs and Meltzer at their best were able to tear off terrific hunks of bombast. There's noise aplenty in rock and rock criticism now, but it's an empty, joyless din. The heart has gone out of the holler.

Vanity Fair, October 1987

The Bollocks

Please Kill Me, Legs McNeil and Gillian McCain

Nothing escapes nostalgia—not even punk rock, which condemned nostalgia as the soft palm of the dead hand of history. Punk rockers felt that the stale old gods of the pop scene would have to go: "No Elvis, Beatles, or Rolling Stones!" the Clash declared in their song "1977." At which the critic Lester Bangs shouted back in print, "Buy all albums by new angry British groups! They stink too!" Punk bands didn't play for posterity; rather, they infested the present, their lyrics as full of lurid horror as tabloid headlines. In punk, everyone and everything appeared shredded: album covers and punk 'zines resembled ransom notes, with their pasted-together photos and words. Despite punk's stabs at immediacy, though, its refusal to look or sound pretty hasn't dated as badly as, say, the paisley shirts and love beads of hippiedom. (Like, wow, man.) Punk rock's influence can be heard in everything from Seattle grunge to sharp new English bands like Elastica. Punk has even entered the higher cultural lexicon: a recent review in the *Times Literary Supplement* compared the shock tactics of T. S. Eliot's poetry with punk rock. Twenty years after the first outbreak of safety pins and rainbow Mohawks in London clubs and Lower Manhattan dives, punk is staging both a comeback and a look-back. It's the return of the undead. Yesteryear's snarling leather boy (and girl) is today's geezer punk. Well, why not? If the culture can accommodate geezer Beats (William Burroughs, Allen Ginsberg), why not geezer punks?

The comeback is led by Patti Smith, who has emerged from a long public twilight to issue a new book and a new album; by the Sex Pistols, who have reunited (minus the late Sid Vicious) to trot out their practiced sneers on a mercenary tour (at their first London concert, the lead singer John "Rotten" Lydon pranced around in a clownish outfit and proclaimed himself "Fat, forty, and back"); and by the Talking Heads, who, minus David Byrne, are releasing a new album with guest vocalists. Other former punks are resurfacing at the cineplex—Deborah Harry as a waitress in *Heavy*, Iggy Pop as a Tiresias-like hag in *Dead Man*. Richard Hell, one of the founding fathers and the author of the nod-out anthem "Blank Generation," has published his first novel, an overblown junkie odyssey called *Go Now*. It was Hell who was alleged to have made punk legend in the seventies by wearing a T-shirt bearing the message "Please Kill Me." Hell now claims that he only created the shirt and made another musician wear it. Whatever. That T-shirt—punk's unofficial flag—supplies the title for *Please Kill Me*, an oral history of punk rock, edited by Legs McNeil and Gillian McCain and published by Grove Press.

The book, an "Edie"-like montage of sound bites, dishes the crud on everyone from punk legends like Lou Reed and Iggy Pop (who, we are reminded, would projectile-vomit onstage and hurl himself into the crowd like a Dionysian sacrifice long before the term "mosh pit" was coined) to now forgotten flame-outs. As someone who was there at the time, I can vouch for how vividly it recaptures the swampy vitality of the New York scene, where the freak show in the audience often outdid the freak show onstage. It was as if everybody became his or her own lab experiment. I remember hearing someone ask the punk chanteuse Lydia Lunch what she'd been up to, and her snappy reply: "Me and my boyfriend spent the weekend drilling holes in each other's teeth." To many, the punk scene had the smell of meat. While Max's Kansas City and CBGB's never held the hot-bodied action of Studio 54 (dancing is always sexier than twitching alone), the book shows how the influx of skinny-boy guitarists with milky skin had gay scenemakers and girl groupies fighting over the chicken bones. Dee Dee Ramone recalls seeing the vision who would become his girlfriend sitting on the hood of a car in a black evening gown and spike heels, filing her nails: "She looked like an ancient vampire countess who was definitely on a mission to capture my soul." Her name is Connie. The next morning, the glow is off and their relationship is clarified: "She was a prostitute, I was a Ramone, and we were both junkies."

Candid, inside, and detailed though it is, *Please Kill Me* is far from being "the definitive work on punk" that its flap copy claims. The book reflects the personal slant of its co-author Legs McNeil, the former mascot of the magazine *Punk*, who preferred fun-guy bands like the Dictators, and had little patience for cerebral ticktocks like the Talking Heads, whose music he dismisses in *Please Kill Me* as a yuppie whine. He's entitled to his opinion, of course. But no book authorizing itself as an official history can afford to give the Talking Heads such a brush-off. Although not strictly a punk band, the Heads were far from being dilettantes. Their lead singer and songwriter, David

Byrne, was (as Pauline Kael noted of Jean Cocteau) one of those aesthetic types who are tougher than they look. While other bands punished the same three or four chords, the Talking Heads evolved from a cute, tentative trio with a Tinkertoy sound to the quartet who conjured and reconfigured African pulsations in *Remain in Light*. The musical thrill that the Talking Heads and Television brought to the scene is relegated to a sideshow in *Please Kill Me*, when in fact that thrill was the main draw at CBGB's, until the Dead Boys learned to upchuck. Television's Tom Verlaine (another transcendentalist) may be the pretentious gargler of French poetry that his detractors claim he is, but the double-helix guitar solos he knitted with Richard Lloyd in the sweatbox of CBGB's at 2 A.M. are what I remember from the scene—not who got head.

The gulf between arty punks and party punks is most funnily demonstrated in *Please Kill Me* when McNeil recounts his half-assed attempt to interview Patti Smith for *Punk:*

Patti was expecting to sit down and do a serious interview. Then I showed up. I didn't have any questions and hadn't done any homework, and I didn't want to hear about art or poetry. I was like, "Hey, Is it true Aerosmith is playing on your record?"

Patti was pissed. She started yelling at me right off, "That was a stupid question, and whoever gave it to you wanted to see you abused, because if I was in a bad mood, if I was feeling like tombstone teeth, you'd be out on yer ass! But yer lucky I like ya."

Then Patti gave me a big lecture on the importance of the underground press, and professionalism, and getting the message out to the people, and how art would save everyone, and then she went off on this sermon about Italian Renaissance frescas. I had no idea what she was talking about.

A decade before Camille Paglia, Patti Smith perfected the art of the interview as intellectual spiel. In interviews to promote her new album, *Gone Again* (so far, she's spoken to *Time Out*, the *Times*, the *Post*, *Details*, *Interview*, *Spin*, *Rolling Stone*, and the Buddhist magazine *Shambhala Sun*), Smith soft-pedals her participation in the punk scene, as if she had simply been holding down the fort until fresh troops arrived. "The truth is, I never really considered that I would go very far myself," she told Lisa Robinson in the *Post*. "I was just trying to inject some energy into the scene." False modesty. Patti shone with messianic purpose back then. Her bare-bulb intensity was like a halation. An androgynous waif, Smith wanted to be Rimbaud, Keith Richards, Anita Pallenberg, Jean Genet, Jeanne Moreau, Joan of Arc, Bob Dylan, Mary Magdalene, Isabelle Eberhardt, and fellow-Jerseyite Frank Sinatra rolled into one human cigarette. From her first days on the downtown poetry scene, she was something of a poseur, constantly eying her own effect. ("Patti would always kiss somebody and then look at you to make sure you'd noticed," Terry Ork, the ex-manager of Television, recalls in the book.) One of the formative movies for her was *Don't Look Back*, the D. A. Pennebaker documentary about Bob Dylan's 1965 tour of England, and as she became famous she sometimes emulated the bad-vibe side of Dylan, who took pleasure in making others squirm (as in his put-down of Donovan in that film). Ron Asheton, a former member of the Stooges, describes bringing Patti and her band flowers and champagne when they played the Whiskey-A-Go-Go, in Los Angeles, only to have his gifts ignored: "Patti treated me like shit. She was with Iggy. They were laughing at me and making fun of me for some reason. It was just a very awkward, bad situation. So I just said, 'Fuck you,' and walked out."

Yet it would be a mistake to dismiss Smith as a walking collage of rock-star ego and cool. She had unique charisma and cocky humor from the outset, and performed unsung acts of generosity (such as getting Television's Billy Ficca a new set of drumsticks when his got ratty). Onstage, she packed so much passion into her poses that she fused them into a kind of physical cry. The sets she performed at CBGB's when she started, in 1975, were punchy and tight, yet lyrical, in-gathering. Her cover of Smokey Robinson's "The Hunter Gets Captured by the Game" provided a quiet cove amid the apocalyptic hoofbeats of songs like "Land." It was only after Patti achieved some public success and began playing larger arenas that she eschewed a hard-rock beat and began free-associating with Kerouacian notions of spontaneous bop prosody. Her song introductions got longer and woollier. I can recall her launching into an ad-lib monologue about the Queen of Sheba—"The Queen of Sheba/Took a shit/And she sculpted that shit/Into a vision/Of the cross"—at a New Year's Eve concert, no less. Once Patti turned shaman on us, she inhabited a circular soundscape meant to evoke spiritual isolation amid Arabian sandstorms and hazy whiffs of ganja.

Lesser mortals reinvent themselves. Patti resurrects herself—not once but as many times as it takes. Her first resurrection came after she was sidelined with a serious neck injury, the result of a fall offstage in Tampa. (Her next album was entitled *Easter.*) She had a mini-resurrection in 1988, when she released *Dream of Life*, after a long quiet spell following her move to Michigan and marriage to Fred (Sonic) Smith, of the protopunk group MC5. When the album received a so-so response, another, longer silence descended, adding to her mystique. As James Grauerholz says in *Please Kill Me*, "Patti actually managed a pretty canny thing. She managed to be a rock & roll death without having to die." With *Gone Again*, Patti has mounted her third and showiest resurrection. The album's cover photo, by Annie Leibovitz, shows Smith, her face averted, wearing black against a black backdrop—in double mourning. The deaths haunting the album are those of her brother, Todd, and her husband, Fred, both of whom died of heart failure in their forties, and it oscillates between personal revival and valediction, as Patti both reintroduces herself and says her good-byes. For every rocker like "Summer Cannibals," with its catchy chant of "eat eat" (Patti as Eucharist), there's a eulogy like "About a Boy" (for Kurt Cobain), or "Farewell Reel" (for Fred), or the title track, which alludes to Jerry Garcia. A Dylanesque album in its intimate geography, *Gone Again* features Patti doing an oddly arrhythmic cover version of Dylan's "Wicked Messenger." But where Dylan is Old Testament in his sensibility, full of fire and reprimand, Patti voices the hope of the New, her lyrics rife with references to air, feathers, clouds, and flight ("And a rainbow appears/like a smile from Heaven"). *Gone Again* is more than a resurrection; it's an ascension. Fred is dead, the album says, but She hath Risen.

I recognize that it's impertinent to intrude upon a private grief, but Patti has made her grief public, incorporating it into the packaging and promotion of *Gone Again*. She's being photographed wearing a cowl, her hands in prayer. Magazine cover lines say "Death and the Rebirth of Patti Smith." At the risk of being offensive, I think she's overdoing her widowhood. There's something pushy about her piety—an ingredient of bad faith or overcompensation. I picked up a spooky vibe about Fred and Patti's relationship when I interviewed Patti during the recording of *Dream of Life*. She phoned me the day after the interview asking that I omit in the article any mention of her having been involved with Sam Shepard and Tom Verlaine. I said, "But that's all public record." Patti said, "I know, but Fred gets upset when he reads that stuff." She mentioned other items that might upset Fred if he read them. She didn't sound like a considerate spouse trying to spare her husband's tender feelings; she sounded nervous, fretful—cowed. (For other reasons, the interview was never published.) Listening to *Gone Again*, I feel that I'm getting a fancy runaround on the real nature of Patti and Fred's relationship—that she's indulging in some automythologizing. When she sings, "Our wild love came from/ above," I want to say, Stop the romanticizing.

A similar impulse arises whenever Patti memorializes the photographer Robert Mapplethorpe, her lover, friend, and role model. In interviews and in her book *The Coral Sea* (a collection of poetic baubles) she paints him as a princely soul and "a pure artist." Fine—then what's that bullwhip doing sticking out of his ass? What about his singling out black men for special abuse, calling them "nigger" and forcing them to eat excrement? So many people around Patti have died of drugs and other forms of suicide that she can't be unaware of the animus coursing through their histories. Yet she blesses these casualties as if little angels had taken them in the night—even Kurt Cobain, whom she never met, and who killed himself with a shotgun. It's as if she'd willed herself back into a state of weary innocence, practicing soul craft from an enlightened perspective. The press has followed her saintly lead, the *Times* reviewer praising "her broader search to find a bridge between holistic thinking and subversive reasoning," and Stephanie Zacharek, in *Salon*, characterizing the album's eulogy to Fred as "a gift from a warrior queen who covers the dead not just with soil, but with blankets of dreams." No wonder Smith's recent sold-out concerts at Irving Plaza resembled a folk Mass or a Partridge family hootenanny (her sister Kimberly and her son Jackson both performed), and kicked into gear only when she threw off her veil of sorrow and tore into rockers like "Free Money" and "Land," proving that her husky voice was a horse she could still ride. The audience bobbed as one, living proof that holistic thinking will never replace a good hard beat.

The New Yorker, July 22, 1996

Postscript

Even though I prefixed it with a candy-ass bit of throat-clearing (if you'll excuse a little metaphor mangling), it was unpardonably insensitive and presumptuous of me to play drama critic regarding Patti Smith's public memorializing of her late husband, Fred "Sonic" Smith, and write, "I think she's overdoing her widowhood." The flak I received for this was deserved, though I still back out of the room when Patti commences a musical dirge, swinging her raspy voice like a rusty scythe.

It isn't as a singer-songwriter that she signifies anymore. It is as a living tarot card icon that Patti has achieved cultural ubiquity over the last two decades. That she's been elevated into the roles of high priestess of lost bohemia and roving ambassador of arts and letters (sanctified by her cameo in Jean-Luc Godard's Film Socialisme *and the worldwide coverage of her shaking hands and laughing with Pope Francis in St. Peter's Square) is a testament to our own sense of loss— our bereavement over the death of the counterculture, of any hope of new rebel energies rising through the thick sediment of money, snark, accreditation, and digital distraction. Art, mischief, and music/dance/ theater guerrilla operations made on the cheap, on the fly, on the sly— gone and never coming back, at least not on the island of privilege that Manhattan has become. Although I find much of Patti's acclaimed bestselling memoir* Just Kids *unconvincing and posterity-posturing, presented with a little too much moisture on the projection lens, it was inspired to frame her brotherly-sisterly soul-mating with photographer Robert Mapplethorpe as a waifish urban fairy tale, endowing the grit of the city with the magic of Cinderella cinders. As the character says in the Whit Stillman film* Damsels in Distress, *after being accused of romanticizing the past, "Well, the past is gone, so we might as well romanticize it." Because rubbishing it would rob us of whatever little idealism we have left.*

The Lives of Albert Goldman

That cagey cat coming down the hall, dressed in the pink windowpane shirt and high-top black Reeboks . . . it's the Big Bopper himself!
pop culture's jitterbug uncle—Albert Goldman, looking like a jovial
disc jockey taking a breather from the booth. Goldman is enjoying
a dry private moment before a public downpour. It is an afternoon
in late July, and he will soon release *The Lives of John Lennon* (William Morrow), his *bombe incendiaire* of Beatles revisionism. It's a mul-
tidirectional blast, covering not only Lennon's phantom phase in the
Dakota but his punk outbursts of fury (the most shocking claim being
that Lennon felt he had caused the death of ex-Beatle Stu Sutcliffe,
whom he had stomped to the pavement with his cowboy boots), plus
the sadomazzie compulsions of manager Brian Epstein. Then there is
the tacky picture of Yoko Ono slipping a cat turd in John's barefoot
path and the more serious accusation that she rigged the arrest of
Paul McCartney on drug charges in Japan. Whether or not Yoko sues,
damage control has already been set in motion.

Unsheathed in October, the month of Lennon's birth, will be the
three-pronged media event *Imagine: John Lennon.* Carrying Yoko's
seal of approval, this film documentary—the other two prongs are
book and sound-track tie-ins—shows us the off-duty Lennon of the
official archives. Mixing newsreel footage and TV interviews with
home movies, *Imagine* memorializes Lennon the house husband,
kneading dough in the kitchen; Lennon the bearded Jesus, conducting peace talks at bed-ins; Lennon the yin to Yoko's yang, finding
oneness by shedding his ego. It contains shrapnel from Lennon's sarcastic wit and a scene in which he has a glaring tantrum in a recording studio. (When he's pissed off at producer Phil Spector, his eyes
look hot enough to spit.) But most of the time it's Lennon hung at
half-mast as hero and martyr. He was a martyr, of course, and a hero
too. But not even *Imagine* will be able to steady the legend of the
sainted John Lennon—Gentle John, laying aside his guitar to bake
bread—on secure pillars. In *The Lives of John Lennon*, Goldman has

blown the pillars, dynamited the bridge. The rushing waters carry a lot of charred debris.

Although Goldman hasn't seen *Imagine*, he's heard from a friend that it will eventually find its rightful place on cable. So this afternoon he's in the catbird seat. But he also knows that heavy rain is headed his way. For his scathing celebrity biographies of Lenny Bruce and Elvis, Goldman has sprouted devil's horns in the press and the laity for being a destroyer, a desecrater, a despoiler. *Elvis*, with its spectacle of the King ringed with fat slowly going gaga in Graceland, made Goldman Public Enemy Number One among rock critics, guilty of felonious assault on a god. MTV has called him an embittered rock hater, and the rock writer Dave Marsh has already predicted that *Lives* will smear Lennon as an uncircumcised faggot junkie. But there are a lot of sides to Goldman, just as there were to Lennon, and the controversy allows a look at Goldman's own various lives.

Contrary to impression, he didn't burst into being on the bandstand at Birdland. "I was born and reared in Mount Lebanon, Pa., which is like a community in the thirties right off the cover of an old issue of *Life* magazine. It had in those days 20,000 people, and I always used to say, 'Twenty thousand Christians and one Jew, me.' I used to work for a black farmer, pulling a wooden plow behind a mule, something Elvis only did in the movies." The death of his father, an engineer and an inventor, was discombobulating. "I was in therapy for years and years in my twenties and early thirties . . . but after all the years of therapy and all the sessions, everything, I've never been able to decide whether my father's death occurred when I was a senior in high school or a junior. It just knocked a hole in my head, you know. And that hole is still there, after all these years."

Goldman's brain kernels didn't really begin to pop until he enrolled at the University of Chicago, which he likens to Laputa, the flying island of intellect in *Gulliver's Travels*. The professors there were into their own performance art. The critic and poet Elder Olson, for example, would "do" Lionel Trilling. "He would stand in the curve of an imaginary piano and puff on an imaginary cigarette and sort of *pule* out Trilling's prose." Ironically, as a graduate student at Columbia, Goldman became the protégé of Trilling and Jacques Barzun. "I was this Sherman tank that had been unloaded from Chicago, and I would like crunch down in the seminars in these arguments . . . and Trilling and Barzun were just cracking up. They loved it."

During a workaholic blitz in which Goldman was teaching at both

Columbia and Brooklyn College, an incident occurred which seeded his subsequent career: he caught a student plagiarizing. Tracking the original source down to a shelf of the student's local library stirred a Sherlock Holmes appetite for the sport of reasoning. Such deduction led to his first authored book. Entranced by an essay by the English Romantic writer and opium eater Thomas De Quincey called "The Last Days of Immanuel Kant," he noticed that passing reference was made to Kant's German biographers. "I said, 'I wonder what those guys were like?' So I went to the Forty-second Street reading room, I sent down for Borowski or whoever the hell it was, and up comes this book that's slowly going back to the tree . . . it looks like a little block of wood. And I open it and blow the mummy dust off the old German print, and I started reading it and I thought, Wait a minute! What the hell is this! It was word for word." The game was afoot. Further reading revealed that about 60 percent of De Quincey's work was either plagiarized or unauthorized. Goldman speedily dictated his findings in a book called *The Mine and the Mint*, which the scholarly press ignored. "Now, here was a major discovery about what in academic terms is a classic, at least. Boo. Nobody said nothing." The lesson for Goldman was that no field appreciates having its crypts disturbed. The caretakers of reputations would rather let the bones rot in their mummy dust.

For years Goldman felt like Schizoid Man, scissored down the middle between the academic drudge who taught freshman English and the cutup who engaged in comedy jam sessions with jazz-crazy characters every Saturday night at his Brooklyn pad. For a time he considered becoming a professional comic. "But I was just scared. Many times in my life I've been defeated by my own fear. I feel that's really been one of my single greatest problems. What's held me back is diffidence, fear, self-doubt. I have a lot of that. Well, at any rate, I didn't do it." Instead he gravitated to criticism, where he found that words on the page are harder to budge than words in the air. Yet he became adept. He covered jazz and classical music for *The New Leader*, rock for *Life*. A compilation of his riffing on rock, comedy, and jazz was briefly preserved in *Freakshow* (1971). One of the best collections of pop criticism ever published, *Freakshow* showcases Goldman as that rare critic who can communicate a dizzy, complex thrill. He opens up the full sensorium for Jimi Hendrix: "I went home and put *The Jimi Hendrix Experience* on the turntable. Tough, abrasive, brutally iterative, the uptake suggested the ironshod tracks of a bulldozer straining against a mountain of dirt. Hendrix's program for the country blues was rural electrification. The end products were futurist symphonies of industrial noise." Unlike most books from rock's chesty youth, *Freakshow* hasn't faded into a dated piece of psychedelia. Out of print, it may even be more apt today. A doomed moonlit glamour still coats the memories of Hendrix, Joplin, Jim Morrison . . . the beautiful dead.

It is the unbeautiful dead from whose skulls our culture continues most deeply to drink. Perhaps Goldman was more inspired than he knows by "The Last Days of Immanuel Kant," because his biographies at their most karmic, flesh-crumbling, and transfixed become The Last Days of . . . Lenny, Elvis, Lennon. He performs high colonics on the addictive psyche. Yet *Lives* didn't start out as a scouring. In part it began as an attempt to atone for the excesses of *Elvis*. Although *Elvis* reads like a comet and has scoops for which Goldman has never received ample due (such as his uncovering of Colonel Parker), his antipathy to his subject gave the book a derisory sneer. The sarcasm that made some of us laugh, others found a cruel affrontery. "It was like running smack into the hunched-up bull with the glaring red eyes at the heart of the American corral, you know?" Goldman says. Some of the critics, he believes, were couching anti-Semitism in their complaints: Who is this *New York Jew* to poach on Elvis's sacred burial ground? Yet the backlash left him somewhat chastened. So when he set to work on Lennon, he thought he would drive out the bad nail with the good by writing about someone "who's really creative and really intelligent and really witty—all the things I saw Elvis as not being." But then he felt a familiar gloom seep in.

"When I began to realize who John Lennon really was, I was horrified and dismayed for two very good reasons. First of all, it was very disillusioning and disheartening; secondly, I could see, 'Uh-oh, here we go again.'" Lennon's mindscape, he discovered, was not merely divided but subdivided. Haphazardly subdivided at that. "I used to say, 'I don't understand. How can he say this one day and do this the next? Be so gung ho and so disillusioned, so active, so passive, so violent, so little-boy sweet, so apparently sexually impelled, so monastic?' Where is the real man in all this?" Stymied, Goldman contacted a young female writer named Lloyd Rose who had written perceptively about Lennon for *The Boston Phoenix*. They met, and for over an hour he tried aloud to separate the tangled noodles of Lennon's personality. When he finished his spiel, he asked her what she made of all this, and she replied, "Well, it all makes sense to me." Her nod was the go-ahead he needed to plunge headlong into his thesis that Lennon had a plural personality. Hence the title.

I asked Goldman what fans and critics are going to resist most about *Lives*. "I'm sure there will be those who can't tolerate the idea that John was violent, because John sang of peace and was a victim of violence . . . indeed, he was martyred to irrational violence. And so the notion that he was violent is something that is going to be jarring. But what people maybe will resist even more is its complement, his extreme passivity. His sort of wimpy side—that he could be so easily influenced and led around by the nose and bamboozled and deceived, and the way he just totally submitted himself to Yoko's dominance in order to achieve a measure of security and also irresponsibility." (Yoko was easier for Goldman to read, because for all her surface mystification—her dark glasses, her Warholesque whimsies—her ambitions always ring clear. She's a doer. Her relation to Lennon evokes for Goldman "the whole doctrine of the external soul, the soul that acts for you.")

After years of arduous research, Goldman has come to believe that Elvis and Lennon, whom he once saw as so radically opposed, are in some sense astral kin. "The dependency and the messianic delusions and the megalomania, the love of death, and the final page, where they're laid out in their bedrooms . . . They were so different in culture and talent and temperaments and everything, who yet converged so much into the common archetype, you ask yourself, Is this really like some deep pattern or logic of this kind of culture? Like a concept of entropy . . . you know, personality entropy.

"See, what people don't realize is that the dynamic, ebullient, brilliant, charismatic pop star of our time, when you get close to him, often seems almost like an angel of death. The closer you get to him, the lower the temperature sinks. And when you get really close to them, you see that these guys are in love with death. Both Elvis and John are very in love with death, very keen on stepping over to the other side. This life doesn't make it for them. They're not really believers in this life. What they want isn't something that you can have here. They have to pass on by, they have to go over, they have to step over into the void." Lennon's genius was making musical origami out of these elliptical, entropic states of mind in such songs as "Strawberry Fields Forever," "I'm Only Sleeping," and "Nowhere Man." (At one time Goldman considered calling his biography *Nowhere Man*.) And in his "primal scream" album, *Plastic Ono Band*, Lennon tried to burn his crutches and purge his past through a bulimic rejection of false idols. *Don't believe in Beatles . . . don't believe in Zimmerman . . .* "I mean, I think John had a great histrionic flair of a kind. He was a great projector of his own psychodrama. You feel that there's always this hysterical child inside him. For example, on that great tape of him at Madison Square Garden [portions of which appear in *Imagine*], he does 'Cold Turkey' and he does 'Mother' and so forth. In 'Cold Turkey' he throws up his hands and he has this hysterical look in his eyes, and you can just see this little child going nuts. And that's one of the powerful projections of Lennon. It's unforgettable." The problem was that he didn't have enough amplification for his anxieties. "He shouldn't have been the Beatles, he should have been the Who."

Yet even riding the rumbling train of Keith Moon's rampageous drumming might not have been enough to keep Lennon from losing himself in the limelight. Though he regrets he wasn't able to explore the idea in the book, Goldman now contends that, contrary to the myth of the rock star as showman and shaman, megastars like Elvis and Lennon aren't truly forgers of their own fates. "Both John and Elvis were radically reshaped by success. John was changed from this red-light-district, tough teddy-boy type into Beatle John. And, similarly, Elvis went from being a tough, roadhouse rocker into a teddy bear. And so it's really the public in a weird way that is the master controller. The public is a Svengali, the public has the energy, the public has the force, the authority."

For Goldman this transference is best allegorized in Thomas Mann's novella *Mario and the Magician*, in which a sinister magician first cracks a whip over his audience like a ringmaster and then eerily submits to its whim. Mann: "Thus he groped his way forward, like a blind seer, led and sustained by the mysterious common will." It's the loony underflap of this common will which insists on believing that Elvis is alive—among the ignorati, Elvis sightings have replaced Big Foot spottings. This collective membrane of wish fulfillment also cushions the reception of star biographies. It's ingrained in the very nature of history versus myth. "History is hard to remember and hard to learn. Myth, on the other hand, is immanent—it comes right out of us." Thus, in time the particularities of history recede into Myth. "And you can never down a myth. If I had written fourteen books on Elvis, I wouldn't have made a dent in the Elvis myth."

Similarly, one suspects that the hot peppers in *Lives* will make little dent in the Lennon myth. Rock critics may still maintain that there was moral and spiritual health within that white womb of heroin. For fans (and rock critics are the ultimate fans), knowledge bows to belief, and *Imagine*, not *The Lives of John Lennon*, is what they want to believe. So why persist? It's absurd to say, as Goldman's detractors do, that it's a matter of greed. If he were in it simply for the money, he could emulate Charles Higham and crank out a cut-and-paste celebrity schlock book a year. No, the man is a manic-obsessive. He puts a mind lock on his subject, and it's a trial maintaining a lock on someone whose mind is going. "The simplest personality when you pour a bunch of chemicals on top of it is going to be very bizarre. I sometimes wonder, when the day comes when everybody is a junkie—what is biography going to be?" Then there is Goldman's own internal turbulence. He has within him the whirlwind nihilism of a Wyndham Lewis. Which is why as racy and racing as his biographies are, they aren't the best chassis for Goldman's free-associative riffing. Once he has strapped himself into the nose cone to re-create his stars' soaring ascent and sputtering fall, he has to spend the duration captive and compressed. He's along for the narrative ride—he can't break loose and boogie-woogie. He wishes that he could have gotten more of Lennon's goonie humor into the book, and his own humor is missing. It's heartening, then, that Goldman's next project will probably be an account of his years covering the drug-smuggling trade, the climax of which came when a cargo plane crashed on his fiftieth birthday and he had to spirit an injured boy out of South America by putting on a Tom Mix hat and pretending to be a rancher. "This is mah boy . . . he burned hisself . . ." With this memoir he can saddle his own vortex rather than trace the line of a dying fall in a space capsule.

Which is not to discount what Albert Goldman has done in *The Lives of John Lennon*. The biggest achievement of *Lives* is not Goldman's prodigious digging for dirt but his powerful composite portrait of Lennon as a far more bewitched, embattled, fractured, tortured, torturing, and lonely man than we'd ever, well, imagined. That achievement will outlast questions or outcries about Goldman's personality, methodology, and presentation. Saints cast a smooth glow, but the psychological fissures of *Lives* will permanently line John Lennon's wan, sad pallor.

Vanity Fair, October 1988

When They Were Kings
The Rat Pack

"I present our hoodlum singer . . ."

With these words of mock homage, an astonishingly young and lanky Johnny Carson introduces Frank Sinatra to the stage of the Kiel Opera House in St. Louis, Missouri. The year is 1965; the event, billed as a "Frank Sinatra Spectacular" and broadcast on closed circuit to theaters across the country, is a benefit for Father Dismas Clark's Half-Way House for ex-cons. Sinatra said, "Be there," and they were there—Dean Martin, Sammy Davis Jr., Trini Lopez, Kaye Stevens, and an amalgamation of two different bands, including members of the Count Basie Orchestra, conducted by a lean cat named Quincy Jones. Joey Bishop was listed on the original program, but had to bow out when he "slipped a disk backing out of Frank's presence," according to Carson, his replacement, who was only three years into his tenure as host of *The Tonight Show*. A recently discovered kinescope of this bash—under the new title, *The Rat Pack Captured*—will be screened this month at the Museum of Television & Radio in New York and at the Los Angeles branch, and will also be broadcast later this year on "Nick at Nite"'s cable channel. The edited 90-minute version of the benefit—featuring Frank, Dino, Sammy, and Johnny—represents the only known full-length video of the Rat Pack in performance. (A two-volume compact disc exists of the Rat Pack performing at the Villa Venice club in Chicago in 1962—a gig they were strong-armed into doing by the mobster Sam Giancana.) The Rat Pack kinescope, found in a closet at the Dismas House, is more than a historical curio. It has the glamorous wham of a championship prizefight. It's an opportunity to catch three of America's greatest showmen in their tigerish prime (with Carson along for the ride), before they became total legends and turned into leather.

There's Dean Martin with his sleepy power, like a leopard in a smoking jacket, finishing his few songs with the words "I'd like to do some more for ya, but I'm lucky I remembered these." There's Sammy Davis Jr., a gleaming revolver of a man, belting out a maudlin Anthony Newley torch song as if he means it, goofing around with "I've Got

You Under My Skin" ("it's a little lumpy, but you're under my skin"), demonstrating the latest go-go dances (the monkey, the jerk, the frug, the mashed potato), and, in a final tour de force, doing quick carbon copies of Billy Eckstine, Nat King Cole, Frankie Laine, Mel Tormé, Tony Bennett, and Dean himself. And then there's Sinatra, confident, not the Adam's apple on a stick he was or the barrel-chested belter he would become, cruising inside the luxury-limousine sound of the Count Basie band, not so much singing the up-tempo numbers ("Fly Me to the Moon," "You Make Me Feel So Young") as riding them home, his rabbit jabs providing the punctuation to his cagey phrasing and eased-off vowels. Frank Sinatra has been called great for so long that it's easy to forget how great he is. Praise becomes platitude. At one point, alluding to Sammy's set, he says that the song he's about to perform makes for "a slight duplication here, but I don't think you'll mind too much," launching into his own rendition of "I've Got You Under My Skin," which he contours and tattoos as if romancing for the first time. Dean amuses, Sammy is mahvelous, but only Sinatra, with his Manhattan-skyline voice, conjures a mood and a spell.

After Sinatra's set comes the usual Rat Pack foolery, some at Dean's expense ("The only reason he's got a good tan, he found a bar with a skylight"), but with Sammy as the primary butt. The racial ribbing, though not as crass or persistent as the kidding on the Villa Venice CD, conveys the edginess of the civil-rights era. Sammy mentions something about getting Martin Luther King Jr.'s permission to appear. Dean lifts Sammy in his arms and says, "I'd like to thank the NAACP for this wonderful trophy." Sammy, who had converted to Judaism, is hailed as the only Jewish Muslim: Irving X. What's interesting about the last segment, aside from the forced joviality of the racial horseplay, is Carson's surfacing irritation as the buffoonery (deliberately bad imitations of Jimmy Cagney, etc.) drags on too long. He feels extraneous on the stage, checking his watch and saying he has to catch a plane, and although he is not nearly the star at that point that Frank, Dino, or Sammy is, he isn't grateful to play stooge to the gods. We see in his broomstick posture and sentry eyes the isolated power that Carson would become. The show ends with all four wailing away at "The Birth of the Blues," with Dean taking a brilliantly timed pratfall just as he wings into his verse.

The excitement that this kinescope has sparked testifies to the unfading legend of the Rat Pack and their streamlined influence on male bravado, which can be observed in everything from the resurgence of "bachelor pad" music and the cocktail hour to the nostalgia for the Vegas of yore in movies like *Casino* and *Bugsy*, when the city still swung and the red lobbies weren't clogged with Mr. and Mrs. Big-Butt America pushing strollers between the slots. The Rat Pack is the Mount Rushmore of men having fun. The designer Mossimo Giannulli keeps a large photograph of the Rat Pack in his Laguna Beach home, like an eternal flame. "These guys are my idols," he told *InStyle* magazine. "They just cruised. They had this great group of people, love and friendship." The fact that the press keeps trying to manufacture fresh new Rat Packs—the acting Brat Pack of Judd Nelson, Ally Sheedy, Andrew McCarthy, Molly Ringwald, and Rob Lowe; the literary Brat Pack of Jay McInerney, Bret Easton Ellis, and Tama Janowitz—indicates the constant itch for a group energy, a moving amoeba of excitement, a scene.

The term "Rat Pack" originally designated not Sinatra and his flying wedge but an informal Hollywood social set revolving around Humphrey Bogart and his pals. Nathaniel Benchley designed the letterhead of the group's stationery, which bore the loyalty oath coined by Bogart, "Never rat on a rat." Sinatra, who idolized Bogart, was a member in good standing, along with Judy Garland and agent Irving "Swifty" Lazar. After Bogart's death in 1957, Sinatra, with his natural charisma and inability to be alone (see Gay Talese's classic study in *Esquire* in 1966, "Frank Sinatra Has a Cold"), filled the social void and then some with his own Rat Pack, also known as the Clan—names Sinatra disavowed as inaccurate and uncouth. "There is no such thing as a clan or pack," he explained. "It's just a bunch of millionaires with common interests who get together to have a little fun." The members of this floating bacchanal included Martin (with whom Sinatra co-starred in *Some Came Running*), Joey Bishop, Sammy Davis Jr., and Peter Lawford, classy dames like Angie Dickinson and Shirley MacLaine, and supporting players like Sammy Cahn, Cesar Romero, Don Rickles, Milton Berle, and the director Lewis Milestone.

It never hit me until now that the Rat Pack formed during the same period that the Beats rolled onto the scene—Jack Kerouac, Allen Ginsberg, William Burroughs, and all those other spontaneous bopsters. (Kerouac's *On the Road* was published in 1957, the year Bogart's Rat Pack gave way to Sinatra's.) At first the two outfits couldn't seem more bizarro-world apart, the Rat Packers showing the money in their sharkskin suits and slick grooming, the Beats bumming around in fleapit pads from Monterey to Morocco on the path to Buddhahood. Yet both were a reaction to the suburban conformism of work-home-family in the Eisenhower era. The Rat Pack, like the Beats, disdained middle-class moderation in their pursuit of freewheeling kicks. ("This [cigarette] ain't got no printin' on it at all," Dean Martin muses in the Rat Pack video.) Like the Beats and their fictional alter egos, the Rat Pack were always in motion, nocturnal creatures partying in a perpetual Now. And like the Beats, the Rat Pack had their own special hipster lingo to winnow out the squares from the truly anointed, a code that sounds like something cooked up by Steve Allen in a jazzy frame of mind. Kitty Kelley provides a glossary in her 1986 biography of Sinatra, *His Way:* women were "broads," "bird" equaled penis (as in "How's your bird?"), "a little hey-hey" meant a good time, "clyde" was an all-purpose noun, and death was "the big casino."

> Nice, France, August 11 (A.P.)—The second wave of Frank Sinatra's Hollywood clan hit the Riviera beaches as cane-twirling Sammy Davis Jr. danced down the ramp of a jet airliner.
> "I would have been here earlier, daddy-ohs, but the hotel clerk in London forgot to wake me," Davis told waiting reporters and photographers.
> —*New York Post*, August 11, 1961

Personal hygiene aside, where the Rat Pack and the Beats parted company was in their attitudes toward power in all its seductive guises. To the Beats—self-educated in the prophecies of William Blake and Eastern notions of nonattachment—the Pentagon, Madison Avenue, and Hollywood were all manifestations of Moloch. "Hollywood will rot on the windmills of Eternity / Hollywood whose movies stick in the throat of God," Allen Ginsberg declared. (And this was before Pauly Shore.) While the Beats were content to woo nodding fields of young minds, the Rat Pack enjoyed the view from the penthouse suite, where sex and money were plugged into the same socket. With Sinatra as their king, their Pope, *il padrone*, the Rat Pack were a royal court, granting and receiving favor. Seas of gawkers parted in hushed wonder when they crossed the lobby of Las Vegas's Sands Hotel, the casino which is the Xanadu of Rat Pack lore. The Sands was where they did their most famous engagements (the double live album *Sinatra at the Sands*, available on CD, preserves the brassy ebullience), drawing the high rollers and their minked molls. Nick Tosches sets the scene in his 1992 Dean Martin biography, *Dino:*

> It was not just the dirty-rich *giovanostri* and *padroni* who were drawn to them, to their glamour, to the appeal of darkness made

respectable. The world was full, it seemed, of would-be wops and woplings who lived vicariously through them, to whom the imitation of cool took on the religiosity of the Renaissance ideal of *imitatio Christi*. The very songs that Sinatra and Dean sang, the very images they projected, inspired lavish squandering among the countless men who would be them. It was the Jew-roll around the prick that rendered them ithyphallic godkins, simulacra of the great ones, in their own eyes and in the eyes of the teased-hair lobster-slurping *Bimbo sapiens* they sought to impress.

Not exactly how I would phrase it, but, hey, man, to each his own bird!

The ranks of Rat Pack wannabes weren't restricted to swarthy men and wives in lobster bibs. Elvis Presley's "Memphis Mafia" was a high-cholesterol Rat Pack. Heavy swingers in their own fields wanted to tap into the electricity. John F. Kennedy was fascinated by Sinatra's chick action. It was at the Sands where JFK, following a Sinatra performance, was introduced by him at a friendly mixer afterward ("blowjobs on the house"—Tosches) to Judith Campbell, whom Sinatra later hooked up with Sam Giancana, thus giving the Mob a direct mouth into the White House. It was Sinatra who triangulated Hollywood, Washington, and the Mafia. The Rat Pack sang "The Star-Spangled Banner" at the Democratic convention that year. Sinatra attended Kennedy's inauguration in top hat, cape, and swallow-tailed coat. Then it all went black. The president, fearful of bad publicity, skipped a visit to Sinatra's Palm Springs spread to stay at Bing Crosby's instead, a snub that infuriated Sinatra. Marilyn Monroe, rumored to have been having an affair with Robert Kennedy, tried to commit suicide at Sinatra's Cal-Neva Lodge in Nevada, a favorite hangout of Giancana's, and succeeded a few days later in Los Angeles. Sinatra, the Kennedys, Monroe, the Mob—for a few short years, it was a dizzying round of musical beds. Perhaps no book captures the dangerous golden-nooky pop-myth glamour of the period better than Norman Mailer's *An American Dream*, which begins with a reverie about double-dating with JFK and ends with a drive to Las Vegas, where the narrator phones his dead sweetheart in Heaven, who tells him that Marilyn says hello. It's an honorary Rat Pack novel.

In the first flush of Camelot, before Marilyn Monroe overdosed, Giancana tried to arrange a hit on Castro, and JFK was assassinated, Sinatra and pals shot a caper movie for his production company that stands as the definitive photo album of the Rat Pack phenomenon, *Ocean's 11*. Other Rat Pack films would follow, such as *Robin and the Seven Hoods*, but this is the one with the *essence de rat*. Shot in 1960, *Ocean's 11* was directed by Lewis Milestone, who had earned his distinction with *All Quiet on the Western Front* and *A Walk in the Sun* before setting aside his taste and dignity to baby-sit these overgrown delinquents. At night the Rat Pack would perform at the Sands and make major hey-hey until dawn, catnap, then slouch before the camera. They look like sirloin in the atomic light of day, while Angie Dickinson, reciting her lines off a blank slate in her mind as Sinatra's long-suffering wife, is pure custard. The guys play military buddies who meet to plan the great heist of all time, knocking out a power line in Las Vegas and hitting the casino vaults during the blackout confusion. (In an enlightened piece of casting, Sammy drives a garbage truck.)

Incidental dialogue reflects the Kennedy euphoria—and its cynical opportunism. Standing around in the game room with pool cues and cigarettes, the gang swaps *Playboy* fantasies about what they'd do with a big score. Sinatra suggests buying out the Miss Universe pageant, "and just sit around and talk to the girls, one by one. Find out how things are in Sweden." Why buy what you could get for free? asks Peter Lawford, who had married into the Kennedy clan. The key, he says, is "turning money into power. . . . Think I'll buy me some votes and go into politics." "*I'm* the one that's going into politics," Dino ripostes. His platform? asks Sammy. "Repeal the 14th and the 20th Amendment, take the vote away from the women and make slaves out of them." "Hey, will it cost much?" Frank asks. "Oh no, we've got the price controls—no inflation on slaves." Lawford, vainly trying to steer them back to the big picture, reiterates that politics is the real racket. "Pay off your own party, settle for an appointment. . . . Hey, fellas, do you have any idea how much money a man can steal if he was something like commissioner of Indian affairs? That's what I'll be, commissioner of Indian affairs!" "That you'll never be," Dean says, " 'cause I'm gonna be secretary of the interior, and *I* won't appoint you." It's a disjointed scene, but the message is clear: money equals power equals male prerogative. Then they quit trading philosophy and gather around the pool table to plan their low-tech, low-IQ operation.

Like Elvis Presley's *Viva Las Vegas*, *Ocean's 11* is one of those dumbbell diversions that have achieved a permanent splotch in the rec room of pop culture. It's a real sixties guy favorite, like *Rio Bravo*, *The Great Escape*, and (my own indefensible must-see) *Hatari!* Its cult status has little to do with quality, more to do with a high kitsch quotient that sticks like chewing gum in the *Mad* magazine of the mind. The schlock highlights include the blaring and much-imitated musical score by Nelson Riddle; Sinatra receiving a backrub in his orange mohair sweater; Dino, backed by a jazz combo (dig those crazy goatees), singing "Ain't That a Kick in the Head" to a trio of cloned-sheep fans; and Richard Conte asking, as his doctor studies his X-ray, "Is it the big casino?" A perfectionist in the recording studio, Sinatra didn't believe in undue strain on the movie set, breezing through as few takes as possible. After Conte buys the big casino, suffering a heart attack as he crosses the street, other members of the gang gather on the street to share the news. Heads nod. Without bothering to change expression, Sinatra then exits the scene as if heading for a sandwich, and Lawford remarks, "He's taking it hard." Not so you'd notice! What rescues the movie from utter plywood is its comic anti-climax, when the scheme runs aground and the money literally goes up in smoke, and the Rat Packers file out of Conte's chapel service across the screen like a lost patrol—past the Sands marquee bearing their names. Their walks have singular style, adding up to an absurdist coda.

Years later, *Ocean's 11* inspired one of the classic movie parodies, *SCTV*'s "Maudlin's 11," in which the *SCTV* regulars trade finger-snapping slang with one another ("Absopositively," "Bingo, dingo!") as they plan a heist with such vocal enthusiasm ("Oh, *yeah!*" "Cool, man, cool!") that everybody in Vegas knows the score. In a takeoff on the *Ocean's 11* strip-club scene, the acerbic Bill Needle (Dave Thomas) belts out the theme from *Exodus*, acknowledging the crowd's flat response with a surly "Thank you for that great round of indifference," kissing off his stripper wife with the words "You're just nothing but a bringdown anyway!" What the *SCTV* parody exuberantly nails is the gee-whiz juvenile giddiness underlying the Rat Pack swagger and camaraderie. Their jive is not the genuine laid-back hip of jazz, but the loud tones and threads of lounge lizards trying to pass as jazzy. Most of the Rat Pack humor is corny, retrograde. The Rat Pack mystique is not about being innately cool; it's about wanting to be cool so much you give each other contact highs. "Oh, *yeah!*" It's white soul, without the soul.

The fascination with the Rat Pack expresses a longing for an every-day masculine style that's cool and crisp, without being James Bond swanky. The Rat Pack video was shot in 1965, before the hippie insurgence feminized men, fluffing their hair and softening the sharp cut

of their wardrobes into more flowing lines. Even the slouchier postures of the Rat Packers (like Dean's modified John Wayne roll) carry
more purposeful thrust than the nudist-colony droop of male hippies.
When unabashed masculinity returned to pop culture, it did so with
a vengeance, pumped up on steroids and so thickened that its meat-
men (Conan the Barbarian, Rambo) could barely speak, or, conversely,
ranted like a neighborhood bully (Andrew Dice Clay). Rat Pack
male-bonding infiltrates such revisionist guy pictures as *GoodFellas* (a
rotting-carcass Rat Pack) and *The Usual Suspects* (the twist being that
the soulful gang leader is played for a fool by the Joey Bishop mascot,
portrayed by Kevin Spacey). Quentin Tarantino's stuff has a perverse
Rat Pack streak. But if the spirit is there, the look is wanting. A lot of
the younger male stars, even when they dress keen, have junkie-dank
skin and sticky, unwashed hair that would have made Sinatra in his
prime drag them through a car wash to straighten out their clyde.

The razor-blade flair of the Rat Pack style gleams best in a time
bubble or a deliberately retro fashion spread. It complements the
overall style of the Kennedy-kaboom sixties; it jibes with the design
and décor—tail fins, stand-up bars, African masks, breezeways, Mon-
drian rectangles, and curvilinear signs. The ladies in this bachelor
paradise sported cocktail dresses and bouffants with enough hair
spray to stop a bullet; when these walking powder puffs made small
talk or indulged in dry laughter, they turned up their wrists just so.
That's all Audrey Hepburn now. The natty extravagance of the Rat
Pack look clashes with shopping-mall functionalism—fern bars, family minivans, video rentals, and computer monitors casting gray death
rays. Clubs have lost most of their dressy cachet; they've become day-
care centers for night owls. (Only in the last few years have cocktails
and cigars made a self-conscious comeback.)

The comedy of trying to emulate a rich Rat Pack attitude in the
downwardly mobile nineties is what animates *Swingers*, a modest cult
hit written by and starring Jon Favreau. The movie, funny but acrid
(burnt around the edges), has also spawned a spin-off book, a *Swingers* manual. Favreau plays Mike, a shlub strictly from Loserville who
mopes over an old girlfriend and gets nowhere fast as an actor in Hollywood. He also MC's at a comedy club on open-mike night. His
best bud, Trent (Vince Vaughn), is his pep coach in cool. "You are
so money and you don't even know it," Trent tells him again and
again. (Vaughn based his characterization on the Rat Pack jargon he
used to make up to amuse his actor-friends.) To get Mike out of his

funk, Trent suggests they go to Vegas. "Vegas, baby, Vegas!" Grabbing the first cocktail waitress they meet, Trent spins her around and introduces her to Mike: "I want you to remember this face here. This is the guy behind the guy behind the guy." Their cover story doesn't translate into clout. They don't rule the blackjack table or command the hospitality suite, but end up in a trailer at dawn with the cocktail waitress and her friend; sex for both couples proves a non-event. It's clear that, for all their front, Mike and Trent are a couple of doobie-doobie-don'ts. They have jangly personas but little genuine personality, which may be the point of the film.

Back in L.A., Trent and Mike don't hold court in a conversation pit, as in *Ocean's 11*, but play video games and cruise dumpy bars looking for "babies" and "bunnies." Having gotten one bunny's number, Mike leaves so many annoying messages that she finally picks up the phone and says, "Don't ever call me again." Mike and Trent want to be finger-snapping free with the ladies, but they lack the hard peanut shell of a Frank or a Dean—they're too sincere and eager to "communicate." Whereas Sinatra described himself as an "18-karat manic-depressive," these guys are passive-aggressive, finky rather than outrageous and flamboyant. Their fear, hostility, and fur trapper's approach to women come out in pissy little gestures, such as Trent's tearing up the phone number of a woman he's just met, Mike's persistent phone calls and snide references to "skanks" (like he's some bonus). As with most passive-aggressives, it's hard to gauge how much of their behavior is intentionally obnoxious and how much is self-centered cluelessness—a not knowing any better. Compared to manic-depressives, with their mighty mood swings, passive-aggressives operate out of a very tight but ambiguous pocket. The true godfather of these swingers is not Sinatra, but David Letterman, smoking a big cigar behind his deflector shield of nervous, impervious irony.

It could be argued that *The Rat Pack Captured* and the backhanded homage of *Swingers* augur a last hurrah. After all, Dean Martin, Sammy Davis Jr., and Peter Lawford are dead; Frank Sinatra has been ailing so long that public radio ran a premature obituary on him in February, which featured an extract from Michael Ventura's novel, *The Death of Frank Sinatra*, and a plea not to flog us with "My Way" over the final credits of his life. The Sands Hotel was demolished last year, to clear ground for a mega-resort. The Vegas the Sands typified is itself extinct, the former sin capital emasculated and deloused by theme parks and chain restaurants ("that Pirate of the Caribbean horseshit," as Trent says in *Swingers*). In time the Rat Pack may be as forgotten as the Ritz Brothers.

But I doubt it. For baby-boomers, the biggest chunk of the population, the Kennedy years will always exert a dark, sexy undertow, in part because the deaths of Marilyn Monroe and JFK still appear mysterious, intertwined. The sixties still seem young, dashing. They say you can't live in the past, but of course you can; that's practically all pop culture does now, is live in the past. The past is a permanent tape loop constantly being sampled and updated to create a new montage. Through the miracle of editing, Fred Astaire now dances with a vacuum cleaner, John Wayne sells beer. We're all Zeligs now. "Let me swing forevermore," Sinatra sings in "Fly Me to the Moon." For better or worse, you got your wish, daddy-o.

Vanity Fair, May 1997

IV: MOVIES

French Fries and Sympathy
Diner

Coffee and Coca-Cola, the crackling hiss of food on the fry, the ring of laughter in a bustling room—*Diner*, written and directed by Barry Levinson, is a bittersweet reverie about the pleasures of noshing and chumming about until the squeak of dawn. An unassuming, small-budget comedy, *Diner* deftly follows the weaving paths of five friends on a Christmas holiday break in Baltimore in 1959, the year the Baltimore Colts played their second championship game against the New York Giants. As Baltimore pretties itself with crinkly gold Christmas decorations and rows of navy-blue Colt banners, Levinson's characters—Eddie (Steve Guttenberg), Shrevie (Daniel Stern), Fenwick (Kevin Bacon), Billy (Timothy Daly), and Boogie (Mickey Rourke)—scheme and gamble, cop cheap feels and mull over impending marriages, blow warmth into their knotted fists, reminisce about high school escapades, razz each other into fits of helpless laughter. But no matter what fun or scrapes come their way, the gang always ends up back at the diner, dipping their fingers into heaps of french fries smothered in gravy. When night gives way to a hung-over, blue dawn, the boys stagger to their cars and reluctantly wheel home.

Not only is the diner an island of warmth and light in the grim, wintry dark, but it's a prime hangout for young men trying to extend their boyhoods with foolish antics and uninhibited bouts of gab. Like the Raccoon Lodge on *The Honeymooners* (where Norton and Kramden fled to escape their wives), the diner is an all-male preserve that allows its members to piddle away the evening without having the women in their lives tugging on their sleeves and reminding them of their—sheesh, groan—responsibilities. Since Barry Levinson himself haunted a Baltimore diner booth in the heyday of Colts Alan Ameche and Johnny U., his movie has an autobiographical savor, but it never turns precious or self-serving; it isn't a portrait of the artist as a young snack fiend. Blemishes and eccentricities are fondly treated as the bumps that give life its character. When a hefty "building with feet" named Earl (Mark Margolis) eats his way through the entire left side of the menu, he isn't snickered at for being a gorging slob; his binge is regarded as a wonderful feat. As Earl ambles across the parking lot, the boys at the diner fire off a round of applause. In their eyes, this big, foolish bear is a waddling hero.

Levinson's script is an idiosyncratic marvel, perhaps the most generous-spirited piece of comic writing for the screen since Steve Tesich's script for *Breaking Away.* Early in the movie a deadpan wiseacre named Modell (Paul Reiser) remarks with picky distaste, "You know what word I'm not comfortable with? 'Nuance.' It doesn't seem to be a real word. Now 'gesture' is a good word. At least you know where you are with 'gesture.'" What's invaluable about Levinson's script is that it is rich in both gesture *and* nuance, reveling in slangy chatter and braggadocio without ever turning into a John Cassavetes exercise in motormouth hysteria. *Diner* is a very talky movie, but the talkiness has shape, point, rambunctious humor. When Eddie and Modell bicker over a roast beef sandwich, it's like listening to an old married couple carry on a gripe session they've had every morning since they were wooing youths—you have the feeling that if the two of them were encased in ice for several centuries, their first words after thawing out would be "Listen, if you *want* the sandwich, just *ask* for it . . ." There's also a hilariously woolly scene in which Eddie's mother, unspooling an ancient complaint of her own, pretends that her son is some sort of sinister changeling. "You *thing*, you," she growls, playfully pressing a kitchen knife to his breast, "where did you come from? You don't even look like me." Levinson is also capable of capping a scene with a crushing flourish. When the sneer-curled, preppie-looking Billy is tossed into the pokey after a scuffle at a Nativity scene, he's accosted in his cell by a weird old coot who dares him to fight. Staring intently into the geezer's eyes, Billy says with withering calm, "You lay a hand on me again and I'll hit you so hard I'll kill your whole family"—a threat that might make even Charles Bronson pale at the gills.

As a director, Levinson may never twirl planets on his fingertips, but he certainly knows how to showcase the alert, natural ease of a talented young cast. As the combustible Eddie, who refuses to marry his high school sweetie until she passes a rigorous football quiz ("Everybody knows that a good marriage depends upon a firm grasp of football trivia," comments Modell), Steve Guttenberg is a sputter of comic agitation, trying to be as suavely cool as his hero Sinatra even as his rubbery cheeks betray ripples of discomfort. He's a creature of simple appetites, Eddie; he falls asleep at Bergman movies but does a flipped-out soul strut on the runway of a strip joint, his entire body pulsating to the boogie-woogie beat. (Keen-eyed rock fans will note that the grind-house drummer is portrayed by Jay Dee Daugherty, formerly the drummer for Patti Smith. *Diner*'s original music is by Ivan Kral, who also once shared the stage with the now reclusive Patti, and Bruce Brody.)

Kevin Bacon, who wades through the suds daily on CBS's *The Guiding Light*, brings an infectious laugh and a bleary, amused scrunch of his eyes to the role of Fenwick, a castoff from a rich family who prefers to cruise aimlessly through life in a boozy haze rather than buckle down and be a proper sober drone, like the brother he so eloquently despises. Bacon's Fenwick is the sort of classic character we've all known but never before seen on screen: the articulate, wise-cracking quick study who never finds a place to channel his intelligence and ends up squandering his smarts in a slumming, drunken frizzle. He could easily grow up to be the sort of amiable barstool philosopher who fumes as poetically as Brendan Behan but never finds time to slap the words down on paper. Daniel Stern, memorable as one of the cutters in *Breaking Away*, shows even more range and subtle tone as the sole married member of the diner clique. With the fellas, Stern's Shrevie is all sass and ingratiation, zinging Eddie and Modell as they wrangle over the last wedge of roast beef on the plate, but when he's home alone with the warden, he's sullen and petulant, his eyes glassing over with rage when his wife misfiles an album in his inviolable record collection. Shrevie is this movie's true splitsoo, a nice guy who saws his wife's nerves to a frazzle over adolescent trifles. When he explains at the top of his lungs that Charlie Parker's albums belong in the jazz section, *not in the rock section*, it's like watching Alan Alda sprout horns and poke Carol Burnett with a pitchfork.

Although *Diner* is a male rite-of-passage comedy, it doesn't toss the women in its cast meager scraps. In a brief but charming role, Colette Blonigan—familiar to most viewers as the model in television's Lip Quencher commercials—uses her ice-blue eyes for amusingly quizzical double takes, and as the stripper who shares the runway with Eddie and his gyrations, Lauren Zaganas is a charming chipmunk with a mop of untidy curls. Best of all is newcomer Ellen Barkin as Shrevie's care-buffeted wife, Beth. With her lipstick tarted up to a loud red gleam, Beth looks like a trapped adolescent trying to persuade herself she's a grown-up. And in a sense she is a pretender: she's a young woman who pushed herself into marriage before her feelings had time to sort themselves out and ripen. So she is pitched into a mire of confusion, unable to talk to her sulking hubby, wondering if her looks are beginning to slide. Barkin captures Beth's doubts and needs with poignant understatement, her face clouding over whenever a passing thought captures her fancy, her nose crinkling in tentative delight when someone assures her that, hey, of *course* you're pretty, what a silly question. Her confidence shattered by her shouting husband, Beth can never again take her prettiness for granted.

Talented as *Diner*'s cast is, one performance peeps out above the others. In *Body Heat*, Mickey Rourke played an arsonist with such ratty, cunning conviction that he seemed to be a creature of damp and rubble, his whiskers twitching in the fading light. As Boogie, a hairdresser who lands himself in the gumbo by not paying his gambling debts, Rourke wears black shirts and salmon-pink ties—the true punk colors. In a way, the character of Boogie is a sly homage to the films of Baltimore sleaze master John Waters, director of (among others) the infamous *Pink Flamingos*, in which a transvestite named Divine eats dog doo-doo. In *Shock Value*, his recent book tracing the roots of his warped imagination, Waters has a nostalgically comic chapter titled "Baltimore, Maryland—Hairdo Capital of the World." Not only is Boogie a hairdresser but his apartment is decorated in kitschy jungle-green drapes and—yes—plastic pink flamingos.

Though Boogie looks like a tattered prince of sleaze (his skin is pockmarked, his brown hair tarnished and unruly), he has slender, soothing hands, and he treats women with soft-spoken courtliness. Indeed, he's the only character who opens doors for women, who murmurs a compliment as he brushes a straying thread of hair back into place. Boogie's low-rent chivalry isn't simply a ploy to entice girls into the sack; he really does have a caring soul. When Fenwick drunkenly punches out windowpanes with his fist, it's Boogie who coaxes him out of mischief, and it's Boogie who curtails a sick prank involving Beth before damage can be done to her tottering marriage. If Mickey Rourke has a crowning moment in *Diner*, it comes when Boogie decks a thuggish bookie and his friends whoop with congratulation. Acknowledging their cheers, Boogie turns and offers a grin that is triumphant yet abashed—atilt with foolish pride. There's no flamboyance or manneristic excess in Rourke's acting; he simply spins across the screen in his own snug groove, hitting notes cleanly without snarling himself in clumps of static. William Hurt may have reaped all the hype for *Body Heat*, but it's Rourke, I think, who's going to emerge as one of the decade's major heart-flutters.

In its depiction of young people monkeying about in the clatter of night, *Diner* is going to remind a lot of viewers of *American Graffiti* and Fellini's *I Vitelloni*, but its unswerving fidelity to time and place gives it an offbeat, original charm. Without making a big deal about it, Levinson throws a nostalgic kiss to the Baltimore Jewish community that whittled him into manhood; it really isn't until Eddie and his girlfriend get married in the movie's final sequence that you notice how many of the characters are sporting yarmulkes. Although the synagogue is decorated in blue and white, the colors of the Baltimore Colts, with the Colts' anthem being piped on the organ as the bridesmaids toe their way up the aisle ("I really think you went too far when you asked the rabbi to wear a striped shirt and a whistle," cracks Modell later), the wedding isn't a vulgar exercise in Jewish self-loathing like the notorious wedding sequence in *Goodbye, Columbus,* in which the guests were caricatured as suburban beasties stuffing themselves into a bloated stupor. Here girls in white gloves flex their fingers in anticipation of the flung bouquet, Earl affably picks his way through the buffet, Boogie and the gang gather around a table (ties loosened, smiles relaxed); the entire sequence has a hushed tenderness in which every character is given his dignified due and then suspended in time, to be remembered only with fondness.

People may come up with dumb reasons not to respond to *Diner,* just as they came up with dumb reasons not to respond to *Shoot the Moon.* (Perhaps I should add that I grew up in Maryland under the shadow of the Baltimore Colts, so the movie touches chords in me that will remain unstirred in others.) But I think that if audiences shake off their tired habits and take a risk on a modest sleeper like *Diner,* they'll discover friendly, intimate pleasures denied them in blowout epics like *Reds* and *Raiders of the Lost Ark.* In one small interlude in *Diner,* a customer in the appliance store where Shrevie works says he doesn't think much of these newfangled color sets on the market. "I saw *Bonanza* the other night," he grumbles, "and the Ponderosa looked faked." Nothing in *Diner* looks flimsy or faked. Its world and feelings have the full crack of life.

Texas Monthly, May 1982

Your Flick of Flicks
My Favorite Year

Peter O'Toole, who swept like a Byronic prince through the sandy wastes of *Lawrence of Arabia* and hobbled like a stick-boned warrior-martyr through television's *Masada*, brings a pickled foppishness to Richard Benjamin's *My Favorite Year*, a comedy set in the first bloom of the Eisenhower era. The revered year is 1954, and O'Toole stars as Alan Swann, a renowned English actor who descends upon Manhattan to make a guest spot on the network variety series *Comedy Cavalcade*. Onscreen, Swann is a swashbuckler in tights who swings from wooden chandeliers and zippily runs his sword through mustachioed villains in the campily brash manner of Burt Lancaster in *The Crimson Pirate*. Offscreen, however, he is a wenching rake who charms women out of their skirts and tanks up on bottles tucked away in coat pockets and bulky valises. Like John Barrymore in his dissolute decline, Alan Swann turns his off-camera life into an episodic succession of careless flings and rough, drunken tumbles.

After arriving in New York, Swann awakens to find himself in the company of two fuzzy-bunny stewardesses, his mind totally befogged with blotto confusion. In a moment of cracked brilliance, O'Toole leans over and does the most inspired alcoholic cough I've ever heard: a thin wheeze that climbs through his chest like a slow rocket and, upon reaching his throat, raspingly explodes. (It's like hearing one of Eugene O'Neill's soulful drunks come undone.) When Swann arrives at the *Comedy Cavalcade* studio, he's a hungover boneless wonder who conks out at meetings and needs to be wheeled to his hotel room, strapped to the top of his luggage. Watching anxiously on the sidelines, wondering if this noble wreck of an actor can be pieced together by air time, is the show's junior writer, Benjy Stone (played by newcomer Mark Linn-Baker). His efforts to keep Swann from coming disastrously unglued turn into a rite of passage, a golden moment that will deposit him on the banks of *mensch*-hood. Sugar-frosted with nostalgia and affection, this movie is the quiet to end at any moment in an eruption of flying books and erasers.

In the smaller roles, Anne De Salvo, who was the hooker in *Arthur*, plays a writer who knows what's what, and beaky Basil Hoffman plays her confederate on the staff, a writer so bashful that he whispers his suggestions and insults into her ear so that she can volley them to the room at large. (His latter role is based on the shy antics of Neil Simon, who got his start on *Your Show of Shows*, where he would relay his ideas into Carl Reiner's ear rather than try to outshout the gang.) In a choice bit part, Selma Diamond brings her famous knowing croak to the role of Lil, a costume mistress who has an untoward meeting with Alan Swann in the ladies' room and ends up as the object of one of his more tenderly profane sallies. Since Diamond was one of television's first and most prolific scriptwriters, her casting in *My Favorite Year* is an endearing grace note, one of many.

Orchestrating the bickering interplay and adorning the scenes with wry, tickling touches is the movie's director, Richard Benjamin. It's quite a directorial debut for Benjamin, who's made his name as the nebbishly suave star of movies like *Goodbye, Columbus* and *Portnoy's Complaint*. Not only does he show a deft touch in the comedy scenes but he also infuses the movie with a generous warmth of feeling without catering to sloppy sentiment.

Even a miracle worker, however, couldn't levitate some of the movie's scenes. Jessica Harper, who plays Benjy's heartthrob, K. C. Downing, should be the sort of catch that Blythe Danner was in *Hearts of the West*—a briskly shrewd career gal whose radiant good sense cuts like a beacon through all the hurly-burly posing of those overgrown boys swaggering before and behind the cameras. But there's something dewy-eyed and cloyingly dear about Harper, and the scene in which Benjy woos her with Chinese food has the emasculated cuteness of Andy Hardy scraping up a date to the senior prom. Jessica Harper was also a soggy deadweight in *Pennies From Heaven;* there just doesn't seem to be anything stirring behind those enameled, beseeching eyes and those Betty Boop cheekbones.

Benjamin does nick by in the movie's most potentially wincing scene, a dinner in the wilds of Brooklyn in which Swann finds himself besieged by Benjy's relatives, a troupe of fleshy opportunists in loud clothes. But disquieting as the scene is, it doesn't bung up the movie unduly. Why not? The key is that Swann betrays no discomfort in their grabby clutches; indeed, he takes in the scene with a faint, gracious twinkle of amusement. He never loses his gentlemanly composure, and his ease sets us at ease. If Alan Swann were being roasted in a pot by cannibals, not a single pop of sweat would undo his aristocratic aplomb.

O'Toole does for this movie what Swann does for the cast and crew of *Comedy Cavalcade:* he swanks in whenever there's a lull in the action and with a dapper flare of his cuffs sets off smiles, sighs, palpitations. Tall and cigarette-slim, O'Toole seems to be riding a zephyr of roguish whim when he enters a room in formal black evening wear, flicking his hellos to old friends and future conquests; he's refined the devilish bisexual flair he flashed as the director in *The Stunt Man.* Even in his cups he seems to hover over mere mortals, nodding like a merry god who's lingered too long at the banquet table. Yet as O'Toole showed in *Masada,* he's capable of revealing the strains of self-laceration without turning into a blowhard masochist, in the slobby manner of George C. Scott or Richard Harris at their most undisciplined. There's a sloshing, corrosive wash of sorrow behind all of Swann's dash and politesse. But O'Toole refuses to wallow in his character's long-nursed griefs, and the stunning thing about his performance is that he shows us a man in pieces, then pulls the pieces handsomely together. Perhaps the crucial exchange in *My Favorite Year* is when Swann drunkenly attempts a bit of derring-do and a rattled Benjy squeals, "This is not a movie, this is *real life.*" To which Swann philosophically replies, "What's the difference?" It's not an idle conceit. By the end of the movie O'Toole's Swann is so large-spirited that he vanquishes the divisions between actor and act, truth and illusion, and sends those puny distinctions wafting like smoke up the crumbling tower of his vanity.

Since *Masada* and *The Stunt Man,* I've become madly partial to Peter O'Toole. I don't know if he's the *best* actor in the world, but I think he's the most lordly, the most generous and pleasure-giving. When *My Favorite Year* ends with a shot of Alan Swann saluting the studio audience by waving his sword in the air, the slow regal sweep of that wave itself seems like a bestowal of greatness. Without Peter O'Toole, *My Favorite Year* would have been an unassuming little item, but with him it tosses off gleams of Shakespearean pluck and vigor, looses stray shafts of daring and mischief. The moist, hard-won gratitude in O'Toole's eyes at the end of the movie becomes an emblem of happiness—his, and ours. Never say that the struggle naught availeth.

Texas Monthly, November 1982

Brian De Palma x Three

The Godfather Goes Slumming
Scarface

Never a shy violet, Brian De Palma really airs it out in *Scarface*, a gangster melodrama set in the flamingo-pink wilds of Miami. Nearly three hours long, *Scarface* features a chain-saw dismemberment; a corpse dragged above the treetops by a helicopter; a machine-gun ambush in a disco, with squeals and shattering mirrors; a handful of assorted killings, with bullets squirting out of silencers; an orgasmic massacre in which the walls receive a fresh coat of blood. All of this violence is scored to a chorus of obscenities and coke sniffles. *Scarface* isn't as slashing as *Dressed to Kill* or as flamboyant as *The Fury* or as steeped in apprehension as *Blow Out*, but its length and aching reach make it De Palma's most ambitious experiment thus far in the chemistry of terror. He's attempting an epic as rich and criminal as *The Godfather* but madder, kinkier. Yet in a curious way the wider scope of *Scarface* (its tropical canvas, its swarming action) seems to have put a crimp in De Palma's camera movements. In scene after scene, his camera, usually so sensuous and wide-circling, descends upon the turmoil with a stately fall. It doesn't take long for those gentle arcs to seem like expressions of creative fatigue—nod-outs.

Like Bob Fosse's *Star 80*, De Palma's *Scarface* piles on the pimp sleaze. A criminal claiming to be a political refugee, Tony Montana (Al Pacino) arrives in this country from Cuba with a bad haircut and a ridge of scarred flesh across his cheek. He's part of the huge influx of Cubans who crowded into Miami following the 1980 Mariel boat lift, a flood of immigrants that included large numbers of Castro's castoffs—junkies, homosexuals, mental patients, and thugs like Tony. (The preface to *Scarface* states that an estimated twenty-five thousand of those Cubans had criminal records.) Detained in a barbed-wire compound, Tony obtains freedom and a green card when he executes a contract killing on a former Castroite. On the outside, he serves in the cocaine trade as courier and enforcer, running his errands in cars with zebra-striped seat covers. Once he has decimated the opposition and become a drug lord, he builds the sort of pimp villa that would have made *Star 80*'s Paul Snider faint with bliss, a ritzy-ditzy pleasure dome with Caesars Palace whorehouse-red decor and gold statuettes that spray water from their upturned nipples. But where *Star 80* was bitterly tight in its condemnation of crass luxury, *Scarface* has pockets of slumming, diabolical humor.

Al Pacino's performance helps. Chimp-faced and uncouth, Pacino's Montana seems to have studied at the *Raging Bull* school of etiquette, sputtering things like, "Don't f—— with me, don't you f——ing f—— with me, or I'll blow your f——ing head off, you f——." He thinks with his crotch, he talks from his crotch; his whole career is a jabbing macho thrust. As a drug trafficker, Montana is fearless, not because he's brave but because he's too much of a hardball fanatic to be frightened. Perhaps the movie's funniest moment comes when Montana threatens to blow the f——ing head off of any piece of garbage that gets in his way, to which his Bolivian supplier says suavely, "I think you speak from the heart, Montana."

Spitting flames, Montana meets his match in Elvira (Michelle Pfeiffer), coke mistress supreme. Pfeiffer, who was an all-American vanilla cookie in *Grease 2*, is an ice maiden here, making a sensational entrance in an electric aqua-green dress that shows off every slicing angle and tossing off rude remarks in a voice that is low, dirty, bored. She's like the white-satin molls Jean Harlow used to play, but without the fighting spunk; leisure and decadence have left her brittle, freeze-dried. On the arm of a rich druggie, Elvira is a breathtaking companion, the ultimate gold accessory, and yet you can't imagine her being anything more than a trinket—lovemaking would disarrange those exquisite bones.

Indeed, we never see Elvira and Montana in carnal embrace; what they share is not sex or even affection but a life of traveling along parallel lines of toot. She licks flecks of cocaine from her lips; he dips his beak into a snow pile at his desk, emerging with a large white smudge. As their alliance comes undone, those lines begin to veer off. In one extended quarrel, Montana soaks in a circular bubble bath in front of a console of TVs, razzing her about being an indifferent lover, while she (as he phrases it) powders her nose. Cocaine is the great, stupid curse of the movie industry, and in this scene De Palma seems to be satirizing the new Hollywood, where baby moguls, who pride themselves on cunning, talk a lot of coked-out dribble. In that circular tub

Montana could easily be mistaken for a hotshot producer, and Elvira is certainly every inch the edgy, adorning starlet. It's wickedly ironic. Tony Montana would probably kill to "go Hollywood," and Hollywood would kill to vacuum up his loose drifts of dope. Their greeds converge at the tip of a single spoon.

If *Scarface* had been conceived as a taut, subversive thriller, it might have had the makings of a classic, but it has been mounted as if it were a Brechtian epic of power mania run amok—a punk-faced *Arturo Ui*. (Not incidentally, Pacino has performed in workshop productions of Brecht's gangster parable.) When Montana wins Elvira's allegiance, he looks out from the balcony, and across the night-blue sky cruises the Goodyear blimp, the words "The World Is Yours" flashing across its belly. It's a funny moment, and eerily beautiful—that blimp seems to be a spectral messenger, dark and majestic. "An auspicious omen!" thinks Tony, who adopts those words as his fighting slogan. We later see in his villa a statue of a goddess holding aloft a globe around which "The World Is Yours" appears in pink neon letters.

Where *Scarface* goes mortally wrong is in spelling out all of its messages in pink neon. Once Tony becomes the Prince of Paranoia, staggering like Elvis through his red velvet hell as his subordinates tremble, the movie's scenes become ever more bloated, disconnected, didactic, and druggily adrift. William Blake to the contrary, the road of excess doesn't always lead to the palace of wisdom. In *Scarface* it leads to the palace of excess, where dead bodies litter the screen in layers, like lasagne. In *The Godfather*, the killings orchestrated around the christening of Michael Corleone's nephew were the result of resentments and grievances that had been subtly pressurized throughout the movie; it was as if all the steam valves had been released, the violence set free. The massacre that climaxes *Scarface*, with Montana blasting a commando force to pieces as he himself spouts blood from every puncture wound, doesn't have that tragic, festering inevitability. It seems nothing more than an opportunity for De Palma to give *Scarface* a big, booming slaughterhouse finale. Hard-core action fans may kick the backs of their seats in delirium, as they do at *Dirty Harry* movies, but the rest of us can only retreat into our tortoiseshells and hope that this proves to be De Palma's final go at rabble-rousing. As a director, Brian De Palma is a nocturnal creature, an owl that keeps sinister surveillance. In *Scarface*, he has come down from the trees, into blinding sunlight, and bloodied his own wings.

Texas Monthly, January 1984

Double Trouble
Body Double

In *Body Double*, a Peeping Tom thriller directed by Brian De Palma, a woman is pinned to the floor and fatally poked with an electric drill—a whirring monster phallus. It's power-tool rape. De Palma seems to have lugged this heavy item in from the hardware store not merely to top himself (in *Scarface*, it was a chain saw wielded with sadistic zeal) but also to drive home his defiance of the feminists and critics and interviewers who have been primed for outrage ever since this project was announced. "You thought I went too far in *Scarface* and *Dressed to Kill*?" De Palma seems to be asking. "Well, take *this*."

As an act of provocation, the murder sequence in *Body Double* carries out its purpose. It had screening audiences on both coasts hissing, and in New York antiporn activists have slapped "This Movie Demeans Women" stickers over the movie's subway ads. True, the movie isn't very inspired, but De Palma doesn't deserve to be buried under a swarm of attackers. For all his bad-boy boasts and scowls, he isn't a slasher with a camera, an enemy of women, a defiler of Hitchcock's tomb, or even just another director who's gotten too big for his safari jacket. He's a fabulously gifted filmmaker who's fallen unsure of his themes and is trying to brazen it out. In *Body Double* he brazens it out badly.

Set in Hollywood, *Body Double* plays peekaboo with reality, taking us into a trompe l'oeil world of painted backdrops and mannequins and blood that oozes like raspberry jam. Jake (Craig Wasson), an actor in a cheapie vampire flick, breaks into a sweat-damp panic when he is stretched out in a cramped coffin—he's too traumatized even to spit out his dialogue. Sent home, Jake discovers his girlfriend in the sack with another guy, and her look of glazed, golden pleasure also undoes him. He promptly packs his things and leaves. He bumps into a fellow actor (Gregg Henry), who offers him a chance to house-sit. The house turns out to be a high-tech, high-rise saucer that features a bar, a revolving bed, state-of-the-art video, and a panoramic view of the twinkling hills; if Hugh Hefner were a space alien, this would be his bachelor pad.

Through a compact telescope, Jake watches the gyrations of his brunette neighbor, Gloria (Deborah Shelton, currently on *Dallas*), who seems to be putting on a private show in her posh negligee. He becomes obsessed with her, even pinching a pair of her discarded panties. One night, however, Jake witnesses a different sort of show—a burglary that turns into a snuff film. Enter the power drill, followed by screams, dog barks, and carnage.

Summarized, *Body Double* is clearly son-of-Hitchcock filmmaking, from its hero's reeling fear (*Vertigo*) to its voyeuristic perspective (*Rear Window*). De Palma also works in recapitulations of his own greatest hits—a sequence in which Jake pursues Gloria through an atrium reminds us of Angie Dickinson's museum visit in *Dressed to Kill*. All this quotation and self-quotation leads to a certain confusion. When Jake and his dream girl spin in a swoony embrace, panting and moaning, is the scene meant to mock Hitchcock or to mock De Palma's emulation of Hitchcock? At times the tone of *Body Double* is so goofily off that the movie doesn't evoke Hitchcock so much as it does Mel Brooks's parody of Hitchcock, *High Anxiety*. (Jake, stricken in that coffin, suffers from low anxiety.)

As an exercise in terror, *Body Double* is too grammatical. We've become too familiar with De Palma's gliding pans and stalking approaches, and in his more obvious flourishes he seems to be retracing his own signature. In a way, he has spoiled us; he has been so fiendish and audacious in the past that it's a letdown when he settles for facile shudders. There's nothing here as sick-fantastic as *Carrie*'s prom-wrecking or John Cassavetes's detonation in *The Fury* or John Travolta's search for a better scream in *Blow Out* or Nancy Allen's throat-clutching nightmare at the end of *Dressed to Kill*. And it's unfortunate that De Palma chose to echo *Vertigo* and *Rear Window*, because Craig Wasson is sure no Jimmy Stewart. He's competent, but he lacks Stewart's distinctive ache and dry-bone twang. He's too singles-bar ordinary.

But De Palma also makes Hitchcockian use of Melanie Griffith, and here he (and she) marvelously succeed. Griffith is the daughter of Tippi Hedren, whom Hitchcock tried to polish into a new Grace Kelly in *Marnie* and *The Birds*. In *Body Double*, Griffith, who made her first appearances in films as a tan-limbed nymphet in *Night Moves* and *The Drowning Pool*, flies as far from her mother's white-gloves-and-pearl-necklace image as is possible. "Ladylike" is not a word that will ever tinkle in her wake. As porn star Holly Body, Melanie Griffith wears black-leather outfits that showcase a holly-green tattoo on her bare cheek and a rooster cut of platinum punk hair. She resembles the real-life porn star Seka, but she's younger and finer-honed; she's a gleaming dagger of illicit sex. What's fascinating—and funny—about Griffith's performance is that she says the most appalling things in a cutesy-pie voice, then scouts the scene with beady, mercenary eyes. In a world of consumer sex, she's a smart shopper. And her own price tag keeps pace with inflation.

Holly Body is an alley-cat parody of a Hollywood starlet (one of her porn efforts is even called *Holly Does Hollywood*), and the porn industry itself is a crazy-house reflection of the studio system. Like Hollywood, the porn factories churn out a product, and they too are plagued by petulant, drugged-out stars, producers who function like pimps, temperamental directors, trimmed budgets. In an age of cable porn, *Body Double* hints, the line between legitimate stars and illegitimate stars is being erased. Someday a porn star like Annette Haven, who coached Griffith for her role, may be regarded as nostalgically as Rita Hayworth.

When Jake duets in a porn musical with Holly, his writhings are intercut with his rapturous embrace of Gloria; he's like a dancer changing partners with each heady spin. (It's also a reprise of Jimmy Stewart's embrace of Kim Novak in *Vertigo*.) Romance and pornography are not diametrically opposed, De Palma is saying in *Body Double*. Both seek heightened states, both have their own conventions and artifices (wind-caressed hair and dewy complexions for romance, black leather and wanton lipstick for porn). Romance may be bloomy and scented, and porn sleaze may be blighted and low, but both are flowerings of the same desire for ecstasy and release. As the man at the piano says in *Casablanca*, a kiss is still a kiss. I only wish that De Palma could have explored the tantalizing interface between Hollywood and porndom more lucidly. The movie is too smoggy and disjointed to get at what's really fascinating about this Sodom of make-believe. Except for Melanie Griffith's stiletto performance, the only thing people will remember about *Body Double* is that damned drill.

I don't mean to peer into Brian De Palma's head, but I think something happened to him after *Blow Out*, and it carried over into *Scarface* and *Body Double*. *Blow Out*, which was a box office flop and an occasion for critical savaging, let its emotions wail in the night, and I think the undeserved pounding De Palma took for the film has shuttered him up. He has gone, that is, from *Blow Out* to burnout, and he doesn't want to court ridicule again. So he is adopting a sullen manner for the press and orchestrating his tensions more abstractly on screen. He certainly has reason to feel galled. It must be maddening to see critics who never praised *Carrie* in the first place now using it to slap down everything he has done since. Brian De Palma hasn't been behaving very well, but I think I understand why he's in his bear costume, growling. I only hope he climbs out of it soon and takes a fresh sniff at what's around. He's too good a director to go into a permanent sulk.

Texas Monthly, December 1984

De Palma and the Women

A case could be made—so why not make it?—that Brian De Palma is the apex predator of American directors, perhaps our greatest living filmmaker. He is undoubtedly the least appreciated. Born in 1940, raised in Philadelphia, De Palma had a ringside seat at the operations performed by his father, an orthopedic surgeon. It was in these tender, formative moments that he developed his keen interest in the fine art of human-parts removal. Majoring in physics at Columbia University, he got the theater bug and took up drama, shooting 16-mm. film shorts. Since the release of his first feature, *Murder à la Mod*, in 1967 (he did an earlier film which surfaced later), De Palma has nosed through our dampest secrets and nightmares, his camera devouring everything before it, digesting on the run. In a telephone interview, De Palma describes himself as someone who "grew up in an era of stunning visual stylists" and now finds himself wondering where everybody went. "Few directors are practicing this," he says, "this" being "pure visual storytelling." Utilizing split screens, instant replay, rhapsodic slo-mo, multiple points of view, and the hovercraft abilities of the Steadicam (a camera that floats and sharks through the air, pursuing figures who themselves seem composed of air), De Palma demonstrates in film after film that reality is simply a rough draft, subject to tricky memories, evidence tampering, drastic re-editing. His prodigious output of twenty-five features in thirty-three years is a virtuoso gloss on the old punch line "Who are you gonna believe, me or your lying eyes?" (*Snake Eyes* deconstructs the footage of a televised assassination to crack open an act of mass deception, a cunning pantomime.) Like his favorite ghost, Alfred Hitchcock, he enjoys playing pranks on the audience that deliver the sting of mortality. Moments of beauty reveal blight at the full arousal of their bloom. Lyrical interludes end with a sprung-trap snap—the hand grabbing from the grave to uncork one last scream in *Carrie*.

Yet nothing he's done previously prepares us for the voluptuous epiphany in his new movie, *Femme Fatale*, when Rebecca Romijn-Stamos plunges daggerlike into water and her clothes magically vanish, her nude body embroiled in blue bubbles. Arms outstretched, feet pointed, her aquatic pose suggests a sexy pinup takeoff on Andres Serrano's *Piss Christ*, crystallizing the movie's sacred and profane intersection of baptism, crucifixion, and resurrection. Full of amazing plenty, De Palma's amoral morality tale is a study of redemption photographed like a Victoria's Secret catalogue, blood drops providing the cherry topping on creamy-vanilla skin trimmed with lace. It's the work of a cheerful, horny man. An anomaly these days.

Which may help explain why De Palma has never earned the honors accorded his peers—his snarky cynicism, hedonism, and jack-in-the-box humor make him seem unserious, lacking in the gravitas that is supposed to go with gray hair. Joker that he is, it's a bad rap. When De Palma has bared the passion of his convictions—in the grief-choked dénouement of the conspiracy melodrama *Blow Out*, his darkest exploration of the politics of perception, and the vale-of-tears Vietnam drama *Casualties of War*—he has been rejected at the box office and snubbed by the tooth fairies who dole out prizes. Like Hitchcock, he has never won an Academy Award for best direction. Of all the seventies directors to storm the pantheon, De Palma is the one most lacking in name-drop cachet, official stature, even minor-celebrity recognition (this, despite wearing a trademark safari jacket for decades: Call me bwana). Martin Scorsese, capable of doing an encyclopedic speed-rap on any director past or present, has become cinema's chief curator through his tireless dedication to film preservation; Steven Spielberg and George Lucas reign as cinema's technocrat aristocrats and visionary entrepreneurs, wedding multiplex franchises to mass merchandise (Spielberg is also becoming fit for a pedestal as a philanthropist); Francis Ford Coppola, tending to his vineyards, is the proud paterfamilias, casting a bulky shadow over a directorial dynasty that includes daughter Sofia (*The Virgin Suicides*) and son Roman (*CQ*); Robert Altman is the grumpy maverick, granted old-master status after putting a pedigree cast through their paces in *Gosford Park*; and Peter Bogdanovich, beating out stiff competition as the most pompous fathead in Peter Biskind's seventies film history, *Easy Riders, Raging Bulls*, received a fond pat from the film community for *The Cat's Meow*, a valentine to pre-talkies Hollywood. Only De Palma has been dumped into the laundry hamper. As he noted in a recent interview, his films have toured the festival circuit worldwide yet never made the slate of the New York Film Festival. "Now there's the irony, that I've never been invited to premiere one of my movies in my hometown festival."

For reasons he can't fathom ("I don't know what I'm doing that's making them so mad," he told me), Brian De Palma is the only artist in his field still being penalized—stigmatized—for the violence of his work. It's as if he's inherited the late Sam Peckinpah's Devil's horns. No denying he's spilled more than his quota of red quarts over the course of his career. The pig's blood dumped on Carrie at the prom; John Cassavetes detonating like a human grenade in the climax of *The Fury*, turning the screen into a splatter canvas; the chain-saw amputation that opens *Scarface* and the baroque massacre that ends it (a Verdi opera performed with assault weapons); and the razor-slashing in *Dressed to Kill*, to name just a few hearty moments, have all helped groom the plausible impression of De Palma as de Sade's darling boy. But if devising ingenious methods of drilling for gore damned a director, he'd have a lot of company on the elevator down. Instead, he rides alone. Scorsese managed to redecorate the wallpaper with ketchup in *Taxi Driver*, squash a head like a melon in *Casino*, and dial up a world of pain in his lurid remake of *Cape Fear* without permanently spotting his nice suits. Critics continue to avert their notepads from the cruel stratagems in Spielberg's work, how he puts the sick squeeze on us for our own good. No one crosses the street when they see carnage specialists John Woo, Robert Rodriguez, or David Fincher approaching (and Fincher's *Seven* was as gruesome as a botched operation). The DVD release commemorating the tenth anniversary of Quentin Tarantino's *Reservoir Dogs*, with its infamous torture-interrogation van Gogh ear slice, was a downright jolly occasion. So what gives?

The difference is that these mayhem artists primarily purvey the violence of men against men locked in mortal combat over money, broads, bragging rights, and local turf—the never-ending battle for numskull supremacy. In De Palma's thrillers, women are the targeted victims. His camera teases, caresses, and prolongs the foreplay leading to the *coup de grâce*, creating complicity between viewer and on-screen stalker, violating the no-fly zone of aesthetic distance. By following the Hitchcockian strategy of shooting his murders as seductions and his seductions as murders, De Palma stands accused of uniting violence and voyeurism, converting pulp into porn, porn into pulp. Some were especially creeped out by how he served up his then wife, Nancy Allen, as a tasty morsel in *Blow Out* and *Dressed to Kill*, as if putting on his own marital peep show (others of us thought it was nice of him to share). The critic Veronica Geng dissented from the consensus, contending that he decoupled sex and violence in *Dressed to Kill*, depicting violence as a shocking, unnatural invasion of the erotic sphere. But the prevailing opinion was that De Palma objectifies women in order to undress and stick pins in his Barbie dolls.

Big pins. Images of impalement recur in De Palma's films. Impalement can be interpreted as a phallic thrust of aggression, a symbolic rape resulting in fatal penetration. I was at the catastrophic public screening of *Body Double* where the audience hissed the notorious low-angle shot of a power drill pointed at a supine woman's body like a steel penis. The image was such a blunt provocation that one suspected De Palma might have been baiting the feminist activists who had urged a boycott of *Dressed to Kill* by upping the ante, saying, in effect, "You thought that was bad?—this'll really get you hopping." If so, it was a foolish miscalculation on his part (he later admitted as much). The hisses switched to boos as the drill bored a hole into the victim and through the floor below, and the drubbing De Palma later took in the press sealed his reputation as "the most vicious woman-hater in Hollywood today" (*Ms.*). It's an ogre image that dogs him still, despite Pauline Kael's championing of *Casualties of War*, with its unflinching depiction of a Vietnamese captive's rape ordeal, as a feminist statement—an anguished cry for mercy and justice. Audiences avoided *Casualties of War*—it was perceived as too much of a downer—and De Palma failed to clear his name with those who had mounted his moose head next to Norman Mailer's in the macho Hall of Shame.

The movie he directed after *Casualties of War* nearly wiped him off the map. In 1990, De Palma began filming *The Bonfire of the Vanities*, based on Tom Wolfe's best-selling novel, which trained a warped monocle on the greed, social climbing, tabloid hysteria, and race-card opportunism of Manhattan in the decade of AIDS, Donald Trump, and taffeta poof skirts. Having made his hoofprint in Hollywood as a horrormeister, De Palma was a curious, controversial choice to direct Wolfe's Hogarthian extravaganza. True, two of his early films, *Greetings* and *Hi, Mom!*, were shaggy, countercultural satires ("*Greetings* must be one of the first movies to take the graffiti generation for granted," Wilfrid Sheed noted in *Esquire*); *Phantom of the Paradise* swung crazily from the rafters; and most of his white-knucklers unsheathed feline moments of sardonic humor. However, "straight" comedy tended to lock De Palma into literal-mindedness. His is a visual, not worldly, sophistication. He had never ungloved the Lubitsch touch required to steer Wolfe's sugar pops and "social X-rays" across a crowded room where the slightest faux pas could trigger a ripple effect, setting off landslides among the face-lifts. The casting also raised caution flags. Tom Hanks seemed too affably normal to play Sherman McCoy, crafty Wall Street bond trader and "Master of the Universe," and rewriting the British hack-journalist character into a role for Bruce Willis and his smirk smacked of idiot expediency. To dampen racial friction, the producers also performed an identity transplant on the crusty Jewish judge in Wolfe's novel, changing him into a black Solomon worthy of Morgan Freeman's noble enunciation. This wasn't enough to placate those who believed that Wolfe, a southern dandy in plantation white, peddled cartoon stereotypes, depicting a wrong turn onto the Bronx's mean streets as a detour into darkest Africa. The production became a battle zone of picket signs and location scrambling. It was also an expensive production: one of the movie's most spectacular shots—the Concorde hazily materializing in an orange sky like a glider mailed from the future—cost more than De Palma's first three films combined.

History shows that a great movie can emerge from the volatile mixture of egos on a troubled set (prime example: *Sweet Smell of Success*, where clashes by day produced a jazzy classic by night). This, however, would not be a triumph of alchemy. A mighty egg was laid. *The Bonfire of the Vanities* turned out to be one of those fiascoes at which even the prophets of doom did a double take. "Bombfire of the Vanities," the film was christened. *Ishtar* was invoked. The almost universally scornful reviews left whip marks on the director's hide. Even De Palma loyalists such as Kael handled the film with tongs, setting it aside as a regrettable lapse. The movie was DOA at the box office. As Julie Salamon writes in *The Devil's Candy*, an inside account of the making of the mess, *The Bonfire of the Vanities* wasn't the only chariot to crash that Christmas season. "Clint Eastwood didn't bring audiences to *The Rookie*, nor did Sean Connery and Michelle Pfeiffer to *The Russia House*, nor did Robert Redford to *Havana*. Indeed, in box office terms, *Havana* was a bigger disaster than *Bonfire*." Yet De Palma's crash site was the one circled by buzzards. And although the director himself is drawn sympathetically in Salamon's book, its publication completed the double whammy to his morale and standing, reminding everyone all over again of how he had fumbled the ball, putting his humiliating setback on permanent record.

"You can't imagine what a disaster that was," De Palma told *Le Monde* earlier this year. "I'd adapted a sacrosanct bestseller, a monument of American literature, and it bombed at the box office. I remained the guy who had made Tom Wolfe look ridiculous, and the critical establishment never forgave me for that." Although De Palma would go on to immortalize Tom Cruise doing heroic jaw-clenching calisthenics in *Mission: Impossible* (a movie I persist in loving, the courtly presences of Kristin Scott Thomas and Vanessa Redgrave bestowing grace notes absent from the Woo-directed sequel), his studio address was still the doghouse. The crushing derision that greeted his space odyssey, *Mission to Mars*—in *Afterglow: A Last Conversation with Pauline Kael*, the retired critic expressed bafflement over how blindly the movie was received ("About half of it is superb, and I can't understand why more people didn't recognize that")—revived the embers of *Bonfire*'s debacle. He awoke from the expensive demise of *Mission to Mars* to find the scarlet letter *L*—for Loser—sewn onto the pocket of his safari jacket.

Two years ago, De Palma beat a tactical retreat to Paris, that refugee camp for orphaned artists, where he needn't fear schoolchildren taunting him on the streets for lousy *Variety* grosses. Unlike most American critics, ingrates too busy eavesdropping on one another in the lobby to formulate their own responses, French film nuts appreciate personalized tapestries. A retrospective of his films attracted full houses at the Centre Pompidou in Paris, and French rappers sample *Scarface* for street cred. Meanwhile, back home he couldn't be more passé. "In the United States, I'm washed up," he informed *Le Monde*. "I'm the biggest subject of ridicule after Jerry Lewis."

"Washed up" isn't a throwaway phrase. It's a Freudian clue. *Femme Fatale*, his first film since making the partial break from America (he divides his time between Paris and his apartment in New York), is drenched in water imagery: a gothic rainstorm, a long bathtub soak, an overflowing aquarium, a dive into the river Styx. The movie is a platform leap into Brian De Palma's state of mind, an allegory for an artist's sinking, near drowning, and splashy resurfacing. Opening with a nude odalisque reflected on a hotel-room TV screen showing Barbara Stanwyck in *Double Indemnity*, their images overlapping (the first of many doppelgänger ploys), *Femme Fatale* announces its creator's intentions when a hood named Black Tie (Eriq Ebouaney) whips open the curtains and spread out below is the red carpet for a gala screening at the Cannes Film Festival. Superimposed on this flashbulb-popping parade of French celebrity is the credit DIRECTED BY BRIAN DE PALMA, De Palma's way of declaring, "Take a look—this is my new playground."

The odalisque dragging herself off the bed is a jewel thief named Laure Ash (Romijn-Stamos, who also plays Lily, the suicidal woman whose identity Laure later assumes). She's part of a crew planning to steal a $10 million diamond-studded solid-gold serpent wrapped as body jewelry around the date accompanying the director of the Cannes entry. As the date, Veronica (model Rie Rasmussen) is the strutting embodiment of forbidden desire, an R-rated Eve entwined by the Garden of Eden's snake, and the movie takes its rhythm from the high-heeled click of these two lithe beauties treating the corridors of the cinema as converging catwalks. A Camille Paglia ode to pussy power made flesh, one deity is blond, the other brunette; nature dictates that they mate. Laure lures Veronica into the ladies' room of the cinema, separating her from her male bodyguards, and without so much as a *bonjour* the two of them proceed to glue their bodies together as if someone rang a bell.

As the notables (among them actress Sandrine Bonnaire) settle into their seats for the screening of *East/West*, whose stark opening shot is a witty distillation of typical festival fare, the two hotties engage in a fast and furious long-limbed lambada. (According to Romijn-Stamos, De Palma lightened her concerns about doing the scene by "casting a friend of mine as per my request." That's one of the upsides of being a supermodel, knowing you can count on a supermodel pal to assist in an on-screen lesbian scorcher.) A panting Laure strips the body jewelry from a panting Veronica piece by piece, each segment replaced with a replica slipped under the stall by Black Tie. The absurd impracticality of this larcenous tryst doesn't slacken its excitement (De Palma demonstrated in *Body Double* that simulated sex has a disco beat that bypasses the brain), pleasure and tension building to a mutual crescendo as the movie intercuts to activity in every corner of the theater, which is beginning to arrow in on that steamy bathroom stall. Scored to a toned-down variation of Ravel's *Bolero*, the tempo of the action racing as if too antsy to wait for the sound track to achieve rapture, *Femme Fatale*'s fifteen-minute multicomponent set piece, with its seduction, heist, double cross, and narrow escape, will send cinephiles into categorical bliss. A mini-masterpiece, it's so meticulously crazed that you want to pause the film, rewind, and watch it again.

Like Hitchcock in *North by Northwest*, Howard Hawks in *The Big Sleep*, and Pedro Almodóvar in his early sex farces, De Palma plays loose and fancy with plot logic in order to follow the wicked bounce of his own inclinations, twirling up each scene into a goody bag of eye candy. "A *noir* story bracketed in a dream," in De Palma's words, *Femme Fatale* seems to have a homing device planted on its cool blonde, tailing her in long, seamless, wordless sequences through the streets and interiors of a Paris that looks airbrushed of tourists and nonessentials, an abstraction of itself, like Woody Allen's Manhattan. Instead of the usual international clamor of ads and logos, the posters pasted on walls and kiosks are figments of that dream, mind tricks. The whole movie is an elaborate, playful trompe l'oeil. Antonio Banderas plays a repentant paparazzo who's assembling a Hockneyesque collage of the view from his balcony—utilizing a split-screen scene, De Palma sets the collage and the real view flush against each other to give the illusion of Laure stepping out of her own zoom shot. What keeps *Femme Fatale* from being a clinical game board of optical gimmicks is the pallor of Eurotrash glamour that Romijn-Stamos flaunts, commanding every scene as if it were a private suite. Her no-nonsense, nicotine line delivery is very *noir*, very funny, and, despite the bitch of a character she plays, strangely likable. When Banderas's photographer pours tender nothings into her ear as he's servicing her from behind over a pool table, she responds, "That's so sweet . . . that's so romantic," in the toneless voice of a call girl counting down the seconds until liftoff. Like Stanwyck's two-timer in *Double Indemnity*, Laure is a cold user—bad, real bad, rotten bad—but Romijn-Stamos imparts an extra karma-chameleon quality to her sullen poses that gives her character a shiny patina. The most iconographically charged moment in the movie comes when Laure appears with her head wrapped in a silk scarf, wearing sunglasses to cover a bruised eye, looking like Grace Kelly, Jackie O., Audrey Hepburn, and Princess Diana fused into a supercomposite sacrificial-goddess cover girl. But the bruise is fake, the badge of victimhood a ruse, and Woman the ultimate winner in *Femme Fatale*, the first chick flick for continentals.

I still have the file folder Pauline Kael once sent me containing the original reviews of *Carrie*. Rereading them was a revelation, one reputable critic after another (Kael herself and Frank Rich being exceptions) snidely dumping on a film recognized today as a pop classic and the sister source of *Buffy the Vampire Slayer*, their eyes shut to its humor, incendiary force, formal design, and teenage-angst pathos. The yellowed clippings are punctuated with Pauline's exclamation marks in the margin, her silent yelps of disbelief. Prediction: in years to come, Brian De Palma's most beautiful unfoldings on film (*Blow Out*, *Casualties of War*, *Femme Fatale*, the best moments of *The Fury*, *The Untouchables*, *Carlito's Way*, *Snake Eyes*) will be as esteemed as *Carrie*. The French aren't always wrong. Jerry Lewis is a genius. So is the guy in the safari jacket.

Vanity Fair, December 2002

Of Vice and Mann

Few movies act as narcotics. Few drop the needle so neatly into the groove that you're held captive if you chance on them while channel-surfing—no matter how many times you've seen them before. The first hour of *Psycho*, for example, always fixates: the drab room where Janet Leigh and her lover have their matinee tumble, Hitchcock's camera pocketing the oddest incidentals (a sandwich left on a plate); Leigh driving in the hypnotic rain, as if fleeing the winged furies of Bernard Herrmann's score; the cozy chat with Anthony Perkins's Norman Bates at the motel, an interchange laced with implications, foreshadowings, petty condescensions, and resentment bared like a sharp incisor; the fatal shower interruptus. Other instant entrancers: *Sweet Smell of Success*, an all-night jag of a movie bulging to the rafters with smoke, bustle, and Clifford Odets dialogue that might be described as Damon Runyon rococo; *The Wild Bunch*—dropping in at any point is like hopping on a moving train; *Waiting for Guffman*, a rare comedy with grainy traction. Unlike narcotics, however, films such as these never numb and dull; they disclose subtle details and subcurrents with each viewing. For me, the movie that sinks the deepest hook of any in the last ten years is Michael Mann's *Heat*, an existential L.A. *noir* that has the ambition, reach, momentum, and grandeur of an (anti)heroic odyssey. Nearly three hours, its duration alone guarantees that the viewer isn't just seeing a movie but undergoing a submersion. The pretentious bits floating around in the script—every Mann-made work has its fancy-schmancy groaners—are the price one has to pay for the rapture of the deep.

Released in 1995, *Heat* is an elaborate redo of a routine made-for-TV movie Mann executive-produced and directed called *L.A. Takedown*. Both were inspired by a story he was told by a law-enforcement officer named Chuck Adamson about having coffee in Chicago with Neil McCauley, a criminal's criminal. Mann told London's *Time Out*, "Chuck had respected this guy's professionalism—he was a really good thief, which is exciting to a detective, and he tried to keep any risks to a minimum—but at the same time he was a cold-blooded sociopath who'd kill you as soon as look at you—if *necessary*. [They] wound up having one of those intimate conversations you sometimes have with strangers. There was a real rapport between them; yet both men verbally recognized one would probably kill the other." The Mamet-like coffee klatch proved prophetic; the two of them did have an appointment to keep. One day Adamson was hailed to the scene of an armed robbery, spotted McCauley, and, after giving chase, shot him dead. (McCauley drew first, but his gun misfired.) Out of this anecdote Mann constructed and stylized an underworld all his own.

In *Heat*, Neil McCauley is played by Robert De Niro, arriving like the Devil's ambassador on a night train shrouded in smoke (the first of *Heat*'s evocative, offbeat touches—who in movies today arrives in Los Angeles by train?). The detective destined to catch him coming around the corner is Vincent Hanna, played at full volume by Al Pacino. Each commands an experienced crew of all-male beef. McCauley's band includes Val Kilmer on assault rifle, Tom Sizemore on fisticuffs, and Kevin Gage as Waingro, your basic long-haired, white-trash, prison-tattooed, crazy-eyed, pervy psychopath who always seems to be picking something out of his teeth. Hanna's includes . . . well, it doesn't really matter. Pacino eclipses them.

Part of the pure kick in *Heat* is seeing two stars at the mid-career peak of their acting studhood, the promise of youth honed into a focused intensity capable of burning holes in casual bystanders. So superbly matched are Pacino and De Niro that the movie seems dual-powered. They're a study in positive and negative charisma. *Heat* finds Pacino at the dramatic top of his "Hoo-ha!" phase (*The Devil's Advocate* was the comedic high), at one point skipping down the stairs like a kid let out of school early. The lean and watchful wolf cub of *The Godfather* has fleshed into a pouchy comedian with a cadaverous skin tone and a snazzy cocktail-bar wardrobe. Whether taking charge of the crime scene, spooking the bejesus out of a sleazeball like Hank Azaria's Marciano (who, wondering aloud why he ever got involved with Ashley Judd's Charlene, the wife of Kilmer's crewman, half jumps out of his chair when Vince bellows, "BECAUSE SHE'S GOT A GREAT ASS!," adding, "Ferocious, aren't I?"), or explaining how he's wired for danger ("I've got to hold on to my angst. . . . It keeps me sharp"—finger snap—"on the edge"—finger snap—"where I gotta be"), Pacino hams it up without ever letting the viewer forget he's playing a hollow obsessive on the express track to personal burnout. Those who dislike Pacino's performance consider it shameless overacting. I prefer to think of it as operatic.

Where Pacino's Vince honks his vowels, De Niro's Neil bites off his consonants. Wearing his dark suits like light armor and rationing his words to minimum daily requirements, he's as anal and aloof as Hanna is oral and outpouring. A ticking time bomb, he holds himself tightly in check until the situation calls on him to unleash, and suddenly he's bashing a guard with a flashlight or slamming Waingro's head on a diner table. Aware of having two great actors share the screen for the first time (they both appeared in *The Godfather: Part II*, but never in the same scene), Mann teases out the anticipation, delaying their first meeting until midway into the movie, when they have a sit-down over coffee and re-create the real conversation Adamson had with McCauley, putting on a world-class acting exhibition of dueling glances and razor-nicked scene inflections, each feeling the other out in a kind of macho flirtation. Like the motel chat in *Psycho*, the Pacino–De Niro face-off repays countless rewatchings because, despite its huge portent, it's shot and staged modestly, naturally, no raised voices, no violent gestures, just two worn tires getting acquainted over the clink of silverware, exchanging confidences, and in civilized tones putting each other on notice as a marked man (or, as Vince puts it, "Brother, you are going *down*"). That settled, they adjourn to spend quality time with their crews.

Perhaps the action director with whom Mann has the most affinity is the other outstanding Mann of American cinema, Anthony Mann (1906–1967), a master of three genres—*film noir* (*T-Men, Raw Deal, Border Incident*), the Western (*Winchester '73, The Naked Spur, The Tin Star*), and the costume epic (*El Cid, The Fall of the Roman Empire*). What the rocky, barren, inhospitable mountain terrain was to Mann I in his Westerns, the urban panorama is to Mann II—the battlefield for a sporadic series of outlaw skirmishes and landgrabs. (The climactic bank robbery in *Heat* escalates from a shoot-out into a stupendous firefight that seems to unfold in real time, the shattering glass, pock-holed cars, and human cries turning downtown L.A. into Mogadishu.) The difference is that Anthony Mann's Martian landscapes are drained and bleached of mystery and poetry, while Michael Mann's cityscapes cast a whory glamour. They beckon only to sour and disenchant. From the Art Deco hotels and cokelord mansions of *Miami Vice* to the Las Vegas casino lairs in *Crime Story* to the minimalist cribs and sleek offices of *Heat*, no living producer-director extorts more mood from locale, architecture, and interior décor than Mann, whose best work shows a lyric appreciation of these lustrous monuments to dirty money. In *Heat*, the fugitive romance has gone cold, sterile: Neil's beach house is a spartan cell suffused with blue nothingness ("I don't know what kind of blue," Nick James writes in his invaluable study of *Heat* for the British Film Institute, "lighter than Matisse blue or Yves Klein blue, but just as intense, and almost phosphorescent"), and the hill-nestled house of money-launderer Roger Van Zant (William Fichtner, always effective in a depraved-yuppie role) is a glass case fit for a human reptile. It isn't what money can buy that compels these hoods—it's the thrill of the hunt, the adrenaline rush. "For me, the action *is* the juice," says Tom Sizemore, uttering the film's key line, and after he exits the bank with a Santa bag of loot, he whoops with laughter, one happy man.

The other signature mood-enhancer in Mann's work is the atmospheric texturing of the music sound track. The two-hour pilot for *Miami Vice* sailed out of the gritty cop genre and into smooth menthol territory the moment Crockett and Tubbs rolled into Uzi battle to the nasal croon of Phil Collins's "In the Air Tonight." *Crime Story* was paced to a Gene Krupa–like drumbeat interspersed with twangy-guitar numbers such as the show's theme song, Del Shannon's "Runaway." Mann's first theatrical film, *Thief*, featured an original score by Tangerine Dream (of whom Lester Bangs wrote, "They sound like silt seeping on the ocean floor"), and the terrifying showdown in *Manhunter* is choreographed to the chunky, relentless plod of Iron Butterfly's arena-rock classic "In-a-Gadda-Da-Vida," perhaps the second-spookiest use of pop music in American cinema. (First prize would probably go to Roy Orbison's "In Dreams" in *Blue Velvet*.) Billy Idol's sneery-lipped cover version of the Doors' "L.A. Woman" served as the anthem for *L.A. Takedown*, but when Mann went back to the drawing board, he mixmastered a sound track that (like *Thief*'s) wouldn't distract the viewer with lyrics, voices, or jukebox memories. A score that would be almost neural, cybernetic. According to Nick James's book, Mann contemplated using Glenn Branca's massed guitar orchestra, but opted instead for a soundscape incorporating the Kronos Quartet's electronically treated strings, Moby's "raging synthscapes," and Brian Eno's ambient brain-wave compositions, bridged with pieces by composer Elliot Goldenthal. The result is a tapestry of electronic pulsations that suggests the uneasy night thoughts of neglected machines. These oscillations never overpower the viewer's attention, as, say, does Philip Glass's score for *The Hours*, but quicken and sustain an almost subliminal tension (as when Eno's

"Force Marker" kick-starts the bank robbery that becomes a battle royal). The Moby piece that balloons at the finale as Vince and Neil seal their death pact bursts and falls like a benediction.

Despite its rising estimation among film buffs, *Heat* hasn't quite achieved full admission into the masterpiece club alongside the personal best of Spielberg, Coppola, Scorsese, Altman, and De Palma (to mention only seventies-era American marvels). True, the film has smudges. It lags here and there, takes on extra baggage. The subplot involving Vince's suicidal stepdaughter—quite unnecessary. The doomed romance between Neil and the young woman he meets in a bookstore—he's carrying a copy of *Stress Fractures in Titanium*, his homework assignment for his next heist—also seems detachable: Amy Brenneman, currently rapping the gavel on TV's *Judging Amy*, doesn't lend much to the skimpy part beyond her usual Victorian glow of womanly understanding. (She's like a reading lamp that cares.) The consoling hug Vince gives a grieving black mother is staged so melodramatically that it smacks of paternalistic grandstanding (as compared with the genuine pathos of the fate of the black ex-con who joins Neil's crew as getaway driver). A couple of coincidences are overly neat, and the police procedures could be better delineated, if you want to get prissy about it. *Heat*'s real handicap, as Nick James notes, is that it's been hindered with an identity crisis. The movie defies easy categorization. Is it a high-tech action film? A human-interest saga? Pulp fiction? Raw realism? A testosterone-pumped fantasy?

It isn't just one of these things, it's all of them, a super-amalgamator. But at its heart beats the metronome of a classic *noir*. Like all true *noirs*, the movie's protagonist gazes into the mirror and sees, gazing back, a stranger living on borrowed time. *Heat* is Michael Mann's ode to mortality—the male midlife crisis as last chance. Each character carries an abyss inside. No wonder Mann fudged what the movie was about to interviewers when the film was released—try laying *that* morbid jive on some snack-dip entertainment reporter. In this twilight vision, Los Angeles isn't a lush playground but a sprawling necropolis, a zombie factory. And in the land of the dead, the living are trespassers. Vince dreams of a mute chorus of homicide victims staring at him "with black eyeballs 'cause they got eight-ball hemorrhages from head-shot wounds." Caught on an infra-red surveillance camera at night, Neil's fist of a face appears to glare from a porthole on the Other Side, and he makes a fatal decision entering the clinical white light of a tunnel, in both scenes becoming a photo negative of himself—a phantom. Neil is Vince's doppelgänger, just as Vince

is his, and a doppelgänger is by definition a ghostly double, the disavowed shadow self.

It's almost inevitable that *Heat*'s haunted endgame should be set
at LAX. In movies, airports often represent the transit hubs of soul
migration. They're where characters are handed their boarding
passes and ferried off into the next world. (At the end of *Bang the
Drum Slowly*, for example, a shiny plane waits to take a terminally
ill ballplayer, portrayed by a goofily young Robert De Niro, to his
final destination, a stewardess poised to serve as the attending angel.)
Giving serpentine chase at LAX, Vince wages a running shoot-out
with Neil on the runway outskirts, the two of them playing lethal
hide-and-seek behind the storage sheds—small, scurrying figures
in an industrial amphitheater of engine roar, runway lights, looming
shadows, cargo containers, generators, and jumbo planes. As Vince
advances on Neil, there's a split-second overhead shot, perhaps the
only one in the movie, and the scrubby vegetation suddenly looks
gothic silver in the light—an overgrown, moonlit graveyard. It's a
kinetic snapshot of the kind Peckinpah used to flick like a wild card
from the deck to throw an unexpected prism-angle on a scene. It's
also unexplainably beautiful.

Although *Heat* ends with a classical tableau, the slayer and the
slain frozen against the dark horizon in a noble-Roman pose, Mann
hadn't quite gotten the night crawlers out of his nervous system. After
making *The Insider* (based on Marie Brenner's *Vanity Fair* article on
tobacco-industry whistle-blower Jeffrey Wigand) and the bombastic docudrama *Ali*, Mann returned to the cracked pavement in 2002
with a new series for CBS, *Robbery Homicide Division*. The show piv-
oted on a neat role reversal. In *Heat*, Tom Sizemore provided muscle
for the heist crew; here, he was the chief of the rob-hom unit, and
in the debut episode he took command of the crime scene in a near
reprise of Pacino's showy entrance in *Heat*. It was a Sizemore physically transformed and electrically recharged. He moved in *Heat* like a
nightclub bouncer, a tank with thick biceps and a swiveling turret for
a head. As the chief honcho in *Robbery Homicide Division*, he bopped
on his heels like a boxer, bobbing and weaving with suspects, infor-
mants, and legal barracudas, taking the other person's measure with
unwavering eye contact, his words fired in combination jabs. He was
an equally active listener—you could see him actually thinking about
what he had just heard rather than idling until his next line—and yet
for all this jazzy input/output he managed to project a quiet inward-
ness that gave his performance ballast. As is typical of a Mann pro-

duction, the supporting cast consisted of rock-solid picks, especially Barry "Shabaka" Henley as Sizemore's jowly, laconic sidekick (he's like a hip Huckleberry Hound).

Where *Heat* employed the full Hollywood arsenal of wide-screen lavishment, *Robbery Homicide Division* was shot on the fly in natural light on high-definition video, making Los Angeles look even more denatured and morally corroded, a teeming bazaar of illicit trans-actions and tribal vendettas. The expediency of the punk aesthetic (fast, smart, cheap, and jagged) has never been put to more expressive purpose, certainly not on TV. *Robbery Homicide Division* was *Heat* in churning microcosm. The most original, gutsy, and expertly written-directed-acted new show of the season, it unfortunately never caught on in the ratings and was lackadaisically praised by the nation's televi-sion critics, who reserved their tail-wagging for the latest shipment of *The Sopranos.* After Sizemore was arrested last December for battery (he has a track record of domestic altercation and substance abuse—it was De Niro who helped him into rehab when he unraveled at the end of making *Heat*), CBS withdrew life support on the series.

The premature burial of *Robbery Homicide Division* was regrettable, to use a polite word, but like *Crime Story* ("a true American epic," claims David Thomson in *The New Biographical Dictionary of Film*) its cult reputation may grow over the years until it finds its rightful spot in the Mann corpus, which is: as the thrashing tail end of a tril-ogy that began inauspiciously with *L.A. Takedown* and went nova with *Heat.* *Noir*'s enduring love-hate relationship with Los Angeles, from Raymond Chandler to James Ellroy, continues to yield an abundance of bitter fruit from this paradise despoiled. In Mann's trilogy, it's as if the ozone layer had been removed and L.A. had been left to bake in its own corruption. His Hollywood lies next door to Hell.

Vanity Fair, April 2003

Sam Peckinpah

Slay 'em Again, Sam

Sam Peckinpah was a walking WANTED poster. He played the part of an hombre to the gills. With his headband, faded denims, dog tags, mirrored sunglasses, and prophet's beard, he resembled a shaman spawned in the dry cracks of the desert. (His nickname was Iguana.) When he entered a room, everything shifted to one side. But Peckinpah's sudden impact couldn't be chalked up solely to wardrobe. The director of *The Wild Bunch*, *Straw Dogs*, and *The Killer Elite* seemed to have a hand grenade for a heart. You never knew what might set him off. One minute he'd be as mellow as a Willie Nelson song, then—*boom*—there'd be pieces of meat flying through the air. He didn't play favorites. He fired his own daughter from *The Getaway*.

Like many despots, he learned to duck. Steve McQueen tried to brain him with a bottle of champagne. Charlton Heston attempted to shish-kebab him with a saber. Yet he also inspired a chain link of loyalty that protected him like love beads. If Peckinpah were ever lost at sea in a crowded lifeboat (it was said), he'd be the last one left alive. As he aged he acquired the hide of a man who had peeled himself off many a dead heap. But his movies remained passionate. He knew how to cater a blowout. Everything flooded and sky-high about Sam Peckinpah emerges in Marshall Fine's *Bloody Sam* (Donald I. Fine, Inc.), a suitable stocking stuffer for the crazed loners on your Christmas list.

Like Garner Simmons's earlier *Peckinpah*, *Bloody Sam* skimps as criticism of Peckinpah's bullet-ridden corpus. Its punch comes from being an oral history of the old buzzard. A product of Fresno, California, Peckinpah was the grandson of a rancher and the son of a judge. Early in life he learned how to simulate a fall. "My father was a gentle man, but he tended to be violent when he was disciplining us kids," Peckinpah's brother, Denny, recalls. "[He] would backhand Sam and Sam would be flying backward before he even hit him. He'd go flying into a wall and hit the floor." It's almost a flash-forward to the reverse dives his film victims would do.

Canned from a TV station for showing a car salesman scratching his balls, Peckinpah enlisted as side arm to the director Don Siegel, doing a bit part as one of the pods in Siegel's cult classic, *Invasion of the Body Snatchers*. It was Peckinpah's crisp work on TV Westerns such as *The Rifleman* that led to *Ride the High Country*. A stately trot up the trail of John Ford and Anthony Mann, *Ride the High Country* honored its elders. The gunmen played by Joel McCrea and Randolph Scott had the courtly bearing and raised chins of commemorative stamps. Aside from *Junior Bonner* (which nobody saw), it's the one Peckinpah film non-Peckinpah fans can stomach.

His manic reputation as "Bloody Sam" began with *Major Dundee*, a cavalry epic climaxing in a massacre worthy of the Charge of the Light Brigade. Way too long, the movie required deep surgery in the editing room. After a preview of the studio cut, Peckinpah stood shaking on the street. His baby had been chopped to bits. "It's just a movie," he was consoled. "It's my fucking life," he said.

He later took a harder hit. Hired to direct *The Cincinnati Kid*, he spent three days shooting a scene written by Terry Southern involving Rip Torn, a caramel-colored hooker, and a sex utensil. The producer freaked. After a snap huddle of the studio brass, Peckinpah was replaced as quarterback. It's rare for a director to be fired from a film in progress. He was now tarred in Hollywood as *non compos mentis*. It would be three years before he could unleash his furies.

Shot in bunghole Mexico ("hot, isolated, primitive, with daily sandstorms and the occasional monsoon"), *The Wild Bunch* was a bitch to realize, a daily horror of skittish horses, ammo problems, foolhardy stunts, and slave-ship morale. More than a third of the crew was fired by Peckinpah, who was puking at both ends. But the result was the most prodigious payload by an American director since *Citizen Kane*. Blood spits from a caldron across a catalogue of knitted details—the white of William Holden's shirt, the hang of Robert Ryan's head—as history seems to draw a dusty blanket over this godforsaken ant farm. The slow motion, much copied, has never been topped as a lyrical shredder except by Peckinpah himself. Some shockers back when become tame in time. Not *The Wild Bunch*. It still has all its thorns.

After a harmonica toot titled *The Ballad of Cable Hogue* (an itchy idyll featuring Jason Robards hopping around in long johns), Peckinpah returned to the pit with *Straw Dogs*, in which a country house in Cornwall plays host to rape and pillage. A thesis film (pacifism is for pencil-necks), *Straw Dogs* has the snarl of a cornered animal, its siege finale escalating into a cruel trance.

It was during this onslaught that he solidified his image as a boozing, whoring, woman-beating, sucker-punching, knife-tossing, paranoia-crazed, tear-ass taskmaster. Peckinpah drank himself horizontal, traumatized Susan George, did the dueling-memos bit with the producer. "By the time of *Pat Garrett and Billy the Kid*, playing the part of Sam Peckinpah was practically a full-time job."

It took its toll. He was a limp rag shooting *Pat Garrett*, a pulpy prose poem which has James Coburn and Kris Kristofferson exchanging heavy nods while Bob Dylan fidgets as if he needs to pee. Reviled at the time, *Pat Garrett* has acquired the patina of a flawed masterpiece. Received opinion is that the movie was crucified by Crass Commercialism at the evil behest of MGM boss Jim Aubrey, a model for Jacqueline Susann's *Love Machine*. Fed up with Peckinpah's tactics, Aubrey ordered his own cut of the film. Peckinpah plotted revenge. Get on a plane to Mexico City, he told photographer John Bryson. "Get a couple of pistoleros. I'll fly them up here first class and they'll kill Jim Aubrey."

Aghast, Bryson refused: "I can't do that, Sam," he said. "That makes me an accessory if they kill the head of MGM."

Peckinpah gave him a cold stare and said, "I thought you were a friend of mine."

But as *Bloody Sam* makes evident, Peckinpah wasn't averse to taking a hike from his own edit. Perhaps he knew no amount of hunkering at the console could supply its missing vital organs. Even in the restored version that played a New York art house to rave reviews, *Pat Garrett* remains a ghost sonata packed in gore.

A better case for critical revise can be made for the appalling *Bring Me the Head of Alfredo Garcia*. As funky as a disco funeral, *Alfredo Garcia* has flies buzzing on the sound track, hit men in flared pants, Warren Oates mildewing the screen like a problem stain. But the movie has a strange Poe-like stupor from the moment Oates awakens after his premature burial following a blow from a shovel to the climactic, silhouetted sweep of bodyguards pumping shots into his getaway car as he slumps behind the wheel. There's no escape, no redemption. No wonder punks considered him a brother-man. *Bring Me the Head of Alfredo Garcia* is the most unreconstructed chunk of slow-death nihilism ever committed on and against film. Talk about *wasted*.

Peckinpah became permanently wasted when he switched from alcohol to cocaine in the seventies. Or so I found when I tried to cover the caravan to nowhere that was *Convoy* in 1977. The temperature in New Mexico was in the triple digits. The movie was over-budget and behind schedule. Trucks sat idle. Stars sulked in their trailers. One afternoon I was summoned to one of the trucks for a Private Audience. Without preamble, he began whispering a story about an old whore's first love. Upon reaching the punch line, he let fall a silence that made clear no more needed be said. He left the cabin as if he were a John Ford hero bidding adieu to the old homestead. Years later I found the story verbatim in a book about Peckinpah. He told everyone that can of corn.

There were times when he was more amenable. He would let his bandanna droop over his eyes, and stagger to actress Madge Sinclair, fumbling for her breasts and moaning, "I'm blind, I'm blind." But another afternoon I managed to get caught in his aerial. I was behaving myself when Peckinpah spun and accused me of being a ball-less wonder content to watch as he put his cock on the line. "The truth is what you *do*," he snapped. "All the rest is illusion." He then stomped off like Achilles to his tent.

To the crew his tantrums had become ho-hum. They were plotting to get him boozing again. As one explained, "Sam's a mean son of a bitch when he drinks, but at least he's in broadcast range. When he's on coke, he's unreachable." How unreachable *Bloody Sam* makes clear. He refused to come out of his trailer to shoot a scene involving three thousand extras and a hundred trucks. His whims continued through the editing process. "His cut had a scene of Ali MacGraw running across the screen upside down," recalls a producer with an ice pack on his head. The best thing about *Convoy* is the opening shot of white dunes, which evoke virgin mounds of cocaine.

Peckinpah was shunned after *Convoy*. He did little but diddle until *The Osterman Weekend*, based on one of Robert Ludlum's wordy blobs. Along with a phenomenal sequence involving bodies plunging into a burning swimming pool, *The Osterman Weekend* boasts an opening unlike anything Peckinpah had ever done, a masturbation scene in which Marete Van Kamp, dazed, glazed, frosted, is murdered by intruders—on video. It's almost a mini-essay on the mystique of the snuff film, with a suspended pang of violation.

It is either a boon or loss to the culture that Peckinpah never photographed sex dead-on, because the evidence of *Straw Dogs* and the *Osterman* intro is that he could have become Andrea Dworkin's worst nightmare, a demon pornographer burning a cigarette hole between hate and lust. He could have whipped a team of male/female whores roughshod into hell. He had the artistry, the Dionysian drive, to thrash all our moral-social-aesthetic criteria regarding the proper doses of pain and pleasure.

He thrived on tumult. Following a heart attack, he had six lawyers hovering around his bed. He became convinced that his pacemaker was a CIA plant that could be detonated at any time. His system finally caved shortly before his sixtieth birthday. At his memorial service in 1985, an actor informed the crowd, "You can tell this is a Peckinpah production. We got started late and nobody knows what's happening." It's amazing what he was able to make of such milling around in his prime. Out of muttering confusion he created a chaos of which he was king. He hurled everything he had into the breach. The unresolved feelings of the speakers in *Bloody Sam* suggest that the debris from his campaigns is still falling. Personally, I found him a heroic presence, even if he did call me a pussy.

Vanity Fair, December 1991

A Fistful of Woodys

The Great White Woody
Broadway Danny Rose

In *Manhattan*, Woody Allen and Mariel Hemingway curled up in front of *The Joe Franklin Show*, and Mariel, with all the bland, piercing candor of youth, wondered why the moribund celebrities Joe interviewed wore such obvious toupees—they look *awful*, she declared. *Broadway Danny Rose*, Allen's latest comedy, is a mellow stroll down the Great White Way, where the sort of celebrities who crowd Joe's sofa wear out their shoesies in search of stardom. Show business for these foot soldiers is not a slick, trim calling; the movie is filled with clinking medallions, fat pinky rings, paunches, chin stubble, and (yes) bad toupees. Indeed, Allen hasn't given us so many harsh, glaring close-ups since *Stardust Memories*. But the two movies have quite different tones. *Stardust Memories* was a long whine about the nuisances of success—the grabbing fans, the idiot critics; *Broadway Danny Rose* is a tribute to the scrounging pleasures of not making it, of plugging on even if it means living on sandwiches and scraps of applause. Failure in *Broadway Danny Rose* wears a halo, a shimmer of beatific innocence. Unfortunately, the movie itself (photographed in b-and-w by Gordon Willis) is bleach-gray and grainy; it looks like a linty pocket turned inside out. Fables, even show biz fables, need warm colors, soft falls of light, a restful sense of "Once upon a time . . ." In *Broadway Danny Rose*, the lightbulbs burn with a fierce, naked leer.

Structurally, *Broadway Danny Rose* is one long, twisting anecdote. At Manhattan's Carnegie Deli a group of veteran comics gathers to reminisce and kibbutz about Danny Rose (Allen), an agent whose client list puts him in the running for Patron Saint of Lost Causes. Told in flashbacks, the movie has funny, bright flares of dialogue, startling images, amusing bit appearances by Berle, Howard Cosell, and the ineffable Joe Franklin, and a friendly, informal air (particularly when those comics are unwinding between bites of pastrami). Yet the laughs don't build and multiply; the humor tapers off into a thin ribbon of noise and sentiment. Allen, who was mum through most of *Zelig*, talks a streak of coaxing bluster here, wheeling his arms like a man unrolling a bolt of cloth as he pushes his clients and preaches optimism. Witty as his lines and inflections often are, Allen seems uncomfortable playing a manic extrovert. The overdone exertion of his arms tells you that he would feel more at home playing a manic introvert (his usual role). Unlike Jack Nicholson and John Candy, Woody Allen doesn't have the uncomplicated spirit to play a man of vulgar gusto; he's too bookish, too self-analytical. Mustard on his collar would bring out his neatnik anxieties.

As his love interest and foil, Mia Farrow is even more out of her element. Packed into a wig and tight slacks, Farrow spends most of this movie in tinted glasses, her eyes and forehead hidden. Like Allen, she's playing against the grain, trading in her shy, schoolmarm manner for a grating voice and a shell of rough experience. Her performance is a stunt, and it's a weird stunt: all of her line readings make for a dead-on imitation of the stand-up comics (among them Sandy Baron, Corbett Monica, and Morty Gunty) idly gathered for eats and laughs. Swapping tales about mutual acquaintances, they eventually light on the legend of Broadway Danny Rose (Allen), who managed some of the most touchingly hopeless, flea-bitten novelty acts in show business history: a stuttering ventriloquist, a woman who dolled up parrots in tiny costumes, a water-glass player. What made Broadway Danny such a mensch, such a saint, was that he *believed* in his acts—he was more sold on them than they were on themselves. His biggest client was a boisterous goombah of a singer named Lou Canova (Nick Apollo Forte), who had a couple of fluke hits in the fifties and is now trying to cash in on the nostalgia craze. When Lou is booked to open for Milton Berle at the Waldorf, he sees it as an opportunity to break out of the small time and into the biggies. But this Italian crooner has a few character flaws—he drinks, boasts, cheats on his wife— and as the big event nears, those flaws turn to fissures. Loyally trying to keep his client from tearing himself in two, Broadway Danny runs errands and takes calming measures, all of which dangerously misfire. In this comedy of errors, Danny finds himself chased by hit men, lost in the flatlands of New Jersey, and thrown into the clutches of his client's tough-cookie girlfriend, Tina (Mia Farrow). It's *Take the Money and Run* without the money. In *A Midsummer Night's Sex Comedy*, Farrow was doing Diane Keaton, and now she's doing Louise

Lasser (Allen's ex, who co-starred with him in *Bananas*). It's an in joke that's so in it's spooky.

Yet there's something poignant about Farrow's impersonations. Although Allen dots *Broadway Danny Rose* with fond close-ups and tracking shots familiar from his previous films, he never quite creates a convincing pull of affection. The most telling moment is when Farrow is standing before a bathroom mirror without makeup, wig, or glasses, and for the first time we can see her eyes, her cheekbones, her beautiful forehead. Stripped of her brassiness, this scene says, she's tender, pure—newborn. And although Farrow *is* beautiful when her character is shorn of affectation, the transformation fails to carry an emotional charge. Woody Allen hasn't found a way to lyricize Mia Farrow on screen the way he lyricized Diane Keaton in *Annie Hall*; there's something muffled about his adoration, something withheld. He seems to dote on her from a distance, approaching her on tiptoe. It's revealing, I think, that in both *Zelig* and *Broadway Danny Rose* the union of Allen and Farrow is established at the end, with a discreet long shot. He keeps us at a distance too.

Patchy and strained as *Broadway Danny Rose* is, it isn't disreputable. A bittersweet funk of honest defeat hangs over the film. Those comedians loitering at the deli—Baron, Gunty, Monica—were once hot young whizzes who appeared regularly on *Merv Griffin* and *Mike Douglas*, wearing skinny ties and avid, wiseacre smiles. Now their features have settled into middle age, their posture is shot, and they've resigned themselves to the fact that they're not going to be megastars like Eddie Murphy and Steve Martin. The biggest problem I had with *Broadway Danny Rose* was that I was more interested in *them*—in their grudges, their pride, their perseverance—than I was in Danny and his slapstick dilemmas. Grown-up versions of the joking kids in *Diner*, these comics have acid, gutty depths that the movie, in its desire to be a wooing fable, never touches. By casting himself as a low-rent, low-echelon manager, Woody is doing penance for *Stardust Memories*, telling us that at heart he's still one of the guys, but kinder, lonelier. It doesn't quite wash, but it's an amiable deceit—and the movie itself is a sweet, mild try.

Texas Monthly, March 1984

Liquid Shimmer

Purple Rose of Cairo

In Woody Allen's *Purple Rose of Cairo*, Mia Farrow is the Poor Little Match Girl of the Depression, a hollow-eyed waif whose bones have been picked clean and bared to the biting cold. Photographed by Gordon Willis, *The Purple Rose of Cairo* is low-skied, bleak, wintry blue—its characters might as well be marooned on one of Ingmar Bergman's frozen islands, waiting for Death to make a chess move. Farrow's Cecilia is married to an out-of-work lout (Danny Aiello), who is as paunchy and rough-handed as she is slender and kind. He pitches pennies and makes smacking noises at other women, and he has his own notions of chivalry. If Cecilia complains about being knocked around, he says, "I never just hit ya. I *warn* ya first." When she's not dodging head shots, Cecilia clears tables at a diner, where her daydreaming and jumpy nerves lead to a clatter of broken dishes. Her only release from that harried grind comes when she takes a pew at the local moviehouse to catch the latest fizz of Hollywood sophistication.

In these movies, everyone is suave and tapered. The men look as if they have been licked clean by kittens, the women sparkle frostily in their snake-hipped gowns, and they all exchange witticisms in arch, fluted tones; they flirt like idle gods. Compared with the slobby crawl of life around Cecilia, these thirties "white-telephone" movies (so called because a white telephone was considered the last word in penthouse elegance) seem cloud-borne and fancy-free, and she drinks them in with choir-girl devotion. Little does she know that one of these movies will soon drink *her* in, like Alice through the looking glass. The line between truth and fantasy becomes a liquid shimmer.

With its characters capriciously popping in and out of the silver screen, *The Purple Rose* recalls Buster Keaton's peekaboo silent *Sherlock Jr.*, and the poignant close-up at the end is a Chaplinesque echo from *City Lights*. But perhaps the strongest influence on *Purple Rose* is the recent Steve Martin–Herbert Ross musical, *Pennies from Heaven*, which also built a staircase to paradise. Like *Pennies*, *Purple Rose* is about how movie-fed dreams and pinch-poor realities collide and mate during a period of economic bottoming out. Mia Farrow functions here the way Bernadette Peters functioned in *Pennies:* as a guiding vision of virgin purity, a lilac angel who dwells among weeds. But where *Pennies from Heaven* says that white-telephone movies are sublime articulations of our yearnings for youth and wealth and streamlined style, *The Purple Rose of Cairo* asserts that such films are jaded come-ons, crass teases. Hollywood, *Purple Rose* suggests, is a pimp who exploits our dreams and shakes the loose change from our pockets.

Pennies from Heaven said that even a blind man has Technicolor dreams, but *Purple Rose* doesn't hold any hope of transcendence. *Purple Rose* also suffers because its black and white movie-within-the-movie proves so much more entertaining than the movie that frames it. It's hilarious to see Jeff Daniels as Cecilia's movie star lover, braving the dance floors of New York in his safari jacket and pith helmet and going starry-eyed over his "madcap Manhattan weekend." Ed Herrmann, who plays a dashing silly, has the perfect delineations of top-hat style for the period (he's one of the few actors you can actually imagine wearing a monocle and spats), and John Wood, as his sidekick, has the antic donkey-braying charm of Edward Everett Horton, that comic bumbler of white-telephone classics such as *Trouble in Paradise* and *The Gay Divorcee.* As a nightclub chanteuse, Karen Akers has scooped cheekbones, a throaty Marlene Dietrich growl, and legs that seem to climb forever. There's also a surly black maid named Delilah (Annie Joe Edwards), who says things like, "You ain't been yourself since you got back from those pyramids." Indeed, my favorite moment in *Purple Rose* is when Delilah, drawing a bath for her stuck-up employer, asks, "Wouldst you be wantin' the big bubbles or the ass's milk?" The hitch is that this romp has such daffy charm that we feel let down whenever we're dumped back into the Depression with that little rag doll Cecilia. We don't want to stand in the soup lines—we want the big bubbles. But Woody Allen keeps emptying the bath.

He certainly drains the tub on Mia Farrow, leaving her with nothing but a long, doting close-up. Allen's camera is tense and protective of Farrow in *Purple Rose*, and there's something creepy about that protectiveness. In his previous film, *Broadway Danny Rose*, Allen paired Farrow with an Italian vulgarian, played by Nick Apollo Forte; here she is married to a low-life vulgarian, presumably Italian (Danny Aiello certainly is), whose snores fill the house. Evelyn Waugh once said of another writer that watching him grasp the English language was like seeing a chimpanzee handle a Sèvres vase, which is what Mia Farrow is in *Purple Rose*—a delicate vase being pawed by an ape.

Aiello isn't permitted an ounce of saving grace, and nearly all of the other characters in Cecilia's world are just as doughy and ill-bred. As a gum-chewing hooker, Dianne Wiest seems to have wandered in from a road company of *Irma la Douce* (she even squints stagily, as if projecting to the back row), and the woman Cecilia catches her husband messing around with is a lump of whory cleavage. No, the message is that Cecilia is too fine for this coarse world, too easily beguiled, and without the Wood Man to embrace her (Allen doesn't appear in *Purple Rose*), she has no kindred spirit to call her own. Farrow looks wonderful, but her characterization is finally too sickly sweet and Victorian. In *The Purple Rose of Cairo*, Allen cups her in his palm as if she were a fluff of feathers about to expire. Perhaps if he released her into the air, she would blaze into new, healthy life. Woody Allen bandages Mia Farrow's wings in *Purple Rose*, and he doesn't let her fly. Or sing.

Texas Monthly, March 1985

Upper West Side Story
Hannah and Her Sisters

Woody Allen's *Hannah and Her Sisters* is an intellectual feel-good massage—a tender kneading for tired brains. Lacily embroidered with culture (quotations from Tolstoy and e. e. cummings, incidental music by Bach and Puccini), *Hannah and Her Sisters* is directed at an educated class of moviegoers that prides itself on understated taste and consumption. Speaking in rapid captions, Hannah's friends and relatives are artsy, rumpled versions of the striped-tie, yachting-club yuppies in William Hamilton's *New Yorker* cartoons, making ever so clever chat around the snack tray. But where Hamilton's brittle Waspy achievers deliver their quips with thin, crumbling grins, Allen's Jewishy characters seem to have a fleeting sense of panic whistling through their ulcers. Their pain isn't on the spiffy surface; it's soul-deep.

As the hypochondriac Mickey, Allen is like a cricket in Tolstoy's ear, trying to eavesdrop on the master's thoughts as the great questions thunder: Does God exist? Is suicide preferable to slow death? But when the thunder dies, we're left with the simple lesson, Be fruitful and multiply. *Hannah and Her Sisters* is a schmaltzy piece of uplift, saying yes to love, marriage, and the consoling power of laughter. Well, it's pretty damned easy to say yes to "life" if life is a beautiful, doting wife, fond, obedient children, and a roomy Upper West Side apartment in Manhattan stocked with cultivated friends (not to mention a silent black maid gliding in to light the dinner candles). *Hannah*'s hard questions rest on soft, downy cushions.

It's amazing that *Hannah and Her Sisters* is being treated as Woody Allen's awake-and-sing movie, because so much of it is a talky rehash of riffs, themes, and predicaments from *Annie Hall*, *Manhattan*, *Interiors*, and *Broadway Danny Rose*. It's hardly a novel spin to make Mickey a hypochondriac—all of Woody's stand-ins have been Felix Unger fretheads with thermometers stuck in their mouths. And when Mickey questions life's final destination, it's a glide path we've flown before with the Wood Man, who has gotten a little beyond-it for all this blabby pseudophilosophizing. A fifty-year-old man shouldn't still be waving his hands and asking, If God exists, then how come there's evil? We used to throw pillows at freshmen who interrupted pinochle games with questions like that.

Allen certainly doesn't shake anything wild and original out of his gifted cast. The luminous Mia Farrow, costumed in mouse-brown clothes as Hannah, looks worthy of one of Barbara Pym's blend-into-the-woodwork spinsters. As her husband, Elliot, Michael Caine hasn't acted so simpering and flustered since he was whomped by that teeny-bopper's breasts in *Blame It on Rio*. It's painful seeing Caine being anything but dashingly droll. In the ludicrous role of Frederick, Max von Sydow fares even worse. A rigid pillar of rectitude, he isn't allowed one light moment—he represents European high culture unleavened by American sass.

Passing from mentor to mentor is Hannah's sister Lee (Barbara Hershey), who is having an affair with Elliot (which explains Michael Caine's jumpiness) after having her fill of Frederick's lecturing bull. With her firm jaw, slender fingers, and moist, coital eyes, Hershey looks great, but her character is a warm, enigmatic zero. Lee's mentor fixation is never explored, and she becomes little more than a parking space for older men's fantasies. In the obligatory Diane Keaton adorable-kook role is Dianne Wiest, wearing a head scarf and a subcontinent of costume jewelry as Hannah's other sister, Holly. Wiest is spikier than Keaton—her porcupine quills of hostility tipped with blood—and her sulky mood swings are quite convincing. But I resent her being the movie's lost-soul mascot. When Mickey tells Holly how much he likes her writing, his face is so strained that he seems to be indulging a woman-child in her hour of need. He, too, is playing mentor.

Hannah and Her Sisters scoots along on its gravel of chatter, and it is marginally entertaining. I laughed when Hannah suggests that Mickey's infertility might be rooted in excessive masturbation, and he cries, "You gonna start knocking my hobbies?" I also liked the scene in which Mickey and Holly meet at Tower Records and zing each other with reminiscences of a horrible date they had; the dialogue has a loose, winging rhythm the rest of the movie lacks. And Lloyd Nolan, now deceased, makes a touching appearance as Hannah's vaudeville-veteran father, whose dignity has settled into a delicate crust. But the movie is so determined to be nice that it can't be anything but minor. If Hannah ever discovered her husband's infidelity with her own sister, for example, the mahogany veneer of these characters' lives would crack—perhaps permanently. Critics keep saying that in *Hannah and*

Her Sisters Woody Allen has made peace with himself and finally kissed off his killjoy anhedonia. But if Woody Allen has learned to accept life, why does he still look as if he were before a firing squad, facing death without a blindfold? All of the "life-affirming" moments in *Hannah and Her Sisters* (the visit to the Marx Brothers' *Duck Soup*, particularly) are contrivances of will rather than expressions of temperament. He is forcing himself to reenlist in the human race, wearing a smile as his insignia. But this isn't the face of someone who is willing to be fruitful and multiply.

Texas Monthly, April 1986

How Green Was My Woody

No male artist seems to have emerged wiser or happier from the sex wars that began in the seventies and continue, sporadically, today. The buckshot lodged in their hides still smarts. Norman Mailer, whose fictional heroes bent women like pretzels and who answered his feminist critics in *The Prisoner of Sex* by hanging Kate Millett out to dry, grumps in interviews about how these harpies have poisoned the culture. Philip Roth—branded a misogynist even before his former wife Claire Bloom depicted him as a cad and a Svengali in her dozy memoir *Leaving a Doll's House*—continues to churn his hostilities and grievances through the blender (most recently in his novel *I Married a Communist*). The results can be hilarious, but his anger seems real, gnawing, not just exaggerated for effect. Even John Updike, a much cooler customer, vents a certain testiness in his recent novels, tweaking the nipples of his feminist hanging jury with acrid descriptions of body parts and caustic one-liners. Perhaps the artist who has curdled the most, however, is Woody Allen. He enjoyed a free ride in the seventies, back when feminists were beginning to catch on to Mailer and company, only to be chased by a lynch mob waving microphones in the nineties. The romance with and subsequent marriage to Mia Farrow's adopted daughter Soon-Yi, the tumultuous breakup with Farrow and her tell-all book, the accusations of child molestation and dirty Polaroids, and the media wilding that all of this unleashed (including merciless op-ed columns by Maureen Dowd in *The New York Times*) have left him feeling beleaguered, defensive, and embittered, if his latest work is reliable evidence. *Mighty Aphrodite, Everyone Says I Love You, Deconstructing Harry*, and, now, *Celebrity*, have a raggedy construction, a choppy rhythm, and an obscene bluster ("Beth Kramer's an aggressive, tight-ass, busybody cunt, and it's none of her fucking business how I speak to my son"—*Deconstructing Harry*). His rooting section—his chief cheerleader, *The New York Times* cultural desk—chalks these films up to a loosey-goosey liberation from narrative constraints and audience expectations (an old pro letting go), but audiences have tended to recoil. This unzipped lip doesn't represent the Woody they once loved.

It's difficult to recall the honeymoon period when Allen was considered a cuddly mascot, the thinking woman's huggy-bear. Like Phil Donahue and Alan Alda, fellow paragons of post–John Wayne manhood, he was quick on the verbal draw and amiably slouchy. He specialized in cajolery and neurosis-juggling. True, he did partake of poppin'-fresh flesh in *Manhattan*, in which Mariel Hemingway played the world's first Amazon nymphet, but most of the female characters in his films were responsive, animated, smart, skittish, ardent grown-ups—former English majors from whom the poetry hadn't yet worn off. Their words carried a quiver of lyricism. His men and women may have gotten on each other's nerves, but their anxieties were equally matched; they clung to the same psychiatrist's couch—the Jewish lifeboat. Since *Mighty Aphrodite*, however, the balance of sexual power has shifted. Now when a woman opens her mouth in a Woody Allen movie, it isn't because speech is required. As Allen's movies have gotten pornier, oral sex has become the favored way to keep women quiet and occupied. In *Deconstructing Harry*, Julia Louis-Dreyfus sinks to her knees before a dried-apple Richard Benjamin, who, after chiding her for using her teeth, says, "C'mon, open wide"—the first of the film's several blowjob scenes. In Allen's new movie, *Celebrity*, which premiered at the thirty-sixth New York Film Festival and reaches theaters nationwide this month, a movie star (Melanie Griffith) bestows her mouth on a grateful reporter (Kenneth Branagh), claiming that her body belongs to her husband but from the neck up she's fancy-free. That's become the feminine ideal in Woody Allen films—the bobbing-head doll.

Increasingly, the women in his movies can be divided between menopausal nuts and coltish sluts. The type of lyrical kook Diane Keaton played in *Annie Hall* has lost her cheekboned shine and is withering into premature hagdom, her thrift-shop wardrobe destined to become bag-lady rags and her hair shot to hell. Bristling with anger and unresolved issues, these biological time bombs cradle themselves as they walk, as if trying to contain their own destructive force. One of the rude shocks in *Deconstructing Harry* is seeing how unattractively lit and drearily costumed most of the women are, save for Elisabeth Shue, the film's designated *shiksa* and emanator of blond rays. They're Jewish-shrewish horrors drawn from Philip Roth's filing cabinet. Kirstie Alley, who plays a woman wronged with thick sobs of hysteria, is a chunkier version of Bea Arthur in *Maude*, Demi Moore is a castration complex come to life, and Judy Davis, as another victim of Harry's infidelity, resembles something torn up by the roots, to borrow a phrase from P. G. Wodehouse.

Davis fares even worse in *Celebrity*. As the ex-wife of a hapless journalist played by Kenneth Branagh, Davis picks and pecks at herself, her sulky head protruding from a teeming anthill of mannerisms. A fearless and feared actress who dared to belittle David Lean on the set of *A Passage to India* when she was still a relative newcomer, Davis has squandered the lioness potential shown in her early work and devolved into a caricature of bug-eyed bitchery. Simmering in *Husbands and Wives*, boiling in *Deconstructing Harry*, she is a veritable triathlete of angst in *Celebrity*, projecting a neediness that could warp gravitational fields. One of the film's cognitive dissonances is that her scatterbrain ineptitudes (bungling her job; having a panic attack when she spots her ex-husband and falling on all fours, pretending to hunt for an earring) are meant to be cute, endearing—bits of screwball comedy. To please her TV-producer boyfriend (Joe Mantegna, giving his roguish eye a workout), she consults a call girl played by Bebe Neuwirth about tricks of the trade regarding oral sex. It's reminiscent of a similar tutorial in *Fast Times at Ridgemont High* involving Phoebe Cates and Jennifer Jason Leigh, without the charm or ease. Practicing on a banana, Davis bites down hard (men in the screening-room audience winced in unison); demonstrating the proper technique, Neuwirth pulls back the peel, slides her mouth over the banana—and then, eyes signaling trouble, begins to gag as a broken-off piece lodges in her throat. Davis has to perform a typically frantic Heimlich maneuver to free it. Meanwhile, I sat there thinking, "So it's come to this."

Some critics have deplored this scene as pandering to the cynicism and voyeurism of the Clinton-Lewinsky scandal. I think the political overtones are simply happenstance. The oral fixation in Allen's films predates the presidential kneepads. It's part of the larger, familiar passive aggression. Aside from whining, the Woody Man has never exerted himself much. Getting head not only liberates him from making any actual effort of his own but allows him to remain lazily detached—to tune out the woman on his lap and holster his precious thoughts. (Not that there are any great brain waves coursing through the screenplay of *Celebrity*, which features clunkers such as "Ask not for whom the bell tolls, or, more accurately, for whom the toilet flushes.") The aggressive half of passive aggression is expressed in finky acts of infidelity which the Woody Man pretends "just happened." After Branagh's Lee Simon has set up house with Famke Janssen's Bonnie, the sexiest, poutiest book editor since Suzanne Pleshette in *Young-blood Hawke*, he lies about going to the all-night drugstore for ulcer medicine in order to meet Winona Ryder—it doesn't matter what her character's name is, since her role seems made up as it goes along. (She's a movie extra and a waitress who moonlights as the translator and companion of a Nobel scientist—a Renaissance waif.) They kiss, and this foolish romantic whim ends up wrecking his relationship. "The heart wants what it wants," Allen famously remarked during the height of the Soon-Yi scandal, which is a mantra for shirking responsibility for one's actions—for pretending one is gripped by a higher power, like an alien abductee lifted by the light.

Whenever a Woody Man is cornered and asked to own up to his feelings or behavior, instant disavowal kicks in, as he waves his arms and sputters in broken sentences. Vagueness is his preferred avoidance technique—his verbal aikido. He tries to toss the women off-balance with the force of their accusations: when Mia Farrow asks Michael Caine in *Hannah and Her Sisters* whether he's disenchanted with their marriage or in love with someone else (he is), he snaps, "My God, what is this, the Gestapo?" Pressed further, a Woody Man gaslights his wife or girlfriend, making her feel her suspicions are paranoid figments of imagination. "What are you, *crazy?*" may be the most oft asked question in the Woody Allen oeuvre. Being treated as crazy eventually makes the women crazy. There's nothing like being lied to to make you lose it. One glass of red wine and these divorcées are ready for combat.

So much for the nuts.

The sluts are all trim physique and no psyche, young yet lacking any higher yearning, too narcissistic to have outside interests or questions to ask. In the past, Allen would mentor the child-women in the films, give them recommendation lists intended to nurture their tender taste buds. The sex was part of a larger instruction, the student-teacher relationship being inherently erotic, according to some academic theorists. This cultural pretense—this cover story—has been pretty much dropped. The molding and marriage of like minds has been replaced by the collision of pure flesh. In *Celebrity*, Charlize Theron plays a model who strides like an upright puma and describes herself as polymorphously perverse; she oozes at the slightest touch. Inexplicably, this wonder honey fastens on Branagh's Lee, who drives an Aston Martin, pretty flash wheels for an aging Josh Freelantzovitz; in the car, her tongue invades his ear like a wet snake (when she asks if he's afraid of catching her germs, he replies, "From you, I'd be willing to catch terminal cancer").

The mercenary beauties *Celebrity* seems to be stockpiling for a nuclear winter represent the high-maintenance end of Allen's prostitute fixation. Since showcasing Mira Sorvino as a hooker with a heart of gold and a Judy Holliday voice in *Mighty Aphrodite*, he has shifted from comic sentimentality into a more low-down appreciation of amateur nymphos and professional whores. Unlike civilian women, with all their needs and entanglements, these passing fancies have an emotional off switch. The most capable of them provide a tidy service. You pop, you pay, they go, as Woody explains to his shrink in *Deconstructing Harry*. Moreover, they don't wear you out with lots of cultural shoptalk. "You don't have to discuss Proust or films," he explains. In Woodyland, literary name-dropping is man's work, dammit—the Eurotrash groupie in *Celebrity* who mentions Chekhov's name after sex is meant to be regarded as a shallow dip.

The primary hooker in *Deconstructing Harry* was played by a black actress (Hazelle Goodman), a casting decision which was perceived by some as a sly "take that" from Allen. For years, he had been criticized for portraying Manhattan as a strictly white upscale wonderland, populated exclusively by psychoanalyzed Jews and lustrous *shiksas*. Now, after two decades of pretending people of color didn't exist (aside from Bobby Short at the piano), he finally inserts a major black character into one of his films, and what is she? Superfly's mama. When Allen's Harry asks Cookie if she knows what a black hole is, she says, "Yeah, that's how I make my livin'." After she (implausibly) accompanies him to an awards ceremony at his alma mater, they're both thrown into the clink; later, he's bailed out, but she's never mentioned. Her fate means nothing to the film, or the filmmaker—it's as if she were not even a person.

A charitable reading would chalk up Cookie's foxy-mama cartoonishness as part of the film's tactical assault on political correctness. After all, Allen didn't hesitate to ruffle fellow Jews: when Eric Bogosian's Orthodox character asks Harry if he believes in the Holocaust, he replies, "Not only do I know that we lost six million, but the scary thing is that records are made to be broken." With *Celebrity*, however, the use of the black characters is too consistently coarse and lowbrow to be rationalized away. Whether it's Branagh stammering to basketball star Anthony Mason, "You must have a huge . . . following," or a minor Italian-American character, in a cringe-inducing compliment, remarking how "cheerful" all black folks are, the movie carries a racist tinge. It's as if Allen can't conceive of black characters as anything other than (sexual) athletes or entertainers. He's dangerously close to Norman Mailer's notion in "The White Negro" that black people have a natural lock on physical prowess—a primitive advantage. The jungle-fever gyration Mason does on the dance floor with Theron hypnotizes Allen's camera maybe more than it ought.

As he's gotten older, Woody Allen has schizzed off into an odd combination of sexual swinger and cultural prig. Not that his cultural tastes haven't always been on the fogyish side. In a famous monologue in *Manhattan*, he enters into his tape recorder his honor roll of things which make life worth living, which include the second movement of Mozart's *Jupiter* Symphony, Louis Armstrong, Swedish films, Flaubert's *Sentimental Education*, Cézanne's apples, Frank Sinatra, and Marlon Brando. Note: Louis Armstrong, but not Charlie Parker; Cézanne, but not any of the Abstract Expressionists. It reveals a cutoff point in Allen's consciousness after which no other influences seem to have entered. "Tradition is the illusion of permanence," Woody says about religion in *Deconstructing Harry*, but it's a nifty line that may apply to culture as well. Cinematically, his enthusiasms haven't advanced beyond the art-house favorites of the fifties and sixties: Bergman, Fellini, Truffaut, Godard (those jump cuts in *Husbands and Wives* and the opening of *Deconstructing Harry*). Musically, his sound tracks have the faded oomph of old gramophone records. Comedically, he remains loyal to the Marx Brothers (especially Groucho—he wore a Groucho mask in homage in *Everyone Says I Love You*), whose tumult of slapstick and wordplay is his touchstone for a redeeming kind of crazy sanity. In *Hannah and Her Sisters*, the Woody character, moping after a medical misdiagnosis plunged him into a funk over death and the meaninglessness of existence, has his spirits restored when he pops into *Duck Soup* at a revival house and is able to laugh again, much as Joel McCrea becomes one with his fellow man in *Sullivan's Travels* as they hoot at a Mickey Mouse cartoon. It's a sweet gesture but a sentimental cop-out—when you're depressed, Marx Brothers humor sounds as hollow as anything else—and shows how desperately he clings to his old tastes, afraid to let go or move ahead.

Unfortunately, the movie world has moved ahead without him. Allen is preaching the Marx Brothers to audiences clued in to the Farrelly Brothers. Allen's heavy intentions don't fly in this period of lighter gravity. Faithfully invoking the Modern Library demigods of modernism who shaped his intellectual development (Proust, Flaubert, Kafka), he's quixotically upholding the image of the artist as the tortured minister of his own complex sensibility in a postmodern culture which is characterized by sampling, pastiche, and multiple scenarios that don't require a single *auteur*. More than any other performer, he made the stand-up-comic persona a pacing novelistic presence on the screen—a focal point of social observation. His best films were X-rays of the *Zeitgeist* at the time and are valuable time capsules now. Indeed, his comedies form one of the main bridges between modernism and postmodernism, linking the bookish neurosis and absurdism of the bohemian fifties and sixties (Freud, Jules Feiffer, Mort Sahl, Nichols and May) to the flippant, noncommittal, nonintrospective, free-floating irony of the yuppie ascendancy (in a word, *Seinfeld*). Without Woody Allen, no George Costanza. Without *Annie Hall*, no Ally McBeal. For that matter, without *Zelig*, no Forrest Gump.

Being able to make movies for decades with minimal interference is a privilege that has allowed Allen to write, cast, direct, and edit without being nitpicked to death by focus groups and studio executives. This elbow room has enabled him to invent an inspired newsreel collage such as *Zelig*, experiment with a German Expressionist allegory such as *Shadows and Fog*, produce a Dennis Potter–like musical such as *Everyone Says I Love You*, even completely reshoot a maudlin sleepwalker such as *September* (another one of Allen's Chekhovian pressings of autumn leaves), and yet make each foray a personal marker in his own artistic pilgrimage. His films never have the tin stamp of Hollywood product. With their trademark white credits against a black screen, they constitute a cinematic uniform edition of Allen's varied output. But this protected status has also made him something of a bubble boy, distorting his view of his fans—as needy gargoyles (*Stardust Memories*) or cheap gawkers (in *Wild Man Blues*, Barbara Kopple's documentary of Allen's European jazz tour, he laments as a fan takes his picture in Venice, "They won't pay 10 cents to see one of my movies, but passing in a gondola, they love it")—and sealing him off from his casts, whom he treats not as collaborators but as patchwork figures, most of whom are fed only the few pages of script they need. God forbid they should get a glimpse of the big picture, or develop their own ideas. It's instructive that the last truly entertaining Woody Allen movie, the last one to get into gear, was 1993's *Manhat-*

tan Murder Mystery, which was co-written with Marshall Brickman (co-author of *Annie Hall*) and reunited Allen with Diane Keaton and Alan Alda (who was hilarious as the vain television producer in *Crimes and Misdemeanors*). *Manhattan Murder Mystery* spritzes along happily, unpretentiously, offering convincing proof that Allen needs collaborators, sidekicks, foils. Somebody—anybody—to interrupt his compulsive conversational comb-overs. (In fairness, austerity moves resulting from the meager box-office returns of Allen's recent work have forced him to toss longtime members of his select circle from the lifeboat, including producer Robert Greenhut, editor Susan E. Morse, and cinematographer Carlo Di Palma. He also parted company with his agent, "the legendary Sam Cohn." His security blanket has been torn to scraps.)

In its own diddling way, *Celebrity* is an admission of Allen's isolation, a study of the unbearable lightness of being a bystander at the passing scene. It's a continuing thread in Allen's work, this persistent sense of having missed out on the party. In *Stardust Memories*, Woody has a Fellini-esque scene about being stuck in a dreary train and observing passengers (including a starlet named Sharon Stone) in another car laughing and whooping it up—having the fun he wishes he were having. He's the eternal outsider, excluded from the festivities. In *Celebrity*, Branagh's Lee covets the statuesque blonde trophy-date a classmate squires to their high-school reunion. He thinks becoming a player will help him nab a better class of babe. At the end of the film, his quest for the golden fleece has been squashed. The author of two disappointing novels (and a third that was pitched into the East River by the woman he betrays), along with a screenplay (which he failed to peddle to a dissolute star played to spooky perfection by Leonardo DiCaprio, whose droogie entourage is Allen's vision of young pagan Hollywood), Lee finds himself at the premiere of a popcorn movie called *The Liquidator*. Alone, bereft, artistically null, a sellout with no takers, Lee stares at the word HELP written across the Manhattan skyline on the screen—a silent cry that mirrors his existential plight. Unlike Woody in *Hannah and Her Sisters* and Joel McCrea in *Sullivan's Travels*, Lee's being in a movie audience—a crowd—doesn't bring him out of himself. It bottles him up and cuts him off as he feels his own insignificance. Woody Allen isn't the first filmmaker to mistake his own drop in morale for a larger cultural malaise (Paul Mazursky, the director of *Down and Out in Beverly Hills*, took a sad, satirical look at his own inability to connect with today's thrill-happy movie audience in an exercise in futility called *The Pickle*), but he may be the first to try to turn it into an Everyman fable. It's a lot to ask of a viewer, to empathize with a loser like Branagh's Lee, that bag of mush, or to accept high-minded editorializing from a director so obviously on booty call. In a line that functions as the movie's thesis statement, Branagh laments "a culture that took a wrong turn somewhere," presumably in O.J.'s white Bronco. Maybe so, but Woody Allen himself is going in circles.

Vanity Fair, December 1998

Death and the Master
Alfred Hitchcock

Movie directors are supposed to be larger than life, Caesars of all they survey. From the birth of cinema—from the silent epics of Sergei Eisenstein, Abel Gance, and D. W. Griffith into the sound era—the film director has doubled as field commander. John Ford re-creating cavalry movements in Utah's Monument Valley, Leni Riefenstahl supervising Nazi parades, Cecil B. DeMille staging biblical spectacles with throngs of costumed extras, David Lean bracing himself against the raging winds (*Ryan's Daughter*) and desert sands (*Lawrence of Arabia*), Sam Peckinpah detonating a horse-crowded bridge in *The Wild Bunch*—of such stuff fearless leaders are made. But there is another traditional role, less grand but equally enduring, of the director as nimble chef, whipping up treats which contain nasty surprises. In this camp, which encompasses practical jokers from Luis Buñuel to John Waters, no one served death as a cold dish with more Jeevesian aplomb than Alfred Hitchcock. A pudgy man who seemed to hold on to his baby fat for protective padding, Hitchcock elevated the voyeurism implicit in all filmmaking into an explicit stare and aesthetic statement. Popularity meant more to him than it did to the field-commander directors, who were content to play God. Long before his name became synonymous with his droll brand of macabre, Hitchcock put his own face on his product, introducing his films in coming attractions, making cameo appearances which his fans learned to anticipate (popping up in a weight-loss ad in *Lifeboat*, walking a pair of dogs in *The Birds*), lending his name to pulp magazines, book anthologies, and board games, and becoming the only legendary director to make himself at home in America's living room as the host of *Alfred Hitchcock Presents*, where his distinguished-penguin silhouette became the most famous profile in television. Introducing each episode, he enunciated his English vowels to suggest a wry mortician talking shop.

Do you have a desire to be remembered?
I don't think so.

I mean, do you think about posterity?
What did posterity ever do for me?
                           —Alfred Hitchcock, interviewed by Peter
                              Bogdanovich, in *Who the Devil Made It*

While Hitchcock was alive, his salesmanship made him suspect in the eyes of some American critics. *The New Republic*'s Stanley Kauffmann labeled Hitchcock "a successful cynic" in the Somerset Maugham mold, chalking up Hitchcock's success to shrewd pandering. "In the country of the bland, the wan-eyed is king," Kauffmann aphorized in 1963. The cultural landscape has been bombed beyond recognition since then, and Hitchcock's name has not only lasted but retained its catchphrase status as a synonym for suspense. Since Hitchcock's death in 1980, posterity has done plenty for him. "Hitchcock is the most intuitive and prophetic of all our popular artists," George W. S. Trow proclaims in his recent book, *My Pilgrim's Progress* (Pantheon), voicing the new consensus. Nineteen ninety-nine marks the one-hundredth anniversary of Alfred Hitchcock's birth, an event that will feature full-scale retrospectives of his work, the publication of *Hitchcock's Notebooks*, by Dan Auiler (Avon Books), and a five-day conference being hosted by New York University's Department of Cinema Studies this October titled "Hitchcock: A Centennial Celebration."

These forthcoming homages amount to an avalanche on top of an avalanche. In his book of interviews with Hitchcock (*Hitchcock/Truffaut*, 1983), Truffaut predicted that before the end of the century Hitchcock commentary would rival that on Marcel Proust, a comparison which sounded fanciful at the time but now appears clairvoyant. No director has inspired more word count on every possible aspect of his personal life, creative output, persistent childhood fears, and embedded psychosexual coding. He has been the subject of standard biographies; collections of interviews; "The Making of . . ." books about individual films; recent memoirs by the actress Janet Leigh (*Psycho: Behind the Scenes of the Classic Thriller*) and the novelist and screenwriter Evan Hunter (*Me and Hitch*); critical studies of his scare tactics and recurring motifs, with special emphasis on "the MacGuffin," his term for the deliberately vague pretext used to set the plot machinery into motion (a stolen briefcase or a microfilm involving unspecified "government secrets"); Lacanian-Derridean deconstructions, such as *Hitchcock's Bi-Textuality: Lacan, Feminisms, and Queer Theory*, by Robert Samuels; scene-by-scene and even frame-by-frame studies of individual films (Camille Paglia's tour de force tribute to *The Birds* and

Stefan Sharff's *The Art of Looking in Hitchcock's Rear Window*); a scholarly newsletter published in Australia called *The MacGuffin* (which has its own Web site, www.labyrinth.net.au/~muffin); and a journal called *Hitchcock Annual,* whose latest issue offers an interpretation of Hitchcock's cameo appearance in *Torn Curtain*—"In *Torn Curtain* we see a progenitorial Hitchcock sitting in an armchair (suggestive of a director's chair) reacting when the infant (an extension of himself, his double, his film, his future) creates chaos in his lap." Chaos being a soggy diaper. The Gore Vidal phrase "scholar-squirrels" applies to the Hitchcockians and their nut-gathering activities as they go theme-spotting and detail-quibbling. That same issue of *Hitchcock Annual* scrutinizes *The Art of Looking in Hitchcock's Rear Window,* correcting the author for saying the newlywed husband is wearing white shorts when "he is actually wearing blue pajama bottoms." Like Trekkies, Hitchcockians have no trivia threshold.

Born in 1899, in a suburb east of London, Alfred Hitchcock was raised Catholic and educated by the Jesuits, a moral education that wedded free-floating guilt to logical rigor, a combination guaranteed to leave one clear-minded but uneasy. In his biography *Hitch: The Life and Times of Alfred Hitchcock* (1978), John Russell Taylor describes the discipline at St. Ignatius College, where corporal punishment— caning—was applied with psychological subtlety. "Once the errant child was sentenced to corporal punishment, he could choose for himself when it should be administered—first morning break, lunchtime, mid-afternoon or the end of the day. Naturally the child put off the fateful moment as long as possible, sweating all day." This desire to postpone inevitable pain as long as possible may have been the source of the delay tactics and wicked teases Hitchcock refined as a director. He made the audience wait for a violent act it both dreaded and desired.

As Hitchcock wrote in an article called "Why I Am Afraid of the Dark" (1960), "In cinematographic style, 'suspense' consists in inciting a breathless curiosity and in establishing a complicity between the director and the spectator, who knows what is going to happen." He distinguished between surprise, which makes audiences jump, and suspense, which keeps them in a state of anticipation. From an efficiency standpoint, suspense is much more time-productive. As Hitchcock explained to Peter Bogdanovich:

> You and I sit talking here and there's a bomb in the room. We're having a very innocuous conversation about nothing. Boring.

Doesn't mean a thing. Suddenly, boom! The bomb goes off and [the audience is] shocked—for fifteen seconds. Now you change it. Play the same scene, insert the bomb, show that the bomb is placed there, establish that it's going to go off at one o'clock—it's now a quarter of one, ten of one—show a clock on the wall, back to the same scene. *Now* our conversation becomes very vital, by its sheer nonsense. "Look under the table! You fool!" Now they're working for *ten minutes*, instead of being surprised for fifteen seconds.

After St. Ignatius, Hitchcock studied engineering and worked as a graphic artist in the advertising department of a manufacturing firm. Drawn to movies, he began designing title cards for Famous Players–Lasky, which set up a British production shop in 1919.

It was here that Hitchcock had his first opportunity to direct. Some of his work was filmed theater (*The Farmer's Wife*, 1928), while other movies, such as *The Lodger* (1926), had intimations of the cat-and-mouse games Hitchcock would later play in *Suspicion* (1941) and *Shadow of a Doubt* (1943). Hitchcock always maintained that silent film was invaluable schooling in how to tell stories without words, through composition, editing, and punctuating detail. He even married a film editor, Alma Reville, whose eye would prove invaluable. Silent film also brought out his resourcefulness regarding optical effects. He devised a trick shot involving a monocle in *Easy Virtue* (1927), had a glass floor built for *The Lodger* so that pacing feet could be shown from below, and developed a muralist's eye for matte backdrops. "The beauty of a matte is that you can become God," he told Bogdanovich. With the introduction of talkies, Hitchcock employed sound as an element to be used as precisely and expressively as any other film element. The lasting triumphs of Hitchcock's English period are *The Man Who Knew Too Much* (1934, remade in 1956 with Doris Day and James Stewart), *The 39 Steps* (1935), which was Phoebe Caulfield's favorite movie in *The Catcher in the Rye*, and *The Lady Vanishes* (1938). In 1938 the producer David O. Selznick invited Hitchcock to Hollywood to direct a movie based on the story of the *Titanic*, which will remain one of those great what-if projects. Hitchcock and his wife left England and relocated to Los Angeles, where he instead directed *Rebecca* (1940), the Joan Fontaine–Laurence Olivier romance, in which he thwarted Selznick's meddling designs by shooting the bare minimum of the script and leaving no alternative takes and angles for outsiders to reassemble. "Hitch's material was a jigsaw which permitted of only one solution: his" (Taylor's *Hitch*). *Rebecca*, which won the Academy Award for outstanding production, was followed by *Foreign Correspondent* (1940), in which Joel McCrea climbed into the trench coat to defend democracy. Alfred Hitchcock was on course to becoming the British institution that America would adopt as its own.

But enough chronology. The arc and highlights of Hitchcock's American career are so well known that they need no narrative recap. What interests me are the misperceptions about Hitchcock and his work which persist to this day. Re-seeing his films, I was struck by how much verbal blockage clogs the drain. Hitchcock told Truffaut, "In many of the films now being made, there is very little cinema: they are mostly what I call 'photographs of people talking.' When we tell a story in cinema, we should resort to dialogue only when it's impossible to do otherwise." Given such an emphasis on fluent storytelling, it's remarkable how often his films bog down in explanatory blather—the psychoanalytical rigmarole of *Spellbound* (1945), the tiresome business about switched keys in *Dial M for Murder* (1954), the long-winded diagnosis of Norman Bates's mother complex at the end of *Psycho* (1960). The entire script of *Rope* (1948) is a witless twitter of Broadway banter; filming it in long, continuous takes was a stunt that didn't make the movie version any less stagy. As late as *Frenzy* (1972), there are comic-relief exchanges in Hitchcock which present the actors like pheasants under glass. Clearly there was something about the enclosure of theater that satisfied Hitchcock more than he would admit.

Another myth about Hitchcock is that he was a perfectionist whose films are models of meticulous pre-production, surface plausibility, and narrative coherence. Using his celebrated storyboards (many of which are reprinted in *Hitchcock's Notebooks*), he would map out the movie like an extended comic strip. The actual filming would be a faithful transference of his sketchbook to celluloid. Hitchcock undeniably did his homework, but his homework often had a lot of holes. Reviewing *Secret Agent* (1936) in the London *Spectator*, Graham Greene noted such laughable absurdities as "the secret agent who loudly discusses his instructions in front of the hall porter of a Swiss hotel and who brandishes his only clue to a murder in a crowded casino," and lamented, "How unfortunate it is that Mr. Hitchcock, a clever director, is allowed to produce and even to write his own films, though as a producer he has no sense of continuity and as a writer he has no sense of life."

Hitchcock's work was always glitchy. The critic Manny Farber cited "a speeding car in which the only thing moving is Ingrid Bergman's overteased coiffure" in *Notorious* (1946); *Rope* has a scene in which Farley Granger, giving one of the worst performances of anyone's career as a member of a Leopold-Loeb pair, smashes a glass he's holding in a moment of fright and soon after sits down at the piano to play, both hands unbandaged (he would have been bleeding all over the keys); and Camille Paglia considered the New England accent of the shopkeeper in *The Birds* (1963), which is set in Bodega Bay, California, "a major gaffe." In Hitchcock's later work—papier-mâché puppetry of Cold War intrigue such as *Torn Curtain* (1966) and *Topaz* (1969)—the fakery (rear projections, tacky sets) showed Hitchcock unable to keep up a good front. Recording such flubs is not to engage in revisionism at Hitchcock's expense but to place his strengths and flaws in perspective. As Manny Farber wrote, "To put Hitchcock either up or down isn't the point; the point is sticking to the material as it is, rather than drooling over behind-the-camera feats of engineering."

Hitchcock's greatness is as a pictorial showman—a creator of billboards—not as a conscientious realist. With the possible exception of Michelangelo Antonioni (whom Hitchcock admired), no director has shown a greater aptitude for framing and pitting actors against architectural surroundings. Buildings in Hitchcock's films have mystery, presence. In so many post-seventies films, the intermediate zone between the actors and their backdrops—the middle distance—is rendered indistinct as directors cram in as much production-value verisimilitude as the screen will hold. In Hitchcock's films, everything is cleanly delineated, angled, emphasized, and juxtaposed. Foreground and background appear scissored and pasted against each other to create a dynamic clash. As he told Bogdanovich, "You see, the point is that you are, first of all, in a two-dimensional medium. Mustn't forget that. You have a rectangle to fill. Fill it. Compose it." He objected to having "air space" around actors' heads and bodies because it padded the screen with useless depth.

The glamorous faces of Hitchcock's stars are legendary façades set against other legendary façades, icons versus sites. A scenic tour through Hitchcock's world would include the Spanish mission in *Vertigo* (1958), groved in shadows, and the museum rooms where the lateral pan of his camera makes the walls look like sliding panels; the office building in the opening sequence of *North by Northwest* (Hitchcock's trains-planes-and-automobiles excursion, in which Cary Grant confronts every mode of transportation), whose windows reflect the streaming bustle of New York City, and the Frank Lloyd Wright-like house perched on a cliff which serves as the enemy agents' HQ, a weaponlike structure with jutting edges; the drab, almost government-issue Phoenix office Janet Leigh embezzles from in *Psycho*, and the Gothic-gingerbread bat house looming above the Bates Motel, where she meets her fate. Hitchcock also made classic use of national monuments—the Statue of Liberty in *Saboteur* (1942) and the presidential faces on Mount Rushmore, down which Cary Grant and Eva Marie Saint skitter in *North by Northwest*. Hitchcock said he wanted to have Cary Grant sneeze in Lincoln's nose. That was the limit of his impudence. Where contemporary filmmakers don't hesitate to demolish national landmarks (the White House incinerated in *Independence Day*, the Statue of Liberty's lopped head sinking underwater in *Deep Impact*), Hitchcock played with American iconography, Pop-art-style. He didn't believe in breaking his toys.

Women are the other wondrous artifices in Hitchcock's work. Not because of their physiques (he wouldn't have known how to handle Marilyn Monroe's milk-shake wiggle), but because of the trim structural integrity of their wardrobes, accented colors, accessories, and hairstyles—their glossy-magazine look. Where a sexpot flaunts her assets, a lady keeps something piquant in reserve. A woman of elegance, he wrote, will never cease to surprise you. Probably a virgin until he was twenty-five, married to the same woman his entire life, Hitchcock practiced a "Look, don't touch" form of female idolatry. Like George Balanchine with his favorite ballerinas, he was a Pygmalion with his leading ladies, fussing over every aspect of their appearance. Preparing *North by Northwest*, he sat with Eva Marie Saint at Bergdorf Goodman's as mannequins modeled outfits, quarreled with Kim Novak over the gray suit he selected in *Vertigo*, and chose a soft-green suit for Tippi Hedren in *The Birds*. He wasn't just playing pasha. The designer Edith Head said that Hitchcock had a "psychological approach to costume," a sophistication that has become almost extinct. (He also had a psychological understanding of coiffure. Seen from James Stewart's point of view, Novak's French twist in *Vertigo* resembles a nautilus shell, a small symbolic vortex.) One of the reasons Hitchcock remakes look so déclassé is that young actresses today don't know how to walk, much less dress. Compare Tippi Hedren's clicky entrance in *The Birds* (to which Camille Paglia pays honor in her book on the film) with Gwyneth Paltrow's mopey slouch in *A Perfect Murder*, the remake of *Dial M for Murder*; or Grace Kelly's pearled sophistication in *Rear Window* with Daryl Hannah's droopy deportment in Christopher Reeve's misconceived TV remake. The gold standard in blondes has been devalued since Kelly. What we have now are pretty doll heads mounted on stems—attenuated girlishness.

If Hitchcock's interest in women had been merely decorative, acquisitive, his work would have dated as badly as an old copy of *Esquire*. It hasn't. Women for him weren't pinups or figurines, but passports into unknown realms. Like Balanchine, Martha Graham, and Ingmar Bergman, Hitchcock placed women at the center of the universe, at the source of creativity, eros, and mortality. One reason that *Vertigo* becomes more haunting with age (aside from the manic-depressive attack of Bernard Herrmann's score, which harks back to Wagner and ahead to Philip Glass) is that it is perhaps the last film to treat woman as archetype and Romantic ideal. James Stewart's shattered Scottie, having lost one woman, tries to remake another in her image, telling her how to dress and fix her hair, much as Hitchcock did with his actresses. Where women in movies today seem expendable, interchangeable, their dewy replacements being bred like guppies on *Dawson's Creek*, *Vertigo*'s lyrical hunger derives from the obsessive belief that there is only one woman—one spiritual-corporeal ideal—who can salvage its hero's racked soul. The movie is a modern Orpheus myth: like Orpheus in pursuit of Eurydice, Stewart reclaims his lost love from the regions of the dead only to lose her again after a dark, treacherous ascent (for Orpheus, the steep trails leading from the underworld; for Scottie, the dizzying, telescoping stairs of the Spanish mission bell tower). For both couples, the brief reunion results in a tragic fall. "Stretching out their arms to embrace each other, they grasped only the air!" (*Bulfinch's Mythology*). The last shot of *Vertigo*, of James Stewart standing bereft with empty, useless arms, is like the final page torn from a dream.

If *Vertigo* is Hitchcock's art masterpiece, *Rear Window* is its entertainment equal. I can't think of any movie I enjoy more and get more out of each time I see it. From the blinds being raised under the credits like curtains on a three-act play, *Rear Window* is a big Broadway production transplanted to a studio set, as James Stewart's globe-trotting newsmagazine photographer L. B. Jefferies ("Jeff"), sidelined in a leg cast, clocks the comings and goings of his courtyard neighbors from his wheelchair. It's summer, windows are flung open in the un-air-conditioned city, and every apartment seems to be putting on a floor show: a dancer, whom he nicknames "Miss Torso," flings herself around to the brassy strains of Leonard Bernstein's *Fancy Free*; an aspiring songwriter in another apartment tries to bat out a hit tune; a pair of cuties sunbathe on the roof (ogled by a helicopter); a newlywed couple conducts an all out honeymoon—the husband leans on the windowsill, looking depleted—while an older couple bickers. "We've become a race of Peeping Toms," says Jeff's physical therapist, Stella (Thelma Ritter), in case we didn't get the point. That's part of the charm of *Rear Window*—it's wittily up-front about its agenda.

As George W. S. Trow notes in *My Pilgrim's Progress*, *Rear Window* is Hitchcock's most theatrical film, the cross-section of lit rooms reminiscent of urban-tenement dramas like *Dead End*. Yet it isn't stage-bound and marking time, like *Rope* or *Dial M for Murder*. The roving eye of Hitchcock's camera follows a perfect diagram across the screen as it tracks the aftermath and cover-up of a murder, creating the illusion of infinite maneuverability within an enclosed setting. Aside from a Toto-like dog who digs up the garden, a subtle nod to *The Wizard of Oz*, the movie's one Cinematic Moment arrives when Grace Kelly's golden-toned face fills the screen for the first time as she bestows a kiss on her undeserving lover, her shadow eclipsing his face like a celestial sphere. Hitchcock uses slow motion to arrest the touching of lips and lend it luxury value. He never needed to follow his lovers into the bedroom. Kisses in his films are climaxes. (Orgasmic fireworks light the sky when Cary Grant and Grace Kelly connect lips in *To Catch a Thief* [1955].)

> JEFF: *Speaking of misery, poor Miss Lonelyhearts, she drank herself*
> *asleep again, alone.*
> STELLA: *Poor soul. Ah, well, maybe one day she'll find her happiness.*
> JEFF: *Yeah.* [Pause.] *Some man will lose his.*
> —Rear Window

Voyeurism is only one of *Rear Window*'s themes; the other is marriage. Jeff and Kelly's Lisa have reached a stalemate: she wants marriage, he doesn't. A Peter Beard type with a tanned hide, Jeff considers socialite Lisa too chic, spoiled, and picture-perfect to share his life of rugged adventure. Why, she wouldn't last a moment on the front lines! "Did you ever eat fish heads and rice? . . . Those high heels, they'll be great in the jungle . . ." Stella, the audience's mouthpiece, thinks he's nuts trying to punt a great girl like Lisa, whose every gown-swirling entrance is a fashion event. Stella's tart advice, Lisa's pampering, the caged birds and newlyweds in the opening sequence, all are part of a conspiracy within the suspense machinery of the movie to undermine Jeff's obstinance—his dumb male pride. His bachelor resistance is no match for the silk web being spun around him. At the end, Lisa, having proved herself a valiant trouper, lounges triumphantly while a recuperating Jeff naps, both of his legs now in casts: her captive. Seeing he's asleep, she sets aside her book, *Beyond the High Himalayas*, which the viewer assumes she's reading for his benefit, and picks up a copy of *Harper's Bazaar*, paging through it as her name is sung on the sound track. The feminine realm has been restored to its rightful order.

The champagne afterglow of *Rear Window* is the reverse image of the romantic desolation of *Vertigo*. It's difficult to think of any director living or dead who could express either joy or abandonment with such a fine wallop, much less both. (Brian De Palma, Hitchcock's most imaginative imitator, can sow devastation—see *Blow Out* and *Casualties of War*—but is too cynical a bystander to portray bliss. He can work only one side of Love Street.) Cool operator though he may have been, Hitchcock worked both extremes of the emotional spectrum.

Unlike field-commander directors, whose ambitions lure them like siren songs toward bigger budgets, wider canvases, all-star casts, and loftier themes (Terrence Malick, for example, breaking his twenty-year sabbatical with the thick vegetation and poetic voice-overs of *The Thin Red Line*), Hitchcock wasn't afraid to divest himself of Hollywood pomp and start with a clean slate. *Psycho* was the cinema-altering product of Hitchcock's experimental primitivism; it's an exploitation film that turns into a threshing machine of Eisensteinian montage. Inspired by the box-office payoff of American International's cheap quickies, Hitchcock decided to do a cut-price horror film of his own, based on a pulp novel by Robert Bloch about a homicidal mama's boy. He and the screenwriter, Joseph Stefano, spent six weeks consulting about the film, piecing it together scene by scene, then Stefano went off and wrote. Hitchcock shot the first draft (something almost unheard of in second-guess Hollywood) with the camera unit from his TV show. The famous shower scene, which took seven days to shoot with seventy camera setups (for forty-five seconds of footage!), was done with a nude body double for Janet Leigh, since nudity didn't conform with Hitchcock's notions of proper use of a star. The movie was shot in black and white "to avoid a wash of Technicolor blood," according to *Hitch*. (That is one reason among many why Gus Van Sant's recent color reproduction was a mistake. Anne Heche's orange outfits were also an affront.)

Psycho is a half-movie which itself is divided neatly in two. The opening sequences of Janet Leigh with her lover lounging in bed after enjoying a matinee, her embezzlement and flight, the rainy drive in the dark (windshield wipers have never had such a threatening rhythm), have a classic *noir* propulsion. Once Leigh steps into the shower of her room at the Bates Motel, the movie enters a different aesthetic dimension. Shadows are banished in a white blare of hospital light. The images are wrested from their social milieu into pure abstraction. The slashing knife, which mimics the editing cuts, introduces a formal virtuosity for which the routine functionality of the embezzlement story has left the viewer totally unprepared. The shower scene isn't just a trap sprung on the unwary; it's an art piece, the shower itself an art installation—an upright sacrificial altar. The Zapruder clip of Hollywood horror, the shower scene is one of the most parodied sequences in cinema (Mel Brooks took a limp stab at it in *High Anxiety*), yet copycat versions and twenty years of slasher films have not dulled its impact.

Critics were divided on the shock tactics of *Psycho* (Dwight Macdonald called it the product of "a mean, sly, sadistic little mind"), but it was a popular smash. One of the interesting finds in the otherwise verbatim tedium of *Hitchcock's Notebooks* is that after the humiliating failure of *Torn Curtain*, a clunker starring Paul Newman and Julie Andrews (a film in which Hitchcock also had a falling-out with Bernard Herrmann), Hitchcock considered another, even bolder return to basics. In 1967, Hitchcock and the screenwriter Benn W. Levy, with whom he had collaborated on his first sound film, *Blackmail* (1929), began planning a film based on the true-life story of Neville Heath, a soft-spoken young man who seduced his victims before murdering them. Suave knockoff artists were nothing new in Hitchcock— Joseph Cotten's "Merry Widow" killer in *Shadow of a Doubt* comes to mind. What would make this treatment unique was Hitchcock's intention to shoot the film on New York City streets cinéma-vérité-style, using unknown actors in natural light and actual locales and showing bohemian nudity, like in them fancy Antonioni films. The most remarkable item is that Hitchcock planned to shoot the film with a portable camera, a radical break from his cinematic principles. As he told Bogdanovich, "Hand-held [camera] is against all the rules of cinema—cinema is montage—it's pieces of film, three frames long if you want it, placed next to other pieces of film." Handheld camera took one into Cassavetes territory, where snapping, unruly heads go in and out of focus and frame. Hitchcock hired the photographer Arthur Schatz to conduct film tests using faster color stocks by shooting a rough draft of the script. "This footage, shot without sound and, to this day, still unknown actors, is an incredible glimpse into what could have been," the author of *Hitchcock's Notebooks* writes. Had this project, originally called *Kaleidoscope*, been produced, "its brutality and cinema verité style would have been ahead of the films from this period that did break down the studios' stylized violence: *Bonnie and Clyde*, even *Easy Rider*. Here was one of cinema's greatest directors (perhaps the greatest) proposing a groundbreaking film that would have eschewed the American studio style for the kind of filmmaking Hitchcock was seeing in France and Italy."

Maybe, though you have to wonder about a script that has the half-naked protagonist, in a moment that anticipates *Beavis and Butt-Head* if nothing else, removing a pinecone lodged in his crevice. "CLOSE-UP—WILLIE'S HAND AND HIS BARE BEHIND." Even if this project weren't the world-beater conjectured by the author of *Hitchcock's Notebooks*, it would have been interesting to see Hitchcock navigate the fleshpots of hippiedom. The proposal was rejected by Universal, which understandably wanted Hitchcock to concentrate on more commercial properties. Instead, Hitchcock tackled Leon Uris's espionage novel *Topaz* and was thrown for a loss. The international cast, led by John Forsythe, appeared to be drowning in aftershave, the sets seemed constructed of office partitions, and none of the several endings shot for the film resolved the confusion. The withering reviews, perhaps the worst of Hitchcock's career, consigned him to the glue factory. "The embarrassment of *Topaz* is that Hitchcock is lazy and out of touch," Pauline Kael wrote. Hitchcock recouped some of his spent reputation with *Frenzy* (1972) and *Family Plot* (1976), pictures that were patted on the head by the favorably inclined when they were released but look wobbly today. Although he continued to sketch out possible films to direct, Hitchcock slowly withdrew into himself, hampered by alcohol and the infirmities of old age, re-emerging to collect honorary awards. (Incredibly, he never won a best-director Academy Award.) He was knighted in 1980, and died in his sleep on April 29 of that same year. His wife, Alma, died two years later.

There's always an unaccountable factor to genius, a shadow area which is never resolved. Fittingly, for a man who made detective films, Hitchcock left behind a lot of clues. Of all his motifs and signature strokes (staircases, keys, birds), the one I find most intriguing is his fascination with falling. Steep falls were his dramatic crescendos. There is a beautiful mountain fall in *Secret Agent*, the death plunge of the Fascist agent from the Statue of Liberty in *Saboteur*, James Stewart's plummeting from ledges in *Rear Window* and *Vertigo*, Eva

Maric Saint's slipping down Mount Rushmore in *North by Northwest,* and Martin Balsam's backward tumble in *Psycho.* The falls are usually photographed from a high angle, the camera often focusing on hands clutching one another for dear life, the figure dropping or about to drop into a whirlpool abyss. (The director Jonathan Demme constructed a whole neo-Hitchcockian thriller around this desperate tug of outstretched hands in his 1979 film, *Last Embrace.*) What do these swoons signify? They occur too often and too vividly in Hitchcock to be mere plot devices. Let's ask the Big Guy.

"Dreams of falling are more frequently characterized by anxiety," Sigmund Freud writes in *The Interpretation of Dreams.* "Their interpretation, when they occur in women, offers no difficulty, because they nearly always accept the symbolic meaning of falling, which is a circumlocution for giving way to an erotic temptation." In Hitchcock's case, fear of falling may symbolize loss of control, letting go. His career was based upon fixing all the variables of filmmaking in advance and leaving nothing to chance, and he personally shied away from confrontation or intrusion that might have had awkward, unforeseen results. He was incapable of hailing his own taxi without becoming white with terror. Physically soft, inwardly unbudgeable, Hitchcock was a meek control freak who plowed himself into his work and used courtesy and "amusing" anecdotes to maintain a protective zone. A supreme sublimator, he made the most of his repressions and avoidance maneuvers—he transformed them into psychosexual cliffhangers and paranoid chases that filled the screen. His movies seem bright and shiny on the surface, jet-age fantasies and merchandise, and yet here we are, on the eve of his one hundredth birthday, still peeling away layers, as if hoping to find encoded messages under the film emulsion. Like Edgar Allan Poe, Alfred Hitchcock is the most obvious of thrill vendors, and the most stubbornly cryptic. Ravens belong on both men's shoulders, perched forevermore.

Vanity Fair, April 1999

New York *Noir*

I love this dirty town.

—J. J. Hunsecker in *Sweet Smell of Success*

Although it had its roots in German Expressionism and the private-eye novel, *film noir* fully emerged like a walking hangover after World War II, a haunted shadow rising from Europe's bombed-out rubble and Japan's radioactive ash—a slice of death drawn from a larger annihilation. Unlike the lusher Hollywood productions of the period, where the light was evenly dispensed and the actors perfectly placed, *noir* had a morbid bent, emphasizing deep focus, skewed camera angles, rain-slick streets, clouded obscurity (smoke, steam, fog), Kafkaesque compositions (a lone figure seated at the end of a long table), and high-contrast black and white. An urban art, like jazz, graffiti, and pulp fiction, *noir* had a neurotic propulsion perfect for the pulse of New York. After all, New York City is the world capital of neurosis—it's almost a matter of civic pride. Freud's late-nineteenth-century Vienna was a mere farm system for the major-league jitters Manhattan came to symbolize in the twentieth century. The city itself stretches across its island slab like a patient on a psychiatrist's couch. The hectic pace, the jarring noise, the struggle for success and the fear of failure, the daily collision of so many smart mouths and hyperactive, hyperanalytical brains—all contribute to the average turnstiler's restless unease. So much thwarted effort is put into daily survival that, as the journalist Seymour Krim wrote, the old idea of peaceful death seems farcical. "All that energy and foxiness spent for nothing? . . . I maintain that every death today is violent." Spoken like a true New Yorker.

As the first port of call for millions of immigrants, New York had a more pronounced sense of uprootedness than Los Angeles, the West Coast capital of *noir*. L.A. *noirs* like *The Big Sleep* and *Double Indemnity* are set in deceptively peaceful groves and quiet bungalows where the corruption and violence snake like evil into paradise. The brush fires in a Ross Macdonald novel carry the same judgment of fire and brimstone on Paradise Debauched that Nathanael West conjured in *The Day of the Locust*. New York never possessed this garden innocence. If anything, it's nature that seems unnatural in Manhattan, Central Park implanted like a green heart in its stony torso. An L.A. *noir* is a horizontal narrative, a serpentine search through beautiful burial grounds; a N.Y. *noir* is a vertical spiral, a climb from the crummy basement to a penthouse view (or vice versa).

Although one New York *noir* was set at the Metropolitan Museum of Art (*Crack-Up*, 1946), another in an office building (*The Big Clock*, 1948)—and let's not forget Chester Himes's Harlem—*noir* is largely a downtown affair. Times Square is the generally agreed-upon cutoff area. At Times Square and below, we find the architectural necessities for *film noir*—a surplus of derelict industrial space (warehouses, underground garages, vacant lots), seedy transient hotels (where even in black and white the lampshades look age-stained yellow), Edward Hopper–esque diners, boxing gyms, nightclubs, pool halls, shoeshine stands. The *noir* city is not the under-construction part of town ready to greet the challenge of tomorrow. It's the atavistic, deadbeat part of town that progress has left behind, where losers, scroungers, and those who prey on them ply their trades. In these dark pockets, the unconscious drives have yet to be civilized. (Which is why the Flatiron Building, with its phallic lift, will always be a *noir* landmark.)

Since the unconscious is often symbolized by water (a liquid bed which swallows its own secrets), many of the New York *noirs* begin or end at bridges and piers. In Jules Dassin's *The Naked City* (1948), which is like a slide show of Andreas Feininger cityscapes narrated by the movie's producer, Mark Hellinger ("The city is quiet now, but it will soon be pounding with activity"), the killer dumps a body off a pier and then is himself tracked down and picked off from the top of the Williamsburg Bridge. Dana Andrews also disposes of a stiff at the docks in *Where the Sidewalk Ends* (1950). In Sam Fuller's *Pickup on South Street* (1953), the pickpocket played by Richard Widmark lives in a waterfront shack, where he keeps his beer cool by submerging it in a case attached to a rope. The common-man spokesmodel for *noir*, Mickey Spillane, opens his Mike Hammer novel *One Lonely Night* (1951) with the sentence "Nobody ever walked across the bridge, not on a night like this," creating a scene of mist, lamplike faces, and latent menace that Ayn Rand would cite as a prize piece of descriptive prose. "I walked and I smoked and I flipped the spent butts ahead of me and watched them arch to the pavement and fizzle out with one last wink." The cigarettes add up when you're waiting to pump some louse full of hot lead.

According to Paul Schrader in his indispensable 1972 essay "Notes on *Film Noir*," *film noir* went through three overlapping phases (the private-eye case/the urban-corruption exposé/the crazed-psycho rampage), peaking in 1955 with Robert Aldrich's wild-man adaptation of Spillane's *Kiss Me Deadly*, which transplanted Mike Hammer (Ralph Meeker) to the West Coast, where a beach house served as the barbecue spot of an atomic blast. With its modern-ape hero, more of a forward-motion machine than a true sleuth (searching for the "great whatzit," Hammer studies every clue as if it had lodged in his paw), *Kiss Me Deadly* packed a primitive wallop while remaining kinetically stylized. Whereas so many of the most notable *films noirs* (*The Naked City*, Anthony Mann's *T-Men*) are minor genre pieces, with anonymous-looking actors, procedural footwork, and instruction-manual dialogue, their chiaroscuro moments opening like magic caverns in the midst of their cardboard constructions, *Kiss Me Deadly* was go-man-go bongo-crazy from its opening titles. Aldrich directed as if each shot were a sneaky uppercut. Instead of femmes fatales in black stockings, *Kiss Me Deadly*'s women were dazed kooks in loose wraps suffering from feline shell shock. The movie's deadpan delirium and bravura nihilistic climax temporarily finished off the *noir* form. An atomic holocaust is a pretty tough act to top.

New York was still a tabloid town, even with the Times *running the show.*
          —Mickey Spillane, *Black Alley* (1996)

The spirit of New York *noir* migrated into other movies, where it mutated and flamboyantly decayed. The neurotic tension which once spiked the atmosphere became a full-blown airborne virus in films directed by Sidney Lumet and Elia Kazan, among others. As the critic Manny Farber noted, "The New York films, which make an almost useless item of the camera, are carried to popularity by the pop-pop-pop type of masochistic acting, which is usually in the hands of Strasberg-influenced performers." In the fifties, Method acting plus Freudian motivation blotted out the charcoal-sketch beauties of New York with overactive faces and sweaty salesmanship. Easily the best of these antsy eye-openers was *Sweet Smell of Success* (1957), in which evil-incarnate tabloid columnist J. J. Hunsecker (Burt

Lancaster) sinks his poisonous fangs into the virgin flesh of Martin Milner and Susan Harrison, the drippiest of virtuous twosomes; as the press agent Sidney Falco ("a cookie full of arsenic"), Tony Curtis gave his verviest performance ever—his needy, opportunistic eyes are the real stars of the film. Shot by the legendary James Wong Howe, *Sweet Smell of Success* opens by following a delivery truck through Times Square (one shot has us inside the truck), then makes the nightclub rounds with its Walter Winchell–ish godfather of gossip. What makes *Sweet Smell of Success* unique in the annals of New York *noir* is the often hilarious hard-boiled verbosity of its screenplay, by Clifford Odets and Ernest Lehman (sample line: "A press agent eats a columnist's dirt and is expected to call it manna"), which is like a John O'Hara nightclub story played at 78 rpm. Even the films made from O'Hara's fiction didn't evoke his sour-ball expertise as did this cold shower of cynicism, which ends with Falco getting roughed up by the police in front of the George M. Cohan monument while a flock of pigeons take flight. Dawn has never looked so gray and dingy.

As more and more movies were made in color, New York began to take on a powdery tint in romances like *Breakfast at Tiffany's* and *The Best of Everything*, and a broad-daylight junk-heap grit in crime dramas like *Serpico, Coogan's Bluff,* and *The French Connection.* These latter films looked like sociology in action, bearing an affinity more to cinderblock TV cop shows like *Kojak* and *M Squad* than to the atmospheric *noirs* of the postwar era. Woody Allen's movies, even those in black and white like *Manhattan* and *Stardust Memories* (with interiors so dim you need a miner's helmet lamp to locate the actors), don't qualify as *noirs*—they have the enclosed jabber of plays. They're not mood pieces, but Ping-Pong tournaments between talkers.

Black had a meaning. It wasn't death. Black didn't represent death no matter what they told you. Grey represented death. Black was the color of ignorance.

—Mickey Spillane, *Black Alley*

It was Martin Scorsese who returned *noir* to New York. Francis Ford Coppola and his cinematographer Gordon Willis may have shrouded the screen in *The Godfather*, but it was a gangster-family saga, and *noirs* are about momentary contact between isolated characters. Asthmatic and cooped up as a child, Scorsese has always been more in tune with isolation than the sociable Coppola. His breakthrough feature, *Mean Streets*, had streaks of *noir* in its impasto of neo-realism; *After Hours*, a black comedy about a hapless yuppie (Griffin Dunne) tunneling through downtown nightlife, revealed the siren slut-pout appeal of Linda Fiorentino (which would be fully exploited in *The Last Seduction*); and *Raging Bull*, shot in black and white, was *Body and Soul* without the soul—a slob slugfest. His *New York, New York* was an old-fashioned Vincente Minnelli–like musical (an homage which encompassed casting Liza Minnelli as Robert De Niro's co-star) suffused with modern disillusionment: a bright smile concealing dark fillings. Scorsese's definitive *noir* statement is, of course, *Taxi Driver* (1976). Its opening shot—a cab whooshing through manhole steam to the swoony blare of Bernard Herrmann's score—established the doomy monotony of making the nocturnal rounds in the urban underworld. In De Niro's Travis Bickle (cabbie by night, nutcase by day), the neurotic loner has hardened into a pathological cipher, acquiring high-powered weaponry and trying out his tough-guy identity in the mirror ("You talkin' to me?"). The movie was made with the knowledge that any two-bit punk could knock off a president, or, failing that, a presidential hopeful. It's a throwback to the third, "psycho" phase of *noir* designated by Paul Schrader, which isn't surprising, since Schrader wrote the screenplay for *Taxi Driver*. Although some of the movie's plot points ring wrong (such as the prudish Bickle taking his date to a porn film) and the final bloodbath is overly stagy, *Taxi Driver* is an invaluable time capsule of seventies New York on the verge of a nervous breakdown. Its lower-depths images of a city have a volcanic verismo. The movie marquees which exploded with white neon in the photographs of William Klein and Louis Faurer are signposts to hell here.

Watching *Taxi Driver* today, one is aware of how much the midtown urbanscape has changed for the better since then. We're not used to improvement in New York—it takes some mental adjusting. Yet it's undeniable: Times Square is no longer the carny Sodom of midnight cowboys, Larry Clark chicken hawks, milk-white whores with blue bruises, and bell-bottomed pimps; the Port Authority Bus Terminal is no longer the fluorescent catacomb of the living dead. Most of the porn theaters and fleabag hotels are as extinct now as the Automats and pawnshops of forties *noirs*. The cabbie hangout in the film, the Belmore Cafeteria, where Peter Boyle offers Bickle advice, closed years ago. Travis Bickle's New York has become a historical figment.

The neo-*noirs* inspired by Scorsese have none of his feverishness and obsessive membrane. They're movies modeled upon other movics rather than ripped from raw life—"attitude" exercises which are closer to Cindy Sherman playing dress-up than Weegee blasting a bunch of potato faces with the flashbulb of his Speed Graphic. The remakes of classic *noirs*—*D.O.A.*, *Kiss of Death*, *Night and the City*, Scorsese's own sadism workout in *Cape Fear*, all of the Jim Thompson adaptations save *The Grifters*—seem gelatinous and gabby compared with the originals. Neo-*noirs* such as *The Last Seduction*, *City of Industry*, and whatever weirdness Abel Ferrara is trying to foist aren't much better, fetishizing the signature mannerisms of *noir* until they become camp (every smoked cigarette becoming a seminar in advanced blow-job technique). It'll take another movie or two before we know whether Quentin Tarantino has anything more than a gift for pop pastiche. One of the few neo-*noirs* to connect emotionally is the mistitled *Bulletproof Heart*, in which Anthony LaPaglia plays a soul-sick hit man and Mimi Rogers his intended victim, who longs for death with voluptuous languor. The deep coloration of the movie expresses its thick, clotted passion, and the final scene is a fatal kiss-off worthy of a forties *noir:* the limp Rogers in her lover's arms as a motorboat heads toward the dock, as if to convey her across the river Styx. *Noir* remains the domain of those who have made an appointment with death.

Vanity Fair, July 1997

The Executioners

You babies make me sick. To you youngsters, the seventies were some kind of joke, one long *Brady Bunch* flashback where white people disgraced themselves and a once great nation by adopting flared jeans, leisure suits, glitter pumps, and Farrah flips, and black folks were no better, with their rain-forest Afros, ruffled shirts, and clanking medallion necklaces. You sit in a window seat at Starbucks, "journaling" into your laptop and daydreaming about that cute blouse Carrie wore on *Sex and the City*, confident that the seventies are just TV and movie nostalgia fodder, their ugly hand-me-downs and sappy cheer good for a chuckle. But to those of us who were there, the seventies were anything but a Cowsills medley. They were mean, scruffy, ratty, riddled with lost illusions, and embittered from the lies and failures of the Vietnam War. The rusty infrastructure was breaking down like the last groan of the dinosaur age. A sense of lawlessness seeped from the White House, where the Watergate coverup cost Richard Nixon his presidency, to the streets, where criminals (conservatives claimed) were being treated as a protected species, coddled by liberal guilt and legal technicalities—particularly the reading of Miranda rights. You'd ride the New York subway just hoping to reach your destination, hell, any destination, suffering claustrophobia from the graffiti-sprayed windows, the lights blinking on and off like a submarine under attack, staring impassively ahead as predators loped from car to car, stalking prey. Urban neighborhoods degenerated into bombed-out, garbage-burning, no-go areas under siege (John Carpenter's 1976 film, *Assault on Precinct 13*, re-staged *Fort Apache* at a Los Angeles police station). Central Park became Club Med for muggers.

Every social disease breeds its cultural antidote, and in the seventies a new kind of antihero rose to play rat exterminator for a country too hamstrung and scared to stand up for itself. He was the movie vigilante, and he went under a number of guises: Billy Jack, Buford Pusser, Dirty Harry, Travis Bickle, Charles Bronson's lone gunman in *Death Wish*, Dustin Hoffman's cuckold husband in *Straw Dogs*.

The message of these films: Push a man too far and the screen will be Jackson Pollocked with blood. It only takes one warrior to turn the tide.

By strict dictionary definition, a vigilante isn't a solo avenger but a member of a committee—a citizens' posse that assumes the powers of apprehending and punishing criminals, meting out its own brand of frontier justice to rustlers and varmints. This sometimes led to innocent victims hanging from a noose. The boozy, hothead barbarity of the lynch mob was a staple in movie Westerns, perhaps the purest example being the classic cautionary tale *The Ox-Bow Incident* (1943). The Western also fostered the masculine mystique of rugged individualism, where the only way to defeat bad guys and restore order was to take the law into your own hands (especially if those wearing badges were themselves in the pay of the local barons, or just plain "yellow"). This countertradition gave us the savior with the quick draw who materialized on the horizon just when needed most, the peacemaker as apostle, such as Alan Ladd's Shane.

In *Billy Jack* (1971), the eponymous hero—a half-breed Indian and Vietnam vet (a former Green Beret, no less) played by Tom Laughlin, who had introduced the character in a biker film called *The Born Losers*—mysteriously rides out of the woods to save a herd of horses from being slaughtered by a fat-cat rancher and local officials. He tells them they're illegally on Indian land. "We've got the law here, Billy Jack," the rancher says, to which Billy Jack replies, encapsulating the vigilante credo: "When policemen break the law, then there isn't any law, just a fight for survival." A strange but potent blend of *Shane*, shamanism, civil-rights activism, role-playing skits, Jungian archetypes, and drive-in melodrama, *Billy Jack* was perhaps the first New Age Western, appealing to countercultural heads and thrill junkies alike. It also had a feminist consciousness that went against the grain of the action genre, which runs on testosterone. In *The New Yorker*, Pauline Kael singled out the scene in which a rape victim articulated her sense of violation for conveying a plainspoken emotional candor never before expressed on-screen. Men may have been women's protectors, Billy Jack recognized, but they were also their brutalizers.

Kael apart, most critics ignored or disregarded the film, whose success was a genuine populist phenomenon back when such a thing was still possible—when a potboiler could excite audiences on a regional circuit before the New York or Los Angeles papers could pronounce judgment. (Today, a "sleeper film" is more likely to be a Sundance entry anointed by the entertainment press based on the decibel level of cell-phone gab after the first screening.) The offbeat attack of Billy Jack wasn't duplicated in the talky, stilted, agitprop sequels, the last of which, *Billy Jack Goes to Washington*, was a notorious dog never released theatrically. But there were other vigilante movies on the warpath. An even cruder incendiary device was *Walking Tall* (1973), starring Joe Don Baker as Buford Pusser, a former wrestler who returns with his family to a rural southern town and finds that the scenic hamlet he once knew has become an illicit honky-tonk. Whores in hot pants turning tricks in trailers, redneck casinos being run in back rooms, black folks getting liquored up on illegal moonshine—this ain't no fit place to raise young'uns! When Pusser tussles with the goons at a sin shack called the Lucky Spot, he's overpowered, brutally carved up with a knife, dumped in a ravine, and left to die. He saves himself by crawling through the rain to flag down a passing trucker. It takes two hundred stitches to sew up his ravaged torso.

Now they've really got Buford riled. He doesn't go bawling for a lawyer like some privileged brat. He whittles himself a hunk of wood and proceeds to clean up this backwoods Babylon by swinging his big stick like a baseball bat, eventually becoming sheriff. He's the Sultan of Swat, the Babe Ruth of whup-ass. Unlike the showdowns in *Billy Jack*, which have an exciting buildup, choreography, and tactical finesse, the brawls here are a one-man stampede through whatever obstacle course of beer bellies and breakable furniture are set in Buford's path. Few tacky anticlimaxes can top *Walking Tall*'s, where the angry townspeople leave the funeral of Pusser's slain wife and converge on the Lucky Spot, ripping out its gaming tables and building a bonfire pile as a grieving, incapacitated Buford watches, blubbing with gratitude. (This spontaneous uprising is staged with all the furor and excitement of a half-price sale at Carpet Barn.) Then, reflecting somebody's idea of class, in wafts the voice of Johnny Mathis as he croons the film's sound track theme, his archangel vibrato never sounding more absurd or inopportune.

Despite this dumbo finale, *Walking Tall* was hugely popular, and not just with backyard barbecuers. It was a guilty pleasure among some cineasts, who considered it a deranged cousin to the rural B-movies of the fifties. The movie had a major asset in Joe Don Baker, whose sideburns and greasy, likable rockabilly grin suggest a larger doughnut version of Elvis Presley. (The sequels to *Walking Tall* starred Bo Svenson, who had none of Joe Don Baker's juicy appetite.) Although *Walking Tall* alarmed liberals with a scene where Sheriff Pusser pummels a suspect as he Mirandizes him ("You got the right not to make a statement without a lawyer"—*wham!*), it, like *Billy Jack*, stood up for the underdog and defied racial prejudice: the razzing, fraternal relationship between Pusser and his black deputy was handled with none of the Hollywood hoo-ha of, say, *In the Heat of the Night. Walking Tall* packed a progressive message in a Popeye can of spinach.

> *I know what you're thinking. "Did he fire six shots, or only five?" Well, to tell you the truth, in all this excitement I've kinda lost track myself. But being this is a .44 magnum, the most powerful handgun in the world, and would blow your head clean off, you've got to ask yourself one question. "Do I feel lucky?" Well, do you, punk?*
> —Clint Eastwood, *Dirty Harry* (1971)

As phallic enforcer, Pusser's bat was rivaled only by the long-barreled persuader extolled by Eastwood in Don Siegel's subversive ode to a modern-day gunslinger. Where *Billy Jack* didactically, idealistically preached a love gospel as it flocked the screen with lustrously shampooed folksinging chicks (one of them Laughlin's real-life daughter, who later sang the excruciating final song in *Billy Jack Goes to Washington*), *Dirty Harry* reflected Hollywood's horror at the Tate-Sebring murders of 1969—the realization that hippiedom bred its own nests of hateful scavengers. The motiveless malignancy in Siegel's film is a Charles Manson sicko called Scorpio (done with drooling abandon by Andy Robinson), who wears a peace-symbol belt buckle, a nasty irony that doubled as a provocation to those itching to attack the movie as reactionary propaganda—an instrument of Nixonian crackdown.

Even those politically and morally repulsed by *Dirty Harry* had to acknowledge its cinematic prowess. A master of the long shot in *The Lineup* (1958) and the crazy adaptation of Hemingway's *The Killers* (1964; the first made-for-TV movie, it was shown in theaters after NBC balked at its violence, including a scene that unintentionally evoked President Kennedy's assassination, which had taken place during production), Siegel used the telephoto lens in *Dirty Harry* like a spectacular trombone. Having no more regard for Miranda rights than Pusser, Harry interrogates the killer in an empty football stadium by grinding his foot into the perp's wounded, bleeding leg as he whimpers for a lawyer. As Scorpio bellows in agony the camera pulls back in a bravura reverse zoom that soars skyward until all we see is a bowl of hazy light floating in darkness. (Following this visual coup is Eastwood's mournful silhouette at dawn as the nude body of Scorpio's victim is lifted from a sewer opening.) Lawyers and judges being somewhat picky about torture, the confession is tossed, releasing the psychokiller to the streets and leaving Harry no alternative but to wipe this human stain off the landscape. One of the film's clever ruses is that Eastwood's rogue cop is constantly accused of being a loose cannon and mad-dog menace, yet it's the supposed representatives of reason and due process who are squawking, irate, and red-faced, while Eastwood maintains his lean, laconic cool. (He's very funny foiling a bank robbery while chomping on a hot dog, not missing a beat.) It's this shrewd micromanagement of facial resources that resulted in the nickname "Clint the Squint."

A sneaky touch of subversion might have added ironic shadings to *Death Wish* (1974) and its sequels, which presented another chipped sculpture, Charles Bronson, his "geological impassivity" (in the critic David Thomson's apt phrase) ennobled by suffering-animal eyes and a surprisingly gentle voice. The joke used to be that a neoconservative was a liberal who had been mugged, and in *Death Wish* the joke is taken to savage extreme. Bronson was improbably cast as a "bleeding-heart liberal"—an architect by profession—who becomes a one-man militia after his wife and daughter are viciously, merrily assaulted by a gang of droogies (one of them played by a goofy young Jeff Goldblum in a Jughead cap). The wife is murdered and the daughter left catatonic after being sexually assaulted and desecrated, her naked bottom spray-painted by her laughing tormentors as the camera itself seems to be lurching around on some acid trip. After such horror-show incitement, how can the audience be anything but psyched for Bronson's scum-removal campaign? Directed by Michael Winner, an unimaginative meat grinder whose credits include such charmers as *The Mechanic*, *The Stone Killer*, *Scream for Help*, and *The Big Sleep* (the worst-ever Raymond Chandler adaptation, with Robert Mitchum glacially drifting through the shamus role as if taking the title literally), *Death Wish* is the one vigilante movie that seems an undiluted act of cynicism and demagoguery, every scene rigged for maximum vile effect. (Winner's idea of comic relief: a shot of a transvestite picking his nose at a diner.) With each sequel, Bronson's quest for vengeance and street justice became more contorted and arbitrary: *Death Wish V* has him warring with "the fashion mafia," and I think we all know what sociopaths they can be, raising and lowering hemlines at whim.

Death Wish spawned dozens of movie clones, but its greatest impact came offscreen. In the film, Bronson iced a couple of cruds who had tried to rob him on a conveniently empty train. On December 22, 1984, the scene was replayed for real. An electronics technician named Bernhard Goetz, who seemed to have "patsy" written all over him, was accosted on the New York subway by four black youths hassling him for money. Instead of handing over his wallet, Goetz drew a .38-caliber Smith & Wesson and methodically shot all four, standing over the body of one victim and reportedly saying, "You don't look so bad, here's another"—then firing another round. The "Subway Vigilante" became a folk hero, especially on AM talk radio. (Bob Grant, on WABC at the time, sounded as if he had a grenade pin clenched in his teeth as he snarled on behalf of Goetz.) That the shooter was white and his victims black added gasoline to the controversy—and a racial division that was a preview of the O.J. trial.

In Martin Scorsese's *Taxi Driver* (1976), the vigilante theme found its grand-opera composer and conductor. It was the culmination of the seventies vigilante wave, its Wagnerian aria and *Summa Theologica*, a character study of a homicidal cipher for whom only violence can fill the vacuum. Cabbie by night, trainee marauder by day, Robert De Niro's Travis Bickle is the classic nobody who makes a name for himself by blasting his way onto the front pages—the sort of soft-spoken psycho who, after he's committed a massacre, is inevitably described in the papers as "a quiet loner who kept to himself." The operating irony of Paul Schrader's script is that Bickle pursues infamy by stalking a presidential candidate, only to shift direction and achieve glory by lavishly slaughtering a pimp and his goons, the message being that the sole difference between a Lee Harvey Oswald and a vigilante hero is the choice of victims. Kill the right people, and society lionizes you. This intellectual conceit, attached to Scorsese's virtuoso technique, De Niro's pencil-sharp persona, and Bernard Herrmann's bombastic score, gave *Taxi Driver* a premium quality other vigilante movies didn't have. Everything lowbrow, blatant, crudely motivated, and thin-textured about *Billy Jack, Walking Tall, Dirty Harry*, and *Death Wish* is aestheticized, pathologized, and dipped in cherry, hellish, bordello red. The racism—the fear of black crime—implicit in so many vigilante films is made snarlingly explicit here. "The movie relishes getting blacks off as malevolent debris that proliferates on the streets. Everywhere the cab moves there is a black marker representing the scummiest low point of city life," Manny Farber and Patricia Patterson wrote in an essay entitled "The Power and the Gory" (reprinted in the expanded edition of Farber's *Negative Space*). They also note that the movie insulates De Niro from the racist smog and keeps him relatively sympathetic by apportioning all of the bristling comments about "niggers" and "jungle bunnies" to the other white characters. "It's [also] not Travis who talks about blowing a woman's pussy with a .44 Magnum." He may be a ticking time bomb, but he's also a gent.

Acclaimed almost unanimously as a masterpiece, *Taxi Driver* seems to me willed, overcontrolled, and schematic—a museum tour of the inferno, stocked with colorful freaks. The movie is heady with the exhaust fumes of its own mythmaking, self-consciously laying on the decadence—a flashy pimp (Harvey Keitel, jiving like the last of the zoot-suiters) and his jailbait princess (Jodie Foster)—and orchestrating the climactic bloodbath as if it were Ravel's *Bolero*. I much prefer the ruthless efficiency and sardonic underplay of *Dirty Harry*. The inadvertent value of *Taxi Driver* is its documentary interest as a time-capsule record of Times Square in the falling-apart seventies. The cesspool panorama of prostitution, rampant drug dealing, architectural dilapidation, and nomadic squalor seen through the windshield of Bickle's taxi is a rebuke to those who romanticize the trashy heyday of Times Square and decry its Disneyfication. Apart from the scenes at Murray Hill's Belmore Cafeteria, a favorite late-night hangout for cabbies and a long-gone landmark, there's nothing here worth being nostalgic about. *Taxi Driver*'s Midtown is a pre-Giuliani mess.

The crime drop in New York under Rudolph Giuliani's mayoral reign was the most visible crest of a nationwide trend as felony rates fell in city after city. Sociologists and criminologists differ over the most salient factor—was it improved policing techniques (such as reversing civic decay by enforcing "quality of life" statutes regarding panhandling, turnstile jumping, etc.), demographic shifts, a booming economy (which spread gentrification to once dangerous neighborhoods), or the crack scourge of the eighties burning itself out like a self-cleaning oven?—but whatever the cause(s), vigilantism receded as a collective gut response. It was no longer necessary, offscreen or on: TV police procedurals such as *Law and Order* and *NYPD Blue* offered weekly confirmation that the good guys were getting the job done. Movie addicts had to import their vigilante eruptions from the Tokyo and Hong Kong action markets, where every film seems like a Quentin Tarantino festival.

[My] deepest reason for hating vigilante films so strenuously is that I'm a rather vindictive person, obsessed with my own impotence, and that I'm drawn to them.
                    —David Edelstein, movie columnist of *Slate*

The movie whose tractor beam Edelstein was resisting with every weak ounce of willpower is *In the Bedroom*, which another reviewer described as "a granola *Death Wish*." But does it truly qualify as a vigilante film? Directed by Todd Field, this study of a married couple (Sissy Spacek and Tom Wilkinson) who desire to avenge the murder of their son sounds like an arty, intensified upgrade of all those Lifetime cable movies about suburban turmoil that are always said to be "based on a true story." From the lyrical transports and fainting spells in the rave reviews, I expected *In the Bedroom* to be a slow-burning, inescapable pressure cooker that built to the bursting fury of Sam Peckinpah's survivalist tract *Straw Dogs* (1972), where Dustin Hoffman's nerdy mathematician reverts to primitive instinct defending a house under siege. (The sweaty rape of his wife, played by Susan George, and the slashing carnage of its human cockfight have a low erotic cunning, razory precision, and shattered beauty that make Peckinpah's reputation among the most unresolvable in movies.) Adapted from a short story by Andre Dubus, *In the Bedroom* is more of a liberal-humanist, literary-sensibility, conscientious craftwork in which the characters are so pristinely drawn they seem like exquisite art-house replications of "real people." (A minority opinion, I admit. I also felt the same way about last year's art-house pet *You Can Count on Me*.) I don't mind a movie's being deliberate, but sitting through *In the Bedroom* as it documented the emotional journey from shock and grief to anger and revenge was like watching a lawn being planted blade by individual blade. The movie will deservedly rack up awards—the acting and direction are impeccable—but it's too much of a chamber piece and prose poem to kick-start a vigilante-movie revival . . .

Vanity Fair, April 2002

Rock Hudson and Doris Day

Lovers Come Back

Now that artists and audiences have defected to the Dark Side—joining clammy hands in a graveyard shift that includes the fiction of Stephen King, Anne Rice, and Joyce Carol Oates, TV's *The X-Files* and *Buffy the Vampire Slayer*, meat-locker films such as *Seven*, *The Silence of the Lambs*, and *Fight Club*, the mime-faced goth of Marilyn Manson and pro wrestling's Sting—what could seem more out of cultural sync, more Republican, than the romantic comedies of Doris Day and Rock Hudson? Even in their heyday, when *Pillow Talk* (1959), *Lover Come Back* (1961), and *Send Me No Flowers* (1964) made them the country's top box-office team, they were considered synthetic material. It was only too apt that the production of *Pillow Talk* coincided with the creation of Barbie and Ken, doll versions of Doris and Rock. Born Doris Von Kappelhoff in 1924, Doris Day graduated from a successful band singer into a blonde chipmunk in the June Allyson mold, a nice girl-next-door type who provided a pert alternative to Marilyn Monroe's creamy overflow. (A favorite quip was "I knew Doris Day before she was a virgin.") Born Roy Harold Scherer Jr. in 1925, Rock Hudson was a sex symbol built to spec in the Hollywood factory. Together, their sex appeal was so merchandisable—her sunny disposition and his toothpaste sparkle so reflective of space-age affluence—that one critic compared their bodies in bed to a pair of parked Cadillacs. Set in a *Breakfast at Tiffany's* Manhattan of martinis, fur muffs, and rat-race bustle (personified by perennial sidekick Tony Randall, with his upset stomach and head-gripping hangovers), the Doris Day–Rock Hudson comedies were among the last holdouts of light sophistication—good clean froth—before the sexual revolution released all of the swingers from the monkey house. Once everything got tribal in the sixties, it was over for the strictly natty. Barbie and Ken could at least update their outfits. Doris and Rock in bugaloo hair and matching bell-bottoms? Unthinkable. No, they were stuck like decals to the era they toasted.

But that era knew how to sell itself. Like Frank Sinatra's upbeat work with Nelson Riddle, Alfred Hitchcock's *North by Northwest*, and

John Frankenheimer's *The Manchurian Candidate*, the films of Doris Day and Rock Hudson have kept their crease and slant. They marshal a spiffy attack which has withstood violent upheavals in fashion and cultural noise levels. Clever, brassy, and stylishly groomed, *Pillow Talk* and *Lover Come Back* (*Send Me No Flowers* is more problematic) are near-perfect valentines. To create a brand-name category on the basis of just two first-rate films is no small doing—people still refer to the Doris Day–Rock Hudson comedies as if they were a long-running franchise, like the *Thin Man* series. I find Doris and Rock more engaging than *The Thin Man*'s Myrna Loy and William Powell, whose screwball banter now sounds ticker-tape and smug, and far superior to Katharine Hepburn and Spencer Tracy, whose movies (such as the Runyonesque *Pat and Mike* and the stagy *Desk Set*) strike me as creaky, talky, and dated. Doris and Rock seem to be more modern now than they did then—they throw off more light, there's more to read in their relationship. I think they're the best romantic-comedy team ever. That they made it look easy is a testament to hard work and sublimation.

Rock

When the future star was five years old, his father left home to find work in California. It was 1930, early in the Depression. His father pledged to reunite the family later, once he was solvent. After two years of waiting and receiving little word, Roy junior and his mother, Katherine, made a bus trip halfway across the country to urge Dad to come home, only to be told, no dice. His new life didn't include them. The bus ride back was like a funeral drive. Katherine divorced and remarried, her second husband a former Marine named Wallace Fitzgerald, who enforced domestic order with his fists, beating his wife and stepson when he had a snootful. Mom had her own manner of pulling rank on her son. "All you had to do, she confided, was to tell him he was stupid. That upset him so much, it was enough to bring him into line," Jerry Oppenheimer and Jack Vitek wrote in their biography of Hudson, *Idol* (Villard, 1986). After leaving the navy in 1946, Roy Fitzgerald, as he was now called, moved to Los Angeles, where he sold vacuum cleaners, made deliveries, and stood around looking studly. Attending a casting call at David Selznick Productions, he was recruited by talent scout Henry Wilson, a dapper operator who stamped his own distinctive cut of T-bone for Hollywood consumption, giving his pinup boys catchy names that smacked of suntan

lotion and peroxide. His stable included Tab Hunter (the former Art
Gelien), Guy Madison (Robert Moseley), and Troy Donahue (Merle
Johnson). Roy Fitzgerald he christened Rock Hudson, after the Rock
of Gibraltar and the Hudson River. In his early films Rock was often
photographed as a scenic landmark or natural formation. He was cast
as hunky Indians (*Taza, Son of Cochise; Winchester '73*), the better to
show off his hairless chest, and dubbed, to his chagrin, "Beefcake
Baron."

Under his athletic build, however, he was a vulnerable softy, his
insecurity being the lifelong result of his father's abandonment and
the physical and psychological battering by his stepfather and mother.
The directors who stroked the most sensitive performances out of
Hudson were those who detected the hurt and worry beneath the
shallow depths of his bland affability. His fear of being considered
inadequate—an inner echo of his mother calling him stupid—helped
offset his thick physique. The soap operas Hudson made with the
director Douglas Sirk, whose windswept allegories of alienation (even
the interiors looked windswept) influenced the lumpy-rain-cloud
fatalism of Rainer Werner Fassbinder, exploited Hudson's sympathetic potential, their very titles soliciting tears: *Written on the Wind,
The Tarnished Angels, Magnificent Obsession, All That Heaven Allows.*

Hudson's screen career evolved into a distorted mirror of the double
life he led off-camera. A closeted homosexual, he suited up in straight
drag. To keep his female fans aflutter and the scandal sheets off his
scent, he upheld the pretense of being a canned-ham Prince Charming even to the point of agreeing to an arranged marriage to one of his
agent's secretaries. A pseudo-documentary called *Rock Hudson's Home
Movies* (1992), directed by Mark Rappaport and narrated by Eric Farr,
decodes his celebrity image in light of what we subsequently learned
about his personal life, sprinkling film clips to make its points. Like
so many products of the Cultural Studies mentality, this celluloid
essay is a smirky exercise in ironic hindsight: we're meant to snicker
knowingly as every back pat and coy bit of eye contact (even with
John Wayne, a swollen monument on horseback) is construed as gay-
guy Morse code. One of the conceits of *Rock Hudson's Home Movies*
is that the homosexual subtext of Hudson's work was lost on most of
Hollywood and America. Yet Hudson was cast so often as an impostor, a dual personality trying to keep the fractured halves together,
that filmmakers must have known or intuited his false façade. Unlike
Marlon Brando or James Dean, however, he didn't have the rebel
reflexes of a born antihero or the acting chops to convert moping and

brooding into a poetic statement. He was too muted. (He audited an acting class taught by the formidable Uta Hagen but couldn't bring himself to take part.) It required a reciprocal force to boost Hudson's confidence and goose him into playing his fears of inadequacy and exposure for laughs—a bundle of positive ions.

Doris

"I grieve for Doris Day and the ignorance that regards her as old-fashioned," the critic David Thomson lamented when the American Film Institute neglected to list her among its top fifty "Greatest Screen Legends." John Updike, another member of her exclusive highbrow fan club, observed with neat understatement, "The words 'Doris Day' get a reaction, often adverse." Once the most popular female star on the planet, Day provokes a gag reflex today from those who equate her with the waxy shine and Waspy complexion of unliberated womanhood in the conformist fifties. Her gumption, optimism, and pep are considered corny, counterrevolutionary. Far from being a perfect sunbeam, however, Day had a personal life as shadowed by adversity as Hudson's. Her father walked out on her mother when Doris was eleven; three years later, a car accident resulted in nearly two years of convalescence; her first husband, a band musician, beat her and later killed himself; her second husband, also a musician, called it quits shortly into their marriage, saying he didn't want to be Mr. Doris Day; her third husband, Martin Melcher, who everyone agrees was a skunk ("an awful man, pushy, grating on the nerves, crass," in the words of bandleader Les Brown), was also a chiseler who shoved her into second-rate productions in which he took kickbacks and then lost their fortune to a swindler, saddling Day with a half-million-dollar debt after his death; her son, Terry, whom Melcher bullied, was nearly a victim of Charlie Manson's gang, who broke into his former residence looking for him and butchered Sharon Tate and three others instead.

Considering the cheerful front she maintained during her career, Day's peachy-keen image is understandable. It wasn't until the publication of her 1975 autobiography, *Doris Day: Her Own Story*, as told to A. E. Hotchner, that she unpacked her troubles in public. Less excusable is the persistent devaluing of her as an all-around entertainer—as a vocalist, comedienne, and romantic lead. She was refreshingly forthright sparring with Clark Gable in *Teacher's Pet*, beautifully still in *Young Man with a Horn* (where Lauren Bacall was the well-bred succubus siphoning the soul out of Kirk Douglas), and the most active ingredient in the musical *The Pajama Game*. To her detractors, she might as well have been performing inside a sack. In an essay published in 1962 called "The Doris Day Syndrome," whose very title indicates that her popularity was a symptom of cultural disease, the critic Dwight Macdonald described her as a shapeless vessel "with highish, smallish breasts and no hips or buttocks to speak of." For once, Macdonald's owl eyes deceived him. Baby had back.

As the producer Ross Hunter relates in *Doris Day: Her Own Story*, with the zeal of someone who has seen the promised land, "No one realized that under all those dirndls lurked one of the wildest asses in Hollywood." We must put that "wild fanny" of yours on-screen! he exhorted Day. Her caboose would be given the luxury treatment. A renowned showman of schlock refinement, Hunter hired the designer Jean Louis to do the snug, elegant costumes, and top stylists to pamper the other end. "After all those early years of suffering at the hands of those Warner Brothers embalmers who posed as makeup men, now I was made up and my hair done as I always hoped it would be done," Day recalled. "In *Pillow Talk*, the contemporary in me finally caught up with a contemporary film and I really had a ball." Day's helmet hair, her career-gal outfits and piquant hats, were a sneak preview of Jacqueline Kennedy's style as First Lady; Hudson's grinning rogues were light, early drafts of JFK. Without knowing it, Rock Hudson and Doris Day were shucking the Eisenhower blahs and ushering in the New Frontier. They were the First Couple of American Pop.

Doris and Rock

Produced by Ross Hunter, directed by Michael Gordon, written by Stanley Shapiro and Maurice Richlin, *Pillow Talk* is a packed sundae of a comedy, its luxury suites and nightclubs shot in bright, soda-fountain colors. Like *Some Like It Hot*, the other knockout comedy that year, it's deceptively casual, scooting along on a solid framework of farce. Jan (Day) is an interior decorator who shares a party line with Brad (Hudson), a callow playboy-songwriter who ties up the line for hours lullabying his harem of girlfriends, blocking her business calls. (He sings the same ditty to each *femme*, slotting in the appropriate name.) When Jan complains, he accuses her of being a dried-up spinster. He soon realizes his mistake when he sees her shimmying on the dance floor in a white gown and muses, "So that's the other end of your party line . . ." (closeup of vibrating fanny). Realizing that he wouldn't get far if Jan knew his real identity, Brad woos her by adopting the persona of Rex Stetson, a shy, strapping Texan who's a mite lonesome in the big city. Being around her does a man good; why, ma'am, "it's like being around a potbellied stove on a frosty morning." (Day's reaction as she processes this compliment is priceless.) Taking the news hard is her hapless suitor, Jonathan (Tony Randall), who utters the mortal cry "Jan, how could you, how could you ever fall in love with a tourist?" Seldom has one man's civic pride been so wounded.

Contemporary critics saw Hudson's Rex Stetson as a parody of the tall Texan he played in *Giant*, an inside joke that hardly registers today. It's the gay subtext that fascinates viewers now, a subtext so blatant it's right on the surface. When Brad casts aspersions on his alter ego, suggesting that the reticent Rex may be the type of man who collects recipes, exchanges bits of gossip, and is "very devoted" to his mother, it's as if Hudson is gay-baiting himself, using the Brad/Rex split to play his public image and private life off each other. He turns the gay closet into his own Superman phone booth, a convenient place to switch identities. The transitions from Brad to Rex are so silky and insinuating that the humor never seems self-hating or crass—Hudson's eyes have too much twinkle. Whenever he slides into that western drawl, it's as if he's opening a private channel of communication, enlisting the audience as co-conspirators. In *Lover Come Back*, he takes gay innuendo to greater absurdity as an adman pretending to be a scientist who is such a sexual naïf that he asks to be taken to a burlesque show to see what he's been missing (the lead stripper is "Sigrid Freud, the 'Id' Girl"). In his big sham dramatic number, he tries to con Day into nurturing him, pressing a wrist to his forehead and racking his brow over his inability to be a man. "Be gentle," he pleads, lying prostrate on her bed. His fake torment is very funny. Although Day carries the stigma of being a virginal trophy cup, it's actually Rock who is the object of deflowering—the overgrown ingenue. (In another scene, he enters a lobby wearing nothing but a mink coat as a bystander mutters, "He's the last guy I would have figured.")

Although *Pillow Talk* and *Lover Come Back* end in matrimony, marriage is used as dramatic punctuation, as it is in Jane Austen, not as bourgeois propaganda or a miraculous cure-all. Despite the entrenched idea that Doris Day's bachelorettes are heat-seeking husband hunters, they don't pursue wedding rings at the price of their own dignity. In both films, Day plays creative professionals who work in high-intensity fields and pride themselves on never betraying

their honor code. White-collar occupations have practically disappeared from women's roles in current movies—it's difficult to imagine Gwyneth Paltrow or Julia Roberts doing anything so gauche as
holding down a job, never mind having to compete. In *Lover Come
Back*, Day is an advertising whiz whose sense of fair play is offended
when she learns that a rival (Hudson's Jerry) is stealing clients with
wine, women, and song. "Believe me," she says, brandishing a client's
product, "the agency that lands this account is the one that shows Mr.
Miller the most attractive can"—cut to a row of chorus dancers shaking their "cans" in a nightclub where Jerry has booked ringside seats.
Day's deportment when she's riled—her executive-battlefield forward
charge, her double takes of disbelief—is a comic revelation. She's
like a popcorn popper on wheels. Day's work ethic and irate propulsion are what make her such a splendid match for Hudson's laid-back,
dreamboat hedonism. The sharp pokes from her fit the soft spots in
him. (One of the reasons the Hepburn-Tracy comedies seem rusty
and backward by comparison is that their relationship falls short of
fifty-fifty. Mugging and cooing and fussing with her damned hair,
Hepburn always seems to be coaxing Papa's approval from Tracy's
granite profile.)

Not as innovative as *Pillow Talk*, *Lover Come Back* is boosted by
a lively spoof of the advertising biz that salutes its mythic spot in
popular culture of the fifties and sixties. (Hudson's Jerry purports
to take a Boy Scout troop to "Inspiration Point" at the top of the
Chrysler Building so that the lads can admire Madison Avenue.) To
get out of a jam, Jerry creates an ad campaign for a made-up product
called Vip; when the ads are mistakenly broadcast by the head of the
agency, an ineffectual heir played by Tony Randall—who resents his
subordinate's rugged advantages ("You had everything going for you:
poverty, squalor")—Jerry is forced to concoct a product to go with
the campaign. Decades before the editors of *The Baffler* formed a collective frown, *Lover Come Back* deftly illustrated the ingenious knack
of capitalism to create and satisfy false needs. "The most convincing
demonstration of the power of advertising ever conceived: You have
sold a product that doesn't exist!" Vip eventually comes on the market
as a candy mint packing the punch of a triple martini. After the first
taste test, a woozy and disheveled Tony Randall waves off someone's
concern with the boast "Don't worry about me—I can hold my candy."

Send Me No Flowers, which completes the Doris-Rock trilogy,
doesn't quite come up roses. Hudson had reservations about the
script, in which he plays George Kimball, a hypochondriac mistak-

enly convinced he's about to die. The role was originally intended for
Tony Randall, who would later immortalize finickiness as *The Odd
Couple*'s Felix Unger. The film's chief fault, however, is not the death-
scare plotline but the domestic setup: Rock and Doris play a married couple living in the suburbs. The producers may have thought
they were advancing the Rock-Doris relationship to the next logical
stage, but having their stars married and bickering across the breakfast table instead of dating and rollicking through the city made for
two layers of wet blankets. Lacking the ritzy production values of
the first two, *Send Me No Flowers* shades into TV sitcom, never quite
rebounding from its drippy theme song and dire slapstick sequence of
Day, locked out of the house in her robe and fuzzy slippers, spilling
groceries on the front porch before climbing through a side window.
She's deglamorized here—this is a film that puts her in hair curlers.
Its central dynamic isn't between Doris and Rock but between him
and his best bud, Arnold, played by Randall, who, miffed at first at not
getting the lead, later applauded the casting against type—having the
scaredy-cat played by someone "built like Tarzan." "He was a moody
person," Randall says about Rock, "but when the mood was on him
he was delightful." Randall may have also been mollified by having
the best lines in the film. When George says he intends to spare his
wife the news about his imminent demise because "she'd probably
go to pieces—all the weeping, wailing . . . ," Arnold sympathizes:
"Yeah, I remember how she was when the *dog* died." Randall tells me
the funniest line for him was in the eulogy his character composed
in advance for the nearly departed: "They needed a good sport in
Heaven, so they sent for George Kimball . . ."

Doris

Doris Day made "Doris Day" comedies with other leading men—
Rod Taylor (*Do Not Disturb, The Glass Bottom Boat*), James Garner
(*The Thrill of It All; Move Over, Darling*), Cary Grant (*That Touch
of Mink*)—but none of these relationships Rocked. In less dashing
productions, the harping on her character's virtue seemed clinical,
almost macabre. The worst may be *That Touch of Mink*, a procession
of coitus interruptus scenes with a glum Cary Grant tiptoeing around
the material and sluffing off his lines as if disavowing his very existence (the Invisible Man with a tan). After duds such as *The Ballad of
Josie* and *Caprice*, Day's movie career stalled. Shortly before he died,

her ogre husband booked her into a TV sitcom, *The Doris Day Show*, which she can barely describe in *Her Own Story* without a shudder. "It was bad enough that I had been forced into television against my will, but what made it doubly repulsive was the nature of the setting that had been chosen for my weekly series. A farm. A widow with a couple of little kids living on a farm. With Grandpa, naturally." Even more naturally, Grandpa was played by that old coot Denver Pyle, who probably had his first pair of overalls bronzed. Later, the series was revamped and made more urban, but it was still an unimaginative grind. After the series folded in 1973, Day began to devote herself almost entirely to the protection of animals, a cause which would reunite her with Hudson one last horrific time.

Rock

Rock Hudson made "Doris Day" comedies without Doris Day, co-starring with Gina Lollobrigida in *Come September* and Paula Prentiss in *Man's Favorite Sport?* (a Howard Hawks film where the gay-baiting does seem demeaning—a dartboard game at Hudson's expense). He also attempted to deepen the double life he played for comedy with Doris Day into psychodrama in John Frankenheimer's *Seconds* (1966), a *Twilight Zone*–like thriller about a schlub who undergoes surgery to change his identity, only to discover that he's still caged inside his own mind. A Grim Reaper of a movie, *Seconds* has some of the middle-class self-contempt that spews out of a John Cassavetes film, where the characters are stripped bare. Hudson needed his protective padding. The pressure of the shooting, the pain the script tapped, drove him into a personal meltdown. When it came time to film a drunk scene in which his protagonist buckles under the strain of leading a double life, Hudson himself broke down sobbing, unable to regain his composure. Frankenheimer called time-out, sent the crew home, and held Hudson as he wept for hours, unable to stop. *Seconds* bombed with audiences and mainstream critics, its poor reception (it has since become a cult favorite) perhaps justifying Hudson's fear that the cost of opening up was private humiliation and public rejection. He would never allow himself to be that unguarded again. Afterward, he stuck mostly to mindless fluff, achieving near helium with TV's *McMillan and Wife*, and adjusting his increasing bulk in turkeys such as *Las Vegas Strip Wars* and *The Star Maker*. The possibility of a sequel to *Pillow Talk* was tossed around in the eighties, but nothing came of it.

QUESTION: *Do you feel different or better now than as a young man?*

HUDSON: *I'm even comfortable with my gray hair and this paunch! But I do—I do look forward to the future. . . . I have confidence, and I hope to see the year 2000.*

—From an interview conducted by Boze Hadleigh, published posthumously in *American Film* (January-February 1987)

As Hudson got older, he became almost a poignant figure on the cruising scene. In Patrick Gale's biography of the gay writer Armistead Maupin, Hudson is recorded venturing into one San Francisco leather bar in a red alpaca sweater, "looking like a tourist from the Midwest." During a make-out session with Rock, Maupin was amazed when Hudson pulled out a popper case initialed R.H. "He had a personalized Rock Hudson popper case! And I completely lost my hard-on." His status an open secret within the gay community, Hudson was unable to be honest about the nature of his illness after he was diagnosed with AIDS in 1984. He seemed to age overnight, losing his looks in the wave of a wand. He did a guest stint on *Dynasty*, his haggard appearance spurring rumors about his health that he continued to deny, claiming that a spiteful producer was the source.

Doris and Rock

In 1985, Hudson accepted an invitation to take part in the promotional launch of *Doris Day's Best Friends*, an animal show she was doing for the Christian Broadcasting Network. A gesture of friendship, it proved to be a tragic folly. "Here was a man with only ten weeks to live," note the authors of *Idol*, "a man who had successfully hidden the secret of his terrible disease for over a year, who had kept the secret of his homosexuality from the world for a lifetime—about to allow it all to disintegrate by appearing at a routine news conference to announce a minor cable-TV show." The press conference took place in Carmel, California, at a lodge near Day's home. A still-perky Day vamped as the reporters and film crews awaited Hudson's arrival. He ran so late that some of the crews packed up their equipment and departed, while other reporters stayed behind in a state of extreme huff. "Their get-tough attitude soon changed. There was an audible, collective gasp—and then a hush—as Rock, his face a virtual death-mask, his body gaunt and hollow under baggy pants and jacket, was ushered into the room." As stunned as everyone else, Day, barely missing a beat, embraced her former co-star. With one arm draped around her, Hudson told the press, "This is just like a stroll down memory lane. I think I can even remember some dialogue from *Pillow Talk*." The next day Hudson and Day taped a segment utilizing *Pillow Talk*'s split-screen technique. Shooting had to be paused when Hudson was too weak to continue. In truth, it wasn't *Pillow Talk* they were reprising, but *Send Me No Flowers*, this time for real, with no last-minute reprieve. History had repeated itself, the first time as farce, the second as tragedy. Rock Hudson survived the taping by only a few months, dying on October 2, 1985. He remains the most famous victim of AIDS, which is probably not how he wanted to be remembered.

And won't be. Enough years have passed for an understanding of the scope of his life to subdue the shock of his death and even out the bumps in between. The showing of his films on Turner Classic Movies and American Movie Classics has contributed to a reverse-aging process. The ravaged features of Hudson's final days have been rewound until he has once again reached smooth Technicolor youth. The buoyancy of his partnership with Day should be a lesson. Since Hudson's death, the Doris-Rock romantic-comedy genre has mutated into the gay man–straight woman buddy flick (*My Best Friend's Wedding, The Object of My Affection, The Next Best Thing*) and the yuppie romance (Tom Hanks and Meg Ryan in *Sleepless in Seattle* and *You've Got Mail*), but the foam is missing. Both subgenres suffer from sincerity, a nagging self-consciousness. Identity—sexual, ethnic, economic—is a burden and a responsibility now, a badge worn on the outside rather than a self-awareness borne on the inside. The psychology of the characters is conveyed not in how they behave with each other, but in how they explain themselves. They simulcast the running monologue in their heads. In the Doris-Rock movies, Tony Randall monopolized the neurosis, enabling everybody else to get on with their shopping. It was the civilized thing to do.

Tony

Near the end of my chat with Tony Randall, I mention that most comedies today are aimed at kids. He offers his own take. "They're aimed at idiots," he says.

Vanity Fair, April 2000

From Fear to Eternity
The Americanization of Emily

As if to make amends for the cheap heroics that Hollywood war movies have flexed over the century—the beachhead assaults led by John
Wayne, squinting with solemn resolve as he clutches the dog tags of
a slain supporting actor; the aerial sagas with bomber crews cracking
jokes in the cockpit as enemy fighters buzz in to spoil their picnic;
Clint Eastwood, a golem of pure gristle, liberating the tiny country of
Grenada in *Heartbreak Ridge*—other filmmakers present the flip side
of playing soldier, the puking realities. They produce antiwar movies
that resemble ghastly hangovers that never lift, nightmares on endless replay. The traditional antiwar movie surveys the mired killing
fields to etch man's inhumanity to man, the cruel caprices of fate that
make a mockery out of recruiting-poster propaganda. (In *All Quiet
on the Western Front*, a hand reaches out from the trenches to capture
a butterfly, a bullet sings, and the hand slumps lifeless, as dead as a
monkey's paw.) They're documents of disillusionment, the horrors
of war inscribed on the ravaged faces of the survivors (Kirk Douglas
marching accusingly toward the camera in Stanley Kubrick's *Paths
of Glory*), or hushed away in the hospital wards where nunlike nurses
attend to maimed limbs and mummied heads (*Johnny Got His Gun*,
which unfolds within the tortured consciousness of a mute, immobile
"vegetable"). Commercially, such movies can be tough sells. Reviewers may applaud such honorable efforts for being uncompromisingly
"grim" and "harrowing," but how many moviegoers want to be grimly
harrowed?

Yet an antiwar film need not traffic in gore and burnt-out cases to
mail its message home. Perhaps the most subversively dovish statement ever crafted in Hollywood barely dallies a moment on the
battlefield and doesn't withdraw into shell-shocked silence—it loves
hearing itself talk too much. It's a true rarity, a *cheerful* tract. It's also
the most unjustly neglected classic comedy of the postwar era—*The
Americanization of Emily*, the greatest Billy Wilder film that Billy
Wilder never made.

By which I mean that the item in question, starring Julie Andrews and James Garner, adapted by Paddy Chayefsky from the novel by William Bradford Huie, and directed by Arthur Hiller (who later gave us *Love Story*, but let's not be punitive), has the signature traits of a Wilder romp—the gift of gab, the bold-stroke characterizations, and the madcap reversals of fortune. Moreover, William Holden, who had won an Academy Award as the cynical heel in Wilder's *Stalag 17*, was originally cast as the male lead. But *The Americanization of Emily* beats Wilder at his own game. Where *Stalag 17* now seems too chuffed with its cocky iconoclasm, a smug complacency that corrodes many of Wilder's comedies as the years go by, *The Americanization of Emily* seems more adult and daring today than when it was released, in 1964. The country around it has changed, its people too. America has become a more brutally sentimental superpower since then, more enthralled with the idea of war as a crucible of national and individual character-building. From talk radio to the Fox News Channel to the neoimperialist bellicosities of historians Victor Davis Hanson, Robert Kaplan, and Max Boot, we've never had so many white men peering through Patton's field binoculars to reconfigure a stronger America. Such armchair centurions drip scorn on those wobblers and weaklings who believe the better part of valor is to heed the call of battle, then run like hell the other way.

The hero of *The Americanization of Emily* is one such yellowbelly.

A naval lieutenant commander, Garner's Charlie Madison, like Holden's Sergeant J. J. Sefton, is a clever racketeer, an expert scrounger. For both, the war is an entrepreneurial arena. But unlike Sefton, who's detested by his fellow POW's for his brash, me-first attitude, Charlie is smooth and outgoing, a slickster with a deft line of patter. An aide to Rear Admiral Jessup (Melvyn Douglas), Charlie is known in the ranks as a "dog robber," whose job is to pamper his boss, keep the old bazoo well fed and lubricated. (A happy admiral is a hazy admiral, less liable to enforce discipline and interfere with his junior officers' recreational pursuits.) Overseeing a high-end retail trade, Charlie procures luxury items from the black market, his bedroom a boutique stashed with lingerie, soap, silk stockings, liquor, fresh fruit, expensive chocolates, and other exclusive treats. Noticing that he stocks the finest French perfume, a pert English widow and navy motor-pool driver named Emily Barham (Andrews) marvels at how Charlie managed to obtain Arpège with the Germans occupying Paris. "There are Germans in Paris, aren't there? There is a war on, I think. You Americans must have heard something about it, I'm sure." To Emily, the Americans came late to the war and made up for their tardy entrance by capitalizing on the deprivation. "Most English families haven't seen that many oranges or eggs in years, but it's all one big Shriners' convention to you Yanks, isn't it?"

Whereupon Charlie lets fly with the first of Chayefsky's rhetorical catapult attacks, a patriotic bucketload worthy of Bill O'Reilly:

> You American-haters bore me to tears, Miss Barham. I've dealt with Europeans all my life. . . . I've had Frenchmen call me a savage, because I only took half an hour for lunch. Hell, Miss Barham, the only reason the French take two hours for lunch is because the service in their restaurants is lousy. And the most tedious of the lot are you British. We crass Americans didn't introduce war into your little island. This war, Miss Barham, to which we Americans are so insensitive, is the result of two thousand years of European greed, barbarism, superstition, and stupidity. Don't blame it on our Coca-Cola bottles. Europe was a going brothel long before we came to town. . . .

So, lay off, Mrs. Miniver.

Apart from the unconquerable tilt of her chin, Julie Andrews's Emily is no Mrs. Miniver, a porcelain cup into which the milk of human kindness has been poured. Beneath her trim uniform and prim manner, she's quite the little minx. A war widow (of a soldier who shipped out to Africa three days after the wedding, never to return), Emily is an angel of death, falling for men on their last night of furlough and sending them off to war with that fondest of farewells, a mercy fuck. Or so the script implies. To some, Andrews was miscast as a trollop, having trilled so wholesomely in *Mary Poppins* (also released in 1964) and *The Sound of Music* (which enchanted the clouds a year later). Her virginal aura seemed to be a permanent light fixture, which accounts for Pauline Kael's putdown in *Kiss Kiss Bang Bang*: "Julie Andrews could play a promiscuous girl in *The Americanization of Emily* and shine with virtue." But is it virtue that shines, or vanity? Andrews invests Emily with the sin of pride. She puts a high price tag on the little that she gives of herself, treating her brief affairs as lovely parting gifts. After Charlie falls in love with her and proposes marriage, she refuses, adopting a pose of noble renunciation. He sees right through her sham. "Well, you're a good woman. You've done the morally right thing. God save us all from people who do the morally right thing. It's the rest of us who get broken in half. You're a bitch."

The acrid bite that Garner puts into the word "bitch" is one of the prize moments in male screen acting in the sixties, comparable to Brian Keith's bon mot in *Reflections in a Golden Eye* after the disastrous party where Elizabeth Taylor whips Marlon Brando with a riding crop—"Well, my god, what a *debacle*." Garner, like Keith, never has gotten his acting due. Those who know him only as the easygoing charmer on the TV series *Maverick* and *The Rockford Files*, where he seemed to hum the story lines as if they were familiar tunes, may be surprised at the barking conviction he imparts to Chayefsky's dialogue, of which there is loads. A normally laconic actor who plays with a payoff line as if it were a poker chip, Garner delivers Chayefsky's long speeches without losing the beat, gathering theatrical force and stature as he goes along.

And what speeches they are. *The Americanization of Emily* represents the sweet spot in Chayefsky's screenwriting career, the juicy midpoint between the kitchen-sink naturalism of *The Catered Affair* and *Marty* (with its sad-sack, singsong refrain, "Whaddya feel like doing tonight, Marty?" "I dunno, wadda you feel like doing?") and the ulcerous invective of *The Hospital* and *Network* ("I'm as mad as hell, and I'm not going to take this anymore!"), where his male-menopause protagonists seemed to be trying to outshout a raging storm.

Over morning tea in the garden with Emily's mother (Joyce Grenfell, perfect in a small part), Charlie reveals that he wasn't always the gutless wonder he professes to be. When war broke out, he did his patriotic duty and volunteered for combat. "My wife, to all appearances a perfectly sensible woman, encouraged me in this idiotic decision." Seven months later, Charlie finds himself hitting the shores of the Solomon Islands to engage the Japanese. "There I was, splashing away in the shoals of Guadalcanal. It suddenly occurred to me a man could get killed doing this kind of thing." All around him his fellow soldiers are being butchered, reddening the water and rending the air with their agonized screams. "In peacetime, they had all been normal, decent cowards, frightened of their wives, trembling before their bosses, terrified at the passing of the years. But war had made them gallant . . ." And what good did their gallantry do them? It didn't make them any less dead.

Later that evening, sopping wet in the jungle, he has an epiphany: "I discovered I was a coward. That's my new religion. I'm a big believer in it. Cowardice will save the world. You see, cowards don't fight wars. They run like rabbits at the first shot. If everybody obeyed their natural impulse and ran like rabbits at the first shot, I don't see how we could possibly get to the second shot. As long as valor remains

a virtue, we shall have soldiers. . . . So, I preach cowardice. Through
cowardice, we shall all be saved."

> *In the 1964* Americanization of Emily, *the filmmakers took a radi-
> cally different approach in putting their antiwar message on the screen.
> They rejected the value of combat altogether and suggested that man
> should perhaps not make the ultimate sacrifice, even for the good of his
> country. In creating its comment on the absurdity of war and the irra-
> tionality of military men,* The Americanization of Emily *became
> the first major Hollywood production to portray an American service-
> man proudly professing the virtues of cowardice. When confronted with
> such a unique portrayal, many reviewers reacted with stunned outrage.*
> —Guts & Glory: The Making of the American
> Military Image in Film, by Lawrence H. Suid
> (University Press of Kentucky, 2002)

What makes *The Americanization of Emily* a radical statement is that
it doesn't take easy outs or make nice concessions. It has a crusty core.
Chayefsky indicts everyone equally for complicity in the enterprise
of war and condemns sentimentality for being as conducive to war as
greed and conquest. "We shall never end wars," Charlie tells Emily's
mother, "by blaming it on ministers and generals or war-mongering
imperialists or all the other banal bogies. It's the rest of us who build
statues to those generals and name boulevards after those ministers.
It's the rest of us who make heroes of our dead and shrines of our
battlefields. We wear our widow's weeds like nuns, Mrs. Barham, and
perpetuate war by exalting its sacrifices." (One can only imagine the
withering scorn Chayefsky would have trained on the limp bathos
of the ubiquitous "Support Our Troops" ribbons adorning America's
family-fun vehicles.)

Chayefsky pays women the honor of not patronizing them as
sainted bystanders and passive victims. He treats them as equal sparring partners, full parties to the folly of war. Wives and mothers who
mourn their losses and build shrines to their slain husbands and sons
are only helping march more husbands and sons into the cemetery.
Including Charlie's own mother, who insists that the death of one of
her three sons at Anzio was a brave gesture even though no heroism
was involved—it was an ordinary, messy death. ("They buried what
pieces they found of him.") With maternal empathy, Mrs. Barham
suggests that taking refuge in such pretense is a harmless enough
consolation. Oh no it's not, says Charlie—because now the youngest

brother in the family can't wait to enlist so that he too can bayonet into battle. "What has my mother got for pretending bravery was admirable? She is under constant sedation and terrified she may wake up one morning and find her last son has run off to be brave." On different decibel levels (Chayefsky's roar got louder as he got older and angrier), *The Americanization of Emily* and *Network* update the advice that Dr. Johnson gave Boswell: "Clear your mind of cant." The lies the government and media tell are amplifications of the lies we tell ourselves. To stop being conned, stop conning yourself.

But can Charlie practice what he preaches? The movie puts his chicken philosophy to a critical test. In a moment of fugue-state madness, Admiral Jessup, determined that the navy won't be denied a public-relations boon from the D-day invasion, bursts into Charlie's bedroom with a brain wave. "The first dead man on Omaha Beach must be a sailor!" he declares. "That's a very piquant thing to say, don't you think?," Emily muses after the admiral leaves. "Yes, I think I'd call that piquant," Charlie agrees. What makes it more piquant is that, through a series of intrigues and betrayals, Charlie ends up being the patsy shoved ashore to be D-day's first dead fish stick. He doesn't realize he's the designated Unknown Sailor until he has forded the gray soup of mist and foaming water, bombs bursting around him, bullets ripping tiny plops in the surf, a camera filming as he tries to retreat to the landing craft and is ordered by his superior officer to turn around. But that's where the shooting's coming from!, a panicky Charlie protests.

Now, at this crucial threshold, years of movie watching have prepared us for Charlie Madison to meet his baptism of fire by summoning something within, proving he's a man of backbone and idealism after all. In *Stalag 17*, Holden's Sefton makes his escape and earns the grudging respect of the other slobs in his barracks. In *Casablanca*, Bogart's Rick, who boasts that he sticks his neck out for nobody, does his bit for the French underground and plugs Conrad Veidt at the foggy airport. In the musical *For Me and My Gal*, Gene Kelly, playing a song-and-dance man who deliberately injures his hand to avoid the draft, redeems himself under fire. I was watching this rerun of *Combat!* (it was obviously a slow night) where guest star Nick Adams, a jazz musician who shied from battle to protect his chops, eventually martyrs himself for the good of the mission. So we know the routine.

But *The Americanization of Emily* stays true to itself, and Charlie remains faithful to his cowardly creed. Graceless under pressure, "bug-eyed with terror" (so says the script), he runs crazy-legged for

cover, doing a broken-field dash across the beach, cutting a vulnerable, ridiculous, poignant figure that shrinks him into a pictograph
on the screen. A land mine explodes, flinging his body several feet
(Chayefsky himself was injured by a mine during World War II), and
a shot shows Charlie sprawled motionless in the sand: "For the length
of this shot, Madison's body is the only body on the long white stretch
of Omaha Beach." A coward in life, he will be converted into a front-
page hero in death, but the movie isn't over, and Chayefsky still has a
joker or two up his sleeve.

Despite favorable reviews from influential sources (Bosley
Crowther of *The New York Times* called it a "mischievously nimble
farce"), *The Americanization of Emily* failed to excite moviegoers when
it was released, except to make some of them "hopping mad," in the
words of director Hiller, who popped into the first public screening
to gauge audience reaction and probably wished he hadn't. To ride
the skirts of Julie Andrews's success in *Mary Poppins* and *The Sound
of Music*, the movie later was reissued with the shortened title *Emily*,
but a "women's picture" this wasn't. In a sense, the movie was a beat
ahead of its time. In 1964, American involvement in Vietnam had
not yet swelled to bulging-anaconda proportion, and the script's paci-
fist creed didn't pack the relevance it would have a few years later,
when draft-card burning became a campus craze. But other movies
limp out of the gate and are rediscovered by film buffs, enthusiasti-
cally adopted, a few aficionados growing into an army of appreciative
eyeballs. Why is *The Americanization of Emily* still so orphaned? In
part, it's because it remains jauntily unclassifiable. It's such an *uncharacteristic* movie for Andrews and Garner, neither of whom has ever
been identified with social commentary, and, as mentioned before, it
nestles shadowed between the ragged peaks of Chayefsky's popular
success. (The obituaries after his death, in 1981, emphasized *Marty*,
Network, and *The Hospital*, lumping *The Americanization of Emily* with
the other, lesser credits.)

But the chief reason the movie hasn't achieved even minor canonical status is because sightings of it are so frustratingly rare. Due to a
vexing copyright issue involving William Bradford Huie's estate, it's
never been released on DVD, and videos are scarce. Writing in *The
Washington Post*, Jay Mathews, a lovelorn *Americanization of Emily* fan,
recounted the scavenger hunt for a glimpse of his beloved that left
him "canvasing the grimier video rental places and scanning the late
night television listings." Though his odyssey was in vain, Mathews
held out the hope that the rights issue could be resolved and the film

would become freely available again. Hope still flickers. Huie's widow, heir to the estate, says she is open to a DVD deal and other repackagings—a musical version of *The Americanization of Emily*, called *Wave Me Goodbye*, was staged in 2002—but hasn't been approached. Someone needs to give the widow a call.

Because we owe it to future generations to spread the gospel of *The Americanization of Emily*. You, me, Rush Limbaugh, Dick Cheney, Tom DeLay, we've had our chance to avoid combat. But think of the kids. Not the video-game junkies who hope to enlist and join "Generation Kill" in the streets of Fallujah or Tikrit, putting their first-person shooting into real-life practice, but those less fortunate—the teenage cowards of today and the timid wussies of tomorrow who *need* a role model to emulate, someone who bravely stands up for the craven impulses that promote self-preservation. It's one thing to fight for what you believe in, another thing to fight for what others believe in, especially if they don't believe it themselves (and harbor other agendas). A war as fraudulently packaged and incoherently executed as the one in Iraq makes it imperative that individuals resist the predations of the state and protect the precious property of their own piddling lives. For even the most piddling life is of momentous consequence to its owner. One of the key perceptions in *War and Peace* comes when Tolstoy enters the group mind of prisoners about to be executed, who cannot comprehend what is about to befall them: "They could not believe it because *they alone knew what their life meant to them*, and so they neither understood nor believed that it could be taken from them" (my emphasis). Charlie Madison experiences that shock of incredulity twice, first at Guadalcanal, then on Omaha Beach. And for him that's twice too many.

Vanity Fair, March 2005

Postscript

Happily, The Americanization of Emily *no longer requires a scavenger hunt to lay eyes on. It's now available on DVD, rentable from Netflix, and streamable from Amazon Instant Video.*

An Unforgettable Face
A Face in the Crowd

Made during the middle slumbers of the Eisenhower era, Elia Kazan's *A Face in the Crowd* marks its fiftieth birthday in 2007 and retains its status as one of the most provocative, unplaceable vagrants—or is it mongrels?—of American moviemaking. It's a perennial in-between. It didn't behave then, and it doesn't quite belong now. It has neither indelibly darkened into a lithographic fable, like Charles Laughton's masterwork, *The Night of the Hunter*, nor faded into parchment. As Richard Schickel observes in his gung-ho biography of Kazan, published in 2005, "The film has never achieved wide popularity, but it has never disappeared, either. It keeps nagging away at us. At some of us, at least." *A Face in the Crowd* was and is a satire for the enlightened minority ("some of us, at least") about the threat posed to democracy when TV personalities achieve magnetic sway over the masses and wield their popularity like a whip. If Fascism comes to America, this film suggests, it'll be wearing the friendly, donkey grin of a good ol' boy. Written by Budd Schulberg (who also did the screenplay for Kazan's *On the Waterfront*), *A Face in the Crowd* is a dark-hued tall tale about a rough-diamond charismatic—Andy Griffith's singer-joker Lonesome Rhodes—who catapults into national celebrity, only to become the puppet of a populist scheme orchestrated by corporate overlords, who exploit his likability as a lever of social control. Rhodes is no innocent buffoon; he's as cynical as his paymasters. He preys upon the yearnings and insecurities of regular folks and plays them for suckers, until he commits career suicide by open mike, the victim of a "Macaca" moment. *A Face in the Crowd* might have become an acrid, worrywart exercise in elitist condescension if it hadn't been for the seams-busting acting of Griffith, who unleashes a moody, gutsy force unsuitable for the future sheriff of Mayberry; Patricia Neal, as the film's abused, bruised conscience; Anthony Franciosa, who has the appetite of a gigolo turned jackal; and, gleaming in her screen debut, Lee Remick.

A Face in the Crowd could have drawn its creative inspiration only

from below the Mason-Dixon line, in the country's moist loins.
Postwar American drama roughly split along a North-South divide.
The North was Arthur Miller country, the Puritan New England of
repression (*The Crucible*) and the urban stronghold of Ibsenite social
conscience (*All My Sons, A View from the Bridge*). Major stress is laid
on the Dignity of Man, with *Death of a Salesman*'s famous injunc-
tion, "Attention must be paid," hoisted as the banner statement of
the period. What hope is there for the little guy when society is so
hierarchical, top-heavy, uncaring, and unsparing? If the North was
the crown of America's superego, crushing the spirit of the little guy
with its demands and duties, the South was the oozy underbelly of id,
its poet laureate of psychopathia sexualis being Tennessee Williams.
("Even those who dislike Tennessee Williams must give him credit
for castrating a hero here, eating one there," Gore Vidal mused in
his famous survey of the fifties theater scene, "Love, Love, Love.")
Where Miller's plays showed flinty integrity, a strong work ethic,
and a vertical horizon, Williams's imagination curled in on itself,
laid up with dreamy memories and a supply of medicinals, its sly
cunning lurking beneath the mingled fragrance of sachet, perfume,
hothouse flowers, and fleshly decay. With *A Face in the Crowd*, Kazan
bridges North and South, scales them, the movie starting out as a
character study in southern depravity and ending up as a northern
message movie complete with sociological commentary by Walter
Matthau's Mel Miller, whose last name can't be a fluke. Outfitted
with a pipe, intellectual spectacles, and an owlish-liberal demeanor,
Matthau's man of reason is virtually a stand-in for Arthur Miller,
acerbically editorializing from the sidelines as Rhodes goes ape. If
A Face in the Crowd has a split personality, the personality that's split
is Kazan's. Unlike, say, John Cassavetes, whose directorial approach
was strictly observational-behavioral, Kazan encouraged brute ferocity in his actors—getting Griffith soused to bellow his big, raging
monologue—but used his movies to espouse ideas, illustrate themes,
and pound home the holy-mackerel truth.

*Slaps are usually choreographed so the actor receiving the slap will pull
back as if actually hit, with sound added later, but Kazan told Patricia
to really haul off and hit the actor. Patricia gave it everything she
had. Franciosa, stunned by the force of the slap, began to cry. Patricia
recalled, "He was utterly fantastic. But when the camera stopped, he
kept on crying and cried all through lunch. I felt terrible. I wanted to*

*tell him what a great job he'd done, but he wouldn't come near me. I'm
sure he thought I was a number one bitch." Unfortunately, the scene
was not used in the film.*

—From *Patricia Neal: An Unquiet Life*, by Stephen
Michael Shearer (University Press of Kentucky, 2006)

Our introduction to the film's antihero comes when "roving
reporter" Marcia Jeffries (Neal) pokes her hated head into the pig-
pen of the county jail to scrounge up amateur talent for her radio
program, *A Face in the Crowd*, which highlights the music and
gab of everyday folk. Caterpillared against the wall trying to get
some shut-eye is Griffith's Lonesome Rhodes (real name, Larry), a
drifter spending the night after a drunk arrest. Remember drifters?
They've gone the way of beachcombers and boardinghouses. These
itinerant souls—"outcasts, hobos, nobodies, gentleman loafers, one-
time or all-time losers," as Rhodes rhapsodizes in jail—used to have
such mystique on stage and screen before they culturally morphed
into serial killers. Drifters factor large in southern lore, these
rogue males embodying the musky threat and Tarzan muscularity
of untamed passion. Materializing out of the dusty nowhere and
traveling light, the lean silhouette of the lone drifter tantalizes
dullsville communities oppressed by torpor, indolence, prejudice,
and a surplus of old farts loitering at the general store. As soon as
a drifter sets foot in town, tongues wag, insects buzz, and young
girls start getting blushing ideas. Think of Paul Newman in *The
Long, Hot Summer*, his cocky insolence the perfect antidote for the
low sperm count that has denied Orson Welles's pug-nosed patriarch his rightful crop of heirs; or as Chance Wayne in *Sweet Bird of
Youth*, reducing that town's petty despot to Rumpelstiltskin stamps
of impotent fury. Think of William Holden hopping off the train
in *Picnic*, his shirtless torso driving Rosalind Russell into a sexual
dither and arousing the narcotic, metronomic beat of Kim Novak's
hips. Think of Marlon Brando in *The Fugitive Kind*, a poetic hunk
who wows Anna Magnani with the melancholy wisdom that "we're
all of us sentenced to solitary confinement inside our own lonely
skins for as long as we live on this earth."

Andy Griffith, fresh from making comedy records such as "What
It Was, Was Football" and cradling a beat-up guitar that he calls
"momma," can't compete with Newman, Holden, and Brando in the
hairless-chest, backwoods-Apollo category—who can? But he owns

a thick mop of curls that screams virility, contrasted against the bald gents infesting the executive suites (he rubs one geezer's scalp and compliments his "fine head of skin"); flaunts a winning manner (his best scenes are the quieter, joshing ones); and cavorts with a lusty energy reminiscent of Burt Lancaster bending invisible bars of steel. The lusty, dusty Rhodes hasn't been emasculated by being held captive indoors, chained to a desk, and bleached white; he still bears a ruddy touch of the barefoot primitive, the roughneck elemental. Hired to tout a product called Vitajex, he pitches this innocuous glucose concoction as a rocket boost to the libido, a jolt of ecstasy that gets the entire country frisky ("Why don't you take Vitajex like Lonesome Rhodes does?" moans a pulp-novel blonde in a nightgown). Everywhere this rascal goes, he incites sexual hysteria, a sea of crazed women and squealing schoolgirls clawing the air to tear at his clothes. The explosive emergence of Elvis Presley probably inspired the pubescent damburst that erupts after Rhodes achieves TV fame, and it's pertinent that the same year that *A Face in the Crowd* was released Presley starred in *Jailhouse Rock*, where, like Rhodes, his character goes from inmate to idol. (And it was a year earlier, in 1956, when Elvis, in his first flush of glory, was filmed walking around Times Square—see the documentary *Elvis '56*.) Sexual hysteria, another fifties artifact (which would crest in the early sixties with the collective orgasm that was Beatlemania), was the flip side of sexual inhibition—pop open the lid, and all that pent-up energy sends wet panties flying. Now that we live in a porny society that's lost nearly all inhibition, such scenes have an anthropological interest. It's like watching tribal footage of our ancestors' Dionysian rites.

"They could all use a good cold shower," Pauline Kael observed of Kazan's cast in her capsule review of *A Face in the Crowd*, finding the frenzy even then a bit much. Erotic heat is always accompanied by heavy humidity in the fictional realm that critic Dwight Macdonald labeled Kazanistan. Set before air-conditioning became the norm in homes and businesses, Kazan's melodramas are drenched in perspiration—foreheads glistening, shirts stained, sheets damp with fetid desire, electric fans swiveling their heads and shifting stale air around in cramped rooms. Where Kazan's women are coated with a thin veneer of sweat, enabling them to maintain a semblance of dignity (before they let themselves go native wild), the men are sopping, whipping up a good lather from all the dirty, itchy thoughts prowling around in their primordial brains. Part of what makes Patricia Neal so sexy in certain roles is that she tidily tends to business even as her appraising glances measure every inch of the man under inspection. Here, playing a Sarah Lawrence graduate with certain refined notions that are going to be put through the wringer, she never gives Griffith's Rhodes as avidly frank a going-over as she does Gary Cooper and his phallic drill in *The Fountainhead* or Paul Newman in *Hud* (her sexiest performance, with her crookedest grin), but she lets you see the layers of her ladylike reserve slide away when he calls on her in an hour of need, and she tends to his need as only a mature woman can in the sanctity of her hotel room.

But a man-boy such as Rhodes has only passing interest in mature women, with their complicated needs and undergarments. A perky pair of devoted eyes gazing up and idolizing him—that's what he's hankering for. Like Elvis, who bestowed his first glance upon his future princess, Priscilla, when she was a mere fourteen, or Jerry Lee Lewis, who married his second cousin when she was thirteen, this cradle robber scoops up a dewy handful of southern delight to be his sister-daughter-lover-missus. The movie's iconic emblem and tasty morsel of wholesome American coquetry is Lee Remick's Betty Lou Fleckum, a drum majorette with a trim, bare midriff, white boots that accent her athletic thighs (not until *Myra Breckinridge* would white boots be used so prancingly), and cheekbones that catch the sun. Every pose she strikes seems perfect for a yearbook photo. A more sparkly and spangly version of Carroll Baker's thumb-sucking nymphet in *Baby Doll* (directed by Kazan from a devilish screenplay by Tennessee Williams), Remick's Betty Lou burned a hole in the film stock as a "sex-bomb miniature living in a small-town nowheres," in the words of critic Manny Farber. Chosen by Rhodes from a bevy of contestants as the winner of a baton-twirling competition ("I been a fan of baton twirling from way back—I think it's an honest-to-God American art form!" he enthuses), Betty Lou so captivates him that they impetuously run off to Mexico together for a quickie wedding ("We dood it in Juarez!"). Upon return, Rhodes introduces his teen dream to America on his smash TV program (he was married once before, to a shrewd dame who's now bleeding him for hush money), where Betty Lou lends a touch of class to the festivities by twirling flaming batons to the scherzo from Beethoven's Seventh Symphony. Inexplicably, the movie then neglects Betty Lou as much as her hillbilly-messiah husband proceeds to do, shunting her back to Arkansas after Rhodes discovers her being unfaithful with his agent

(Franciosa, with whom Remick would be re-united a year later, in *The Long, Hot Summer*). Her departure is a loss for the movie, depriving it of peppermint-stick candy and substituting a stern diet of bitter pills of wisdom to be forced down the gullet.

Rhodes gets too glory-hound full of himself, and when a man gets too full of himself in a Hollywood film, he's ripe for a fall. (As the author of *The Harder They Fall*, Schulberg was an old hand at bringing a protagonist to the brink and then waving good-bye.) Fed up with this louse and his Svengali hold over his fans, Neal's Marcia works a lever in the studio control room so that the parting words Rhodes shares with his cronies under the closing credits are broadcast to those watching at home. Leering at the camera, he conspiratorially sneers, "Those morons out there . . . you know what the public's like?—a cage full of guinea pigs . . . good night, you stupid idiots, good night, you miserable slobs. They're a lot of trained seals—I toss them a dead fish and they'll flap their flippers." Ma and Pa Kettle, the ladies' bridge club, the bedridden, the construction guys with their safety helmets and lunchboxes—these trusting goops don't appreciate being bad-mouthed by the low-life they held in such high esteem. (Flanked by a seedy pair of bellboys, Rhodes's slatternly ex-wife, the one he married before Betty Lou, rues, "I knew he'd open his big yap once too often.") In the film's wittiest visual touch, Rhodes's rapid plunge in popularity is signaled by the panel lights in the elevator as it descends from floor to floor ("The Lonesome Rhodes Express, going down!" roars the elevator operator)—by the time it reaches the lobby, Rhodes's career has hit flat bottom. Stunned, stung, disoriented, he retreats to his Manhattan penthouse lair, where his punny name takes on ironic significance: he learns it's Lonesome at the top. In fifties films, nothing symbolizes how lonely it is at the top better than a penthouse suite from which love has flown. A spectacular view of the skyline, sure, but with no one tender to share it, no one to cuddle, it's just a highrise mausoleum filled with the canned laughter and applause of imaginary crowds (courtesy of a laugh-track machine installed to stoke Rhodes's ego). Shot from an ominous low angle, Rhodes's apartment building looms like the castle tower in *Frankenstein* (only the penthouse windows are lit), its monster shorn of a mate. Just as Burt Lancaster's J. J. Hunsecker is bereft in his eagle's aerie after his sister leaves him to his rotten devices in *Sweet Smell of Success*, Griffith's Rhodes is reduced to frantic pleading after Marcia flees his palatial pad, lashing out like a wounded beast and rending the night air with the anguished cries of her name. "Marcia, don't leave me!" The last shot enshrines the cursive neon of the Coca-Cola sign in Times Square as light reflects off the hoods and windshields of the heedless traffic, not a face in the crowd to be seen.

A time capsule from the pioneer days of television, when the cameras and sets looked Soviet-bulky and the production values were strictly Salvation Army, *A Face in the Crowd* grits with a documentary charm, presenting cameo appearances by then familiar granite heads such as Walter Winchell, John Cameron Swayze, and Mike Wallace (who has outlived *everybody*), postcard snaps of Norman Rockwell small-town Americana, and anxious political palaver whose sinister tone seems drawn from the demagogic specter of Red-baiting senator Joe McCarthy, who died the year *A Face in the Crowd* was released but whose influence lingers today, an enduring toxin in the bloodstream. *A Face in the Crowd* peered into a glass darkly at the prospect of a mob mentality that might rise from the mud and follow the tune of a malignant Pied Piper. While contemporary reviewers scoffed at the prospect of a hayseed fireball like Lonesome Rhodes becoming a national sensation, Kazan-Schulberg's depiction of the packaging and marketing of fake authenticity now looks prophetic, if a trifle overcooked. In 1990, Kazan told biographer Schickel that the film anticipated the rise of Ronald Reagan, and Schickel adds, "It also anticipates George W. Bush's manipulation of the crowd." These days we pride ourselves on being more sophisticated in perceiving image manufacturing and media manipulation, but I would argue that it's the average voters who have savvied up over the last half-century and the Beltway pundits who have become the rubes, regressively dumber with each political cycle. They're suckers for a "man of the people" more than the people themselves are! It's the Beltway cognoscenti who fetishized Bush's likability, harping on how much more fun he'd be to have a drink with than the cardboard Gore (never mind that Gore won the popular vote), lionize John McCain as a no-guff maverick (never mind his rampant reversals and shameless backflips to court favor with the Republican far right), and keep fobbing off Newt Gingrich—that Uriah Heepish fraud—as a bubbling fountain of futuristic intellect instead of the flagrantly opportunistic manure spreader he has shown himself to be over the last two decades. It was the majority of the American people who kept "Monicagate" in sensible perspective while archdeacons of capital wisdom such as David Broder worked themselves up to a fine moral lather, and it was the majority of the American people who faced reality and turned against the war in Iraq while the archdeacons frittered and fence-straddled. The militant gullibility and brassy confidence of today's elite opinion-makers produce more harm and folly than anything conjured in *A Face in the Crowd*. Because they possess influence. They're *professional* dupes.

Vanity Fair, March 2007

V: BOOKS, AUTHORS, CRITICS

Knowledge Is Good?
The Intellectual Killer Elite

Saratoga Springs, April 10. Lining the streets of North Broadway are the sort of threatening-looking trees that pelted Dorothy and Toto with apples on their way to Oz. After hanging a left, the visitor finds himself in the bosom of Skidmore College, where squirrels carelessly frolic and "Knowledge Is Good." Before long, however, the true cheery horror of campus life comes flooding back: Frisbees! beer busts! student elections! (Pinned to a bulletin board in the student lounge was a sign that read "Simon Sez: Vote for Garfunkle.") What could possibly lure an unsuspecting soul into this godforsaken wilderness?

The back cover of the literary quarterly *Salmagundi*'s winter issue announces the following:

Salmagundi
15th Anniversary Conference
American Civilization: Failure in the New World?

Participants:

George Steiner
Christopher Lasch
Stanley Kauffmann
John Lukacs
Bharati Mukherjee
Robert Garis
Dwight Macdonald
Gerald Graff
Susan Sontag
John Gagnon
Leslie Fiedler
Ben Belitt
Ronald Paulson
Robert Boyers
& others

This intellectual Killer Elite would participate in nine sessions concerning the current state of American culture—"the civilizational perspective/the novel/poetry/the idea of history in america/dance/theatre/film/character types in american social science/painting." . . . When I read the announcement, chapel bells pealed in the distance and a host of doves fluttered against the windowpane: omens beckoning me to Saratoga Springs. So off to Skidmore I scooted, keen on seeing whether or not American Civilization would be given a send-in-the-lions thumbs-down.

I

Inside Filene Hall, murmurs, gossip. At stage right, a man fiddled with knobs behind a portable console, taping the weekend's proceedings for National Public Radio; near him stood a lectern, and left of the lectern a foldup table with microphones taped to its top. Except for clusters of Skidmore coeds (strawberry-haired pretties in jeans and sneaks), the audience was infested with the sort of young academics who haunt the classified pages of *The New York Review of Books:* A Witty, Erudite Sybarite snuggled up to a Warm, Appealing Scorpio; behind them, a Woody Allen Admirer in a patched-elbow corduroy jacket scanned the room for Sensitive Wasps (no fatties please). . . . Suddenly a door flipped open and out trooped the *Salmagundi* allstars: and a grimmer group of gangsters I've seldom seen. LESLIE A. FIEDLER went to his seat with the defiant waddle perfected by Norman Mailer in *Maidstone;* STANLEY KAUFFMANN looked as if he had just emerged from a Marguerite Duras double feature; and on the panelists' table converged CYNTHIA OZICK, CHARLES MOLESWORTH, JOHN LUKACS, and HENRY PACHTER. Holding forth at the lectern was host and moderator ROBERT BOYERS. And who, squeaks a voice from the back of the room, is ROBERT BOYERS?

ROBERT BOYERS is a bearded young academic with a peculiar fondness for salmon-pink ties. Sleeplessly industrious, BOYERS assembles lit-crit anthologies, teaches English at Skidmore, contributes to London's *Times Literary Supplement*, and edits not only *Salmagundi* (a deep-think quarterly modeled on *Partisan Review*) but *The Bennington Review* (a large handsome graphics-oriented slick). He has also composed book-length appreciations of critical mentors R. P. Blackmur, F. R. Leavis, and Lionel Trilling. The Trilling study is jawbreakingly titled *Lionel Trilling: Negative Capability and the Wisdom of Avoidance*, and there are those of us who feel Trilling might have been wiser had he accepted more and avoided less. Shabbier mortals might smoke in the balcony or root in the bleachers; Trilling apparently spent every evening brooding on the cliffs of Dover Beach. (Mused art critic Harold Rosenberg, "When I first encountered the gravity of Lionel Trilling I did not get the joke; it took some time to realize there wasn't any.") In March 1974, BOYERS convened a two-day symposium at Skidmore to discuss Trilling's *Sincerity and Authenticity*, a gray cerebration lightened only by Trilling's brief rumination on the nude-running craze—"We won't go into the sincerity or authenticity of streaking, which is a very ambiguous thing," he observed. Lionel Trilling could find ambiguity in the damnedest places.

Even with Trilling hovering like the Holy Ghost above its pages, *Salmagundi* manages issue after issue to be one of the few quarterlies worth a serious skim. It isn't as lively as *The Hudson Review*—which has a bullpen full of hard-throwing critics (Marvin Mudrick, William Pritchard, Roger Sale)—but it has far more juice and rigor than the now-moribund *Partisan Review*. Ironically, *Salmagundi* represents a chaste retreat from the flirtation with pop culture indulged in by *Partisan Review* contributors in the late sixties, a flirtation which provoked culturally conservative powerbrokers like Philip Rahv to make grousing remarks about nihilistic "swingers." Instead of meditations on camp, the Beatles, and the significance of Muhammad Ali, *Salmagundi* entices its academic audience with articles like *The Extraterritoriality of Siegfried Kracauer, Johan Huizinga—The Historian as* Magister Ludi, *"Shipwreck, Autochthony, and Nostos": An Approach to the Poetry of John Peck*, and (a real pearl, this) *Performance as Transformation: Richard Schechner's Theory of the Play/Social Process Knot*.

After welcoming us to Skidmore, BOYERS announced that the keynote speaker—GEORGE STEINER—was too ill to attend, and that he would read STEINER's paper on the parched emptiness of American culture—"Archives of Eden." A thankless task, though BOYERS made things easier on himself by slicing STEINER's speech from two hours to one. STEINER sent word through BOYERS that the "awkward" and "vulnerable" paper we would hear *was* his presence—a lightly sounded note of mock humility. In Clive James's comic epic about the London literary world, *Peregrine Prykke's Pilgrimage*, GEORGE STEINER appears as "Doc Stein," a pompous polymathic whiz whose vocabulary consists of "words a cockroach uses to its mother/And *Barthes* and *Levi-Strauss* use to each other." Early on STEINER lived up to his reputation as "Doc Stein" by sprinkling his paper with phrases like "relevant antinomies" and "quotidian awareness" and "Puritan theodicy." He also indulged in his notorious flair for namedropping, unbuckling the velvet rope that separates the gum-chewing rabble from the great to usher in Nietzsche, Kafka, Heidegger, Sartre, Goethe, Mann. ". . . I take it that American culture has no extraterritoriality to time . . . densities of obtuseness . . . howl with the wolves of the so-called counter-culture . . . from Thoreau to Trilling . . . make excellence fully accessible to the vulgate. . . ." Imagine a village in which, one by one, the lights are going out—that's what happened to the audience as "Archives of Eden" snuffed the flame from their minds. Coughs began to echo coughs like yodels across Alpine crags.

The paper was, in short, a Pseud Masterpiece. STEINER's argument: America has not created a rich, loamy culture, but serves as the custodian of European art and thought. Our museums display the sculpture and paintings of Euro-masters, our libraries house their manuscripts; America itself, however, has created little of lasting value in art or literature or mathematics or metaphysics. According to STEINER, this country was founded by immigrants with pinched minds who "opted out" of history to create a New Eden. Instead, they created a gluttonous empire teeming with goopy, provincial Babbitts—"In the New Eden," he intoned, "God's creatures move in herds." As damning proof of America's philistinism, he sourly observed that the country has a Hall of Fame for baseball players but no classic editions of American writers. In Europe, he told us, a good student carries Gramsci in one pocket, another carries Bonhoeffer; and the best will carry both. He concluded: "It is the book in the pocket that matters." Which made me a touch sheepish, since the book in *my* pocket was a P. G. Wodehouse entertainment in which Bertie Wooster fretted about spending a weekend with Sir Roderick Glossop, a loony-bin doctor who sits on his patients' heads. Sir Roderick might have cocked an inquisitive eyebrow had he heard STEINER's speech, which was filled with references to schizophrenia, sclerosis, contagion, infection, cancer, and leprosy. Perhaps (thinks Glossop, stroking his chin thoughtfully) it's not Western civilization but STEINER's psycho-somatica which makes him think everything has turned to rot and ennui.

After this soul-sick lamentation came a panel discussion, and it was something of a shock to hear panelist CYNTHIA OZICK proclaim s.'s speech a "thrillingly stupendous" voyage that carried her along on waves edged with "a snowy plenitude of flakes." Gifted as she is, OZICK is something of a flake herself. In D. A. Pennebaker's film *Town Bloody Hall*, she draws a big laugh when she confronts Norman Mailer with a quote he made about writing with his balls—Norman, she wanted to know, exactly what color ink do you dip your precious testicles into? When not being mischievously cute, OZICK enjoys playing the pixie-victim; she told the Skidmore audience that she suspects her apartment is the target of vandalism because she's the only one in her working-class neighborhood who frequents the library and has a kid who doesn't use double negatives. Though OZICK coyly poor-mouthed herself as a "philistine scribbler," she launched an analysis of STEINER that was as tortuously academic as an article in, well, *Salmagundi*. Quarreling with STEINER's concept of the artist as a Romantic sufferer, OZICK climbed a spiral staircase in her mind, step by creaky step, arriving at the top only to flick on a small dim switch marked "Irony." Had the Skidmore audience been in a rebellious mood, OZICK might have been bonked on the beezer with a well-aimed avocado, but she read from her notes for a half hour without a single missile whistling through the air. After she concluded her incomprehensible rebuttal, several couples grabbed their coats and bolted for freedom.

CHARLES MOLESWORTH, a professor of English at Queens College who has a too high regard for the later poetry of Robert Lowell, wisely kept his comments brief, noting only that STEINER's attack ignored the contributions of Duke Ellington and IBM. Just as the goggle-eyed audience began to resemble a netful of contaminated fish, JOHN LUKACS slapped some life into the evening. LUKACS, a Hungarian emigre whose books include *Historical Consciousness* and *The Last European War*, didn't needle STEINER with irony, as OZICK had done; he demolished him with a scorn that can only be called Nabokovian. After a funny discourse on the Puritan heritage and that "medieval Levittown" known as Massachusetts, LUKACS ridiculed the notion that the mass of European immigrants "opted out" of history, or that the emigre intellectuals so admired by STEINER nourished America with their greatness. Einstein, with his baggy trousers and "astral hair," played the role of genius long after his genius had been tapped; George Lukacs (my namesake, LUKACS ruefully noted) was "a Weimar Age fossil" dug up by fatuous lefties; and Paul Tillich—well, Tillich devoted his sacred days to pornography and other unsavory pursuits (Hannah Tillich, in *From Time to Time*: "One of the nudes came to our table, where we placed a silver coin. She turned around and took it with her sphincter muscle"). LUKACS unsettled some people with a contemptuous aside about "the vomitorium of Brecht," but his attack on universities that have turned the Holocaust into a "cultural industry" had heads nodding with vigorous approval. After praising

American pop composers like Johnny Mercer and George Gershwin, LUKACS cited a passage in STEINER's speech in which he lamented that a Washington museum houses a roomful of Stradivariuses. To STEINER, this roomful of unplayed violins is damning proof that America is a custodian and not a creator of fine culture; to LUKACS, it proves that the country isn't bound to a desiccated classicism. "The violins may be mute," he concluded, "but the fiddler is still on the roof."

When LUKACS was finished, STEINER's thesis lay in a smoking, bone-hacked heap, a burnt offering to the Homeric gods. Unfortunately, the evening was not yet done. HENRY PACHTER, an author and historian who reminds one less of Nabokov than of one of his bewildered academics (Pnin, perhaps), dawdled for 10, 15, 20 minutes, dropping pellets of scorn on STEINER's loftier conceits. Fingers began to twitch with fear and boredom, for PACHTER is one of those speakers who never reaches a full stop but keeps connecting clause to clause to clause, his sentences forming a string of boxcars stretching endlessly into the night. Finally, mercifully, the caboose whistled off, and the audience began to volley forth comments. Two seats away from me, a Passionate, Caring Young Intellectual complained about the absence of a Marxist perspective on the panel, saying that the dialogue lacked a "dialectical dimension." When PACHTER said that "dialectical" was one of those intellectual buzzwords that ought to be retired, the Passionate, Caring Marxist Pseud snapped, "*Excuse* me, sir, but I didn't interrupt *you* while you were speaking, so please don't interrupt *me*." Before I could reach over and smack the twerp over the head with my clipboard, BOYERS diplomatically cooled things down by saying that the spirited comments were "well taken" (whatever that means). Before the session adjourned, there was an odd exchange between OZICK and FIEDLER. FIEDLER, sitting in the front row, cheerfully remarked that GEORGE STEINER "aspires to snobbery" but lacks the confidence to be a true snob. (He's wrong, I think: STEINER has a snootful of confidence.) "Are you a snob?" asked OZICK. "Yeah," answered FIEDLER with a Mailerish growl, adding, "*I* live in a working-class neighborhood and feel at home."

The next afternoon the two of them would again lock antlers.

II

As Friday spread its colors with the glory of a Ronald Firbank epiphany ("The turquoise tenderness of the sky drew from her heart a happy coo"), American Civilization seemed secure: The opening address had been trampled beneath a stampede of ridicule, and the Holiday Inn stood undisturbed, a symbol of everything STEINER and the Steinettes despise in our materialistic wasteland. Legging it out of the Inn, I arrived at Skidmore shortly before LESLIE FIEDLER's well-rehearsed attempt to rehabilitate the reputation of the American Novel.

When the spotlight is on, FIEDLER doesn't waddle or slomp. Riding his stomach like a chariot, he rolls past mere worldlings like a Jewish Sun God. His untidy locks and bulging brow may remind one of the bust on Linus's piano, but the manner is Steps of the Pentagon 1967: jovial, combative, ironically grandiloquent. Like Mailer, FIEDLER enjoys teasing the audience by suggesting that the air is alive with existential possibilities—that his talk may swerve around unanticipated corners. The title of his address: "The Death and Rebirth of the Novel." He began by saying that he wasn't sure what he was going to say until a few minutes before he arrived. Which seemed a trifle disingenuous, since he contributed a paper to John Halperin's 1976 anthology *The Theory of the Novel: New Essays* titled "The Death and Rebirth of the Novel," and has been fanning the flame of the phoenix since *Cross the Border—Close the Gap.* "The novel," FIEDLER announced, "is dead as a final form; as an end itself." And from that RIP he wandered down familiar paths, tracing the novel from its humble beginnings as Bourgeois Entertainment to its ascendence into its various subgenres (Jewish-Feminist, Neo-Colonial SciFi, etc.). Echoing Gore Vidal, FIEDLER noted the proliferation of University Novels: novels which exist only to be taught, explicated, embalmed. And, again echoing Vidal (V.'s essay on the best-seller list in *Matters of Fact and of Fiction*), FIEDLER observed that most novels these days have their roots not in Parnassus or Grub Street but in Hollywood, as future movie projects. Stale as most of this news was, FIEDLER was never less than engaging: he embroidered his talk with comic anecdotes and odd bits of fact about Saul Bellow, Samuel Clemens, and *Uncle Tom's Cabin.* Resistance, however, began to percolate on the panel.

OZICK declared, "The sociology of the novel is of no interest to me," explaining that what did interest her were paragraphs, punctuation. "The colon is dead," she lamented, to much applause. GERALD GRAFF, a humorless scold whose new book, *Literature Against Itself*, tries to fend off the semiotic police, tugged on his mustache and did some earnest huffing about "values" and "content." When he reminded the audience that Shakespeare's work has "a humanistic dimension," a hundred pair of eyes rolled heavenward in exasperation. Watching his rivals committ harakiri, FIEDLER buoyantly lit up a long thick cigar, a foul-smelling number that had the panelists turning darker shades of green.

It took SUSAN SONTAG (who was sitting in the front row wearing baby blue cowboy boots) to say what sorely needed saying: that Fiedler's categories not only have lost their usefulness but now clutter his (and our) vision. At one time his heady love of myth and genre and archetype allowed him to detect patterns in American literature that had eluded less foolhardy critics. FIEDLER's unashamed love of pop— sci-fi, comic books, Russ Meyer flicks—was also liberating at a time when academic critics tended to be ponderously Olympian (Lionel Trilling), hyperaesthetically gnomic (I. A. Richards, R. P. Blackmur), or sneeringly severe (F. R. Leavis and the *Scrutiny* spear carriers). In recent years, however, FIEDLER's love of pop has turned into a love of a love of pop. He extravagantly admires his appetite for trash; it's his way of proving that he isn't a prissy academic prig—that he's one of the kids. Similarly, FIEDLER's schlock-Freudian methodology is now used onanistically—his allegiance is not to the artist but to his own technique. An artist who doesn't fit FIEDLER's archetypes has his limbs lopped off.

In FIEDLER's new book, *The Inadvertent Epic*, a study of race melodramas from *Uncle Tom's Cabin* to *Roots*, he unleashes a squadron of archetypes—Good Good Nigger, Good Bad Nigger, Black Rapist, Wicked Slavedriver, Old Testament Mother. When a black artist like Ishmael Reed criticizes such stereotypes or tries to subvert them in his own fiction, FIEDLER dismisses him as the darling of "elitist critics," adding that Reed's reservations "are clearly cued by the fact that [*Roots*] not merely outsold but obliterated his own book [*Flight to Canada*]." For FIEDLER, success is the only thing that matters—the roar of the masses imbues even the shoddiest work with mythopoeic power, leaving losers like Ishmael Reed to chew on their spite. *The Inadvertent Epic* concludes with FIEDLER's by-now familiar celebration of the privileged insanity and "dionysiac, demonic" ecstasies released by such books. "But it doesn't occur to him [writes Marvin Mudrick of another would-be Dionysian] that nothing in life or literature is more exciting than goodness: that Troilus, Criseyde, and Pandarus are all both good and wonderfully interesting; so too Elizabeth Bennet, Anne Elliot, Sophocles's Antigone, Pushkin's Tatyana, Trollope's Plantagenet Pallises, Lawrence's Tom Brangwen . . . when someone takes *me* to the zoo I want to see the swans."

SONTAG didn't toss crumbs to the swans or snip roses from the hedges of *Mansfield Park*, but she did come to the defense of OZICK, who became teary-eyed after FIEDLER made sport of her endangered colons. She said OZICK was one of the *few* good writers in America; an *unclassifiably* good writer. With the smell of FIEDLER's stogie polluting the room, the session broke up, Skidmore students dashing to the exits for gulps of fresh air.

After a brief breather, a panel on film and theater convened, hosted by *Salmagundi*'s film critic, ALAN SPIEGEL, an eager young blister who dresses in a manner FIEDLER would doubtless describe as Academic Funky (earth-colored corduroys, rolled-up shirtsleeves, scuffed Hush Puppies). At his side were STANLEY KAUFFMANN of *The New Republic*, dance critic ROBERT GARIS, and that legendary dreadnought, DWIGHT MACDONALD. Speaking first was KAUFFMANN, a movie critic who has an unhealthy respect for alienation, whether it's packaged as American lower-depths naturalism (*Wanda*) or European art-house asceticism (*The Left-Handed Woman*). A connoisseur of anomie and artful fatigue, KAUFFMANN isn't a writer who surfs on the crest of giddy passion; his sentences drip and dribble, forming stagnant pools of commonplace opinion. Like Trilling's gravity, KAUFFMANN's "gentlemanly" tact is taken as the proud disinclination of a fine mind to lose its mooring. In other words, Inertia equals Integrity. Happily, the energy missing in his writing is spurtingly present in his public appearances. Here, he talked about how America gave film to the world, and, during a discussion of the impact of movies on private lives, fondly reminisced about receiving his first kiss from an impetuous lass—"As she kissed me, she turned into Joan Crawford."

After KAUFFMANN came MACDONALD, once described by Norman Mailer as conceivably the world's worst public speaker: "It was true Macdonald's authority left him at the entrance to the aura of the podium. In that light he gesticulated awkwardly, squinted at his text, laughed at his own jokes, looked like a giant stork, whinnied, shrilled, and was often inaudible. When he spoke extempore, he was some-times better, often worse." Friday was one of MACDONALD's better days. After saying that he wasn't used to being at events where words like "antinomian" were bandied about so freely, he declared that STEINER's speech and OZICK's da capo recapitulation "turned me off culture—and I don't know when I'll get back to it." Admitting that only a few films had pleased him in recent years—*Amarcord, Tree of the Wooden Clogs*, Coppola's two *Godfathers*—MACDONALD wondered if he had really missed anything by hanging up his spikes as *Esquire*'s movie critic in 1966. Suddenly the session (weirdly, comically) turned into a discussion of what MACDONALD should have done with his career, the panelists serving as guidance counselors. *Well, Dwight, maybe you should have hung in there until Fassbinder squeezed into his first leather jacket. . . .*

As the afternoon waned, KAUFFMANN played the Soul of Liberal Reason, MACDONALD the curmudgeonly crank. After KAUFFMANN said that he didn't wish to speak slightingly of "the popcorn crowd," MAC-DONALD barked, "Aw, go ahead." KAUFFMANN: "No, no; Ingmar Berg-man has remarked that those who go to see a Doris Day film—forgive me, is she still alive?—may go to see one of his films the following week. Often in the same theater." MACDONALD: "They shouldn't be allowed to."

The afternoon's climax came when a woman in the audience com-plained that in this session on American film and theater, the-ah-tur had gone totally undiscussed. ("Fine with me," someone muttered, and several heads nodded in agreement.) Well, said KAUFFMANN, Ameri-can playwriting is in a sorry state; there are, however, interesting pro-ductions around. And he lauched into an aria over Elizabeth Swados's "Passover Cantata," *The Haggadah.* As KAUFFMANN explained that the show's Moses is played by a half-black, half-Chinese nine-year-old named Craig Chang, MACDONALD began shaking his storky head in disbelief. Then, spreading his arms wide, KAUFFMANN said that the work possessed "a beautiful efflorescence"—which was too much for MACDONALD. "Stop! stop" he sputteringly pleaded, teasing KAUFFMANN with the word ("efflorescence . . . *efflorescence?*") as K. tried vainly to defend Swados. KAUFFMANN explained to the audience that MACDON-ALD comes from the H. L. Mencken generation which believes that a resounding No is always more convincing than a Yes. "Deliquescence, maybe," chuckled MACDONALD amiably, "but efflorescence . . ."

III

Saturday, April 12. After a short break, the symposium's grand finale commenced: an audience participation session featuring FIEDLER, KAUFFMANN, GRAFF, MACDONALD, SONTAG, and CHRISTOPHER LASCH. In this press conference setup, the audience could sharply probe the panelists' minds and feelings on the current drift of American culture.

It was a Luis Buñuel nightmare, invisible hands gripping us to the chairs as swallows chirped in Esperanto—a subcommittee meeting at the United Nations couldn't have been more soul-stifling. It wasn't all boredom: SONTAG, after needlessly fluffling her feathers to inform us that she had slaved "five years on the six essays" in *On Photogra-phy*, spoke at some length about the Americanness of American pho-tography: FIEDLER, ebullient as Falstaff in an ale-house, claimed that a male sexist conspiracy was responsible for Harriet Beecher Stowe being denied her great due (sighs, groans); and GRAFF stirred the audi-ence to hisses when he told them they didn't ask good questions. As if to prove his point, a Vietnam veteran who had asked a question the previous day complained that his query hadn't been satisfyingly answered. KAUFFMANN said, Excuse me, I thought I *had* answered your question; no, said SONTAG, I don't believe you did, Stanley. Well, why don't you ask your question again? said KAUFFMANN, the Soul of Lib-eral Reason. And, dropping a needle into a groove, the man said, "I'm a Vietnam veteran . . ." and reasked his question word for tiresome word. Later, a man in the last row who assured us all that he was a friend of Michael Herr said that a lot of young Americans had the time of their lives in Vietnam. "I don't think the Vietnamese had as much fun as the Americans," SONTAG dryly remarked. And from a conversation about the political emptiness of Vietnam films ("Wasn't there a film called *The Deer Hunter*?" wondered MACDONALD), the dis-cussion detoured into the cultural impact of feminism. By this time, the panelists were leaning on the table with such bad posture that they looked like a truss advertisement, their spines bending under all the weight and wisdom and guilt of Western Culture. And then SON-TAG said something startling: Responding to a comment from one of the feminists in the peanut gallery about her being the only woman on the panel, she half-ruefully confessed, "I've spent all my life being the only woman on the panel."

As a question from the audience tediously unraveled, the Only Woman on the Panel slipped her arms into her coatsleeves, signaling that this glorious occasion was about to end. After FIEDLER suggested that from now on serious drinking should be done *before* the sympo-sium, panelists and acolytes trudged like a defeated army over to the Surrey Inn, a dark, cozy cove across the street from the Skidmore campus. Conviviality reigned: ALAN SPIEGEL made "cheese" smiles for James Hamilton's camera; CHRISTOPHER LASCH curled his fingers to form shadow-graphs on the wall (". . . this is a duck, and *this* is a bunny"). Somewhere across the Atlantic, however, an embittered GEORGE STEINER was lining antinomies up like toy soldiers, contem-plating a fresh assault upon the New World.

The Village Voice, May 5, 1980

On the Ropes

Selected Letters, Ernest Hemingway

Dropped from a modest height, Ernest Hemingway's *Selected Letters* (Charles Scribner's Sons, $27.50) could capsize a canoe, flatten a toiling peasant, leave a brick-sized hole in a patch of damp cement. At 948 hefty pages, the book represents perhaps the last big bang of the Hemingway industry [no such luck—JW], the last log to be kindled in his honor. Along with Hemingway's own memoir, *A Moveable Feast* (published posthumously in 1964), there have been volumes of reminiscences from a brother, a wife, friends, rivals, casual bystanders, and disgruntled spear-carriers. Time and time again we've heard Hemingway quiet F. Scott Fitzgerald's qualms about the size of his penis (which Zelda slighted as being a touch wee) and seen Fitzgerald forgetfully let a round go long, enabling Morley Callaghan to send Hemingway sprawling on the canvas in a Paris gym (the fullest account appears in Callaghan's bittersweet *That Summer in Paris*). If stags could talk, they would dictate memoirs describing the tremulous moment Hemingway's bullet grazed their antlers.

Yet this streaming cataract of books hasn't been enough to keep Hemingway's reputation from slipping—slipping so dramatically that in 1967 critic Malcolm Cowley felt compelled to write a cannonade for *Esquire* called "Papa and the Parricides," which chided those whittling away at Hemingway's reputation. Eloquent and impassioned as Cowley's essay was, it failed to shore up Hemingway's slide. As Wilfrid Sheed observed, "[Hemingway's] serious admirers had retreated . . . to defending the early short stories and parts of *The Sun Also Rises* and snippets of *A Farewell to Arms*, and retreat usually leads to rout in these matters: the short stories could not hold out by themselves forever."

I'm afraid this volume of letters isn't going to give Hemingway's reputation a thrilling lift. Profane and briskly gossipy at their best, these letters have a scrappy, dashed-off bluster: they lack the full-flowing humorousness of Flannery O'Connor's great letters, the teasing, pugnacious rigor of Edmund Wilson's correspondence (to name only two of Hemingway's contemporaries). As editor Carlos Baker notes in his foreword to *Selected Letters*, Hemingway's letter-writing was a way of unwinding, of shooting off steam. The screws of concentration, so tight when he was writing prose, could be comfortably loosened to offer buck-up advice to Fitzgerald or to spread a bit of malicious dirt ("[Gilbert] Seldes, his sphincter muscle no doubt having lost its attractive tautness has left the Dial. An aged virgin [poet Marianne Moore] has his place"). Hemingway was always full of bluff and braggadocio, and his letters are crammed with accounts of insults given and deflected, punches triumphantly thrown. In a letter to Sara Murphy, Hemingway describes a bash-up with Wallace Stevens, who broke his hand on Hemingway's jaw: "Tell Patrick [Sara's son] for statistics' sake Mr. Stevens is 6 feet 2 weighs 225 lbs. and that when he hits the ground it is highly spectaculous." *Timmmbeeeer!* you can almost hear Hemingway shouting.

Statistics play a prominent role in Papa's correspondence. When not totting up the weekly kill of fish, elk, and bear, Hemingway keeps a careful watch on the day's word count. Writing to his publisher in 1949, Hemingway delivers a progress report on *Across the River and into the Trees:* "House count on book is Monday 802, Tuesday 379, Wed. 314, Thursday 688." In a postscript, H. adds, "Did 388. Plenty for the week. Adds up to 2516." Hemingway was both rooster-proud and touchy about his output. "I'll never forget," he writes Max Perkins, "Sinclair Lewis calling To Have etc. [*To Have and Have Not*] a 'thin screaming of only 67,000 words!' May have the number of words wrong. He himself writes a hoarse scream of never less than 120,000. But if I wrote as sloppily . . . as that freckled prick I could write five thousand words a day year in and year out." Everything needs to be tabulated, even one's wounds: "It is never in the papers," he complained in a letter to Robert Cantwell, ". . . that you were wounded on 22 different occasions and have been shot through both feet, both legs, both thighs, both hands and had six bad head wounds due to enemy action." In his fiction, Hemingway enshrines the *texture* of experience—the bone-white purity of pebbles in a stream, the iridescent gleam of trout writhing on the hook; in Hemingway's letters, reality is endowed with a sense of authority and of snaillike progress only when it can be racked up in tidy columns.

Watching Ernest Hemingway add a modest amount of words to his weekly mound is not the stuff of enthralling heroic drama, however. It's like watching a toy skyscraper going up, brick by tiny brick. But what finally wears the reader out is Hemingway's monotonous bravado. Readers familiar with Lillian Ross's needle-sharp 1950 *New*

Yorker profile of Hemingway will wince with embarrassment when they come across Papa's thumping his chest once again about which literary giants he could lick in the ring. "I tried for Mr. Turgenieff first and it wasn't too hard," he writes Charles Scribner in 1949. "Tried for Mr. Maupassant (won't concede him the de) and it took four of the best stories to beat him." The author of *Daisy Miller* and *The Golden Bowl* isn't worth even a halfhearted poke: "Mr. Henry James I would just thumb him the first time he grabbed and then hit him once where he had no balls and ask the referee to stop it."

Yes, Hemingway was the founding father of the the-bulge-in-my-pants-is-bigger-than-the-bulge-in-your-pants school of criticism, and he doesn't content himself with sizing up the dead. Unnerved by the acclaim given *From Here to Eternity*, sensing perhaps that James Jones might be a contender for the throne of Official Great American Writer, Hemingway spat out his distaste in a letter dispatched to Charles Scribner. Jones, he tells Scribner, is a "wide-eared jerk" and screw-up who will probably kill himself someday: "I hope he kills himself as soon as it does not damage his or your sales. If you give him a literary tea you might ask him to drain a bucket of snot and then suck the puss out of a dead nigger's ear." It's a festering sore of a letter, so ugly and obsessive in its details that it casts a stomach-lurching pall over the rest of the book. After reading the slash at Jones, I felt like tossing the book aside and taking up something pleasurable—a P. G. Wodehouse novel, perhaps, or a volume of Pepys. Only duty drove me on to the end.

Not all of these letters are spiteful and self-inflating, of course; many—most—of them are kind, generous, salty, astute (for example, Hemingway's unfooled analysis of Fitzgerald's flimsy, glamour-smitten *The Last Tycoon*). But even at their most congenial, these letters chip away at Hemingway's stature as an artist. By now it's a ritual bugle note in Hemingway criticism to lament that his swaggering as Papa blurred and tarnished the fine, true achievement of his early fiction, but with the publication of *Selected Letters* the mournful note must be sounded again—for these letters further conceal the cool, rippling lyricism of Nick Adams's big two-hearted river behind a tangly, thorny thicket of gossip and bragging chatter. Blasted Hemingway!—he was always his own worst enemy, right up to the bloody end.

Esquire, May 1981

Stop Me Before I Write Again

A Bloodsmoor Romance, Joyce Carol Oates

Under the doorframe Joyce Carol Oates's *A Bloodsmoor Romance* insidiously creeps, oil-black and oozesome. Like the monster that caused Steve McQueen such distress in *The Blob*, Oates's new novel—her fourteenth—is a near-unstoppable sprawl of renegade force, fattening itself on the bodies of the sleepy and slow-footed as police officers futilely pump shots into its rubbery maw. The novels of most so-called serious writers are usually exercises of craft and care, but *A Bloodsmoor Romance* seems a freak of circumstance, a speck of inspiration that somehow metamorphosed into a word-goop with a ravenous case of the eaties. After the psychological gusts and rages of her previous novel, a contemporary tale of revenge entitled *Angel of Light*, Oates has again laced up her rain bonnet and returned to the mock-gothic storminess of her greatest success, *Bellefleur*. A chronicle of twenty grief-tossed years in the lives of the Zinn family of Pennsylvania, *A Bloodsmoor Romance*—blood on the moor; bring on the Brontës!—is intended to be a subversive takeoff of the brand-name gothics cluttering up the nation's paperback racks, all those Harlequin and Regency and Coventry romances so treasured by dream-hungry housewives. But crowded as it is with showy episodes (séances, virgin snatchings, sadomasochistic tussles), *Bloodsmoor* wants to be more than a fond, romping satire. It's a feminist gothic, a demonstration of how the fripperies of ladylike propriety—corsets and ribbons, parasols and cinches—served as the bonds of erotic repression, leading to madness and lunatic excess. In the heart of every shy maiden is a snow leopard of desire waiting to leap free and bloody its claws.

Tidily put, *A Bloodsmoor Romance* tracks the steps of five vestal pretties and the ways their lives tempestuously stray. On a dusky evening in 1879, Deirdre Zinn, the adopted daughter of the eccentric genius inventor John Quincy Zinn, is plucked from the lawns of Kiddemaster Hall in an outlaw balloon and carried off into the azure. Left on the ground gawping are her half-sisters Samantha, Octavia, Malvinia, and Constance Philippa, too astonished by the sight of this black apparition to toss aside their crochetwork and summon aid. Deirdre's surrealistic abduction becomes the departure point for *Bloodsmoor*'s parade of period kink, as the Zinn sisters fling to the winds their girlhood inhibitions and abandon unwanted husbands, consort with actors, even trade in their sex for a new gender. Although each fallen peach in the Zinn family is given her due, Deirdre seems to be the author's stand-in, not only because she's such a pale wisp of injured feelings—a classic spurned duckling—but because she turns out to be a seeress, a psychic whose head is full of unruly voices. (Oates, as we shall see, often describes the creative process as an invasion of voices.)

But if Deirdre is Oates's fond fancy, the pivotal figure in *Bloodsmoor* is Deirdre's great-aunt Edwina Kiddemaster, who churns out volume after volume of instructional Christian uplift—books with titles like *A Guide to Proper Christian Behavior Amongst Young Persons* and *The Young Lady's Friend: A Compendium of Correct Forms*. Pious and exacting, Edwina Kiddemaster might have sprung from the pages of *The Feminization of American Culture*, Ann Douglas's 1977 study of Victorian sentimentalism and its influence on mass culture. In her starched proprieties, Great-Aunt Edwina isn't unlike Sarah Hale, a magazine editor described by Douglas as "the most important arbiter of feminine opinion of her day, [who] frequently reprinted clerical injunctions to women with obvious approval." Armed with hindsight, Oates makes light amusement of the tropes of maidenly woe, all those swoonings and fretful blushes. She mocks their faith, their fears, their candied politenesses, their snippy sarcasms, their adoration of mustachioed swells. She's using pop literature to unmask pop literature—subverting the conventions of feminine fiction to reveal how those conventions shrouded the true appetites of women in layers of silk and fluff. Like John Barth's *Giles Goat-Boy*, *A Bloodsmoor Romance* is deliberately wordy and antique, a stony artifice carpeted with plastic moss.

Although *A Bloodsmoor Romance* has the fixings of a provocative antinovel, Oates's inability to turn off the babble once again plunges her into the gumbo. In a typical Oates novel, the reader is treated—if that's the word—to a series of Big Scenes connected by a lot of flimsy, careless doodle. Her fans probably drum their fingers patiently during the drowsier passages, knowing that Oates will soon barbecue a new fright for their snacking pleasure. (In Oates's *Wonderland*, a doctor broils and dines on the uterus of a female cadaver. You can't get much freakier than that, and you wouldn't want to try.) In this novel, however, the vamping tap steps leading up to the show-piece horrors are so busy and arch that there's no way for the reader to take a breather between rumbles. To unravel this family saga, Oates has taken on the narrative voice of a flustered old biddy and the results are—well, ruinous. The text becomes an orgy of italics and apostrophes and dithering digressions.

> *That I, as the narrator, am not to* blame *for the sordidness of this particular enterprise, and that the sophisticated reader well comprehends this fact does very little, I confess, to alleviate my sense of both* revulsion *and* guilt. *Nor does the fact that, in seeking to illumine the duplicitous ways by which the eldest Zinn girl, Constance Philippa* [she of the wayward gender], *alter'd herself, or was alter'd, into the outlaw Philippe Fox, I freely—nay, proudly—confess myself* I am ignorant of all detail, and wish to remain so. *For is not the artist, as I have argued earlier, obliged to serve the higher moral truths, in his or her craft? Is he not obliged to* better *the world, and not merely* transcribe *it?*

Beats me; but I do know that fluffing one's petticoats for over 600 pages is of a coyness not to be endured, even (I suspect) by those most devoted to Oates's bumblebee flights.

Perhaps the key to Joyce Carol Oates's fiction is her phantasmagorical fear of sex, her revulsion from the flesh's treacheries. Sex in her fiction is seldom a tender idyll, a bit of lingering play, or even a collision of will and temperament (as it is in, say, Mailer's notorious story "The Time of Her Time"). Sex is instead a ghoulish prank, a corporeal meltdown. In *Bloodsmoor*, one man who has the misfortune of marrying a Zinn daughter doesn't realize that his bride has made a bolt until he's finished rogering a mannequin—"no woman lay beside him, no trembling Constance Philippa, nay, not even a human being, but a *dressmaker's dummy:* headless, armless, and possessing no nether limbs!" (The message: men, in their blind brute lust, aren't smart enough to know whether it's live or Memorex.) Another, who has a thirst for bondage and self-mortification, dies in the saddle when his wife, Octavia, too severely tightens a noose during one of their coupling sessions, snapping off his oxygen supply. Almost needless to add, these slapstick entanglements send Oates's narrator into a nervous tizzy. She even worries that men of base appetite may use her chronicle as an excuse to dash off and have an irresponsible wank. "... I am heartsick, at the distinct possibility, that, amidst my readership, there may well be, here and there, those persons of the masculine

gender, who, lacking an intrinsic purity of character, may, by labori-
ous effort, and much unseemly exercise of the lower ranges of the
imagination, *summon forth a prurient gratification*, from these hapless
pages!" Before reaching for the smelling salts to revive Oates's wilting
authoress, note how the commas in the above sentence slow down the
action like speed bumps, forcing the reader to brake, press down on
the gas pedal, then brake again. Sentences that fitful won't inflame
anyone's libido, as Oates surely knows. She's simply giving herself a
tickle.

At times, the novel *A Bloodsmoor Romance* most resembles is *Fanny*,
that pastiche of naughty whimsies slapped together by the inde-
fatigable Erica Jong. Jong, too, peppered her pages with exclamation marks—"I wrote and burnt and wrote and burnt! I would pen
a Pastoral thro'-out three sleepless Nights only to commit it to the
Flames!" etc.—and turned sex into grunting slapstick. Indeed, both
books take mischievous delight in dragging famous authors through
the bedsheets. In *Fanny*, Pope and Swift descended in hot pursuit of
Fannikin's cunnikins, and in *Bloodsmoor* it's Mark Twain who turns
satyr. After an evening spent shoveling in oysters, pork, and tripe,
Mark Twain makes for the four-poster with Malvinia, only to have
her turn into a spasm-racked tigress: she slaps Twain about, pinches
and bites, then yanks on *"his masculine organ of regeneration!"*—which
of course leaves the old boy rather winded. As comedy, this scene is
about as imaginative and subtle as a whoopee cushion slipped under
the circus fat lady, but what makes it truly disagreeable is Oates's
shameless zeal—her willingness to do *anything* to tart up her book,
even turn a writer as great as Twain into a pornographic buffoon. But
there's probably no point in blaming Oates for her lapses in taste and
consideration. She doesn't seem able to help herself. Voices knock, the
wind whistles, and off Oates floats, into the Twilight Zone . . .

She seems aware of her plight, poor thing. In earlier interviews,
Oates used to pooh-pooh the idea that she wrote too much, claiming
that she frittered away most of the day in idle reverie. "Most of the
time I do nothing . . . ," she told Joe David Bellamy in *The New Fiction*
(1974). "There are not enough hours in the day. Yet I waste most of my
time, in daydreaming, in drawing faces on pieces of paper. . . ." Now
that Oates is the author of fourteen novels, eleven collections of short
stories, three volumes of criticism, and countless poems, prose poems,
letters to the editor, and reviews, she can hardly remain faithful to the
notion that she dribbles away her afternoons at the sketch pad. In a

recent essay in the *Hudson Review* entitled "Notes on Failure," Oates
obliquely defends her frantic beavering away at literature by invoking
Virginia Woolf: *"This insatiable desire to write something before I die, this
ravaging sense of the shortness and feverishness of life, make me cling . . . to
my one anchor*—so Virginia Woolf, in her diary, speaks for us all."
Impressive-sounding as this is, it somehow fails to convince, at least
as far as Joyce Carol Oates is concerned. Virginia Woolf, with death
pressing down on her brow, may have written with feverish haste, but
her novels are models of shape and discipline—she didn't slop words
across the page like a washerwoman flinging soiled water across the
cobblestones. Oates's books, however, are wonders of reckless energy
and dishevelment. Although Oates's poetry is hardly ringing or memorable, it's easier to take than her prose because in writing poetry
she's compelled to choose this word, that. But in writing fiction she
doesn't seem to spiff up her sentences before dispatching them into
the world; ragtag and motley, her phrases are thrown into the breach
like waves of ill-prepared soldiers, a doomed multitude. She ought to
spend more time revising and paring down, but she seems incapable
of trimming away her wordy flab, or unwilling. Perhaps she *prefers* to
drift high and free in the transcendental ether.

What *A Bloodsmoor Romance* makes clear is that writing, for Oates,
is not a vocation or a calling but a semidivine compulsion. To her, the
writer is a shortwave set receiving and beaming messages into the far
reaches of dreamland. "The practicing writer, the writer-at-work, the
writer immersed in his or her project, is not an entity at all, let alone a
person," she writes in "Notes on Failure," "but some curious mélange
of wildly varying states of mind, clustered toward what might be
called the darker end of the spectrum: indecision, frustration, pain,
dismay, despair, remorse, impatience, outright failure." Yes, uneasy
lies the head that wears a crown of thorns, and even branching off
into criticism offers no surcease of woe. She writes in her preface to
the lit-crit collection *Contraries*, "The critic is a pilgrim, an acolyte, a
translator; a gnostic intermediary fueled by the need to bring metaphors from one system to another." (She seems to have picked up a
lot of highfalutin static from Harold Bloom.) To all this worry and
bother I would counter with a remark from Nabokov, who wrote in
his novel *Glory* that his hero sought in literature not the humdrum
obvious but "the unexpected, sunlit clearings, where you can stretch
until your joints crunch, and remain entranced." Even when Joyce
Carol Oates is in a playful mood, her writing fails to provide patches

of sunlit ease; she's too self-mesmerized to tune out the racket in her head and clear away a pool of summery calm, preferring instead to heap on the rubble, the noise, the piles of broken glass. She doesn't write books now, the books write her. She's like an obsessive pianist who even in her sleep practices arpeggio runs, her fingers rippling up and down a phantom keyboard. Snap to, Ms. Oates. It isn't too late. Wake up, wake up, wake up!

Harper's, September 1982

Richard Ford
Guns and Poses

He-man American writers have a heavy appetite for ammo. "Don't just stand there, *shoot* something" is one of the unofficial mottoes of our literature, burned into the bark of trees by James Fenimore Cooper's heroes, perforated into the stomachs of sharks massacred by Ernest Hemingway, advertised on the rusty sides of pickup trucks in the wild New West of Hunter Thompson and Tom McGuane. Birds spatter in flight, fish crimson the sea, corpses soak the carpet, all in the quest by the writers and their heroes for risk, assurance, clarification. Yes, clarification. To those of us not in on the thrill of the kill, all this shooting may seem a smoky blur, but to those behind the gunsight, their purpose is as pure as a crystal drop at the tip of a syringe. Stalking death with lidless eyes, these great white hunters use bullets to nail destiny to the cross.

The novelist Richard Ford is no stranger to high-caliber consecration. Visited in Tennessee by the journalist John Seabrook for *Interview* magazine, Ford was asked if he would like to take a walk in the woods. His reply: "I don't walk. I hunt. Something dies when I stroll around outside." Well, now we know who killed Bambi's mother! It was Richard Ford on one of his death strolls. Yet Ford is no beer-gut bump-on-a-log. He has a parson's high forehead. Acute, pained eyes. And, according to Seabrook, a "prayerful" voice. He's a *sensitive* deerslayer.

Ford occupies an ever larger place of honor on the fiction scene. He isn't a chic hustler, chasing after the latest craze; he gives off a grounded air of goodness. More than admired, he's revered by reviewers (rare enough) *and* his peers (rarer still). He's even received the embrace of the cultural establishment with his recent induction into the American Academy of Arts and Letters. And yet he still appears a man apart, a pale rider. For years (I realized), I had read more about Ford than I had actually read him, an oversight I decided to remedy. Now, after reading reams of his writing, I find myself older but little wiser to his lean mystique. He certainly isn't the Eagle Scout he was advertised.

Edgy and expansive, Richard Ford's writing resembles a road map in all its arteries and creases. It's a road map inked with his own rest-less travels. With his wife, Kristina, he has lived everywhere from Vermont to Montana to Manhattan to his native Mississippi. His first novel, *A Piece of My Heart* (all of his books are available in Vintage Contemporaries paperbacks), was a long ride on a raw road, a dog-gone odyssey through America's dragging underbelly. One morn-ing Ford's Robard Hewes walks out on his wife, Jackie, with barely a word, never to return. In his truck he wheels thousands of miles to Arkansas, where he has been summoned by his cousin Beuna. What is Beuna's hold on Robard? Firm and handy. One night at a ball game she had "fished her hand in his trousers and squeezed him there until he felt a noise down in his throat that wouldn't come loose." It's a noise repeated in the novel like a refrain. On the road Robard assists a stranded woman and she too takes the Nestea plunge into his pants. " 'I'm tired of talking,' she said, watching her hand tour around in his trousers as if it were after something that wouldn't keep still." When Robard finally reunites with Beuna, having ditched the other woman in a dusty, nowhere town—well, it's as if they had never been apart. "She thrust her hand in his trousers and got a fierce grip on him." By the end of this fierce, gripping novel, it's a wonder Robard can do anything but squeak in falsetto.

There's a lot of loose pussy out there is the lesson Robard the human stick shift learns in *A Piece of My Heart*. (Loose, yet con-trary and snappish—nearly every woman seems to be working off a grudge.) But what lesson does the reader learn? Why *does* Robard dump his wife to unfold the road map of his soul? As one character tells him, "If you just wanted to cadge a little pussy you didn't have to drive three thousand miles. You could just go *home*, or down the road, or next door." The only answer Robard supplies comes when he's asked what's more important than a piece of ass, and he replies, "Another piece." Certainly Beuna is portrayed as nothing more than a cheap piece. Her breasts poke out of her blouse, she talks trash in the take-me, hurt-me sound bites of a James M. Cain roadside attraction ("I want to do it in the back of the truck in the dirt and the rocks and the filthiness"), and she has Jell-O for brains. Her exit from the novel is meant to be the shaming exposure she has earned. Fed up, Robard boots Beuna out of the truck and into a patch of mud, where she lands with "her gauze skirt up over her waist, showing her bare behind to the rain." No, Beuna was never worth all this mileage, and Robard's obdurate motivation remains obscure. His whole trip seems a wind-blown, overblown whim—the puzzle pieces of his search are never fitted together. Ending in aimless death, *A Piece of My Heart* is motored by the aversion to women that marks wilderness-flight novels from the beginning of our literature.

"Women and guns" are what John Seabrook says he and Ford discussed when he was a creative-writing student of Ford's. Women and guns are entwined in Ford's work, emblems of entrapment and treachery and dangerous release. Women suffocate; guns ventilate. Ford's second novel, *The Ultimate Good Luck*, is an attempt to fuse these conflicting forces into a single true shot. The scene: Oaxaca, Mexico. The temperature: hot. The mood: itchy. Inside a bungalow a girl suffering from "mescal willies" is peddling Ford's female brand of feel-bad sex: "I sucked you off, right? And I don't even know your name." His name is Harry Quinn; his mission in Mexico, to spring his girlfriend's brother from prison before drug baddies ice him. The girlfriend—Rae—isn't a vivid presence on the page, but she's sane and stalwart, an advance over the skags of *A Piece of My Heart*. In other ways this second novel is an improvement over the first. Structurally, *The Ultimate Good Luck* is the most compact of Ford's novels, with keen inhalations of dread and decay, implosive tension, explosive terror. But like many novels trying to update the James M. Cain/ Jim Thompson canon, *The Ultimate Good Luck* suffers from too much cornstarch in the dialogue. Primitive itches give way to existential emoting. " 'You're never ironic, Harry,' she said airily. 'That's really what's wrong with you. You need to be more ironic.' "

Ironic Harry isn't. A Vietnam veteran, he's the hard works. But like Robard in *A Piece of My Heart*, Harry is opaque, his motivation filed down to a-man's-gotta-do-what-a-man's-gotta-do. And what a man's gotta do in this situation is blow holes in bodies. Don't just stand there, *shoot* something. "Shooting somebody raised your personal importance level," he thinks, and after a shoot-out that leaves three dead, he slips into the *film noir* rain. "He wondered, as he walked, if he'd perfected something in himself by killing three people he didn't know, when he had come at the beginning, simply to save one, and if now he had pleased anybody anywhere. Though he thought that if he hadn't pleased anybody, at least he'd tried to, and had performed it under control, and he hadn't coped so bad all by himself at the end. He thought, in fact, that he'd done fine." Or as Mickey Spillane's Mike Hammer (like Quinn, a battle vet) put it more colorfully in *One Lonely Night*, "I was able to prove that I wasn't a bloodthirsty kill-happy bastard with a mind warped by a war of too many dawns and dusks laced by the criss-crossed patterns of bullets." Killing with steady hands is satisfying *and* sanctifying. Baptized in blood, Quinn has been symbolically reborn.

Set over an Easter weekend, Ford's third novel, *The Sportswriter*, is even more baptismal than *The Ultimate Good Luck*. But this is no baptism of blood or fire. Waves of words baptize America's brow as Ford pipes his prayerful tone from a portable pulpit. His narrator is—ah, but let him introduce himself. "My name is Frank Bascombe. I am a sportswriter." Author of a book of short stories, Bascombe finds himself treading air as a fiction writer. Admitting defeat on that front, he adapts to covering the thrill of victory/the agony of defeat for a magazine modeled on *Sports Illustrated*. The red-eyed fan fever of sports—the noise in the stands, the cabalistic fascination with stats—is rinsed clean in this novel. Sports in *The Sportswriter* are what movies are in Walker Percy's *The Moviegoer*, thin spectacles that allow the narrator to hang his sagging doubts on the line. (As if to acknowledge kinship, Percy provided a blurb for *The Sportswriter*.)

If the men in Ford's earlier fiction lacked interior life, Frank Bascombe overflows with it, flooding every situation with informal address. Something of a self-portrait, Bascombe represents the loneliness of the long-distance writer. His sense of isolation is heightened by the still-haunting death of his son. Bascombe's direct pleas to the reader and his Everyman plight help make this the most poignantly accessible of Ford's novels. And it's probably the only novel of his which has crossover appeal to women. More than popular, *The Sportswriter* is considered by many critics a modern classic. A masterpiece of malaise.

This Cub Scout finds *The Sportswriter* maddening. The novel does have humor, scope, shifting scenery, slip-sliding moods. It doesn't paw a small patch; it swings for the fences. But it's also swimming up to its ennui-soaked eyeballs in a bookish banality and condescension doing its best to pass itself off as bruised wisdom. On nearly every page is the plop of platitude: "A change to pleasant surroundings is always a tonic for creativity." "A life can simply change the way a day changes—sunny to rain, like the song says. But it can also change again." "Some life is only life, and unconjugatable, just as to some questions there are no answers." "Being a man gets harder all the time." Hey, tell me about it. Don't worry, Bascombe will and does, dropping clichés into the slot until he gets the click of a dead phone at the other end of the line. *The Sportswriter* probably has more message units than any novel this side of Saul Bellow, but at least Saul

Bellow's characters are brainy oddballs—their messages carry a static buzz. Frank Bascombe, however, prides himself on being a dreamy blur, lonely as a cloud. "Dreamy people often do not mix well, no matter what you might believe. Dreamy people actually have little to offer one another, tend in fact to neutralize each other's dreaminess into bleary nugatude." (Nugatude: the chewy candy three out of four alienated intellectuals prefer.)

Ford's sportswriter presents himself as a representative case. Divorced, two kids, adrift. Oh, he ponders new roots. He has a nurse girlfriend named Vicki. "Maybe we'll get married in Detroit, fly back and move out to Pheasant Run, and live happily like the rest of our fellow Americans. What would be wrong with that?" Nothing— everything. The sentiment seems snide and insincere. The phrase "our fellow Americans" carries too much ironic snot, and the character of Vicki is smeared with too much cheap lipstick. Everything about her screams no-taste, including her name. "Vicki sounds like a name you'd see on a bracelet at Walgreen's," she complains. A minty airhead, Vicki seems to have Tic Tacs rolling around like BBs in her brain. She's not as coarse as Beuna, but she doesn't seem much more substantial. So what is her attraction for a man who uses "nugatude" in a sentence? "She is a girl for every modern occasion, and I find I can be interested in the smallest particulars of her life," he explains patronizingly. Her charms are more basic than that. Cut to the hotel room: "I have a good handful of her excellent breast now, and what a wonderful bunch she is, a treasure trove for a man interested in romance."

Ass or breast, a piece is just a piece, at least to a Ford hero. And although other women appear in *The Sportswriter*, it's Vicki whose shortcomings carry metaphorical import. You have the feeling that this is what Ford thinks America is: a tacky bimbo. She epitomizes the tawdry future. In his epilogue, Bascombe confides, "From Vicki Arcenault I have not heard so much as a word, and I wouldn't be surprised to learn that she has moved to Alaska and reconciled with her first husband and new love, skinhead Everett, and that they have become New Agers together, sitting in hot tubs discussing their goals and diets, taking on a cold world with *Consumer Reports*, assured of who they are and what they want. The world will be hers, not mine." As a parting shot, he speculates that Vicki will someday discover that she never liked men anyway and then parade this hostility in public.

What a gent. And this, *this!* is the character saluted by Tobias Wolff as "a bird rare in life and nearly extinct in fiction—a decent man."

Afloat in bad faith, Frank Bascombe isn't a decent man, he's a sensitive creep pulling the long face of a decent man. It's a pious impersonation that fooled the critics, and maybe Ford himself. He allows the sportswriter's podium to become a pedestal.

For some readers the real Richard Ford is to be found not in the novels but in the stories, where he compresses the wayward strains of life out West into a crushed snowball shaped like a heart. In the stories collected in his most recent book, *Rock Springs*, he chronicles lives undone by a single misdeed or bad bounce, avoiding the canned soup of *The Sportswriter* for a clearer broth. The ghosts of Hemingway and Raymond Carver and the badlands ballads of Bruce Springsteen haunt the gun barrels of these stories, in which the characters find themselves courting trouble or cornered by it, caught without consolation or shelter. The limited space of these tales leaves less room for Ford to inflate. Yet here too there are problems. Perhaps it's an easy out built into the short-story form, but many of the stories in *Rock Springs* pump with action, only to step back in the last few paragraphs, pause—and punt. These afterthoughts have a lot of hangtime. Sometimes they're affecting, as in "Communist," where the narrator memorializes his mother's voice. (Ford, whose mother died the year he started *The Sportswriter*, strikes his most sorrowful notes when he mourns missing or ineffectual mothers—mourns the warmth their absence has withdrawn from their sons' lives.) But some of these fade-outs fog the action with rhetoric. At the end of the title story, for example, a car thief cases a Pontiac in the parking lot of a Ramada Inn. He looks back at the motel and sees two lighted rooms, one of them his. And the other? Perhaps he's being observed.

> And I wondered, because it seemed funny, what would you think a man was doing if you saw him in the middle of the night looking in the windows of cars in the parking lot of the Ramada Inn? Would you think he was trying to get his head cleared? Would you think he was trying to get ready for a day when trouble would come down on him? Would you think his girlfriend was leaving him? Would you think he had a daughter? Would you think he was anyone like you?

No, I'd probably be wondering if some sum'bitch is trying to break into my car.

Nevertheless, through such stories Ford has become a symbol of rootless America. Evidence of this was the appearance of his face in the May issue of *Money* magazine to illustrate an essay-meditation on motels. The article itself read like *The Sportswriter* checking into a clinic and getting the shakes. "If there's a gaunt sinking feeling comes over us when we push our bag through the doorway and peep inside, a feeling of bearable indignation, of inconsequential undoing, of losing things we know we can't lose . . ." etc. To Ford, low-cost motels are space stations of soullessness, orbiting in oblivion. "And Lord knows, if I couldn't in such a room even force myself to tweak the woof on the hand towels or pull the drapes to take the view or check the rate card on the door—if all devolved to erasure and denatured spirit—what chance could frail desire ever have? Or mystery? Or illusion?" Ma, it's that damned prayerful tone again. That Ford would climb upon such stilts to write about motels in *Money* means that he's come to accept his role as scarecrow to the masses. What a joyless vigil!

Moral seriousness does lend a certain aura, however. After reading Richard Ford's books in succession, I've come to the notion that it's the *idea* of Richard Ford that accounts for his success as much as his writing. Like his late friend Raymond Carver, Ford brings news of spiritual breakage from the far horizons of the heartland while still harboring hope. And like Carver, he isn't meretricious. (Ponderous, pretentious, but not meretricious—he doesn't take shortcuts in his fiction to sure responses.) Loaded with ammo, Ford has the Hemingwayesque part down pat. Who else could fit the bill? Tom McGuane and Barry Hannah are too weirdly flip, James Dickey too baroque. Ford's American Gothic features provide a living testament to his craft and calling, his laconicism sliced not from ham but from some leaner stripe of manhood. His whole outlook on life doesn't do much for me. But then, I've never wanted Bambi's mother on my conscience. When I walk in the woods, I'm content to look.

Vanity Fair, August 1989

Three Critics

Manny Farber's Termite Art

As a movie critic, Manny Farber always packed his pieces with rock salt. The spray of his densely packed sentences left a wide pockmark. Kissing off the early work of Elia Kazan and Sidney Lumet, for example, Farber wrote, "Though the screen is loaded with small realities— flickering hands, shadows, grunts, squirms, spinal sag, lip-clenching, an old brassiere in a bum's suitcase . . . the New York films seemed to shriek for one ordinary casual action, realistically performed, such as Bogart's succinct repairs on the overpopulated tank in *Sahara*." Born near the Mexican border in Douglas, Arizona, in 1917, Farber reviewed movies in the forties and fifties for *The New Republic*, *The Nation*, and *The New Leader*, branching off into more impressionistic forays for *Artforum* in the sixties. (A selection of his reviews appeared in hardcover under the title *Negative Space*. The paperback reprint was called simply *Movies*.) He built his cult reputation on the championing of tobacco-spit American directors who earned their calluses like honest ranch hands—Howard Hawks, Anthony Mann, Raoul Walsh, Sam Fuller, Don Siegel, and William Wellman.

"For instance, Wellman's lean, elliptical talents for creating brassy cheapsters and making gloved references to death, patriotism, masturbation, suggest that he uses private runways to the truth, while more famous directors take a slow, embalming surface route." The surface route Farber called "white-elephant art," the private runways he heralded as "termite art."

Slangy and butch, Farber's style wasn't new to movie criticism. His predecessor at *The New Republic*, Otis Ferguson, could also bulge his biceps and spin wisecracks on a dime. What *was* new was Farber's action-painter zest and impasto layering of language. For Farber was not only a B-movie nut but an art critic and an artist who chummed with painters in the downtown bustle of postwar Manhattan. In 1945, he wrote an electrically sympathetic riff on Jackson Pollock: "The paint is jabbed on, splattered, painted in lava-like thicknesses and textures, scrabbled, made to look like smoke, bleeding, fire, and painted in great sweeping continuous lines." It's this charged-up visual kineticism that gives Farber's criticism its special cast. Sometimes he watercolors a movie in a single sentence. On other occasions he lays on the strokes until he has a full sitting portrait. Nothing could be fuller than his portrait of the Andy Warhol superstar Brigid Polk.

> When Brigid Polk, hippopotamus of sin, sprawls in a bathtub in white bra and blue jeans, and talks to someone just outside camera range about the drug-curing scene in different hospitals, the image is free, for itself, and wide open: the spectator, as well as the actor, can almost vegetalize inside the frame. Everything is stopped as the movie engulfs itself in a fuck-off atmosphere. With giggling hysteria, fag expressions, the most pathetic bravado voice, she explodes the screen outward by giant abandon and cravenness. The camera milks the paleness of her slack flesh, a cheap cotton brassiere cuts into the doughy torso, the image is the most underrated phenomenon in films: a blast of raw stuff.

I've used the past tense to describe Farber's film criticism because he's done piddling-few reviews since the mid-seventies (and those required the service of a co-author—his wife, Patricia Patterson). Always a slow crawler when it came to deadlines, Farber seems to have used up his momentum and hit a complete stop. But if he is no longer adding a sleek black finish to his favorite gangster films, he's keeping expansively busy assembling his own movie-saturated big-wall artworks. When I was in Los Angeles recently, the Museum of Contemporary Art held a major exhibition of Manny Farber's paintings and cutouts, and the result was pretty mind-zapping. True to his termite loyalties, Farber hasn't attempted to create masterpieces by slaving over "an expensive hunk of well-regulated area," but has emptied out his pockets and his memory and littered the field with his fidgety, collectible whims. Tobacco tins, candy-bar wrappers, unsharpened pencils, pillow-book illustrations of Japanese lovers at play, chess-piece arrangements of Liquid Paper bottles, self-admonishing memos ("Go for tricks," "Get it finished," "Keep blaming everyone"), vased flowers and pitted fruit—Farber arranges all of these items as if he were sort-ing out his favorite toys on an angled plane. He's hovering in a helium balloon above a lifetime's accumulation of precious clutter.

It's no surprise that many of Farber's paintings are named after movies, but it is surprising how he extricates bits of lore from the sweep and violence of those films and plants them like toy trees on a model-railroad set. Sam Peckinpah's *The Wild Bunch* was described by Farber in *Negative Space* as "a virile ribbon image, often an aerial view, of border life in 1914 Texas," and his paintings based on Peckinpah's Westerns are aerial views in which the ribbon images (train tracks, red ants, mammoth trucks rounding a curve) have been snipped and pasted askew. Railroad tracks also wind and run like hedges through Farber's pictorial tributes to Anthony Mann, Howard Hawks, *Claire's Knee*, Laurel and Hardy, and *Honeymoon Killers* (this last collage is a virtual badlands of cheesy philandering).

Not all of Farber's movie paintings are hospitable to locomotives. His *McCabe and Mrs. Miller* features a broken bar of Hershey's choco-late, and *The Films of R. W. Fassbinder* so trims the fat from Fassbind-er's blobby corpus that what's left is a pair of toilets, a telephone cord and receiver stretched across an empty bed, a giant beer bottle, and a magazine spread on Hanna Schygulla. What Farber has done in his movie paintings is release the superconcentrated images of his critical writing with a dice-rolling dare. His random effects soon take on their own loose, jazzy rhythm. His paintings have a goofy syncopation.

Large in scale, the paintings have a no-big-deal air about them; they mess around in their own diversions the way that Henry Miller's watercolors did. Farber, who once accused Michelangelo Antonioni of wanting "to pin the viewer to the wall and slug him with wet towels of artiness and significance," keeps his own stuff dry and crinkly-light. His details don't flog but tickle. For me, Manny Farber always adhered too rigidly to a macho code of honor to be a truly great movie critic—like Otis Ferguson, he seemed to shrink from anything he feared was too uncool or sissy. His responsiveness, that is, was intense but narrow. The paintings, however, have a reaching, acquiring, fid-dling spirit. They're American homemade.

It's a pity that Manny Farber's paintings aren't better-known (espe-cially on the East Coast), but if they were he might be in danger of becoming a white elephant himself, jewel-encrusted with acclaim. Termites have to find their own subterranean eating lanes. Farber: "The best examples of termite art appear . . . where the spotlight of culture is nowhere in evidence, so that the craftsman can be ornery, wasteful, stubbornly self-involved, doing go-for-broke art and not caring what comes of it." The scale of Farber's recent work suggests that he's found a major feeding route. He paints lovely pears.

Vanity Fair, May 1986

The Stand-Up Critic

Mudrick Transcribed
Classes and Talks by Marvin Mudrick

Marvin Mudpie, we called him at *Harper's*. (This was 1981–83, when Michael Kinsley was the editor.) His banzai cry riffling the back pages of the *Hudson Review*, where he wrote about books regularly for over thirty years, Marvin Mudrick didn't curtsy before the niceties of criticism. He was a mudslinger. Hardly anyone high or low escaped his spatter. Shakespeare was a woman-loathing lord high executioner swanking his carnage in purple plumage, the dear Samuel Pepys of the diaries was a "churchy jerkoff and mad secret fucker," John Cheever was an aging funkster veiling "past, present, and future in a fine gray spittle of arbitrary disillusion." John Gardner was a postnasal drip. Philip Roth an unstrung poseur ("Poor Roth has lost not only his bearings but his marbles"), structuralism a conehead con job, led by that "inept wizard" Lacan. Even when Mudrick elevated a writer, he leveled the supporting cast, lopping off heads if need be. Saluting Edmund Wilson as sturdy sentinel on literature and seminal ideas, for example, Mudrick made him appear to have been the only sane man standing in the 1940s and 1950s. "Pound had since gone round the bend," he writes. "Trilling sounded like T. S. Eliot after shock treatments," and "Leavis seemed—well, a mite touchy . . ." Magisterial understatement, that!

And applicable not only to F. R. Leavis. Marvin Mudrick also was—well, a mite touchy. He regarded editing from the perspective of Poe's prisoner in "The Pit and the Pendulum." At the mere mention of cuts in his copy, he saw a hissing blade bearing down upon him, slicing air, paper, skin. About editing he was what Malcolm Muggeridge once called a minimomaniac. With angry pinpoint recall he could detail every punctuation change, altered title, transposed sentence, dropped paragraph, and rejected manuscript perpetrated in the pit over the last thirty years.

His testiness didn't stop at the margins. In argument he could go from zero to boiling in seconds, his spectacles filming with steam. He seemed to go out of his way to add a stitch or two to his hurt feelings. He would come to New York, neglect to tell anyone at which hotel he was staying, then later complain that no one bothered to call him. He was one of criticism's rare hard-core impossibles. And yet—there was more to his criticism than abuse, more to his personality than baby squalls shot with paranoia. Products of close reading and open response, the best pieces in his review collections—*On Culture and Literature, The Man in the Machine,* and *Books Are Not Life But Then What Is?*—have a humor, gallop, and hunger for elation virtually absent from criticism today. (Absent as well from Mudrick's last collection, *Nobody Here But Us Chickens,* where he let his bad temper over Shakespeare get the best of him, though there is a hilarious put-down of Hamlet called "The Unstrung Zero.") "Criticism talks, fiction dramatizes," Mudrick declared, and if he read with a razor's edge, he wrote as if he were talking off the top of his head. He turned litcrit into a spinoff of stand-up comedy. An erudite spiel.

Mudrick Transcribed documents what a blast-off artist Marvin Mudrick could be. Edited by Lance Kaplan, the book preserves from tapes classes and talks given by Mudrick at the University of California, Santa Barbara, where he taught literature and was the founder of its College of Creative Studies. As major mover at the College of Creative Studies, Mudrick was, no surprise, controversial. To some outsiders he was worse than a mischief-maker—he was a horned warlock seducing his students into infidel error. (One onlooker claimed he indoctrinated his students into believing that the only novelists worth reading were Lady Murasaki and Jane Austen.)

But if Mudrick was a warlock, he couldn't have collected a more industrious or supportive cabal. A former student of Mudrick's, Kaplan supervised the transcribing, proofreading, and typesetting of these taped sessions (his preface lists students and former students who assisted in the grunt work), eye-squinting drudgery done out of abiding admiration. Full of go, *Mudrick Transcribed* charges along with unchecked enthusiasm, unafraid of the bumps and blind curves of fast discourse. The impromptu reactions of Mudrick and his students aren't always tidy or apropos, but they have a torn-free adrenaline. As Mudrick himself once wrote, "Such impudence! it's like being alive."

Raised in an Orthodox Jewish family of Russian extraction, Mudrick began early as a bookworm. Even as a child he was in the throes of thick books with pee-wee print. "When I was a kid, when I was seven years old, I could remember going to the library and looking with positive *lust* at big fat books [*laughter*] which would *last* me." "I mean, the weekly walk to the library—infinite riches in a little room—unbelievable." Reading for him wasn't a passive pastime but a passionate escape. "Because reading was great fun, it was extremely entertaining. It's true that Nobody Loved Me [*laughter*] . . . I was All Alone . . . I was very unsocial, and so I read."

As a teacher he expects his students to read too. "Why in the world else would you be a lit major?" So for the first week's assignment in his class on Eighteenth-Century English Prose, he assigns Boswell's *Life of Johnson*. A lost cause, because he knows that for his students reading isn't a lust that lasts:

> [I]f you say to me, Do you seriously expect all of us to read the *Life of Johnson* by next Tuesday? Of course I don't. Most of you are phonies anyway as far as literature is concerned. You've never even read a Shakespeare *play* which has been assigned to you in one week, and that you should be able to read in an hour and a half. *I* know all that, and if you think I'm going to act as a kind of a policeman over you, you really *are* out of your mind.

Mudrick insists that his students swim the torrent and swallow foam even if much of what they read is over their heads. "The worst thing that's done in these classes that you take is that the pretense is that you're going to understand everything you read. If you understood everything you read, you don't belong in school, you belong in heaven."

To read is to plunder. "You take a class like this because you get a chance to plunge into some of the juiciest material in the world in books. The eighteenth century, I have come to be more and more convinced, is the most important century in human history. Everything comes to an end there, and everything has a beginning." For Mudrick the eighteenth century was pivotal not because of abstract historical forces but because of the fascinating *people*. "I'm inclined to think that probably there were more individual great men in the eighteenth century than in any other century."

Sociable men, they didn't hole up in their studies. "It is an amazing age, in the sense that you get the impression that practically anybody in it could talk to anybody else, however different their opinions were—and there was a *very* wide range and diversity of opinion. And the person who is the catalyst, the go-between, the facilitator, and the accommodater, is Boswell!" Rousseau, Voltaire, Hume, Gibbon, Burke—Johnson's biographer pestered them all, provoking them in drawing rooms, taverns, even on their deathbeds, writing between his whoring the truest account of camaraderie ever committed.

Mudrick has no truck with the stale conceit that Boswell was simply a silly bugger, Bertie Wooster to Johnson's Jeeves. Using Boswell's account of an impromptu debate at the Literary Club over emigration, Mudrick demonstrates that Boswell was literature's ace transcriber. Quoting Boswell's account of the parrying between Burke, Sheridan, and Johnson, he tells his students. "What's so astonishing to me about this—I'm sure you don't make much sense out of it, but consider the intellectual effort required to get down this stuff! I mean Boswell is sitting there, he doesn't know any shorthand, he's participating in a conversation himself—you can't really be writing this fast."

And he isn't putting words into anyone's mouth either. "He is not inventing their arguments—he *couldn't* invent their arguments." It's a remarkable, perhaps unrepeatable feat. "I don't think it's ever been done before or since, certainly not reporting the conversation of such extraordinary and extraordinarily different men." What was so touching about Boswell was that he *knew* he was sifting through twilight. After an evening with Johnson and Goldsmith, he wrote in his journal. "I felt a completion of happiness. I just sat and hugged myself in my own mind." And not because he was a groupie among stars. "Words cannot describe our feelings. The finer parts are lost, as the down upon a plum; the radiance of light cannot be painted. . . . It was somehow like being in London in the last age."

It was with Samuel Johnson that Boswell found his big bass drum. "Boswell has his own greatness, but it's very different from Johnson's, and when you begin to read the journals of Boswell you realize how different this is. Boswell doesn't have the wit, he doesn't have the force, he doesn't have the economy of statement that Johnson has." Mudrick isn't blinded by that authority, however. One of the most iconoclastic sections in *Mudrick Transcribed* comes when Mudrick inspects Johnson's *Lives of the Poets*, enthroned by English departments everywhere as Johnson's most enduring achievement. For Mudrick, it doesn't quite pass muster. Generous and frank as Johnson personally was, "the quality that Johnson displays . . . surprisingly and disconcertingly often in the *Lives of the Poets* is *not* compatible with generosity of spirit," Mudrick argues.

He takes as his text the Life of Pope. Compiling Johnson's little digs at Alexander Pope's vanity and affectations ("And here we're involved with the moral nature of two of the major figures in English literature, one of whom happens to be writing about the other—and writing uncharacteristically"), Mudrick reaches a hilarious climax with Johnson's pooh-poohing of the grotto Pope had built on his estate:

> Seems fairly harmless, doesn't it? Would you think there was anything wrong with making a grotto of that kind? . . . [Pope] went around and said, *You know, when I'm in my grotto I feel terrific, and if you'd come down with me to my grotto you'd feel terrific.* And Johnson says *Bullshit. A grotto is not a place where anybody feels terrific.* He's tried grottos. [*Laughter.*] You've seen one you've seen them all [*laughing*]. You hear the fucking stagecoaches rattling over [*laughter*]—it's like being in a tunnel under the airport!

Not that Mudrick sympathizes with Pope or his showy, self-perpetuating style, which he compares to a bicycle without a rider. He prefers Swift. "Swift gains in comparison because Swift is a real nut. It's funny how you can accept a real nut and a pervert and a jerk by comparison with somebody who pretends to be the Second Coming of Jesus Christ." Swift was a cussed man who never compromised. "He bullied and bluffed and browbeat everybody, and beat them all down." A man after Mudrick's own mudpie heart.

Yet Mudrick didn't want to be considered completely "anti-." He found being cast in the role of curmudgeon a bore. "My next-door neighbor . . . greets me always by saying, 'Whom have you been attacking lately?' [*Laughter.*] I think he's being jolly, I think he thinks he's being jolly." All echo, a jolly man is one who laughs at his own lame jokes, an audience of one. Mudrick wanted to make others laugh. Hence the compliment he cherished most came from a young woman at the *Hudson Review* who told him, "You're the funniest writer I've ever read":

> I could live the rest of my life on that compliment. [*Laughs.*] I don't care whether it's true; I love it. That's what I *want* to be. If I had the choice, that's what I would be: the funniest writer you have ever read.

Except for maybe H. L. Mencken, what other literary critic would express such a hope? Since Matthew Arnold, critics have sought to be thought of as worthy, committed, subtly troubled . . . captains on the dark horizon. Not for Mudrick these frown lines etched in settling cement. He didn't care where he slammed the puck as long as he loosened some laughs.

Not all of *Mudrick Transcribed* finds him on such a rollicking roll. The sections in which he describes the purposes and workings of the College of Creative Studies are little more than departmental chat. The chapters in which his class on narrative prose dissects students' stories for freshness of approach and falseness are somewhat inbred too. It's a shame that there isn't more talk about contemporary writers, considering how many of them Mudrick had covered in the *Hudson Review.*

And one chapter points up a major limitation in Mudrick's maverick manner—his inability to accommodate any critical tack other than his own. In a talk titled "Litcrit: If You Haven't Tried It Don't Knock It," he says that the three great critics of the twentieth century are Sir Donald Frances Tovey, B. H. Haggin, and Harold Rosenberg. "And some of you will be interested to note that none of them is a literary critic." (Though he does note that Rosenberg practiced litcrit part-time.) Leavis, Trilling, Eliot, Wilson, they all faded for him. Philip Rahv, Frederick Crews, V. S. Pritchett, R. P. Blackmur, Dwight Macdonald, Mary McCarthy, Allen Tate, Wilfrid Sheed, and Seymour Krim don't even make his roll call.

And how could Cyril Connolly's shining example have slipped his mind? Months earlier Mudrick had published a stunning tribute to Connolly in *Harper's,* extolling him as the best book reviewer on the block for nearly half a century. "What Connolly has more of than any other reviewer, and what (plus intelligence, wit, style, and a prodigious range of reading) a reviewer needs most, is the confidence of the moment." Mudrick too had the confidence of the moment, but in his college talks he resists attributing such confidence to anyone else. He felt compelled to act like the one beating heart in a roomful of department store dummies.

Yet if you're susceptible to Mudrick's wayward style, that solitary beat is inspiriting. I met Marvin Mudrick only once and found him wary, subdued. *Mudrick Transcribed* is Mudrick unsubdued. It shows the wild, expansive side of him we non-students never saw. Without a Boswell by his side, a tape-recorder proved the next best friend. It caught him on the fly, when he hadn't a care, when he was in a courting mood with literature, music, and love:

> . . . The excitement is so tremendous—I can remember, for instance, waiting for a performance by Toscanini of the *Eroica,*

say, and not being able to stop *trembling* while waiting for it,
I mean trembling with nervous excitement, with *pleasure*, with
what I think can only be described as a kind of sexual pleasure,
though it's not directly that. And if you're interested in having
experiences which will last you for a lifetime in the arts, you've
got to do your damnedest to find your way to that kind of experience. How you do it I do not know. If you don't do it you're
wasting your time in the arts and the only thing that will ever
happen is that you will have topics for cocktail party conversation and it won't be of any—forget it. If you don't have that
experience, forget it. You're wasting your time.

The New Republic, August 21, 1989

Seymour Krim
Foreword to *What's This Cat's Story?*

I never met Seymour Krim. But when I was writing for *Harper's* in the early eighties, I began receiving brief communiqúes from the excitable owl. He was pleased that I had quoted him favorably in one of my columns. It made him feel as if his out-of-print books hadn't been buried forever in footlockers at the bottom of the sea . . . that somehow his thought-bubbles had surfaced. He didn't make dialogue easy, however. I had heard that he was a secrecy buff (translation: paranoid nut), and his postcards did seem to have been pushed through slits when no one was looking. They would arrive with only a mailbox number for a return address (as if including a home address would leave him open to hit squads), and many of them were signed simply, cryptically, "Krim." At the time his articles bore the same terse byline. But the communiqués themselves were anything but clenched. Like his journalism, they were funny, offhand, yet intensely felt. I remember one card asking me to check out the reruns of the *Dean Martin Show*, which featured Dino (Ol' Hair Oil himself) crooning on the couch surrounded by the Gold Diggers, a harem of go-go girls in white boots drooping beneath their huge, butterfly lashes. He wasn't recommending the show simply as candied kitsch. He found Dean Martin a hidden rock formation of fascination. Because Krim kept up his defenses, the two of us never got the cha-cha rhythm of a real correspondence going. But when I shifted magazines, the postcards followed me to *Vanity Fair*, one disagreeing with me over my rough treatment of Arthur Miller's autobiography, another kindly asking me to contribute a foreword to a collection of his best work that he was cobbling together. "Pleased to," I replied. It amused me, the idea of beating the bongos on his behalf. But I was also touched, since we were still technically strangers. I knew him only through his jamming prose.

As a critic Seymour Krim started straight, then went woolly. His skull housed a lot of crisscross lightning. Born in 1922 and raised in Manhattan, he wanted to attend the rolling freight of the big American night. For him this meant walking in the big boots of Thomas Wolfe.

He attended Wolfe's alma mater at the University of North Carolina for that very purpose, beating a retreat after a year. Back in Manhattan, he straddled the market, editing a slew of cheesy magazines while publishing in the choicest literary quarterlies. He wanted to be both a conscientious caretaker of culture and a classic howl who couldn't be housebroken. In his debut collection, *Views of a Nearsighted Cannoneer*, he published both his earnest apprentice efforts at traditional litcrit and his crazy-leg runs toward daylight. As a Greenwich Village Jewish intellectual in the bohemian forties and fifties, Krim suffered the oppressive awe of the Modern Library Giants—Kafka, Mann, Joyce, Proust, Melville, Yeats—and their interpreters at the *Partisan Review*. It was an intimidating period. You couldn't get by with being a small original bullet. Your talent had to have scope. You had to have a handhold on the seven types of ambiguity, plus an ability to spot the columned ranks of historical inevitability streaming like ants out of *Das Kapital*. Sheesh! "I knew gifted, fresh, swinging writers who told me in moments of confidence that they knew they weren't 'great' or 'major' and their voices were futile with flat tone when they confessed this supposed weakness: As if the personal horn each could blow was meaningless because history wasn't going to faint over them." They were all sucked-dry supplicants to the "self-deceiving chic snobgod of genius." Krim couldn't keep up the gladiator pose. He lay down his armor, though not his sword.

What Krim's criticism has is a frank absence of game-face certainty. Many critics treat their minds as a cloud of steel wool fixed for all time. They've long since squeezed doubt from their mental makeups. Their books are walled fiefdoms. The *Partisan Review* crowd aspired to be commissars. F. R. Leavis maintained his authority by laying down permanent tracks for his disciples to follow, allowing no deviation, even when he himself deviated (reversing himself on Dickens, for example). Edmund Wilson regarded his own growls as law, even when he was farting around with eugenics in "A Piece of My Mind." Most of their literary work offers a sound legacy of integral reading and thinking. It exalts literature to the utmost power. But for that reason it can be killingly correct. "Life is greater than literature, and the man who enriches life is greater than he who enriches literature," Krim wrote in honor of Thomas Wolfe. As a critic Krim comprehends that even the most word-mad among us can't spend all of our time craning up at monuments. Consequently he doesn't build his essays on a classical pyramid of thesis-evidence-conclusion, QED. He jawbones like a jazz soloist, jumping right into the frenzied rush, springing a punchline or a major perception in the middle of a sentence, as much a practitioner of spontaneous bop as his other great hero, Jack Kerouac. (About Kerouac—"a White Storefront Church Built Like a Man, on wheels yet"—no one has written better than Krim.) The hubbub he created was his alone. For a critic to establish a school and train disciples, he has to have a settled body of opinions that can be transmitted. With Krim nothing could be settled, because he was always staring at *himself* through a kaleidoscope. He couldn't pretend to be disinterested, in the Matthew Arnold–Lionel Trilling tradition. It was his own psyche hanging by a thread on the suicide hotline.

As Krim argued in *Nearsighted Cannoneer,* the creative self could no longer be a mere faithful recorder of common reality. The outer bombardment of stimuli was too big, the inner hungers for recognition too raw. The nervous breakdown and suicide attempt he describes in "The Insanity Bit" represented an inability to ride herd on these bursting galaxies of new sensations and formulate an artistic response. He didn't suffer the steady drip-drip-drip of depression. It's as if the stitching in his head unraveled as the ball was in flight. He needed to reconstitute himself. Years later in the collection *You & Me,* he wrote, "Our secret is that we still have an epic longing to be more than what we are, to multiply ourselves, to integrate all the identities and action-fantasies we have experienced . . . Let me say it plainly: our true projects have finally been ourselves." And what better assembly plant than New York? "Throughout the jumping metropolis of New York," he writes in the essay "Making It!," "one sees vertical fanaticism, the Thor-type upward thrust of the entire being, replacing pale, horizontal, mock-Christian love of fellow Christian love of fellow-creature; the man or woman who is High Inside, hummingly self-aware, the gunner and gunnerette in the turret of the aircraft that is Self, is watching out for number one with a hundred new-born eyes."

High Inside is where Krim aspired to be. He wanted success to massage him with a mink glove until he spurted gold. Crown me king, kiddo! But he was barely able to put one soiled foot into the penthouse suite. Although an early advocate of the New Journalism, he never found a nonfiction project to bring his giant lens into focus. His career became a long vagabondage, a thing of threads and patches. Perhaps the low point was when he was sued by Jimmy Breslin over an article he wrote for *The New York Times Book Review* and fired from the copy desk at the *International Herald Tribune.* A telex from Breslin sitting in the *Trib* office read, SEYMOUR, WHO DO YOU THINK YOU ARE? YOU'RE A

LITTLE, RESENTFUL FAILURE, GOING AROUND JUDGING EVERYONE ELSE'S LIFE AND ABILITIES AND YOU HAVE NONE OF EITHER. Krim considered suicide again, but snapped out of it when James Jones offered to loan him the gun. There are slower ways to go. He indulges in self-pity and petty feuds. In a couple of his books he even reprints his letters to the editor, a sure sign of a crackpot. He cultivates the image of being an overgrown dropout. On the cover of his collection *Shake It for the World, Smartass*, he's photographed (by Diane Arbus) as a bedbug, sprawled under the covers in a one-man sleep-in. He found himself fighting the glare of Mailer's fame and forced to digest the realization that it was Mailer who'd seized the reins of sky chariot over America, not him. A decade later Krim wittily rues that no writer now holds the reins. Our age belongs to bummed-out actors who can barely avoid bumping into the walls. "Yes, the 'player,' whom muttering writers for the past zillion years have usually treated like an infantile textbook case, your ultimate ditzy narcissist, has walked right into history with the authority of a new nose job." Tough enough competing with Mailer. But these cream dreams from central casting! To be a word man in an image age is to be farmed out to the minors.

Failure to reach the majors is the great refrain of Krim's writing. Failure to become a star slugger, a literary stud, a Modern Library Giant. Failure still seems a taboo subject, despite *Sister Carrie* and *Death of a Salesman*—it has a foot-odory pathos right out of the poorhouse. America the Beautiful is based on positive thinking and material reward. His effort to emulate the epic mileage of Wolfe, Whitman, and Kerouac and encompass America the Blemished in his mammoth prose poem "Chaos" became an ode to futility. Despite brilliant passages, its inner rhymes take on a finger-snappin' daddy-o syncopation that isn't sustainable for a longer stretch—symphonies require fuller orchestration. And yet his willingness to face failure first thing in the morning is what gives Krim's writing its tremendous tender sense of fraternity. After all, most people aren't favored by the gods to drip with pearls and drop *bon mots* as Superman holds our coat. It may be lonely at the top, but it's crowded at the bottom. There are millions more in the trenches than in the penthouse suites. One of Krim's *You & Me* essays was titled "For My Brothers and Sisters in the Failure Business," which found him huddling on the sidewalk, fingering the holes in his pockets, trying to figure out where his promise went. There was something Old World about Krim with his cloth cap and kvetching. He had an immigrant's soul. A man whose mother and father died young, he would always crave body warmth.

As I say, I never got to meet him. It wasn't until his death in 1989 that I realized that he and I lived within hollering range of each other in Manhattan's East Village. If only he hadn't been such a Secret Agent Man, obsessed with maintaining his cover! With the simplest exchange of words, we could have met for egg creams at the Gem Spa, haggling over writers and writing in person instead of postcards. Like you, I have to make do with his written words. What joyous, fighting words they are. In this collection we can hear him stepping up to the typewriter and taking his best cuts. For all his flopsweat, Krim was furiously funny, which is no small matter, and no small reward. Wisdom is for statues. Humor uncaps our inhibitions, unleashes our energies, seals friendships, patches hurts. Laughing is probably the most alive you can be. The happy kick that comes from reading Seymour Krim is irresistible, unless maybe you're a statue. If so, move aside, baby—you're blocking traffic!

Foreword to *What's This Cat's Story?:*
The Best of Seymour Krim (Paragon House, 1991)

R. I. P.

Edie: An American Biography, Jean Stein

For a brief spell in the mid-sixties, Edie Sedgwick was the debutante princess of piss-elegance, an Andy Warhol "superstar" whose fashion trademark was a snowy white mink draped over a dimestore T-shirt. Edie was always abuzz with debbie enthusiasm—as Warhol himself put it, even when she was asleep, her hands were wide awake. But the all-American Edie was soon eclipsed on the Warhol scene by the icily cosmopolitan Nico, whose moody, ghostly voice adorned the music of the Velvet Underground. Like Nico, Edie had a fondness for soothing candlelight, but where Nico could bathe by candlelight without setting off fire alarms Edie nearly torched herself twice—once in her East Side apartment, the next time in her room at the Chelsea Hotel. She also banged herself up once in a traffic accident, engaged in monkey-wild bouts of indiscriminate sex, and spent a number of stretches in the swankier and, later, rattier loony bins.

But it was drugs that finally cashiered Edie Sedgwick. After years of skinpopping acquaintance with amphetamine, after years of rooting through her pocketbook for loose pills, Edie expired in a barbituated daze in 1971 at the age of twenty-eight, perhaps the most notable name in that string of casualties from the Warhol camp which includes Candy Darling (cancer), Andrea Feldman (suicide), and Eric Emerson (rumored overdose).

In life, Edie Sedgwick may have been the crowning ornament of the Warhol entourage, but in death she's being elevated into the company of Jim Morrison, Brian Jones, and Jimi Hendrix—that pop cavalcade of the beautiful slain. Not long ago, *Rolling Stone* ran a cover photograph of a pouty, surly Jim Morrison with the headline, "He's hot, he's sexy, and he's dead." Edie Sedgwick too is now a hot, sexy slice of necrophilia—an exploitable piece of nostalgia for those who miss the unruly, dissolute swagger of the sixties. *Edie*, by Jean Stein and George Plimpton, is not only her catapult into the celestial big time but a small, brightly lit shrine. It may be pop journalism's first compact, disposable death kit.

Excerpted in *Rolling Stone*, *Edie* is on one level another saga of golden lives gone astray, a countercultural *Haywire*. Even with all its golden-doomed allure, however, Edie Sedgwick's life would at first glance seem a rather slender bough on which to hang a full-scale biography. With her stalky legs and silver hair and long, swinging earrings, Edie was perhaps the forerunner of new-wavish pop stars like Patti Smith (who's interviewed in *Edie*) and Blondie's Deborah Harry (who, not incidentally, used to waitress at Max's Kansas City, chief hangout for the Warhol scenemakers). But that is at best a trickling influence, and it can hardly be argued that Edie actually *did* anything beyond dressing up and having a giggle; Diana Cooper she certainly wasn't. Indeed, she emerges in *Edie* as little more than a likable, spoiled ditz who allowed herself to be ruled and then ruined by a barrage of bad chemicals. And despite *Edie*'s subtitle—"An American Biography"— there's nothing peculiarly American about her demise: English debs, too, have been known to slump over at parties, their pretty little arms punctuated by needletracks.

But for all that, *Edie* is fascinating, if only because Jean Stein and George Plimpton have pulled off something provocative and novel in biography writing. Instead of sifting through details and probing into motives, *Edie*'s authors offer a smartly edited weave of recollections, with the testimonies of Edie's friends and kin presented without comment in small quick doses, like clips in a documentary. The book is all chatter, the chapters are brief and snappy, the photographs plentiful. Other books have been programmed for those readers with short attention spans, but except for the best pages of Mailer's *The Executioner's Song*, none had *Edie*'s ingenious intelligence and eye for the succinct, telling detail. It's a technique best suited for a marginal figure of glamour like Edie—someone whose greatest deliberations were over which makeup to apply, which party to adorn. Were Edie a more driven, ambitious, and rounded-off heroine—an actress of rich accomplishment—the reader would expect to delve into the wellsprings of her calling. But Edie futilely splashed on the surface, and the disturbed surface is where *Edie* (thick on behavior, thin on psychology) stays. For better or ill, *Edie* is a spring forward in the televisionization of the prose narrative.

The book begins with a powerful, haunting image. "Have you ever seen the old graveyard up there in Stockbridge?" asks John P. Marquand, Jr. Sedgwick Pie, he explains, is where the descendants of Judge Sedgwick are buried in concentric circles, with the Judge and his wife Pamela at the commanding center. "The descendants of Judge Sedgwick, from generation unto generation, are all buried with

their heads facing out and their feet pointing in toward their ances-
tor. The legend is that on Judgment Day when they arise and face the
Judge, they will have to see no one but Sedgwicks." *Edie* then takes us
on a tour through the layered crusts of that pie, from the illustrious
members of the line (like Ellery Sedgwick, who served a formidable
term as editor of the *Atlantic Monthly*) to the more eccentric (Charles
Sedgwick, who used to wander about the farm lecturing to the live-
stock). As the tour progresses, you have a sense of will and energy
being held in clenched fists, then squandered, then—by the time we
get to Edie herself—flung away with reckless insolence.

Casting the longest and most damaging shadow by far in *Edie* is
Edie's father, Francis. Nicknamed "Fuzzy," Francis was anything but
an adorable huggy-bear. A novelist of modest distinction (*The Rim*),
Fuzzy was a bullying hunk of beefcake who paraded about like a
water-dwelling god, plucking the virtues of awed girls. Attending a
wedding at the Sedgwick ranch in California in 1954, Susan Wilkins
recalls, "It was a stud farm, that house, with this great stallion parad-
ing around in as little as he could. We were the mares. But it wasn't
sex. It was breeding . . . and there's a difference, of course. The air
was filled with an aura of procreation. Not carnal lust, but just breeding in the sense of not only re-creating life but a certain kind of life, a
certain elite, a superior race." To those not fitted to sup with the gods,
Fuzzy could be belittlingly cruel. Edie's sister Saucie reports, "For me,
life at Corral de Quati was one long degradation. In front of anyone—
guests, cowboys—my father would say I was fat, or stupid, or a liar."

So the Sedgwick line, once rich in culture, rectitude, and achievement, degenerated into a blight of small tormenting rancors and self-
loathing mortifications. If Edie can be believed (she was given to lurid
exaggeration), her father once tried to seduce her, and she in turn
tried to lure her brother Jonathan into the sack years later. She was
also an anorectic binger, bolting down food, then shooting off to the
bathroom for a heave. Her brother Minty flipped out and eventually
committed suicide, hanging himself with a necktie; another brother,
Bobby, died when he cracked his motorcycle into the side of a bus, a
daredevil stunt that might be labeled a near-suicide. (Characteristi-
cally, he wasn't wearing a crash helmet.) Anorexia, incest, suicide, all
of it played out in the grassy splendor of life among the well-bred—
small wonder reviewers are going to see F. Scott Fitzgerald's famous
green light blinking in the distance, summoning the Sedgwicks to
excess and orgy. But it is in its *absence* of lyricism, its fidelity to unfinished, grinding fact, that *Edie* is most convincing. Were the book

more artful and polished, it might have succumbed to swoons of lamentation. Like Warhol's films, *Edie* is an emission of tarnished, silver-gray cool.

The book's one interlude of carefree indulgence comes when Edie skips off to Cambridge and becomes the darling of Harvard's homosexual dandies. "Edie loved the very nitroglycerine queens, the really smart ones who knew everything," remembers René Richard. "She wanted high, very brilliant faggot friends who posed no threat to her body." Perhaps the most plumishly brilliant was the infamous Cloke Dosset, a lecherous aesthete who draped his walls in satiny black and gave cocktail parties attended mostly by men who gave women the silent treatment. Says Patricia Sullivan, "Many of them had these wonderful names which Cloke would give them: Columbine Streetwalker, Halloween Pederast, Gardenia Boredom, and Gloriana, which is the name of Spenser's Faerie Queene, and Appassionata von Climax. The girls did not get nicknames."

Clearly Cloke Dosset's brilliance consisted of prunings from Ronald Firbank, and clearly too these frolics served Edie as a run-through for the Warhol whirlwind, where the girls *did* get nicknames (Ingrid Superstar, International Velvet) and she would find herself cavorting through a shrill, fruity trashing of Catholicism which married Firbank to the fleshier side of gay stud-dom. *Edie* isn't unaware of these connections. Another one of Edie's friends at Cambridge recalls that the hallowed hangout for the nitroglycerine set was the Casablanca bar, located downstairs from the Brattle movie theater. "When one came through the plywood door, it was into her total world, and what heightened the experience, was that one often had come down from the Brattle—that factory of illusions." So from there it was but a skipping-bounce to Andy Warhol's factory of illusions.

For many readers, the account of Edie's brief sputter of incandescence at the Factory will be the most absorbing section in the book, so spiked is it with gossip, drugginess, and bitching malice. Perhaps I'm turning a trifle jaded, but the anecdotes of amphetamine dementia in *Edie* struck me as tired and familiar—stories about "superstars" thwacking each other in the backsides with syringes and tossing screaming tantrums are now as stale as those fabled accounts of F. Scott Fitzgerald and Hemingway in the men's room together, comparing thingies. Too familiar also are the darts aimed at Paul Morrissey for mousing his way into Warhol's confidence and commercializing the Factory's operations. What's new are the details, which are far more blotched and gruesome than even the particulars

of skin-puncturing abuse served up by Warhol and Pat Hackett in
their sordidly entertaining memoir *POPism* (Harcourt Brace Jova-
novich, 1980). Needle after needle is inserted into the asses of speed-
freaks until their bottoms are eroded into crusty ridges.

Edie was no stranger to needles—as a child, she received Vitamin
B shots in the behind like a sickly animal at the vet's—and she too
developed scar tissue. In an excerpt from the tapes for a pseudo-
documentary film called *Ciao! Manhattan*, Edie does a riff about the
perils of amphetamine.

> You want to hear something I wrote about the horror of speed?
> Well, maybe you don't, but the nearly incommunicable torments
> of speed, buzzerama, that acrylic high, horrorous, yodeling, rep-
> etitious echoes of an infinity so brutally harrowing that words
> cannot capture the devastation nor the tone of such a vicious
> nightmare.

But then Edie does a fast flipflop, testifying to the raptures of speed.

> It's hard to choose between the climactic ecstasies of speed and
> cocaine, they're similar. . . . That fantabulous sexual exhilara-
> tion. Which is better, coke or speed? It's hard to choose. The
> purest speed, the purest coke, and sex is a deadlock.

So surfing on the curve of one hopped-up high after another, Edie
became a rattled, radiant wreck. Henry Geldzahler: "She was very
nervous, very fragile, very thin, very hysterical. You could hear her
screaming even when she wasn't screaming—this sort of supersonic
whistling." And, in a puzzling comment, Diana Vreeland notes that
when Edie modeled for *Vogue*, she had lovely skin-tone, "but then I've
never seen anyone on drugs that didn't have wonderful skin." (God,
I have.) Curiously, *Edie* skimps most on what matters most in sizing
up Edie's true measure of fame and attraction—her antics on film.
The one keen paragraph on Edie's film legacy comes from Norman
Mailer. "One hundred years from now they will look at *Kitchen* and
see that incredibly cramped little set, which was indeed a kitchen. . . .
You can see nothing but the kitchen table, the refrigerator, the stove,
and the actors. The refrigerator hummed and droned on the sound
track. Edie had the sniffles. She had a dreadful cold. She had one of
those colds you get spending the long winter in a cold-water flat. The
dialogue was dull and bounced off the enamel and plastic surfaces. It

was a horror to watch. It captured the essence of every boring, dead day one's ever had in a city, a time when everything is imbued with the odor of damp washcloths and old drains."

Mailer's evocative comments aside, *Edie* shows a lazy hand in trying to nail down what was *special* about the Sedgwick mystique—what made her bob higher in the esteem of the hiply knowing than those in the Warhol stable who gave it a much heartier go. The best pin-down of Edie's appeal I know of appears in Stephen Koch's 1973 study of the splendors and miseries of Warholiana, *Stargazer.* How did Edie Sedgwick carve out a calm nook for herself in all that shriek and squalor?

> . . . [Edie] was unique among the women superstars because she never played the female clown. All the others—Baby Jane Holzer in the grotesquerie of her voguishness; Ingrid Superstar, a perfectly conscious comedienne forever varying on the theme of the dumb blonde; Tiger Morse (who appeared more often at Max's Kansas City than in films), camping and squealing like a schoolgirl; Viva, with her interminable frizzy-haired account of schizophrenia, lascivious priests, and a badly damaged ego—all of them were in one way or another involved in a more or less comic display of their fears and weaknesses and overcompensations as women. But Sedgwick always kept her cool. When she spoke she made sense; her response to a contretemps on screen (and part of the technique was to create those contretemps) was never the customary hysteria but a visibly intelligent effort to cope. . . .

Koch then swerves his attention to Warhol's *Beauty No. 2,* in which Sedgwick perches on the edge of a bed, "ice cubes in her glass tinkling (one associates tinkling with her presence, of ice cubes, jewelry, and her voice and eyes). . . ."

> Lithe and small-breasted, she's wearing a pair of black bikini panties, her long legs alternately girlish and regal. Her movements are nothing but the merest business: sipping her drink, fiddling with her pack of cigarettes, patting the overly friendly dog, until such small stuff at last resolves itself into an attempt at love-making with the silent Gino Peschio (who, shortly after the opening of the first reel, strips to his underwear).

But throughout, there is a continuing and largely inaudible conversation with [Chuck] Wein and [Gerard] Malanga out of frame. The visual field is assailed by their disembodied voices provoking the astonishingly various and precise textures of Sedgwick's responses, the nagging intrusions on her peace that proceed to make her portrait come alive. But those remarks being made at her are also ideal illustrations of a much favored directorial mode in the Factory at that time: Taunt and betrayal. . . . Under the influence of this technique, the conversation in *Beauty No. 2* moves from trivia to desperation. There is even a terrible moment near the end in which Sedgwick . . . speaks more or less inaudibly, but from real fear, of her horror of death. In other places, certain things are said off camera (I have been unable to decipher them) that plainly hurt and offend her (some others provoke the small miracle of her laugh); later, as the lovemaking demanded by the scenario begins, a series of cutting, catty remarks from the kibbitzers at last make her abruptly pull herself up, fold her arms around her knees and stop in unflustered, but visible, fury.

Koch's comments are worth quoting at such length not only because they frame Edie Sedgwick's film manner in sharp-focus perspective but because such appreciations appear nowhere in *Edie*, which is rich in idle chat—*wow, fabulous, fantastic*—and slim on critical insight. *Edie*, taut as it is, is composed of rather stringy fibers.

Once Edie splits with the Warhol sect, her life becomes a tailspin of speed binges, casual ruttings with dopers and bikers, recuperations in the hospital, sweet enthusiasms, and futile hopes. She becomes a noisy blur in the book, a crackle of laughter and energy at the edge of the party. When Edie finally does die, in bed with her husband, her death stirs in the reader little more than a small, fond sadness—small, because Edie's death seems so tediously inevitable. With bones and mannerisms as birdlike as hers, a ravenous appetite for drugs and kicks could only lead to a racking toll on her stamina, a fluttering collapse. She seems to have been fitted for a life both brief and flaring. Had she lived, she might—might—have become a housewifey recluse (like Patti Smith), but she also might have turned into a bloated caricature of herself, banging her head against the crib in one of John Waters's suburban travesties, the "small miracle of her laugh" coarsened into a fag-hag cackle.

According to *Edie*, when Warhol heard of Edie's death, he greeted the news with shrugging small talk. Death or recovery, it's all the same to the Prince of Ether, he admits with rare candor in *POP-*

ism. After Ondine kicks speed and becomes a calm, normal person, Warhol offers a sigh of regret. "Sure, it was good he was off drugs (I supposed), and I was glad for him (I supposed), but it was so boring: there was no getting around that. The brilliance was all gone." To be wired-up is to be dramatic, and Warhol's parenthetical asides indicate that he preferred having those around him laced up with drugs and like cockatoos to their loitering about in the quiet. Edie Sedgwick was wired-up before she met Warhol, and wired-up after she left him, but Warhol created a theater of heightened sensations in which her own brittleness could take on a self-consuming sparkle. Like Fuzzy, Cloke Dosset, and the acid doctors that followed, Warhol was a careless father-figure allowing his daughter to cast about with wolves. Andy Warhol didn't destroy Edie Sedgwick, but he did make destruction seem like a glorious goof, an acrylic high—the ultimate buzzerama. And he left his camp-followers with nothing to cushion their falls.

Of course, Warhol himself is now a dazed whisper of death with a dubious thatch of ash-white hair—"the ghost of a genius," as Taylor Mead describes him in *Edie*. So feyly out of it is Warhol that it's pointless to expect him to express deep feelings of loss or regret over Edie's death: he's lived in the pop of flashbulbs for so long that his emotions are flaked and scattered, bleached-out. If anything, he might feel a sliver of perverse pride at having a book like *Edie* dish the dirt on the lurid doings at his dream-factory. Warhol was always starstruck, his moviemaking tricked-out Hollywood myths in topsy-turvy drag, and now, with *Edie*, he's inspired a book which rakes through the muck and intrigue of his passive reign like a thinking man's *Hollywood Babylon*, with Edie Sedgwick as the waif tossed upon the smoking slag-heap. Edie Sedgwick's death received a curt paragraph in the postscript to *POPism*, and the value of *Edie* is that it cracks open that paragraph to capture the arc of a life in its dying fall. For all its babble and gossip, for all the time spent with its eye glued to the keyhole, *Edie* is a serious, painstaking enterprise.

And it has a disquieting symmetry. If the dead at Stockbridge were to rise from their graves, they would find themselves ringed about Judge Sedgwick, but, reading *Edie*, you feel that *these* dead—Candy Darling, Eric Emerson, Andrea Feldman, Edie Sedgwick—will find themselves staring at Andy Warhol. Poor wayward Edie, she deserved better fathers, a better fate.

The New York Review of Books, July 15, 1982

Life Among the Ninnies

The Diary of Anaïs Nin, Volume Seven (1966–1974)

Art teaches us how to levitate, Anaïs Nin was fond of saying, and in Volume Seven of Nin's *Diary* her toes seldom touch earth. It isn't art that's keeping her aloft, however, it's fame, favorable reviews, rapt adoration. Volume Seven covers the final years of Nin's life, as she emerges from the whispering shadows of cultdom to glide from lectern to lectern in her new role as the counterculture's Lady Oracle. (Nin died in 1977, after a long bout with cancer.) In the closing pages of Volume Six, Nin celebrates the cloudburst of approval which greets the publication of the *Diary*'s first volume in the spring of 1966. Lawrence Ferlinghetti showers her with rose petals in a Berkeley bookshop, love letters crowd her mailbox, and reviewer Robert Kirsch swoons at length about her "poetic and supple" prose in the *Los Angeles Times*. As Volume Seven opens, Nin is still soaking happily in the ironies of success: "The same publishers who turned down my work beg for my comments on new works they are publishing," she notes with rueful pride. Even media personalities lower their knees in homage. "Television interview with Arlene Francis very deep. She knew my work. She is enormously intelligent and wise." Once you've tasted the wisdom of Arlene Francis, lesser fizz won't do.

Her genius vindicated, Nin finds herself constantly on the wing. She travels to Morocco, Japan, Germany, Bali, Cambodia; she descends upon hundreds of campuses, giving sixty lectures in a stretch from autumn 1972 to spring 1973; she stars and tours with a documentary by Robert Snyder titled *Anaïs Nin Observed*; and everywhere she goes she's bombarded with love. In Paris, Nin and Jeanne Moreau discuss a film adaptation of Nin's novel *A Spy in the House of Love*. Though *Spy* was never made, Moreau later directed and starred in *Lumière*, a film that (unwittingly, one assumes) captures the haughty narcissistic glamour of life among the Ninnies. Surrounded by women who adore her and men who worship her unblemished soul, Moreau's Sarah Didieux also seems to be exaltedly aloft. "At the end of the week," writes Pauline Kael in her review of *Lumière*, "she wins something like the Academy Award, except it's at a ceremony where she is the only one being honored, and her girlfriends and boyfriends are all there, gathered around, to be happy for her." Like *Lumière*, Volume Seven of the *Diary* is a cozy get-together. Sandlewood incense wafts through the air, wind-chimes tinkle, and into Nin's hands tremulous coeds press flowers, cookies, rice cakes, unfinished novels. The self-trumpeting climax of this celebration begins on page 200, where Nin lists tributes from readers whose lives have been transformed by the *Diary*. Sample comments:

> When I read the Diary, it took wings! All was transcended. Like some immense swan, it took me on its back lifting me into the air—that now familiar air of your vision which I draw in like strength, like purity, like invisible draughts of growth.

> You speak rain words which fill the saucer eye of a parched insomniac.

> May you know whom you have touched, awakened, raised from the dead. May you know the legacy you have already left, the soil you have watered, the seeds planted, all the solar barques you have launched toward the sun.

> Through your words, your refractions of experience, I have come upon the thresholds of my soul.

and my favorite:

> You have revived the intuitive, caring woman in me and I feel I'll be a better therapist for it.

All that sensitivity—a roomful of Thurber harpies couldn't be more frightening. (Or perhaps one should invoke Jules Feiffer—a therapist inspired by Anaïs Nin sounds like one of Feiffer's more twisted fancies.) In *Anaïs Nin Observed*, the most pleasing thing is the contrast between Nin's gracious French chirpiness and her friend Henry Miller's Brooklyn rasp; but in the *Diary* every voice throbs with the same fruity lyricism. Nearly all of Nin's correspondents sound like Nin herself, something she's proudly aware of. "There was no ego in the Diary, there was only a voice which spoke for thousands, made links, bonds, friendships. . . . There was no *one* self. We were all *one*." As Nin and her admirers trade confidences on astrology and self-realization, scattering showy adjectives like "luminous" and "labyrinthine" through their letters, the book becomes a choral hymn to hazy-mindedness.

Occasionally a few rude notes ruin the harmony. Nin is unnerved when "aggressive" feminists give her the raspberry during her talks. She complains to artist Judy Chicago, "At Harvard, three hostile, aggressive women prevented me from finishing my talk. Really psychotic! I was ashamed of them." One woman, described by Nin as "fat and gross and aggressive," corners her after a lecture and says she works fifty hours a week and doesn't have time for a fancy-schmancy inner journey. Nin never seems to realize that feminists resented her influence not because they were envious but because they considered her Aquarian Age go-with-the-glow dreaminess "feminine" in the most softheadedly reactionary way. With their love of the ineffable sublime, the Nin cultists aren't much different from the P. G. Wodehouse heroine who believed that bunny rabbits were gnomes in attendance on the Fairy Queen. "Perfect rot, of course," grumbled Bertie Wooster in *The Code of the Woosters*. "They're nothing of the sort."

Even more troublesome to Nin than feminists are treacherous reviewers and fellow novelists. To Nin, critics are little more than fiends pitch-forking innocent babes into the furnace. ("Gore Vidal is now a critic, which means he is cremating people," she observes sourly in Volume Six. Vidal, whose memorable pan of Nin appears in *Homage to Daniel Shays*, is also the villain of Volume Seven.) In the winter of 1970–1971, Nin meets Edmund Wilson at the Princeton Club to receive his permission to print portions from his "portrait" in one of the diaries. To her surprise, Wilson not only chuckles at the passages she assumed would anger him, but later sends a letter saying how charming he found her company. Sniffs Nin: "Of course I never asked him why, after praising *Under a Glass Bell*, he never mentioned me again."

What makes the *Diary* such a comedy is that though Nin comes on as an ethereal yenta, gathering coeds like chicks beneath her silky wings, she's so relentlessly, *spitefully* competitive. After saying a few kind words about Marguerite Duras in Volume Six, for example, Nin can't resist quoting someone who praises her for being "more genuine, more human" than Duras. Even old friends like Lawrence Durrell get their knuckles rapped.

> While Henry [Miller] and Larry incensed each other, the women discovered me.

Larry talked about a discussion with Joaquin [Nin's brother] in the thirties on wanting to achieve polyphony. Joaquin said it could not be achieved in writing: "Don't try to be a Mozart." But Larry did try and describes it in an interview as "palimpsest." Is he aware that I have done it? He has gone into intellectual abstractions (*Tunc*). He is sterile. With time could I have reconnected him? His defenses, humor and impersonality are slippery.

The image one has is of Nin bending under the hood of Durrell's psyche, screwing in new spark plugs.

Decades before the *Diary* was published, Henry Miller claimed that Nin's confessions would someday be ranked with those of Augustine, Petronius, and Rousseau. Yet as chronicle and gossip, the *Diary* is little more than a long tease, a fluttering of veils. In the diaries of Dorothy Wordsworth and Virginia Woolf, small moments inch across the page—visitors sip tea, frost forms on the windowpane—and yet one is always aware of an acute intelligence reaching beyond the day-to-day. Not so in Nin. When she travels to Bali and Fez, she revels in the exotic sensations of new aromas, new fabrics; but otherwise the details of her life are obscured by a perfumey mist. She doesn't seem to *see*—a Dorothy Wordsworth snowfall is worth a dozen descents into the labyrinth—and she uses clusters of adjectives where a single metaphor might do. And except for the large-scale portrait of Henry Miller and a few vivid glimpses of Artaud, Wilson, and Tennessee Williams, Nin seldom writes about people with novelistic exactness—she shrouds them in language too pretty to be anything but platitudinous.

Of Marguerite Young (*Miss MacIntosh, My Darling*), she enthuses, "Her hair weeps, her eyelids weep, but when her voice takes up the rhythmic spirals of her writing it is the female soul of Joyce, Joyce without the male ego, the intellectual juggler with language, it is the waves, the ocean of myths . . . ," and upward Nin spins in her own rhythmic spiral. Famous Names serve to confirm or deny her genius; unfamous admirers, like the mostly homosexual clique of "transparent children" in Volume Four, circle Nin, then ungratefully scatter. Flattery and betrayal form the *Diary*'s alternating currents.

Now that this final *Diary* has joined Nin's novels, essays, and prose poems on the shelf, it's clear that her great gift was not for literature but for friendship and persuasion. For letters, lunches, blurbs, and lectures. Her surrealism is tame, a grazing of lazy centaurs. Even more embarrassing are her attempts at moist, hot sensuousness, not only in erotic entertainments like *Delta of Venus* and *Little Birds* but in a more ambitious effort like *A Spy in the House of Love* (only a writer beyond shame and taste could describe sexual intercourse as "a joyous, joyous, joyous, joyous impaling of woman on man's sensual mast"). But her career—her *life*—was a masterpiece of self-promotion.

The Nin industry will undoubtedly continue the promotion through tributes, analyses, reminiscences, photograph albums, and collections of letters; friendly critics will persist in trying to persuade us that she was a Proustian enchantress; but I suspect the hilariously vain *aperçus* of Volume Seven will do more damage to her reputation than the cruelest slice from villainous Vidal. "So I shall die in music, into music, with music," she writes near the end of her struggle with cancer. Foolish sibyl that she was, Anaïs Nin gives herself a graceful send-off in the book's final pages, and her admirers will probably cling to their affection for her long after they've outgrown these Diaries.

The New York Review of Books, June 26, 1980

Philip Larkin's Enormous Yes

I don't much fancy photographs of writers—Walt Whitman balancing a butterfly on his finger has always seemed the height of sham, rivaled only by those shots of Hemingway on safari—but there's one photograph that makes me smile with fondness and admiration. It's a photograph of the poet Philip Larkin that appears in a birthday chorus of tributes entitled *Larkin at Sixty*. While most poets feel duty bound to look fierce-souled and picturesque, Larkin is the very picture of quiet, clerkish reserve. Wearing spectacles and a checkered jacket, Larkin (who once described himself as looking like "a bald salmon") leans on a border marker that says in simple, large letters ENGLAND.

Larkin's air of calm and restraint, his solitariness, his indifference to bohemian fashion, his essential Englishness—all this is captured in that photograph, which has the emblematic simplicity of a postage stamp. What's missing from that snapshot is any hint or glimmer of the mischievous humor that leaps with claws from Larkin and his work. Philip Larkin is often spoken of as a connoisseur of doom, a gin-and-tonic Thomas Hardy, but even in the shadow of fate and extinction his wit refuses to surrender. Like the novelist Barbara Pym (a longtime pen pal of Larkin's), Larkin makes music of sighs and murmurs—a music interlaced with laughter.

Philip Larkin is a writer of austere output, an Anthony Burgess in reverse. Since the release of his first volume of verse, *The North Ship*, in 1945, Larkin has published but three slim poetry collections (*The Less Deceived, The Whitsun Weddings, High Windows*), two novels (*Jill* and *A Girl in Winter*—both full of bruised, pensive longings), and a book of jazz criticism (*All What Jazz*). In this compact body of work, death and enfeeblement certainly figure large. Death is described by Larkin in various poems as a spread of evening in which no lamps are lit; a black-sailed ship towing "a huge and birdless silence"; an anesthetic "from which none come round." And with this creep of death comes a slackening of flesh and vigor. In "Sad Steps," the narrator parts the curtains after a trip to the john and is "startled by/The rapid clouds, the moon's cleanliness." With mock bombast, he apostrophizes the moon—"Lozenge of love! Medallion of art!"—then draws back shivering, sobered by the moon's cool appraisal.

> *The hardness and the brightness and the plain*
> *Far-reaching singleness of that wide stare*
> *Is a reminder of the strength and pain*
> *Of being young: that it can't come again*
> *But is for others undiminished somewhere.*

"The Old Fools" of Larkin's famous poem don't even have this level of awareness or perspective. They're completely out of it, pissing themselves, drooling, carrying lighted rooms in their heads ("and people in them, acting"). All of this dilapidation might be tolerable if there were the hope of transcendence, but Larkin dismisses the consolation offered by the promise of a hereafter. In an uncollected poem entitled "Aubade," he refers to religion as "That vast motheaten musical brocade/Created to pretend we never die. . . ." It's a pretense with which Larkin has never collaborated. Death is a one-way ticket he was issued at birth.

Larkin has been affectionately tweaked for clutching that ticket so intently. The playwright Alan Bennett begins his toast in *Larkin at Sixty* by wondering if such a toast is even suitable. "A volume of this sort is simply a sharp nudge in the direction of the grave; and that is a road, God knows, along which he needs no nudging." Bennett also fails to be impressed by Larkin's senior-statesman status. "Apparently, he is sixty, but when was he anything else? He has made a habit of being sixty; he has made a profession of it. Like Lady Dumbleton he has been sixty for the last twenty-five years. On his own admission there was never a boy Larkin; no young lad Philip, let alone Phil, ever." Larkin has abetted such characterizations by describing his childhood in a poem as "a forgotten boredom," adding in interviews that he's always found children a rather detestable lot.

Yet if it's difficult to imagine the infant Larkin banging a spoon against his oatmeal dish, another contribution in *Larkin at Sixty* does remind us that its subject was once a young man of green enthusiasms and aversions. Kingsley Amis, who met Larkin at Oxford in 1941, describes their ardent discovery of jazz artists like Bix Beiderbecke, Count Basie, Fats Waller, and Sidney Bechet (whom Larkin later immortalized in "For Sidney Bechet"—"On me your voice falls as they say love should,/ Like an enormous yes"). After the heady honks and ripples of jazz, literature was something of a letdown. When Amis is forced to burrow through *The Faerie Queene*, he uses a library copy previously in Larkin's possession. "At the foot of the last page of the text he had written in pencil in his unmistakable, beautiful, spacious hand: 'First I thought Troilus and Criseyde was the most *boring* poem in English. Then I thought Beowulf was. Then I thought Paradise Lost was. Now I *know* that The Faerie Queene is the *dullest thing out. Blast* it.'"

Amis and Larkin share more than a love of pre-Coltrane jazz. Both display a wary disregard for things un-English. Amis once pretended in print not to know who Kierkegaard was, and when Larkin was asked in a recent interview about Jorge Luis Borges, he replied, "Who is Jorge Luis Borges?" (This attitude seems to have seeped down from Evelyn Waugh, who considered even Edmund Wilson a wog.) Both are also distrustful of the attempts of government and the universities to help germinate art. Amis has gone on record against government support of the Muses; Larkin, striking a more playful tone, once told a teacher of creative writing, "There's too much poetry on this campus. I'm relying on you to stamp it out. Come down *hard* on them!" Squash those couplets—take no prisoners! To top it off, Larkin is also anti-Romantic and antimodernist. Anti-Romantic in that he doesn't believe that we carve out our destinies willy-nilly in life—tumbling the chambermaid, deposing the king—but that life itself deals the cards. In the abrupt, stark ending to "Dockery and Son," he writes,

Life is first boredom, then fear.
Whether or not we use it, it goes,
And leaves what something hidden from us chose. . . .

Antimodern?—antimodern in that he resists fauvist forays into self-conscious technique, whether it's John Coltrane drilling through the brickwork with an interminable solo or Samuel Beckett pitching his characters neck-deep into the dustbin. Larkin prefers the steadiness of the sane and the true. When a novel of Barbara Pym's was rejected by Faber and Faber in 1965, Larkin wrote to his publisher that he couldn't believe that a writer in the tradition of Trollope and Jane Austen wouldn't find a receptive audience (how prescient he was!). "Why should I have to choose between spy rubbish, science fiction rubbish, Negro-homosexual rubbish, or dope-taking nervous-breakdown rubbish?" he asked with some exasperation. "I like to read about people who have done nothing spectacular, who aren't beautiful or lucky, who try to behave well in the limited field of activity they command, but who can see, in little autumnal moments of vision, that the so called 'big' experiences of life are going to miss them. . . ." Larkin's complaint against the modernists—he cites particularly Pound and Picasso—is that they throw up a din of noise and images that make difficult such moments of clear-sightedness. Modernism is for him a showering of violent debris.

The remarkable thing about Larkin as a poet is how much expressive, lyrical force he can muster even after armoring himself against romanticism, modernism, trendiness, and myth ("As a guiding principle I believe that every poem must be its own sole freshly created universe, and therefore have no belief in 'tradition' or a common myth-kitty," he once wrote, and added recently in the *Paris Review*, "I am not going to fall on my face every time someone uses words such as Orpheus or Faust or Judas"). Everyone knows the assured, colloquial, snap-to-attention openings of Larkin's poems: "They fuck you up, your mum and dad" ("This Be the Verse"); "Sexual intercourse began/In nineteen sixty three . . . /Between the end of the *Chatterly* ban/And the Beatles' first LP" ("Annus Mirabilis"); "When I see a couple of kids/And guess he's fucking her and she's/Taking pills or wearing a diaphragm . . ." ("High Windows"). (For a lot of readers, Larkin's openings are *all* they know of his work, which is one of the reasons I'm writing about him in this, my last column for *Harper's*.) Then there are the famous clinchers, like the widely quoted—and misunderstood—finish to "A Study of Reading Habits":

> *Don't read much now: the dude*
> *Who lets the girl down before*
> *The hero arrives, the chap*
> *Who's yellow and keeps the store,*
> *Seem far too familiar. Get stewed:*
> *Books are a load of crap.*

What saves Larkin from sounding merely like the saltiest wit in the alehouse is his genius for observations that have an almost caressing regard. There is the girl whose maiden name is like an abandoned melody ("Its five light sounds no longer mean your face,/Your voice and all your variants of grace"), the parents who have been pushed to the side of their own lives in "Afternoons," the hand-linked lovers carved in faithful repose in "An Arundel Tomb," the once famous racehorses in "At Grass" who huddle in anonymous shade "till wind

distresses tail and mane. . . ." While other poets spill words promiscuously, Larkin keeps his on such firm rein that these climbing,
enfolding moments of emotion seem all the more dramatic. Amaz-
ingly, there are still critics who accuse Larkin of being a poet of wan
resignation and thin feeling, perhaps because he doesn't thump out
his feelings with exclamation marks, like a Beat bard. O tremulous
ether! Abode of angels! No, that's not where Larkin's poetry lives.

Rereading Larkin's verse (and Larkin is the only contemporary
poet that I find myself reading again and again, with deepening pleasure), I was struck by how often the word "happiness" recurs in his
work. Larkin's attitude to happiness seems to have been shaped by a
slight speech impediment that dogged him as a child and bungled
any hope of social ease. "I stammered badly," he told an interviewer,
"and this tends to shape your life. You can't become a lecturer or anything that involves talking. By the time you cure yourself—which
in my case was quite late, about thirty—all the talking things you
might have done are lost." Such losses are for Larkin irrecoverable.
Pressing at the rear of his verse is the belief that the rewards of adult
life can't and don't compensate for that which was held back from us
in youth—that spring comes only once, and the springs that follow
only bear false witness. (In "The Trees," he says that the greenness
of leafing trees is a kind of grief, an intimation of mortality—"Is it
that they are born again/And we grow old? No, they die too/Their
yearly trick of looking new/Is written down in rings of grain.") It's
this sense of estrangement that has inspired critics to think of Larkin
as a morbid old sourball who, in Alan Bennett's words, gets depressed
when he sees fifteen-year-olds necking at the bus stop. There's some
truth to this caricature, but the larger truth is that Larkin doesn't
deny that there's happiness in the world (the newlyweds of "Whitsun"
are happy, as are the seaside vacationers of "To the Sea"), only records
his detachment from it. He not only isn't a necking teenager now, he
never was.

Where Larkin strikes the deepest and most responsive chord—in
me, at any rate—is when he argues that happiness is finally an uncer-
tain bargain we strike with ourselves. There's a little-discussed poem
in *The Less Deceived* that looks at this bargain from twin perspectives.
"Reasons for Attendance" begins with the narrator watching a group
of young dancers, "sensing the smoke and sweat,/The wonderful feel
of girls." Making, perhaps, a reference to the isolation brought about
by his stammer, Larkin spells out what it means to ford your way
through life unaccompanied.

. . . Surely, to think the lion's share
Of happiness is found by couples—sheer
Inaccuracy, as far as I'm concerned.
What calls me is that lifted, rough-tongued bell
(Art, if you like) whose individual sound
Insists I too am individual.
It speaks; I hear; others may hear as well,
But not for me, nor I for them; and so
With happiness. Therefore I stay outside,
Believing this; and they maul to and fro,
Believing that; and both are satisfied,
If no one has misjudged himself. Or lied.

That final equivocation, an uncoated pill, catches with a click in the throat.

Harper's, November 1983

Amis Père et Fils

The Old Devil
Difficulties with Girls, Kingsley Amis

Lunchtime in London. Ambling toward the lobby of the Savoy hotel is the author Kingsley Amis. He has a recognizable stride. It's the boulevard stroll Fred Mertz had in the episode of *I Love Lucy* where Fred, top hat atilt, chugged into a nightclub as an English duffer, doncha know. Not that there's anything ersatz about Amis's dash or demeanor. Seated in the bar of the Savoy for a brief chat about his new novel, *Difficulties with Girls* (Summit), he is every stitch and seam the English gent. A portly gent, it should be said—his belt now takes a long ride around the rotunda. But his face, that of a leading man sliding into character parts, has a distinguished glaze. For someone as fond of drink as Amis is (he's written numerous books on the topic), he shows no signs of the puffy, floaty discoloration often caused by longtime submersion in the sauce. Nothing fishy about his eyes either, which are scrupulous, keen—twin sentries on alert. His eyes man their stations even as he enters a relaxation mode. Amis nurses a nonalcoholic starter called a pussyfoot, then, with a flip of his wrist to consult his watch, announces it is time for a *real* drink: large bourbon with ice. At the thought of having a serious gargle, he immediately perks up, like a houseguest who has heard the ding-ding of the dinner bell. Liberation is at hand.

Kingsley Amis has entered an Indian summer of acclaim. It is as if his deck chair were stationed sunward to catch the dusk. In his late sixties, Amis is mellow proof of the adage that the important thing is to outlive the bastards. With an eclectic output which includes everything from a survey of sci-fi, *New Maps of Hell*, to a James Bond adventure, *Colonel Sun*, from a study of Kipling to a roundup of his own verse, he has secured a wide berth on the shelf, but at the cost of some suspicion that slumming had stuffed his sinuses as a serious comic novelist, reducing his characters' outbursts to a chronic wheeze. The success of *Stanley and the Women* wounded that notion and *The Old Devils* dealt it a deathblow. A lopsided look at love and liquor among the Geritol set, *The Old Devils* won the Booker Prize in 1986.

Amis's acidic rebirth in late age has helped take the steam out of his iconoclasms as a young devil. The tempests that once swirled over *Lucky Jim*, Amis's status within the Angry Young Men, his championing of genre fiction and rejection of F. R. Leavis's great tradition (with characteristic overkill, Leavis supposedly reviled Amis as "a pornographer"), have been construed over time into the settled dust of academic recap. Even the boil over his political shift from Labour left to Tory right has leveled to a low simmer. He has become, in short, an institution—an underlying asset.

In a floating exchange rate where various flavors of the month are up, down, sideways, drifting, Kingsley Amis represents the gold standard in English literature, as Evelyn Waugh did before him. Like Waugh, his belly seems designed to cushion him against runs on the bank. Evidence of his asset value is a compilation of his favorite poems published in England last year called *The Amis Anthology*, a bedside keepsake suitable for preserving crushed rose petals. (The notes retain Amis's thorny touch, however. Apropos of a John Betjeman poem about golf, he remarks, "For the record, I am bored by golf to the point of hatred.") Although Amis appreciates the kind attention he's received in recent years, he's mildly miffed that reviewers keep treating him as a serial mugger, preying on one protected species after another. "What people tend to get wrong is this 'target' thing. 'Who is he in for this time? You know, this last time he had it in for women. This time he has it in for queers. And he has it in for . . .'" Jews, wogs, make a list.

On that list women occupy the top spot. Despite having written sympathetically from the female point of view in the Trollopian *Take a Girl Like You*, Amis has acquired the reputation of behaving in print like a sour-ball SOB beset by bitches. It's a somewhat dubious rap and rep. True, at the end of the labored satire *Jake's Thing*, his impotent Jake chooses to remain limp rather than lay himself open to women and their irrational mood mongering. And then there is Exhibit A, *Stanley and the Women*. After its tough go at finding a publisher in America, accusations were made that feminist cabals had sought to blockade Amis's brand of woman bashing from our beaches. But following much ado in the *TLS* and other places, *Stanley and the Women* belatedly made it ashore. It remains one of Amis's most problematic novels—almost Jamesian in its implicative asides and askew point of view. When I first tried reading it, I found it thick, gray, and wrinkly, a hunk of elephant hide hacked from a lumbering attack of misogynist ego. But in a bitter funk I picked the book off the shelf, began browsing, and suddenly his warped account of dissonance between the sexes all made *perfect sense*. It is a novel that you don't so much read as surrender to as a chill narcotic—you have to be in a susceptible state of disappointment to receive its needle. *Stanley and the Women*'s paranoid premise, persuasively dramatized, is that women everywhere are mad and maddening. Their unavowed aim is to make men's lives a steaming muddle. "Not enough of a motive?" shouts a doctor at Stanley, trying to put him wise. "Fucking up a man? Not enough of a motive? What are you talking about? Good God, you've had wives, haven't you?"

But the male bonding that takes place in *Stanley* (us against all them crazy dames) is a funny parody of drunken guy talk, not meant to be taken as gospel. Complaining about women is how Stanley and his chums loonily let off steam. There are worse ways to let off steam. Unlike D. H. Lawrence, whose bearded prophecies leave Amis cold, he doesn't see strife between men and women as an apocalyptic contest of will and submission—blood consciousness, phallic worship, and the eternal feminine battling it out beneath the snake-coiled tree where Eve was tempted. He veers away from absolutism and violence. He doesn't decapitate women in his fiction, like Norman Mailer, or sniff at their flesh as if it were tainted meat, like Saul Bellow and John Updike. He achieves a rough equivalence. His men are hardly prizes. The amoral shittiness of men is as constant in his fiction as the moral shiftiness of women. And those men often get their comeuppance, like the pub owner in *The Green Man* who stages a ménage à trois only to have the two women get so entwined that he's extraneous. Amis's women certainly aren't weaklings. They have far more spike and spunk than the meek mice in Margaret Drabble and Anita Brookner. "What makes you such a howling bitch?" asks the narrator in *Girl, 20* of the horrid Sylvia, who's been carrying on with his married pal, Roy. Her reply:

> I expect it's the same thing as makes you a top-heavy red-haired
> four-eyes who's . . . impotent and likes bloody symphonies and

fugues and the first variation comes before the statement of the theme and give me a decent glass of British beer and dash it all Carruthers I don't know what young people are coming to these days and a scrounger and an old woman and a failure and a hanger-on and a prig and terrified and a shower and a brisk rub-down every morning and you can't throw yourself away on a little trollop like that Roy you must think of your wife Roy old boy old boy and I'll come along but I don't say I approve and bloody dead. Please delete the items in the above that do not apply. If any.

Any man reading such a passage will check afterward to see if he still has his scalp.

Girl, 20 is middle-period Amis. There was a tailing off of interest after that burst of verbal hostilities, into the implausible mystery of *The Riverside Villas Murder* (great seduction scene, though), the arthritic collapse of *Ending Up*, and the alternative-world fantasizing of *The Alteration* and *Russian Hide-and-Seek*. Amis seemed to be in a long slough. What brought him out of his slide? It's been intimated that it was the breakup of his marriage to the novelist Elizabeth Jane Howard that cracked open the raw, cathartic emotions which found their flow in *Stanley and the Women*. (He currently lives in a curious arrangement with his first wife and her third husband.) It may have been a healing catharsis, for his next novel, *The Old Devils*, had a ravishing presence named Rhiannon and a tremendously romantic ending. "The poem, his poem, was going to be the best tribute he could pay to the only woman who had ever cried for him." For his characters it's the heaviness of being that's unbearable. Lightness is for the young and the dead.

Difficulties with Girls is a drier, lighter affair. It doesn't knock dentures around like hockey pucks, as *The Old Devils* did—it wears a toothpaste smile that's yellowing at the edges. A sequel to *Take a Girl Like You*, *Difficulties with Girls* concerns the marriage of a young couple, Patrick and Jenny Standish, as they cope with the swinging sixties. They're coping better than one of their neighbors, Tim, who convinces himself after his difficulties with girls (in bed he loses his erection presto) that he's a latent case. He tries to acclimate himself to the homosexual lifestyle to the point of acting "poofy" at the local pub. Only a night on the town with a homosexual couple down the hall finally frightens Tim back to the straight and narrow. Amis's mild and unmalicious depiction of the gay couple has drawn a few flurries.

"One reviewer, who I won't name and who's male, said the trouble with the portrayal of these males, you know, he put it like that, is that it's based on hearsay and not on actual experience. Oh, sorry about that, yeah. Hmmm. Thank you. You know, the trouble about Mr. Shakespeare's portrayal of Cleopatra, it's not based on experience."

No one disputes Amis's authority when it comes to man-woman wrangling. Perhaps the funniest exchange in *Difficulties with Girls* comes after a spot of adultery one afternoon. Patrick, who has just given a married woman named Wendy a spin in the sack, basks in the belief that he's thrummed her lute, uncorked an inner glow. Her hard-set look soon tells him he's quite mistaken.

> "I don't understand. You drove at me so remorselessly, so . . . implacably. You seemed tormented by some kind of hatred, for me, for yourself, whatever, I don't know, I'm just baffled. What is it with you, darling? Won't you tell me, for the love of God?"
>
> If he had not felt slightly indignant at the thought of all that good work going for nothing, he might not have said, as he did, "I know I've asked you this already, old thing, but are you absolutely *sure* you're not an American?"

From *Lucky Jim* to Sylvia's tirade in *Girl, 20* to this postcoital spat in *Difficulties with Girls*, the best parts of his fiction have been playable—actable. Amis learned from Anthony Powell, Evelyn Waugh, and especially P. G. Wodehouse the importance of capturing character through dialogue, framing the action, keeping the staging simple. But much of his histrionics came right out of his own hammy spirit. His handsome actor's face houses big-screen lights and shadows. The poet Philip Larkin has paid tribute to Amis's pantomimic skill in their student days at Oxford, mentioning a photograph showing Amis contorting his face into a fierce scowl as he crouched on the grass with an invisible dagger, miming the role of—Japanese soldier. Even more striking than Amis's jawline jujitsu were his vocal air raids. He was a master of sound-track noises (gunfire, static, pigeons, geese) and foreign gibberish. One of his classics was a morale-boosting speech by FDR fighting to be heard on a faulty radio against an incoming front of interference and band music.

Writers are often mimics, trying on attitudes like masks. But when Gore Vidal, say, imitates Richard Nixon or Ronald Reagan on TV, it's a suave simulation, a parlor trick meant to raise at most a titter. Sweat doesn't bead his marble mask. Amis's classics are more Artaud. Larkin: "Kingsley's masterpiece, which was so demanding I heard him do it only twice, involved three subalterns, a Glaswegian driver and a jeep breaking down and refusing to restart somewhere in Germany. Both times I became incapable with laughter." His son Martin Amis seconds the incapability part, saying that after his father's routines there isn't a dry cheek or dry pair of trousers in the house. "The great mimics are very vehement. I mean, he does one of an airplane taking off, but by the time he gets to the pilot he's completely purple in the face. Putting even his body at risk."

I met with Martin Amis, no stranger to vehemence himself, one night at his home in London. "I don't have to wear nappies," one of his sons told him, "not on Tuesday I don't." Ah, the inimitable logic of children! Martin was staying with his two blond boys while his wife went out to a concert. Dinosaur toys lined a shelf downstairs. Martin himself appears in his father's fiction in *I Like It Here*, asking questions about big beasties. "If two tigers and a lion fought a killer whale, who would win? And him going, 'It just could never happen.' Yeah, but who would win?" He also remembers the thrill of checks arriving. "I used to run upstairs with the mail and say, 'There's a check,' and sit around and open it. It was incredibly exciting. It was a check for £700 or something, which would buy you a house." In later boyhood Martin Amis had his own literary difficulty with girls—smart and sarcastic, his first novel, *The Rachel Papers*, was considered a little too inclined to panty sniffing. (A somewhat sanitized version of the novel was being filmed in England when we met.) It was the addictive-minded *Money* (money as sex, money as maintenance, money as obsession) that put Martin on the map in America.

In his father's house his writing is still a submerged landmass, however. "He doesn't read my stuff. He can't get on with it. The last one he read, I think, was *Success*, thirteen years ago." His father had read a chapter of *Money* when it was printed in a magazine, but showed less patience with the complete novel. "I knew the exact moment he sent the novel windmilling across the room: when a minor character named Martin Amis showed up in the book. He has very firm rules about that."

Kingsley Amis resists and resents self-referentialism in fiction not only because he thinks it's trendy but because to him its tricks are dated. "Because my first novel, which was never published, had a hero called Kingsley Amis." Its title? "*The Legacy*. It's a writer's title. *The Legacy*? Who wants to know about that?"

Writerliness Kingsley Amis abhors. To be a writerly writer is to be cerebral, cliquish, enclosed, exiled to a bookish realm, be it a Borgesian maze or a Nabokovian hall of mirrors—literary with a capital *L*. To be a readerly writer is to be literary, lowercase. Although Martin clearly admires his father's fiction and his dedication to book reviewing ("He believes in putting something back into literature"), he seems less enthused about the lowercase slack in the recent work. Of *Difficulties with Girls*, he comments, "It's sort of tacky, as if it's being told to you at a pub, that novel." For his part, Kingsley looks with amusement at his uppercase son. "My son's next novel is going to be very long—it's called *London Fields*. Now, that's a writer's title. That's the sort of thing that great novels are called." (The novel is also set in 1999, another sign of greatness calling.)

The tentative title of Kingsley Amis's next novel is more reader-friendly. "I think it's going to be called *The Folks Who Live on the Hill*. After that, you know, bloody Bing Crosby record." Only these are not Bing Crosby's idea of folks. One husband is desolated when his wife runs off with another woman—he wants her back. Another character is a woman with a history of alcoholism. "Anyway, she's off the bottle, you think she's very nice. She's going to say, 'Harry, you see those people walking on the street there?' 'Yes, dear.' 'I'd like them to be in a *war*.'" There are also dead-end discussions in which two baffled men try to figure out exactly what it is lesbians do. From the bits Amis recited, the book sounds like a swing back to the crust and brio of *The Old Devils*. He's at home with these crocodiles.

After *The Folks Who Live on the Hill*, Kingsley Amis is considering his memoirs, to be structured not as a chronological account of his life but as an ABC of anecdotes. "My memoirs are not going to be an autobiography, but an alphabiography, putting them in alphabetical order. Because there are only two things I have a good memory for, poetry and anecdotes. I've got lots and lots of anecdotes." As an example, he mentions the black musician Rex Stewart, cornetist for eleven years in Duke Ellington's band. "I said to him, 'Did you know that King George VI'—actually, it wasn't King George VI, it was Prince George, the Duke of Kent, but I didn't know that then—'had a complete collection of Ellington records on their original American labels?' 'Yes,' he said. 'We all knew that,' he said. 'When we were refused hotel service in Charleston, somewhere like that, we'd say, "Well, George likes us. George likes us." ' "

Like the jazz masters he admires, Amis has learned to pace himself, keep his whistle wet, bend to the notes. He has a shorthand fluency, a flair for slang phrasing that's like the stop-start of fast music. Even a minor novel like *Difficulties with Girls* has a sad moan at the back of its metallic chimes. And there's little danger Kingsley Amis will go God on us, as Evelyn Waugh did. He's wedded to the human stew. Its incessant bubble.

Vanity Fair, April 1989

Kingsley's Ransom

Late this summer, a literary crime was committed in London: if the victim had been a woman, it might have been called "granny bashing." The elderly gentleman being ganged up on was Kingsley Amis, who, at seventy-three, had brought out his twenty-fourth novel, *The Biographer's Moustache*, to little acclaim. The majority opinion was that this book revealed sad evidence of diminished capacity. The *Observer*: "'The Biographer's Moustache' is reflex writing, full of Pavlovian pedantry." The *Sunday Times*: "A stale, flat, savourless affair." The *Daily Mail*: "Banal, boring and extremely silly." Terribly dated, nearly everyone agreed. Amis, having been a pooh-bah on the public scene for decades, had become an overstuffed father figure, and father figures are made to be toppled. (After beating up on the father figure, the London press then smacked the son figure around, taking special glee in the failure of Martin Amis's much hyped *The Information* to be short-listed for the Booker Prize.)

If the reviews of Kingsley Amis's new novel reached a hostile decision (Pack it in, Pops), the interviews intended to promote it were even nastier. They literally added insult to injury. In August, Amis had one of the all-time bad months. His old friend the solicitor Stuart Thomas died; Amis spoke at the funeral service. At the time, he was a guest at the Swansea, Wales, home of his friends Michael and Virginia Rush, and in none too fine repair himself. When a *Guardian* interviewer, Joanna Coles, and her photographer arrived, Amis joked about a groin pull and grumbled about being dislodged from the sofa to have his picture taken in better light. You might think an interviewer would sympathize with the plight of a septuagenarian in obvious discomfort, but no, Amis was treated as if he were a prima donna holding up production. A more damning portrait was drawn by Glenys Roberts, for the *Daily Telegraph*, who likened Amis to "a cross between Winnie the Pooh and the misogynist American comedian W. C. Fields" and then complained that she was able to tweeze only a few quotes from him. That morning, Amis had taken a serious spill on the stairs, landing on his back, and as he waited on the sofa for the doctor, he sloughed off her questions. "It isn't often one goes from London to Swansea to meet a famous figurehead and encounters such a lack of civility for one's pains," Roberts fumed. No, it probably isn't. Given that Amis was physically racked, and dispirited about the death of his friend, he would probably have been better off canceling the interviews instead of staring out into space in long, Pinteresque silences. The reviews of his interviews proved more scathing than the reviews of his book. The *Evening Standard* took a stern line with the geriatric juvenile delinquent: "Journalists should not let him get away with it. . . . If it is not possible to come up with anything remotely new or interesting, newspapers should not print this stuff."

Amis's oft-quoted line about bad reviews is that they ruin his breakfast but not his lunch. Yet such a battery of setbacks, public and private, may have been a serious blow even to an old curmudgeon with a thick crust. Amis had cracked a couple of vertebrae in his fall, and shortly afterward he suffered a stroke and ended up in the intensive-care unit of a London hospital. "I fear he may be on the way down," one longtime friend says.

I had no knowledge of this when I read the hostile notices of *The Biographer's Moustache*. At the time, I merely found myself experiencing such cognitive dissonance that I ordered the book from England toot sweet. For many of the very sentences that reviewers had singled out as examples of slack execution, faltering powers, or rabid prejudice made me laugh. One critic was baffled by the line "A girl of about thirty answered his ring apparently clad in an excerpt from the Bayeux Tapestry." Another was offended by the sentence "Wishing he had been drunk, Gordon got on a bus apparently reserved for winners and runners-up in some pan-European repulsiveness contest." Another cited this supposed clunker: "Gordon got to his feet as Louise had done and grappled with her briefly in an amatory way, at the end of which she disengaged herself without hostility and telephoned for a minicab." This deadpan diagram struck me as inspired—a perfect Etch-A-Sketch drawing of the activities of a pair of stick figures. Admittedly, I'm favorably predisposed. As someone who has read virtually everything Amis has written, including such little-known curiosities as his study of Rudyard Kipling, I always look forward to the latest Amis novel not as a separate and detachable artwork but as an opportunity to spend time in his mental company.

For better or worse—mostly better—Amis loosened the collar of English prose. He loosened its tongue. Not that he did it alone:

Anthony Powell mastered the art of taking a sentence the long way round; Ivy Compton-Burnett hung thick nettings of domestic discourse; Henry Green dropped petals in the unimpeded flow of his characters' consciousness. But it was Amis who invested writing with the largest volume of chat. Beginning in 1954, with *Lucky Jim*, he made a performance art of the right inflection, and not just in his fiction. The journalistic reviews collected in *What Became of Jane Austen?* and *The Amis Collection* have a slangy, matey tone that is a deliberate slap at both the grim specter of F. R. Leavis, the forbidding Cambridge don who was said to have decried Amis as a "pornographer," and the belletristic legacy of Bloomsbury, wherein books were discussed in terms of breeding and palate. Amis opinionized in an off-duty mode, his manner frank and relaxed. He would discuss Keats not as a doomed Romantic immortal but as a chap who sometimes got a little flowery. According to Harry Ritchie, a contributor to a 1991 Amis Festschrift, Amis's reviewing has had a powerful influence on postwar English criticism. Now, he wrote, "the democratic wise-cracking of critics such as Clive James and John Carey, inspired by Amis's example, constitutes a new orthodoxy."

Amis's deceptively casual approach was more than a tactical ploy, a way of sneaking in punches; it expressed his conviction that language loses its responsive energy and observant value when it becomes over-jewelled and forcibly sublime. He deplored Nabokov's aestheticizing of the mother's car death in *Lolita*. After quoting the description of "a porridge of bone, brains, bronze hair, and blood," he remarked, "That's the boy, Humbert/Nabokov: alliterative to the last." He made sport of Evelyn Waugh's *Brideshead Revisited* in a review smartly titled "How I Lived in a Very Big House and Found God," deploring how Waugh's abject awe of religion and the aristocracy turned his once pristine prose into slosh. He even took Jane Austen to task for turning priggish in *Mansfield Park*. He saw literature not as a mountain range of Towering Masterpieces but as a series of individual involvements that engage us at eye level and can be divided into those books we fancy and those we don't. Or, as he wrote, "Importance isn't important. Only good writing is."

And good writing can be found anywhere, in any genre. Amis was one of the first active practitioners (as opposed to pop-cult theorists) to see that the traditional literary novel has no monopoly on art. He monkeyed with the class system in literature, treating the categories of high-, low-, and middlebrow fiction as rough equals. Along with his serious comedies (*Take a Girl Like You, Stanley and the Women, The Old Devils*), he wrote an innovative mainstream treatise on science fiction (*New Maps of Hell*) and an uncondescending study of James Bond (*The James Bond Dossier*), and later tried his hand at his own post–Ian Fleming Bond novel (*Colonel Sun*). He has also plowed the horror graveyard (*The Green Man*), played "what if?" with history (*Russian Hide-and-Seek, The Alteration*), and dabbled in walking the detective beat (*The Crime of the Century*). Always an antimodernist, Amis rebelled against the role of the artist as deep-sea diver of the inner universe (Flaubert, Joyce, Woolf, Proust, Beckett: take your exemplary pick). He preferred to cast himself as a versatile pro running a modest amusement shop. His stance reflects not only a practical Everyman approach to writing but the distinctive English aversion to looking pretentious. But to Amis's detractors his pretension-avoidance was just a facet of his inherent philistinism and hostility to anything that smacked of cultural enhancement. (Translation: He thinks we're sissies!)

In his new book, Amis plays footsie with fact and fiction: *The Biographer's Moustache* was written parallel with the completion of the authorized biography of Amis by Eric Jacobs, which was published in England earlier this year. The biography, a dutiful, uninspired job, did turn up an interesting fact about Amis's childhood—that his mother, worried about his nourishment, spoon-fed Kingsley his meals until he was twelve or thirteen years old. "Then a new regime took over, though only slightly more adult," Jacobs writes. "After some minutes toying with the food on his plate, Kingsley would say, 'Mum, would you sort it out for me?' Mum then divided what was left into two parts, the food that definitely must be eaten and the rest that Kingsley could leave if he wished." This mollycoddling explains Amis's reliance on others for his routines, and his sense of himself as a little monarch. The critic Paul Fussell saw much of Amis in the sixties; he and his then wife, Betty, who is a food writer, knew what it was like to live under his rule. Betty Fussell recalls, "Kingsley's rituals. We all lived by them when we were with Kingsley—man, woman, and child—because we had to. They were the order of the day, as inviolable as military commands or church liturgies." Even on holiday, people had to abide by Amis time. She writes, "Breakfast with the papers was punctually at 9 A.M., even if Kingsley had fallen dead drunk into bed at 4 A.M. after a liquid intake that reduced the rest of us to Jell-O for the next 24 hours."

Kingsley's maintenance routine has continued despite changes of address. He shares a house in north London with his first wife, Hilly, and her third husband, Lord Kilmarnock—an odd living arrangement, which Amis himself has admitted smacks of an Iris Murdoch novel. Hilly brings him dinner every Monday, Wednesday, Friday, and Sunday. On Tuesdays and Thursdays, his daughter Sally pinch-hits. And what Amis's critics didn't seem to appreciate is that Jimmie Fane, the biographical subject in *The Biographer's Moustache*, is also something of a stuffed goose. Like his creator, Fane has a lot of bluff in his makeup. Paul Fussell, who has written a thorny valentine to Amis called "The Anti-Egotist: Kingsley Amis, Man of Letters," told me that one of his chum's most admirable traits is that, "compared to Americans, he doesn't have an ounce of sincerity about him—everything he says is figurative." Likewise Fane. Everything he does is for foggy effect.

In this portrait of the artist as aging matinée idol, Amis is mostly making fun of his own inflatable persona—puncturing his own gas-bag. Fane is a toady to the rich, a meal sponger, a wine snob, and a word bore ("These days I'm told the creatures have the impertinence to call themselves *gay*, thereby rendering unusable, thereby destroying a fine old English word with its roots deep in the language"). He diverts himself by playing pranks on his hapless biographer, the aforementioned Gordon—one of those earnest nonentities who make useful foils in English fiction. Gordon's abuse at the hands of Fane and his brief, wrenching affair with Fane's wife, Joanna, serve as his sentimental education. Never again will he partake of aristocratic nooky. At the end, Gordon recognizes Jimmie Fane for the shit he is—a "massive and multifarious shit." Nor does Fane's fiction pass inspection; the seemingly rich ambiguities of his early prose are laid bare by Gordon as "abject piss, well beyond any excuse of a comprehensive change of taste, simple passage of thirty years or more, etc." It's as if Amis were imagining the worst that could be said about his own output—imagining himself consigned to limbo.

A number of reviewers complained about the lack of engine in the novel's narrative. Fair enough; yet story has never been Amis's strength. (The plot of *Lucky Jim* didn't roar down the railroad tracks.) Amis's non-genre novels have always been ambulatory exercises in mulling things over. Where so much of current literary fiction either aims for damnation, combing the alleys in search of sex demons and serial killers, or strives for affirmation, seeking the rainbow over the bridges of Madison County, *The Biographer's Moustache* muddles through the middle latitudes of normalcy, which are laced with random nuttiness. Amis's characters don't scan the world through photo-realist lenses, putting a price-tag on every item of furniture and fashion; they take things in a general lump.

But beneath their surface inertia is what Fussell calls Amis's "highly rapid ironic intelligence." Amis's novels are always operating at two speeds simultaneously—a slower narrative speed and a faster judgmental clip. Behind their putty faces, Amis's characters formulate thoughts and store grievances; they mimic "all's well" even as their minds articulate like mad. The machinery of *The Biographer's Moustache* is sleepy, and the invective is more contained (though there is a passing reference to "his bloody lordship and his piss-artist elephant's-bum-faced four-eyed boiler of a wife"), but the book transports the reader along to a brilliant set piece in the ancestral home of a dotty duke—a sort of P. G. Wodehouse Blandings Castle novel in compact form. Here Jimmie introduces Gordon to sylvan haunts similar to those of his youth:

> The view before them was certainly unusual in that, to the eye of a town-dweller at least, it contained nothing of the twentieth century, no power lines, no metal fences, no machinery, no advertisement. . . . Nevertheless the scene made no more than a puny appeal to Gordon personally. It was green, brown here and there but mostly green, motionless, silent, unpopulated and asking for the addition of a passage in curlicued italics about man's quest through the ages.

This country interlude saves *The Biographer's Moustache*. It reminds you that a novel is not a blueprint for better living or a spiritual guidebook but an organism, with its own breathing patterns. For all the talk of Amis's patented misanthropy, the book is almost suspiciously free of malice.

The Biographer's Moustache is agreeable minor Amis, somewhere below *Lucky Jim* and *Stanley and the Women*, and above *I Want It Now* and *Difficulties with Girls*. Given his age, drinking habits, and shaky health, it's a wonder Amis bothers banging out a book at all. It isn't as if he had anything additional to prove. If you pick up *Lucky Jim* today, you're impressed by how much it has retained its original fizz. Written over a period of seven years, during which Amis was peppered with encouragement and advice from the poet Philip Larkin (to whom the novel was dedicated), this academic comedy, published in 1954, about Jim Dixon, a young instructor at a podunk college, remains the classic test case: how does a bright mind cope with creeping boredom? Trying to pass as a capable young man, Dixon indulges in a full repertory of facial expressions (hearing his name called, he makes his "shot-in-the-back face") and anti-cant exercises. (When he reads a paper that begins, "In considering this strangely neglected topic . . . ," he asks himself, "This what neglected topic? This strangely what topic? This strangely neglected what?") *Lucky Jim* also contains Amis's prototypical hangover scene: "His mouth had been used as a latrine by some small creature of the night, and then as its mausoleum."

After a spotty period in the early eighties, in 1986 Amis won the Booker Prize for *The Old Devils*, that jangly group portrait of lust and swollen livers among the Geritol set, and then, in 1990, he was knighted. With one eye on the exit, he published his *Memoirs*, which mixed anecdotes he had dined out on for years with a few revisionist put-downs. The Russian expert Robert Conquest, an old friend of Amis's and his collaborator on *The Egyptologists*, told me that he'd noticed an anecdote about himself in the manuscript of Amis's memoir which wasn't true; after he pointed this out, Amis substituted Philip Toynbee's name—"which I don't think was accurate, either."

Amis has recently completed a new nonfiction book, and he was deep in the bag of yet another novel before his illness. Very few American writers continue to plug away past the point of glory, but Amis has been harnessed to his work habits. He would rise each morning for a small meal of yogurt and honey, put in three hours of work, break for lunch, then write for another hour in the afternoon. "That's four hours a day, every day, seven days a week," he informed the *Guardian*. Yet this steady application is more than a sturdy example of neo-Victorian work ethic, akin to the production schedule Trollope kept. Morale is a fragile mechanism. The diligence of Amis's daily routine expresses a strong psychological drive to keep the motor running, as if Amis believed that if he came to a halt a greater power would seize possession: his life would be impounded. "The moment you stop writing, you're turning your face to the wall," he told Joanna Coles, of the *Guardian*.

One of the most interesting revelations in the grudging interviews Amis gave was that he still dopes himself to sleep at night. "I pill myself up. Very relaxing, pills and Scotch. I sleep very well. It's partly drugged sleep, of course. But better drugged sleep than no sleep." On being asked if he could sleep without his dosage, he replied, "I don't know, I'm not going to take the risk. I don't like lying in bed tossing and turning. I used to be scared of the dark." (Readers of *The Old Devils* will recall the character Charlie, who suffered from this same fear.) By giving himself knockout drops at night, Amis is hastening sleep and blotting out intimations of mortality before they can muster an appearance. He chooses a small oblivion to ward off a bigger one. If his fiction sometimes reads like a groggy dream with the cobwebs still clinging, perhaps this is because it's the product of so much fermented anxiety. Like Hemingway near the end, Amis, in recent photographs, resembles a desolate hulk; his body has become a haunted house. "There is no personal God. There is no point to life," he told Glenys Roberts, of the *Telegraph*, with "utter finality," adding, "Though there is a point to art." And what is the point? To give other people pleasure, he said, with what Roberts deemed "uncharacteristic generosity."

In the current climate, beauty and pleasure are doomed to be obscured by character issues, which are in turn governed by attitudes toward race, class, sex, and politics. The posthumous reputation of Philip Larkin has been pitted by the publication of his letters and Andrew Motion's biography, which document his racist jingles, reactionary gibes, miserliness, damp palm for soft porn, and unwillingness to commit to the women in his life, all adding up to an image of a mama's boy in a dirty old man's raincoat—not the picture of a lyric poet you want to carry in your locket. Even Fussell, a staunch cultural conservative, says that he has become "disaffected with Larkin's character," which he now finds "hateful." Amis has always been more open about his cranks and antipathies than Secret Agent Larkin, so there'll be less shock at whatever indiscretions are later divulged, but not necessarily lighter reprimand. Inklings of the toxic leakage to come can be found in Jacobs's biography, a prize exhibit for future prosecution being a photograph of Amis on the beach which shows the words written in lipstick on his back by his wife Hilly, who was fed up with his philandering: "I FAT ENGLISHMAN I FUCK ANYTHING." The caption notes, "They split up shortly afterwards." Amis went on to marry the novelist Elizabeth Jane Howard, with whom he had been having an affair. When that marriage dissolved, years later, the divorce was bitter and public. Robert Conquest recalls Howard's denouncing Amis in the press: "You'd pick up the paper one day and there'd be the headline 'How Kingsley Ruined My Life.' Then a few days later would be the headline 'How Kingsley Ruined Our Holidays.'" The Jacobs biography also reprints the draft of an unfinished, unpublished poem Amis sent to Conquest, a Kiplingesque ditty that ends:

The usual sort of men
Who hold the world together
Manage to face their front
In any sort of weather.
With rueful grins and curses
They push the world along;
But women and queers and children
Cry when things go wrong.

The paradox is that it's often easier to pardon true, frothing bigots, like Céline or Ezra Pound, because they seem so lashed by pathological furies; their sort of prejudice can be analyzed as the black ash of a charred heart. Next to them, Amis and Larkin merely sound cheeky. They're firing poison blow darts.

Yet compared with such hearties on this side of the Atlantic as Hemingway and Norman Mailer, Amis isn't so macho. The Amis man does not seek conquest of women and dominion over his shining field of endeavor; like his creator, the Amis man wants to settle into a comfortable rut. He is a longtime combatant in the sex wars, who no longer has the energy or the inclination to do more than kvetch about the minor irritations of his captive fate. (The last page of *Stanley and the Women* declared a domestic truce.) And a small rivulet of remorse trickles through the rut the Amis men travel from home to office to pub. It springs from Amis's personal history, from his persistent sorriness over the breakup of his marriage to Hilly. He snapped at the *Guardian* reporter who asked if he ever wondered whether things could have been otherwise: "Of course it could have been otherwise, but you don't think of that at the time, do you?"

No, you think of it later, and try to make amends. In the final line of *The Old Devils*, Malcolm sits down to write a poem to an old love— "The poem, his poem, was going to be the best tribute he could pay to the only woman who had ever cried for him." Amis's biographer notes that the novel *You Can't Do Both*, the predecessor of *The Biographer's Moustache*, is an extended note of regret addressed to Hilly, and a subplot in *The Biographer's Moustache* involves restitution to a woman from the past. But it is more than guilt that sends Amis's heroes on these goodwill missions. They're also expressing a fear attendant on death. The saddest fate in an Amis novel is to be alone, ailing, and unvisited. Amis men may resent being dependent on women, but they would miss having someone to talk to even more. Kingsley Amis has kept writing because he knows that death is when you reach the end of your words.

The New Yorker, October 30, 1995

Postscript

The last sentence of this tribute was in the present tense because Amis was still alive, but not for long, dying on Sunday, October 22, 1995, the day before the magazine appeared on the newsstands in New York.

The Amis Papers

The Setup

In the mid-1990s, Martin Amis's fame blew up in his face. After twenty years of maintaining a stony cool in public and perfecting his pout, Amis became the victim of a journalistic pile-on, buried alive beneath a squirming mound of jealous hacks. What incited the mob? Never underestimate the ugly thrill of spite. A literary sex symbol since his debut with *The Rachel Papers* in 1973 at the age of twenty-four, Amis struck some as a spoiled child of fortune. His being a son of a famous writer—Kingsley Amis, the creator of *Lucky Jim*—gave his first novel (a goyish *Goodbye, Columbus* recounting the seduction of a junior bitch goddess) pedigree, curiosity value, and brand-name recognition. He seemed heir to a going concern. Small but perfectly formed, to borrow a put-down from the satirical magazine *Private Eye*, Martin made up what he lacked in height by projecting a wide sweep of rock-star glamour. His was the scowl of a new generation. His floppy mop of Mick Jagger hair and mod duds were an advertisement for the bad-boy swagger and electrical spurt of his prose. He made writing look insolently easy, tossing off bravura passages as if they were guitar licks. His precocious, no-sweat flair gave rise to a popular joke that a strong candidate for Most Unlikely Book Title was *My Struggle*, by Martin Amis. He may not have struggled, but he didn't coast. His subsequent fiction traveled offbeat channels. *Dead Babies* (1975), a dark parody of the English-country-house novel in which a group of guests indulge in an orgy of sick jokes and abused body parts, lived up (or down) to its punk title. *Other People: A Mystery Story* (1981), an allegory about a woman with amnesia trying to re-piece her identity, was so pure in execution it seemed written in white ink. *Money* (1984), the novel that propelled him into the majors, was a scathing monologue machine set to Nabokovian overdrive about a human vacuum cleaner named John Self who hoovers up everything in his path (women, drugs, booze, smokes) . . . capitalist consumption on an oral rampage. Pioneering the advent of "lad's mags" such as

Maxim and *FHM*, he was a matey writer, shooting pool, playing tennis, writing a nonfiction book about the video game Space Invaders.

After a bachelor tear as a "sack-artist" (one of Amis's pet phrases), during which he dated journalistic starlets such as Emma Soames, Julie Kavanagh, and Tina Brown, Amis married an American, Antonia Phillips, in 1984. He settled down and seemed to have it all: fame, money, marriage, children (two boys), a house in London, the respect of his peers, and popular appeal on both sides of the Atlantic. He even kept his girlish figure. Other writers of his generation and acquaintance such as Ian McEwan and Julian Barnes may have won more awards or sold more books, but everyone understood that Amis was the one with charisma to burn. Consolidating his powers for a productive middle age, he seemed geared to make the transition from golden boy to steady beacon. Newspaper profiles testified to the maturity and moral responsibility fatherhood had conferred: his interviews and fiction now concerned themselves with the fate of nations under the dangling sword of nuclear destruction rather than mapping out underwear stains. On the occasion of the launch of *London Fields*, a dark-night-of-the-millennium novel about a sexy enigma who arranges her own murder, he was given the usual ointment application on Melvyn Bragg's *South Bank Show*, complete with dramatized excerpts featuring some sultry babe swanking about in lingerie. Coinciding with that lovefest, Mary Harron—who went on to direct *I Shot Andy Warhol* and *American Psycho*—and I did a parody of *London Fields* for BBC's *The Late Show*, where I impersonated an unctuous Bragg, re-enacted Martin's first day at Oxford (an angelic chorus rising as he sets foot on the quadrangle), and, lacking lingerie models, used salt and pepper shakers to demonstrate scenes from the book. What I was struck by most then was the undisguised glee in London when *London Fields* wasn't short-listed for the Booker Prize. At the Groucho Club and elsewhere, faces that were usually overcast glowed with delight at the news. The novel's merits and demerits were a side issue. There was a sense that Amis already had more than his fair share, that he didn't need any more petting, he was puffed up enough as it was—give some other sod a break. This scattered chorus would become a full-blown posse as Martin Amis, who seemed incapable of misstep, became tangled up in blue.

The Takedown

Although Martin Amis might be accused of hubris, what happened to him in the mid-nineties went beyond the lowered boom of Greek drama. It was more like a cosmic inversion. It was as if the roof had fallen in on him, then the sky, followed by pieces of satellite debris. He was hit with everything in God's cupboard. His losses compounded until life itself seemed x'd out.

In 1994 his cousin Lucy Partington, who had vanished in 1973, was discovered to have been a victim of the serial killer Frederick West when her dismembered remains were exhumed. The press swooped down on the relatives as the mystery of Lucy's disappearance was solved as a tragedy. "The Pain Vultures," as Lucy's sister, Marian, called them, had landed, and around Amis they would continue to flock. That same year he ditched his longtime agent, Pat Kavanagh, and signed with Andrew Wylie, a pact that lost him the friendship of Kavanagh's husband, Julian Barnes, who sent Amis a flying tomahawk of a fuck-off letter. When Wylie secured a mind-boggling $800,000 advance for Amis's next novel, *The Information* (1995), and a collection of short stories, the London literary scene let howl. A. S. Byatt, the author of *Angels & Insects* and *The Matisse Stories*, called Amis one of the "strutting boys of the book world," and mentioned the expensive dental treatments Amis was undergoing in New York. What had been literary-world gossip was now front-page blab. This repairwork was considered yet another sign of his swollen vanity and narcissistic preening. When *The Information* was also snubbed by the Booker Prize committee, the vindictive glee was like a victory dance.

In 1995 his father died at the age of seventy-three. The Amis family was robbed of the opportunity to mourn in peace when Kingsley's authorized biographer, Eric Jacobs, sprinted to *The Sunday Times* to tattle on Kingsley in his dotage. Furious that Jacobs would use his position as a family friend to cash in before his father was laid to rest, Amis insisted Jacobs withdraw the diary from publication, rescinded his invitation to the funeral, and, the sharpest slap, relieved him of the honor of editing his father's collected letters. When the offending diary was offered again to *The Sunday Times*, Jacobs added new material in which he asserted with the blithe assurance of someone who is thoroughly mistaken that Kingsley's daughter, Sally, was the only family member who wept at the funeral ("Everybody cried," Martin writes in *Experience* [Talk Miramax/Hyperion], his newsmaking memoir). This would lead to another kung-fu round of recriminations. Complicating matters was that not only was Martin the chief book reviewer of *The Sunday Times*, a post he resigned as soon as the serialization began, but the agent who brokered Jacobs's serialization was Andrew Wylie's London partner, Gillon Aitken. It was like a Jacobean court with all this daggered betrayal. (The Aitken-Wylie agency itself was split asunder when Wylie broke with Aitken to set up a separate shop in 1996.)

That same year, Amis and his wife divorced after he had left her and his two sons for another woman, the author and heiress Isabel Fonseca, nicknamed "Isabel Funseeker." A child of divorce himself, he had pledged never to put his children through what his parents had put him and his siblings through—and now this! He stood condemned of double infidelity, first betraying his friends for money, then his wife for another woman. To some, this last development cinched the case that Mr. Nuclear Worrywart was just another out-for-himself hustler. In *The Sunday Times*, Toby Young crowed, "It's difficult to suppress a hint of *Schadenfreude* on hearing the news about the collapse of his marriage. . . . To have abandoned his wife, Antonia, and their children for a younger woman, particularly after droning on about the joys of fatherhood, makes it that much harder to take him seriously. For those of us who find literary novelists insufferably self-righteous, this is undoubtedly a source of real pleasure." As the kid says in the last sentence of the Hemingway story "My Old Man," "Seems like when they get started they don't leave a guy nothing." Small wonder Amis spoke of moving to America, where envy springs less green and abundant (or so he thinks). As if all this turmoil weren't soap-opera enough, a shadowy suspicion lurking at the back of Amis's mind for decades was confirmed in the flesh. A daughter of whom he had only the smallest inkling announced her existence. Her name was Delilah Seale. At the age of eighteen, Delilah learned that the man who had raised her as his own child—her mother, with whom Amis had had a brief affair, had committed suicide when Delilah was two—was not her biological father. She now wanted to meet the man who was. At a hotel bar in Knightsbridge, Amis awaited the arrival of a young woman wearing a softer likeness of his face. Their reunion too would generate ink.

The Sound-Off

"I can't remember the details of all those months of crucifixion in the press," Amis writes of his time on the cross in *Experience*. Marketed as a literary hullabaloo so frank and blazingly humane it has to be kept in a Domino's Pizza carrier, *Experience* is a Lazarus act of self-resurrection. Contradicting Amis's cold-fish image, it's a confessional strip search, personalized with schoolboy letters and family-album photos—a portrait of the artist as a battered man reborn. Also brought back from the dead this spring is the cantankerous voice of his father in *The Letters of Kingsley Amis* (HarperCollins), a mammoth compendium which resembles a sunken tanker retrieved from the ocean floor, barnacled with footnotes. The books form a dynastic set. The cover of *Experience* shows a boyish, sun-blond Martin striking a tough-guy pose with a cigarette stuck in his mouth; the cover of the letters shows a dashing Kingsley wielding a cigarette between extended fingers. Father and son, united in devilry. But if the photos rhyme, the affections inside run asymmetrically. *Experience* is an expansive gesture of fealty to the father. Kingsley, a touchy panda, takes up a lot of room on the page. Even when he behaves like an Evelyn Waugh knockoff ("I've finally worked out why I don't like Americans . . . because everyone there is either a Jew or a hick"), he has presence, scope. But his emotional stinginess, fortified by age, fat, and alcohol (toward the end he was like a pickle jar with a stuck lid), leaves Martin on the bad end of a lopsided deal. It's as if he views his father in close-up while his father miniaturizes him. In the letters, Martin is referred to as the "little shit."

Hopscotching across time, *Experience* is a montage of regrets, anguishing moments, and sad farewells that is part hair shirt, part memorial quilt. Those expecting ripped-panties revelations about Amis's bachelor romps and extracurricular activities will feel cheated and perhaps ashamed of themselves—cheap inside. (I know I did.) For example, Amis adopts a tone of High Propriety describing his all-too-fleeting love affair at Oxford with future buzz-czarina Tina Brown. "Tina, pointing to a lacuna in my emotional repertoire, would later say that I had never had my heart broken. And I can now recognise that I somewhere harboured an unconscious distrust of love (to this I will return)." When he alludes to the dissolution of his first marriage, it is in the Clintonesque "Mistakes were made" mode, the testimony of a stricken bystander rather than an active player. Similarly, he doesn't lay out the telephone tag that must have led up to his dropping Pat Kavanagh as his agent, he simply relates the aftershocks while managing to insert a catty comment about Julian Barnes's being "uxorious." Considering that Amis's best novel may be *Money*, where cash infusions have the kick of cocaine, he's notably reticent discussing his own itchy wallet.

In *Experience*, he eschews any dynamic capework as seducer, careerist, and bankroll artist to offer himself in the passive role of sufferer. He tailors his tone to his crucifix, presenting himself as steadfast, forsaken. All those he holds dear show him their backs: Julian Barnes ("It was said that I turned away—and I don't do that. I won't be the one to turn away," Amis writes); his father when he visits him in the hospital ("'I don't want to see *anyone . . . Anyone*,' my father says, and turns emphatically on his side"); his baby daughter ("My daughter, revolving on her axis for the first time in her life, and turning away from me. I hate it when they turn away"). There's almost a rhythmic lilt to his sorrowful refrains. Progressively, *Experience* becomes a lyrical crying jag. Amis weeps at movies (the floating landscapes of faces affect him), he and his father weep over a passage from Primo Levi, he weeps over Lucy, he weeps on the airplane for hours after visiting his sons in America, he weeps over his father's death, he weeps "tears of pure misery" after reading Jacobs's diary. The waterworks in the opening pages of *The Information*, an aerial view of men sobbing in bed in the throes of their mortality crises, are in full flood here. If the book becomes a hit, it will be in large part because readers find themselves weeping in tune. It's a cry-along.

Amis's unsparing account of his dental agony should prove chastening to all those jokesters who made light of his predicament at the time, and provoke sympathetic flinching. Since childhood he had suffered from poor choppers—"Observational evidence soon established that *everyone* had better teeth than me: football hooligans, junkies, tramps"—and in 1994 his teeth were in such poor fettle he was reduced to "using about 8 per cent of my mouth." The descriptions of his dental operations in Manhattan, performed not to purchase Amis "a Liberace smile" but out of grim necessity, have a transfixing horror—a Frankenstein poignance. When he looks in the mirror, it's as if he took a hockey puck in the mouth, an oral cave-in which is instantly aging (death's peephole). He's forced to wear a device he calls The Clamp, which is like having a horseshoe inserted in the jaw. It's slim consolation that he has joined a select group of cavity-prone prodigies. "Question: How many of these three noted stylists—James Joyce, Vladimir Nabokov and Martin Amis—suffered catastrophic tooth-loss in their early-to-middle forties? Answer: All three." Suddenly we are out of the clinic and in the classroom as Amis inevitably cites the well-known bit from Nabokov's *Pnin* in which the hapless hero's "fat sleek seal" of a tongue flops among the rocks of his ruined teeth. "What else did Nabokov and Joyce have in common, apart from the poor teeth and the great prose? Exile, and decades of near pauperism." We don't need this little seminar, and Amis's modest disclaimer at the end of it rings coy. "Still, I claim peership with these masters in only one area. Not in the art and not in the life. Just in the teeth. In the teeth." Well, he certainly can't claim to share their pauperism!

The Overhang

To Martin Amis, Vladimir Nabokov is the supreme example of god-like genius amusing itself by breathing illusion into iridescent bubbles. The "noble Nabokov," he calls him, "in whose veins raced the grape blood of emperors." To Kingsley Amis, Nabokov was a heartless show-boater, a stylemonger who would stoop to tarting up the description of a traffic accident for baroque effect. He deplored Nabokov's influence, telling the poet Philip Larkin that it was what was wrong with half of American writing "and has fucked up a lot of fools here, plus, or including as you might wish to say, my little Martin." In *Experience*, little Martin defends himself and his grape-blooded hero against the charge of empty show by arguing that style isn't fancy topping or exotic plumage but the very inscription of character and intention. "I would argue that style *is* morality: morality detailed, configured, intensified." Style is identity.

But what does Martin Amis's style say about him? Amis's early work was fast, mean, and vernacular, a sporty convertible capable of darting through traffic and turning on a hair. With fame and maturity his prose has lost its racing stripes. The slang and noise-density of his early work have been replaced with leather upholstery and a parliamentary drone. Plain statement is sacrificed to Listerine-gargling locutions. "There is murk, there is poor visibility, in the motives of literary ambition—*nostalgie*, acidic isolation . . ." "Only once, when I was turning thirty, did I find myself entertaining the prospect of a *froideur*." "On the auriferous arcades of midtown I would constitute an embarrassment to the social scene." "It was my notion to buy some [astronomy] books that would transport me from the quotidian, the merely sublunary, the bluntly dental." He can't describe a beach holiday without turning it into an Updikean meditation. "On the first morning, as your quivering, death-grey foot broaches the sand, you think only of your shocking etiolation—the stripped creature, so pale, so parched. Then, after a while, the body becomes the focus of a cautious complacency. How one primes it with oils and unguents, how one braces it with the alerting asperities of sand and salt and solar fire . . ." Solar fire, no less! The only pages bristling with unrehearsed life are those in which his friend Christopher Hitchens (a *Vanity Fair* contributor) louses up a dinner with Saul Bellow and his wife by launching into a greatest-hits list of Israel's sins against its neighbors. Amis hurts his foot kicking Hitchens's shins under the table, to no avail.

Hitchens's diatribe might have cost Martin a Great White Father figure, which isn't so easy to come by these days. Crosscut in *Experience* is the loss of a patriarch and the courting of a spiritual replacement. Amis not only has to reckon with the death of his father but the near-demise of "my friend, mentor and hero Saul Bellow [who] was on a breathing machine in an intensive-care unit with both his lungs whited out." When Martin extolled Bellow's fiction in print and appeared on TV with him in a documentary love-in, it seemed another way to tweak his father, who dismissed Bellow as an upmarket butcher of the English language. In an essay in his collection *What Became of Jane Austen?* (1970), Kingsley wrote: "John D. MacDonald is by any standards a better writer than Saul Bellow, only MacDonald writes thrillers and Bellow is a human-heart chap, so guess who wears the top-grade laurels?" With his father dead, the reverent nods in *Experience* to the "radiance of *Ravelstein*"— *Ravelstein*, that *Tuesdays with Morrie* for highbrows—and the "brilliance" of *More Die of Heartbreak* ascend to intimate rapture. He addresses Bellow:

> Do you remember I called you on the day my father died? And you were great. You said the only thing that could have possibly been of any use to me. The only thing that would help me through to the other side. And I said dully, "You'll have to be my father now." It worked, and still works. As long as you're alive I'll never feel entirely fatherless.

> It is still working, in 1999. But I mustn't encroach on the territory occupied by Gregory, Adam and Daniel—and by a fourth child, expected at the end of the millennium. I feel it is okay to quote from a letter I wrote Janis [Bellow's fifth wife] . . . because I am only quoting my father: "The greatest difficulty is believing in the baby's resilience. But they *are* resilient, fanatically

resilient. . . . You do know this, don't you, about Saul? You will have a bit of him, half of him, for ever."

It may be a lacuna in my emotional repertoire, but I find all this gooey and unseemly. Martin Amis is a little old to be Brandon de Wilde chasing after Shane.

The Underpass

As an admirer of Kingsley Amis (I interviewed him for this magazine in 1989), I dreaded the prospect of his published letters even as I was pawing to get at them to see whom he slagged. After all, the publication of his pal Philip Larkin's letters in 1992 muddied Larkin's reputation, transforming the poet laureate of late-night loneliness ("Deprivation is for me what daffodils were for Wordsworth," he famously remarked) into a dirty lech panting after naughty-schoolgirl porn and teeming with jolly prejudices. ("Keep up the cracks about niggers and wogs," he encouraged Amis.) If Larkin's letters gave high-minded sorts the sniffies, Kingsley Amis's were certain to be even more liberal-repellent, because he had devoted so much more print space during his career to needling women, minorities, and left-wing nobs. His hazy and rudely uncharitable *Memoirs* of 1992 offered the spoutings of a beached-whale Tory. Also, there is the matter of sheer quantity. As Amis himself once formulated, "MORE will mean WORSE." Where Larkin's letters ran 790-some pages, including index, Amis's balloon to 1,200-plus packed pages, scrupulously annotated by Zachary Leader to the point of insanity. (When Amis compliments his hosts for a corn dish served at dinner, a footnote informs us that it was "fried mealie (maize) bread"—stout work, Sherlock!) When Amis refers to an all-women's college as "that cunt-only place," or to his penis as his "pork sword," one's forebodings return.

Most of the humor and invective in the letters from Amis to Larkin are in the classic English saucy-bottoms tradition that stretches from Chaucer to Benny Hill to the cartoon mag *Viz*. They end most of their letters to each other by attaching the word "bum" to the end of some current cliché or platitude, such as "Anthony Burgess's gusto and exuberance springs [*sic*] from his brilliant bum" and "The Inner Cities are full of frustrated blacks looking for bum." All-cap phrases such as "DREADFUL STENCH OF ANUS" and "A PORRIDGE BOWL FILLED WITH OTTER SHIT" suddenly boom, along with brisk bulletins

such as "Have just delivered a reeking billet of turd into the lava-
tory pan." The lavatorial byplay in Larkin's and Amis's letters can be
defended in theory. The concentration required for creative work—
superconcentration where poetry is concerned (recall that, along with
being the premier comic novelist of his generation, Amis was also
a superb poet)—causes an engine-room buildup of mental pressure
that seeks release in gossip, puns, smut, parodies, and in-jokes, such
as dubbing Anthony Powell, the distinguished author of the multi-
volume series *A Dance to the Music of Time*, the "horse-faced dwarf," or
"h-f dwarf" for short. Amis chides Larkin, "It is very wrong of you to
call him that—*quite inaccurate* and *off-key* to start with—and makes
me laugh no end." It makes me laugh too, and I love Powell's work.
But in practice most of the rude jests in Amis's letters to Larkin and
to the historian Robert Conquest are stale patties because they were
throwaway remarks meant to pass the time and perk up the other
party rather than to be entered into posterity. To outsiders (you, me,
and everybody else), their reflex jocularity can't help but seem forced,
a bunch of old duffers flapping their elbows. The intellectual muscle-
flexing in *Experience* is matched by the anti-intellectual posturing
in the letters, whose relatively few bits of literary comment become
disproportionately welcome. "Have you read the new Waugh? It's a
tour de force: he's taken all the most snobbish and boring and soft-
headed parts out of *Brideshead*, and all the most unfunny and boring
and snobbish parts of *Put out more flags*, and put them all together into
one book, and called it *Men at arms*."

The letters won't win Kingsley many female fans. *Stanley and the
Women*, his fun-house-mirror novel about men at the mercy of their
mad wives, had difficulty securing an American publisher because of
its reputed misogyny, but he was never the hearty combatant in the
feminist wars that Norman Mailer became in the seventies, when he
grew devil's horns and butted heads with Germaine Greer and Kate
Millett. Amis, a regular at the all-male Garrick Club, lobbed insults at
feminists from a remote easy chair. He wanted mostly to be left alone
to get quietly soused. Women interfered with that. To him, most of
them were radios missing an "off" knob. The letters confirm the final
kiss-off paragraph of *Jake's Thing*, which diagnoses women's most
vexing trait to be their aikido ability to personalize every conversation and flip it to their advantage. They wear men down over time
through tireless word-erosion. Writing to Larkin, Amis describes
attending "an incredibly drunken funeral in Wales" for John Aeron-
Thomas, "who I doubt if you ever met, prematurely killed off by his

drunken incessantly-talking wife's drunkenness and incessant talk."
He later relates the sighting of a Dylan Thomas groupie gone to seed.
"A tall bottle-nosed of-course-unstoppably-talking (I met her) Jewess
with jet-black dyed hair and a small bald patch at the crown." The
comic high point of Amis's exasperation is when he meets the writer
Iris Murdoch (whom he likes) and finds that she too has "joined the
swelling ranks of the free-associators." He presents a sample of their
non-sequitur conversation before concluding, "In other words like
TALKING TO A BLOODY WOMAN."

The irony is that the peak moment in both volumes of Larkin and
Amis letters comes when they're championing a woman writer. To the
editor Charles Monteith, whose house (Faber and Faber) had in 1965
just rejected the latest novel by Barbara Pym, Larkin wrote, "I like
to read about people who have done nothing spectacular, who aren't
beautiful or lucky, who try to behave well in the limited field of activity
they command, but who can see, in little autumnal moments of vision,
that the so called 'big' experiences of life are going to miss them; and
I like to read about such things presented not with self pity or despair
or romanticism, but with realistic firmness & even humour, that is
in fact what the critics wd call the moral tone of the book." Larkin, a
legendary tightwad, even offered to write an introduction for the book
for free if that might turn things around. Faber still said no. (Pym's
novel *An Unsuitable Attachment* was rejected by twenty-one publishers;
she spent the next twelve years in limbo, until she was named one of
the most underrated twentieth-century writers in a 1977 *Times Literary Supplement* survey, which sparked a Pym revival on both sides of
the Atlantic. She died in 1980.) In Amis's case, chivalry rears its hooves
when the journalist Paul Johnson scoffs at the inclusion of the writer
Elizabeth Taylor's *Angel* among the "Best Novels of Our Time." In
retort, Amis wrote:

> Elizabeth Taylor herself gave her status no help by having no
> public life, not being seen on television, not pronouncing on the
> state of the world and not going round explaining that her under-
> lying subject was the crisis of bourgeois conscience. It was hard
> to believe that this rather ungregarious wife of a businessman
> living in no great style in the Thames valley, fond of a gossip over
> a gin and tonic, could be the author of any kind of novel, let alone
> an important one. And *Angel* is not important in the usual sense:
> it inaugurated nothing, summed up nothing, did nothing outside
> itself. But importance isn't important. Good writing is.

The Touchdown

Importance resonates like a gong through every page of *Experience*. With its quotations from Kafka and Borges, its Nabokovian parallels (Eric Jacobs, Kingsley's prize-booby biographer, is compared to the clueless Kinbote of Nabokov's *Pale Fire*), and its fondling of Saul Bellow's brain, the book seems to be making Literature's Last Stand against the pygmy tribes of press snoops. It's a lonely-at-the-top epistle, where the only company apart from family members seems to be other beleaguered big-league writers, such as Salman Rushdie. With a half-century now under his belt, Martin Amis has drafted a summation statement that clears the deck for the missions that lie ahead in his new persona as "human-heart chap." According to an item in *The Guardian*, which reportedly paid more than $150,000 to serialize his memoir, Amis recently returned from California, where he was attending a literary conference and researching the porn industry. "His inquiries in relation to the latter were thorough enough to have included an encounter with an ageing pornographer who specialised in videos devoted to anal sex—'the arse man of the millennium.'" They must have had a lot to share.

Vanity Fair, July 2000

The Yob That Failed

Lionel Asbo: State of England, Martin Amis

Martin Amis has reached that not entirely enviable plateau in an emi-
nent literary career where he (and we) might be better off if he gave up
writing novels and just granted interviews from now on. He could air
his observations on issues throbbingly relevant in the republic of letters, then retire to his den for a nip or a nap. Giving up fiction would
lighten his workload considerably, and take the pressure off having to
re-prove himself to the growing sector of the literary punditry that
treats him with such jaded familiarity.

Since *London Fields* or so, I find myself anticipating the profiles,
chat sessions, and drink visits promoting the novels more than I do
the results themselves—reminiscent of the patch in Mel Brooks's
career when his guest spots on *The Tonight Show* plugging his latest
self-wallow were funnier, jazzier, and more turned-on to the audience
than the actual releases, as any bleary survivor of *Spaceballs* or *Robin
Hood: Men in Tights* can attest. The Q&A format seems to smoke out
more reverie from Amis, unclenching his clam-tight control. Not that
he puts on a command performance for the journalists who gingerly
approach, fretful of running afoul of a verbal scowl, however gra-
ciously he offers them a suitable beverage. Nearly every Amis interview expresses the wary, battle-weary tone of a veteran interviewee
hiking Boot Hill again. But within this monochromatic range he is
far more engaging, perceptive, interesting, and adept at cultural land-
scaping than he is in the novels themselves, the forced labors of *Night
Train, Yellow Dog, House of Meetings.*

By accident or by design, Amis has developed a knack for initiat-
ing a first wave of publicity that provokes a backlash that triggers a
counterwave, a ripple field of controversy that has little relation to
the novel coming out but keeps its title and his name in play. Shortly
before the release of *The Pregnant Widow*, he mused that a "silver tsunami" of ga-ga geezers threatened to engulf society, "a population
of demented very old people, like an invasion of terrible immigrants,
stinking out the restaurants and cafés and shops." He proposed the
possibility of street corner "euthanasia booths," where the wrinklies

could receive a martini and a medal for offing themselves as a public service rather than dragging out the inevitable. This Swiftian thought experiment did not endear him to the nearly departed, though in follow-up remarks Amis was eloquently emphatic and empathetic about the misery that Iris Murdoch and his stepfather, Lord Kilmarnock, went through in their drawn-out demises. And after all, as he pointed out, he himself was a junior member of the silver tsunami.

In the run-up to the publication of *Lionel Asbo*, his new novel, Amis gave a drove of interviews in which he discussed aging, smoking, parenthood, grandparenthood, the torrential corrosion of porn (porn-concern is often a sign of spiritual arthritis—see John Cheever's later outbursts), his and his wife's recent move to Brooklyn, and the weight of the loss of his longtime friend Christopher Hitchens ("it's hard to make progress with grief"), to whom the book is dedicated—so many unfailingly interesting interviews that it got to the point where I could almost hear his murmurous voice in my ear, like a grumpy lullaby. It is the acute articulation of Amis in offhand performance—the phrase-measuring, chopstick darts of insight, the ponderous buildup to a lethal-jab punchline—that makes the inattentive drift and dawdle of *Lionel Asbo* such a discomforting shock.

It isn't just that Amis's heart doesn't seem to be in it with this book. His brain seems to be hanging back, too, somewhat reluctant and hazily disengaged. Strictly as narrative, *Lionel Asbo* doesn't overexert itself, fading in and out of time, breaking into exclamation marks for no apt reason ("And guess who they ran into. Jon and Joel!" [Jon and Joel are dogs]), ending sections with weather summaries worthy of Scandinavian noir ("The winters were unsmilingly cold," "The winters were medievally cold," "the winter in between was petrifyingly cold"), and outfitted with comic riffs that manage to be unfunny to the point of bafflement, such as the changes that Amis tries to ring on the conceit of a brace of sons being named after the Beatles, leading to dialogue exchanges such as: "'Plain as day,' said John. 'Open-and-shut,' said Paul. 'Common sense,' said George. 'No-brainer,' said Ringo." It's like listening to coconuts conk heads.

The Pregnant Widow revealed that Amis had lost a bit of velocity on his wicked curve—the delivery of the wisecracks seemed just a hair off—but it had a firmer handle on itself, a coherent small-scale time and place. This novel's subtitle—*State of England*—promises a diagnosis of the condition of the country that he has left behind, an allegorical heft, but the dysfunctional city in which it is set—Diston, "with its burping, magmatic canal, its fizzy low-rise pylons, its buzzing waste"—never seems anything more than a rear projection, an urban collage. It's an anywhere nowheresville.

Amis has reiterated in interviews and in an article for this magazine that the decision to leave England was based on familial concerns and not a desire to flee that celebrity-whore, junk-food hellhole before it went celebrity clockwork orange. I believe him, since it is the polite thing to do and because this novel doesn't have the kick of a true kiss-off. Had *Lionel Asbo* been fired by the sort of fury that drove D. H. Lawrence to damning indictment—"Curse the blasted, jelly-boned swines, the slimy, the belly-wriggling invertebrates, the miserable sodding rotters, the flaming sods, the sniveling, dribbling, dithering palsied pulse-less lot that make up England today"—it would have had more blood, bubble, and compulsion than this sketchpad of disdain.

The slothful state of England in *Lionel Asbo* is drawn through a kitchen-sink portrait of yob life that is often played for grotesque travesty in pop culture, as in the Monty Python sketch "The Most Awful Family in Britain Annual Awards," where the third-worst brood spent their mornings slagging each other off and discussing their bowel irrigation ("Wilkinson's Number 8 Laxative Cereal. Phew. That one went through you like a bloody Ferrari"), and the winning clan was so ghastly they couldn't even be shown on TV. More recently, we have the British cartoon magazine *Viz*, which bacterially teems with flatulent slobs and fat slags, and the Channel 4 series *Shameless*, set on a Manchester council estate, an ode to squalor and chemical waste from the neck up that has been Americanized for Showtime cable. In Amis's book everything rotten about busted-ass Britain is pressed into the cookie dough of Lionel Pepperdine, a bulk-sized bully, a layabout and criminal whose chief ability is "disseminating tension," an intimidation factor amplified by the pair of "psychopathic pitbulls" he owns who move "like missiles of muscle."

Amis's protagonist earns the handle "Lionel Asbo" due to the mini-reign of terror he began spreading as a mere toddler. At the age of three he smashed car windshields with paving stones. Generic cruelty to animals escalated into an attempt to burn down an entire pet shop. "Had he come along a half generation later, Lionel's first Restraining Directive would have been called a BASBO, or Baby ASBO, which (as all the kingdom now knew) stood for Anti-Social Behavior Order." A bad seed sullenly intent on getting even better at being bad, Lionel sports his ASBOs as badges of honor.

In an unsigned notice of Amis's non-fiction collection *Visiting Mrs. Nabokov, and Other Excursions* that long ago appeared in the satirical fortnightly *Private Eye*, the reviewer mentioned the chapters in which Amis interviewed John Updike, played snooker with Julian Barnes, and eulogized Philip Larkin, who went about their belletristic business with routine flair. "Unsurprisingly, Mart's much better when he's writing about darts or football, subjects that allow him to do what he does best. Oddly, what Mart is *really good at* is patronizing the working classes. Those darts players, those fat bastards with fisted lagers and piggy eyes! Just watch Mart take them on, that's all!" He's still patronizing them, despite protests to the contrary. In the interview with *New York* magazine, Amis declared that "I love the working class, and everyone from it I've met, and think they're incredibly witty, inventive—there's a lot of poetry there. . . . A lot of thwarted intelligence."

There may be poetry there, but there isn't any poetry here. From beginning to end, *Lionel Asbo* is a whale spout of clichés and commonplaces—"Of women in general, Lionel sometimes had this to say, More trouble than they worth, if you ask me"—and about as witty as a brick to the skull. A repository of ruthless, shortsighted self-interest, Lionel encarcasses a slit-eyed cunning capable of sniffing out enemy betrayal and craven dissembling, suggesting Tony Soprano two rungs down on the evolutionary ladder, but his rare attempts at self-improvement and appearing clever are feeble, risible. "Says he read a whole dictionary." "Which dictionary?" "Pocket Cassell's, but still." The counterpoint to Lionel is his nephew Des, an industrious lad who goes to the library to do actual reading and whom Amis has described as the nicest character he has ever created. He is also the dullest. Granted, Des has been having sexual relations with his grandmother, but within the welter of mouth-breathing pathologies at prey here, afterschool incest seems an almost tender sin, though it leads to terrible reckonings.

The big turn in the novel is an undeserved reversal of fortune. While in prison, Lionel wins the lotto—a whopping 140 million pounds, catapulting him from just another belligerent bald head bobbing in a sea of blobs to an instant-notoriety "Lotto Lout," whose exploits and excesses are covered like King Kong's swing through Manhattan. As with Roseanne in the desperate last season of her sitcom, when her family hit the jackpot for $108 million, Lionel doesn't acquire taste or refinement with his windfall. His yahoo appetite simply gets greater legroom to sprawl, a larger funnel to feed its greedy maw, whether he's feasting like Henry VIII on a bucket of KFC or more fancily dining: "Propped up on silken pillows, Lionel Asbo sat in the great barge of the four-iron four-poster with the gilt breakfast tray resting on his keglike thighs."

Lionel becomes a buffoon parody of a country squire presiding over "Wormwood Scrubs," named after his favorite prison, a thirty-room Gothic pile surrounded by manicured lawns and protected with the fortress security of a Colombian drug lord. His wealth and anti-charisma attracts a trophy girlfriend-adviser-tabloid-siren named Threnody, whose "famous boobs" are "more like pottery than flesh." Threnody is clearly modeled on Katie Price, a famous-for-being-famous human blow-up doll whom Amis once dismissed as "two bags of silicone," though he later issued a lukewarmish endorsement of her memoirs, for whatever inscrutable reason. The name Katie Price of course means nothing in America, where we have plenty enough big bazoomy bubble-butted no-talent reality-TV dirigibles of our own to keep us occupied without importing additionals. As an it-came-from-the-lower-classes celebrity freak and a symbol of the fall of empire, Lionel himself seems rather dated and quaint compared with our locally grown Honey Boo Boo and her go-go juice.

Doing a caricature of a gross caricature risks redundancy unless you go all the campy way with it, and *Lionel Asbo* is too drizzly gray for hot-pink and gash-gold vermilion. Even exaggeration requires a certain exactitude, and nothing here comes across as investigated on foot, or personally eyewitnessed. Whatever one thinks of Tom Wolfe's novelistic powers and execution, when Wolfe curates the palatial excesses of arrivistes, the blinding kitsch of pimped-out bling, he escorts the reader on an interior-decorating tour that didn't derive from a catalog or a magazine spread. Always on the go, Wolfe remains America's oldest boy reporter. *Lionel Asbo*, however, reads like a tabloid saga observed from the perspective of an educated broadsheet reader, an arched-eyebrow exercise in armchair editorializing.

Aiming downward narrows Amis's vision, targets easy pickings. It's the old joke—"Sire, the peasants are revolting" "They certainly are"—played straight. Horrendous taste in decoration and piggy manners are depicted as a defective chip in the lumpenprole Homer Simpson donut brain when some of the most godawful eyesores have been planted on the landscape by billionaire hedge fund managers and Russian oligarchs, not lotto winners who happened to hit the lucky numbers. The ASBOS aren't the ones running the casino. The power they wield only extends as far as they can swing a bottle.

The state of England in this book mirrors the state of Amis's morale (moribund), and the shellacking the novel has received on both sides

of the Atlantic can have done nothing to improve it. I watched Charlie Rose's interview with Amis, and, despite Amis's contention that he
doesn't read reviews, his subdued, sparkless manner was that of a battery victim. But morale can always enjoy an upswing and moving into
a new house can renew and release creative energies, as Gore Vidal
observed in relation to Henry James and the shift to Lamb House
(from which came *The Wings of the Dove*). Perhaps Amis's new vantage
point in Brooklyn will re-invigorate this most American of British
writers into becoming the *American* American rhythm ace he aspires
to be, though it's somewhat dismaying that he has already sneak-
previewed his next book to an interviewer from the *Telegraph* as "my
second visit to the Holocaust"—well, we can't say we weren't warned.

Like his friend and fellow expat Salman Rushdie, Amis finds himself in the tricky predicament of a high-altitude author of literary
fiction in a pop-genre landscape that prizes accessibility. Name recognition is not enough anymore. In his youthful past Amis may have
done the punk-inflected *Dead Babies*, an erudite fanboy ode to video
games (*Invasion of the Space Invaders*), and the frazzled, adrenaline jag
of *Money*, but *Lionel Asbo* shows that he doesn't have the storytelling gifts to compete with the program grid that television has laid
in our heads. When *Lionel Asbo* attempts to crank up horrible apprehension in its third act—through a melodramatic bit of crosscutting involving Lionel's pit bulls and an infant in danger of becoming
their next doggy dinner, a gruesome dingo-ate-my-baby scenario—I
found myself thinking, "This is the sort of sick grabber *Breaking Bad*
does so much better." That I kept being thrown out of this novel
into television shows may say something about my easily diverted and
derailed attention span, but it also indicates that there wasn't much in
the writing-thinking-perceptualizing of *Lionel Asbo* to keep the brain
seatbelt-fastened.

The novel reads like the work of a writer who has become bored
with his own voice, and who can blame him? Whatever well-deserved
vanities Amis cradles as an author, he does not strike me as someone
completely in love with the sound of his own drone. Next year will
note the fortieth anniversary of his debut novel *The Rachel Papers*, a
brilliant showpiece of young-man bravado that had the snap of Mick
Jagger's belt-whip in "Midnight Rambler." It would have been a
tough number for any writer to follow, but not for Amis, who refined
and extended and textured his aspish voice until reaching the white
cocaine blaze of *Money* in 1984, a decade-definer marred only by a
doppelgänger device that was like having Nabokov stick his nose into

the peepshow booth. (By drawing too neat a line from *The Rachel Papers* to *Money*, I'm doing an injustice to *Other People*, a strange cross between Val Lewton's cinematic hauntings and Craig Raine's "Martian" poems that is so unrepresentative an Amis work that it's become something of a ghost in his oeuvre.)

Amis was never the sort of cozy writer who could settle into a plummy mellow maturity—as in *Time's Arrow* and *The Information*, his mature voice bears the mortal freight of history's horrors and of personal extinction—and as he keeps sharp watch on the chipping away of body and mind by aging's cruel elves, going full curmudgeon isn't really an option. His father beat him to it with his fussing about language and his reactionary effusions, and the son is too adventurous to revive that crusty vaudeville act. Another model offers itself: his hero and mentor Saul Bellow, who managed to maintain up to the end a sly, clued-in voice that had an octopus reach of everything around it—a confidential monologue at the service of Bellow's wraparound curiosity and cagey parsing of others' motives, which became so embracing that his later novellas turned into conversational suites. But dialogue in Amis's novels, which certainly is plentiful, stays stuck on the platform, since he is less interested in the intimacies of characters than in the ideas or the conceits that they envelop, and there is no dialectic between his cut-out dolls, no Shavian jousting. *Lionel Asbo* ends with a domestic note of renewal, of new life coming into the world, but it is an unconvincing, hackneyed exit, because Amis is not really engaged in new life coming in but in old life going out, the twilight shimmer before the curtain drop. He hasn't found a way to voyage into it yet, as Bellow did and Philip Roth ragingly has. He's got time, but the hour is late.

The New Republic, October 19, 2012

Updike x Three

Running on Empty
Rabbit Is Rich

John Updike has dug himself into a fine funk in *Rabbit Is Rich* (Knopf, $13.95), the third installment in the moribund saga of ex–basketball whiz Harry "Rabbit" Angstrom. Updike, whose last novel was that Nabokovian kaleidoscope *The Coup*, usually rides a chariot through the clouds, showering the reader with waves of silver flakes. *Rabbit Is Rich*'s prose is familiarly silver-flaked—Updike's metaphors still give off their expensive wink and sheen—but the mood of the book is grumpy and despairing, swollen with forlorn rue. It's 1979, a year of soaring gas prices and serpentine lines at the pumps, and Rabbit, lucky chump, is running a Toyota franchise near his home in Brewer, Pennsylvania. "Or rather he co-owns a half-interest with his wife Janice, her mother Bessie sitting on the other half inherited when old man Springer died five years back." Now, with Americans antsy about gas mileage, Japanese compacts are all the rage, and Rabbit sits in his office watching gas nibbler after gas nibbler get whisked off the lot. No longer is Rabbit a figure of Rodney Dangerfield seediness; not only is he making a tidy bundle, he's getting respect from old school chums who used to give him the snub. And yet . . . success fails to bring with it an unfolding of happiness and serene ease. No banners of joy ripple from the pages of *Rabbit Is Rich*. This novel flies at half-mast.

The curious thing is that Rabbit is less shackled by fortune or circumstance than he is lashed to the mast of Updike's theme. True, Rabbit's life is haunted by ghosts from earlier novels: his infant daughter, Becky, who drowned in the tub in *Rabbit, Run*, and poor, pale Jill, who went up in flames at the climax of *Rabbit Redux*. And sharing the same ceiling with Janice and her mother is hardly a patch of heaven on earth. But the ghosts of remorse and the minor annoyances of the day-to-day grind fail to account for the vague air of doom that hangs over Rabbit's head like a misty blue halo. Rabbit may be rich, but he isn't free; he's impaled on the pike of Updike's grim sense of purpose. Curious, this: Updike is usually a rather dandyish writer, squinting with fey amusement at man and beast through a raised monocle, like *The New Yorker*'s cover boy, Eustace Tilley. In this new *Rabbit*, he's dropped his butterfly coyness and pumped himself up with all the woe of Theodore Dreiser contemplating a boulevard of crushed souls. Slipping his head into the yoke, Updike plows home his message—oh, how he plows it home.

The message? Everything is running down . . . entropy reigns supreme. The point is established in the novel's opening sentence, when Rabbit looks at the trickle of traffic outside his window and observes that the country is running out of gas. Running out of gas becomes Rabbit's theme song: "A lot of topics, [Rabbit] has noticed lately, in private conversation and even on television where they're paid to talk it up, run dry, exhaust themselves, as if everything's been said in this hemisphere."

Everything is petering out: gas, conversation, conviction, hope, lust. Flesh is turning to flab, metal to rust, money to scrap, nature to moist rot. In *Rabbit Is Rich*, mortality doesn't rap gently at the door, it knocks the mother off its hinges. Iodine-bottle skulls seem to peep out from every placid face as once-blooming skin turns to crinkling parchment. Even a Sunday-afternoon outing on the golf course brings Rabbit no sense of nourishment: "Every blade of grass at his feet is an individual life that will die, that has flourished to no purpose." Yeah, well, that's one way of looking at it.

To Rabbit's weary eyes, gravity and the erosions of time have taken their greatest toll on the women in his life. Not that Rabbit himself is any trim bargain. His belly has ballooned to a forty-two-inch waist, and the skin beneath his chin has converged into a "chaos of wattles and slack cords." But since the novel reflects Rabbit's pinched consciousness, less attention is paid to his shabby flesh than to the cobweb wrinkles sprouting in his field of vision. Time and time again Rabbit recoils from a glimpse or whiff of women in their sagging decline, and Updike, sharpening his metaphors to a piercing edge, makes certain that we recoil too. When Rabbit is in the sack, reading *Consumer Reports* (his favorite magazine), his wife makes a lurching entrance and stabs her tongue into his mouth: "He tastes Gallo, baloney, and toothpaste while his mind is still trying to sort out the virtues and failings of the great range of can openers put to the test over five close pages of print." Granted, this is a sticky attempt at comedy—as is the appallingly cloying scene in which Rabbit, aroused by wealth, tries to insert a Krugerrand into his wife's vagina—but it isn't much fun watching Updike parade these women as if they were blue-ribbon pigs or cows. Once Janice has fouled Rabbit's mouth with her kisses, she climbs into bed: "Her breasts hang down so her nipples, the color of hamburger, sway an inch above his furry bloated belly." Elsewhere, Rabbit has a reverie about how Sealtest ought to consider marketing a woman's most intimate aroma as an ice-cream flavor; later, after indulging in cunnilingus, he thinks that maybe it isn't such a hot idea.

No, face it: Except for ripe chippies, women are sloppy, smelly nuisances, peeling off your skin in long, cruel strips with their demands and complaints. Sex is the lure, entrapment the fate. When Rabbit's sulky crybaby son, Nelson, gets a girl named Prudence pregnant (one of the novel's dinkier ironies), Nelson's acorn-size brain seethes with indignation:

> He didn't ask her to conceive this baby, nobody did, and now that he's married her she has the nerve to complain he isn't getting her an apartment of her own, give them one thing they instantly want the next. Women. They are holes, you put one thing after another and it's never enough, you stuff your entire life in there and they smile that crooked little sad smile and are sorry you couldn't have done better, when all is said and done.

Like father, like son. Both see women as agents of ruin, black holes that suck men in, then spit their useless remains, like pits, into the void.

Of course, Updike is capable of writing a comedy of bad nerves, a novel in which men's complaints about women build to an absurd fury (Philip Roth carried it off in *My Life as a Man*). But you need some pull of wills, a clash of temperament and cunning that allows fevers to rise, skirmishes to escalate. *Rabbit Is Rich*, however, is dramatically static—Updike provides a few soap-operaish shudders (a near-miscarriage, wife-swapping, a whisper of incest), but the force of entropy bends all the action to a futile droop. His characters droop too, as potted in their sour disappointments as those poor sods planted in Samuel Beckett's ash heaps. Encamped poolside at the country club, Rabbit's friends lubricate their tonsils and bitch about the slumping Phillies and the gouging Arabs ("'Jesus, those Arabs,' Buddy Inglefinger says. 'Wouldn't it be bliss just to nuke 'em all?'"). As the afternoon wanes,

Rabbit himself tells bad jokes and tosses off tired remarks, squatting like a better-off Archie Bunker on his pile of slob opinions.

As a piece of prose, *Rabbit Is Rich* resurrects many of the excesses of Updike's supernal naturalism—excesses that turned his 1968 novel *Couples* into such a dripping display of vainglorious ooze. Reviewing *Couples* in *The New York Review of Books*, William Gass neatly pinned down the book's showy flaws—its pseudo-Joycean interior mono-logues, strained symbolism, theological moonings, and empty exten-sions of significance "unfolding like collapsible tin cups." Those tin cups make an unholy racket in *Rabbit Is Rich* as Updike goes for grand symphonic effects, never striking a modest bell when he can send all cymbals acrashing. He even revives those Joycean monologues, to numbing effect. Here is Rabbit idling away at the office:

> Average eight hundred gross profit times twenty-five equals twenty grand minus the twenty-five per cent they estimate for salesmen's compensation both salary and incentives leaves fif-teen grand minus between eight and ten for other salaries those cute little [expletive deleted] come and go in billing one called Cissy a Polack a few years ago they got as far as rubbing fannies passing in that awkward hall and the rent that Springer Motors pays itself old man Springer didn't believe in owning anything the banks could own but even he had to pay the mortgage even-tually boy the rates now must kill anybody starting up and . . .

Et cetera. That's what John Updike's naturalism in *Rabbit Is Rich* comes down to: telling you every dumb thing that is on Rabbit's mind.

Yes, as always, there are beautiful sentences here, metaphors and images that have the soft, preening splendor of flowers photographed by Irving Penn. But these are flowers scattered across brackish water. I suppose what I find disagreeable about Updike's book—and it is easily his most unattractive book (off-novels such as *Marry Me* and *A Month of Sundays* are mere lollipops by comparison)—is the way Updike uses the muscle of his talent to keep dunking his characters in the brine. The novel is prefaced with a quote from Sinclair Lewis's *Bab-bitt*, and the barbecuing ironies of *Rabbit Is Rich* indicate that Updike is trying to forge affinities between Rabbit and his rhyming ances-tor. But *Babbitt*, for all its blaring crudeness, is a far more tenderly comic examination of philistinism American style than Updike's tour of the Angstrom libido. And Lewis, whopping tub-thumper that he often was, at least spared us all the invocations of the Lord above that

Updike throws up in order to hammer home how antlike and pitiful we are under His pitiless gaze.

As in *Couples*, whenever Updike wants to tone up a passage, he whistles for God. All Updike's worst tendencies in this novel—his vulgarity, his wistful lyricism, his aching after religious epiphanies—come together in a brief incident near the end of the novel. Rabbit learns that a woman with whom he was once intimate has had a breast removed: "Breast he had sucked. Poor old Peggy. Flicked away by God's fingernail with its big moon." There's something almost *hatefully* clever about using a minor character's mastectomy as an opportunity to toss off a dapper phrase—it's taking almost inhuman delight in showing off one's flash technique.

Rabbit Is Rich has a certain plodding integrity—except for a few slapstick episodes, it's a stoically grim affair, every footfall leading to the grave—but watching John Updike screw Rabbit's head into a vise of cosmic resignation hardly provides a lift to one's love of art or life. Updike is better skating along the cool edge of his gifts, as in the wonderful *Bech: A Book* and in his best stories. Once he dons Martin Luther's robes, he disappears into their solemn folds, from which he makes oracular mouse peeps about women's aromas and God's fingernail. *Rabbit Is Rich* has its head in the stars and its feet in the gutter, and at neither extreme is Updike's droll talent comfortably at home.

Esquire, October 1981

Caretaker/Pallbearer
The Widows of Eastwick

John Updike's unfailing geniality and fluent industry appear to get on a fair number of nerves, of which he's slyly aware. (Is there anything he isn't slyly aware of? That foxy grin conceals volumes.) When Updike was but a sprig, apprenticing at *The New Yorker* and carving out a little piece of Pennsylvania as his literary duchy, his gleaming facility was found suspect by some detractors, its satin finish the imposture of a fair-haired boy out to impress his elders with the fine flick of his exquisite perceptions and deflective modesty. "*The New Yorker* and John Updike are both deeply immersed in the image of man as trivia," Alfred Chester wrote when panning Updike's short story collection *Pigeon Feathers*. "Reading Updike, like reading *The New Yorker*, gives one the impression that the pages would turn to ash at the mere suggestion that life was other than a negative-positive mosquito buzzing in the ear of a total vacuum." Where Norman Mailer set out to bend the future with his telepathic powers and the Beats sought to hot-wire the American psyche (at the risk of frying their own circuits), Updike wrote as if he were doing fine draftsmanship under a cone of light, honoring creation and the American plenty. He was the ideal son of a platonic union between John Cheever and J. D. Salinger, with Nabokov attending the christening as fairy godfather. Apparent lack of inner struggle and purring efficiency made it possible to take him for granted. "No one has ever sat around worrying about Updike, the way one apparently worried about Wolfe and Fitzgerald and Hemingway, as if they were all soloing the Atlantic with each book, to see whether he's lost his touch or his nerve or his fastball," Wilfrid Sheed wrote in *Essays in Disguise*. "We know damn well he'll have his touch this time and next: we just want to see whether we like what he's done with it."

Now that Updike's an elder statesman in the world of letters, an elfin figure pared down to a David Levine caricature of himself, a newer generation of detractors (replacing the ones that died off) has reserved him a room at the retirement home and seems irritated that he won't take the hint. In recent interviews and articles he acknowledges the testy impatience his lingering presence provokes in some strict quarters. Some nerve he has, refusing to vacate the stage and vanish into a silver cloud, insisting instead on bringing out one new book after another, no matter how fine a steam rises from the dome of James Wood. (Writing in *The New Republic*, Wood welcomed Updike's best seller *Terrorist* into the world by wishing it had been aborted: "John Updike should have run a thousand miles away from this subject—at least as soon as he saw the results on the page.") Then there is Michiko Kakutani of *The New York Times*—"every writer's friend," he refers to her with laconic rue in *Updike in Cincinnati*—who often recoils from his fiction ("chauvinistic," "voyeuristic") as if she's been pawed on the subway by an old lech.

It isn't only critics who've developed cricks in their necks. Younger novelists have voiced disgruntlement with the solipsism and literary penis-wagging of Updike's generation of privileged males. Updike may have been praised for his missionary work on behalf of the Sexual Revolution in *Couples*, *Marry Me*, and other tales from the commuter line, but the generation that followed were the children of divorce—the collateral damage of those adulterous games of musical beds. In 1997 the phenomenally gifted David Foster Wallace caused a ruckus in the pages of the *New York Observer* when, between wallops at Updike's *Toward the End of Time* ("a novel so mind-bendingly clunky and self-indulgent that it's hard to believe the author let it be published in this kind of shape"), took it on himself to be spokesman for the injured party. "I think the major reason so many of my generation dislike Mr. Updike and the other G.M.N.s has to do with these writers' radical self-absorption, and with their uncritical celebration of this self-absorption both in themselves and in their characters." A decade later, Wallace is no longer with us, but two of the Great Male Narcissists he cited, Updike and Philip Roth, are still displaying their self-absorbency and depriving tender young empaths of valuable column inches.

With an almost audible sigh, Updike concedes that the pups have a point. "He or she may feel, as the gray-haired scribes of the day continue to take up space and consume the oxygen in the increasingly small room of the print world, that the elderly have the edge, with their established names and already secured honors," Updike recently observed in "The Writer in Winter," an essay published in the American Association of Retired Persons' bimonthly magazine. "I don't mean to complain. Old age treats freelance writers pretty gently. There is no compulsory retirement at the office, and no athletic injuries signal that the game is over for good." And unlike other writers who grew old with and at *The New Yorker* (Perelman, John O'Hara, Thurber), Updike hasn't undergone the indignity of having his work rejected, his relationship tapered; his byline, like Roger Angell's, is one of the magazine's most comforting standbys. A writer's true adversaries are those that eat from the inside. It's the rust that accretes, the synapses that no longer fire, the fading of acuity—the deep wide focus necessary to keep track of the moving parts of a long narrative. "An ageing writer wonders if he has lost the ability to visualize a completed work, in its complex spatial relations," Updike observes. "He should have in hand a provocative beginning and an ending that will feel inevitable. Instead, he may arrive at his ending nonplussed, the arc of his intended tale lying behind him in fragments. The threads have failed to knit. The leap of faith with which every narrative begins has landed him not on a far safe shore but in the middle of the drink."

Curiously, the opposite occurs with *The Widows of Eastwick*, the sequel to 1984's *The Witches of Eastwick*. It doesn't land in the drink, it starts out in the sand trap, and takes its sweet time digging itself out. It's understandable that Updike would wish to establish a suitable pace to reintroduce us to the coven of former playmates and arrange a proper reunion. Having put Rabbit Angstrom to rest and closed the book on Henry Bech, Updike understands the formalities of reintroducing characters who have been kept in storage. It's been more than two decades since the original novel and the mental picture of its warlock and witches was colonized by the movie version, remembered most vividly for the leering satyr eyebrows and pagan gusto of Jack Nicholson as the warlock Darryl Van Horne (the self-described horny little devil), sharing an orgiastic hot tub with Cher, Michelle Pfeiffer, and Susan Sarandon. Only the passage of time could compete with their spanking charms. So here we are in the new millennium, which so far has been a distinct let-down. The witches are widows now, geographically dispersed grandmothers going about their own paltry business and needing a psychic tug to pull them together again.

Updike's narrative device is to make one plus two equal three. He contrives a triplet of travelogues—a solo excursion, then a duo outing, then all three united in the passengers' lounge. In the first junket, Alexandra, "the oldest in age, the broadest in body" (I'm picturing Vanessa Redgrave for the film sequel), embarks on a ten-day tour of the Canadian Rockies, an opportunity for a fine medley of scenery sketches done with Updike's droll mastery: "Beyond the trees across the lake, the Rockies bared themselves; they were a pleasing dove-gray, a giant geological sample of Canadian understatement." If only Other People didn't insist on crowding the landscape and interposing themselves; a previous vacation to St. Thomas had been ruined for Alexandra and her late husband when their rental car was besieged in traffic, "surrounded by black drivers who took a racist pleasure in tailgating them." Here Alexandra has to contend with the milder nuisance of a stock Asian couple who snap photos non-stop and murder their "l"'s. "You rost, too!" they exclaim when Alexandra strays from the tour group and can't find her way back. Pointing at her cold feet, they cry: "Code feet!" What this pair of Charlie Chan rejects is doing in the novel is a puzzlement, but a more sour question mark hangs over the treatment accorded another tour member, a soft-spoken gent named Willard, who expresses condolences to Alexandra over the loss of her husband, adding in his "sugary, melancholy voice" that he lost someone too: "My partner passed last year. We'd been together for thirty-seven years."

A tiny bell rings in the parlour of Alexandra's brain.

Partner. One of the new code words, usefully bland. Willard was one of those. She'd been fooled before. She felt some relief and some resentment. This fag had been wasting her time.

(This what?)

"That's a long time," Alexandra said. She did not add, *for a pair of fairies.* Who notoriously flit around, breaking each other's hearts with their infidelities, their unchecked attraction to younger fairies.

Flitting fairies? That Alexandra was "sucked into the orbit of a homosexual man" and "betrayed" way back when in Eastwick seems a slim reed on which to drape sneering contempt toward a character whose sole trespass is to engage in conversation and extend sympathy—whose presence has no bearing on the storyline, slack though that is. When Willard materializes a few pages later, again courteous to a fault, Alexandra can't resist, noting: "His studied lumberjack costumes seemed, in retrospect, faggy." Between the Asians talking funny (at least they didn't order "flied lice"), the dried-fig widower modeling the latest in lumberjack attire, and the other load-bearing women annoying her on the tour ("boring, overfed human does"), Alexandra would seem to be less than the ideal traveling companion, but the novel proceeds to hook her up with her former co-conspirator, Jane, who proposes a fun trip to Egypt, and off they go: pyramids, tombs, bustling bazaars, majestic floats along the banks of the Nile, camel rides, the whole bit, complete with tour-guide patter: " 'The great dam at Aswan,' she explained, 'has raised the water levels in the Nile valley.' " Yes, it's almost as boring as being there, the witchy widows enjoying cocktails after a long hot day shlepping the eternal sands, their thoughts turning reflective:

> "Why are Egyptians so happy?" Jane asked Alexandra from her adjacent deckchair.
> "I don't know. Why?"
> "They're in de-Nile."
> —"Ouch."

Ouch is right, and Updike in his methodical cruelty doesn't spare us Jane's twaddlings on Egyptian mythos, moistened by her sibilant hiss.

> Really, *ss*weetie, those old Egyptian priests must have laughed themselves silly, thinking of the nonsense they put over on everybody, not for a day or a week but for *millennia*! What did the guide at Edfu tell us? The Temple of Amun at Thebes was given 1500 square kilometers by Ramses III alone? Ten percent of all the cultivatable land at the time? No wonder the Nubians and Hyksos and whoever kept pushing in. It was a very *ss*ick situation.

Galumphing through this travel brochure come to life and listening to heavy earfuls of pharaoh lore affords the two the opportunity to contemplate "the solemn ponderosity of death," but mortality's dark fingers are already rooted so deep in the corporeal decay of the characters that they (or we) hardly need Egyptian eschatology to remind us of the black door waiting at the end of the hall.

Even more extraneous is the final leg of the wiccans' world tour, which finds the remaining member of the hot tub sorority, Sukie, joining Alexandra and Jane for a trip to China. I groaned inwardly at the prospect of the Great Wall, the visit to Mao's mausoleum, the Yangtze river, the history lessons about to unfold ("China within their memory-span had taken various forms: a fabled land of starving children, Pearl Buck peasants, dragon ladies, rickshaws and comic-strip pirates; a friendly democracy ably led by Chiang Kai-shek and his glamorous Soong-sister wife"—come back, Pearl Buck! All is forgiven!), the tacky cavalcade of fellow Westerners in their native garb ("Sukie asked a plump American, a grotesque barbarian in Bermuda shorts, billed baseball cap and running shoes, to take their photograph"), Updike's running commentary all the more runny because he has shared his impressions of China before, in his essay "Back from China" (reprinted in *Due Considerations*), which ended on a confessional note of existential fright, one of the few times he's allowed his suave mask to slip. On their return from China, the widows waste a few pages playing phone tag trying to determine where their next passport to adventure should lead, vetoing Mexico, Ireland, and the Caribbean ("'*Ss*aint Croix is a *ss*illy suggestion,' she hissed") before arriving at the inevitable answer, the reason we're reading this novel, the original scene of their sins and crimes—the witching grounds of Eastwick, Rhode Island.

Here's my philistine advice, straight from the donkey's mouth. Skip the first third of the novel, flip to page 121 in the hymnal, and begin there. Because from the first sentence—"News that the damnable trio were back in town percolated from ear to ear like rainwater trickling through the tunnels of an ant colony"—Updike is in his native element, his eye and mind the greatest notational devices of any postwar American novelist, precision instruments unimpaired by age and wear. Abroad, Updike is still only a glorified sightseer, a Keen Observer, but in his native land he blends the roles of novelist, historian, social critic, civics teacher, randy theologian, anthropologist, dermatologist, photorealist illuminator of drugstore aisle and automobile showroom (every shiny accent in place), and caretaker/pallbearer of the *New Yorker* tradition of scrupulous observation salted with a proper measure of irony, acerbity, dismay and regret, depending on the circumstance or site under inspection:

> The new wing of the Eastwick Public Library was larger than the original, a 19th-century benefaction of lumpy brownstone that had sat with a certain touching self-importance at the center of a gentle dome of public green. The glass-and-concrete addition took up again as much space and had caused a new driveway and a generous parking lot to pave over swathes of grass where children and dogs used to play. The much-vaunted auditorium, with its lobby and adjacent function room, extended beneath a main floor devoted, table after table, to computers where town idlers

played video games and ingeniously searched for pornography. The section of children's books, once a modest nook of colorful slim volumes presumed to be transitional to adult reading, had greatly expanded, into tall cases of inch-thick walnut, as if to memorialize the end of reading for all but a few of the library's patrons. The concert-and-lecture hall, optimistically conceived to hold improving events almost every night, betrayed its subterranean condition with stifled acoustics that to spectators in the back corners gave tonight's concert a spectral, mimed aspect.

It's quite an observatory Updike houses in his brain, his characters sometimes appearing as small and blank as the human figures positioned around an architectural model or a railroad set. It's interesting—almost inspiring, really—how entertaining *The Widows of Eastwick* manages to be once its plot mechanisms get into motion, despite its prattle, awkward stretches, and artifice. The return of the three witches to the village they once vexed tees up the settling of a personal and cosmic score and the making of amends. In the first novel, the trio trained their wrath on Darryl Van Horne's fiancée with a fatal spell. "We killed Jenny Gabriel, that's what we did," Alexandra reminds Jane, providing a recap for the reader. "After bewitching Clyde's wife so that he killed her with a poker and then hung himself." Eh, so what, is Jane's response. Ancient history. But Jenny's aggrieved brother Chris is lurking in the shadows ("Older, fatter, faggier," Jane reports) and taking retaliatory measures, armed with some sort of electromagnetic shock device inherited from Van Horne. Electricity is the omnipresent rogue force in Eastwick, where even the clicking of laptop keys coats the air "with a furtive film of panic." Jane is knocked sideways by a bolt of energy near a telegraph pole and suffers acute abdominal pains; Alexandra sickens and undergoes a cancer scare, feeling as if she's been invaded by an alien army, "eaten alive from within by tiny hatching spider babies." Only Sukie is unaffected, her sexual vitality still potent enough to fend off evil ions and make old lovers lick their chapped lips. She's proof that just because you're a prime candidate for hip replacement doesn't mean you have to retire to a private nunnery, like some wilted daffodil in Anita Brookner declining the solace of an after-dinner mint. Late-life celibacy is no automatic character-improver or cleansing agent:

Sukie had imagined before turning old that quirks—bad traits and mannerisms—would fall away, once the need to make a sexual impression was removed; without the distraction of sex, a realer, more honest self would be revealed. But it is sex, it turned out, that engages us in society, and keeps us on our toes, and persuades us to retract our rough edges, so we can mix in.

To stay on her toes, Sukie goes down on her knees. That's how things are done in the fallen world of geriatric erotica. No Updike novel seems quite complete without a fancy cumshot, as they say in the porn trade, the artistic blowjob in *Seek My Face* earning a runner-up citation in the 2003 Bad Sex Awards ("his pale semen inside her mouth, displayed on her arched tongue like a little Tachiste masterpiece"), and his larger body of work garnering him a Lifetime Achievement Award this year. The BJ performed here is a bit less refined than *Seek My Face*'s nimble juggling feat, but luminous as only an Updike emission can be: "Her face gleamed with his jism in the spotty light of the motel room, there on the far end of East Beach, within sound of the sea." A sloppy facial set to the "rhythmic relentless shushing" of the sea—it may not be the stuff of Gershwin romance, but it'll do until creaky infirmity takes even Sukie out of commission, round about the year 2016.

Although *The Widows of Eastwick* is unsparing in its topographical study of bodily decay, inventorying every wattle, welt, wrinkle, sag, liver spot, varicose vein, flaky patch and set of receding gums, it finds no hopeful influx of romping, coltish vigor from the generations below. What a let-down the widows' middle-aged children and their spouses are: a lumpy, dumpy, grumpy, sullen, sallow, lax bunch of softies rebelling against the Sexual Revolution by becoming risk-averse little hobbits. "Why are children so disappointing?" Alexandra laments. "They take your genes and run them right into the ground." Into the ground is where everything in *Widows* is irreversibly heading, its former libertines bony and graveyard-bound, the country that produced them past its postwar peak and in poky decline, gathering moss as it lumbers downhill. Heavy on mortality, light on morbidity, Updike elegizes entropy American-style with a resigned, paternal, disappointed affection that distinguishes his fiction from that of grimmer declinists: Don DeLillo, Gore Vidal, Philip Roth. America may have lost its looks and stature, but it was a beauty once, and worth every golden dab of sperm.

The London Review of Books, January 1, 2009

The Prince of Finesse
Hugging the Shore

"He ought to write with a crystal pen on silver paper," observed Hazlitt of the Irish poet Tom Moore, and the same might be said of John Updike, who also writes with a rich, streaming ease, spraying the air with foam flecks of dazzle. But just as Hazlitt found the "strawberry-ice" scintillations of Tom Moore a touch too ineffable ("His imagination may dally with insect beauties, with Rosicrucian spells; may describe a butterfly's wing, a flower-pot, a fan: but it should not attempt to span the great outlines of nature, or keep pace with the sounding march of events"), critics have always harbored suspicions about the true reach and muscle of Updike's art. To some, he is an air-dancing dandy, the most regal butterfly ever to hover before Eustache Tilley's monocle. "Need Updike's fine mind be so much in evidence?" asked Alfred Kazin in *Bright Book of Life*, irked by the crush of "brilliant images" in *Rabbit, Run,* and in his review of *Couples* William Gass found much in Updike's style to make him wince (though he did concede that at his best Updike can "condense an image until it becomes a hard fist of meaning").

In recent years, however, the suspicions about Updike have subsided. Of his recent fiction, I found *The Coup* too lush and *Rabbit Is Rich* an elaborately faked orgasm of sour feeling; but those are definitely minority squawks—to most, Updike's hard fist of meaning has never been more in solid evidence. And now, as if to rout all straggling hints of dandyism, comes by far his biggest book—*Hugging the Shore,* a volume of criticism, reflections, and asides that runs to nearly 900 pages. Hefty as the book is, it lands in the reader's lap with an agreeable, almost coquettish bounce.

Clearly, no living American novelist can match Updike in the range and responsiveness of his reading. Norman Mailer is scathingly shrewd when he takes the measure of his rivals in the room, but has seldom strayed beyond the combat arena; Gore Vidal has shown far more curiosity, roving from Italo Calvino to the *Oz* books to the thickets of structuralism, but in recent years he's become an irritable scold, forever flogging the shanks of his most hated hobby-horses (America, academe). Styron? Bellow? Roth?—their scattered criticisms have tended to be investigations intended to enrich their work as novelists. Anne Tyler seems to see book reviews as opportunities to let her mind coast. Diane Johnson and Elizabeth Hardwick are dartingly astute when they catch a whiff of something hidden and dubious in a cultural phenomenon, but in praise both are given to a certain diffuse niceness, their lanterns casting a soft yellowy glow. No, almost alone John Updike has kept his sane, disinterested bearings and managed to write about literature with a generous sweep of attention and a fine, probing focus.

Now and then his conscientiousness goes beyond the call of duty— why, for example, did he insist on lugging a pair of (my God) *German* novels on holiday? They didn't exactly brighten his afternoons. "I took these two slim volumes"—i.e., Gerhard Roth's *Winterreise* and Hans Joachim Schädlich's *Approximation*—"with me on a week in the Caribbean and must confess that, brief as both are, it took all the bracing counter-effects of sun, sea, and shuffleboard to get me through them." On such occasions Updike doesn't seem so much hugging the shore as lashed to the mast. But most of the time he is content scanning the horizon, there by choice and not obligation.

Two Nobel prizewinners—Saul Bellow and Günter Grass—earn a large chunk of Updike's attention in this collection. With deft, polite scalpeling, Updike peels away the rugged prettinesses of Bellow's style (which he rightly admires) and locates the "agitated sluggishness" that makes *Humboldt's Gift* so busy and yet so inert, the "firm, simple center" that *The Dean's December* sadly lacks. In both novels, shape, drama, and character development have been embedded in a fat of "worldly mass" as the narrator cocks nervous glances at the heavens and makes with wheezing ruminations. The result is talky, static. "Corde [Albert Corde, the dean of *The Dean's December*] is too closely tied to his creator to be free, to fall, to be judged in the round, to have anything much happen to him. No stark Greek fate is going to flatten this coddled agonist, we can be sure."

As Bellow's novels have gone baggy, Günter Grass's have taken on a terrible bloating. There's something comic about Updike's mannerly tone as he makes his way through *The Flounder* and *The Meeting at Telgte*, his tolerance for boredom sorely tested. On *The Flounder*:

> Grass has not bitten off more than he can chew, for he chews
> it enthusiastically before our eyes. But, as he chews, our own

empathetic relish dulls; my consumption, at least, of large portions of *The Flounder* was spurred on by no other hunger than the puritanical craving to leave a clean plate.

Finally, confronted with *Headbirths; or, The Germans Are Dying Out* (a book as dire as its title), Updike's tolerance snaps and he brings the two Nobel prizewinners together for an instructive show of contrast.

It is hard to imagine an American writer of comparable distinction publishing a book so unbuttoned in manner, so dishevelled in content. Saul Bellow, his head as spinning with ideas as Günter Grass's, yet dresses them up in fictional costume, as in *The Dean's December*, or else presents them straightforwardly as journalism, as in *To Jerusalem and Back*. These are clean headbirths; Grass gives us pangs, placenta, and squalling infant all in a heap, plus a damp surgical mask and a bent forceps.

Updike tries to end his review on a more considerate note, but those bent forceps are pretty damning.

Indeed, one of the unexpected pleasures of *Hugging the Shore* is seeing the Prince of Finesse occasionally dip into his quiver for an acid-tipped arrow. John Updike will never be considered a member of the slash-and-burn school of criticism ("Bring forth your maidens!"), but he is given to fits of eloquent pique.

While reviewing a posthumous collection of prose works by Flann O'Brien, Updike wonders, "First, why is it called, on the title page, 'A Richard Seaver Book'? Mr. Seaver's personal contributions to the volume are nowhere specified, so his name presents itself as a purely territorial assertion. . . ."* With this prickliness comes a searching eagerness to dig beneath the hype and confetti of a book's reception and discover a writer's true strengths and hollows. While all about him were losing their heads over Milan Kundera's *The Book of Laughter and Forgetting*, Updike captured the political evasiveness underlying Kundera's beguiling musicale.

---

* This is an echo of F. R. Leavis's famous complaint, in *The Common Pursuit*, regarding Harry T. Moore's temerity in dedicating a collection of D. H. Lawrence's letters. "Who is Professor Harry T. Moore, one asks, and what standing does he suppose he has in relation to the genius of whom he has taken academic possession, that he should dedicate a collection of Lawrence's letters?"

The Communist idyll he youthfully believed in seems somehow to exist for him still, though mockingly and excludingly.
He never asks himself—the most interesting political question
of the century—why a plausible and necessary redistribution of
wealth should, in its Communist form, demand such an exor-
bitant sacrifice of individual freedom. Why must the idyll turn,
not merely less than idyll, but nightmare? Kundera describes
the terrors and humiliations of the intellectual under totalitari-
anism with crystalline authority, yet for all he tells us these bar-
barities are rooted in the sky, in whims beyond accounting.

(Socialism holds no spell for Updike. When a character in a Hein-
rich Böll novel says that socialism must come, must prevail, Updike
aptly comments, "As if it had not already crushingly prevailed over
hundreds of millions. . . .")
And while still other critics were bemoaning the fact that the
director Joseph Losey was unable to raise sufficient funds to film
Harold Pinter's adaptation of Proust's *Remembrance of Things Past*,
Updike took a thoughtful look at the Pinter screenplay and noted that
Pinter's paring down turned Marcel into "a surly stick" and garbled
his involvement with Albertine. "As the novel frames the case, it is
Albertine who is resolved on escaping, and the narrator's cruelties
are pathetic maneuvers to forestall her. In the Pinter version, Marcel,
drained of the child's vulnerability and sexual tentativeness that he
carries through the novel, becomes—with kissing closeups and bare-
shouldered bed scenes—a standard cinema stud, a stag at bay in the
woods of sexual freedom, a trapped lover tossing over his latest dolly."
He also notes, tartly, that "Saint-Loup would not breezily introduce
his friend to his mistress with 'This is Marcel. Marcel—Rachel.'"
(Which has the rhythm of a Henny Youngman routine: "Take my
mistress—please.") Since Updike knows intimately every blade and
pebble in Proust, he can alight like a robin and spot the worms in
Pinter's adaptation, removing them with a few light tugs.
   This feathery fineness does result in a certain lack of heat and
force. Essentially, John Updike is an appreciator, but not in the high-
voltage style of Randall Jarrell, whose electric enthusiasm could send
readers rushing to the shelves for confirmation. (Reading Jarrell on
Whitman, you couldn't wait to crack open Whitman to share the
sublime buzz in Jarrell's head.) Updike's manner of appreciation is
softer, more murmurous, more a matter of sighs and attentive ahhhs,
but before his tone can turn too melting he pulls himself up and fixes

the writer with an arresting phrase or judgment. He polishes the glass case of Nabokov's butterfly collection, hops along the broken circuits of Henry Green's neglected novels, shines a flashlight into Céline's steaming gutter, takes tea with Barbara Pym and sandwiches with M.F.K. Fisher, inhales the fragrance of Colette, and discerns a tenderness of feeling beneath John O'Hara's vain, gruff bravado—"To perceive the atrocity in Scott Fitzgerald's flirting with his insane wife took moral imagination and courteous instincts; this sensitivity, one suspects, set O'Hara a little apart from the boys even during his roistering days."

In the company of his favorites, Updike's eyes gleam with admiration and gratitude, but every now and then his hand starts to doodle. When Updike writes about Anne Tyler, for example, he expresses his small qualms about her work with such Jamesian tact and hesitation that he seems to be standing above Tyler with a drink in his hand, fearful of spilling a drop. "It is true, no writer would undertake to fill a canvas so broad without some confidence that she can invent her way across any space, and some of Miss Tyler's swoops, and the delayed illuminations that prick out her tableaux, have not quite the savor of reality's cautious grind." But although I would prefer more plainspokenness, even a whiff of woodsmoke from the old slash-and-burn, I can respect Updike's disinclination to thump the table and scold. It isn't simply a matter of decorum on Updike's part. In his previous collection, the lewdly entitled *Picked-Up Pieces*, Updike wrote, "If a harsh Providence were to obliterate, say, Alfred Kazin, Richard Gilman, Stanley Kauffmann, and Irving Howe, tomorrow new critics would arise with the same worthy intelligence, the same complacently agonized humanism, the same inability to read a book except as a disappointing version of one they might have written, the same deadly 'auntiness.'" So when Updike backs off it isn't because he lacks steel but because he doesn't want to be a sour geezer in the grandstand, shouting complaints through a megaphone. At ease among his equals, he has no need to raise his voice or issue marching orders. And his love of the luminous saves him from the frumps of "agonized humanism."

In a book this crammed with goodies, there are trivial pieces that Updike might better have discarded. His salutations to other *New Yorker* writers are a little too kissy, becoming what we used to call in high school Public Displays of Affection; and he needn't have displayed his medals in the book's afterword, where he reprints acceptance speeches and whimsical self-interviews. And, as in *Picked-Up Pieces*, he flips over a blonde fluff-bunny—in *Pieces*, it was Erica Jong who inspired his mooniest prose ("On the back jacket flap, Mrs. Jong, with perfect teeth and cascading blond hair, is magnificently laughing")— here it's Doris Day, whom Updike dotes upon with eyes as dewed as Bambi's. He pretends to be clear-sighted about her accomplishments, but like Norman Mailer on Marilyn Monroe he goes a little gaga— e.g., "The particulars of her life surprise us, like graffiti scratched on a sacred statue." But in bracing contrast to the candles lit in honor of St. Doris of Day, Updike's long meditation on the career of Herman Melville ("Melville's Withdrawal") is lucid, sympathetic, informative, spiced with bright observations, and handsomely thought out, the very model of an expansive literary essay.

Not that long ago Gore Vidal said with some justification that in the age of rock and apocalypse, the very word "literature" seemed paltry and weak. But reading Updike's essay on Melville, warming my lap with this book's pleasing weight, I felt—feel—that literature has managed to weather the last two decades rather well, and that it's rock and apocalypse that have come to seem thin, flimsy, forced. Which is not to say that literature will ever again regain its cultural preeminence, just that its walls and brickwork seem sturdy enough to survive even the blinking dither of the Age of Video. It's a house with many mansions, and in *Hugging the Shore* Updike gives a splendid, striding tour.

Harper's, September 1983

Postscript

If it please the court, I ask that it be stricken from the record that I ever mocked/denigrated John Updike for his devotion to Doris Day, which I have come to share, though perhaps not with the same lambent intensity.

It's Still Cheever Country

Cheever: A Life, Blake Bailey

If a tinge of melancholy haunts the cocktail hour, if a croquet mallet left derelict on the lawn evokes a broken merriment, if the bar car of a commuter train gives off a stale whiff of failed promise and bitter alimony, pause and pay homage to John Cheever. Light a bug candle on the patio in his honor. For Cheever—novelist, master of the short story, prolific diarist—is the patron saint of Eastern Seaboard pathos and redemption, the Edward Hopper of suburban ennui, preserving minor epiphanies in amber. Despite his patrician patina, Cheever was no saint in his personal life and not quite one of nature's noblemen. The publication in 1991 of *The Journals of John Cheever* put a permanent wrinkle in that façade, publicizing Cheever's previously cloaked bisexual appetites and polecat propensities, along with a lesser host of miseries, vanities, and maunderings that left an oily residue. A greater smirch on Cheever's name recognition was inflicted a year later, on an episode of *Seinfeld* where George Costanza (Jason Alexander) discovered that his prospective future father-in-law was a former lover of Cheever's, hoarding a secret stash of letters from the dear man. Millions of viewers who may never have read a single story of Cheever's now had his identity branded into their brains as a gay punch line.

But if some of the mahogany richness has worn off of Cheever's individual reputation following his death, in 1982, the influence of his imagination and sensibility has swum ever deeper into the cultural bloodstream, its unique formula of magical elixir and embalming fluid winding its way through everything from *Ordinary People* to *The Ice Storm* to *American Beauty* to *Far from Heaven* to *Revolutionary Road* to TV's *Mad Men*. Nearly every stylized retro examination of the hidden tooth decay of the American Dream owes Cheever symbolic royalties. As this country edges into the prospect of losing so much of what it once had, a vast devaluing of everything it took for granted, the bittersweet pang of Cheever's nostalgia and the bleak apprehension underlying idle chitchat have never been more apropos—perfect timing for the publication of Blake Bailey's *Cheever:*

A Life (Knopf), a biography of monumental heft and picky asides that certifies Cheever's enduring relevance while smacking his wrist with a nun's ruler. After one of Cheever's typical lyrical effusions, his biographer chides, "Perhaps, but the fact remained that he was impotent, and often drunk before lunch." Even when you're dead, you can't get away with anything.

> *My God, the suburbs! They encircled the city's boundaries like enemy territory, and we thought of them as a loss of privacy, a cesspool of conformity and a life of indescribable dreariness in some split-level village where the place-name appeared in the* New York Times *only when some bored housewife blew off her head with a shotgun.*
> —John Cheever, *Esquire*, July 1960

In the halo'd circles where the craft of fiction is a devotional calling, Cheever is held up as an exemplar of a writer's writer, tending to his tiny plot of fallen paradise. First published at the age of eighteen, with an account in *The New Republic* of being expelled from Thayer Academy (a private school), Cheever had the good fortune to land under the aegis of *The New Yorker*'s fiction editor William Maxwell, whose solicitude and self-effacement were the stuff of Vatican legend. In 1938, Cheever, who had published a few stories in the magazine under Katharine White's editorial wand, was lateraled off to Maxwell. "Maxwell's attentiveness was all the more flattering—and his editorial advice valuable—because he himself was already, at age thirty, the author of two well-regarded novels, *Bright Center of Heaven* and *They Came Like Swallows*," Bailey writes. "For most of his career, though, his own reputation would be eclipsed by the greater fame of the writers he edited: Nabokov, Salinger, Welty, and (as Maxwell put it) 'three wonderful writers all named John'—O'Hara, Updike, and Cheever." Under Maxwell's tutelage, Cheever produced a basket of golden eggs, stories that by the late forties—"miraculous years for Cheever"— placed him near the top tier of the fiction writers at *The New Yorker*, an exclusive fraternity that included O'Hara, Nabokov, Salinger, and Irwin Shaw. But literary cachet didn't stock the pantry or cover the dry cleaning, especially during dry spells. "In his journal Cheever wrote, 'We are as poor as we ever have been. The rent is not paid, we have very little to eat. . . . We have many bills.' Determined to write 'a story a week,' he was rejected four times in a row by *The New Yorker*, which meant he wouldn't be receiving a yearly bonus either. Faced with dire poverty, and forced into writing 'lifeless and detestable' fiction, Cheever chided himself for entertaining an 'unreason-able' degree of petulance."

A petulance inflamed into a rash of envy by the thumping success of his friend Irwin Shaw's World War II epic, *The Young Lions*. It was like being slapped across the face with a fancy wallet listening to Shaw, who was raking in screenplay money on the side as the royalties rolled in, flaunting his jackpot status as postwar fiction's newest golden boy. "For Cheever, it was exquisite agony to hear Shaw complain, blithely over lunch, about how much money he'd have to make this year in order to pay taxes on his earnings from last year." This as Cheever prepared to attend *The New Yorker*'s twenty-fifth-anniversary gala in a secondhand tuxedo. Cheever would later feel overshadowed and outmaneuvered at *The New Yorker* by J. D. Salinger (which was like being upstaged by the Invisible Man), Donald Barthelme, and that ingenuous pup, John Updike.

Reading Bailey's biography reconfirms an impression of Cheever that I've carried around in my locket for years—that the man had a lot of ham actor in him, which he served pretty thick. Like illustri-ous glazed hams of stage and screen such as John Barrymore, Charles Laughton, and Jack Nicholson, Cheever enlisted his audience as co-conspirators, calculating his effects down to the last Noël Coward drop of sherry. His role-playing began out of social necessity as he went through the motions of keeping up appearances, like a character in a minimalist cartoon strip or a Jacques Tati comedy. After Cheever, his wife, Mary, and their daughter, Susie (who would grow up to be an author in her own right), moved into an apartment on Sutton Place that they could barely afford, he took pains to pass himself off as a member in good standing of the corporate rat race. "Almost every morning for the next five years, he'd put on his only suit and ride the elevator with other men leaving for work; Cheever, however, would proceed all the way down to a storage room in the basement, where he'd doff his suit and write in his boxers until noon, then dress again and ascend for lunch." He might as well have been wearing prison stripes, so regimented was his routine, and Cheever wouldn't discover his real, breathing persona until he dropped this cookie-cutter pose of uniformity and moved to the suburbs, where his inner Wasp could unbend and spruce up its affectations. His wardrobe selection was shabby chic before the phrase and style became voguish. His accent beautified into a veritable flute. "When appearing on *The Dick Cavett Show*, or putting an impudent barkeep in his place," Bailey writes, "Cheever became almost a parody of the pompous toff ('like Thurston

Howell III on *Gilligan's Island*,' the writer James Kaplan observed, 'or Chatsworth Osborne in *Dobie Gillis*'), but at other times—relaxed, cracking jokes—he sounded not unlike a boy from the South Shore with an English mother." Our literary life would be poorer without its theatrical touch-ups, and Cheever's are no more to be begrudged and censured than the pile of buttermilk batter that James Dickey became or Isak Dinesen's eye shadow. A little shamming doesn't hurt as long as it doesn't become the last line of brittle defense. But as Cheever grew older and his drinking spun into a kamikaze spiral, his mannerisms developed a desperate flutter and hollow ring, as if echoing from a cracked shell. He might fool his fans with fustian eloquence, but he couldn't bluff the psychiatric staff of Manhattan's Smithers Alcoholism Treatment and Training Center, where he was admitted in 1975 after a binge that left him "naked and incoherent." They weren't there to humor his lordship. Bailey writes:

> Bullied at every turn for his "false light-heartedness" and "grandiosity," Cheever retreated into a vast, fraudulent humility. "Oh, but of *course* you're right," he'd mutter (in so many words) when challenged. Nobody was fooled or amused. Carol Kitman, a staff psychologist, remarked that Cheever reminded her of Uriah Heep: "He is a classic denier who moves in and out of focus," she wrote in her progress notes. "He dislikes seeing self negatively and seems to have internalized many rather imperious upper class Boston attitudes which he ridicules and embraces at the same time."

It was in his erotic life that Cheever constructed his most ornate artifice, subject to erosion. Although he would stray from the marriage bed that he often found so cold and forbidding for sexual interludes with men, he prided himself on maintaining a masculine front with no minty accents. Swish he abhorred. "Although he loved men," Susan Cheever writes in her biographical memoir of her father, *Home Before Dark*, "he feared and despised what he defined as the homosexual community; the limp-wristed, lisping men who are sometimes the self-appointed representatives of homosexual love in our culture. Men who run gift shops, sell antiques, strike bargains over porcelain tea sets."

Fear of effeminacy and disdain for adorable bric-a-brac drove Cheever to police the premises like a butch watchdog in his role as patriarch, browbeating his poor son, Ben, over any fey infraction, according to Bailey. "You laugh like a woman!," Cheever would snap at the boy when he giggled (interestingly, the Smithers staff were struck by Cheever's own chronic tittering), and he accused his son of pampering himself like some starlet when he took bubble baths. Ben literally had to watch his every step. "[Ben] liked to dance in front of the bathroom mirror—pretending he was a gunslinger who could dance so well he could dodge bullets—until one day his father walked in: 'That,' said Ben, 'was the end of my dancing in front of the mirror.'" And with it the promise of being a future Billy Elliot.

What besmitten Cheever to his young protégé Max Zimmer, an aspiring writer whom he had met while visiting the University of Utah, was that he wore cowboy boots and "had none of the attributes of a sexual irregular," such as rampant antiquing on weekends. Using his clout as literary wizard, Cheever championed Zimmer's work and got him a spot at the artists' colony Yaddo, in Saratoga Springs, New York, and he expected something nice in return. "I knew before I left for Saratoga," the Mormon-raised Max realized with a heavy heart, "that I'd have to give him another hand-job." Although Cheever insisted he had no intention of feeding upon Max's cowpoke innocence like a praying mantis, he was a wily cuss when it came to getting his way. Whenever Zimmer brought a manuscript to the master for appraisal and advice, Cheever, who believed that sexual arousal sharpened his eyesight and concentration, would ask that Max assist in unblurring his vision. Sigh; it was time to give the old handle another crank. I am irresistibly reminded of the comedian Louis C.K.'s requiem for a half-hearted wank: "That hand job was probably the saddest thing that ever happened in America. There should be a monument to that hand job, with a reflecting pool, where you just sit and think, 'God that was fucking sad.'" It was more than sad for Zimmer. It had an air of gentle coercion. As a cautionary lesson, Cheever would invoke the example of an earlier protégé, Allan Gurganus, who would earn best-selling success with *Oldest Living Confederate Widow Tells All.* "Gurganus . . . was often invoked for Max's benefit, both as the embodiment of *true* homosexuality ('he suffers acutely from the loss of gravity that seems to follow having a cock up your ass or down your throat once too often') and as living proof that it was unwise to spurn Cheever's advances. As he told Max more than once, he'd helped get 'Minor Heroism' published in *The New Yorker;* but now that he'd withdrawn his patronage, Gurganus would *never* appear in the magazine again." And Gurganus didn't appear in *The New Yorker* again while Cheever was still alive.

It can't be said that Cheever played coy in his maneuvers with the opposite sex. He carried on an intermittent flurry of an affair with the actress Hope Lange (the star of *The Best of Everything* and TV's *The Ghost & Mrs. Muir*) about which he crowed far and wide, countenancing her advancing years with a courtly twirl, confiding to his journal: "That her voice may be shrill, that her looks may be passing, that there is very little correspondence in our tastes are things I know and don't care about at all." There is so much one is willing to overlook when one is diddling a celebrity. But it wasn't reciprocal, this forbearance, as ice formed on Hope Lange's higher slopes. "The decisive episode had occurred after a recent lunch when, returning to her apartment, Cheever had dropped his pants and waited. 'I can't help you,' she said, and made a phone call." Leaving him dangling. Even coarser than Cheever's crude shortcuts through the art of seduction (enter room, drop drawers) was the swarmy way he extolled womanly charms to his fellow cavaliers. To Frederick Exley, the author of *A Fan's Notes*, with whom he went rollicking at the Iowa Writers' Workshop, Cheever wrote, "We seem to have something basically in common, something more lambent, I hope, than hootch and cunt." And to Max Zimmer he exulted in the afterglow of a gala dinner celebrating the publication of *The Stories of John Cheever* that was held in his honor at Lutèce, where he was seated between the actresses Lauren Bacall and Maria Tucci (the wife of the collection's editor), "bask[ing] in that fragrance of beaver we both so enjoy." I'm sure the evening was a treat for them too.

> *Oh, those suburban Sunday nights, those Sunday night blues! Those departing weekend guests, those stale cocktails, those half-dead flowers, those trips to Harmon to catch the Century, those postmortems and pickup suppers!*
> —John Cheever, "O Youth and Beauty!"

Now we come to the inevitable station stop in the piece where we say, But enough about the Life, with all its gauche lapses and unkempt complications—what about the Work? The Work holds. The Work withstands. As Bailey observes, Cheever—whose 1977 novel, *Falconer*, scored him the cover of *Newsweek* (due in large part to daughter Susan's editorial role at the magazine) and whose collected *Stories* lionized his place in letters ("not merely the publishing event of the 'season' but a grand occasion in English literature," marveled John

Leonard)—"died almost at the pinnacle of his fame." And despite the biographical and autobiographical disclosures since, Cheever retains a pinnacle aura. His worth as author has not suffered the steep drop-off of his fellow John, O'Hara. It isn't simply that Cheever wrote more handsomely than O'Hara, but that his best stories have an emotional reach and regretful ache that the more stonyhearted O'Hara was incapable of, so intent was he on laying out the real inside dirt on his country-club louses. Whatever inside dirt Cheever extracted on the secret vices of suburbanites was gold-flaked with a tender idolizing of the clouds, wind, sun, rain, swimming pools, tennis courts, and elegant greenery that composed their miniature kingdoms. In the best Cheever stories (his novels I find too hodgepodgy), there's always something wild ready to break loose once the leash of propriety snaps, which often takes only a few drinks and a bared bra strap. Like F. Scott Fitzgerald, Cheever was a besotted romantic who might slop around in person but who kept a taut rein on his lyrical gifts, striving for an exalted precision of perception that would infuse his descriptive passages with enough rapture to keep the demons temporarily at bay. Despite the epic boozing ("You drink like Siberian worker!" he was once hurrahed) and other dissipations, Cheever had a tremendous stamina that saw him through to the triumphant finish. A stamina and missionary zeal worthy of the protagonist in his classic story "The Swimmer," who swam from pool to pool in a quixotic quest to reach home: "He was not a practical joker nor was he a fool but he was determinedly original and had a vague and modest idea of himself as a legendary figure." Not a bad epitaph for Cheever himself, whose vague modesty was all part of the act.

Vanity Fair, April 2009

Ayn Rand
Rand Inquisitor

Long before Madonna was a material girl, Ayn Rand was the material guru. Her very name had the clink of coinage. Born Alice Rosenbaum in St. Petersburg, Russia, in 1905, Ayn Rand took her last name from a famous make of typewriter, an apt choice for someone who herself became a word machine, a sacred monster of super, staccato output. As for Ayn—she pronounced it to rhyme with "mine," also apt. For Ayn Rand's entire career was based on the belief that no one has the moral right to mess with what's mine. Individualism is utmost. I outweighs we. I *certainly* outranks y'all. Shucking the dead skin of collectivism (her novel *Anthem* anatomizes a closed society where only "we" is permissible), she unshuttered her soul to the clear blue of capitalism. Money for her was not a dirty pile of dead presidents but the shining sky-high symbol of man's unshackled mind. For her, $ marked the spot. When she died in 1982, her body lay next to a six-foot dollar sign, a floral arrangement donated by an admirer. Capitalism mourned its patron saint. But the bones of a saint are often up for grabs, and her bones have been picked clean in memoirs written by her closest sidekicks, Nathaniel and Barbara Branden. The resulting rumble over the reputation of Ayn Rand has rattled her skeleton.

Although Rand wrote filmscripts, stage plays, and polemics, her reputation rests on two power fantasies in prose fiction, *The Fountainhead* (1943) and *Atlas Shrugged* (1957). In both novels she expounded and dramatized the philosophy of objectivism, an iron-supplement-for-tired-blood regimen of reason and unreined will. The hero of *The Fountainhead* is Howard Roark, an architect who unfurls his blueprints over the shrinking masses like Moses descending from the mountain with stone tablets. His integrity is tamperproof. He blows up a building he has designed rather than have his original plans prostituted. Howard Roark with his stick of dynamite for a phallus was a prototype for John Galt, the hero of *Atlas Shrugged*, who brings the world to a screeching halt by leading a strike of smokestack America's illuminati.

If Rand's novels were simply he-man handbooks on how to make enemies and influence people, they wouldn't have had such a healthy shelf life. But for all of her philosophical grounding, she had a mad pop instinct. She wrestled with Kant and Hegel, but also found time to follow Perry Mason, Ian Fleming's James Bond, and the novels of Mickey Spillane. Absurd, unstoppable, *The Fountainhead* and *Atlas Shrugged* lumber along on tilted stilts, dinosaurs of thematic import with big, tall drive-in-movie images, slow yet fast, the heartbeats of her characters as loud as kettledrums as they hurtle down the tunnel and up the express elevator of her action sequences.

Even today, when Rand's buckshot rhetoric on behalf of capitalism finds far more assent in the mainstream (sugar-coated by such free-enterprisers as George Gilder and Michael Novak), her novels still have the unlicensed crackle of pirate broadcasts. They show both the extended reach of her energy and its focused firepower. She spent two years writing John Galt's sermon in *Atlas Shrugged*, and during a homestretch run on *The Fountainhead* worked nearly nonstop for thirty hours. Irony, doubt, ambiguity would have gummed up the whirring gears of her motorized mechanisms. Historically, Ayn Rand may be seen as the last industrial novelist, the last to lyricize the urban might of stone and metal. After her came plastic, suburbia, and postmodernism. No wonder she loved the work of Mickey Spillane! They were the last of the shameless hot dogs, biting off big parts of the night.

At her most idealistic, Ayn Rand was the apostle of ascendancy. Street life and local color were not her concern. She preferred the rarefied heights. Even when she pictures society going to rot, she envisions it not at the sinking bottom (as Dickens did), but at the tainted top.

> The clouds and the shafts of skyscrapers against them were turning brown, like an old painting in oil, the color of a fading masterpiece. Long streaks of grime ran from under the pinnacles down the slender, soot-eaten walls. High on the side of a tower there was a crack in the shape of a motionless lightning, the length of ten stories. [*Atlas Shrugged*]

But most of the time she scanned the sky for inspiration. So it is not surprising that her romantic fancies reflected this craning view. Her dream lover was a man she could look up to. The essence of femininity, she once wrote, was hero worship, and her own hankering for a superior being was half Nietzsche, half Hollywood. Unfortunately, her husband, Frank O'Connor, didn't fit the bill, even though he looked the part. Kind and supportive as O'Connor was, he was too laid-back and laconic. She sought mastery. She jokily admitted that the sex scenes in *The Fountainhead* had their source in wishful thinking. Asked about the rape of Dominique by Roark, she replied that if it was rape, it was rape by engraved invitation. So Ayn Rand wanted more than a loyal plank to prop her up against adversity—she wanted a hunka, hunka burnin' love, a Howard Roark to emerge from the quarry and answer that engraved invitation. A primitive man with a superior mind.

Enter Nathaniel Branden, destiny's dimpled darling. In 1950, at the age of nineteen, he visited Ayn Rand as a fan at her California house. One look into her eyes was instant conversion. They talked until dawn. He staggered home in a daze. On his second visit he brought his girlfriend, Barbara, whom he later married and divorced. She too was mesmerized. For years Ayn and her husband, Frank, Nathaniel and his wife, Barbara, formed a string quartet of philosophical fiddling. It was when the fiddling got physical that their perfect little harmony was ruined. The story of that dissolution and its divisive effect on objectivism's cadre of true believers has been amply documented, first by Barbara Branden in *The Passion of Ayn Rand* (Doubleday), and now by Nathaniel Branden in *Judgment Day* (Houghton Mifflin). Their overlapping accounts show Rand in the full sweep of her mood swings. She emerges as one tough bird, an eagle to her fans, a buzzard to her foes.

For a time Nathaniel Branden was Rand's top salesman, pitching her philosophy as if it were the shiniest new model on the showroom floor. He founded the Nathaniel Branden Institute, devoted to the discussion and dissemination of objectivism. Rand deputized him as the only person allowed to speak for her. "I felt myself standing in the spotlight of history," he says about being designated her intellectual heir. But then, Branden often writes in *Judgment Day* as if a spotlight were following him around on the page. This soliloquizing is what elevates his story into the realm of camp, despite all the pain he felt and inflicted.

The heartache began when Rand slipped out of her mentor role into a more comfortable mode. One night as they cuddled in the backseat of a car, their talk took on a lovey-dovey tone. Acknowledging their attraction to each other, Rand and Branden convened their spouses and carved out a schedule of private time together, sessions which they promised would be platonic. The promise was soon broken. Into bed they fell. Me Ayn, you mine. Under a sexual spell, they met regularly to do the wild thing. "I recalled the day last winter when, returning to Ayn's apartment after lunch, I had made love to her in the living room, both of us dressed, Ayn still in her fur coat. I heard myself saying, 'I've always wanted to make love to a woman in a fur coat,' and her answering, 'Next time, without the dress, just the coat.'"

Each round of bliss boosted their self-esteem. Satisfying a younger man made her feel more womanly, satisfying an older woman made him feel more manly. It was almost French, their scenario. Yet sex wasn't a softening experience for them, as it is for many people. They didn't bump into strangers with cloudy smiles on their faces. Sexual collaboration encased their egos like mortar shells. As *Atlas Shrugged* added more and more recruits to the ranks of objectivism, Rand began enforcing an even stricter roll call. She assumed the dictatorial airs of a warden in a correctional institution. To like the wrong composers (Wagner, Beethoven) or the wrong painters (Rembrandt, the Impressionists) invited censure. In the field of ethics she verbally wasted those who waffled. And woe to him stuck with the stigma of being a "social metaphysician," Rand's label for the lost soul who draws his values from other people rather than his own upright I. Such a person had his very psyche stretched on the rack, with Nathaniel Branden turning the screws. Heady with success in the sack and at the lecture stand, he became the Grand Inquisitor's grinning assistant.

But the spotlight glare of being Ayn Rand's pretty accessory began to make her prince wilt. Adultery, even above-board adultery, taxes the nerves. Damn-all as he wanted to be, Branden brooded with bourgeois guilt over the hurt he was causing Barbara and Frank. And there was that inescapable age gap (Rand was twenty-five years older than Branden), which seemed to widen with every wrinkle. His engines slowly cooled. After a long layoff following the publication of *Atlas Shrugged*, during which Rand submerged into an extended funk, she surfaced with the desire to reconnect their sex lives. Branden stalled. "I still worshiped her as a goddess of reason," he writes. However, he no longer wished to do the bump with bad mama, especially now that he had a new sweetheart named Patrecia.

After years of deflecting Rand's queries as to why her hunka, hunka burnin' love had turned into an elusive icicle, Branden decided to write a kiss-off letter stating that he was not in love with her and considered the gap in their ages too large for them to resume hanky-panky. Unwisely, he even tossed out that last scrap lovers leave for the spurned, the hope that they might still be friends. She didn't take it well. " 'You *bastard*,' she kept shrieking, 'You bastard, you bastard! You nothing! You fraud! You contemptible swine!' "

And she was just getting revved. When she learned that she had been supplanted by a younger woman, that she had been misled for years about the true nature of his affections, she summoned him to her lair: *"Get that bastard down here, or I'll drag him here myself!"* Enter Branden, ass sorely dragging. *Sit*, she said, indicating a chair near the door. "I don't want you in my living room," she explained. A whipped dog, he obeyed. Barbara Branden was present at her husband's humiliation. She reports that Rand just couldn't bring herself to wish Nathaniel and Patrecia the best.

> The choked voice spat out its last terrible sounds. "If you have an ounce of morality left in you, an ounce of psychological health— you'll be impotent for the next twenty years! And if you achieve any potency, you'll know it's a sign of still worse moral degradation!" The voice stopped too abruptly, as if stunned by its own words. There was silence.
>
> Suddenly, with a sound that rang through the room like a shot—a shot fired at Nathaniel's heart and her own—Ayn's open hand arced through space to slash across Nathaniel's upturned face. It retreated, arced again—slashed again. And then once more.
>
> "Now get out!" ordered a stranger's voice.
>
> Nathaniel rose to his feet. Three red welts scarred his face. He had not flinched. He had not uttered a word. His glance flicked, once, to me. Then he turned and left the room. And left Ayn's life forever.

Nathaniel Branden records only two shots upside his head and reverses the chronology of Rand's impotence curse (placing it after the slaps), but otherwise his account jibes with his ex's. It's a confrontation worthy of a Rand novel in all its hair-raising hysteria. The hysteria didn't subside with Branden's exit and exile either. Ayn Rand continued on the warpath. The Nathaniel Branden Institute was dismantled. An open letter from her appeared in *The Objectivist* newsletter, casting both Nathaniel and Barbara Branden into the outer darkness. They fired off a counterblast to *The Objectivist*'s subscribers. It was civil war in the ranks of reason's ragtag army. Friend broke with friend, marriages split down the middle, the sidewalks of Manhattan became a battlefield of huffy looks and averted gazes. The schism that split the objectivist movement resembled the zigzag of motionless lightning cracking the tower in *Atlas Shrugged.* Those dwindling few who remained faithful to Ayn Rand have never forgiven the Brandens for riling the goddess of reason. Barbara Branden laments, "To this day, my cousin and friend, Leonard Peikoff, has refused to deal with me or discuss the events of 1968." Some friend!

Cousin Lenny is the editor of a posthumous collection of Ayn Rand's articles and speeches entitled *The Voice of Reason: Essays in Objectivist Thought* (New American Library). Depicted in Nathaniel Branden's book as a loyal nerd, Peikoff does nothing in his afterword, "My Thirty Years with Ayn Rand," to dispel the impression. "[If] I am to go down in history as her apologist or glamorizer, then so be it. I am proud to be cursed as a 'cultist,' if the 'cult' is unbreached dedication to the mind and to its most illustrious exponents." What a winky-dink. But the anthology Peikoff has assembled is useful in showing how strong, perverse, and unassimilable Rand was as a writer. For example, "Of Living Death" is a prime humanist and feminist document, a ripping response to the papal encyclical "Humanae Vitae (Of Human Life)" and a ringing defense of one's right to control reproduction. "Abortion is a moral right—which should be left to the sole discretion of the woman involved; morally, nothing other than her wish in the matter is to be considered." Such a passage is a reminder of why Ayn Rand never conformed to the religious right, especially the Catholic right exemplified by William F. Buckley. She saw religiosity as a retarding check on human progress. She would have viewed the crucifix bouncing between Madonna's breasts on MTV as a sign of backwardness.

An essay in *The Voice of Reason* extolling the flight of *Apollo 11* is extra evidence that Ayn Rand was never more in control of her effects than when she aimed high. The rocket's red glare immortalized by Francis Scott Key was born again above the launchpad of *Apollo.* "The dark red fire parted into gigantic wings, as if a hydrant were shooting streams of fire outward and up, toward the zenith—and between the two wings, against a pitch-black sky, the rocket rose slowly, so slowly that it seemed to hang still in the air, a pale cylinder with a blinding oval of white light at the bottom, like an upturned candle with its flame directed at the earth." This was no mere spectacle, no votive offering to the eye of the moon, but a demonstration of Promethean ardor and American know-how. She expresses the hope that before America sinks into sloth and stupor it will plant its flag on Mars or

Jupiter. A hope characteristic of the spirit of a woman who studied algebra at the age of seventy-six to better understand its relation to metaphysics and epistemology, and who declared a few months before her death that she would love to see the year 2000. In a retro age, Ayn Rand was one of the last intellectual futurists.

Her legacy? The epilogue to Barbara Branden's *The Passion of Ayn Rand* updates the whereabouts of her closest disciples. (The most highly placed is Alan Greenspan, head of the Fed.) Across the Atlantic, Margaret Thatcher appears a bossy offshoot of the goddess of reason if one substitutes a £ for a $. Yet Ayn Rand's influence is more than a matter of alumni notes and ripple effects. Learning of Ayn Rand's death at the end of *Judgment Day*, Nathaniel Branden, still licking his wounds, suggests that the secret of her hold on people was that she tapped into the "need to experience an ecstatic state of consciousness." It was not a passive Nirvana she proposed, a druggy dropping out, but an *engaged* ecstasy. She wrote as if the Force were with her.

To those in her immediate circle who quaked every time she cleared her throat, her human failings may have cost them plenty, but to us distant bystanders it's just thunder. That's why the personality defects that the Brandens record—her tantrums, her tyrannies, her rewritings of her own history, her humorlessness—finally seem rather so-what, pesty bug specks on a space capsule eating up stars. She was an impossible woman and often an impossible writer. But she wrote a pair of pop-cult classics that have stood the test of time without arti-ficial respiration from the Eng.-lit. establishment, renegade gospels hewed from granite. She recognized the mythic knack animating the paperback heroics of Perry Mason, James Bond, and Mike Hammer because she too had a mythic knack. A touch of immortality. Like Perry Mason and company, her heroes are unslayable. *She's* unslay-able. It could almost be said with skywriting. AYN RAND LIVES.

Vanity Fair, June 1989

Kerouac's Lonesome Road

Jack Kerouac, who died thirty years ago this October at the age of forty-seven, committed suicide on the installment plan. He took his time at the checkout line, drinking himself numb. As a young man Kerouac was blessed with a handsome jaw, a dark, virile Superman forelock, an athletic build (he played football for Horace Mann), and a raft of life experience which set him apart from the baby owls in academe trying to emulate T. S. Eliot's dry-sherry manner. (Such as Allen Ginsberg, whom he met in 1944 at Columbia University, where Ginsberg was a student of the distinguished literary critic Lionel Trilling, the J. Alfred Prufrock of the English department. Kerouac met the other member of the Beat trinity, William Burroughs, later that year.) Kerouac's most famous achievement as a writer—*On the Road*, one version of which was typed on a 120-foot scroll of wire-service paper during a three-week Benzedrine-and-caffeine binge—was as much a physical feat as a creative splurge, the work of a powerful locomotive. Add to this a movie-star name (it even rhymed!) and a tough, wounded masculinity reminiscent of Marlon Brando, and it was no wonder fame found Kerouac a natural. But far more swiftly than Brando, Kerouac turned to bloat. As he wrote in a ditty called "Rose Pome," "I'd rather be thin than famous . . . / But I'm fat. Paste that in yr. Broadway Show."

When Kerouac died on October 21, 1969, of massive abdominal hemorrhaging in St. Petersburg, Florida, where he was visiting his mother, he was fat and mostly forgotten. "He was a very lonely man," his third wife, Stella, told the Associated Press. The portrait of Kerouac's last days was captured in an illustration for *Esquire* magazine (March 1970) which showed a beer-gut has-been slumped in an armchair surrounded by a stack of *National Review*s and a scatter of empty bottles: the king of the Beats on his crumb-bum throne. Once a charioteer hurtling toward the horizon, his car radio tuned in to the cosmos, Kerouac had degenerated into a test model for *All in the Family*'s Archie Bunker, grumbling about hippies, Commies, and Jews. The year 1969, remember, was also the year of *Easy Rider*, whose shock climax of bikers bushwhacked by rednecks spelled the end of the wind-whistling romance of freedom and acceptance celebrated in *On the Road*. At the time, it seemed plausible that his rebel yell would fade into a historical footnote, but thirty years after his death, Jack Kerouac still broods over the landscape, larger than ever. Kerouac lives.

Not only does he live in the minds of readers, he remains a wanted man, one of the few writers worth stealing. Like a saint's relics, his books attract thieves. At the St. Marks Bookstore and the Union Square Barnes & Noble in lower Manhattan, his paperbacks are so prey to shoplifting that they're kept behind the counter. Skyline Books, a secondhand store in Manhattan's photo district, offers a section of Beat memorabilia, a humble shrine which occasionally stocks back issues of *Holiday*, *Evergreen Review*, and *Escapade* containing articles by Kerouac. The Kerouac cult is part of the larger unquenchable fascination with all things Beat. For a group of writers who exalted and peddled drug highs, jazz sensations, spontaneous kicks, transient moods, Oriental-rug visions, and other wordless transports, it's ironic that they not only amassed mountains of their own pesky words but also inspired a beaver community of hangers-on, historians, critics, former lovers, and idolaters whose output threatens to dwarf the original peaks. Hundreds of titles have been published on the Beats from every personal-critical-psychosexual angle. A larger irony, given how heavily the Beats stressed the Zen Now, is the persistent backwash of nostalgia they left behind, a beckoning piano concerto of typewriter keys striking the page rivaled only by Hemingway's Paris in the twenties. The Beats have proved such an enduring beacon and monument on the pop-culture scene that even those who might be called children of the Beats, such as Patti Smith and Bob Dylan, have become sacred elders, presiding over their own flock of crows. The permanent Beat cult isn't strictly a literary phenomenon, even though the reading of *Howl*, *Naked Lunch*, and *On the Road* has become a classic rite of passage for every restless kid staring out the window at school. It's an initiation into a mythic tribe.

Kerouac was the heart and soul of the Beat operation. He coined the term "Beat"—beat as in worn, beat-down; beat as in beatific—and was its true apostle. William Burroughs, with his banker's suits and vampire demeanor, was the surrealist of the group, dishing up pristine cuts of rotting carcasses in *Naked Lunch*. Allen Ginsberg was the chief propagandist, a Jewish Buddhist huggy-bear devoted to good works and street theater (the attempt to levitate the Pentagon in the 1967 antiwar march, a quixotic magic act immortalized in Norman Mailer's *The Armies of the Night*, had Ginsberg written all over it). The great outlaw inspiration was Neal Cassady, Kerouac's model for Dean Moriarty in *On the Road* and the title character of *Visions of Cody*. An autodidact, pool shark, jailbird, satyr, and roustabout, Cassady bulleted through life with none of the inhibitions or Sorrows of Young Werther that plagued undergraduate bookworms like Kerouac and Ginsberg. (Burroughs, an old soul with no illusions to rend, always plotted his own pirate course.) Without the example of Cassady goosing them into action, the Beats might have remained a Romantic offshoot, a homegrown version of Rimbaud, Blake, and Shelley syncopated to the incantatory lines of Walt Whitman, never getting beyond the chatterbox stage.

Kerouac led the way out. He did what Cassady was unable to do—translate fugitive experience into what the critic and Beat-scene maker Seymour Krim dubbed Action Writing. In *On the Road* (1957), Kerouac piped the license and movement he found in Cassady through his own tenor-sax prose. It's become fashionable to say that *On the Road* doesn't "hold up," that it's dated and sentimental and backtracking. The issue of whether *On the Road* holds up is irrelevant to a kid cracking it open for the first time; to him (and it's usually a him, Kerouac's disciples being overwhelmingly male, in my experience), the novel isn't a literary artifact to be judged against the inner gold of other artifacts, but a personal saga and broadcast that bypass normal communication. To newbies, Kerouac's exploits aren't filtered through layers of critical analysis but come at them point-blank, just as Ginsberg's haranguing lines in *Howl* manage to hit new generations of readers full blast. Kerouac writes as if he's right there with you, a fellow passenger. (Kerouac himself seldom drove.)

> *Everything in life is foreign territory. Kerouac—he's my teacher. The open road, my school.*
> —Xander (Nicholas Brendon), brandishing a copy of *On the Road* in an episode of *Buffy the Vampire Slayer*

It would be unfair to leave the patronizing impression that *On the Road* appeals only to untapped minds. I recently reread it, not having dipped into it since high school, and was bowled over by its superabundance of incidents, energy, open-pored passion, and canine devotion. Like his literary hero Thomas Wolfe, whose cathedral detailing and rhetorical swollen glands provided the model for Kerouac's first novel, *The Town and the City* (1950), Kerouac had America mapped in the palm of his hand. (Together, Wolfe and Kerouac helped father

Bob Dylan, who rattles off place-names in his lyrics like a train conductor.) The lifeline in this palm is the Mississippi River, "the great
brown father of waters rolling down from mid-America like the torrent of broken souls." As Kerouac's Sal Paradise caroms like a pin-
ball from one bank of city lights to another ("with the radio on to a
mystery program, and as I looked out the window and saw a sign that
said USE COOPER'S PAINT and I said, 'Okay, I will,' we rolled across the
hoodwink night of the Louisiana plains . . ."), the novel flickers with
snapshots of the poor and neglected in an ongoing montage which
evokes not only Wolfe's night-watchman reveries but also the photographs of Robert Frank. (Kerouac did the foreword for Frank's *The
Americans*, the most evocatively shrouded book of postwar photog-
raphy.) Although *On the Road* was published in 1957, its action takes
place ten years earlier, tinged with a sepia-toned longing for a pre-
TV America which retained vestiges of vagabond individuality. *On
the Road* is a paradise-lost elegy but—here's its secret—a buoyant one,
not some limp flag of commemoration.

The energy is rooted in misfit comedy. Often forgotten today is
what a funny writer Kerouac was. The humor doesn't spout from
dyspeptic one-liners (Burroughs's specialty) or facile absurdism, but
finds release through the sheer collision force of all these human can-
nonballs smacking together. The section in *On the Road* where we're
introduced to Bull Lee, the William Burroughs character, is a comic
lithograph of Tristram Shandy–like eccentricity, from the pet ferret
Lee used to keep in his "well-appointed rooms" to his drug tinkering
("He also experimented in boiling codeine cough syrup down to a
black mash—that didn't work so well") to the following psychological
checklist:

> He had a set of chains in his room that he said he used with his
> psychoanalyst; they were experimenting with narcoanalysis and
> found that Old Bull had seven separate personalities, each grow-
> ing worse and worse on the way down, till finally he was a raving
> idiot and had to be restrained with chains. The top personality
> was an English lord, the bottom an idiot. Halfway he was an old
> Negro who stood in line waiting with everyone else, and said,
> "Some's bastards, some's ain't, that's the score."

Driving fast and fighting sleep, Kerouac's road warriors are trying
to outrace their own nervous breakdowns and demons as they gulp
the scented night air. The novel eventually veers off to Mexico, as all

salvation tours must, because that's where the madonna-whores are, tiny crosses dangling between the tawny bosoms on which our heroes can rest their mangy heads until it's tequila time.

Despite that legendary scroll, *On the Road* wasn't published hot out of the typewriter. The novel took years to gel; draft after draft was rejected by various houses, the standard edition trimmed and massaged into shape by the editor and critic Malcolm Cowley over Kerouac's foot-dragging objections. For years afterward, Kerouac and Ginsberg complained that Cowley's commonsensical Yankee approach took the snap out of the novel's serpentine spirit, taming its pulsating swing for a more straight-ahead story line. Instead, they should have shown some gratitude, for *On the Road* prospers and endures precisely because Cowley found a way to bottle the lightning. It's the one Kerouac book that seems fully assembled and guided. In a letter to John Clellon Holmes, the author of the Beat novel *Go*, Kerouac championed "*wild form*, man, *wild form*"—but without an authorial design or editorial oversight Kerouac's writing tended to taper off into wispy formlessness. Even novels graced with epiphanies of pencil-sketch portraiture (*The Subterraneans*) or nature worship (*The Dharma Bums*) suffer from a noodling-doodling lack of dramatic emphasis. It's like listening to a musician tune up, only words are more than notes and sounds: they signify and convey meaning. Without somewhere useful to go, they lie there orphaned, mere jottings, providing evidence for Truman Capote's famous gibe, "It's not writing, it's typing." For all its hoots and yelps, *On the Road* is undeniably writing.

With the publication of *On the Road*, Kerouac awoke one morning to find he had won the literary lottery. After a rave review by Gilbert Millstein appeared in *The New York Times*, Kerouac's publisher arrived bearing champagne, and the phone began ringing with congratulations. Kerouac, however, wasn't ready for his screen test. Where Burroughs and Ginsberg knew how to joust with the press and were foxy enough to create brand-name personae (Burroughs was doing jeans commercials shortly before he died), Kerouac stumbled into traffic like a tourist, lost in the oncoming lights. His radio and television appearances took mumbling beyond Method acting (he sat and moped), his public readings were amateur hour (he never developed Ginsberg's bardic showmanship), and a famous panel discussion featuring Kingsley Amis, Ashley Montagu, and James Wechsler, among others, reduced him to clown antics. He seemed to regard tabloid ink as if it were his own spilled blood. The fame and all its goodies that most writers chase like an ice-cream truck sent Kerouac literally reeling in the other direction. His drinking intensified, turning Superman into Stuporman, his blackouts a foolhardy way of blotting out the world's now insatiable demands. At the height of the *On the Road* hullabaloo, Kerouac told Jerry Tallmer of *The Village Voice* that he was splitting this crazy scene. "I'm going down to my mother's in Orlando. Always go back to my mother. Always."

A grown man living with Mom, what could be squarer? Who did he think he was, Liberace? (Kerouac's mother was no sweetheart, either—Mémère read her son's mail like a prison snoop, refused to let Ginsberg into her house because he was a drug user and homosexual, and was so nasty that even the unflappable Burroughs considered her a minor form of evil.) Kerouac wasn't kidding, though. He unplugged himself like a neon sign. The drastic U-turn Kerouac made in his life—from gypsy preacher of Beat prophecy ("a White Storefront Church Built Like a Man, on wheels yet," in Seymour Krim's majestic estimation) to stay-at-home hermit—has a pathos and rotting integrity worthy of a Eugene O'Neill play set in a dim interior. One of the reasons Kerouac is such an unresolvable case three decades after his death is that by chucking it all he turned his hunched back not only on fame but on the entire notion of a literary career. Even writers who have shrouded themselves in secrecy (J. D. Salinger) or move among us like the Invisible Man (Thomas Pynchon) have produced a recognizable body of work which they zealously safeguard. Kerouac, however, seemed to tear up the books he had within him into many pigeon scraps. Alcohol may have so hollowed him out that all he could hear were echoes of what he had done before and of those he had left behind. Jack McClintock, a newspaper reporter who visited Kerouac in St. Petersburg in his last few months, speculated in *Esquire:* "It was almost as if Kerouac, in the last years, had burrowed farther and farther back into his personality, back into the dense-packed delights and detritus of a life, and then turned around, and was peering out at the thronged world through the tunnel he made going in. Perhaps being back there clarified his sight in some ways, focused it more clearly on the things he could see. Perhaps it just gave him tunnel vision. I don't know."

After Kerouac died, his body was shipped to Lowell, Massachusetts, for burial. Vivian Gornick covered the funeral in an affecting piece for *The Village Voice*, recording the dignity of Allen Ginsberg and his lover Peter Orlovsky, the generous heft of the townspeople, and the sight of Kerouac in his open casket, waxy and remote, "stripped of all his ravaging joy." Kerouac seemed roadkill from a bygone era when he was put to rest, but over the succeeding years he rose to the stature of Hank Williams and James Dean and other saints of the celestial highway. Ginsberg and Dylan made a pilgrimage to his grave site during the Rolling Thunder tour of 1975, providing one of the few grace notes to the film *Renaldo and Clara.*

In 1988 the city of Lowell erected an elaborate memorial for Kerouac, an event which had the neoconservative commentator Norman Podhoretz shaking his fist at the temerity of officials honoring this hooligan. As a climbing young critic, Podhoretz had written a much-reprinted essay thirty years before called "The Know-Nothing Bohemians," which accused the Beats of being storm troopers in sandals (their marching orders: "Kill the intellectuals who can talk coherently, kill the people who can sit still for five minutes at a time, kill those incomprehensible characters who are capable of getting seriously involved with a woman, a job, a cause"—kill, kill, kill!). So he at least had the virtue of being a consistent crab. To Podhoretz and other cultural declinists, the Beats were nihilists responsible for the hedonistic disarray of the sixties, never mind that Kerouac himself repudiated Abbie Hoffman and his Yippie followers. He once removed an American flag Allen Ginsberg had wrapped around his, Kerouac's, shoulders like a shawl, folding it properly, and explaining, "The flag is not a rag." Which didn't deter Podhoretz from fuming in the *New York Post*, "Dropping out, hitting the road, taking drugs, hopping from bed to bed with partners of either sex or both—all in the name of liberation from the death-dealing embrace of middle-class conventions. . . . This, then, is what the City of Lowell is inescapably honoring in building a monument to Kerouac," those heathens.

What really bothers Kerouac's killjoy detractors is that a memorial for the Beat King is a victory for reckless creativity over critical rigor. In Podhoretz's Manichaean mind, it's reason, coherence, tradition, Judeo-Christian ethics, and monogamous maturity versus risk, itchy impulses, immediacy, Eastern mysticism, and dirty feet on a bare mattress, and guess what?—*his side lost.* O, the inequity of it all, mastering the nuances of modernism only to be shunted aside by this bony army of hairy armpits! Deeper than the Culture War or an Alamo defense of literacy and even more vexing to those suffering from Beat antipathy is the knowledge that replenishing waves of readers love Kerouac—no other word will do—love him despite himself, despite his drunkenness, racist insults, and unreliability (he's the deadbeat dad everyone's decided to forgive). Kerouac is loved and mourned for the loneliness that penalized him most of his life and for the rugged reflection he left in the hard surface of American life. "America is where you're not even allowed to cry for yourself," Kerouac observed in *Visions of Cody,* and he may have been the last American writer without a trace of cynicism or protective guile. (Of those who came after, only Raymond Carver tiptoed around similar heartbreak.) It was a tragedy for him and for American fiction once he was no longer able to articulate the tempests he felt. He withdrew, suffered like a saint, and prematurely aged, yet some part of him stayed rockabilly to the end. "The only time I saw him with his hair combed," Jack McClintock wrote in *Esquire,* "was in his casket."

Vanity Fair, October 1999

Remaking It

New York Days, Willie Morris; *Kafka Was the Rage*, Anatole Broyard

It must be nice getting lionized twice. Maybe, like love, it's even sweeter the second time around. During the sixties, Willie Morris was lauded as the editor of *Harper's*, where he published Norman Mailer, Irving Howe, David Halberstam, Joan Didion, and Bill Moyers, among others. He dazzled New York and New York dazzled him. He became a regular at Elaine's and a popular partygoer, exchanging chitchat with such screen favorites as Lauren Bacall ("Betty, we all called her"), Deborah Kerr, Richard Widmark, and Shirley MacLaine.

Now, more than twenty years later, Morris is being feted again for his memoir *New York Days*, in which he recounts how he published Norman Mailer, Irving Howe, David Halberstam, Joan Didion, and Bill Moyers, among others, became a regular at Elaine's, and exchanged chitchat with such screen favorites as Lauren Bacall, Deborah Kerr, Rich- . . . well, you get the idea. It's déjà vu all over again, a coy recital akin to Comden and Green doing a Broadway show of their old Broadway hits. Morris's former cronies can hardly contain themselves. The back cover of the book features blurbs from Bill Moyers, George Plimpton, and Joseph Heller. On the front page of *The New York Times Book Review*, Elizabeth Hardwick called the book "a star-crossed romance on the boulevard of broken dreams." Given the drinking habits of Morris and company, it's more like the boulevard of broken bottles, but never mind: starry-eyed Willie Morris still is.

Time and memory have not shrunk his sense of wonder. He goes through the entire book agape and agog, the Thomas Wolfe of the three-martini lunch. The editor of *Harper's*! He still can't get over it, or himself, or this unfolding miracle we call life. As he strolls one January day in 1969, he tells himself:

> I am the editor of one of the most respected magazines in the history of America, and the most long-lasting. The best writers will write for us and not for the money. *Harper's* is what this

town calls "hot"; I cannot but remember that *Esquire* citation in '63 of its being "Squaresville." It is the kind of moment that I have come all my life for. We are making a difference in the way the most powerful civilization in the history of the world perceives itself, the sexiest, richest, most self-conscious society ever conceived. I have at my touch the best and the brightest. Is not Halberstam, at this very moment, writing for us on that subject, but with a certain irony? What killer idea will be pursued today? Everyone who matters wants more. Why has Jack Valenti of Hollywood called to have dinner at the "21" Club tonight? What's shaking in D.C.? Whose cage should be rattled? I am on my way to lunch in the Plaza with Seymour Hersh, who has an important story to tell. Or is it Styron, who will describe the Polish girl with the Auschwitz tattoo he knew just after the war in Flatbush? Or Lizzy Hardwick, about going home to Kentucky? Or Vermont Connecticut Royster, editor of *The Wall Street Journal*? Or the precocious tycoon with Macmillan who wants to talk about something? Or Joan Didion fresh in from L.A.?

Whoever his Mystery Date will be, he or she will be brilliant, the conversation will sparkle, the waiters will smile knowingly and Morris will be released into the street shiny new. "These are the New York days, the fabulous and limitless and halcyon days, and I think we will surely be young forever."

A native son and current resident of Mississippi, Morris wrote a book a couple of decades ago called *North Toward Home*, which touched on the experience of being editor of *Harper's*, but spoke more of the isolation, the anxiety and the culture shock of being a soft-spoken Southerner in a city of combat-ready sophisticates moving at twice his speed. Nothing had prepared him for the verbal fisticuffs of even casual conversations. The book had a sleepy subduedness, as if it had been written between naps, or during. Although I haven't opened the book in twenty years or so, I can still recall his description of a drive up the New Jersey turnpike, where even the sunrise (or was it the sunset?) looked venereal. Everything that was personally observed and proportionate in *North Toward Home* is pumped full of hype and portent in *New York Days*. Morris writes as if he were intoning into a microphone, the Manhattan skyline at his back. "The people. The places. The neighborhoods. Anything could happen in the city, bizarre juxtapositions, prodigal confrontations."

Of course, the action wasn't all in New York. The sixties were a traveling circus. Whether it was Hunter S. Thompson stomping with the Hell's Angels, Tom Wolfe hanging with car buffs and surf bums, John Sack training with the troops, Truman Capote offering the anatomy of murder or Joan Didion taking the pulse of the L.A. freeway, the best writings during and about the decade are those in which the writer was in the weird thick of it, taking in the madhouse scene as if his or her head had multiple lenses. Morris had a more bird's-eye view of the decade:

> From the summit of the cultural capital and in my extensive travels as a writer and editor I bore witness to a broader America sundered with its internecine tensions and angers and extremes, its enveloping conflicts, and I had a consuming ache and fear for my country then, for its dire tempers and unraveling excesses, and for the incredible prodigal clashing voices of a crazy mass democracy, and for "the fragility of the membranes of civilization," as Arthur Schlesinger, Jr. wrote then, "stretched so thin over a nation so disparate in its composition, so tense in its interior relationships, so cunningly enmeshed in underground fears and antagonisms."

That's the recipe for *New York Days:* reheated punditry, smothered with quotation. Given Annie Gottlieb's *Do You Believe in Magic?*, Morris Dickstein's *Gates of Eden*, the various books on Woodstock and the rest, yet another helicopter tour of the sixties yields well-chewed terrain. Morris has nothing original or revisionist to say about the decade:

> As we approach the fin de siècle, I recall Professor Schlesinger's Hegelian tides in our history, the coming and going and coming again in cycles of retrenchment and vitality. Is this protean, unpredictable, malleable, bifurcated and sometimes frightening nation slowly approaching another such crossroads? I look forward to knowing.

In the meantime, I think I'll have me some of that lemonade.

The vulgar truth is that the sole selling point of a book like this has to be its gossip. As Morris waxes Proustian about his days at Oxford ("Yet, slowly, the spell of Oxford grew, until one was suffused with it, with its majesty and largesse"), or plays pop sociologist ("Rock and roll as a presage of the 1960s dissidence had always fascinated me"), you find yourself muttering: yeah, yeah, get to the good stuff. The negative surprise of the book, aside from its gaseous prose, is how little good stuff there is. As Louis Menand noted in *The New Yorker*, Morris's account of how he became editor of *Harper's* doesn't jibe with his earlier tale in *North Toward Home*. The office lore, such as how *Harper's* writers would bug David Halberstam by sending him crank letters, was more amusingly told in Larry L. King's *None But a Blockhead*. The book's big set piece—Morris arriving at a posh party for Senator McGovern with dog doo stuck to his shoe ("the excrement, which possessed the creamy consistency, say, of overcooked mashed potatoes, began squishing in my shoe, a soft but not negligent whish")—becomes an urban folktale of almost room-clearing whimsy. Even the chapter on the dissolution of his marriage, which finds him spying on his wife's psychiatrist and promises some personal revelation, trails off into platitude. "Finally, I have learned how difficult love is, how hard to achieve and sustain, no matter who the person or how felicitous the circumstance."

Wilfrid Sheed accused Norman Podhoretz of padding the index to *Making It* with the names of his famous friends. When it comes to padding, Podhoretz (a schmucky minor character in *New York Days*) is a piker compared to Morris, whose paragraphs sometimes read like invitation lists. He namedrops about those he saw at Elaine's. "Woody Allen, producer, director, writer, latter poet of the city, began to frequent Elaine's, accompanied by one or another of the movie actresses, Mia Farrow or Diane Keaton or Meryl Streep. . . ." He namedrops about those he didn't see at Elaine's. "In my time in the city I never once saw Eudora Welty in Elaine's, or Walker Percy or Shelby Foote, to mention a few Southerners, or Saul Bellow or Bernard Malamud or Isaac Bashevis Singer, of urban dwellers. . . ." He namedrops about those who might have enjoyed Elaine's, had they not been dead. "From what I know of them, the young Hemingway would have come to the place if it had existed then when he was out of sorts in the town, and Fitzgerald, and Steinbeck, and for that matter Dreiser and St. Vincent Millay." When Morris takes reluctant leave of Manhattan—his harsh, glittery mistress—he finds that Long Island, too, offers a living pantheon:

> Only later, beyond the purview of this memoir, would I come to
> know and spend time with some of the finest writers who would
> choose out of love for this land to live here: Peter Matthiessen, Joseph Heller, Jean Stafford, Shana Alexander, Kurt Von-

negut, Jr., Wilfrid Sheed, Betty Friedan, Budd Schulberg, John Knowles, Craig Claiborne.

Craig Claiborne!

The real story of *New York Days*, the story that Willie Morris seems too mesmerized to tell, is how the sixties turned even serious people into starfuckers. The one person in the book who refuses to be wowed is Robert Lowell, who, when asked by Morris what it feels like being on the cover of *Time*, shrugs and replies: "It doesn't feel [like] anything, really. It doesn't amount to anything either." It's a lesson lost on Morris, who keeps chugging through *New York Days* as if being on magazine covers, mentioned in articles, and invited to the right parties amounts to everything. It's as if he fears that if he doesn't flatter his friends and if they don't flatter him, the world will come to a dead stop, and he'll be left standing alone in the middle of the room, spotlighted as a Southern boy who doesn't belong.

Once he's ousted as editor of *Harper's* (corporate shortsightedness and falling circulation aggravated by his refusal to include the owners in his clique), his worst fears are realized. Instead of taking another job, he leaves New York for Long Island's South Shore, where he ponders away the winter. "Why would the hurt and anger and guilt, the tangible and continual sense of loss, last so long, so far into my adulthood? Someday I would know." But that "someday" doesn't occur in *New York Days*. He still seems mystified by his oversized sense of failure. He eventually winds his way back down to Mississippi, where he writes a book about the football sensation Marcus Dupree and plants his prose in what he thinks is Faulkner soil. It smells and sounds like the same old Southern bull.

None of this diminishes what Morris accomplished at *Harper's*. Publishing Seymour Hersh on My Lai, Jeremy Larner on Eugene McCarthy, Joe McGinniss on the selling of the president, not to mention springing Norman Mailer on the Pentagon, the 1968 conventions, and feminism (*The Prisoner of Sex* appeared complete in the pages of *Harper's*, the longest single magazine article since John Hersey's "Hiroshima"), displayed a nerve, an instinct, and a capacity for encouragement rare among editors. Each issue was proof that writers will settle for less money, if less money means more freedom and space.

But I'm sure that Morris himself would admit that the triumphs of *Harper's* weren't isolated flourishes. Flipping through magazines then was like spinning the AM radio dial and hearing a succession of hit singles. *Esquire* was in its heyday under Harold Hayes. *The Vil-*

lage Voice ran free under Dan Wolf. *The New Yorker* offered powerful coverage and commentary on Vietnam. *Rolling Stone, Ramparts, Evergreen Review,* and the underground rags offered the latest fleabites of hippie radicalism. From Theodore Solatoroff's literary *New American Review* to I. F. Stone's scrappy newsletter (the true forerunner to desktop publishing), the written word was weapon, omen, summons, catcall, put-on. Every hotshot writer seemed hooked up to his own amplifier. Now that the noise has died, it isn't evident how much of this work will endure.

Indeed, the argument has been made by Joseph Epstein and others that the fifties, long belittled for their blandness and conformity, were actually a far more incubative period for lasting writing than the gloryhound sixties. Where the sixties placed a premium on public posture, the fifties still retain the scuff marks of offstage activity. It was a time when writers lived like poor students. One thinks of Saul Bellow's description of Isaac Rosenfeld's kitchen, the cockroaches leaping from the toaster with the slices of bread. The intellectual center of bohemia was Greenwich Village. (The creative center was wherever Jack Kerouac happened to be.)

Its neighborhood bars now as varnished in legend as the Paris cafés that Hemingway frequented, the Village of the fifties has been fictionally satirized by Dawn Powell and Wallace Markfield, replayed like a nostalgic newsreel in Dan Wakefield's *New York in the '50s,* reduced to a cigarette flicker in Herbert Gold's *Bohemia: Where Art, Angst, Love & Strong Coffee Meet,* restaged like a Strindberg play in Leonard Michaels's *Sylvia.* It's a period easy to caricature. (Goatees! Spade chicks! Orgone energy!) Yet there was a balled-up mental hunger beneath all the sponging and posing.

Where the star bylines at Elaine's honked their horns all night long about politics and publishing deals, the Village intellectuals were browbeaten by the feverish demands of modernism. As Seymour Krim, a veteran of the scene, wrote:

> What had happened was that each outstanding single achievement of the recent past—by a D. H. Lawrence, Picasso, Stravinsky, Gerard Manley Hopkins, Melville—was linked with the other to create a vocabulary of modernity; familiarity with great work was as casually expected of a person as familiarity with the daily paper; . . . this stitching-together of extraordinary achievement provided the background for all conversation, friendship, feuds, affairs. . . .

Parties became verbal jam sessions. Woe to him or her who couldn't keep pace. "The stuttering crudenik who couldn't come on in public and didn't understand or like Kafka . . . would have been slaughtered if he stuck his head in a jumping living room where my teachers and I mapped and remapped the world by the second."

The very title of Anatole Broyard's posthumous memoir, *Kafka Was the Rage*, supports Krim's claim. Back from World War II, during which he and a large crew scraped clay-hard human dung off the dock at Yokohama, Broyard left his family in Brooklyn and moved to Greenwich Village, where he opened a secondhand bookstore:

> I realize that people still read books now and some people actually love them, but in 1946 in the Village our feelings about books—I'm talking about my friends and myself—went beyond love. It was as if we didn't know where we ended and books began. Books were our weather, our environment, our clothing. We didn't simply read books, we became them.

Delmore Schwartz, for instance. "Like many other New York writers and intellectuals of his generation, Delmore seemed to me to have read himself right out of American culture. He was a citizen only of literature. His Greenwich Village was part Dostoyevski's Saint Petersburg and part Kafka's Amerika." Schwartz even had a European walk, zigzagging down the street like Dr. Caligari. The critic Richard Gilman was another creature of osmosis:

> In his reading, for example, he was a serial monogamist. He'd fall in love with a particular author and remain faithful to him alone, reading everything by and about him. He would become that author, talk like him, think like him, dress like him if possible. He took on his politics, his causes, his eccentricities. At one point in his D. H. Lawrence phase—this was after his Yeats and Auden phases—Dick actually went to Mexico and tried to find Lawrence's footprints in the dust.

Unlike Schwartz or Gilman or Krim's jazzy crowd, Broyard wasn't a Jewish superbrain pitting himself against the Modern Library giants. He didn't carry his head on a pedestal. Handsome, copper-skinned, Catholic by religion, hedonist by nature, an exotic import from the French Quarter of New Orleans, Broyard tested ideas on his skin. Pleasure was the only truth you could trust. His memoir rings directly from Broyard's pleasure centers, free of bloat, abstraction, and second-guessing. It has the unpretentious ease of John Glassco's classic *Memoirs of Montparnasse.*

Where Willie Morris has to paint the side of a barn to make a point, Anatole Broyard can recapture in a single burst the excitement of Meyer Schapiro lecturing on Picasso ("When he said that with *Le Demoiselles d'Avignon* Picasso had fractured the picture plane, I could hear it crack") or the pent-up libido of the postwar period: "When a girl took off her underpants in 1947, she was more naked than any woman before her had ever been." Her nakedness was an event, because the entire culture said "No." Women were taught to wait. "One of the things we've lost is the terrific coaxing that used to go on between men and women, the man pleading with the girl to sleep with him and the girl pleading with him to be patient."

Broyard had a reputation for being quite a coaxer. Introducing a story of his in the anthology *The Beats*, Krim claimed that Broyard had "fascinated enough New York chicks to start a war between himself and the rest of Mankind." But every man meets his match. Leonard Michaels had his manhood twisted into a pretzel by his wife Sylvia, a mad downtown version of *la belle dame sans merci.* Broyard's femme fatale is the earthy, ethereal Sheri Donatti, a painter who invites Broyard to share her walk-up apartment in the Village, complete with bathtub in the kitchen. Ample below the waist, slender above, her figure denoted a divided self. "Her waist was so small, it cut her in two, like a split personality, or two schools of thought."

Sheri was a disciple of Anaïs Nin, the novelist and diarist who distilled art into a delicate perfume that left strong men dizzy. When Broyard is presented to Nin, he receives her hypnotic rays. "I could feel her projecting an image of herself, one that was part French, part flamenco, part ineffable. When she said, 'You are Anatole,' I immediately became Anatole in a way I hadn't been before." But there's something cornball about Nin's high-priestess act and her head-scratching pronouncements. Sheri, however, was literally the latest craze, embodying "all the new trends in art, sex and psychosis." So enslaved is Broyard by Sheri's rampant body and unreachable mind that when she complains of a heart condition, he decides to spare her any undue exertion. "From then on, whenever we went anywhere, whenever we came back to the apartment, I carried her up the stairs. I delivered her, conveyed her. I became her porter as well as her lover."

At first he doesn't mind ("I liked the idea that she was portable"),

though he does gets winded toting her to parties. He eventually realizes that there's nothing wrong with her heart. Her wish to be carried
is a comic form of hysteria expressing a deeper depression. One night
he awakens to find her naked in the kitchen with her head resting on
a towel on top of the stove. All the gas jets are going. He shuts off the
gas in time to save her life, but it's a deathblow to her hold on him. He
finds another apartment, other women, a flock of shadows.

He insists that his interest was more than physical. "Although their
bodies were often beautiful to me and their personalities as appealing as our inhibitions allowed them to be, it was ultimately with girls'
souls that I grappled. No matter what we said or did, I couldn't get
away from their souls." The book ends with Broyard walking down
the street with Milton Klonsky, perhaps the most brilliant of Village
bookworms (a poet, local historian and Blake scholar), when he spots
an attractively packaged soul.

> She must have seen the admiration in my face, because she
> smiled, a little conspiratorial smile. I broke off in the middle of a
> sentence and ran after her, which enraged Milton. I could never
> make him understand that, at the moment when she smiled, I
> saw her as the incarnation of meaning.

Such crooning lures us away from the central mystery of Broyard's
career. He's filtering his past through a silk stocking. While Broyard
may have made a name for himself downtown as the last of the incur-
able romantics, a moist sensualist amidst all the broomstick intellectuals, he had a larger public reputation as a writer of (oh, dread
word) promise. In the fifties he published stories, including a couple
of unforgettable ones about his father, that impressed readers and fellow writers alike. When Norman Mailer torched his contemporaries
in *Advertisements for Myself,* he reserved a favorable nod for Broyard,
saying he would buy a novel by him the day it appeared. But no novel
ever did appear. Neither did a collection of short stories. Instead he
taught at the New School, where he had a racy reputation for running
around with his students, and became a book reviewer at *The New
York Times,* collecting his articles under the throbbing title *Aroused by
Books.* (A title that did a disservice to the book, which is full of light,
biting perceptions.)

An inveterate sweet-talker, Broyard was tone-deaf to feminism,
incapable of understanding that women might find courtly phrases

a cover for the same old tired come-on. His charm did carry specks of condescension. His reasoning with women had a smooth layer of coaxing. More militant women refused to play coy. I once saw Germaine Greer, grouchily leonine, behead him with a single bite on *The David Susskind Show*. He tried to call a truce with his collection *Men, Women and Other Anticlimaxes*, but the static between the sexes was too tense for his worldly tone. His last book was a punchy but lyrical account of his cancer called *Intoxicated by My Illness*, where he cast off pride and shame and intellectual armor. He had no problem with illness as metaphor. "Perhaps only metaphor can express the bafflement, the panic combined with beatitude, of the threatened person. Surely Ms. Sontag wouldn't wish to condemn the sick to Hemingway sentences." *Intoxicated by My Illness* is a moving farewell, a suitable monument to Broyard's career. Yet the fact remains that he never became the fiction writer that he might have been, fit company for Vidal, Bellow, Mailer.

Almost nothing of his thoughts and his feelings about his writing or unfulfilled hopes appears in *Kafka Was the Rage*. It's as if he thought he would snap the spell if he alluded to anything so mundane as work. But if he harbored any disappointments, he wasn't dour about it. Unlike Delmore Schwartz, he didn't build a scarecrow out of failure (and unlike Morris, he wasn't tempted to write and rewrite testimonials to his own fleeting success). Or perhaps Broyard was mature enough about his limitations and modest achievements not to haunt himself over what might have been. The one time I met him, he struck me as that rare bird among writers, a happy realist. His eyes were clear panes. In *Intoxicated by My Illness*, he pays homage to a friend named Paul Breslow who spent the last few months of his life trying to write a novel. Although Breslow had done everything— published books, collected art from the African bush—he convinced himself that his life would be a failure if he didn't finish his novel. "Though he covered quite a few pages with his slackening fingers," writes Broyard, "he never finished his novel, never reached that final satisfaction. He was anything but a failure, though, because the style is the man and literature isn't everything."

The New Republic, November 15, 1993

The Truman Show

Truman Capote, George Plimpton

Truman Capote was the most extraordinary literary exhibit of the talk-show era. Bizarre as he looked and sounded (his high-pitched voice could scrape paint), he was perfect for TV. In a medium which prizes close-ups, Capote was all head, and what a head, a magic lantern lit with mischief. Its bulging size and lolling movement, offset by his baby-blond hair and the lizard flick of his tongue, fixated the camera and filled the screen. He was more than telegenic. A debauched angel with a bourbon drawl, the likes of which had seldom been spotted outside of Tennessee Williams's swamp mists, Capote had a knack for the swift kill of the sound bite. On David Susskind's *Open End* show, he dismissed Jack Kerouac's work with the still-quoted remark "[It] isn't writing at all—it's typing." Years later, he rollicked Johnny Carson's audience by claiming that the author of *Valley of the Dolls*, Jacqueline Susann (with whom he was feuding), resembled "a truckdriver in drag"—a wisecrack that sent Susann and her husband reeling to their lawyer, Louis Nizer. As Capote grew older, his mind aslosh with alcohol and drugs, he lost pinpoint control of his poison darts. In one of his late-seventies TV appearances on New York's *Stanley Siegel Show*, he affected a fey Rip Torn persona ("I'll tell you something about fags, especially southern fags. We is mean. A southern fag is meaner than the meanest rattler you ever met . . .") and laced into his former friend Lee Radziwill, his face puffy, his diction gummy, his words seeming to wander off on their own. The TV screen, which had been his vanity mirror, turned into a CAT scan of a mind in public ruin.

These three TV appearances correspond to the three stages of Capote's career, as he himself conceived it. Act I was the golden-cherub period of *Other Voices, Other Rooms*, published in 1948 (the year of such heavy clompers as Norman Mailer's *The Naked and the Dead* and Irwin Shaw's *The Young Lions*), culminating in the critical and popular success of *Breakfast at Tiffany's* a decade later; Act II was the arduous climb and *excelsior* cry of *In Cold Blood*, which brought him wealth, magnified fame, and critical acclaim; Act III, the mandarin phase, was pledged to *Answered Prayers*, his magnum opus about the emaciated courtesans of the ruling class that would be his Proustian feast for posterity. As his performance with Stanley Siegel suggests, Act III proved to be a bitter anticlimax; instead of a grand finale, the curtain came crashing down on Capote's head. Not only didn't he complete *Answered Prayers* (boogying the night away at Studio 54 may have unfastened the girdle of his Flaubertian resolve), but the parts that were published cost him the friendship of the Fine Bone Structure socialites Capote called his "swans"—most prominently, Nancy "Slim" Keith and Barbara "Babe" Paley. He was ostracized and traumatized. His last years were a sad muddle of blackouts and ambulance rides.

This doesn't dampen interest in Capote. If anything, the opposite. For many, the fizzle of *Answered Prayers* and his personal tailspin offer a spectacle more engrossing than the perfect arc of a distinguished life. A dignified exit may be desirable in principle, but if you can have your subject bumming around in his bathrobe in public, then you've got yourself a Cautionary Tale. There but for the grace of God and an empty liquor cabinet go I. Capote's star-crossed life, chronicled in a superb biography by Gerald Clarke published in 1988, is being examined under the celebrity spotlight again this month in George Plimpton's *Truman Capote* (Nan A. Talese/Doubleday).

I know what is being said about me and you can take my side or theirs, that's your own business.
          —The opening sentence of Capote's first published story, "My Side of the Matter," *Story* magazine, 1945

Like *Edie*, the biography of Edie Sedgwick that Plimpton edited with Jean Stein, *Truman Capote* is an oral documentary which consists of quotes from interviews edited into snack-size sound bites: Memory McNuggets. What's eerie is how many of these remembrances issue from the ether. Diana Vreeland, Slim Keith, Leo Lerman, Herb Caen, Diana Trilling, Kathleen Tynan, Irving "Swifty" Lazar, the team of Arthur Gold and Robert Fizdale—all have died since the interviews were conducted. With its ghostly chorus, the book is both a séance and a memorial service—a memorial service for Capote himself and a requiem for the pre-hippie postwar era, before hedonism hardened into decadence, when society still had a capital *S* but had begun to loosen its pearls and swing. Like *Breakfast at Tiffany's* Holly Golightly, Capote's most enduring creation, Capote was a starry-eyed opportunist, but unlike her he didn't drift up, down, and sideways like a stray boa feather. His social ascent, which carried him from the swimming holes of his native Alabama to luxury yachts anchored in the Mediterranean Sea, was one of the great solo guerrilla operations of the century.

Act I

Born in 1924, Capote grew up in a small town in Alabama, next door to Harper Lee, who would later write *To Kill a Mockingbird*, basing one of its characters on him. Divided natures are nothing new to artists (who, more than most people, are both subject and object, civilian and spy), but Capote was figuratively and physically split in the middle. As the writer John Malcolm Brinnin recounts in Plimpton's book, hereafter known as *T.C.*, "Willowy and delicate above the waist, he was, below, as strong and chunky as a Shetland pony." A centaur with a Napoleon complex, Capote combined the dreamy hypersensitivity of a poet with the push and stamina of a Balzacian upstart from the provinces. Forced to fend for himself after his mother, Nina, left him behind to glam it up in New York (his biological father wasn't really in the picture), Capote "never had a center in his life," according to one of his aunts, and the archivist Andreas Brown says that "Truman's whole life was haunted by abandonment." This sense of isolation made him adaptable, fanciful (he was always thinking up stories), and as acutely observant as only those who take nothing for granted can be, but it also robbed him of any inner anchor. He would complain later of lifelong "free-floating anxiety"—what Holly Golightly called "the mean reds."

Being the center of attention at least gave him a fixed position. When Capote was in the second grade, he learned that he would be leaving Alabama to live up North with his mother. "He said he wanted to throw a party so grand that everybody would remember him," Jennings Faulk Carter, a cousin, recalls. He decided to host a Halloween costume party, and created elaborate games for the other children to play. The party was nearly stampeded by a visit from the Ku Klux Klan, who had heard tell that there might be Negroes present and set upon one scared (white) boy dressed as a robot, whose cardboard legs prevented him from fleeing. After Harper Lee's father and other powerful townsfolk gave the sheeted rednecks the big stare, the Klansmen slunk off to their cars. With its giddy buildup and unexpected drama, this going-away party was the forerunner to the masked Black and White Ball Capote would host for Kay Graham in 1966, a night of operatic intrigue which was the Woodstock of the tuxedo brigade. (Don DeLillo devotes a chapter to its mythos in *Underworld*.)

While still in his teens, Capote was hired as a copyboy at *The New Yorker*. The editor, Harold Ross, looked askance at his flouncing down the corridors "like a little ballerina," in the words of one spectator. The cape Capote wore in the office also probably added an inch or two to Ross's porcupine hair. Copyboys and girls come and go at *The New Yorker*, they flicker like fireflies, so it was a shock to some of the old gray mares at the magazine when Capote's debut novel, *Other Voices, Other Rooms*, was published and they realized that this pop-pet had such confident prose in him. A precocious marvel when it appeared, *Other Voices, Other Rooms* has been severely marked down in recent decades (Cynthia Ozick took a mallet to the novel in her collection *Art and Ardor*, pounding it as paste jewelry), part of a general devaluation of the whole school of Southern Gothic, whose carnival-sideshow grotesqueries seem rather faded and clown-forlorn now. The stories in *A Tree of Night* (1949) and the novel *The Grass Harp* (1951) were likewise gaudy and impressionistic. If Capote had continued manufacturing pathos and plastic honeysuckle, he might have occupied the same small but durable niche today that Carson McCullers (*The Heart Is a Lonely Hunter*) does. His book of travel essays, *Local Color* (1950), an attempt to widen his compass, was a series of exquisite watercolors in prose—the descriptions so preciously sweet, he seemed to be writing with a peppermint stick.

Breakfast at Tiffany's was Capote's Houdini escape into open air. Originally set to be published in *Harper's Bazaar* until an officious dolt in the Hearst hierarchy interfered (it could be said of him what was said of the editor who rejected Poe's "The Raven": Congratulations; you goofed), the novella, although set in the forties, conveys the champagne fizz and sparkle of fashion magazines in the fifties, the infusion of frisky new energy into old money. It's all surface, but the surface dances. A call girl and gold digger, Holly Golightly tears through the lives of those around her like a small duster, her flighty narcissism making her as hard to lasso as the most enigmatic European beauty emoting for eternity. *Breakfast at Tiffany's* captures that period in everyone's life in the city when new acquaintances offer fresh avenues to experience, and even bad experiences feel like initiation rites. Critics drew parallels between Holly Golightly and Christopher Isherwood's Sally Bowles, but the desperate yearning enveloped in Holly's wheedling charm expressed Capote's own desire to be admitted into the VIP room. The writing is eager and limber, drained of southern (mil)dew, offering the prospect that Capote might become the *petit maître* of cosmopolitan tales, a Maupassant of the cocktail hour. It was not to be. He had a masterpiece to hammer.

Act II

On November 15, 1959, a couple of lowlifes named Dick Hickock and Perry Smith descended on the Kansas farmhouse of Herbert Clutter and his family. The two jailbirds had been tipped in prison that there was a large stash to be taken from the farm, but robbery turned out to be incidental. They slaughtered the Clutter family, leaving blood and hair on the walls, escaping with a measly forty or fifty dollars. On assignment for *The New Yorker,* Capote went to Kansas to investigate the case (which at that point was still unsolved), accompanied by Harper Lee. *In Cold Blood* would take six years to research and write, its publication delayed not only by the reporting involved but by the need for dramatic resolution. Capote befriended Hickock and Smith (some say fell in homoerotic love with Smith), but friendship be damned—for the good of the book, for the sake of justice and symmetry, they'd have to die. The composer Ned Rorem recounts that in 1963 Capote confided that his book "can't be published until they're executed, so I can hardly wait." Two years later, he was still pacing. Kathleen Tynan, the wife and biographer of the critic Kenneth Tynan, says, "In the spring of '65 Ken met Truman, I think, at a Jean Stein party. The decision had just been made that the guys would be hanged and Truman, according to Ken, hopped up and down with glee, clapping his hands, saying, 'I'm beside myself! Beside myself! Beside myself with joy!'" When he witnessed the actual executions, Capote went wobbly and wept, and his description of the executions in the book has a penitential dolor. But his original jig can't be ignored. Critics and pundits interpreted the book, and the movie made from it by Richard Brooks, as a statement against capital punishment—sheer piety.

In Cold Blood is self-consciously classical in its structure and presentation. It has a churchly sense of its own high aspirations. Capote wanted to prove that he could be the interpreter of the invisible eye of God, that he could divest himself of literary plumage and delve into evil and death. The Clutters—mom, pop, son, daughter—are ready-made symbols: the model American family, America in microcosm, their murders a blow to the heartland and a desecration of the American Dream. Such elaborate foreplay went into the promotion of *In Cold Blood* (Capote was a crowd teaser as well as a crowd pleaser) that the book was heralded years before it was even finished. When *In Cold Blood* was serialized in *The New Yorker*, it was the closest thing the publishing world had seen to Beatlemania. The four issues broke the magazine's newsstand-sales record. The reviewers went hoarse with hyperbole. "He now broods with the austerity of a Greek or an Elizabethan," proclaimed Conrad Knickerbocker in *The New York Times Book Review*, though he didn't specify which Greek or Elizabethan. A notable dissent was Stanley Kauffmann's review in *The New Republic*, which deplored the compressed goo of Capote's Reddi-wip prose and contended that for all the book's heavyweight flexing it was psychologically slight and "residually shallow." It's a complaint echoed in *T.C.* by Norman Mailer. "I was unsatisfied when I read it. I thought, 'Oh, there we are again, that goddamn *New Yorker*, always ready to put a headlock on everything.'" But Kauffmann's and Mailer's astute gripes place them in the minority camp. Most readers, then and now, maintain an almost religious attachment to Capote's text.

The tumultuous success of *In Cold Blood* was the making and breaking of Capote. Some say that the shock of witnessing the executions left an existential hollow in his soul, others that all the fame and glory expanded an already swelled head. There's little doubt that certain tendencies in his character became more pronounced. His lying, for example. Like many writers, Capote had always been an embellisher, trying out things for effect; now his lies took on a brazen grandiosity. He claimed that everybody, male and female alike, found him irresistible. Albert Camus, Errol Flynn, Greta Garbo—all succumbed to his honeyed tongue. His friend Leonora Hornblow (now, there's a name) recalls, "He said he'd seduced Norman Mailer. My husband got up and went out of the room. . . . Norman Mailer? I wouldn't believe that if I saw it on this carpet!" Me neither, but it makes for a vivid picture. Capote devotee Joanne Carson (one of Johnny Carson's ex-wives) claims that Truman's lies were harmless fantasies—"In Truman's mind, he doesn't lie, he makes things the way they *should* have been"—but Gore Vidal takes a sterner, Montaignesque line, believing that Capote's lying was hostile and intended to harm others.

Accompanying the lying was an inflammation of snobbery. Capote, schooled in prissiness under Cecil Beaton, had come too far to consort with nonentities. The Black and White Ball was a lavish exercise in pomp and exclusivity, the delight being in deciding who made the cut. Leo Lerman: "One of the things he adored saying was 'Well, maybe you'll be invited and maybe you won't.'" One of the *Rashomon* moments in *T.C.* comes from the conflicting testimonies of the glittering guests, some of whom thought the party never got off the ground and others who seemed to have spent the night blissfully levitating. Some outsiders (like firebrand Pete Hamill) thought it was in poor taste to conduct such opulent revels during the Vietnam War—it smacked of Marie Antoinette. The furor only heightened Capote's status as the little potentate of the ladies who lunch, making him "the most lionized writer since Voltaire, socially" (so sayeth the jewelry designer Kenneth Jay Lane). But at what cost to the quality of his brain? In his sixties diary, Edmund Wilson reports on a party starring Jacqueline Kennedy and Tennessee Williams at which "Truman Capote kissed all the ladies mushily with an 'Mm-mm-mm, Sarah,' etc." Multiply that a few thousand times and you're talking major sappiness. Babe Paley and Slim Keith may have been charm personified, but many of the rich twits he sought to amuse must have been studies in taxidermy. One of the comedies in both the Clarke and Plimpton books is the spectacle of Capote staying as a guest on his friends' yachts and being browbeaten to see historic ruins ("some big old bunch of fucking rocks," he complained). Culture bored him blind. He wasn't interested in the great works of the past but in the daisy chain of infidelities that made up the secret annals of society.

Act III

Answered Prayers was intended to be the ark that would survive Capote's lifetime and be his canonical legacy. For all his worldly success, he lacked full literary-establishment embrace. Incredible as it seems, *In Cold Blood* won neither the National Book Award nor the Pulitzer Prize. Both honors would go to Norman Mailer years later for *The Armies of the Night*, which infuriated Capote ("Norman Mailer, who told me that what I was doing with *In Cold Blood* was stupid and who then sits down and does a complete ripoff"), who grumbled about a "Jewish mafia" that had it in for him. *Answered Prayers*, its title taken from a possibly misattributed quotation from Saint Teresa of Avila ("More tears are shed over answered prayers than unanswered ones"), would be his masterpiece and silencer. It would have the sanctity of art, the dazzle of showmanship, the savage bite of an inside scoop. Only problem was, Capote was frozen at the console. Having compiled notes and spoken of the book since 1958, he conjured such a dense, shimmering mirage in his mind that the actual writing of the book seemed inadequate, like straining the Sahara through an hour-glass. Deadlines to deliver the book came and went. Finally, in the mid-seventies, he began to peddle portions of the unfinished novel to *Esquire*—a strategic gamble, since an adverse reaction can cripple a writer's morale.

The first glimpse, "Mojave," went over well. Then Capote gave *Esquire* "La Côte Basque, 1965," which would prove the blunder of his life. The chapter is a suite for voices, a cutthroat string quartet, narrated by Capote's protagonist P. B. Jones, a writer–masseur–male prostitute (busy, busy, busy), but dominated by his lunch date, Lady Ina Coolbirth, a coarse version of Slim Keith, with Carol Matthau and Gloria Vanderbilt eavesdropping at a nearby table and providing bitchy counterpoint. The dialogue about face-lifts and fat legs is serrated and overrehearsed, Capote's society swans sounding more like vultures picking over a carcass—"Shit served up on a gold dish," in the words of the art historian John Richardson. The set pieces within this set piece are two long anecdotes by Ina, the first involving the shotgun killing of her husband by Ann Hopkins (a thinly disguised Ann Woodward), an alleged murder that was ruled accidental; the second recounting an adulterous episode in which a powerful businessman beds a governor's wife, a "porco" with the mouth of "a dead and rotting whale," who "punishe[s] him for his Jewish presumption" by leaving his sheets sopping in menstrual blood. Unable to summon assistance, he spends frantic, sweat-drenched hours trying to scrub the blood from the sheets before his wife arrives home. Forget the misogyny that informs all of the unfinished *Answered Prayers*—that women are vulgar messes. The shock of recognition that rocked the Capote circle was that the cheating scrubber was clearly based on CBS boss William Paley, and the unsuspecting wife on Capote's longtime friend Babe Paley. He put filth into the mouth of one friend to slime the husband of another. As an act of betrayal, that counts as a twofer.

Speculation was that "La Côte Basque" was Capote's revenge for being treated as a court jester by his jet-set friends. However, court jester was a role Capote sought, not one he had clamped upon him; he prided himself on being able to "sing for his supper." And Capote didn't seem to realize he was playing with dynamite until he blew off his hands. When it was first broached with him that his friends might take offense, he said, "Nah, they're too dumb." Days before the issue hit the newsstand, Ann Woodward committed suicide, indicating that the import of the story wasn't lost on her. After Liz Smith did a cover article for *New York* magazine on the brouhaha, providing a scorecard to all the players, a caught-off-guard Capote tried desperate double-track diplomacy. Publicly, he not only defended the sacred right—nay, duty—of a writer to rat out those near and dear to him, but promised even juicier carvings to come. (A subsequent excerpt in *Esquire* featured Capote on the cover, fingering what looked like a stiletto.) Privately, he funked. *All my rich, idle friends have deserted me!* Too old and obvious to make new rich, idle friends, he tried to patch things up with the former ones. He had his boyfriend, John O'Shea, phone Slim Keith as he listened on the extension. He wrote letters to Babe Paley. He professed his innocence to those who could serve as intermediaries. Running into Leonora Hornblow, he asked, "Did you really think it was Babe? Did you really think it was Slim?" She replied, "Truman, come on," and quoted the line from *Born Yesterday*, "Never crap a crapper." He had grace enough to laugh.

During this crisis period, Capote said to Diana Vreeland, "Oh, honey! It's Proust! It's beautiful!" It was a line of defense seized by others at the time, that all literature is gossip, and didn't Proust leech off and tattle on his aristocratic coterie? Yet no sane person reads *Remembrance of Things Past* for tawdry tidbits on long-dead duchesses; its trance power derives from the opium jag of its reveries and perceptions. Gossip can be the germ for fiction, the initial trigger, but gossip shorn of any other purpose is belittling and petty. It reduces the complexities of character and motive into gotcha moments of shame and hypocrisy. In an essay on gossip that appeared in *Clinical Studies: International Journal of Psychoanalysis*, Sergio C. Staude observes that gossip serves a dual function—to spread a secret and to safeguard it by enlisting the listener as an accomplice. "[Gossip] will reveal something, but, following the rule of furtive dissemination, will prevent it from reaching the public. When it does, we are in another domain: that of news, of information, of the exhibitionist boast, that of treason or outrage." Cries of treason and outrage buffeted Capote, and as subsequent installments of *Answered Prayers* emerged, it became evident that he had no ulterior design to justify the gossip as social criticism or artistic license. He reported gossip without reimagining the participants. "Kate McCloud" featured cameo appearances by Tallulah Bankhead and Dorothy Parker as drunken bags; "Unspoiled Monsters" is littered with sneering references to lesbians ("pock-marked muffdiver" and "slit-slavering bitch") and score-settling shots at Ned Rorem ("a queer Quaker") and Arthur Koestler ("an aggressive runt"). *Answered Prayers* was probably bitched from the start, to use a phrase of Hemingway's, not only because Capote put his faith in the fool's gold of gossip and chose a narrative persona whose pissy attitude robbed the book of expressive range (it's hard to convey disil-lusionment through a hero-whore who sounds jaded from the get-go) but because his lyric gift couldn't withstand such elongation. As the writer Marguerite Young puts it in *T.C.*, "Like many American writ-ers, he existed in tidy vignettes of limited dimensions. . . . But just stringing them together doesn't make an epic. An epic has to have a vast undertow of music and momentum and theology."

It's possible that the publication of "La Côte Basque" was semi-deliberate self-sabotage—an unconscious act of suicide. Capote's mother, Nina, who longed to be accepted into café society, com-mitted suicide by swallowing pills at the age of forty-eight. Capote, who was accepted by society, may have harbored a resentment and self-loathing that compelled him to push the self-destruct button in a similar desire for oblivion (or a gesture of solidarity with his dead mother). For in detonating himself he precipitated a renewal of the very abandonment he had felt in his childhood and feared all his life would happen again. Even Lee Radziwill, treated kindly in "La Côte Basque," dumped him, refusing to intercede in a legal battle between him and Gore Vidal, telling Liz Smith, "Liz, what difference does it make? They're just a couple of fags." No one as canny as Capote could do something this convulsive without deeper forces at play. His weep-ing disbelief at the misery and havoc the story caused him and oth-ers suggests a profound psychological disconnect. The phrase "social death" has never been more apt. Capote killed himself off in the eyes of others and rolled downhill in a slow twilight of pills and drugs.

His last days were comic horror. Bereft, running on inertia, a social lion turned social leper, he found refuge in the Los Angeles household of Joanne Carson, who kept a bedroom for him which later became a kitschy shrine. She mommied him in his hour of need; she created a protective bubble and kept the bad people away. "When Truman was here, I put my answer phone on and I was not available to anybody, because my time was so precious." They drove to Malibu and flew kites—kites are a recurring motif in Capote's fiction—or took imagi-nary trips together. Joanne Carson:

> He'd call me from New York and say, "Tomorrow we're going to Paris." I would pick him up at the airport; we would come home, I would put my answer phone on, and cancel anything I had for the next day, and when I would wake up in the morning he would bring in a tray with croissants and sugar cubes from the Ritz Hotel and little jars of marmalade from the Hotel Crillon, which

of course he'd lifted. Then we'd take out books from the Rodin Museum, books from the Louvre, and we'd take a trip there. "Now we're going to have lunch," he'd say; he'd pick a restaurant and we'd have a French-style cuisine here to match, and so we would spend a whole day in Paris without moving. We did the same thing with China. We went to Spain; we went to Mexico.

All without ever leaving the house. Doesn't it sound charming? Doesn't it sound insane?

On Saturday, August 25, 1984, Capote expired at Carson's house, though Joan Rivers wickedly speculated that he had died on the lawn and she dragged him indoors. His funeral would have made a fitting sequel to Evelyn Waugh's *The Loved One*. The service was held at noon at the Westwood Mortuary on a day so hellish you can practically hear a giant fly buzzing on the sound track. Robert Blake, who costarred in *In Cold Blood* but was more famous as the streetwise cop in *Baretta*, babbled in actorspeak about himself. The bandleader Artie Shaw went off on an endless tangent about Duke Ellington's funeral. Joan Didion: "We were watching and suddenly a glaze came over Artie's face and he realized he was far afield. So he got a grip on himself, and he said, 'And many of the same lessons apply. These were some of the same thoughts that were in my mind today!'" Didion's husband, John Gregory Dunne: "This thing was a fucking nightmare. Absolute nightmare. Then Joanne Carson got up with great rivulets of mascara coming down, like a couple of rivers, and she read from one of the stories, gulping away like people who can't control their tears." The last speaker was Christopher Isherwood, who said that the wonderful thing about Truman was that he had always made him laugh, a remark that some found winning and others (the *Rashomon* effect again) found coy. In the latter camp was Carol Matthau, who told Plimpton, "He said, 'Every time I think of Truman, I laugh.' And he laughed and laughed. I think he was tinkling in his pants. It was a debacle."

Capote's divided nature followed him into beyond death. According to Joanne Carson, his wish was to be cremated and have "half of his ashes kept in Los Angeles and half in New York, so he could continue to be bicoastal." Truman Capote—terminally chic.

Epilogue

But let's not end on a snotty note. Although he's been dead more than a decade, Truman Capote doesn't seem a dated figure, unlike so many writers of his generation (James Jones and Irwin Shaw, to name two). His iridescence has kept his reputation alive. Capote had a tabloid mentality with a slick-magazine gloss, which made him one of the most representative writers of his (and our) time, a roving ambassador between the last remnants of the Beautiful People and the celebrity photon chamber of *People* magazine, where new famous nobodies are covered weekly. Like Andy Warhol, whom he worked with at *Interview*, he understood that in the media universe real fame and bogus fame occupy the same lustrous plane, or at least adjoining booths on *The Hollywood Squares*. Capote's tragedy was that he came to value the spoken word over the written word, believing that he could sweet-talk his way out of anything because he had sweet-talked his way in. He was both the snake charmer and the snake, toying with toxic insinuation until the spell snapped and he was bitten by his own sound bites. In a chapter of *T.C.* called "In Which the Reader Is Let In on TC's Secret," we learn that Capote kept a small studio apartment where he maintained a collection of snakebite kits, which he decorated with collages and cryptic phrases, like Joseph Cornell boxes. It was his private stash of voodoo, an attempt (like his fiction) to make something lasting and celestial out of loneliness, menace, and fear. I bet they're beautiful.

Vanity Fair, December 1997

William Shawn
The Love Bug

In late-twentieth-century New York, three men have enjoyed the unofficial honor of being identified as "Mr."—a verbal nod that is both a form of respect and a sign of affection. Each an exemplar in his own field, together they form a trinity of culture, achievement, and metropolitan style. The big three are George Balanchine, the chief choreographer and artistic director of the New York City Ballet; Geoffrey Beene, the preeminent American fashion designer; and William Shawn, the legendary editor of *The New Yorker*: Mr. B., Mr. Beene, and Mr. Shawn. The first two possessed and possess a seamless, flowing genius, and the last—the last remains an enigma. Mr. Shawn is a Zen koan that hasn't been solved. The more we read about him, the deeper his secret self retreats into its shell. "Elusive pimpernel!" Tom Wolfe cried in 1965, and it's still true, even as the testimonials about him begin to mount.

> *"Hello, may I speak to Miss Ross?"*
>   *"Whom should I say is calling?"*
>   *Whum, dramatic, grammatic pause—whisper—"Mr. Shawn."*
>   *Zonk! Mr. Shawn! . . . He slipped in under the tympanic membrane with the whisper. One of the four or five most prominent men in Communications!*
>   *Unrecognized in his own office!*
>   —Tom Wolfe, "Tiny Mummies! The True Story of the
>   Ruler of 43rd Street's Land of the Walking Dead!" (the
>   *Herald Tribune*'s *New York* magazine, April 11, 1965)

William Shawn outfoxed his contemporaries and outstripped his rivals. As the successor to Harold Ross, the founding editor of *The New Yorker*, Shawn was mocked by Tom Wolfe and others as a mere caretaker, a shuffling mortician. Where Henry Luce, the founder of *Time*, *Life*, and *Fortune*, preached anti-Communism and the triumphal arc of "the American century," Shawn seemed to lower the blinds to half-mast, consecrating himself and his magazine to the intricate craft of writing. He was less concerned with the influence words could have than with their inner music and structural integrity. His desk was an altar where the ideals of accuracy, clarity, and understated elegance were held sacrosanct. Every article, no matter how ephemeral, was groomed like a French poodle. This ultra-finesse often resulted in preciousness (sentences neatly buttoned, facts lined up like little gentlemen), and *The New Yorker*, inhabiting a parallel universe of scrubbed perfection, could look quaint. Yet during Shawn's tenure *The New Yorker* published some of the most far-reaching and deep-rippling journalistic prose of the postwar era—Edmund Wilson's criticism and reporting, Rachel Carson's *Silent Spring*, James Baldwin's *The Fire Next Time*, Hannah Arendt's *Eichmann in Jerusalem*, Truman Capote's *In Cold Blood*, and Dwight Macdonald's review of Michael Harrington's *The Other America*, which helped inspire the War on Poverty. (It was also Shawn who, as Harold Ross's second-in-command, succeeded in persuading Ross to devote an entire issue to John Hersey's *Hiroshima*—a defining event in the magazine's history, and perhaps the most famous magazine article ever printed.) He didn't need feminism to push him into publishing a pride of lionesses— Mary McCarthy, Rebecca West, Arlene Croce, Pauline Kael, Lois Long, Andy Logan, Renata Adler, Elizabeth Drew, Muriel Spark. The editorials he ran about Vietnam and Watergate had a ferocity and sting that cost the magazine advertising but made *The New Yorker* the flagship of mainstream dissent.

To Shawn, such achievements were important and nice, but not really the point. When he was obliged to step down as editor in 1987 after thirty-five years, a Lou Gehrig streak in a revolving-door world, the farewell statement he drafted for the staff didn't recap old glories and pat the magazine on the back. Instead, he bared his heart. He heralded *The New Yorker* as a house of love. "Love has been the controlling emotion, and love is the essential word. We have done our work with honesty and love," he wrote. Unable to let the word go, he ended his letter, "I must speak of love once more. I love all of you, and will love you as long as I live." He faded into retirement and died almost six years later. An editor's legacy is usually buried with the back issues, but the legend of Mr. Shawn, like the legend of Harold Ross before him, has been magnified over time. A shrinking violet when he was alive, Shawn is now being regarded as the tree of life.

A posthumous revival is in full swing. Nineteen ninety-eight is the summer of Shawn, and the summer of love. Two attention-getting books have just been published about Mr. Shawn, part of a larger flood of Shawniana (the fashion writer Kennedy Fraser devoted a chapter of her 1996 collection, *Ornament and Silence*, to her experience of writing for Shawn, and Alison Rose, a current staff writer at *The New Yorker*, is completing a memoir tabulating the office affairs she has had there with married men—which should perhaps be called *Carpets and Desktops I Have Known*), and in both books, "love" is indeed the essential word. In Ved Mehta's *Remembering Mr. Shawn's New Yorker* (Overlook Press), the author recalls "sitting anxiously by the phone waiting for Mr. Shawn's call, as if I were in love." When he and Mr. Shawn agree to meet for lunch, he quivers inside like a teenager on a first date, worrying that he might order the wrong sandwich and chew too loud. He decides to order whatever Mr. Shawn orders, just to be safe. "I am aware that I sound as if I had fallen in love with Mr. Shawn," Mehta admits, but insists it was a healthy, platonic puppy love, one of a nervous rookie for a generous, consoling mentor.

Lillian Ross's *Here but Not Here: A Love Story* (Random House) is a more intimate and frilly valentine. "'Love' isn't a word I take lightly or tire of today," Ross writes, and true enough, she uses the word or its variant seven times in her opening paragraph. Understandably, she feels entitled. The author of *Picture*, an account of the making of John Huston's adaptation of *The Red Badge of Courage*, and the classic *New Yorker* profile of Ernest Hemingway, Ross was long rumored to be Shawn's companion (Tom Wolfe drops hints in his piece). The revelation of her memoir is that for forty years Ross was more than Shawn's companion, she was his faithful mistress, his wife in all but name, maintaining a separate household for him while he continued to live with his wife, Cecille, and his two sons, Wallace and Allen. The title *Here but Not Here* plays off the title of Brendan Gill's best-selling tour of the premises, *Here at The New Yorker* (Random House, 1975), and refers to Shawn's transmigration from his marital status. "I am there, but I am not there," he would say over and over again of his home life. According to Ross, Shawn, with his wife's knowledge, even had a bedroom phone put in to which only she had the number; they would ring each other on the Bat-phone and talk snookums late into the night. They took romantic trips together (she provides snapshots), and she assures us that as a lover Shawn was a veritable Bob Dole on Viagra—"After forty years, our love-making had the same passion, the same energies . . . ," et cetera, "as it had in the beginning." Their glow followed them around. "When Bill and I sat together in his office to go over the editing of my stories, we worked seriously and professionally, but the atmosphere of love was not suspended; it enhanced the pleasure that we shared in our work." She adopted a son on whom Shawn doted (more snapshots), and who many thought was Shawn's biological son. That Lillian Ross would publish such kissy-face indiscretions while Shawn's widow is still alive, a book in which Ross postures as Shawn's real wife, his true joined spirit, only compounds the act of betrayal many feel she has committed.

For decades, *New Yorker* writers regarded any intrusion into the internal workings of Mr. Shawn's magazine or his psychological makeup as impertinent. At the mention of Mr. Shawn's name, they would huddle under what was known on *Get Smart* as "the Cone of Silence." When Tom Wolfe published his infamous satire "Tiny Mummies!" in 1965, a giant spitball composed of a combination of wild X-ray vision and wicked speculation, the shock effect was immediate. It was as if, Mehta writes, the magazine had been mugged. Renata Adler flew to Chicago to check court documents (one of Wolfe's floated rumors was that Leopold and Loeb had targeted the young Shawn as their original victim), Dwight Macdonald drew up a rebuttal for *The New York Review of Books*, and even J. D. Salinger came out of hibernation to complain. Ten years later, Brendan Gill's *Here at The New Yorker*, published to coincide with the magazine's fiftieth anniversary, was also considered by many an act of gaucherie, the bon vivant Gill being constitutionally incapable of grasping Shawn's delicate wiring. But no outside detractor or breezy raconteur, no illiterate baboon, has violated Mr. Shawn's privacy and dignity with the snappy assurance of Lillian Ross in *Here but Not Here*. She has taken the Cone of Silence and turned it into a megaphone. "I'm sure he would be proud to read this story," she writes. If anything, he'd probably die all over again, this time of embarrassment. (After all, Shawn himself disapproved of memoirs about Harold Ross. Kennedy Fraser writes of Ross's ex-wife Jane Grant's book: "The publication of *Ross, The New Yorker, and Me* seemed painful to Mr. Shawn. . . . 'It was a mistake,' he said, tersely.")

To understand why people feel she's violated such trust, it is necessary to understand that the preoccupation with Mr. Shawn is more than the product of a personality cult. It's part of the long-standing, ongoing (but eroding) fascination with and veneration of *The New Yorker* as an institution. Founded by Harold Ross in 1925, *The New Yorker* served as the house organ of the Algonquin Round Table, whose members—among them, Dorothy Parker, Robert Benchley, and Alexander Woollcott—bannered their quips with theatrical flair.

(Harold Ross himself was considered stagestruck.) With the Algonquin group, writers became show people—nearly all of them wrote, performed, or reviewed plays—and the bright lights of the period continue to cast a nostalgic shine out of all proportion to their actual achievement (the great writing of the period having been done by Faulkner, Hemingway, Eugene O'Neill, and other nonjoiners). No matter how many times the Algonquin group is debunked, there remains a longing for a time when parties were parties and not networking opportunities, and people were poured into taxis. After the Depression and the inducements of Hollywood dispersed most of the original gang, *The New Yorker* thrived as an open-air bazaar for the omnivorous eyes of writers such as A. J. Liebling, Joseph Mitchell, and Emily Hahn. Humor writing didn't vanish from its pages, but after the Depression and the Second World War, no longer could *The New Yorker* raise a champagne glass in the name of frivolity. As E. B. White wrote in a *New Yorker* "Comment" in 1945, "We feel like a man who left his house to go to a Punch-and-Judy show and, by some error in direction, wandered into *Hamlet*."

After William Shawn succeeded Ross in 1952, *The New Yorker* became less of a flying fortress and even more of an anxious castle. The atomic jitters and the suburban boom left *The New Yorker*'s audience well-off but wary. A spiritual malaise lurked behind the new-product shine. J. D. Salinger and John Cheever were the representative fiction writers of the period, nimble maneuverers across the hairline intimations of acedia among the prep-school set. Assured of itself if not of the world around it, *The New Yorker* formalized its editorial procedures and became a self-producing machine. Its multilayered editing (galleys upon galleys annotated with marginal comments), its fact-checking department, its scrupulous attention to grammar and usage, its extreme courtesy to its contributors, its fastidious distaste for slang and coarse language, its refusal to chase fashion, pursue celebrity, or simplify complex subjects—all this made *The New Yorker* the weekly chalice of sweet reason. To some, this distillation tasted of formaldehyde. In the early sixties, Seymour Krim consigned the magazine to squaresville—"the diehard editorial neoclassicists, the punctuation castratos who have gone to bed with commas for a quarter of a century, are living in a world that no longer exists." Contributors, too, cracked under the incessant niggling. In *Here but Not Here*, Lillian Ross describes how Shawn left a meeting with the philosopher-historian Hannah Arendt shaking in his shoes. Arendt, incensed at

The New Yorker's "stupid" editing methods, demanded that the magazine stop torturing her with questions. "She called me names, horrible names," Shawn told Ross.

> "Is she demented?" I asked. "Maybe something pushed her over the edge. Call Susan Sontag." I didn't know Susan Sontag, but I figured there might be something mysterious that only another high-powered intellectual could account for.

It's pretty funny, the notion that intellectuals are transmitters that can communicate only with each other as the rest of us scratch our heads.

Outbursts such as Arendt's (Mary McCarthy also chafed) were a tribute to the magazine's unique character as an exclusive club and to the discipline imposed by its protocols. Talent alone wasn't sufficient. One didn't simply write for *The New Yorker*; one had to be worthy—chosen. Hence *New Yorker* memoirs have become a distinct genre, with their own ritualistic formula. First, there is The Initiation, in which a phone call from Mr. Shawn emanates like a faint tap from the Holy Ghost. (Bill McKibben, receiving a call on April 1, thought it was a practical joke.) Then follows The Induction, in which one meets Mr. Shawn in his office, basks in his beneficent rays, and is shown to one's own modest cell. ("It was Mr. Shawn himself who showed me, on my first day on the eighteenth floor, the eight-by-twelve-foot room that was to be my 'office,'" recalled Kennedy Fraser. "He stood in the doorway smiling and picturing the Good Writing I might conceivably produce on the old Underwood with its chipped round keys.") As one begins to feel at home and form relationships with the other figments floating down the halls, comes the long honeymoon of Identification with the magazine and all that it represents. (Lillian Ross: "In the elevator, going up, I was afraid that other people could hear the din inside my body. The wonderful reporters and writers I met in the dimly-lighted corridors were now my *colleagues*.") Then, for some, arrives the wrenching moment of Tribal Separation, when, for whatever reason (being let go, falling out of favor, feeling suffocated), one bids farewell to the old homestead and braces oneself for the outside. (Hello, cruel world.) One's belongings are boxed for removal and one experiences a sad sense of erasure, a *petite mort*. The last phase is the *Brideshead Revisited* stage of Bittersweet Reflection, in which the author muses on a grandeur that has fallen into desuetude but is thankful for the small kindnesses and treasured anecdotes. On the final page, the author puts his reluctant lips to the bugle, and blows.

Mehta and Ross stick to the script, studying *The New Yorker* solely through the opera glasses of their own experience. Even charting *The New Yorker* from within, however, they suffer from cramped perspective. They judge the magazine's health by how well they're doing. To Mehta, *The New Yorker* began to show signs of decline when it had the nerve to start cutting his copy. As a young man Mehta published voluminous profiles and articles in the magazine on topics ranging from English philosophers to the life of Gandhi; a new department called "Personal History" was created to accommodate his reminiscences of India and Oxford. Shawn personally oversaw most of Mehta's work, which spoiled him for others. Mehta survives the razor hands of Gardner Botsford ("He was known among the people in the makeup department, who saw his proofs regularly, as the Slasher"), and is perturbed years later when novice editor Jonathan Schell prunes his manuscript, "causing some of the deeper resonances in the piece to sound hollow." In both cases, he ran to Daddy ("I ran to Mr. Shawn") to have his resonances restored. When Robert Gottlieb becomes editor of the magazine in 1987, Mehta loses this higher court of appeal. One of Gottlieb's first acts is bumping yet another of Mehta's book-length serials to publish a piece by Doris Lessing, explaining, "I am the editor now, and I think Lessing is a very important writer." With a *tsk*, Mehta writes, "His use of the word 'important' reinforced my feeling that all of us writers and artists were now living in a different world—a world where the notoriety of the writer would, for the first time, be a factor in what was published, and even take precedence over the quality of the writing." (As if Doris Lessing were some sort of floozy.) Gottlieb not only reduced Mehta's series by two-thirds "but also cut out any intellectually demanding material, such as a favorite quotation of mine from the 'History of Philosophy' by the German philosopher W. Windelband." The unfeeling brute! Mehta even objects to Gottlieb's democratic gesture of installing a coffee machine in the office. "There was something inviting but also offputting about the smell . . ." By the time Gottlieb has departed, *The New Yorker*, to Mehta, is already a lost cause.

Like Mehta, Ross consigns the Gottlieb era to the memory hole, but for a different reason. To Mehta, Gottlieb's arrival is the beginning of the end—a fade to black. To Ross, Gottlieb's tenure was a bothersome interruption between the glacial grandeur of the Shawn administration and the sprightly cheek of the current editorship—a twilight period. She sees the magazine now as happy and thriving because she still participates. Indeed, Ross is under the enchantment that Mr. Shawn himself would be tickled by the drastic changes at the magazine and the flamenco dance being done on his grave, though it is highly dubious that Shawn, who recoiled from obscenity and any reference to bodily function, would applaud Richard Avedon's necrophiliac photos, or the use of the f-word five times in a single sentence in a slack-jawed appreciation of Robert Redford, or cartoon captions featuring references to "boners" and an adult man announcing "I just did a huge one in my diaper." Ross was encouraged to do her memoir by the current editor of *The New Yorker*, who is cited in the acknowledgments for "her cheerful understanding of love," a new one on me. (For the record, I wrote for the magazine from 1992 to 1996.) Articles in *New York* and *Newsweek* have speculated that this nudge was rooted in a desire to pollute and undercut the moral high ground of the Shawn era, which the present regime finds burdensome. Tarnishing Shawn's halo makes recent shenanigans look less whory, or so the theory goes. Whatever the validity of this Machiavellian scenario, *Here but Not Here* reveals that Shawn was slated to meet with the current editor, Tina Brown, to discuss a possible role as consultant. For the occasion, Ross and her adopted son, Erik, bought Shawn a new blue suit at Brooks Brothers. Later, at a restaurant, Shawn tried on the jacket, and all seemed well. But "when we walked outside with him to his car, I noticed that his eyes, strangely and frighteningly, were no longer blue. They had become black, deep black." Shawn died shortly after this sudden downturn and before the meeting could take place.

Enveloped in love-mist, Lillian Ross renders Shawn indistinct in *Here but Not Here*. She purrs of love and serves the reader slush. " 'We must arrest our love in midflight,' Bill once said. 'And we fix it forever as it is today, a point of pure light that will reach into eternity.' " Although they were together for more than forty years, their relationship is never vivid, and most of Shawn's quotes are vague expressions of Prufrockian unease, such as "Why am I more ghost than man?" and "Who am I? Am I really here?" Despite such existential moans, Shawn exerted as much control over his personal relationship with Lillian Ross as he did over the magazine—and to much the same effect. He verbally massaged both into complete compliance. According to Ross, it was he who did the wooing, pursuing her with a persistence (cards, poems, phone calls, standing in front of her apartment building at night) that might be construed as sexual harassment today. He was so won't-take-no-for-an-answer that when she went to Paris in 1953 to detach herself from him he not only dogged her with phone calls and cables but gave her an itinerary of sights she should see—the places he had visited in Paris with his wife in 1929. And she went! She can't explain why she obeyed, why she stayed with a man who wouldn't leave his wife for her (even after his children were grown), stressing again and again how unintrospective she is. Whatever her man wanted was good enough for Mama. "Bill disliked the odor of cigarettes. I immediately gave up smoking. He was afraid of 'drinking.' I gave up martinis." Over the years the verve of Ross's writing was slowly leeched away by their liaison, cuddled to sleep. What made her Hemingway profile a fabulous coup then and an exciting read today is that it was so untypical a *New Yorker* profile. It has a spontaneous, dialogue-driven, wide-eyed wonder that eventually ebbed in *New Yorker* profiles as a genre, which became waxwork exhibits as bleached and starched as a eulogy by Dr. Johnson. Aside from *Picture*, Ross seldom wrote again with the same present-tense drive. Ross says she doesn't mind, she never wanted to write major works, but in their relationship the sacrifices made for love seem to have all been made on her side.

Even with its mealymouthed snobberies and false modesties ("Many of my *New Yorker* colleagues and I, in the manner of Mr. Shawn, always let our work speak for itself, and were satisfied as persons to fade into the woodwork"), Mehta's book does a better job of conveying Shawn's workhorse ethic and thoughtful consideration—his calm center amid orbiting writers. Where Shawn's wife, Cecille, is a mere name attached to marital duty in Lillian Ross's memoir, a blank looming outside their love bubble, she carries her own smack of personality in Mehta's. He describes a dinner at their house where the theater critic Edith Oliver rips into James Thurber's 1959 memoir of Harold Ross.

> "The book is trash," Edith said. She had a smoker's hoarse voice, and her remarks came out sounding like little barks. "It's all untrue. He might as well be writing about his mother."
> "Have a melon ball, Edith," Mrs. Shawn said.

Admired through a beauty lens of hero worship (Mehta), romantic love (Ross), and daughterly devotion (Fraser), Mr. Shawn emerges rounded and complete, a deskbound Buddha who is peaceful, humble, and wise. None of these tributes to Shawn do justice to the powerful contradictions of his seemingly passive manner and the psychological strain of this makeover. Like the narrator in the Philip Larkin poem "The Life with a Hole in It," it wasn't a matter of Shawn's always doing what he wanted as much as never doing what he didn't want. Here was a man who was afraid of heights and enclosed spaces (he had his own elevator in the *New Yorker* building and, according to Ross, wouldn't visit his sons' apartments, because they were too small), yet had no problem visiting the fifteenth-floor apartment he and Ross originally secured as a love nest. Here was a man who professed he couldn't travel, yet hopped into a Triumph sports car with his mistress and tooled off for the Catskills. Here was a man who played jazz to unwind, and removed every ounce of improvisation from his magazine. A man considered a moral beacon who lived the life of a bigamist. Within the limitations imposed on him by his various phobias, Shawn flexed enormous force. His psychic cage kept him in a constant state of concentration. In his own way, Shawn was as willful, poignant, and imprisoned a self-creation as Richard Nixon, with Nixon's bureaucratic mastery (and, blessedly, without Nixon's paranoia).

Born William Chon in 1907, the son of a Chicago stockyard vendor known as Jackknife Ben, he changed his last name to Shawn because, according to Ross, Chon sounded too Chinese. He made himself inconspicuous around his father, of whom he was afraid. "Unlike my brothers and sister, who might do things to make my father angry, I just tried not to be noticed by him." (And he grew up afraid of expressing anger.) Jewish on both sides of his family, Shawn over time gentrified himself into a Henry James figure with warm milk for blood—industrious, refined, cushioned against any extremity of word or deed by invisible cobwebs of implication and deflection. Like James, he was a comma addict, dimpling even the most casual remarks with carefully crafted hesitation. Although Shawn published Jewish authors of note (Isaac Bashevis Singer, for example), *The New Yorker* maintained an upscale Wasp persona, evoking Connecticut lawns, riding stables, prep schools, and Dad having a spiritual crisis over cocktails. The earthiness and pungency of Jewish expression— its mother-wit—offended him, unless it was couched in nostalgia, as in the dialect humor of Myron Cohen. In my presence, Shawn was visibly wounded at the mention of the comedian Alan King's name. Vulgarity to him wasn't crude vitality or loud manner, but a kind of violence against civilization—a hostile clowning. And one thing on which all those who came into contact with Shawn can agree is that he shrank from all forms of violence. ("She was so emotionally *vio-*

lent," he said after Hannah Arendt's tantrum.) Like most pacifists, he aspired to sainthood.

> *He eagerly read passages to me from Dr. Cohn's writings in* The Psychoanalytic Quarterly. . . . *Bill was especially taken with the following: "Saintly people have submitted to a life of the dead, renouncing all possessions, and thus surrendering to a lifetime transfiguration. Their present must have seemed irrelevant to them, an existence suspended in time. We ordinary people of our time imagine ourselves to be well protected against such a philosophy."*
> —Lillian Ross, *Here but Not Here*

The great paradox of Shawn's career is that he practiced the art of self-effacement while making himself central, dug-in, and indispensable. Channeling himself, he was most present when he was bodily absent—over the telephone. Kennedy Fraser says that all other life froze when Mr. Shawn was on the line. Within the small theater in which he operated, his egolessness was all-conquering. Nowhere in the memoirs of Shawn appears the nickname I heard given to him: The Iron Mouse. Meek yet implacable, he carried the workings of *The New Yorker* in his head. Others had pieces; he alone knew the whole puzzle. He did the major assigning, chose which articles would run and when (some would sit in the "bank" for years until being summoned on deck—a John Updike piece was said to have waited for eleven years), determined how writers would be reimbursed, decided who would be hired and how long they would remain, deemed which words were "appropriate." Shawn resisted outside pressure and internal dissension, both to preserve the integrity of the magazine and to consolidate his tender choke hold on the decision-making process. Not only did he strenuously fight a union movement at *The New Yorker* (ironic, given the magazine's New Deal liberalism in all other regards), but, as Gigi Mahon reports in *The Last Days of The New Yorker* (McGraw-Hill, 1988), he shafted the top echelon in the editorial department by unilaterally denying "key" writers and editors access to stock grants, insisting that everyone at *The New Yorker* was equal. Shawn refused even to discuss stock options with his subordinates. He decided for them that they didn't deserve a bonus. *The New Yorker* was a patriarchy, and father knew best. So when the magazine's stock was later sold and the proceeds distributed, the business side enjoyed a windfall and the editorial side got nothing. Mahon writes, "Even some who wouldn't have benefited felt cheated by what they saw as Shawn's stinginess. Says one bitter staff member: 'Shawn kept [the writers and artists] deliberately poor. Shawn kept control by impoverishing' them." When more straightforward salaries were instituted under new management, some still clung to their begging bowls. "Getting a salary lowered our anxiety level but also had the effect of somewhat corrupting our austere ways," Ved Mehta writes. (Ved, have a melon ball.)

Paternalism breeds dependency, and dependency breeds pathologies. While Shawn kept a strict account of the word flow, he conducted a policy of benign neglect toward much of his staff. Writers often dangled for years without being published, wandering the ward like Ancient Mariners while younger writers were hired and left equally unattended. The result was an institutional outbreak of mental itch. Wilfrid Sheed wrote: "One had a picture of *New Yorker* writers (whom one seldom saw) vying with each other in feats of hypochondria and shyness: also of flinching and shrinking, jumping at small sounds, and holing up in the country. American writers will compete at just about anything." Others dropped out of the race entirely, their downfalls tragicomic. The evocative short-story and "Talk of the Town" writer Maeve Brennan (she was "the Long-Winded Lady" who covered the city as if writing home from home) became a sort of bag lady in the building. Another staff writer was a notorious kleptomaniac, stealing items off other writers' desks; still another set fires in the ladies' room. Perhaps the saddest case study in Mehta's book is Penelope Gilliatt, a fiction writer and film critic who had been married to the playwright John Osborne and became increasingly alcoholic and wobbly. Despite Gilliatt's obvious disarray, no concrete action was taken until she was caught plagiarizing, and she was put on medical leave. What's odd and noxious about Mehta's book is that he can see how nonintervention didn't improve Gilliatt's condition ("At another magazine, Penelope would have been put in the care of a doctor and not been allowed to continue her column until her condition improved"), yet he can't bring himself to blame Shawn, and takes swipes at those who do show some backbone. He says that Gilliatt's film colleague, Pauline Kael, perversely turned against "art and gentleness." Kael practiced critical kung fu, and, worse, had the gall to argue face-to-face with Mr. Shawn. The little sneak (Mehta, I mean) recounts waiting outside Shawn's office as he tried to reason with her—"Pauline's voice loud and strident, Mr. Shawn's calm and persuasive." Not only is this vignette sexist, but it makes anyone who resisted Shawn's namby-pamby control mechanisms and phony coddling seem like an ingrate. (In the preface to her greatest-hits collection, *For Keeps*, Kael relates how Shawn assumed the mantle of martyrdom as his guilt-trip device.) There's a prim authoritarian streak in Mehta, as there was in Shawn, who was part Yoda and part yenta. (Which is why Shawn resented Kael's comparing Gandhi to a Jewish mother.)

For all his mystic mildness ("Some people saw Bill as submissive, but I saw him as genuinely meek, in the beatitudinal, the biblical sense"—Ross), Shawn hardly practiced nonattachment when it came to his position at *The New Yorker*. As a former *New Yorker* editor, Dan Menaker, once said to me, "The hardest thing in the world is to walk away." Shawn couldn't face the plank. He wanted to stay forever at a job he loved, which is understandable, and choose a successor who would carry on his mandate, which was foolhardy. (No one controls their aftermath.) Shawn so identified himself with *The New Yorker* that he couldn't imagine one without the other. Having created a power vacuum which he alone filled, Shawn elaborately stalled forever on picking a successor, diddling with candidates and delaying the inevitable. He caught his staff off guard by anointing the humorless, idealistic Jonathan Schell as the heir apparent (a staff rebellion made Shawn withdraw); devised an unworkable co-managing editorship with Charles "Chip" McGrath and John Bennet, which (according to Mehta) left them both sitting awkwardly on the sofa in Shawn's office, auditing meetings; and urged William Whitworth to stay without offering him any monetary inducement or necessary assurance. Ad pages sank, articles seemed as long as tapeworms, the issue of successorship remained unresolved, and finally the dark day came when Shawn was told to pack up his pencils. Lillian Ross led a staff revolt in which a letter was drafted imploring Bob Gottlieb not to accept the job, to no avail. Although a few writers quit in sympathy when Shawn departed, he believed there would be more of a mass exit—in Mehta's words, "that, as soon as Gottlieb came over, all of us who signed the protest letter would go down in the elevator and never come back." He later recognized he was being romantic, but still, it must have hurt.

Mehta and Ross present quite different slants on Shawn's retirement years. Mehta claims that a disheartened Shawn couldn't bear to read *The New Yorker* he had left behind. "I had the impression that, except for separating himself from the office, giving up reading *The New Yorker* was the most painful thing he had ever done." Not so, Ross contends. "He had never fully stopped looking at *The New Yorker*, but now he was reading it with new interest." Mehta has Shawn plodding away on a novel about an old pianist living alone in a fleabag hotel—a maudlin exercise—while Ross relates how the two of them collaborated joyfully on a pair of screenplays, including a satire of the magazine biz called *Info*. Mehta, who continued to submit his works in progress to Shawn, insists Shawn wanted to be wanted by the writers he had once edited, whereas Ross has Shawn wishing they would go away. Finally, the hell that is old age wore him into infirmity. He became shrunken, frail. He died on December 8, 1992, at the age of eighty-five—almost forty-one years to the day after Harold Ross had died. God's way of saying the circle had been joined and *The New Yorker* they had created was truly gone.

On paper, William Shawn seems to have had a successful life. He was a man who got his way without being a bully. He had a wife and a mistress, children, grandchildren, the best editing job in magazines, the adoration of writers who dedicated books to him, good health, and longevity. Like Maxwell Perkins, he will be remembered as the last of the gentleman editors. Yet toward the end, stumped at writing fiction, Shawn complains to Ross, "I'm not writing what I wish to write," and "There's just too much I am not free to say." When the two of them see Cecille on the street and Shawn neglects to go over to his wife (even after Ross urges him to do so), Ross cries, "For God's sake, Bill, at this point along the line we all know what's happened. Why can't we live, just *live*?" Shawn nods in agreement even as he says no. "It's too complicated. There's just too much I can't say." Repressed all his life, Shawn was never able to unburden himself, to express everything he had stashed inside. In his eighties, he was still afraid of being anything but careful. For me, the mystery of William Shawn is: When he died, did he feel he had ever really lived? Was sainthood worth it? Those are Rosebud questions probably no one can answer. But when I look at photographs of Shawn, I don't see love, I see an unreachable loneliness.

Vanity Fair, July 1998

Norman Mailer
The Norman Conquests

What an active afterlife Norman Mailer has led! He's left us behind and yet here he buzzes, a prodigious gossip item from beyond the grave. A writer who never stopped making news—from the age of twenty-five, when his best-selling novel *The Naked and the Dead* captured the first beachhead of postwar American fiction, until his death at the age of eighty-four in 2007, when the critical ruckus over his final novel, *The Castle in the Forest* (a metaphysical proctology probe of the incipient evil of Adolf Hitler), shook the branches yet again—Mailer was too warrior-minded to let his words do all the talking. His fists and penis also played principal roles. Perhaps the most highly publicized American author of the modern era, the inheritor of Hemingway's heavyweight-division machismo and cult of experience (taste that salty sea air, inhale that tarty perfume!), he punched his way through the paper walls of print to test himself on stage and screen (as scriptwriter, actor, and director), in the TV studio (behaving like a wrathful thundercloud in his infamous faceoff with Gore Vidal on *The Dick Cavett Show*), on the feminist battlefield ("I'm not going to sit here and listen to you harridans harangue me," he barked in the 1979 documentary *Town Bloody Hall*), at the political racetrack (he ran for mayor of New York in 1969), and inside the boxing ring (sparring with José Torres on *The Dick Cavett Show*). Violence attended a life driving forward along the knife edge of one's nerves. Mailer made shock headlines for stabbing his second wife, Adele Morales, at a party after she called him a "faggot," and for cosponsoring the release of prisoner Jack Henry Abbott, who, shortly after parole, stabbed a waiter to death in the East Village. By the time Mailer's life neared its end, however, the fevers he had aroused had mostly burned off, dissipating into the winter sky, his hair and reputation glinting with statesman-like silver. More modesty entered his manner, yet the scale of his intentions remained overarching. Unlike some novelists as they enter the wind-down phase, Mailer didn't miniaturize his ambitions in his senior years, aiming instead high and wide with mammoths such as *Harlot's Ghost*, *Oswald's Tale*, and the first installment of the Hitler prose epic, *The Castle in the Forest*, conceived as a Thomas Mann–ish seven-volume swan song. He intended to go out the way he came in: big.

After death comes inevitable shrinkage, a diminution of interest that can taper off into near-total indifference. (When's the last time Jerzy Kosinski's name lit up the board?) An admirable support system and a prolific publishing rollout have kept the Mailer enterprise from suffering a similar posthumous dip. Founded in 2003, the Norman Mailer Society sponsors conferences and publishes a thick annual issue devoted to Maileriana, and Mailer's former home in Provincetown, Massachusetts, has been converted into a writers' colony, with scholarships offered. Reissues of his works pound off the presses, including *The Faith of Graffiti* and an extravagantly illustrated edition of *Of a Fire on the Moon*, titled *MoonFire*. Excerpts from Mailer's tremendous correspondence have been published in *The New Yorker*, *Playboy*, and *The New York Review of Books*, and a new biography is being written by Stephen Schiff, a former contributing editor at *Vanity Fair*. All very fitting and worthy. But now some of the old bumps in the night have come back to bite, raising unwelcome questions.

Three memoirs have been published this year alone about contending with being inside the particle collider of Mailer's company and charisma, testaments ranging from the doting and domestic *Mornings with Mailer*, by Dwayne Raymond, Mailer's cook and assistant at the house in Provincetown, to the glittery but trauma-racked *A Ticket to the Circus*, by Norris Church, Mailer's statuesque, pale-moon widow, to the score-settling *Loving Mailer*, by Carole Mallory, one of Mailer's countless extracurricular hotsies. Although diametrically opposite in tone and texture, the last two books bear the puncture marks of Mailer's satyr horns.

Like so many conquering heroes of his literary generation (a male fraternity to which the critic Vivian Gornick has devoted so much frowning attention), Norman Mailer had a "woman problem" that bedeviled his reputation while he was extant and may have cost him sales—half of a potential audience is a lot of alienation of affection to risk—and will do it few favors with future readers and literary reckoners. It isn't simply a matter of sensitive types recoiling when Mailer or one of his Don Draper alter egos imposes his will on women and the world with a firm sausage, as with the spirited buggery of the German maid in *An American Dream*, his bestowing the title of "Retaliator" on his cock in *The Prisoner of Sex*, or the alchemical qualities he ascribes to male ejaculate in the Marilyn Monroe biography. ("He sees it as a one-way process, of course," wrote Pauline Kael in her review, mocking Mailer's magic-squirt-gun theory.) Being a male chauvinist isn't an automatic disqualifier in the fiction department, and there are novelists tagged with the misogynist label who have rendered sympathetic, perceptive, full-dimensional portraits of female characters (crusty Kingsley Amis's Rhiannon in *The Old Devils*, John Updike's Joan Maple in the Maples stories). The crippler is that in his writing Mailer was psychologically, creatively, empathetically tone-deaf when it came to women, his female characters a creamy mélange of angel-whores whose lipstick was ripe for smearing—a Playboy Bunny mansion of haughty bitches and breathy ditzes whose dialogue bore no resemblance to indoor speech. One of the imponderables about Mailer's career is that even though he bobbed and deep-sea'd in an ocean of women—six wives, countless mistresses and casual flings, five daughters—he doesn't seem to have actually learned anything from them, because he never really listened. Because who needs to listen when you insist on and succeed in getting nearly everything your own way? Genius has its privileges, and male prerogative provides extra thrust.

It's difficult to forgive Mailer for the wringer he put Norris Church through, even if forgiveness isn't ours to withhold or grant. In *A Ticket to the Circus*, the former teacher and model describes her unlikely romance and marriage with Mailer in a memoir that is generous, sweet, well observed, harrowing in its recounting of a rape and a miscarriage, and occasionally waspish, but never unkind. Although Mailer serenaded her with love letters the likes of which Abelard never wrote Eloise ("Darling, I just had a picture of how you look in the morning with that incredible beauty in your face as if you'd been fucking a stag in your dreams and he said something lovely as he left you in my arms"—fancy that, a talking stag!), prominent bystanders, wise to Norman's ways, waved caution flags to warn her of heartbreak ahead. Elizabeth Hardwick, novelist and essayist, cautioned "with that croaky little giggle she had" not to let him get her pregnant, and Congresswoman Bella Abzug, whose voice, Mailer once wrote, could boil the fat off a cabdriver's neck, gave Norris her phone number as a twenty-four-hour personal emergency hotline. Norris shooed away such well-intended, buttinsky advice, and her May-December romance with Norman resulted in a marriage whose installments became a staple of the gossip columns and celebrity spreads, her Junoesque height and his howitzer stare embossing them as one of New York's most totemic eighties couples, matching accessories. Unlike

Mailer's previous marriages, this one looked as if it would be his climactic toreador turn in the matrimonial ring, his final Picasso period. Asked which Mailer wife was she, Norris would tartly reply, "The last one," and so she proved to be.

But at what a bruising and exacting price, a long season of blight and betrayal that cannot fail to leave discolored memories that even death can't entirely pacify. It began with a twitchy suspicion, a bit of dodgy behavior from Mailer during a trip to California (an uncharacteristic late-night phone call in which "he was vague and defensive and obviously had been drinking"), along with credit-card receipts from Chicago, which hadn't been on the itinerary. He claimed he had made the unscheduled stop to meet with Saul Bellow about a joint project, a fib so preposterous that it collapsed as soon as the Alpha-Bits sputtered out of his mouth. Busted, Mailer confessed to meeting with an old girlfriend, but it was no one-off for auld lang syne; Norris tugged on the loose string in the evidence chain and found herself deluged by a balloon drop of floozies, a Clinton-esque bimbo explosion. (Interestingly, Norris reveals in the book that she had a brief tryst with the future president.) Mailer's desk bulged with letters, notes, gifts, and photographs from girlfriends, including a stack of nudies from "an aging porn star," the kind of tender keepsake with which so many men would find it difficult to part. Mailer's rationale for his furtive rampage of satyriasis was that he had begun living a double life and was conducting covert operations in the sack while working on his CIA epic, *Harlot's Ghost*, a writer's version of a Method actor getting into character. "It was an imaginative excuse. I do give him credit for that," Norris writes. But given the long gestation of *Harlot's Ghost*, this meant that for half of their marriage up till then, eight out of the sixteen years, "he was totally, blindingly, a cheat." Adding insult to infidelity, she finds herself bumping into her husband's former harem partners on book tours and at parties, forced to restrain herself from whipping out Wonder Woman's golden lasso on one of these hussies for fear the paparazzi would have a field day. "Why had I been so consumed by this old, fat, bombastic, lying little dynamo?," Norris Church asks in the reeling aftermath. But they patched themselves together and toughed it out until the last round, through the faltering arc of his infirmities and her unsparing bouts of cancer, kidney pain, and intestinal operations, bound by devotion, attrition, and too much shared history to declare their marriage kaput.

What has this to do with Mailer's literary legacy? Not listening to women in general handicapped Mailer's fiction and not listening to Norris in particular was a literary felony, like refusing to ask for directions and driving hundreds of miles into the mouth of mounting despair. She implored him to junk the interminable narrative detours in *Harlot's Ghost* that took the novel so wearily astray, losing readers in droves, and lobbied in vain for him to fix the clangers in his screenplay of his pulp novel *Tough Guys Don't Dance* (including the immortal howler "Oh, man, oh God, oh man, oh God, oh man, oh God, oh shit and shinola," uttered by Ryan O'Neal, looking as if he wants to enter a witness-protection program for mortified actors). Raymond's *Mornings with Mailer* records that Norris was none too enthused by the prospect of her husband's Hitler opera cycle and of having the top floor of their house converted into something resembling "a Nazi propaganda vault": "Her feeling was that any subject floating around in the house that was so inherently evil could not be good." How right her premonitions were, given the dense spoilage that *The Castle in the Forest* became. If only he had heeded her!

But heedlessness was what helped propel this human cannonball into the highs of *The Armies of the Night* and the other daredevil triumphs as well as the belly flops into the sawdust where he wildly, erratically overshot. For better (brash, brilliant, generous, ebullient, defiant) or worse (stubborn, bullying, hyperbolic, coarse), he was what he was, and to wish otherwise is to play nursemaid in hindsight. Still, this woman thing—it's a stickler. Literary scholarship has peeled away Hemingway's hearty bluster to reveal an androgynous side hidden under his safari jacket, but I don't see that happening here.

Vanity Fair, June 2010

Bow. Wow.
Gore Vidal, Fred Kaplan

"I love dead, hate living," intones Boris Karloff's monster in *Bride of Frankenstein*. He's not alone. "I prefer my subjects dead," Fred Kaplan confesses in the prelude to his ambitious biography of Gore Vidal. Kaplan, a professor of English in New York whose taxidermies include Henry James, Dickens, and Carlyle (they hardly get deader than Carlyle), understands that it's much easier to get the paperwork done if you don't have the living-breathing item second-guessing you at every turn or trying to use you as a ventriloquist's dummy. It's also easier getting friends, former lovers, fellow writers, and disgruntled airline attendants to open up once so-and-so is out of the picture. (No one wanted to cross Lillian Hellman while she was still alive and smoking.)

Of course, the primary reason for waiting for the subject's death transcends tactical considerations. Only after the final curtain can the life be properly framed, its dramatic arc seen in its entirety. Its volatile elements need to settle before the sorting-out process can begin. The cause and circumstances of death, the reaction of the survivors, the nature of the will, the tone of the newspaper obituaries, the survival of diaries or other private papers—absent these and any biography is doomed to be a progress report, an interim statement. (Contemporaries mostly took Hemingway at his macho word and accepted the *Life* magazine image of him as a bearded king. It took the shock of his suicide to show the thin ice on which his sovereignty stood, and the black depths below.)

Despite the formal and practical advantages of waiting, financially it is better to strike while the body is still warm. Editors and agents are falling out of their East Hampton hammocks signing up biographies of high-profile authors such as Saul Bellow, Susan Sontag, and Norman Mailer (three thus far, along with a memoir by one of his former wives, with other exes waiting in the wings to take their whacks). The irony is that publishers seem more eager to bring out books about golden-oldie authors than books by them, gossip about literary life being thought more marketable than the original horsehide. (Lack of publishing enthusiasm piqued Bellow to bring out some of his recent novellas as paperback originals.) Kaplan's *Gore Vidal* captures the flagging winds of literary fashion, as even the bestselling author of *Myra Breckinridge* and *Burr* finds himself shunted aside, a lion in winter. Unfortunately, Kaplan's biography—the second to be authorized by Vidal (the first was stillborn when its author, Walter Clemons, died)—will do little to restore Vidal's roar in the marketplace or boost his profile, just as the biographies of Mailer have only added to a general fatigue. The American reviews have been so sour and testy that Vidal and his sympathizers have blamed *The New York Times* for pursuing a vendetta that dates back to its snuff job on Vidal's gay-themed novel *The City and the Pillar* in 1948. Vidal's sly mockery of Michiko Kakutani, the paper's leading book reviewer, may have goaded them into arthritic action.

Yet the grumpy reaction to this book is partly—largely?—Vidal's own fault. He has generated a Gore Glut which even the most skillful wave of Kaplan's wand could not have whisked away. With the deft, evocative strokes of a Japanese brush-artist, Vidal has been dolling up the pages of *The New York Review of Books* for decades with mini-memoirs about his childhood in Washington, DC (his grandfather was a U.S. senator) and his delight aloft as a boy pilot (his father was a pioneer in aviation and a business partner of Amelia Earhart, who doted on young Gore), his serio-comic encounters with Tennessee Williams, Eleanor Roosevelt, and Orson Welles, and his holidays in the sinister sunlight of Hollywood as a hired hand (there's still controversy about how much homoeroticism he snuck into the screenplay of *Ben-Hur*—"I suspect that Heston does not know to this day what luridness we managed to contrive around him"): essays which were reprinted in various collections and have finally come to rest in *United States: Essays 1952–92*, a lap-buster of nearly 1,300 pages.

In 1995, Vidal wove his memoirs into a dance of the seven veils called *Palimpsest*, which, unbound by the boring chronology that constrains the average biographer, superimposed past and present in a Proustian montage. "Ravello. Province of Salerno. Italy. Twenty-two years ago, at this table and in this room, I wrote the last sentence of the novel *Burr*." The supporting cast in this séance included Marlon Brando, Greta Garbo, André Gide, the Beat poets, the Kennedys, and the Sitwells. To follow a triumphant vanity production like *Palimpsest* with an authorized biography is a bit too-too. It's as if Vidal were commissioning a monument to fit inside the scaffolding that he's already built. He wanted a biography to appear in his lifetime and Kaplan did double duty, not only complying with Vidal's wishes but editing the anthology *The Essential Gore Vidal*.

What's interesting—almost touching—is how determined Vidal is to establish and fortify his legacy before the vultures dip. Given that so much of his fiction ends in fiery extinction ("when time stops and the fiery beast falls upon itself to begin again as dust-filled wind"— from the novel *Two Sisters*), given that he has a stoical outlook which views man as a bundle of atoms destined to disperse into the void, given that he sees writing as a noble exercise in futility in the age of idiot mass distraction (he's bid literature so many adieus his lips are chapped)—given all these givens, one would have thought he had made his peace with his words and famous name leaving a faint trace. Compared to such beating pulsars as Mailer or Bellow, he seemed resigned to the indifferent clockwork of the cosmos (perhaps the best anecdote in Kaplan's book is when Bellow asks if he can introduce his son to Vidal, explaining that "I want him to meet someone *really cynical!*"). But here he is, primping for posterity, enlisting Kaplan's awkward assistance in trying to secure his place in the literary pantheon and stage-manage his exit. He even invites his biographer to accompany him and his longtime companion Howard Austen as they stroll through Washington's Rock Creek Park Cemetery to pick out burial plots. Kaplan accepts, crafting his own angle. If Vidal expires before he completes his book, he reasons, he can use this tour as material. "It is one of the rewards for having foregone my preference that my subject be dead." Kaplan is being ironic in that academic-twinkly way that can really grate.

All the tricky devices at his disposal can't compensate for the fact that Kaplan entered this project hopelessly outclassed and outfoxed. How does any biographer compete with an autobiographer and professional raconteur who has already dished out his life in such leafy, elegant detail? How does he breathe fresh life into such twice-told tales as Vidal's breaks with the Kennedys, Anaïs Nin, and his own mother? There are a few embarrassing moments in which Kaplan tries to channel Vidal and Set the Scene with his own lyric touches that echo the master's prose. One chapter begins: "Dogs running on the beach and barking in the sunlight. Sand. Water." (Bow. Wow.) But for the most part Kaplan meets the challenge of Vidal's cagey wit by bearing down even harder, giving him the full Leon Edel– Matthew Bruccoli filing-cabinet treatment. For years Vidal has made fun of "scholar-squirrels"—myopic trivia buffs who comb the lives of

Hemingway and Fitzgerald hoping to find the one itty-bitty piece of factual lint no one else has—and here comes Kaplan, gathering nuts in May. Passage after passage is devoted to travel and lodging arrangements. When Vidal takes a swing through Italy, we're told every town on his itinerary. It isn't enough that Vidal should fly to Rome, we have to know that he flew via Switzerland. "The previous December, Howard and Gore had flown eastward from Rome on Singapore Airlines, at what seemed a bargain first-class rate, around the world." (That "seemed" sounds suspicious. Did Howard and Gore mistakenly pay full fare?) Kaplan also keeps tabs on Vidal's ground transport. "From Gulfport he took the bus back to New Orleans, from which at the end of February he went by bus back to Houston, presumably to pursue the now totally unremembered romantic object."

Such haziness on Vidal's part is understandable, given how many forgotten lads have slipped through his lukewarm embrace. The photographs in Kaplan's book remind you of a time when male writers looked fetching in swimming trunks and frisked like seals. In *Palimpsest*, Vidal informs us that he notched more than a thousand sexual liaisons by the time he was twenty-five. To Vidal's irritation ("What, that you don't already know, he asked, would you learn from of a list of the boys I had fucked?"), Kaplan insists on taking his own inventory, monitoring Vidal's sex life like a meat inspector. "Apparently, though, Gore had little difficulty making up for his Egyptian abstemiousness. In a short while he had all the usual one-incident pick-ups, most of them French trade, and at least one affair in which the affections if not the heart were touched." "At parties, at bars, in New York or wherever he traveled, there was the expectation of erotic excitement, of one-night or even fifteen-minute pick-ups, none likely to have any emotional content. As he had told John Lehmann, 'I freely admit to having no romantic notions about trade.'" "Their residence in Paris in spring 1965 made clear to both Howard and Gore how much more they preferred Rome. Nightlife and cruising were easier, more casual there, and there were the 'beautiful Italian boys.'" Near the end of *Gore Vidal*, Vidal, fed up with Kaplan's literal-minded sleuthing, finally lets fly. "Goddamn it, I think you'll never get it through your head that these sexual things aren't what my life's about and that you'll never understand how we deal with these things in my world." Kaplan, frustrated by Vidal's refusal of emotional access, tells him "immediately, and with equal expressiveness, that he was wrong." Vidal, wrong? Never!

It is Kaplan who is on the wrong track, failing to comprehend how necessary it is for some people to compartmentalize, to keep work and recreation, business and friendship, in separate holds. For them, extracurricular activities provide the safety valve—the steam release—which makes the intense, extended concentration that writing demands possible. Despite his priapism, prodigious drinking, and gluttony (his ballooning waistline practically becomes a separate character in this book—see the index entry for "physical appearance"), Vidal has secured his talent in a leak-proof container and protected it from the violent ups and downs to which flesh is heir. He may not have the "heart" of writers aching to be loved (Thomas Wolfe howling to the heavens), but his cool eye has proved an invaluable instrument. From his precocious debut with the war novel *Williwaw*, in 1946, up to the present moment, his focus has been keen, individual and unwavering. A thoroughbred workhorse, he keeps his sentences well-groomed no matter what the format. A stickler for language, he's no snob when it comes to the launch-vehicles for his copy: along with the historical novels for which he is best known (*Julian, Burr, Lincoln*), Vidal has written television plays, Broadway comedies, mystery novels under the pseudonym Edgar Box, speculative fantasies such as *Messiah* and *Kalki*, campy romps such as *Myra Breckinridge* and *Duluth*, political dramas (*The Best Man, An Evening with Richard Nixon*), and TV travelogues (*Vidal in Venice*). With the exception of John Updike, no American novelist of the postwar period has shown as much disinterested devotion to criticism as a regular practice (as opposed to an easy way to keep your name in print between books). He introduced Calvino to American readers, diagnosed the influence of French theory on metafiction in "American Fiction" (where he got off memorable shots at John Barth and Thomas Pynchon, among others), gave the now unfashionable Somerset Maugham and William Dean Howells their dues, and resurrected the novels of Dawn Powell from neglect.

Confronted with reams of words which speak so forthrightly for themselves, Kaplan resorts to academic robot-talk, wading into a minor comic escapade like Vidal's novel *Myron* (the sequel to *Myra Breckinridge*) with lead boots: "Like *Myra Breckinridge, Myron . . .* focused on issues of sexuality, gender, politics and culture, and it especially dramatized the relationship between the divided mind of the culture and the divided psyche of the individual, an attempt by the author to create a novel that reflected his own hard-earned but still not totally secure sense of a unified and autonomous identity." Clobbering themes together to make a Statement isn't how playful minds like

Vidal's function, and it's difficult to imagine he has ever fancied his identity as anything but autonomous.

The shatterproof Plexiglas of Vidal's persona has survived more than forty years of public exposure (including two unsuccessful runs for political office) with barely a scratch or drawn mustache. His literary ascent coincided with the advent of television in the 1940s and 1950s. Indeed, he and TV were a splendid debutant couple. Vidal—handsome, fluent, on loan from some higher cultural sphere—was the perfect cool smoothie for a cool medium. He spoke as if he had the world at his fingertips at a time when the television airwaves were flattered by a few well oiled syllables. (Today, writers are relegated to the "death slot" on celebrity talk shows.) The liveliest stretch of Kaplan's biography arrives when the political and cultural wars of the 1960s erupt across the airwaves, inciting writers to drop the civilities and engage in sneering mouth-to-mouth combat. As commentators for ABC News at the 1968 Democratic Convention in Chicago, where the police went on a headbanging rampage against hippies and Yippies amid clouds of tear-gas, Vidal and his conservative rival William F. Buckley Jr. blew their own fuses and made television history. When Vidal called Buckley a "crypto-Nazi" (he meant to say "crypto-fascist" but words for once failed him), Buckley responded: "Now, listen, you queer! Stop calling me a crypto-Nazi or I'll sock you in your goddam face and you'll stay plastered." Yipes; the technicians in the control booth nearly popped their headphones. As Kaplan records, Buckley's angry use of the word "queer" was so jolting and unprecedented that ABC canceled the time-delayed West Coast feed of the telecast and used static to obscure the offending word on its archival tape. Like spit on the sidewalk, this spat would have evaporated had Buckley not decided to revive the incident in the pages of *Esquire*, semi-absolving himself of fag-bashing before offering Vidal an apology as warm and sincere as a dead-fish handshake. Unmoved, Vidal composed a withering rebuttal, exposing some allegedly anti-Semitic hijinks by the Buckley clan, and Buckley whistled for his lawyers. Years of litigation followed as the case turned into a tar baby to which everyone was stuck.

The Buckley-Vidal fracas was a tune-up match for the legendary broadcast of *The Dick Cavett Show* in 1971 in which Norman Mailer, furious at a review by Vidal in *The New York Review of Books* that linked him and Henry Miller to Charles Manson ("The Miller-Mailer-Manson man, or M3 for short, has been conditioned to think of women as, at best, breeders of sons; at worst, objects to be poked, humiliated, killed"), decided to take his gripe to the source. It was evident that there would be more than a frank exchange of ideas when Mailer head-butted Vidal in the green room and Vidal punched him in the stomach. It was rumored at the time that Vidal had recently had a facelift which Mailer's head-conk threatened to undo. Lesser men would have fled, but as Vidal is fond of saying, there are two things to which one always says yes: sex and appearing on TV. The show itself turned into absurdist theater as Mailer turned his fuming wrath not only on Vidal but on the diminutive Cavett and *The New Yorker*'s even tinier Janet Flanner, who had known Hemingway and thus was no stranger to macho posturing, but who was nevertheless aghast. Although Vidal's conflation of Mailer and Henry Miller with Charles Manson was a low blow, Mailer's cryptic verbal shorthand cut the audience out of the loop and made the natives restless. Vidal won the evening by not losing his temper or, quaint word, manners. Years passed before these two literary lions tussled again, this time at a party thrown by Lally Weymouth, an altercation Vidal later dubbed "the night of the small fists." When not fending off Mailer, Vidal found himself trading insults with Truman Capote, a verbal slapfight which—like the one with Buckley—degenerated into an ugly legal tango.

Apropos, the one occasion I met Vidal was in a television studio where the wife of the talk-show host David Susskind, attempting to launch a separate career, was presiding over her own prospective talk show. Taking part in the pilot were Vidal, the movie critic Pauline Kael, the actor Ed Asner (TV's Lou Grant), and myself. Before the taping, Vidal and I chatted about the then-hot slander suit involving Lillian Hellman and Mary McCarthy. "When you get to a certain age," Vidal said almost wistfully, "a juicy lawsuit is sometimes the only thing that gets you up in the morning." We watched on the monitor as Asner repeatedly wondered aloud if the microphone attached to his sweater was picking up his stomach rumbles. It was one of life's little moments.

It's unhappy now, twenty some years later, seeing Vidal still making the promotional rounds on *The Late Show with David Letterman* or *Late Night with Conan O'Brien*, defensively folding his arms across his chest and making self-deprecating jokes about his weight to an audience of young yahoos who never knew the slim him and have the attention span of fleas. The portly, senatorial Vidal who does cameo appearances in cinematic claptrap such as *Bob Roberts* and *With Honours* (where his character was upstaged by a wise bum played by Joe Pesci—faux Hollywood populism at its worst) is a stationary ham with none of the Zorro slash of the duellist in days of yore.

The later chapters of Kaplan's biography make for wan reading, as

Vidal is deprived not only of a dynamic connection to a responsive, literate audience but of the supportive feedback every writer needs from his immediates. He breaks with his longtime friend, editor, and fellow foodie Jason Epstein, with whom he binged on eating tours through the finest restaurants in France, over Epstein's halfhearted-to-frankly-hostile responses to his more far-out fiction—e.g. the soap-opera satire *Duluth* (which Kaplan rightly considers underrated) and *Live from Golgotha*. Although, like most rational minds, Epstein prefers Vidal the essayist to Vidal the novelist, he was curiously reluctant to back *United States* at Random House. Another editor was assigned to the book, which subsequently won the National Book Award for criticism. Awards, though nice, don't compensate for the wound to one's pride of being nudged out of the spotlight. Vidal's most recent novel, *The Smithsonian Institution*, was released with small fanfare and a jacket kitschy enough to suggest goo. Its reviewers seemed baffled and mildly apathetic. Their attentions have shifted elsewhere.

Before Vidal is mothballed in the geriatric ward of fading matinee idols, consider this. He may be an obscure fogey to young TV viewers and an unknown quantity in college lit. courses (where his novels are considered too commercial for the syllabuses), but his political espousals have never been more in vogue on the activist front. His constant drumbeats against American imperialism, the corruption of the democratic process ("The corporate grip on opinion in the United States is one of the wonders of the Western world"), the permanent war machine, and the ecological destruction wreaked by multinationals have instructed and helped motivate those tattered insurgents mobilizing against globalization. (One of his pamphlets appears in the same series as several titles by the greatest voice of no! in thunder, Noam Chomsky.) His radicalism, which seemed to many like cushy armchair socialism with the requisite cocked eyebrow of Bloomsbury snobbery, has now achieved street credibility. The protesters who gummed up the works at the WTO meeting in Seattle are Vidal's ideological children, or grandchildren. Whether they know it or not, they're on his wavelength. From his observation post in Ravello, where he has lived since 1972, Vidal must take a certain satisfaction in knowing that decades of admonishing his countrymen have not been in vain. Somewhere someone was listening. He has become, in his own fashion, a Founding Father. As for his fiction, well, it will just have to fend for itself, like everybody else's.

I Adore Your Mustache

Selected Letters of William Styron

Big bash at the Styrons—Lennie Bernstein in an orange shirt, some sort of exotic "prayer" shawl draped over his expressive shoulders, smoking away, talking to eager young girls. Mike Nichols, the serpent in the garden . . . Claggart to the life, said not enough money was coming in just now, wanted to get unused to the money. Arthur Miller a bit tight addressing me as usual on the subject of his latest openings. Benevolent, even comradely in a Jewish-1915 way, but would never think of saying a word, *asking* a word, about anyone else's work . . . Caroline Kennedy (Schlossberg) was there. The Pete Gurneys, daughter a graduate of the Yale English school, now a financial officer at the ad agency whose long name still ends in Benton and Bowles. That little rat, Jerzy R. Kosinski, thought Conrad was a good subject to bring up with him, but it didn't interest him very much. All the while, host Bill Styron looking a bit subdued as usual these days; we talked about Randall Jarrell's possible suicide, Bill's own depression. And I talked to him about William James's own breakdown and his resuscitation through faith.

What in hell am I doing with all these theatre types?

Alfred Kazin's journals, December 26, 1986*

Discount Kazin's weary, load-bearing sigh in this characteristic entry from his journals, which record him enduring party after party, decade after decade, as if it were his suffering duty, a Calvary of cocktails and canapes. Had Kazin not been invited, he would have been even sorer, nursing a fine, bitter grudge, his other favorite hobby. Guest lists meant something then. The novelist William Styron and his wife, Rose (respected worldwide as a human rights activist), had drawing power as party hosts, the cultural cachet to net compos-

---

* *Alfred Kazin's Journals* edited by Richard Cook.

ers, playwrights, directors, ratfink fabulists, and a former president's daughter to toast the holidays and air out their egos. Such dos were among the last hurrahs of the postwar literary era dominated by heap big novelists now facilely grouped as a cetacean school of Great White Males (Styron, Norman Mailer, James Jones, John Updike, Saul Bellow, Gore Vidal, J. D. Salinger, Joseph Heller, the recently retired Philip Roth), whose ghostly father and bearded Neptune disturbing the liquor cabinet deep into the night was Ernest Hemingway. Even those least influenced by Hemingway's style couldn't fail to register the impact of his hold on America's consciousness: he established the coordinates of celebrity and masculinity that turned literary life at the highest level into a spectator sport. Styron would enjoy his first taste of fame at a party thrown in 1952 by Leo Lerman, who decades later became the editor of *Vanity Fair* and whose own journals, *The Grand Surprise* (2007), are the aesthetic flipside of Kazin's. Lerman, who had written about Styron's clarion debut novel, *Lie Down in Darkness*, for *Mademoiselle*, asked the young author to a little thing he was hosting. Who was there? Oh, you know, the usual crew: Tennessee Williams, Laurence Olivier and Vivien Leigh, and Hemingway's great chum, the one he called "the Kraut": Marlene Dietrich. "You could have knocked me over with a pin," Styron wrote to his aunt Edith, "when Leo took me over to meet Dietrich and she took my cold clammy hand in hers and said she had not only 'rad' *LDID*, but 'lawved' it! It was pure Elysium, I can tell you that."

If the literary histories of the future have less wattage, it will be because such parties (mingling writers, movie stars, choreographers, socialites and theater folk from *All About Eve*) have disappeared in a spiral of cigarette smoke, replaced by book festivals and literary panels, where nothing interesting ever happens between judicious sips of bottled water. Friends of the playwright Lillian Hellman, whom Edmund Wilson would describe in his journals as the queen bee of the Martha's Vineyard "cocktail belt," Styron and Rose would become champion party-throwers themselves up in Roxbury, Connecticut, between work-slogs. But by the year of Kazin's Christmas report, the festivities had begun to fray, private shadows creeping into the social minglings. A year earlier, on December 15, 1985, to be exact, Styron had entered a mental hospital for suicidal depression, a nosedive precipitated by a sudden cessation of alcohol intake and the effects of Halcion medication. He emerged from treatment a couple of months later shaken and depleted, but optimistic in the belief that depression in most cases was "self-limiting" and eventually runs its course "until the victim comes out the other end of his nightmare more or less intact. In the meantime, however, it's Auschwitz time in the heart of the soul—a form of madness I wouldn't wish upon a literary critic." A few years later Styron wrote about his bout with what Churchill called "the black dog" in a memoir, originally published in *Vanity Fair*, called *Darkness Visible: A Memoir of Madness* (1990). It was an instant best seller with staying power. "Curious to think that a slender little volume about lunacy may provide a meal ticket for my superannuated years," Styron muses in *Selected Letters*, edited by his widow with R. Blakeslee Gilpin. The irony of Styron's career is that as a literary son of Faulkner, Wolfe, and Hemingway, he expended massive energy and mountaineering stamina into making himself a major prestigious novelist—and succeeded!—yet that "slender little volume" has left its big brothers behind. It is the one book of Styron's that everyone can relate to, a modern classic of despair and endurance, like Viktor Frankl's *Man's Search for Meaning* and Joan Didion's *The Year of Magical Thinking*. Without it, Styron's reputation might have joined his pal James Jones's, bobbing in and out of the purgatory of posterity, big-novel authors in danger of being dragged down by their own bulk.

I was never a fan of Styron's fiction or his well-oiled, august persona. Each attempt at fording his fiction left me stranded somewhere in the marshy thickets, pushing the canoe, up to my armpits in sonorities. As a student at Duke in 1943, Styron loaded his literary imagination with the brawny prose of Balzac, Faulkner, Hemingway, the Wolfe of *Look Homeward, Angel* and *You Can't Go Home Again*, John Dos Passos, and similar colossi. (Women writers the young Styron found a little too pale and pastel for his white-heat liking, a men's club mentality that he never really outgrew. And mostly a straight men's club at that, if the patronizing reference to "that nice faggot John Ashbery" is any indication.) For such an aspirer at such a time, with the entire world engulfed in war, beautiful miniatures—glass menageries—were out of the question: life was to be absorbed in great gobs and gulps in lusty pursuit of masterpieces. A Marine stationed at Parris Island, South Carolina, in 1945, Styron wrote to his father about the difficulty of tackling war as a subject:

Now the crux of the situation lies in the fact that, to the writer, war is a gigantic, inexorable, relentlessly terrible panorama which, although at every hand fraught with mists of beauty and pathos, swirls about him so swiftly and chaotically that he is unable to find a tongue to utter his thoughts. And after the war, if he has extricated himself from the whole mess with a sound mind and body, he is usually so terribly cynical and embittered that those golden words turn to dust. To be platitudinous, it changes one's viewpoint immensely. Like Wolfe's Eugene Gant I see "Time, dark time, flowing by me like a river"—and that is all one can say.

As the critic Wilfrid Sheed wryly noted, everybody's writing got a little windy around the Second World War, so blowsy with intoning radio-drama pronouncements and humanistic platitudes that even Hemingway's white-boned prose acquired loose flaps. Two years later, still stricken with Thomas Wolfe elephantiasis, Styron sends haunted dispatches from the asphalt jungle. "New York is vast, hideous and strewn with the wrecks of lost and fidgeting souls." Unlike so many others of his word-besotted WW II–vet generation, he would retain this Old Man River rumble in prose, a purple majesty. As the titles of his books indicate—*Lie Down in Darkness* (taken from Sir Thomas Browne), *Set This House on Fire* (John Donne), and *Darkness Visible* (Milton)—he strove for canonical grandeur and stature, never dallying in quick-buck genre fiction, as Jones and Norman Mailer would do with *A Touch of Danger* and *Tough Guys Don't Dance* respectively.

He had a clairvoyant gift for launching long-range assaults on major themes from a counterintuitive angle: the leather hide and audacity required for a Southern white novelist to take on a black slave legend in *The Confessions of Nat Turner* and then the Holocaust with *Sophie's Choice*. That both of these novels became blockbuster successes doesn't mean that they were cynically, commercially conceived. Styron had no way of knowing way back in 1952 when he began contemplating "a novel based on Nat Turner's rebellion"—with literary soul brother James Baldwin's blessing, no less—that Black Power would be waiting to shake its fist at him when the book was finally published in 1967, that militant black authors and radical honky critics from the burning ghettos of academe would consider him a presumptuous carpetbagger. He couldn't appear on a college campus without an uproar ensuing and in 1968 the novel was the target of an almost unprecedented counterblast, *William Styron's Nat Turner: Ten Black Writers Respond*, which whammed him from every angle. (Styron, reading the galleys, goes down the checklist: "I'm a racist, a distorter of history, a defamer of black people, a traducer of the heroic image of 'our' Nat Turner.")

Sophie's Choice, published in 1979, was a more calculated risk, the non-Jewish author having to know he was juggling nitro in using a non-Jewish victim—a Polish Catholic—for tragic universality. In March 1979, Styron wrote to his daughter Susanna that sinister mutterings had reached him that at least one powerful Jewish organization had it in for him, "that *Sophie* was violently anti-Semitic and would be 'dealt with' accordingly." Not the sort of news a novelist wants to hear on the eve of publication. "Can it really be that the furor over *Nat Turner* is going to be duplicated?" The furor turned out to be less than he feared, the most withering attacks originating from the high parapets at *The New Yorker* and *The New York Review of Books*, but resentment would recur like a rash. In 1997, *Nat Turner: Ten Black Writers Respond* was reprinted under the even angrier title *The Second Crucifixion of Nat Turner*. Eventually a younger generation of African-American scholars, prominent among them Cornel West and Henry Louis Gates Jr., came round and paid respects to *The Confessions of Nat Turner*, and some even designated Styron the inadvertent father of the postmodern slave narrative, but by then he may have been so bruised by the initial beatdown that it wasn't much consolation. In 1999, Cynthia Ozick published an essay in *Commentary* imposingly titled "The Rights of History and the Rights of Imagination" that called Styron's intent into suspicion. "The investigation of motive is history's task, and here a suspicion emerges: that Sophie in Styron's novel was not conceived as a free fictional happenstance, but as an inscribed symbolic figure, perhaps intended to displace a more commonly perceived symbolic figure—Anne Frank, let us say." That's a pretty loaded insinuation. As late as 2005, Ozick, speaking at Harvard, was still condemning Styron's decision to position a non-Jewish protagonist at the narrative center, thereby diluting, obscuring, and ultimately expunging "the real nature of the Holocaust."

My own problem with Styron's ennobled potboilers was not his subject matter, point of view, historical accuracy, pale-male effrontery, or any other heavy carbs, but the sheer awful self-conscious succulence of the prose, a fruit orchard in every scene-painting description. In her memoir *Reading My Father*, Styron's youngest daughter, Alexandra, describes dipping into *Sophie's Choice* when she was twelve years old. She's embarrassed by the lubricity of an erotic reverie recounted by Stingo, her father's narrator and alter ego in the novel, over a recently deceased maiden. Here's the passage:

For now in some sunlit and serene pasture of the Tidewater, a secluded place hemmed around by undulant oak trees, my departed Maria was standing before me, with the abandon of a strumpet stripping down to the flesh—she who had never removed in my presence so much as her bobbysocks. Naked, peach-ripe, chestnut hair flowing across her creamy breasts, desirable beyond utterance, she approached me where I lay stiff as a dagger, importuning me with words delectably raunchy and lewd. "Stingo," she murmured. "Oh, Stingo, fuck me." A faint mist of perspiration clung to her skin like aphrodisia, little blisters of sweat adorned the dark hair of her mound. She wiggled towards me, a wanton nymph with moist and parted mouth, and now bending down over my bare belly, crooning her glorious obscenities, prepared to take between those lips unkissed by my own the bone-rigid stalk of my passion.

In the absence of Maria, our hero might have diddled one of those undulant oaks.

Like Susan Cheever's *Home Before Dark* and Kaylie Jones's *Lies My Mother Never Told Me*, Alexandra Styron's *Reading My Father* is further evidence that growing up as the daughter of a famous writer can mean growing up feeling like a background drawing, even an impediment to the full flex of Daddy's genius. Once Styron was deep into the black lagoon of his latest project, everyone was on verbal tiptoe, prohibited from bugging Daddy with questions about what he was working on, and from idle chatter. For the youngest daughter these heavy-hung silences were often preferable to her father's idea of funning, which was terrorizing her with stories about the nearby institution for the mentally retarded ("When we drove by the rolling campus, I gripped the door handle, or pushed myself back into the car seat. 'Some of the really dangerous ones,' Daddy liked to tell me, 'they escape and do *vile* things . . . They're imbeciles. *Deranged*'"), or joking about having her favorite pony put down, claiming it was now the new law. As a former Marine, Styron may have felt he needed to toughen her up—so Alexandra speculates—but why does a young girl need toughening up, and when in the history of child-rearing has sadistic teasing done anyone any good? Surly, sullen, selfish, alcoholic, Styron could be far from the Southern gent he presented to the gallery. Submerging herself in the vortex of letters that readers wrote to her father regarding *Darkness Visible*, relating their own tales of depression or asking for counsel, Alexandra writes that she "thought, not for the first time, of the exquisite irony embedded in my father's relationship with his readers, an irony I was still trying to reconcile as I worked to make sense of the man after his death: how could a guy whose thoughts elicit this much pathos have been, for so many years, such a monumental asshole to the people closest to him?"

Given the grandiloquent gunk of so much of his prize-winning prose and the mottled portrait of his character that has surfaced since his death, the *Selected Letters* offer a surprising, substantial, likable lift, an act of literary restoration that shows us the dedicated man inside the sacred monster and doubles as a time machine traveling through a championship season of American letters, when writers were more than content-providers and had the medals and scars to prove it. The novelists and poets in these pages—the stellar cast includes Lillian Hellman, Mary McCarthy, Truman Capote, Robert Lowell, Elizabeth Hardwick, Robert Penn Warren, Peter Matthiessen, Philip Roth, Irwin Shaw, and the always vivacious William Burroughs ("He is an absolutely astonishing personage, with the grim mad face of Savonarola and a hideously tailored 1925 shit-colored overcoat and scarf to match with a gray fedora pulled down tight around his ears. He reminded me of nothing so much as a mean old Lesbian")—may have drunk, drugged, whored, boasted, feuded, flipped out and plowed their talents into misbegotten mammoths (Jones's *Some Came Running*, Mailer's *Ancient Evenings*), but, even through a distorting lens, larger-than-life beats the small-time pantomime we have today.

Styron's later immodesty was hard-earned. He paid his apprentice dues and the early letters to his father, William Styron Sr., and his writing professor, William Blackburn (whose creative writing program taught and mentored Styron, Reynolds Price, Mac Hyman, Fred Chappell and Anne Tyler), show a commendable respect, seriousness, idealism, and work ethic. Right at the start he zeroed in on his weakness as a writer, his overreliance on rhetorical trumpets, and even in the acutely self-conscious larval stage of young author he establishes kinship with those also at the starting gate, membership in the guild. "Before I left Whittlesey House"—a publisher where Styron had been briefly employed—"I asked Diarmuid Russell to let me be the first to read Guy Davenport's novel," he writes to Blackburn. "I stayed up for seven hours last night reading it, and I think it's an overwhelming, sorrowful, beautiful job of writing, and I frankly went to bed at 5:00 in the morning disturbed, shaken and humble in the light of its unmistakable signs of true, burgeoning genius." If Guy Davenport doesn't become one of America's best writers in the next decade or so, Styron declares, his faith in the gods will be shattered. Davenport's novel—*Effie Garner*—went unpublished; it was shorter fiction and

criticism where he would make his name, justifying Styron's preco-
cious talent-spotting (a posthumous anthology, *The Guy Davenport
Reader*, will appear in 2013). It was a gift that didn't desert him later
in his career. With younger authors, among them Frederick Exley (*A
Fan's Notes*), Philip Caputo (*A Rumour of War*), and Michael Mewshaw
(*Walking Slow*), he is the encouraging old pro, spreading the largesse.
He recognized and recommended Richard Yates (*Revolutionary Road*),
"an all-around swell cat."

The literary shoptalk in these letters is free of jargon and brimming
with embattled fellow-feeling. Commiseration and comradeship are
the dominant chords, although the competitive drive to be the king of
the ring led to verbal scufflings that threatened to brew into genuine
fisticuffs, as witness the ugly falling-out with Norman Mailer. Mailer
entered the heavyweight division of postwar novelists with his debut
novel, *The Naked and the Dead*, in 1948, but at the time of his episto-
lary back and forth with Styron, his ranking had slipped badly. He
was in danger of becoming publishing's version of box-office poison.
Barbary Shore, his second novel, was a cramped political allegory that
creaked as slowly as a Val Lewton movie (without the dream languor),
and his third, a sun-bleached scroll of Hollywood decadence called
The Deer Park, suffered agonies of editorial rebuff and Benzedrine-
fueled rewrites; it was met by a spate of mortifying reviews ("Love
among the Love-Buckets" was how *Time* magazine headlined its
beating of the book), a shredded-nerves saga Mailer would recount
in *Advertisements for Myself*. In the beginning Styron and Mailer buck
each other up, forming a party of two. Thanking him for his praise of
The Long March, a novella which Mailer called "as good an 80 pages as
any American has written since the war," Styron confesses: "I swear,
I can hardly read any of our contemporaries. I'm either deafened by
them, or find them practicing onanism in the corner." An editorial
footnote informs us that "practicing onanism" means "masturbation,"
in case anyone thought it referred to oboe lessons. One of the offending onanists was their mutual irritant Gore Vidal, another WW II
prodigy (with the novel, *Williwaw*, written when he was nineteen),
whom Styron refers to as "that talentless, self-promoting, spineless
slob you mentioned," a compact marvel of mischaracterization, except
for the self-promoting part. Courtesy of the postal service, Styron/
Mailer share not only dislikes, but confidences, expressions of vulnerability. When Mailer begins a letter admitting he's been "kind of
depressed lately," Styron owns up to his own low spirits, lifting the
curtain on his depressive sloughs. "Perhaps I'll change some as I get

older but it seems to me that life (and I wonder how closely it parallels the experience of other men) is a long gray depression interrupted by moments of high hilarity." It is Styron's fraternal affinity for Mailer's creative funks that enables him to discern the underlying mood of *The Deer Park*. "Anxiety runs through the book like a dark river—the true torturous anxiety—and gives to the book this deep sense of depression, which is totally divorced from purely literary concerns." Styron proceeds to address those literary concerns with a tactful candor:

> Here, then, is my final pompous verdict: you've written a book like sour wine, a lethal draught bitter and unlikeable, but one which was written with a fine and growing art, and about which I think you can feel proud. It doesn't have the fire of "Naked" but I think has primer and maturer insights. It is not an appealing book, but neither does it compromise, and for that alone you should be awarded a medal. If lacking the large universe of "Naked," it doesn't have "Naked"'s impact, it is also a book which burns with a different, somehow keener light. I don't like the book, but I admire the hell out of it, and I suppose that's all I have to say for the moment—or until I can talk to you face to face.

Four years later, in March 1958, Mailer would propose a very different "face to face," one in which he would mail his fist into Styron's meretricious mug. The friendship had gone south with a vengeance. The provocation was word from a "reliable source" that Styron had spread disparaging remarks about Mailer's wife, Adele, whereupon Mailer challenged Styron "to a fight in which I expect to stomp out of you a fat amount of your yellow and treacherous shit." Styron responded to this vivid proposition with a raised chin or two of Southern Yankee pride, declining to trade knuckle sandwiches over such a calumnious accusation, "so utterly false, that it does not deserve even this much of a reply." Despite the starchy stage exit on which his note ended, Styron had in fact attached a list of point-by-point rebuttals to Mailer's accusation which his wife and others urged him not to send. He didn't, but the addendum is included in the *Selected Letters* and its closing item is Styron's surmise that "something is, and must have been, *eating* you that has nothing to do with the 'viciousness' you so meanly and falsely saddle me with." Styron is being a bit Scarlett O'Hara here, because, as he admitted decades later, he probably *had* been badmouthing Adele, but he was also right that something else was eating Mailer: status envy. Mailer may have been the greater literary lion, but as a social lion Styron left him back at the watering hole.

After the dissolution of diplomatic relations following the Adele affair, Mailer reamed Styron something fierce in *Advertisements for Myself,* and Styron retaliated by caricaturing Mailer in *Set This House on Fire* (1960), using a variant of the treacherous-shit-stomping threat. The mayhem escalated. In a notorious St. Valentine's Day massacre of his literary rivals in *Esquire* in 1963 called "Some Children of the Goddess," Mailer not only performed a gruesome autopsy of *Set This House on Fire*—"the magnum opus of a fat spoiled rich boy," "a bad maggoty novel" where "four or five half-great short stories were buried like pullulating organs in a corpse of fecal matter"—but also sought to jam a crowbar between Styron and James Jones, of whose friendship he was jealous, revealing that Styron had hosted a gathering where the evening's entertainment consisted of reading aloud choice execrable passages from the galleys of *Some Came Running* for everyone's merriment. It was a little low of Mailer to squeal on Styron's perfidy, since he had been at the party and joined in the laughter at Jones's clunkers, albeit with a somewhat sick feeling that was presumably his conscience calling. But he wasn't going to let a little bit of hypocrisy arrest his trigger finger. The anecdote fitted too nicely into the evidence folder of Mailer's bill of indictment, which charged Styron with being a first-class literary operator oiling the levers of influence and laying on the flattery with forked tongue—a courtly racketeer. Given Mailer's own prodigious politicking—"I have been running for president these last ten years in the privacy of my mind," he wrote in *Advertisements for Myself*—Styron's real offense wasn't that he played the insider game, but that he was so good at it. Styron had married a woman of means, the former Rose Burgunder, whose parents owned a department store in Baltimore (they first met at a graduate seminar at Johns Hopkins University), and, despite heavy turbulence, the two remained married for more than half a century. Whereas Mailer would find himself batting out magazine assignments for money and pulling a wagon train of alimony payments, unable to afford Styron's luxury of discreet pauses between novels lasting years at a time.

What perhaps rankled most was Styron's fleshy proximity to Camelot and Jacqueline Kennedy's Chiclet cool. The *Selected Letters* feature an amusing, theatrical account of the Styrons' attendance at a White House dinner hosted by President and Mrs. Kennedy in honor of Nobel Prize winners. After the "splendid" meal, "there was a boring reading by Fredric March of a garbled and wretched piece of an unpublished Hemingway manuscript; it was done in semi-darkness, and most of the Nobel Prize winners—many of whom are over 70—nodded off to sleep." The reading completed, reprieve seemed at hand. But then the Styrons are invited to the president's private quarters ("Aha! It's just as I suspected. The son of a bitch is after my wife"), and up they troop, joined by March, Robert Frost, and Lionel and Diana Trilling, not exactly the snappiest bunch. "Diana Trilling had the look of a woman who had just been struck a glancing but telling blow by a sledgehammer," Styron notes. The evening's coup: "I spent most of the hour talking with Jackie, who I must say has a great deal of charm, and I treasure her promise to take us out on the presidential yacht when we are across the Sound from Hyannisport this summer."

The injustice of it all! First Arthur Miller captures Marilyn Monroe—or, in Styron's words, "that sexually endowed barrel of pineapple Jello, Miss Mmmmarilyn Monroe"—and then that boll weevil Bill Styron becomes the literary darling of Camelot, yachting with the president and the First Lady, who dispense with formalities. "We were sitting around a big table in the open cockpit and occasionally she would put her feet up in JFK's lap and wiggle her toes, just like you'd imagine the wife of the president to do." With his famous bugle-call essay in *Esquire*, "Superman Comes to the Supermarket," Mailer could justifiably feel that he had emblazoned the Kennedy mystique on the American consciousness, yet it was the pullulating-organ donor who was granted a season ticket to Camelot after Mailer bungled whatever chance he had to ingratiate himself with the First Lady with an ill-considered comment about the Marquis de Sade. (That far even a Francophile such as Jackie wasn't willing to go.) It might have made Mailer's mustard even hotter had he known that a few years later, after the president was assassinated, Styron would be water-skiing with Jackie and rubbing "a good deal of Sea n' Ski foam on the widow's thighs," thighs to which Mailer would never be granted visiting privileges. Styron and Mailer would eventually lower their sabers, as Mailer and his archvillain adversary Gore Vidal would do, setting aside their differences in the wintry satisfaction of outlasting the other bastards.

Knock each other as they may in print, old-pro novelists harbor a crusty collegiality borne of the awareness of the attrition involved in pushing that cannon up the hill, enduring false starts, racking fatigue, spent livers, sunken eyeballs, crises of faith, year-round seasonal affective disorder, and carpal tunnel syndrome, only to stagger into publication day and have Michiko Kakutani of *The New York Times* nail them in the neck with a poison blowdart. Kakutani, referred to in these pages with an ethnic slur that needn't be repeated, is one of the many bête noire reviewers and critics against whom Styron vents, from the "spineless, gutless parasites" of the *Partisan Review* to "deadly young squirts" such as Norman Podhoretz (who fermented into a deadly old squirt, forsaking criticism largely to devote himself to hawkish fist-waving and falling out of friendships), to the literary rabbis scolding Philip Roth for breaking curfew and playing his bongos too loud. As authors, Styron and Roth broadcast on two very different wavelengths, but they bonded over the scuffmarks both nursed from critics trying to stuff them into boxes.

The Styron-Roth correspondence gets off on a jaunty, racy note. "I ever so much enjoyed seeing you up here," Styron writes, "and I have a confession to make. I adore your moustache and have had a single incredible fantasy: suppose I was a girl and you were going down on me with that moustache. What would it be like? Please destroy this letter." It was the 1970s, after all, the decade when porn 'taches came into furry fashion, and a fine bromance was born. After Roth suffers a tag-team shellacking in the pages of *Commentary* from Norman Podhoretz and the redoubtable Irving Howe, Styron rallies to Roth's beleaguered side by recounting his own pummelings at the hands of Stanley Kauffmann and Richard Gilman over *Nat Turner* before zeroing in on the Jewish-elder paternalism—"an old-fashioned Jewish *defensiveness*"—that seems to animate Howe's distemper. Howe makes Roth look guilty of some woeful act of frivolity, literature being serious business, not some branch of vaudeville.

> His entire attack on *Portnoy*, for instance, is to me nearly incomprehensible since it fails to acknowledge the fact that whatever its defects the book *works*: the animating spirit behind the novel is of such vigor as to make it quite academic whether the book is a group of skits, or has imperfect "development," or whatever. This is why earlier on [in the letter], rather self-indulgently, I made the comparison with Gilman's treatment of *Nat*. The point is that, whatever its flaws, *Nat Turner worked* in a very special way for people.

And once something clicked with the public and catapulted into a media phenomenon, it overshot the strictly literary jurisdiction of stern disciplinarians such as Howe, Podhoretz, Gilman, et al., and if there was one thing the high-minded pulpits of the time couldn't abide, it was middlebrow acclaim and the money that formed the comet tail. Critics with their daily crab haul of niggling complaints would never know what it was like to roll big.

> February 25, 1971 Roxbury, CT
> Dear Philip:
>   What has happened about your super country Joint? Let me know. We need some friendly neighbors. This is a great house.
>   I too have been brooding about mortality and have been filled with Kierkegaardian despair believe me.
>   In the midst of this Angst, I found the solution. I bought a $9,000 XJ36 Jaguar, and feel much better.
>   Stay in touch,
>   W.S.

If you're keeping tabs, that would be about $50,000 or so in today's money. Perhaps it doesn't signify, but the coruscatingly brilliant poet-critic-novelist Randall Jarrell, whose descent into depression and possible (probable) suicide haunted the literary world, was also a sports car guy, owning a Mercedes and an MG. Speed only gets you so far.

With the publication of *Darkness Visible* in 1990, the last portion of the *Selected Letters* tails off (only two letters from 1991, for example, just one from 1993), even though Styron lived for another decade and a half. He extends birthday wishes to the editor, author, and fellow Southerner Willie Morris, who had just turned sixty, welcoming Willie to the wonders that the sixties hold: meet your new nemesis, your prostate gland, and "learn the pleasures of slow motion, like the three or four minutes [it takes] to get out of the front seat of a car." And he informs the critic Robert Brustein that "according to our friend Philip Roth, it is only the prospect of the Nobel Prize that keeps Arthur Miller alive October to October." Between these sporadic letters loom large blanks of time. Alexandra Styron's memoir traces the bleak trajectory of these years of public acclamation and King Lear unraveling, but for readers of the *Selected Letters* a brief editorial note tolls the bell: "In the spring of 2000, Styron's depression returned, much more seriously than ever before. He ended up having shock treatments against his will and was contemplating suicide." In the letter that follows this insertion, dated June 14, 2000, Styron apologizes to a friend for requesting a suicide cocktail ("a half insane idea of mine") and adds a PS: "Do call me, though. I'm suffering." This plain statement of pain is the most piercing moment in the book.

The final letter included here is dated February 11, 2002, after which falls a cliff drop of silence until Styron's death in 2006, the book concluding with a posthumous note addressed to the readers of *Darkness Visible*: "I hope the readers of *Darkness Visible*—past, present and future—will not be discouraged by the manner of my dying. The battle I waged against this vile disease in 1985 was a successful one that brought me 15 years of contented life, but the illness finally won the war." He must have been hell to live with, especially toward the ragged, drawn-out end, but the worst hells can be within, and the visible darkness he showed us may have been only the tip of the abyss.

The London Review of Books, January 24, 2013

Acknowledgments

A proper roll call for a collection such as this would require one of those scrolls in the end credits of summer blockbusters where all of the crew members, technical wizards, and behind-the-scenes players receive their due. So many editors, researchers, copy editors, and fact checkers to name and thank at the magazines and newspapers where these pieces first appeared, from the fight club of *The Village Voice* to the *Starship Enterprise* of *Vanity Fair*—special thanks as always to Aimee Bell and the great Graydon Carter—and the pleasurable stops in between, specifically *Harper's, Esquire, Texas Monthly, The New York Review of Books, The London Review of Books,* and *The New Yorker.* In lieu of a movie scroll, let me express how grateful I am for everything everyone has done in making the words come together on the printed page and sent out into the world—I've never taken any of it for granted.

This book wouldn't have been possible without the encouragement, guidance, enthusiasm, and dedication of its editor, Gerald Howard. Every writer should be so fortunate. His former assistant, Hannah Wood, and current assistant, Nathaniel Sufrin, helped make this happen as well, and Kristin Anderson did stellar Lara Croft research work digging out the streaky, smudgy difficult-to-find *Village Voice* clips from the bat caves. And a special shout-out of appreciation to my literary agent, the peerless Elyse Cheney.

About the Author

JAMES WOLCOTT is a longtime columnist and blogger for *Vanity Fair*. He is the author of a novel, *The Catsitters*, the nonfiction work *Attack Poodles and Other Media Mutants*, and the memoir *Lucking Out: My Life Getting Down and Semi-Dirty in Seventies New York*. He lives in New York with his wife, the critic and novelist Laura Jacobs, and their two ocicats, Henry and Veronica.